A
Middle East
Mosaic

Map of Istanbul from Happelius, Die Kurze Beschreibung der Gantzen Turckey, *1688.*

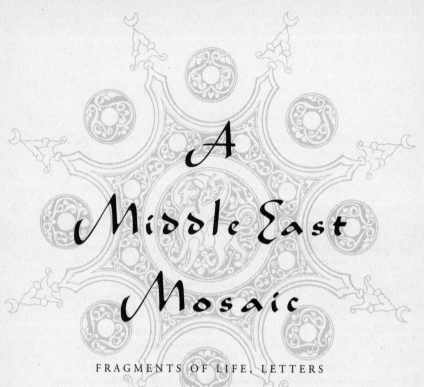

A Middle East Mosaic

FRAGMENTS OF LIFE, LETTERS
AND HISTORY

Selected and Presented by

BERNARD LEWIS

THE MODERN LIBRARY

NEW YORK

2001 Modern Library Paperback Edition

Copyright © 2000 by Bernard Lewis

All rights reserved under International and Pan-American Copyright Conventions.
Published in the United States by Random House, Inc., New York, and simultaneously
in Canada by Random House of Canada Limited, Toronto.

Originally published in hardcover by Random House, Inc., in 2000.

MODERN LIBRARY and colophon are registered trademarks
of Random House, Inc.

Owing to limitations of space, acknowledgments of permission
to reprint previously published material and photographs appear on pages 467–69.

Library of Congress Cataloging-in-Publication Data
A Middle East mosaic: fragments of life, letters and history / selected and presented by
Bernard Lewis.—Modern Library pbk. ed.
p. cm.—(Modern Library classics)
Originally published: Random House, 2000.
Includes bibliographical references and index.
ISBN 0-375-75837-2 (pb.)
1. Middle East—Relations—Europe—Quotations, maxims, etc.   2. Europe—
Relations—Middle East—Quotations, maxims, etc.   I. Lewis, Bernard.   II. Series.
DS63.2.E8   M53   2001
956—dc21   2001037412

Modern Library website address: www.modernlibrary.com

Printed in the United States of America

4689753

First Paperback Edition

Book design by Caroline Cunningham

To Buntzie

". . . along with me . . ."

A man will turn over half a library to make one book.

—SAMUEL JOHNSON (1775)

Preface

oward the middle of the tenth century, an Arab geographer and cosmographer from the great city of Baghdad wrote an account of the known world in which he included a few words about some of the strange, wild people beyond the northwest frontier of civilization—that is to say, of the Islamic empire of the caliphs. Of the northernmost of these peoples, he observed, "Their bodies are large, their natures gross, their manners harsh, their understanding dull and their tongues heavy. Their color is so excessively white that it passes from white to blue. . . . Those of them who are farthest to the north are the most subject to stupidity, grossness and brutishness."

In 1798 an Ottoman secretary of state wrote a memorandum to inform the Imperial Council about the recent troubles in Paris. He began his description of the events which, in the West, came to be known as the French Revolution: "The conflagration of sedition and wickedness that broke out a few years ago in France, scattering sparks and shooting flames of mischief and tumult in all directions, had been conceived many years previously in the minds of certain accursed heretics. . . . The known and famous atheists Voltaire and Rousseau, and other materialists like them, had printed and published various works, consisting . . . of the removal and abolition of all religion, and of allusions to the sweetness of equality and republicanism, all expressed in easily intelligible words and phrases, in the form of mockery, in the language of the common people."

During the nine and a half centuries that intervened between these two reports, the level of information about Europe among Middle Eastern visitors and observers had improved considerably. The basic attitudes of contempt and certitude, however, remained substantially unchanged. Much the same may be said about Western attitudes toward the Middle East. Though in general rather better informed, medieval and early modern Western observers of the Middle East, including travelers, show a similar self-satisfied ignorance in their discussions of the places they visited and the peoples they met.

The rise and spread of Islam brought the Middle East into contact—and sometimes into collision—with other regions and cultures: in the east with India and China, in the south with Africa, in the west and north with Christendom. The last of these, seen by Islam as its only serious rival both as world faith and world power, gave rise to the most sustained and most traumatic of these encounters. It began with the advent of Islam in the seventh century and the irruption of the Muslim Arabs into Palestine, Syria, Egypt and North Africa, all until then part of the Christian world. Three major areas of European Christendom were for a while lost to Islam: the two peninsulas at the southwestern and southeastern corners of Europe, Iberia and Anatolia, and the vast plains of Russia. The first was conquered and ruled by Arabs and Moors, the second by Turks, the third by Islamized Tatars. The loss of Anatolia proved permanent. The attempt by the Crusaders to reconquer the Holy Land failed. But in both Russia and the Iberian Peninsula, the Christian inhabitants were in time able to defeat and expel their Muslim rulers, and, in the flush of victory, even pursued them whence they had come—from Russia to Asia, from Spain and Portugal to Africa and beyond. The reconquest grew into conquest and began the great expansion of Europe, from both east and west, which in time brought most of Asia and Africa into the European orbit.

The relationship between the Middle East and the West has not been limited to war and its consequences—fear and mistrust, resentment and hatred, and a readiness to invent and believe the most absurd of calumnies. As well as fighters and preachers, there were others who looked at the people beyond their religious frontier with sometimes puzzled, sometimes eager curiosity. By turns amused and bewildered, they reflected in their books and in their letters home a range of envy, respect, hostility and—very rarely—admiration.

With the expansion of commerce during and after the crusades, European diplomats began to establish permanent missions in the coastal cities of the Ottoman Empire. Trained to observe and ready to comment on their hosts, their colleagues and (with deep mistrust) their interpreters, diplomats traveling in both directions provide some of the best accounts we have of the habits and customs of those with whom they were sent to negotiate. Merchants in the Middle East, as elsewhere, discussed commodities, prices and their competitors. European Christian merchants defied papal and national bans to sell arms to Saladin fighting the Crusaders and, centuries later, to the Turks advancing toward the heart of Europe. Constructive engagement has a long history.

European travelers in the East discovered such delights as coffee and polygamy. An Italian pilgrim in fourteenth-century Alexandria describes his joyous discovery of the banana; an Egyptian sheikh in nineteenth-century Paris describes the French postal system and observes how it is used, among other purposes, for assignations. Inevitably, there are more negative comments—on the position of women, the punishment of crime, the conduct of war.

Much has been written of late about Western misperceptions, through negligence and prejudice, arrogance and insensitivity, and sheer lack of interest. Some have gone so far as to argue that Western views of the Middle East are largely the result of such attitudes and that misperception has frequently been aggravated by willful misrepresentation, serving a Western desire to dominate and exploit. Certainly, there is no lack of ignorance and prejudice in what Westerners, through the centuries, have written about the Middle East. But the same is true about much of what Middle Easterners have written about the West, in the phases of both their advance and their retreat.

Some territorial definition may be useful. The term Middle East has never been precisely demarcated and extends, for some purposes, as far west as Morocco. Broadly speaking, it applies to the countries of southwest Asia and northeast Africa, with vague and ill-defined extensions at both ends—from Iran into Central Asia and beyond to the borders of China; from Egypt into Africa, westward to the Atlantic and southward up the Nile as far as the Islamic faith and the Arabic language predominate.

The words "Europe" and "West," in common use in Europe and the West, were not in the past used in the Islamic Middle East, where "West" meant their own west, North Africa and for a while Sicily and Spain. The term "Europe" occurs very infrequently, in a few translations of Greek geographical works. These regions and their inhabitants were usually designated either by religious terms—infidels, pagans, Christians—or by ethnic terms—Greeks and Romans in the adjoining Mediterranean lands, Slavs and Franks in eastern and western Europe.

For a long time, the peoples of Europe used similar designations, referring to their southern and eastern neighbors by religious terms, as infidels or Mohammedans, or by ethnic terms, as Moors, Saracens, Turks and Tatars. The terms "Near East" and "Middle East" came into general use at the turn of the nineteenth and twentieth centuries. Clearly, they reflect a view of the world from a Western vantage point—more specifically, from Western Europe, then rapidly extending its rule, and to an even greater extent its influence, in the rest of the Old World.

In Greco-Roman antiquity and medieval Christendom, the region which we now call the Near and Middle East was simply the East, with no need for more precise identification. It was known by a series of names, all meaning "sunrise"—the Greek *anatolê* (whence Anatolia), the Latin *oriens,* the Italian *levante,* and their derivatives. In Greek and later in Latin writings, these names often carried with them a suggestion of something exotic and barbaric, sometimes also effete and luxurious. At most times the East was seen in Europe as hostile and dangerous, the dark hinterland from which came the invading armies of the great kings of Persia and their many successors. The last of these, the Ottoman Turks, confronted Europe with what came to be known as "the Eastern question" in its two phases: first the menace of the Ottoman advance, second the problems posed by the Ottoman retreat.

When a new and more distant Orient was perceived, the old and familiar East—Anatolia, the Levant—seemed much nearer. It was the new awareness of a remote and unknown Far East that led Europeans to rename the countries around the eastern Mediterranean the Near East, and those immediately beyond them the Middle East.

It is easy to understand how these terms came into European usage. It is more difficult to understand why they still remain in common use at the present time, when European domination of the East has decisively ended and Europe itself—apart from the Greenwich meridian—is no longer the principal point from which the world is viewed.

The Middle East, along with China and India, is one of the three most ancient regions of civilizations in the world. Yet it differs significantly from the other two in its pattern of diversity and discontinuity. This diversity goes back to remote antiquity and surely owes much to the geographical configuration and situation of the region. Its division into valleys separated by high mountains and cultivated plains separated by vast and impassable deserts encouraged cultural polycentrism. It was the meeting place of the very different peoples and cultures of Asia, Africa and, in the later stages, of Europe, all of which helped to produce a region of striking contrasts.

From the earliest times we see not one but several centers of civilization: in the river valleys of Egypt and Mesopotamia, on the high plateaus of Iran and Anatolia, in the mountain ranges that go from north to south, from Taurus to Sinai, and on their slopes, facing westward to the coastal plain and the Mediterranean, eastward to the desert and to Asia. These were inhabited by different peoples who spoke different and often unrelated languages, wrote in different scripts, worshiped different gods and created different, sometimes contrasting, societies and polities. Relations between them developed in antiquity from minimal to hostile.

The discontinuity of Middle Eastern history was the result of consecutive phases of conquest and conversion—the one bringing a restructuring of power and authority, the other a reorientation of religion and culture. There were four major phases, beginning with the Hellenization of much of the region after the conquests of Alexander the Great, and continuing with the extension of Roman imperial authority to all of the lands of the eastern Mediterranean. Hellenization and Romanization prepared the ground for two great waves of religious conversion, first to Christianity and then to Islam.

All four processes have left their mark on the present-day Middle East. Of the four, the last is undoubtedly the most comprehensive, the most profound and the most enduring, and gave the peoples of the Middle East the only shared perceived identity they have ever known. To this day, the term "Islam" is used as the equivalent of both "Christianity" and "Christendom," to designate both a religion and a civilization. The cumulative effect of these four cataclysmic changes was to obliterate the religions, the cultures, the languages and, to a large extent, even the nations of the ancient Middle East and to replace them with a new faith, a new political system and a new set of languages and loyalties.

Since the advent of Islam and the Arab conquests in the seventh century, there have been three major languages in the region: Arabic, Persian and Turkish. Some other languages survive. Kurdish and Berber are both spoken by numerous peoples, though neither has evolved a standard written language or literature. Older literary languages still in use are Hebrew, Armenian and Georgian, while others survive in a vestigial form as spoken dialects in a few remote villages, or as the scriptural and liturgical languages of minority religions. The other ancient languages of the region—Sumerian and Elamite, Assyrian and Babylonian, Egyptian, Hittite and Old Persian, together with the literatures written in those languages—were lost, literally buried and forgotten until modern times, when they were exhumed, deciphered and interpreted, mostly by Western Orientalists, and restored to the historical self-awareness of the remote descendants of those who had created them.

Some civilizations, including a few that might be seen as very advanced, have regarded history as unimportant, preferring to live only in the present. Others have attached great, at times even religious, significance to the past—that is, of course, their own past—and have devoted great effort to creating, preserving, and interpreting a record of events.

Their purposes were varied, and the presentation, even the selection, of events varied accordingly. The ancient kings were at great pains to provide written, publicly displayed narratives of their victories and achievements for the edification of their subjects, their rivals and posterity; their modern successors use modern media for the same purpose. But the three major Middle Eastern religions saw history in a different light and created a historiography of universal significance. In the historical books of the Old Testament, history is the record of the working out of God's purpose for mankind, and this required a level of honesty rarely equaled in other historiography. King David, the founder of the royal house of Judah and the greatest of Jewish heroes, is depicted with brutal frankness: his weaknesses, his pettinesses, his sins both great and small. And the rest of the kings and leaders of the Jews, present as well as past, fare no better at the hands of Jewish historians.

Much the same spirit inspired the classical historians of Islam, who saw their task as a sacred trust. The Sunna, the practice and usage of the past and more particularly (though not exclusively) of the Prophet and his companions, was accepted as a source of binding law; it was therefore a religious duty to preserve an accurate record of that past. An immensely rich and varied historical literature attests the fulfillment of that duty.

Though the early religious motivation no longer applied, concern with history and with historical accuracy remained, and every Muslim society, however remote or undeveloped, produced and preserved some kind of historiography. The three major historical literatures of the Muslim Middle East provide a remarkably full record.

Their concern was with what they saw as meaningful history, that of God's community, i.e., themselves. As is the common way of mankind, until very recently they showed little or no interest in what were, for them, the meaningless gyrations of infidel barbarians. Some examples of this perception are given in the pages that follow.

The greater part of what follows consists of excerpts from a wide range of Middle Eastern writings, as well as letters, documents and books from outside the region. Books on history and travel have obviously formed a major source of information. I have also drawn on memoirs and works of literature in the narrower sense of that term. A poem is as much a document of a people's history as a letter or a treaty.

The evidence thus assembled is arranged by topic, by source and by period. There are sections on travel and diplomacy, government and war, commerce, women, arts and letters, food and drink, wit and wisdom. Humor is at once the most universal and the most parochial of human expresssions. The Middle East has its own rich tradition, with a marked predilection for the short, sharp anecdote and the pungent aphorism. Despite, or rather because of, its importance, there is no separate section on religion. In Middle Eastern perception, shared by the various communities of the region, religion is not a part or compartment of life, separated or separable from the rest; it rules and suffuses the whole of life and thus appears in all sections. I have drawn to some extent on the scriptures of the three main Middle Eastern religions, the Old and New Testaments and the Qur'ān, and also on what Muslims call *ḥadīth,* the actions and sayings attributed by Muslim tradition to the Prophet Muhammad. These traditions were transmitted orally for generations before being committed to writing and brought together in major collections. They are numbered in the hundreds of thousands, and their authenticity was critically examined, almost from the beginning, by Muslim religious scholars, who developed a set of standards by which they assessed the reliability of traditions and classified them on a scale ranging from sound through good to weak and defective.

Middle Easterners, for millennia, have devoted much effort to foretelling the future, in the form of prophecy, apocalypse and, latterly, simple prediction. The volume concludes with a selection of such predictions, ranging from the strikingly accurate to the egregiously wrong.

The selection, as in any anthology, is inevitably personal, reflecting the reading, interests and tastes of the compiler. I have, however, tried to make this something more than purely personal choice. As a child of one civilization trying to present a portrait of another, I thought it wise to begin with a display of prejudices and stereotypes—ours about them, theirs about each other and their neighbors. As a counterbalance, a sampling of Middle Eastern views of the West follows, and then a discussion of loanwords of Middle Eastern origin. The remainder deals with some major aspects of public and private life as perceived or exemplified both inside and outside the region. There is some discussion of antiquity and of the present day, but most of the excerpts relate to the period between the advent of Islam and the coming of modernity.

Interaction between Islam and the West is a major theme, but I have also tried to illustrate, more briefly, relations between the Islamic world and its other neighbors and, more important, relations between the different regions, peoples and social groups within the region. Much of the material is translated from Middle Eastern languages. Where suitable translations exist and were available, I have used them and cited the name of the translator. For the rest, I have made my own translations and cited the originals. Dating the excerpts has at times proved something of a problem, especially with premodern texts. In general, the excerpts are headed with the known or estimated date at which they were written. An exception was made for accounts of major military events, which carry the dates of their occurrence.

At the end of the book I have added three appendixes which I hope may help the reader. The first is an explanation of the structure of Middle Eastern personal names and the transcription of Middle Eastern systems of writing, both markedly different from those customary in the modern West. The second and third consist of a listing of the authors cited, with brief biographical notes, and a bibliography of the works from which the citations are taken. I have not thought it necessary to list well-known Western literary figures such as Shakespeare, Dickens, Milton, etc. I have, however, included a few, such as Mark Twain, Herman Melville and W. M. Thackeray, who traveled in the Middle East and left some written account of their adventures and impressions.

There remains the pleasant task of thanking those who have helped in various ways in the preparation and production of this book: my editor, Joy de Menil, whose combination of a sharp mind and gentle manner, of vision and vigilance, have made this a much better book than it would otherwise have been; my daughter, Melanie Carr, who found, chose and arranged the illustrations; my former research assistants, Michael Doran and Michael Reynolds, for help of various kinds in the collection and preparation of the material; Nancy Pressman Levy, of Firestone Library, for invaluable help in tracking down some of my sources; and finally, my assistants Annamarie Cerminaro and Robin Pettinato, for the skill and care with which they handled the many versions of this book, from first draft to final copy.

CONTENTS

ix   Preface

PART I

A Bundle of Prejudices   1

5   ANCIENT PREJUDICES—A Byzantine Misapprehension—Sayings Attributed to the Prophet

7   ON NATIONAL CHARACTER: SOME MEDIEVAL JUDGMENTS: A Persian View of the World—An Iraqi View—A View from Jerusalem—Another Arab View—Another Persian View—Ibn Khaldūn on Subjugation—A Consumer's Guide to Servants

10   SOME WESTERN PREJUDICES: Literary Stereotypes (Shakespeare, Marlowe, Milton, Congreve, Chateaubriand, Byron, Moore, Austen, Hugo, Dickens, Carlyle, Twain, Thackeray, Shaw)—Some Religious Prejudices (Martin Luther, *The Book of Common Prayer,* John Wesley)—And Some Political Judgments (Rycaut, Hume, Washington, Hamilton, Tocqueville, Engels)—Five British Views of the Arabs (Nightingale, Bell, Douglas, Lawrence, Jarvis)—And Some American Prejudices (Diplomatic, Military)—Dr. Johnson on Orientalism

PART II

As Others See Us   21

27 IN DARKEST EUROPE: An Embassy from the Arab Ruler of Cordova to the Vikings—Rome c. 886—The Northern Barbarians—Whaling in the Irish Sea—Northerners, Seen from Andalusia—England and Ireland—Franks in Syria—The British Isles—The Franks According to al-Qazvīnī—Rashīd al-Dīn on European Languages—Ibn Khaldūn on European Science—The State of Nature in Ireland and England

35 THE MYSTERIOUS OCCIDENT: Emperor Leopold I in Vienna (1665)—Frederick the Great (1763)—A Moroccan Ambassador's View of Spain (1690–91)—A Turkish Ambassador's View of Paris (1720)—Parisian Commerce (1777)

38 TWO REVOLUTIONS: Revolution in America (Report from a Moroccan Ambassador in Spain)—The French Revolution: Contemporary Turkish Reactions; The French Revolution Observed; The French Revolution Refuted; An Ottoman Historian; From the Letters of a Turkish Ambassador in Paris

43 THE WESTERN MENACE: A Visitor's Guide to Western Europe (c. 1799–1803)—An Egyptian in Paris Discovers Newspapers, the Mails and Advertising (1826–31)—An Egyptian Lady on Shopping in Paris (1879–1924)—On Causes of the Progress of Europe and the Backwardness of the Orient, Though the Human Race is One—Western Dancing (1903)—Germans in Turkey (1914–18)—English Women and Men (1918)—A Turkish View of Freedom and Eccentricity (1933)—An Egyptian View of Western Civilization (1933)—Plagued by the West (1961)—Working Women: A View from Afghanistan (1998)

PART III

Migratory Words   59

Alcove—Amber—Aryan—Assassin—Baksheesh—Carafe—Caravan—Cassock—Caviar—Check—Chicane—Crimson—Divan—Gala—Harem—Hashish—Hazard—Lute—Magazine—Odalisque—Orange—Ottoman—Pajama—Paradise—Seraglio—Sugar and Candy—Zero

PART IV

Travelers   *73*

79   ON TRAVEL AND TRAVELERS—Hints to Travelers in the East—Salute to the Orient

84   LOOKING THE OTHER WAY: India and China—An African Adventure—Ibn Baṭṭūṭa, the Traveler of Islam, in Turkey, Iran and India

91   QUARANTINE: Contagion—Symptoms—Prayer—Departure from Europe: Crossing the Sava River

94   WESTERN TRAVELERS: Bernard the Wise, Pilgrim (867)—The Misadventures of an Italian Pilgrim (1384)—A Rabbi on the Road (1481)—Time and Space in Sixteenth-Century Turkey—A Spiritual Exercise: The Pilgrimage of Ignatius Loyola (1523)—Letter from a Jesuit Missionary (1700)—Testimony of Two English Slaves (Seventeenth Century)—On the Habits and Character of the Inhabitants of Syria (1782–85)—A Philosopher at Sea (1785)—Napoléon in Egypt (1798)—A Swiss Pilgrim in Medina (1814)—Kinglake's Travels—Damascus (1835 and 1845)—Persian Jews (1846–55)—Flaubert's Travel Notebook (1850)—Richard Burton's Arrival in Mecca (1853)—Melville on Missionaries (1856)—An Innocent Abroad: The Travels of Mark Twain (1867)—Jerusalem (1877)—Fraternizing with Orientals (1894–96)—Gertrude Bell in Praise of Gardens (1894)—On Punctuality (1947)—Saul Bellow Facing History in Jerusalem (1975)—A Journey to the Islamic Revolution (1981)—Interview with Qaddafi (1986)

PART V

Diplomats   *125*

132   RULES CONCERNING AMBASSADORS: How to Test an Ambassador, from an Arabic Manual of Statecraft (Ninth Century)—From a Persian Manual of Statecraft (Eleventh Century)—How to Write a Letter to Europe, from an Egyptian Guide for Officials (Fifteenth Century)

136   RECEPTION AND NEGOTIATION: An Offer of Marriage and Friendship, Apparently Unrequited, from a Frankish Queen (905–6)—A Letter from the Ottoman Grand Vizier Siyavush Pasha to Queen Elizabeth of England (1583)—An Organ for the Sultan (1599)—The Appointment of an Ottoman Ambassador to India (1653)—

The Manner of Reception of Foreign Ambassadors Among the Turks, and the Esteem They Have of Them (1667)—Sir Paul Rycaut on the Dangers of Interpreting (1667)—An Orientalist's View (Eighteenth Century)—James Porter's Advice on Negotiations; Interpreting Treaties; Thoughts on Book Learning and Intelligence, Credulity and Pedantry (1768)—A Turkish Ambassador in Spain (1787)—Petition from a Dragoman—The Dragoman System in the Levant: A Foreign Office Memorandum (1838)—The Etiquette of Embassies (1824–27)—A Lesson in Pride (1833)—Reception and Reform (1867)—An English View of an American Consul-General (1898)—Advice to a Vice Consul (1837)—And a Warning from an American Visitor (1856)

160 MODERN DIPLOMACY: A Persian Mission to England (1838–9)—Nāṣir al-Dīn Shah in Europe (1873)—Letters from Persia: Harold Nicolson to Vita Sackville-West—Politics in Syria Under the French Mandate: Two Foreign Office Memoranda (1934)—Diplomacy and War: The Siege of Baghdad (1941)—An American Diplomat in Baghdad (1944)—The Mad Hatter's Tea Party (Jordan, 1948)—Dean Acheson's Mosadeq (Tehran, 1951)—President Nasser and King Hussein: The Impressions of Henry Kissinger (1969)

PART VI

Women   177

183 INTERPRETING SCRIPTURES: Men and Women: A Qur'ānic Verse in Translation

187 MIDDLE EASTERN VIEWS: Aphorisms (Eleventh Century)—A Consumer's Guide (Eleventh Century)—Two Tales (Fourteenth Century)—On Beauty (Fifteenth Century)—An Egyptian View of Marriageability (Seventeenth Century)—A Traveler's Tale from Vienna (1665)—French Influences (1800–1801)—Frenchwomen, and a Note on Ballroom Dancing (1826–31)—The Need to Educate Women (1867)—The Koltuk Ceremony (Early Twentieth Century)—Lessons and Learning—Atatürk in Praise of Women (1923)

195 EUROPEAN VIEWS: A Wedding (1384)—A Peek at the Harem (1599)—In Praise of Polygamy and Concubinage (1656)—Women's Quarters (c. 1667)—The Tales of Lady Mary Wortley Montagu (1717–18)—On the Domestic Life of the Inhabitants of Syria and Why There Is So Little to Envy (1782–85)—A Physician Visits the Harem, with Notes on Certain Feminine Concerns (1824)—The Price of a Slave (1824)—The Second Wife—Florence Nightingale's Thoughts on Polygamy (1849–50)—The Superior Sex (1858)—Women in Muslim Law (c. 1900)—Behind the Veil (1923)

211 FOUR CLASSICAL LOVE POEMS: Waddāh al-Yaman—Rūdagī—Yehuda Halevi—Fuzuli—Last Word from a Turkish Lady

PART VII

Government   215

219 THE THEORY AND PRACTICE OF GOVERNMENT: Wisdom of the Rabbis (First Century B.C.E.)—From the Qur'ān—Sayings Attributed to the Prophet—The Severity of Ziyād (Seventh Century)—Cutting Bureaucracy (Eighth Century)—A Letter to Secretaries (Eighth Century)—Maxims on Statecraft (Seventh–Ninth Centuries)—Advice on Government from the Vizier Ibn al-Furāt—Al-Fārābī and the Democratic City (Tenth Century)—Three Views of Kingship—A Turkish Rule of Statecraft (1269)—A Bureaucratic Parody (Eleventh Century)—On Taxation and Its Effects—Decline and Fall: Ibn Khaldūn on the Lifespan of Empires—A Connoisseur's View of Kingship (1532)—Another View, Some Time Later (1786)—An Ottoman Official Offers Advice and a Warning to the Sultan (1630)

229 CRIME AND PUNISHMENT: Requisites of a Judge (Twelfth Century)—Justice in Damascus (1384)—Ottoman Advice on Trust and Fear (Mid–Seventeenth Century)—An English Merchant Reviews Methods of Execution (1600)—Turkish Justice (1650)—Summary Justice in Syria (1782–85)—Comments of a Military Adviser (1785)—Flaubert on the Bastinado (1850)—Thackeray on the Rules of Roguery in Cairo (1898)

237 ASPECTS OF REFORM: Despotism, Democracy and Human Rights: Reflections of an English Conservative (1832)—Florence Nightingale on Politics Here and There (1849–50)—Reform and Emancipation: A Turkish View (1856); An English View (1867)—Two Comments from a Turkish Liberal (1868–72)—An Ottoman View of Ottoman Officials (1872)—Persons and Institutions: A British View (1878)—Education: A Memorandum to the Sultan (1880)—Encounter with Freedom (1878)—A Young Turk's View of Old Turk Government (1897)

244 IMPERIAL SIDELIGHTS: Britain in Egypt (1883)—The Leisure of a [British] Egyptian Official (1921)—Trouble in Palestine (1920–22)—Glubb Pasha on Arab Prospects for Self-Government and Democratic Institutions (1941)

247 INTELLECTUALS AND THE STATE: Dependence (1978)—Words Versus Deeds (1986)—Reflections of an Egyptian Statesman (1997)

248 REVOLUTION: Tehran, August 1906—Istanbul, 1908—Three Poems of
Revolution—Atatürk on the State of the Union (1921–27)—Khomeini's New Year's
Message (1980)—Turkey and Iran Look at Each Other

PART VIII

War   267

271 WAR AND PEACE: Scriptures—Sayings Attributed to the Prophet—On
Suicide—Abū Bakr on the Rules of War—St. Augustine on the Desire for Peace—
Two Views on the Origins of the Crusades: Machiavelli and Ibn al-Athir

276 TERRORISTS IN THE HOLY LAND: Crusader Encounters with the Assassins (Twelfth–Thirteenth Centuries)—Murder and Paradise (1192)—A Social Call
on the Assassins (1198)—Plus Ça Change (1250)

279 THE PROPER USE OF SPIES: The Spies of Moses—The Qur'ān on Pri-
vacy—Catching Spies and How to Deal with Them: Two Legal Views (Eighth Century)—A Pilgrim's Progress (721–27)—Advice to Kings on How to Use Spies: Iraq
(Ninth Century)—Iran (Eleventh Century)—Egypt (Fourteenth–Fifteenth Centuries)—USA (1997)

284 OTTOMAN ADVANCES AND RETREAT: The Battle of Lepanto
(1571)—Turkish Imperial Orders after Lepanto (1571)—The Struggle for the Heart of
Europe: Skirmishes in Bosnia and Croatia, an Ottoman Account (1592–93)—Spoils
of War: Defeat at the Gates of Vienna (1683)—Modernizing the Ottoman Army
(1757)—General Bonaparte in Egypt: Campaign Plans and Proclamations
(1798–1801)—The French in Cairo: A Contemporary Egyptian View (1799–1801)—
The Outbreak of the Crimean War: A Contemporary Marxist View (1854)—Balance
of Power in Central Asia: A View from London (1873–4)

300 THE FIRST WORLD WAR AND THE ARAB RISING: The War in
Syria: Impressions of a German General (1918)—Calculations of the Ottoman
Commander (1916–18)—T. E. Lawrence Before and After: Handling Hejaz Arabs
(1917); Reflections After the War (1921–22)—Lawrence and Clemenceau at the
Versailles Peace Conference (1919)—The Lawrence Legend: An Arab View
(1969)—Mustafa Kemal and the Turkish War of Independence: A Churchillian
View (1929)

309 THE SECOND WORLD WAR AND AFTER: De Gaulle in Cairo (1941)—Count Ciano's Diary (1939–43)—The Battle of El-Alamein: An Egyptian View (1942)—An Anglo-French Interlude (1945)—Declaration of a Jihad (1998)

320 THE POETRY OF WAR, AND OF WAR WEARINESS

PART IX

Commerce and Trafficking   323

327 EARLY ISLAMIC VIEWS: Sayings Attributed to the Prophet—A Clear Look at Trade (Ninth Century)

328 TRAFFICKING WITH THE ENEMY: Saladin Defends Constructive Engagement (1174)—An Egyptian Ruler Condemns It (1288)—Contraband of War: A Papal Bull of 1527—The Turkish Trade (1606–7)

330 BUSINESS AS USUAL: Trade in Damascus (1522)—A Business Letter (1586)—An Errant Vice Consul; Some Businessmen Complain (1596)—Diplomatic Reports on English Trade in the Levant (Some Illegal) to the King of Spain (1568–1606)—Advantages of Free Trade with the Ottoman Empire (Mid–Seventeenth Century)—Business Correspondence from Voltaire (1771)—Trade in Baghdad (Nineteenth Century)

338 THE SLAVE TRADE: Letter from the Sultan to the Ottoman Governor of Baghdad (1847)—Slavery and Diplomacy: From a Debate in the House of Lords (1960)

342 THE BUSINESS OF OIL: Possibilities of Petroleum: An American Report (1887)—Striking Oil in Persia (1908)—Oil Comes to Kuwait (1937)—The Oilmen Come to Arabia (1984)

PART X

Arts and Sciences   349

355 CHOICE OF A PROFESSION

355 SCIENCE AND MEDICINE: A Guide for Physicians (Ninth–Tenth Centuries)—A Syrian View of Crusader Medical Practice (Twelfth Century)—A Hospital and Asylum in Baghdad (1165–73)—Physicians in Constantinople: Customs and Costumes (c. 1551)—The Perils of Printing: Advantages of a Turkish Education (1656)—A Visit to the Observatory (1748)—A View of Western Science (1947)

363 MUSIC: An Appreciation (Early Tenth Century)—Western Music (Tenth Century)—Turkish Chamber Music (1717)—Paris Opera (1720)—Musical Diplomacy in Spain: A Turkish Ambassador Reports (1787–89)—"If It Had Not Been for Lehar" (1916)

366 ARTS AND LETTERS: A Well-Turned Thought (Ninth Century)—The Power of Poetry (Twelfth Century)—Lady Mary on Turkish Scholars (1717)—Ancient Arabian Poetry: Four Western Views

369 PRECURSORS: Conversations in Heaven and Hell with Pious Houris and a Pagan Poet (Eleventh Century)—Growing Up on a Desert Island (Twelfth Century)

371 PERSIAN QUATRAINS (Daqīqī, Sanā'ī, Mujīr, Khāqānī, 'Ubayd-i Zākānī)

PART XI

Food and Drink   373

378 RULES: A Medieval Muslim Guide—A Modern Guide

382 MIDDLE EASTERN VIEWS: The Discovery of Rice (Seventh Century)—Tales of a Wine Bibber (Eighth Century)—Warnings (Ninth Century)—In Praise of Wine (Thirteenth Century)—Watching People Eat: A Turk in Paris (1720)—An Egyptian Shaykh Discovers the Restaurant (1826–31)

386 WESTERN VIEWS: Table Manners in Cairo (1384)—Discovering the Banana in Alexandria (1384)—Street Vendors in Damascus (1384)

387 DINING IN TURKEY: Orders from the Sultan (1573–85)—A Turkish Palace Feast, and Its Disappointing Menu (1582)—Lady Mary on Spices and Soop (1717)—Dinner-Dance in Istanbul (1785)—Dinner with the Kapudan Pasha (1829–31)

393 COFFEE AND TOBACCO: A Turkish Cure for Melancholy (1621)—Coffee and Tobacco in Istanbul (c. 1635)—The Sin of Smoking (c. 1869)

PART XII

Wit and Wisdom   397

401   Sayings of the Rabbis—A Saying Attributed to the Prophet—Friends and Enemies—Classical Arab Wit and Wisdom—Dicts and Sayings—The Wisdom of Al-Watwāṭ—Thoughts from a Persian Satirist—Servant Problems—Fuad Pasha

PART XIII

Prophecy and Retrospect   413

417   **PROPHECY AND EMPIRE:**   The Ottoman Lands (1837)—The Dangers of Balkan Nationalism (1862)—New Zeal (1876)—A Prophecy at the Turn of the Century (1900)—Intimations of War (1912–14)—"The Death-Knell of Ottoman Dominion"—A Turk in Hyde Park (1933)

420   **PROPHECY AND THE HOLY LAND:**   Return to Judea (1843)—Jewish National Home: An Ottoman Prophecy (1917)—Visons of Arab-Jewish Cooperation and Confrontation at Versailles (1919)—Another Opinion (1920)—"We Will Sweep Them into the Sea" (1948)

424   **WAR AND PEACE:**   The Future of King Hussein (1958)—The Coming War (1967)—Cairo: A Visitor Predicts Sadat (1969)—Lebanon's Future (1975)—The Rising Tide of Discontent (1986)—Saddam Hussein (1991)—There Must Be Something

429   What Is Your Name, and How Do You Spell It?

432   Cast of Characters

442   Bibliography

452   Index

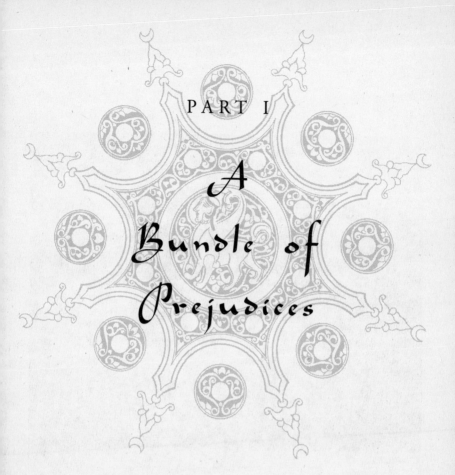

PART I

A Bundle of Prejudices

I am, in plainer words, a bundle of prejudices—
made up of likings and dislikings.
—CHARLES LAMB

Jonah about to be thrown into the sea by fellow passengers of diverse origins, including some in European dress. Iran, late seventeenth century.

Introduction

In our time and place, negative generalizations about ethnic, racial or religious groups are taboo. The only permitted victims are those groups that are currently or were recently dominant in a society. These are regarded as fair game and are sometimes even willing to accept such hostile comments as a reluctant tribute to their present or previous dominance.

It was not always so—indeed, it is still not so in many parts of the world and in some layers of society. In the past, the practice of stereotyping was almost universal, and it seems to have been a common human habit to define and dismiss the Other in terms of some real and exaggerated or imagined characteristic. Otherness is, of course, variously defined—by creed or sect, by race or tribe or nationality, by caste or class or profession, by country or region or neighborhood.

The Middle East, a region of extraordinary ethnic, racial and cultural diversity, has produced—and inspired—a rich crop of stereotypes. Already in antiquity, the Greeks and Romans were moved to surprise or derision by the strange ways of the Jews, who, contrary to the norms of the civilized world, worshiped a single, invisible God and rested from their labors on every seventh day. For the Roman satirist Juvenal, they "worship nothing but the clouds . . . and give up every seventh day to idleness." Seneca comments that "by introducing one day of rest in every seven [the Jews] lose in idleness almost a seventh of their life." Cicero, in a glancing blow, dismissed "Jews and Syrians [as] nations born for servitude." And the poet Horace, in a famous line, expressed his hate for what he called "Persian luxuries."

What follows is a selection of stereotypes, perceptions and misperceptions, some from outside, some from inside the region. The first group comes from the late Roman and Byzantine Empires and expresses their views of their eastern and southern neighbors. Notable among them is the Byzantine emperor Constantine X, who in his manual of kingcraft, written for his son, discusses the Muslims at some length and offers an unfamiliar (and wholly false) explanation of the familiar Muslim war cry *"Allahu Akbar,"* God is greater. This is followed by a group of medieval texts translated from Arabic and Persian, beginning with a selection of sayings attributed by tradition to the Prophet. Many, perhaps even most, of these traditions are apocryphal, but they illustrate some attitudes not of the founder of Islam but of the second and third centuries of the Islamic era, when most of them came into circulation. These and the following texts show how the different peoples of the region regarded themselves and one another. The third and last section derives from the West and illustrates the changing view of the Islamic world and its peoples as seen from Christendom. It includes such religious figures as Martin Luther and John Wesley; poets and writers such as William Shakespeare, Christopher Marlowe, John Milton and Lord Byron; philosophers and wits such as David Hume and Voltaire; voices from the New World such as George Washington and Alexander Hamilton; and finally travelers, diplomats and adventurers who actually visited the region and met some of its people.

We live in an age when ethnic generalizations of any kind are tantamount to blasphemy—or rather have supplanted blasphemy as the ultimate unspeakable offense, in the most literal sense of that word. Some of these relics from earlier ages, expressing sentiments that would be equally unacceptable in academic and polite society, may shock the modern reader. But they deserve attention as preserving a faithful record of the opinions and prejudices of those ages and of the ideas and emotions that inspired them and thus helped to shape the actions of those who held them.

Most of these generalizations are negative, though a few reflect positive stereotypes. Both kinds are equally unreliable as guides to Middle Eastern peoples and cultures.

Ancient Prejudices

On Levantine Immigrants in Rome

The Syrian Orontes has long since poured into the Tiber, bringing with it its lingo and its manners, its flutes and its slanting harp-strings; bringing too the timbrels of the breed, and the trulls, who are bidden to ply their trade at the Circus.

Some who have a father who reveres the Sabbath, worship nothing but the clouds, and the divinity of the heavens, and see no difference between eating swine's flesh, from which their father abstained and that of man . . . for all of which the father was to blame, who gave up every seventh day to idleness, keeping it apart from the concerns of life.

—Juvenal (translated by G. G. Ramsey)

India . . . lies far to the East . . . beyond the learned Egyptians, beyond the superstitious Jews and the merchants of Nabataea, beyond the children of Arsaces in their long flowing robes, the Ituraeans to whom earth gives but scanty harvest, and the Arabs, whose perfumes are their wealth.

—Lucius Apuleius (translated by H. E. Butler)

Why do the Massagetae eat their fathers and the Jews circumcise themselves and the Persians preserve their nobility by begetting children of their mothers?

—Sallustius Neoplatonicus (translated by A. D. Nock)

The Saracens . . . whom we never found desirable either as friends or as enemies, ranging up and down the country, in a brief space of time laid waste whatever they could find, like rapacious kites which, whenever they have caught sight of any prey from on high, seize it with a swift swoop, and directly they have seized it make off. . . .

. . . a number of Egyptians, a contentious race of men, by custom always delighting in intricate litigation, and especially eager for excessive indemnification if they had paid anything to a collector of debts, either for the purpose of being relieved of the debt, or any rate, to bring in what was demanded of them more conveniently by postponing it; or eager to charge wealthy men with extortion and threaten them with court proceedings. All these, crowding together and chattering like jays, unseasonably interrupted the emperor himself, as well as the praetorian prefects, demanding after almost seventy years moneys that they declared they had paid, justly or otherwise, to many individuals.

—Ammianus Marcellinus (translated by John C. Rolfe)

A Byzantine Misapprehension (Tenth Century)

And they pray, moreover, to the star of Aphrodite, which they call Koubar, and in their supplication cry out: "Alla wa Koubar," that is, "God and Aphrodite." For they call God "Alla," and "wa" they use for the conjunction "and," and they call the star "Koubar," and so they say "Alla wa Koubar."

—Constantine Porphyrogenitus (translated by R. J. H. Jenkins)

Sayings Attributed to the Prophet

Love the Arabs and desire their survival, for their survival is a light in Islam, and their passing is a darkness in Islam.

Those who revile the Arabs are polytheists.

Love the Arabs for three reasons: because I am an Arab, because the Qur'ān is in Arabic and because the inhabitants of Paradise speak Arabic.

If the Arabs are humbled, Islam is humbled.

If God intends something gentle, he reveals it to the ministering angels in courtly Persian; if He intends something severe, He reveals it in clarion Arabic.

The people with the greatest share in Islam are the Persians.

If faith were hung on the Pleiades, the Arabs would not reach it, but the men of Persia would.

Who speaks Persian gains in love and loses in manhood.

The ruin of the Arabs will come when the sons of the daughters of Persia grow up.

May God curse both lots of foreigners, the Persians and the Byzantines [Rūm].

Leave the Ethiopians alone as long as they leave you alone, and keep away from the Turks as long as they keep away from you.

Arabs are the equals of Arabs [in marriageability], and non-Arabs are the equals of non-Arabs, except for weavers and cuppers.

Do not marry women for their beauty, which may destroy them, nor for their money, which may corrupt them, but for religion. A slit-nosed black slave woman, if pious, is preferable.

On National Character: Some Medieval Judgments

A Persian View of the World (Sixth Century?)

[Iran] is the navel [of the world], because our land lies in the midst of other lands and our people are the most noble and illustrious of beings. The horsemanship of the Turk, the intellect of India, and the craftsmanship and art of Greece; God (blessed be His realm) has endowed our people with all these, more richly than they are found in the other nations separately. He has withheld from them the ceremonies of religion and the serving of kings which He gave to us. And He made our appearance and our colouring and our hair according to a just mean, without blackness prevailing or yellowness or ruddiness; and the hair of our beards and heads neither too curly like the Negro's, nor quite straight like the Turk's.

—*The Letter of Tansar* (translated by Mary Boyce)

An Iraqi View (Early Tenth Century)

A man of discernment said: The people of Iraq have sound minds, commendable passions, balanced natures, and high proficiency in every art, together with well-proportioned limbs, well-compounded humors, and a pale brown color, which is the most apt and proper color. They are the ones who

are done to a turn in the womb. They do not come out with something between blond, buff, blanched, and leprous coloring, such as the infants
dropped from the wombs of the women of the Slavs and others of similar
light complexion; nor are they overdone in the womb until they are burned,
so that the child comes out something between black, murky, malodorous,
stinking, and crinkly-haired, with uneven limbs, deficient minds, and depraved passions, such as the Zanj, the Ethiopians, and other blacks who resemble them. The Iraqis are neither half-baked dough nor burned crust but
between the two.

—Ibn al-Faqīh

View from Jerusalem (Late Tenth Century)

The most elegant country is Iraq. It is the one which most lightens the heart
and sharpens the mind and in which the soul is most at ease and thought is
most refined, if means suffice. . . .

The country where the people and the merchants are smartest and
where there is most vice is Persia.

The fiercest in heat and drought and with the most palm trees is Arabia.

The richest in blessings, righteous people, holy men, and holy places is
Syria.

The richest in worshipers, Qur'ān-readers, wealth, trade, special features, and corn is Egypt. . . .

The country with the most uncouth, doltish, and dishonest people, the
most numerous cities, and the vastest territories is North Africa.

—Al-Muqaddasī

Another Arab View (Late Tenth Century)

The Chinese are people of furnishings and handicrafts, with neither thought
nor reflection. The Turks are wild beasts for the fray. The Indians are people of fantasy, of legerdemain and conjuring and tricks. The Africans are
feckless cattle.

The Persians have statecraft, civility, rules, and etiquette; the Byzantines
have science and wisdom; the Indians have thought and reflection and nim-
bleness and magic and perseverance; the Turks have courage and impetuosity; the Zanj have patience and toil and merriment; the Arabs are intrepid,
hospitable, loyal, gallant, generous, protective, eloquent, and cogent.

These qualities are not found in every individual of these nations but are

widespread among them. Some, however, may be bereft of all these qualities or even marked by their opposite. Thus there are Persians who are ignorant of statecraft, lacking in civility—ruffians and rabble; there are Arabs
who are cowardly, boorish, fickle, miserly, and tongue-tied; and likewise
with the Indians, the Byzantines, and the others. And so, if the people of
merit and excellence among the Byzantines are compared with those
among the Persians, they meet on the Straight Path and differ only in the dimensions of merit and extent of excellence; and this does not distinguish
but unites them. Likewise, if the flawed and vicious of one nation are compared with the flawed and base of another, they meet on one track; and they
differ only in the merits and defects. . . . It is clear that all nations have their
share of merits and defects, by both innate compulsion and intellectual
choice. The rest is mere argument among people, according to their places
of origin, their inherited customs, and their aroused passions.

—Abū Ḥayyān al-Tawḥīdī

Another Persian View (Twelfth–Thirteenth Centuries)

Among the classes of nations, the Arabs are distinguished for their speech,
their eloquence and their ingenuity, but they are also noted for harsh nature
and powerful appetite. The Persians, on the other hand, are distinguished
by intelligence, quickness, cleanliness and sagacity, albeit noted for cunning and greed. The Byzantines are distinguished for loyalty, trustworthiness, affection and competence, but noted for stinginess and meanness.
Indians are distinguished for strength of feeling, and of intuition and understanding, but noted for conceit, malevolence, guile and a tendency to fabrication. The Turks are distinguished by courage, worthy service and fine
appearance, but noted for treachery, hardness of heart and indelicacy.

—Naṣīr al-Dīn Ṭūsī (translated by G. M. Wickens)

On Subjugation (Fourteenth Century)

[Injury has been done] to every nation which has been dominated by others
and treated harshly. The same thing can be seen clearly in all those persons
who are subject to the will of others and who do not enjoy full control of
their lives. Consider, for instance, the Jews, whose characters owing to such
treatment have degenerated so that they are renowned, in every age and climate, for their wickedness and slyness.

—Ibn Khaldūn (translated by Charles Issawi)

The only people who accept slavery are the blacks, owing to their low degree of humanity and their proximity to the animal stage.

—Ibn Khaldūn

A Consumer's Guide to Servants
(Fifteenth-Century Iran)

Again, the species of servants are three: 1st, The free by nature; 2nd, The menial by nature; 3rd, The menial by incontinence. Of these the first are to be treated like children, the second like cattle and beasts, and the third to be encaged for our pleasures, and employed as occasion requires. As to their species, considered nationally, Arab servants are noted for language, eloquence, and acuteness; but stigmatized for their troublesome dispositions and strong passions. Of these, again, the Abyssinians possess acknowledged integrity and steadiness of behaviour; but their haughtiness and intolerance of indignity is equally certain. Those of the Middle Asia have great good sense, conduct, good-humour, and discrimination; but as much trickery, knavery, and pretence. Romish ones are esteemed for integrity, probity, and exactness; but disapproved for parsimony and sordid feeling. Hindus are recommended by aptness of conjecture, and induction; but censured for spitefulness, conceit, and fraud. Turkish ones are remarkable for bravery, generosity, usefulness, and dashing exterior; but notorious for perfidy, hardness of heart, and unconcern for their employer's safety.

—Jalāl al-Dīn Davānī (translated by W. F. Thompson)

Some Western Prejudices

Literary Stereotypes

—in Aleppo once
Where a malignant and a turban'd Turk
Beat a Venetian and traduc'd the state
I took by the throat the circumcised dog,
And smote him thus.

—Shakespeare, *Othello*

This is the English not the Turkish Court.
Not Amurath an Amurath succeeds
But Harry, Harry.

—Shakespeare, *Henry IV, Part II*

Wine lov'd I dearly, Dice, dearly; and in Woman,
Out-paramour'd the Turk.

—Shakespeare, *King Lear*

What? Think you we are Turks, or infidels?
Or that we would, against the form of law,
Proceed thus rashly in the villain's death?

—Shakespeare, *Richard III*

Well fare the Arabians who so richly pay
The thing they traffic for with wedge of gold.

—Christopher Marlowe, *The Jew of Malta*

Now Turks and Tartars shake their swords at thee,
Meaning to mangle all thy provinces.

—Christopher Marlowe, *Tamburlaine the Great, Part I*

If an Englishman, forgetting all laws, human, civil and religious, offend against life and liberty . . . he is no better than a Turk, a Saracen, a heathen.

—John Milton, *The Tenure of Kings and Magistrates*

To drink is a Christian diversion
Unknown to the Turk or the Persian
Let Mahometan fools
Live by heathenish rules
And be damned over tea-cups and coffee.
But let British lads sing
Crown a health to the king
And a fig for your sultan and sophy!

—William Congreve, *The Way of the World*

What above all distinguishes the Arabs from the peoples of the New World is that through the roughness of the former one can still see something of delicacy in their manners and customs: one feels that they were born in this East from which came all the arts, all the sciences, all the religions. . . . In a word, in the American, everything proclaims the savage who has not yet reached the level of civilization; in the Arab, everything shows the civilized man who has relapsed into savagery.

—Chateaubriand, *Itinéraire de Paris à Jérusalem*

'Tis said they use no better than a dog any
Poor woman, whom they purchase like a pad:
They have a number, though they ne'er exhibit 'em,
Four wives by law, and concubines "ad libitum."

—Byron, *Beppo*

A Persian's Heaven is easily made;
'Tis but black eyes and lemonade.

—Thomas Moore, *Intercepted Letters*

The turban'd Turk who scorns the world,
May strut with his whiskers curled,
Keep a hundred wives under lock and key,
For no one else but himself to see,
Yet long may he pray with his al Koran,
Before he can love like an Irishman.

—Jane Austen, "The Irishman"

The Turks have passed that way. All is ruin and mourning.

—Victor Hugo, *Les Orientales*

It's over, and can't be helped, and that's one consolation, as they always say in Turkey, ven they cuts the wrong man's head off.

—Sam Weller, in Charles Dickens, *The Pickwick Papers*

The unspeakable Turk.

—Thomas Carlyle, letter to G. Howard

The people of this region in the Bible were just as they are now—ignorant, depraved, superstitious, dirty, lousy, thieving *vagabonds*.

—Mark Twain, *Notebooks and Journals*

The much-maligned Orient, I am confident, has not been maligned near enough; for the good reason that none of us can tell the amount of horrible sensuality practised there.

—William Makepeace Thackeray, *Eastern Sketches*

WARWICK: I am a soldier, not a churchman. As a pilgrim I saw something of
    the Mahometans. They were not as ill-bred as I had been led to believe.
    In some respects their conduct compared favorably with ours.
CAUCHON   (displeased): I have noticed this before. Men go to the East to
    convert the infidels. And the infidels pervert them. The Crusader comes
    back more than half a Saracen.

—George Bernard Shaw, *Saint Joan*

Some Religious Prejudices

Antichrist is the Pope and the Turk together. A beast full of life must have a
body and soul. The spirit or soul of Antichrist is the Pope, his flesh or body
the Turk.

For the Last Judgment draws nigh, and the angels prepare themselves for
the combat and to strike down Turk and Pope into the bottomless pit.

The Turks are the people of the wrath of God.

—Martin Luther, *Table-Talk*

Jews, Turks, Infidels, and Hereticks.

—*The Book of Common Prayer,* Good Friday, Third Collect

. . . as absolutely void of virtue as any Jew, Turk or heathen that ever lived.

—John Wesley, *Diary*

And Some Political Judgments

The Maxims of the Turkish Polity (1667)

If (Reader) the superstition, vanity, and ill foundation of the Mahometan Religion seem fabulous, as a Dream, or the fancies of a distracted and wild
Brain, thank God that thou wert born a Christian, and within the Pale of an
Holy and an Orthodox Church. If the Tyranny, Oppression, and Cruelty of
that State, wherein Reason stands in no competition with the pride and lust
of an unreasonable Minister, seem strange to thy Liberty and Happiness,
thank God that thou art born in a Country the most free and just in all the
World; and a Subject to the most Indulgent, the most Gracious of all the

Princes of the Universe; That thy Wife, thy Children, and the fruits of thy Labour can be called thine own, and be protected by the valiant Arm of thy fortunate King: And thus learn to know and prize thy own Freedom, by comparison with Foreign Servitude, that thou mayst ever bless God and thy King, and make thy Happiness breed thy Content, without degenerating into Wantonness, or desire of Revolution. Farewell.

—Sir Paul Rycaut

Greeks and Turks (1741)

The integrity, gravity and bravery of the Turks form an exact contrast to the deceit, levity and cowardice of the modern Greeks.

—David Hume

A View from America (1774)

Are not all these things self evident proofs of a fixed and uniform plan to tax us? If we want further proofs, do not all the debates in the House of Commons serve to confirm this? And has not General Gage's conduct since his arrival (in stopping the address of his Council, and publishing a proclamation more becoming a Turkish bashaw, than an English governor, declaring it treason to associate in any manner by which the commerce of Great Britain is to be affected), exhibited an unexampled testimony of the most despotic system of tyranny that ever was practised in a free government?

—George Washington

A Model of Despotism and Voluptuousness (1787–88)

Here the writers against the Constitution seem to have taken pains to signalize their talent of misrepresentation. Calculating upon the aversion of the people to monarchy, they have endeavored to enlist all their jealousies and apprehensions in opposition to the intended President of the United States; not merely as the embryo, but as the full-grown progeny of that detested parent. To establish the pretended affinity, they have not scrupled to draw resources even from the regions of fiction. The authorities of a magistrate, in a few instances greater, in some instances less, than those of a governor of New York, have been magnified into more than royal prerogatives. He has been decorated with attributes superior in dignity and splendor to those of a king of Great Britain. He has been shown to us with the diadem sparkling on his brow and the imperial purple flowing in his train. He has been seated on a throne surrounded with minions and mistresses, giving audience to the envoys of foreign potentates in all the supercilious pomp of majesty. The

images of Asiatic despotism and voluptuousness have scarcely been want-
ing to crown an exaggerated scene. We have been almost taught to tremble
at the terrific visages of murdering janizaries, and to blush at the unveiled
mysteries of a future seraglio.

—Alexander Hamilton

On Democracy (1835)

Muhammad brought down from heaven and placed in the Qur'ān not only
religious doctrines but also political maxims, civil and criminal laws, and
scientific theories. The Gospels, in contrast, speak only of the general relations between man and God and among men. Apart from this, they offer no
teaching and impose no belief. This alone, among a thousand other reasons, suffices to show that the first of these two religions could not long
dominate in times of enlightenment and of democracy, while the second is
destined to prevail in these as in all other periods.

—Alexis de Tocqueville

Pirates and Bourgeois (1848)

The conquest of Algeria has already forced the Beys of Tunis and Tripoli,
and even the Emperor of Morocco, to enter upon the road of civilisation.
They were obliged to find other employment for their people than piracy,
and other means of filling their exchequer than tributes paid to them by the
smaller states of Europe. And if we may regret that the liberty of the
Bedouins of the desert has been destroyed, we must not forget that these
same Bedouins were a nation of robbers,—whose principal means of living
consisted of making excursions either upon each other, or upon the settled
villagers, taking what they found, slaughtering all those who resisted, and
selling the remaining prisoners as slaves. All these nations of free barbarians
look very proud, noble and glorious at a distance, but only come near them
and you will find that they, as well as the more civilised nations, are ruled
by the lust of gain, and only employ ruder and more cruel means. And after
all, the modern *bourgeois,* with civilisation, industry, order, and at least
relative enlightenment following him, is preferable to the feudal lord or to
the marauding robber, with the barbarian state of society to which they
belong.

—Friedrich Engels

Five British Views of the Arabs

1850

Why is there not national like individual progression? Does it not seem as if the greatest amount of progress would be secured by the *same* nation continuing to carry its own on, and profiting by its own experience? It cannot be a law that all nations shall fall after a certain number of years. God does not work in that sort of way: they must have broken some law of nature which has caused them to fall. But are all nations to sink in that way? As if national soil, like the soil of the earth, must lie fallow after a certain number of crops. And will England turn into Picts again, after a certain number of harvest years, as Egypt has turned into Arabs? Or will a nation find out at last the laws of God by which she may make a steady progression?

However that may be, I really think a traveler should consider the question, whether it is not less painful to him to travel in America, where there is no Past, an ugly and prosperous Present, but such a Future! or in the East, where there is such a past, no Present, and, for a Future, one can only hope for extinction!

—Florence Nightingale

1907

There is no nation of Arabs; the Syrian merchant is separated by a wider gulf from the Bedouin than he is from the Osmanli, the Syrian country is inhabited by Arabic speaking races all eager to be at each other's throats, and only prevented from fulfilling their natural desires by the ragged half fed soldier who draws at rare intervals the Sultan's pay. And this soldier, whether he be Kurd or Circassian or Arab from Damascus, is worth a good deal more than the hire he receives. Other armies may mutiny, but the Turkish army will stand true to the khalif; other armies may give way before suffering and privation and untended sickness, but that of the Sultan will go forward as long as it can stand, and fight as long as it has arms, and conquer as long as it has leaders. There is no more wonderful and pitiful sight than a Turkish regiment on the march; greybeards and half-fledged youths, ill-clad and often barefoot, pinched and worn—and indomitable. Let such as watch them salute them as they pass: in the days when war was an art rather than a science, of that stuff the conquerors of the world were made.

—Gertrude Bell

1912

The chief mental exercise of the Arab, they say, consists in thinking how to reduce his work to a minimum. Now this being precisely my own ideal of life, and a most rational one, I would prefer to put it thus: that of many kinds of simplification they practise only one—omission, which does not always pay. They are imaginative, but incredibly uninventive. How different from the wily Hindu or Chinaman, with his almost preternatural sagacity in small practical matters! Scorn of theories is one of their chief race-characteristics, and that is why they end in becoming stoics—stoics, that is, as the beasts are, who suffer without knowing why.

But I observe a defect in the eyes of all Arabs, namely, that they seem to be unable to utilize them as a means of conveying thoughts; they have no eye language, even among each other, and must express by words or by some gesture what other people can make clear with a glance. The best-looking youth or maiden has eyes which, beautiful as they are, might be those of a stuffed cow for all the expression they emit. They cannot even wink.

—Norman Douglas

1926

Semites had no half-tones in their register of vision. They were a people of primary colours, or rather of black and white, who saw the world always in contour. They were a dogmatic people, despising doubt, our modern crown of thorns. They did not understand our metaphysical difficulties, our introspective questionings. They knew only truth and untruth, belief and unbelief, without our hesitating retinue of finer shades. . . .

They were a people of spasms, of upheavals, of ideas, the race of the individual genius. Their movements were the more shocking by contrast with the quietude of every day, their great men greater by contrast with the humanity of their mob. Their convictions were by instinct, their activities intuitional. Their largest manufacture was of creeds: almost they were monopolists of revealed religions. Three of these efforts had endured among them: two of the three had also borne export (in modified forms) to non-Semitic peoples. Christianity, translated into the diverse spirits of Greek and Latin and Teutonic tongues, had conquered Europe and America. Islam in various transformations was subjecting Africa and parts of Asia. These were Semitic successes. Their failures they kept to themselves. The fringes of their deserts were strewn with broken faiths.

—T. E. Lawrence

1938

I give the Arab the highest marks, for he plays the right cards and plays them, moreover, with the most consummate skill, so that if there is such a thing as an Arab-Jew or an Arab-Assyrian or an Arab-Anything-Else problem the British officials on the spot are almost invariably pro-Arab to a marked and most disconcerting degree and continue as such long after retirement has come to stultify and warp their activities.

It is to the skilful application of the right sort of flattery that the Arab owes most of his adherents and by means of it has won to his cause Englishmen and women who are almost prepared to die for it, and this amuses the Arab intensely.

—C. S. Jarvis

And Some American Prejudices

Diplomatic (1887)

It is often very difficult to distinguish a Jew, an Armenian, a Turk or a Greek, one from the other. To do so you must be very observant. You want to know the man first. The genteel haughtiness of the Turk will soon enable you to tell that the man whom you are addressing has not the cunning subtleness of the Greek. His manner distinguishes him from the Armenian, Jew or Arab.

The Armenians are the sharpest people in the world. They are the Yankees of the Orient, with much additional acuteness. They are divided also; some, as will appear, lean to the Catholic faith, and some to their own Church; and both away from Greek Orthodoxy.

The Levantines—the descendants of the French, Italian, German and other settlers of European origin—are also among the shrewdest of people. They are a class by themselves, and mingle very little with the Greeks or the Armenians.

It is a mooted question as to which race is paramount for sharpness, or, as we call it, smartness. I will not attempt to debate that question. Certainly, the Turkish is not the one, although it is the ruling power. The Frank or the Levantine is not the one; nor the Greek, nor the Jew. It is a common saying, and likely has some basis in fact: that it takes the wit of four Turks to overreach one Frank; two Franks to cheat one Greek; two Greeks to cheat one Jew; and six Jews to cheat one Armenian.

—Samuel S. Cox

Military (1943)

Reflections of an American general in North Africa.

It took me a long time to realize how much a student of medieval history can gain from observing the Arabs.

All members of our oil-daubed civilization think of roads as long slabs of concrete or black-top, or at least as dragged and graded thoroughfares full of wheel ruts. As a matter of fact, roads, or perhaps it is better to call them trails, existed thousands of years before the earth-shaking invention of the wheel was even dreamed of, and it was along such roads that our sandaled or barefoot progenitors moved from place to place just as the Arabs do today.

Viewed from the air, the Arab road is a gently meandering tracery of individual footpaths. Where the going is good, this collection of paths may spread to a width of twenty to forty yards, while, where rocky outcroppings must be circumvented or defiles pass through the wandering tendrils, they come into focus and form a single path, only again to spread out when the going improves. Nowhere is a wheel track or a heelmark, because the Arabs wear heelless slippers or go barefooted; their animals are unshod—there are no vehicles.

In the waterless districts, the roads are generally straight, but not in the brutal mathematical meaning of the term. They are straight only as a man would walk from one point to another, or as the dried slime path where a snail has crossed the sidewalk. . . .

It takes little imagination to translate the Arab on his white stallion and the men and women on donkeys into the Canterbury pilgrims, while the footman, equipped with a large staff and poniard, can easily be mistaken for Friar Tuck, Little John, or Robin Hood. This similarity not only applies to their dress, save the turban, but also to their whiskers, filth, and probably to their morals; and they are all talking, always talking. They have no other recourse. Few can read, there are no books, no newspapers, no radios, to distract them. Only the spoken word, and truly they are "winged words" with a daily rate of from forty to sixty miles, as we learned during the battles in Tunisia by checking the known origin of a rumor against the time we heard it.

Of course the rumors were not factual, but were in general little less garbled in transmission than some of those received by radio. In the rumors, tanks often were reported as trucks and trucks as tanks, and always the number attained astronomical proportions; but that is natural. Once I asked a farmer in Virginia how many soldiers had passed him, and he replied, "Ah don't know for sure, but Ah reckon about a million"—and he could read and write and had a radio.

For a long time I was greatly intrigued by constantly seeing groups of Arabs squatting in the dust or mud—how they avoid piles is a mystery— gossiping. Then I got the answer from a chance remark by a soldier who referred to such a group as "the morning edition of the daily news."

—General George S. Patton, Jr.

Dr. Johnson on Orientalism

A generous and elevated mind is distinguished by nothing more certainly than an eminent degree of curiosity; nor is that curiosity ever more agreeably or usefully employed than in examining the laws and customs of foreign nations. (1734)

There are two objects of curiosity,—the Christian world, and the Mahometan world. All the rest may be considered as barbarous. (1783)

—James Boswell

PART II

As Others See Us

O wad some Pow'r the giftie gie us
To see oursels as others see us!
—Robert Burns

The images of an embracing European couple on a cup from a hookah bowl. Iran, nineteenth century.

Introduction

From time to time, travelers from the Middle East braved the dangers of darkest Europe and ventured into the lands of the infidels, some of them penetrating even as far as the remote islands beyond the coast of France. But these travelers do not compare, in numbers, range and variety, with the endless flow of European visitors to the Middle East.

The reasons for this disparity are obvious. Unlike European travelers to the Middle East, Middle Easterners had no holy places in European hands— no sacred shrines to visit as pilgrims or to reconquer as crusaders. Christians and Jews from Europe had to venture into the lands of Islam in order to visit their holy places in Jerusalem. For Muslims, their holiest places—Mecca and Medina, the site of the Prophet's career on earth and the revelation of the Holy Qur'ān—were and had always been in Muslim hands.

Nor did trade offer any great incentive. Western Europe, in the days when the Islamic caliphate was the greatest and richest power on earth, offered little attraction. Its people were poor and backward, its resources minimal. While the fabulous and more particularly the real treasures of the East tempted needy and greedy traders from the West, the Europeans, with few exceptions, had nothing to sell and no money to buy. It was not until centuries later that Europe became interesting as a market and a supplier— and by then the European supremacy in the trade between Christendom and Islam was well entrenched.

It was not only a lack of incentive that kept Muslims from visiting Europe; there was also the active discouragement of their religious teachers. For most of these, a journey to the lands of the infidels was a curse to be avoided if at all possible. Some authorities forbade it altogether; others permitted it only in special circumstances—to ransom captives, to buy supplies in times of dearth, and the like. And even for these, such journeys created serious problems. Where, for example, could one be sure of finding food in conformity with the Muslim dietary laws? Where would one find Muslim places of worship? The Christian or Jewish traveler to the East would, ex-

cept in the holy land of Arabia, have no difficulty in finding churches or synagogues among the local Christian and Jewish minorities. But in medieval
Europe no Muslim presence was tolerated.

For most Middle Easterners, as one can see very clearly from the references in historical and geographical writings, western Europe was an outer
darkness of barbarism and unbelief, inhabited by primitive peoples with
nasty and dirty habits, whom they saw much as Victorian Englishmen might
have seen the inhabitants of the central African jungles or the tribes beyond
the northwest frontier of India.

But there were some travelers, and a few of them left accounts of their
adventures and impressions. Sometimes these are preserved as written.
More often, they survive only as quoted by later Arab, Persian and Turkish
historians and geographers.

These visitors fall into several groups. One group are what one might
call the involuntary visitors—those captured in warfare or raiding who afterwards managed to return home and convey some impression of their
captors. Very few are known, and even fewer have left any record. In this
they differ markedly from the vast and varied literature produced by ransomed or escaped captives in Muslim hands—the many soldiers and sailors,
merchants and passengers who were taken by Muslim armies on land or by
Muslim corsairs at sea. But the few that we have are of interest and, together
with translated fragments of Greek geographical literature, provided the
first information available to Muslim readers about western Europe.

Another group are the diplomatic visitors—envoys who, from time to
time, were sent on a mission to a Christian ruler. Presumably, they reported
to their masters on what they had seen, heard and done, but until Ottoman
times no such reports are known. Occasionally, however, a head or member of a mission wrote a more general account.

From the sixteenth century, Europe, by its growing power and increasing wealth, was forcing itself on the attention of the Middle East and indeed
of other parts of the world. Three major Muslim rulers—the sultan of
Turkey, the shah of Persia and the sultan of Morocco—entered into diplomatic relations of a sort with European rulers, sending a special envoy when
circumstances required it.

The opening of resident embassies in the last decade of the eighteenth
century gave a limited number of Middle Eastern men the opportunity to
live for a while in a European city. This bold initiative was followed by a second and even more portentous one: the sending of student missions to European countries. It was not until the eighteenth century that Middle Eastern
governments came to the conclusion that Europe might, after all, have
something important to teach. At first they imported European teachers,
mainly of the arts of war; later, Middle Eastern governments began to send

Muslim students to European countries to acquire the skills needed for survival in a Europe-dominated modern world.

The message these students brought home with them from Europe—for example, from Paris in 1848—soon led to a third category of long-term Middle Eastern visitors: political refugees. As more and more Middle Easterners learned Western languages for the first time, they also translated Western books into Middle Eastern languages and inaugurated the massive importation of ideas, persons and commodities that has continued to the present day.

The following presents a sampling of what was available to Middle Eastern readers anxious to know something about the West in premodern times.

The first is a very unofficial early report of an ambassador from Muslim Spain to an unnamed Viking court in about 845 C.E. The envoy told his story to a friend who committed it to writing. That version was lost but survived as quoted by a later author. The second is by Hārūn ibn Yaḥyā, an Arab captive who was taken to Rome in about 886 C.E. His impressions are preserved by later writers. He alludes to the Anglo-Saxon heptarchy and gives what must surely be the earliest extant description of Anglo-Saxon immigration controls. By the tenth century Muslim geographical literature—in other respects rich and well informed—begins to include some scraps of information about the West, most of them secondhand. Some examples follow. One of them, a description of whaling in the Irish Sea, is cited on the authority of a tenth-century diplomatic envoy who actually visited Europe.

The arrival of the Crusaders in the East and the establishment of Western principalities in the Levant brought new contacts between Westerners and Middle Easterners. In the intervals between wars, these were often reasonably friendly. A Syrian gentleman of the twelfth century records some impressions of his new neighbors. But these, if anything, confirmed the rather negative impression that Middle Easterners had about the West. As late as the fourteenth century no less a man than the great Ibn Khaldūn, in a general history of science and learning among mankind, had only a few dismissive remarks to make about Europe.

For a while Middle Eastern visitors to the West were mainly diplomatic. Evliya Çelebi was not himself a diplomat but went to Vienna as part of an Ottoman diplomatic mission. His description of the emperor is clearly intended to amuse rather than to inform.

There were other visitors from the lands of Islam. Some came from the newly acquired empires of the Western powers, trying to learn something of the home life of their new masters. One such was Mīrzā Abū Ṭālib Khān, an Indian Muslim of Perso-Turkish background who visited England and France between 1799 and 1803 and gave his impressions, in a book written in the Persian language, of the new masters of India. He does not mince his words.

One of the most interesting firsthand accounts of a Western country was a book written by an Egyptian shaykh, Rifā'a Rāfi' al-Ṭahṭāwī, who was in Paris between 1826 and 1831 with an Egyptian student mission. He was not a member of the mission but accompanied them as their religious preceptor and moral guide. He seems to have learned more than any of his wards. His book attracted considerable attention and was even translated from Arabic into Turkish—a rare distinction at the time.

The French expedition to Egypt in 1798, the first armed incursion of Westerners since the Crusades, opened a new chapter and a profoundly new relationship between the Middle East and the West. The remaining excerpts in this section illustrate some different Middle Eastern responses to this experience. They include some contemporary comments on the French Revolution and its ideas and on the behavior of the French in Egypt; the impressions of a Persian shah, an Egyptian lady and a Turkish journalist; a Persian critique of Middle Eastern Westernizers; and, in conclusion, two contrasting reactions to Western civilization, one from an Egyptian scholar and scientist, the other expressed in a very modern form—on a Web site by the antimodernist Taliban of Afghanistan.

In Darkest Europe

An Embassy from the Arab Ruler
of Cordova to the Vikings (c. 845)

When the envoys of the king of the Vikings came to Sultan 'Abd al-Raḥmān to ask for peace after they had left Seville, had attacked its surroundings and had then been defeated there with the loss of the commander of their fleet, 'Abd al-Raḥmān decided to reply accepting this request. He commanded al-Ghazāl to go on this mission with the envoys of their king, since al-Ghazāl possessed keenness of mind, quickness of wit, skill in repartee, courage and perseverance, and knew his way in and out of every door. . . . The envoy of the Viking king went on ahead and informed him of the arrival of the envoys. At this he rejoiced and sent for them, and they went to his royal residence, which was a great island (or peninsula) in the ocean, with flowing streams and gardens. It was three days' sail, that is, three hundred miles, from the mainland. In it are Vikings too numerous to be counted, and around the island are many other islands, large and small, all peopled by Vikings. The adjoining mainland is also theirs for a distance of many days' journey. They were heathens, but they now follow the Christian faith and have given up fire worship and their previous religion, except for the people of a few scattered islands of theirs in the sea, where they keep to their old faith, with fire worship, the marriage of brothers and sisters and various other kinds of abomination. The others wage war against them and enslave them.

The king ordered his people to prepare a fine dwelling for them and sent out a party to greet them. The Vikings thronged to look at them, and they wondered greatly at their appearance and their garb. They were then led to their lodgings in an honorable manner and spent a day there. After two days the king summoned them to his presence, and al-Ghazāl stipulated that he would not be made to kneel to him and that he and his companions would not be required to do anything contrary to their customs. The king agreed to this. But when they went to him he sat before them in magnificent guise and ordered an entrance, through which he must be approached, to be made so low that one could only enter kneeling. When al-Ghazāl came to this, he sat on the ground, stretched forth his two legs, and dragged himself through on his rear. And when he had passed through the doorway, he stood erect.

The king had prepared himself for him with many arms and great pomp. But al-Ghazāl was not overawed by this, nor did it frighten him. He stood erect before him and said, "Peace be with you, O King, and with those whom your assembly hall contains, and respectful greetings to you! May you not cease to enjoy power, long life and the nobility which leads you to the greatness of this world and the next, which becomes enduring under the protection of the living and eternal One, other than whom all things perish, to whom is the dominion and to whom we return" (Qur'ān 28/88). The interpreter explained what he had said, and the king admired his words, and said, "This is one of the wise and clever ones of his people." He wondered at al-Ghazāl's sitting on the ground and entering feet foremost, and he said, "We sought to humiliate him, and he greeted us with the soles of his shoes. Had he not been an ambassador, we would have taken this amiss."

Then al-Ghazāl gave him the letter of the Sultan 'Abd al-Raḥmān. The letter was read to him, and interpreted. He found it good, took it in his hand, lifted it and put it in his bosom. Then he ordered the gifts to be brought and had the coffers opened, and examined all the garments and the vessels that they contained, and was delighted with them. After this, he permitted them to withdraw to their dwelling and treated them generously.

Al-Ghazāl had noteworthy sessions and famous encounters with them, when he debated with their scholars and silenced them and contended against their champions and outmatched them.

Now, when the wife of the Viking king heard of al-Ghazāl, she sent for him so that she might see him. When he entered her presence, he greeted her; then he stared at her for a long time, gazing at her as one that is struck with wonderment. She said to her interpreter, "Ask him why he stares at me so. Is it because he finds me very beautiful or the opposite?" He answered, "It is indeed because I did not imagine that there was so beautiful a spectacle in the world. I have seen in the palaces of our king women chosen for him from among all the nations, but never have I seen among them beauty such as this." She said to her interpreter, "Ask him: is he serious, or does he jest?" And he answered, "Serious indeed." And she said to him, "Are there then no beautiful women in your country?" And al-Ghazāl replied, "Show me some of your women, so that I can compare them with ours." So the queen sent for women famed for beauty, and they came. He looked them up and down, and he said, "They have beauty, but it is not like the beauty of the queen, for her beauty and her qualities cannot be appreciated by everyone and can only be expressed by poets. If the queen wishes me to describe her beauty, her quality and her wisdom in a poem which will be declaimed in all our land, I shall do so."

The queen was greatly pleased and elated with this, and ordered him a gift. Al-Ghazāl refused to accept it, saying, "I will not." Then she said to the interpreter, "Ask him why he does not accept my gift. Does he dislike my gift or me?" He asked him—and al-Ghazāl replied, "Indeed, her gift is magnificent, and to receive it from her is a great honor, for she is a queen and the daughter of a king. But it is gift enough for me to see her and to be received by her. This is the only gift I want. I desire only that she continue to receive me." And when the interpreter explained his words to her, her joy and her admiration for him grew even greater, and she said, "Let his gift be carried to his dwelling; and whenever he wishes to pay me a visit, let not the door be closed to him, for with me he is always assured of an honorable welcome." Al-Ghazāl thanked her, wished her well and departed.

Tammām ibn 'Alqama said, "I heard al-Ghazāl tell this story, and I asked him: 'And did she really approach that degree of beauty which you ascribed to her?' And he answered: 'By your father, she had some charm; but by talking in this way I won her good graces and obtained from her more than I desired.' "

Tammām ibn 'Alqama also said, "One of his companions said to me, 'The wife of the king of the Vikings was infatuated with al-Ghazāl and could not suffer a day to pass without her sending for him and his staying with her and telling her of the life of the Muslims, of their history, their countries and the nations that adjoin them. Rarely did he leave her without her sending after him a gift to express her goodwill to him—garments or food or perfume—till her dealings with him became notorious and his companions disapproved of it. Al-Ghazāl was warned of this and became more careful, and called on her only every other day. She asked him the reason for this, and he told her of the warning he had received. Then she laughed and said to him, "We do not have such things in our religion, nor do we have jealousy. Our women are with our men only of their own choice. A woman stays with her husband as long as it pleases her to do so and leaves him if it no longer pleases her." It was the custom of the Vikings before the religion of Rome reached them that no woman refused any man, except that if a noblewoman accepted a man of humble status, she was blamed for this, and her family kept them apart.' "

When al-Ghazāl heard her say this, he was reassured and returned to his previous familiarity.

—Ibn Dihya

Rome c. 886

Rome is a city governed by a king who is called the pope [al-Bāb]. It is forty miles long by forty miles wide. A river flows towards it from west of the city and cuts through its streets. The bed of the river is paved with copper; its two banks are also built of copper, and they have built copper bridges across it. In the center of the city is the great church.

From this city you take ship and sail for three months, until you reach the
land of the king of the Burjān [Burgundians?]. You can also travel through
mountains and valleys for one month, until you reach the land of Franja,
and from there you set forth and travel another four months, until you reach
the city of Baratiniya [Britain]. This is a great city on the shore of the Western Sea, and it is ruled over by seven kings. At the gate of the city there is an
idol, and when a stranger tries to enter, he falls asleep and is unable to enter
until the people of the city seize him and ascertain his purpose and his aim
in entering the city. They are Christian people, and theirs is the last of the
lands of Rum. Beyond them there is no inhabited place.

—Hārūn ibn Yaḥyā

The Northern Barbarians (c. 947)

As regards the people of the northern quadrant, they are the ones for whom
the sun is distant from the zenith as they penetrate to the north, such as the
Slavs, the Franks and those nations that are their neighbors. The power of
the sun is weak among them, because of its distance from them; cold and
damp prevail in their regions, and snow and ice follow one another in endless succession. The warm humor is lacking among them; their bodies are
large, their natures gross, their manners harsh, their understanding dull and
their tongues heavy. Their color is so excessively white that it passes from
white to blue; their skin is fine and their flesh coarse. Their eyes too are
blue, matching the character of their coloring; their hair is lank and reddish
because of the damp mists. Their religious beliefs lack solidity, and this is
because of the nature of cold and the lack of warmth. Those of them who
are furthest to the north are the most subject to stupidity, grossness and
brutishness.

—Al-Masʿūdī

Whaling in the Irish Sea (Tenth Century)

It is said that on their shores they hunt the young of the whale, which is a
very large fish of which they hunt the young and eat it as a delicacy. It is said
that these young ones are born in the month of September, and they are
caught in October, November, December and January, in these four
months. After that their flesh grows tough and is unfit to eat. As regards the
manner of hunting them, al-ʿUdhri says that the hunters assemble on ships,
taking with them a large iron hook with sharp teeth. On the hook there is a
large, strong ring, and in the ring a stout cord. If they come upon a young

whale, they clap their hands and shout. The young whale is diverted by the clapping and approaches the ships in a sociable and friendly manner. One of the sailors then leaps onto it and scratches its brow vigorously. This gives pleasure to the young whale. Then he places the hook in the center of the whale's head, takes a hammer of strong iron, and with it strikes the hook three times with the utmost vigor. The whale does not feel the first blow, but with the second and third it becomes greatly excited, and sometimes it hits some of the ships with its tail and shatters them. It goes on struggling until it is overcome by exhaustion. Then the men on the ships help one another in dragging it along until they reach the shore. Sometimes the mother of the young whale perceives his struggles and follows them. For this case they prepare a great quantity of ground garlic, which they mix into the water. When she smells the odor of the garlic, she finds it revolting, turns around, and goes back. Then they cut up the flesh of the young whale and salt it. Its flesh is as white as snow, and its skin is as black as ink.

—Ibn Ya‘qūb

Northerners, Seen from Andalusia (1068)

The other peoples of this group who have not cultivated the sciences are more like beasts than like men. For those of them who live furthest to the north, between the last of the seven climates and the limits of the inhabited world, the excessive distance of the sun in relation to the zenith line makes the air cold and the sky cloudy. Their temperaments are therefore frigid, their humors raw, their bellies gross, their color pale, their hair long and lank. Thus they lack keenness of understanding and clarity of intelligence and are overcome by ignorance and apathy, lack of discernment, and stupidity.

—Ṣā‘id ibn Aḥmad al-Andalusī

England and Ireland (1154)

The first part of the seventh climate consists entirely of the ocean, and its islands are deserted and uninhabited. The greatest of its islands is the island of Ireland, which has already been mentioned. It is a large island; between its topmost point and the land of Brittany there is three and a half days' sailing, while between its lowest point and the empty peninsula of Scotland there is two days' sailing. The author of the *Book of Wonders* says that there are three cities there, and that they used to be inhabited, and that ships used to call there and put in there and buy amber and colored stones from the natives. And then one of them tried to make himself ruler over them, and he made war against them with his people, and they fought back against him; thus enmity arose among them, and they exterminated one another, and some of them migrated to the mainland. So their cities were ruined, and no inhabitant remained in them. That is all concerning this section, and praise be to God the Lord of the Worlds.

This deals with the second section of the seventh climate, containing a part of the Ocean in which is the island of Angleterre—England. This is a great island shaped like the head of an ostrich; in it are populous cities, high mountains, flowing streams, and level ground. It has great fertility, and its people are hardy, resolute, and enduring. The winter there is permanent. The nearest land to it is Wissant, in the land of France, and between this island and the continent there is a strait twelve miles wide.

—Al-Idrīsī

Franks in Syria (Twelfth Century)

Among the Franks there are some who have settled down in this country and associated with Muslims. These are better than the newcomers, but they are exceptions to the rule, and no inference can be drawn from them.

Here is an example. Once I sent a man to Antioch on business. At that time, Chief Theodore Sophianos [an eastern Christian] was there, and he and I were friends. He was then all powerful in Antioch. One day he said to my man, "One of my Frankish friends has invited me. Come with me and see how they live." My man told me, "So I went with him, and we came to the house of one of the old knights, those who had come with the first Frankish expedition. He had already retired from state and military service and had a property in Antioch from which he lived. He produced a fine table, with food both tasty and cleanly served. He saw that I was reluctant to eat, and said: 'Eat to your heart's content, for I do not eat Frankish food. I have Egyptian women cooks and eat nothing but what they prepare, nor does swine flesh ever enter my house.' So I ate, but with some caution, and we took our leave.

"Later I was walking through the market, when suddenly a Frankish woman caught hold of me and began jabbering in their language, and I could not understand what she was saying. A crowd of Franks collected against me, and I was sure that my end had come. Then, suddenly, that same knight appeared and saw me, and came up to that woman, and asked her: 'What do you want of this Muslim?' She replied: 'He killed my brother Hurso.' This Hurso was a knight of Afamiya who had been killed by someone from the army of Hama. Then the knight shouted at her and said, 'This man is a *burjāsī* [bourgeois], that is, a merchant. He does not fight or go to war.' And he shouted at the crowd and they dispersed; then he took my hand and went away. So the effect of that meal that I had was to save me from death."

—Usāma ibn Munqidh

The British Isles (Thirteenth Century)

Among the islands in the seas deriving from the Western Ocean is the island of Britaniya in the sea of Bordeaux, that is, the sea that lies beyond the north of Spain. There is only rainwater in this island, and it is by rainwater that they grow their crops. The islands of Britain are eleven in number, and among the famous islands is the island of Inkiltere (and some say Inkeltara). Ibn Sa'īd says: The ruler of this island is called al-Inkitār in the history of Saladin and the wars of Acre. His capital in this island is the city of Londres. Ibn Sa'īd also says: The length of this island from south to north, with a slight deviation, is 430 miles. Its breadth at the center is nearly two hundred miles. In this island there are mines of gold and silver and copper and tin. They have no vineyards because of the great cold. The people transport the produce of these mines to the land of France and exchange them for wine. That is why the ruler of France has such abundance of gold and silver. They make fine scarlet cloth there from the wool of their sheep, which is as soft as silk. They cover their sheep with cloth to protect them from the rains, the sun and the dust. Despite the wealth of the English king and the extent of his kingdom, he is subject to the suzerainty of the French king. On ceremonial occasions he expresses his vassalage by offering him a vessel of food. This is an ancient, inherited custom.

To the north of the island of Inkiltere is the island of Irlanda. Its length is some twelve days' journey, and its breadth at the center about four days, and it is famous for its multiplicity of dissension. Its people were heathens and then adopted Christianity in imitation of their neighbors. They export much copper and tin.

—Ibn Sa'īd

The Land of the Franks (Thirteenth Century)

. . . a mighty land and a broad kingdom in the realms of the Nazarenes. Its cold is very great and its air is thick on account of the excess of cold. It is full of good things, of fruits and harvests, rich in rivers, plentiful of produce, possessing tillage and cattle, trees and honey. There is a wide variety of game there, and the swords of Franja are keener than the swords of India.

Its people are Nazarenes, and they have a king possessing courage, great numbers, and power to rule. He has two or three cities on our shore of the sea in the midst of the lands of Islam, and he protects them from his side. Whenever the Muslims send forces to them to capture them, he sends forces from his side to defend them, and his soldiers are of mighty courage and in the heat of combat do not even think of flight, rather preferring death.

But you shall see none more filthy than they. They are a people of perfidy and mean character. They do not cleanse or bathe themselves more than once or twice a year, and then in cold water, and they do not wash their garments from the time they put them on until they fall to pieces. They shave their beards, and after shaving they sprout only a revolting stubble. One of them was asked as to the shaving of the beard, and he said, "Hair is a superfluity. You remove it from your private parts, so why should we leave it on our faces?"

—Al-Qazvīnī

On European Languages (Early Fourteenth Century)

The Franks speak twenty-five languages, and no people understands the language of any other. All they have in common is their calendar, script and numbers.

—Rashīd al-Dīn

On European Science (Fourteenth Century)

We have heard of late that in the lands of the Franks, that is, in the country of Rome and its dependencies on the northern shore of the Mediterranean, the philosophic sciences are thriving, their works reviving, their sessions for study increasing, their assemblies comprehensive, their exponents numerous, and their students abundant. But God knows best what goes on in those parts. "God creates what He wishes, and chooses" (Qur'ān, 28:68).

—Ibn Khaldūn

The State of Nature in Ireland and England
(Early Fourteenth Century)

Opposite Spain and in the middle of the ocean there are two islands. One of them is Iberniya [Ireland], and it is a peculiarity of the soil of the country, that venomous vermin die. In that country no mice are born. The men there are long-lived, red-faced, tall, powerful of build and courageous. There is a spring of flowing water, such that if a piece of wood is left in it, within a week its surface is turned to stone.

The name of the second, bigger island is Anglater [England]. It contains many mountains and numberless mines of gold, silver, copper, tin and iron, as well as great variety of fruits. One of the wonders of that land is a tree which grows a bird as its fruit. It happens in this way: at blossom time a pouch, looking like an apple, emerges, with the shape of a bird inside it. As it grows, it comes to life and comes out of the pouch. They eat the fruit and keep the bird until it reaches the size of a large duck. The meat of the inhabitants of that country comes chiefly from this bird. It is reported that among the Christians who eat no meat on fast days, there is disagreement as to whether this bird may be eaten. Some consider it a plant because it grows on a tree, others as an animal because blood comes from it. In both islands they have ewes from the wool of which woolen cloth and scarlet are made.

—Rashīd al-Dīn

The Mysterious Occident

Emperor Leopold I in Vienna (1665)

As seen by a member of a Turkish embassy.

One may almost doubt whether the Almighty really intended, in him, to create a man. . . .

He is a young man of medium height, beardless, narrow-hipped, not really fat and corpulent, but not exactly haggard.

By God's decision he has a bottle-shaped head, pointed at the top like the cap of a dancing dervish or like a gourd pear. His brow is as flat as a board, and he has thick, black eyebrows, set far apart, under which his light brown eyes, round as circles and rimmed with black lashes, gleam like the orbs of a horned owl.

His face is long and sharp, like a fox, with ears as big as children's slippers, and a red nose that shines like an unripe grape and is as big as an eggplant from Morea. From his broad nostrils, into each of which he could stick three fingers at a time, droop hairs as long as the mustachios of a thirty-year-old swashbuckler, growing in confused tangles with the hair on his upper lip and with his black whiskers, which reach as far as his ears. His lips are swollen like a camel's, and his mouth could hold a whole loaf of bread at a time. His

Young European gentleman, by the Turkish court painter Levni, early eighteenth century.

teeth too are as big and as white as a camel's. Whenever he speaks, the spittle spurts and splashes over him from his mouth and camel lips, as if he had vomited. Then the dazzlingly beautiful page boys who stand by him wipe away the spittle with huge, red handkerchiefs. He himself constantly combs his locks and curls with a comb. His fingers look like cucumbers from Langa.

—Evliya Çelebi

Frederick the Great (1763)

As seen by an Ottoman ambassador to Berlin.

The king is an adept in the arts and sciences and especially in history. Day and night he studies the achievements of such bygone rulers as Alexander and Tamerlane and seeks to emulate their ways and their wiles in battle. Unperturbed by family concerns, uninvolved in religious affairs, all his thoughts are devoted to the expansion of his realm and the increase of his fame and glory.

—Ahmed Resmi

A Moroccan Ambassador's View of Spain (1690–91)

The Spaniards still own many provinces and vast territories in the Indies, and what they bring from them every year makes them rich. By the conquest and exploitation of the Indian lands and the great riches they draw from them, the Spanish nation today possesses the greatest wealth and the largest income of all the Christians. But the love of luxury and of the comforts of civilization have overcome them, and you will rarely find one of this nation who engages in trade or travels abroad for commerce as do the other Christian nations such as the Dutch, the English, the French, the Genoese and their like. Similarly, the handicrafts practiced by the lower classes and common people are despised by this nation, which regards itself as superior to the other Christian nations. Most of those who practice these crafts in Spain are Frenchmen. Because their own country offers them only a poor livelihood, they flock to Spain to look for work and make money. In a short time they make great fortunes.

—Muḥammad ibn 'Abd al-Wahhāb, al-Wazīr al-Ghassānī

A Turkish Ambassador's View of Paris (1720)

The city of Paris is in fact not nearly as large as Istanbul, but its buildings have three, four and often seven floors. A rabble of families and their children live on every floor. The people on the streets look more numerous, since the women are always in the streets, going from house to house and never staying at home. With this mixture of men and women the city looks more crowded than it is. It is the women who sit in the shops and haggle and bargain and deal.

—Mehmed Efendi

Parisian Commerce (1777)

This city, the capital of France, is of great size, it is said to be fifteen miles round. Its streets and squares are wide enough for two coaches to pass each other with ease, even though foot passengers are walking along the sides of the roads. The city is served by its river, the Seine, over which there is a great bridge, long and wide, called the "Pont Neuf," that is to say, the "New Bridge." All day long, and all though the night, without ceasing, pedestrians are wending their way over it. Here stands the clock "la Samaritaine," which is surrounded by water. There is a saying that never in the twenty-four hours is there an instant without a white horse, a monk and a prostitute at this spot. The city is of great beauty and everything is to be found in it, but all at a very high price, except prostitution, which is very cheap and openly displayed; there are said to be thirty thousand public prostitutes inscribed on the registers, without counting the thousands who are not public and offered to all comers. There are academies in great numbers, and every kind of manufacture is carried on.

—David Azulai (translated by Elkan Nathan Adler)

Two Revolutions

Revolution in America (1779–88)

Report from a Moroccan Ambassador in Spain

The English ambassador left Spain because of the war that broke out between the Spaniards and the English. The cause of this was that the people of America were subjects of the English, and thanks to the revenue which he collected from them he was stronger than all the other Christian peoples. It is said that he increased the burden of taxes and imposts upon them and sent them a ship laden with tea and compelled them to pay for it more than was customary. This they refused and asked him to accept the money that was due to him from them but not to impose excessive taxes on them. This he refused and they rose in rebellion against him, seeking independence. The French helped them in their rebellion against the English, hoping in this way to injure and weaken the English king because he was the strongest of the different races of Christians on the sea.

—Muḥammad ibn 'Uthmān al-Miknāsī

The French Revolution:
Contemporary Turkish Reactions

The French Revolution Observed (1798)

It is one of the things known to all well-informed persons that the confla-gration of sedition and wickedness that broke out a few years ago in France, scattering sparks and shooting flames of mischief and tumult in all direc-tions, had been conceived many years previously in the minds of certain ac-cursed heretics and had been a quiescent evil which they sought an opportunity to awaken. In this way: the known and famous atheists Voltaire and Rousseau, and other materialists like them, had printed and published various works, consisting, God preserve us, of insults and vilifications against the pure prophets and great kings, of the removal and abolition of all religion, and of allusions to the sweetness of equality and republicanism, all expressed in easily intelligible words and phrases, in the form of mock-ery, in the language of the common people.

Finding the pleasure of novelty in these writings, most of the people, even youths and women, inclined toward them and paid close attention to them, so that heresy and wickedness spread like syphilis to the arteries of their brains and corrupted their beliefs. When the Revolution became more intense, none took offense at the closing of churches, the killing and expul-sion of monks and the abolition of religion and doctrine; they set their hearts on equality and freedom, through which they hoped to attain perfect bliss in this world, in accordance with the lying teachings increasingly dis-seminated among the common people by this pernicious crew, who stirred up sedition and evil because of selfishness or self-interest.

It is well known that the ultimate basis of the order and cohesion of every state is a firm grasp of the roots and branches of holy law, religion and doctrine; that the tranquillity of the land and the control of the subjects can-not be encompassed by political means alone; that the necessity for the fear of God and the regard for retribution in the heart of God's slaves is one of the unshakably established divine decrees; that in both ancient and modern times every state and people has had its own religion, whether true or false. Nevertheless, the leaders of the sedition and evil appearing in France, in a manner without precedent, in order to facilitate the accomplishment of their evil purposes, and in utter disregard of the fearsome consequences, have removed the fear of God and the regard for retribution from the common people, made lawful all kinds of abominable deeds, utterly obliterated all shame and decency, and thus prepared the way for the reduction of the people of France to the state of cattle.

Nor were they satisfied with this alone, but, finding supporters like themselves in every place, in order to keep other states busy with the protection of their own regimes and thus forestall an attack on themselves, they had their seditious declaration which they call "The Rights of Man" translated into all languages and published in all parts, and strove to incite the common people of the nations and religions to rebel against the kings to whom they were subject.

—Memorandum from Chief Secretary
Atif Efendi to the Imperial Council

The French Revolution Refuted (1799)

In the name of God, the Merciful and the Compassionate.

O you who believe in the unity of God, community of Muslims, know that the French nation (may God devastate their dwellings and abase their banners, for they are tyrannical infidels and dissident evildoers) do not believe in the unity of the Lord of Heaven and Earth, nor in the mission of the intercessor on the Day of Judgment, but have abandoned all religions and denied the afterworld and its penalties . . . so that they have pillaged their churches and the adornments of their crucifixes and attacked their priests and monks. They assert that the books the prophets brought are clear error and that the Qur'ān, the Torah and the Gospels are nothing but fakes and idle talk . . . that all men are equal in humanity and alike in being men, none has any superiority of merit over any other, and every one himself disposes of his soul and arranges his own livelihood in this life. In this vain belief and preposterous opinion they have erected new principles and set new laws, and established what Satan whispered to them, and destroyed the bases of religions, and made lawful to themselves forbidden things, and permitted themselves whatever their passions desire, and enticed into their iniquity the common people, who are as raving madmen, and sown sedition among religions, and thrown mischief between kings and states. . . . With counterfeit books and meretricious falsehoods they address themselves to every party and say, "We belong to you, to your religion and to your community," and they make them vain promises and utter fearful warnings. They are wholly given up to villainy and debauchery, and ride the steed of perfidy and presumption, and dive in the sea of delusion and oppression and are united under the banner of Satan. They compelled those who would not obey or follow them, so that the other nations of the Franks were thrown into confusion and disorder by their iniquities; the French, baying like dogs and biting like wolves, gathered against those nations and communities, seeking to destroy the foundations of their religions and to plunder their women and their property. Blood flowed like water, and the French gained their objective and ruled over them with injustice and evil.

—Ottoman Imperial Proclamation

An Ottoman Historian (c. 1801)

The newly established republic in France is different from the other Frankish polities. Its ultimate basis is an evil doctrine consisting of the abandonment of religion and the equality of rich and poor. . . .

The deliberations . . . of the republic are like the rumblings and crepitations of a queasy stomach. . . .

[In Turkey] certain sensualists, naked of the garment of loyalty, from time to time learned politics from them; some, desirous of learning their language, took French teachers, acquired their idiom, and prided themselves . . . on their uncouth talk. In this way they were able to insinuate Frankish customs in the hearts and endear their modes of thought to the minds of some people of weak mind and shallow faith. The sober-minded and farsighted, and the ambassadors of the other states, foresaw the danger of this situation; full of alarm and disapproval, they reviled and condemned these things both implicitly and explicitly and gave forewarning of the evil consequences to which their activities would give rise. This malicious crew and abominable band were full of cunning, first sowing the seed of their politics in the soil of the hearts of the great ones of the state and then, by incitement and seduction to their ways of thought, undermining—God preserve us—the principles of the Holy Law.

—Asim

From the Letters of a Turkish Ambassador in Paris (1803–6)

I ask you to pray for my safe return from this land of infidels, for I have come as far as Paris, but I have not yet seen the Frangistan that people speak of and praise; in what Europe these wonderful things and these wise Franks are found, I do not know. . . .

Glory be to God, the minds and beliefs of these people! It is a strange thing that this Frangistan, with the praises of which our ears have for so long been filled, we found to be not only unlike what was said but the reverse. God knows, their minds and their comprehension are such that the difference between them and the people of Islam is like the difference between boatmen and scribes among us. Their stratagems and policies are crude; before they even formulate an intention, one can understand what they are going to do; these successes they have won arise only from our own lack of zeal, for they have no soldiers as brave as ours, no ministers like our ministers, and our artillery officers are more competent than theirs. Their capital consists of nothing but talk. God knows, I am of the opinion that if, as an emergency measure once every three or four years, 25,000 purses of aspers were to be set aside and five factories for snuff, paper, crystal, cloth and porcelain, as well as a school for languages and geography, set up, there would be nothing left for them to hold on to, since the basis of all their current trade is in these five commodities. May God bestow some zeal on our masters. Amen.

If anyone, with the intention either of intimidating you or of leading you astray, praises Frangistan, then ask him this question: "Have you been to Europe, or have you not?" If he says, "Indeed I have been there, and I enjoyed myself awhile," then assuredly he is a partisan and a spy for the Franks. If he says, "No, I have not been; I know it from history books," then he is one of two things—either he is an ass who takes heed of what the Franks write, or else he praises the Franks out of religious fanaticism.

Since the French had no king, they could have no government. Furthermore, as a result of the interregnum that occurred, most of the high positions are held by the scum of the people, and, though a few nobles remain, effective power is still in the hands of the vile rabble. Thus they were unable to organize a republic. Since they are no more than an association of revolutionaries, or in plain Turkish a pack of dogs, it is in no way possible for a nation to expect loyalty or friendship from these people. . . .

Since neither Bonaparte nor the "ministers" he employs are cognizant of the language and the usage of government, they behave like brigand chieftains. Not knowing how either to show respect or to give an effective answer, they strive to settle everything by force. Even Talleyrand, though better born than the rest of them . . . is just a spoiled priest. . . . The usages followed between nations are strange to him, and he is very treacherous.

Bonaparte, rebellious against fate and in a lust for domination, strives day and night like a fiercely biting dog to bring diverse mischiefs on the surrounding lands and to reduce all states to the same disorder as his own accursed nation.

—Halet Efendi

The Western Menace

A Visitor's Guide to Western Europe
(c. 1799–1803)

*Mīrzā Abū Ṭālib Khān was the first nondiplomatic Muslim visitor to western
Europe who has left a detailed account of his travels and impressions. An
English translation of the Persian original was published in London in
1814.*

Some Defects of the English

The first and greatest defect I observed in the English, is their want of faith
in religion, and their great inclination to philosophy. The effects of these
principles, or rather want of principle, is very conspicuous in the lower orders of people, who are totally devoid of honesty. They are, indeed, cautious how they transgress against the laws, from fear of punishment; but
whenever an opportunity offers of purloining any thing without the risk of
detection, they never pass it by. . . .

The second defect, most conspicuous in the English character, is pride,
or insolence. Puffed up with their power and good fortune for the last fifty
years, they are not apprehensive of adversity, and take no pains to avert
it. . . .

The sixth defect of the English is their throwing away their time, in
sleeping, eating, and dressing: for, besides the necessary ablutions, they
every morning shave, and dress their hair; then, to accommodate themselves to the fashion, they put on twenty-five different articles of dress: all
this, except shaving, is repeated before dinner, and the whole of these
clothes are again to be taken off at night: so that not less than two complete
hours can be allowed on this account. One hour is expended at breakfast;
three hours at dinner; and the three following hours are devoted to tea, and
the company of the ladies. Nine hours are given up to sleep: so that there remain just six hours, out of the twenty-four, for visiting and business. If they
are reproached with this waste of time, they reply, "How is it to be avoided?"
I answer them thus: "Curtail the number of your garments; render your dress
simple; wear your beards; and give up less of your time to eating, drinking,
and sleeping." . . .

The eighth defect of the English is vanity, and arrogance, respecting their
acquirements in science, and a knowledge of foreign languages; for, as soon

as one of them acquires the smallest insight into the principles of any science, or the rudiments of any foreign language, he immediately sits down and composes a work on the subject, and, by means of the press, circulates books which have no more intrinsic worth than the toys bestowed on children, which serve to amuse the ignorant, but are of no use to the learned. . . .

Virtues of the English

I fear in the foregoing Chapter, I have fatigued my Readers with a long detail of the vices, or defects, of the English; I shall, therefore, now give some account of their virtues; but, lest I should be accused of flattery, will endeavour to avoid prolixity on this subject.

The first of the English virtues is a high sense of honour, especially among the better classes. This is the effect of a liberal education, and of the contempt with which those who do not possess it are regarded. . . .

Their second good quality is a reverence for every thing or person possessing superior excellence. This mode of thinking has this great advantage—it makes them emulous of acquiring the esteem of the world, and thus renders them better men. . . .

The third of their perfections is a dread of offending against the rules of propriety, or the laws of the realm; they are therefore generally content with their own situations, and very seldom attempt to exalt themselves by base or nefarious practices. . . .

Their seventh perfection is plainness of manners, and sincerity of disposition: the former is evinced in the colours of their clothes, which are generally of a dark hue, and exempt from all tawdriness; and the latter, by their open and manly conduct.

Their other good qualities are good natural sense and soundness of judgment, which induce them to prefer things that are useful to those that are brilliant; to which may be added, their perseverance in the acquirement of science, and the attainment of wealth and honours.

The Irish

The Irish, by reason of their liberality and prodigality, seldom have it in their power to assist their friends in pecuniary matters: they are generally in straitened circumstances themselves, and therefore cannot, or do not aim at the comforts and elegance of the English: neither do they take pains to acquire riches and honours like the Scotch, by limiting their expenses when in the receipt of good incomes, and paying attention to the Great. In consequence of this want of prudence, they seldom attain to high dignities, and but few of them, comparatively, make much progress in science. . . .

The rich expend a vast deal in wine; and the common people consume immense quantities of a fiery spirit, called whiskey, which is the peculiar manufacture of this country and part of Scotland.

The French and Their Women

I had been so long accustomed to English cookery, that during the whole of my residence in France and Italy I could never relish their culinary process. Their roasted meats are burned up, and retain not a drop of gravy: the boiled meats were also overdone, and quite stringy. The French are exceedingly fond of mixtures, that is, meat stewed with vegetables, and a great quantity of garlic, spices etc. On this account I have frequently risen hungry from a table of thirty dishes, on the dressing of which much pains had been bestowed, and principally on my account. The only good dinners I ever ate in these countries were at the houses of English or Americans, who had taken pains to instruct their servants in the proper mode. Neither could I relish their pies or tarts, etc., as an inspection of their pastry-cooks' shops had prejudiced me strongly against them. . . .

The men in France are I think better looking than the English; their clothes are made to fit the body, and are of more lively colours; many of them also wear ear-rings and other ornaments.

The French women are tall, and more corpulent than the English, but bear no comparison with respect to beauty. They want the simplicity, modesty, and graceful motions of the English damsels. Their fashion of dressing the hair was to me very disgusting, as it exactly resembled the mode practised by the common dancing-girls in India; that is, by dividing the hair into ringlets, two of which hung on the cheeks in an affected careless manner. They were also painted to an excessive degree, were very forward, and great talkers. The waists of their gowns were so short and full-bodied that the women appeared hump-backed; whilst the drapery in front was so scanty as barely to conceal half their bosoms. Although I am by nature amorous and easily affected at the sight of beauty, and visited every public place in Paris, I never met with a Frenchwoman who interested me.

—Mīrzā Abū Ṭālib Khān (translated by C. Stewart)

An Egyptian in Paris Discovers Newspapers, the Mails and Advertising (1826–31)

Men learn about what goes on in the minds of others from certain daily sheets called *Journal* and *Gazette*. From these, a man may learn of new events that occur both inside and outside the country. Though he may find in them more lies than can be counted, nevertheless they contain news by which men can acquire knowledge; they discuss newly examined scientific questions or interesting announcements or useful advice, whether coming from the great or the humble—for sometimes the humble have ideas which do not occur to the great. . . . Among the advantages of these sheets are: if a man does anything good or evil and it is important, the people of the *Journal* write about it so that it may become known to both the great and the common people, in order to win approbation for men of good deeds and condemnation for men of evil deeds. Likewise, if a man is wronged by another, he writes of his grievance in these sheets, and everyone, the great and the common people, become aware of it and know the story of the oppressed and his oppressor, exactly as it happened, withholding or changing nothing, so that the affair reaches the place of justice and is judged according to fixed laws, so that this may be a warning and an example to others. . . .

In Paris there are many kinds of vehicles with different shapes, names, speeds and uses. There are vehicles made to carry goods from Paris to the provinces, called *roulages*. There is another kind made to carry passengers, called *diligence*. There are small vehicles to travel to places near to Paris, called *coucous*. In these one pays a fixed amount per head as when traveling on a ship. In Paris there are also vehicles which one can hire for a limited time: a day, a month or a year. The usual vehicle in Paris is the *fiacre*. This contains two benches, facing each other, seating six people and drawn by two horses. There is also the *cabriolet*, which represents the half of a *fiacre* with only one bench. One may hire a *fiacre* or a *cabriolet* by the hour or by the distance from one place to another for a fixed price which can be neither increased nor decreased. There are more of these vehicles in the streets of Paris than donkeys in the streets of Cairo. They have now invented a new kind of larger vehicle called *omnibus,* a word that means "for everybody." These are large vehicles holding many people. On the door it is written that it is going to such and such a street. . . .

The mail, which the French call "post," is one of the most useful services for commercial and other purposes. It makes it easy to keep other people informed by correspondence, which goes promptly and is answered within the shortest time. Its organization and operation are among the most admirable things that can be. The letters sent to a town or a district reach the addressee without any doubt because all the houses are numbered and the numbers are written on them, so that it is possible to tell them apart. When you address a letter to someone, you put it into the mailbox situated in every neighborhood. The mailman comes, takes it, and the letter arrives at its destination, as does the reply, by return, the same day.

The French show great respect for the mails. Nobody may open a letter addressed to another person, even if that person is under suspicion. Because of this respect, letters exchanged between friends, colleagues and, above all, between lovers abound, since everyone knows that his letter will be opened by no one but the addressee. When a lover declares his love to his beloved, he does so by correspondence. It is also by correspondence that they make their rendezvous. . . .

Another thing that is very useful for business is the newspaper. There they write at length in praise of useful and good-quality merchandise, to promote sales and inform people about them. The owner of the merchandise pays something for this . . . sometimes the merchant, with a view to promoting his merchandise, prints numbers of small pieces of paper which he sends with servants to all the houses and distributes free to passersby in the streets. On these papers he gives his name, the name of his shop, what he sells and the prices of his goods.

In a word, in Paris they sell everything in the world, both precious and base. Among the most admirable things are the shops of the apothecaries, stocked with all kinds of ready remedies and all the drugs in the world that are known by name and quality.

Everybody in Paris loves earning and trade, the rich and the poor alike. . . . If their earnings were not stained with usury, they would be the best businesspeople in the world.

—Shaykh Rifā'a Rāfi' al-Ṭahṭāwī

An Egyptian Lady in Paris (c. 1924)

Two things about Paris that I did not like were the odour of absinthe and cigarette smoke in the cafés, and the smell of the crowds leaving public places or mingling in the streets. The pushing crowds dismayed me because I had thought the French were always courteous. I shall never forget the first time I entered a shop in Paris during a special sale. Seeing the crowd at the front door, I paused to let some people enter, out of politeness as we do in the East, thinking someone in turn would allow me to enter. Unfortunately, not a soul was aware even of my existence. Suddenly, I was swept along by the crush of human bodies, pushed and pulled in a churning mass until I was about to cry. When I finally found myself in front of a counter and gently reached for a piece of material, as a lady would do in the East, someone snatched it from my hands. Once again I was on the verge of tears but held them back to avoid ridicule. Finally, using my arms like oars I made my way through the human sea and escaped from the shop. Upon reaching the curb I hailed a taxi. Before I could enter, however, a bystander jumped in without so much as a word of apology.

—Huda Shaarawi (translated by Margot Badran)

On Causes of the Progress of Europe
and the Backwardness of the Orient,
Though the Human Race Is One

From the eighteenth century onward, Middle Easterners became painfully aware of the growing disparity between European power and wealth and their own weakness and poverty. Many explanations were offered, and many remedies suggested. The following is by an Egyptian writer in the late nineteenth century.

Some say that climate determines human behavior, dooming Easterners to laziness and inaction in the work of civilization, as it directs Europeans to action and enterprise. This argument is disproved by the record of the past. The East too had its periods of science and civilization, from which Europe derived its own civilization, at a time when it was much more backward than the East is today.

Some say that the Islamic religion obstructs progress and that this is the prime cause. . . . They forget that the East is full of other religions beside Islam, with adherents far more numerous than the Muslims, and these are not less but more backward than the Muslims in civilization and science. . . . If it were Islam that obstructed progress, we would see India and China as advanced as Europe, whereas in fact these two countries are much more backward than the Muslims. . . .

Each of the dynasties established in Europe unified its religion and imposed it on its subjects, shedding much blood to achieve the religious unity of society, so that no other religion should survive and give rise to dissension, internal struggles and external intervention. Indeed, Europe was obsessed with religion, filling its schoolbooks on whatever subject with religious words and inscribing the cross, a revered religious symbol, on clothing, crockery, glasses, carpets, bedclothes, utensils, visiting cards and buildings, and even on the lintels of doors, so that a man could hardly look at anything without seeing this holy image—ensuring that religion would be present in everyone's mind at every moment. . . .

Europe did not content itself with religious unity at home. Europeans formed religious associations, trained thousands of priests for them, spent millions in gold on them, and sent them to the East under the protection and the care of their governments. These traveled all over Asia and Africa, propagating their religion. . . .

Europe excelled in corrupting the kings of the East and sowing hostility among them by lies and deceit. . . .

Europe gave writers the freedom to spread their ideas among the nations, so that the ideas of the common people might be enlivened by contact with those of the intellectuals. By this means writers shaped nations, educated them, and brought them up from the depths of ignorance and darkness to the peak of science and light. In this way, states found competent men without it costing them a penny to educate them—writers and scientists educated them. . . .

The European nations having entered upon the paths of knowledge and progress, the men of wealth among them joined to open the strongboxes of finance. From small beginnings they acquired much money and they invested it in factories and trade. Governments helped them by restricting foreign products and trade, so as to promote local products and keep wealth inside the country. By this means wealth grew, the poor were raised to the level of the rich and the states vied in the prosperity of their people and the abundance of their finances.

The Easterners did not follow this path. They amassed fortunes to bury them in the ground or to squander them on pleasure and dissipation. They let their own products perish and used those of Europe. Thus they ruined both crafts and craftsmen and sent their wealth to Europe. . . .

When the states of Europe realized that illiteracy could lead a nation only to ruin and loss of independence, they established education and made it compulsory, so that there are few illiterates even in large states. Each state took measures to standardize education. The nation thus learned the religion and history of its people, its language, manners, and customs and its unifying civil law; the history of the kingdom, the rights of the king and the duty of defending the realm. . . .

The Easterners did not enter this path. They let their nations blunder in blind ignorance, in the absurd belief that educated people would oppose them in what they did. But it was by entrusting authority to the ignorant and the stupid that they achieved this result. So Eastern nations slumbered in negligence and heedlessness, and science and scientists perished. . . .

When the European governments observed that in acting autocratically they often made mistakes, they created councils of ministers and consultative assemblies by which they were ostensibly bound. Responsibilities were placed on notables and elected deputies of the people, to benefit from their ideas. . . .

The Easterners, because of their general ignorance, did not follow this path. Their kings did not trust their notables and did not wish to see the number of intellectuals increase, for fear lest these latter overcome them.

—'Abdallāh Nadīm

Western Dancing (1903)

8th February, 1903. Hamoud Bey, the Mufti's brother, was here today. He has been seriously ill of late through overwork at his legal business. He has been recently given the rank of Bey, and in virtue of his new title was invited the other night to the Khedive's ball, as to which he gave us a naive and amusing account. "I went," he said, "with two friends, men like myself in the legal profession, and we arrived among the first, none of us having ever been at such an entertainment before. As we were depositing our coats and umbrellas, for it had rained, at the vestiary, suddenly I saw in a mirror a sight reflected such as I had never in my life beheld, two women who were standing behind me, naked nearly to the waist. I thought it must have been some illusion connected with my illness and I was very much frightened. Their faces and arms and everything were displayed without any covering, and I thought I should have fallen to the ground. I asked what it meant and whether perhaps we had not come to the right house, but my friends took me on into the ball-room, where they showed me a number more women in the like condition. 'Who are they?' I inquired, and they told me, 'These are the wives of some of our English officials.' 'And their husbands,' I asked, 'do they permit them to go out at night like this?' 'Their husbands,' they answered, 'are here,' and they pointed out to me Mr. Royle, the Judge of Appeal, before whom I had often pleaded, a serious man and very stern, as the husband of one of them. This judge I saw dancing with one of these naked ladies, gay and smiling and shameless, like a young man. 'And he is here,' I said, 'to see his wife thus unclothed? and he dances with her publicly?' 'That,' they answered, 'is not his wife, it is the wife of another.' I was dumbfounded with shame for our profession. Just then I saw Lord Cromer pass by. His coat was unbuttoned and showed his shirt down to here (pointing to his stomach). I did not see Lord Cromer dance, because as I was looking the Khedive entered the room leading another of these ladies, and there was a crush of those near me to look at him. I found myself jammed close to two of the naked ones, their shoulders and bosoms pressed against me. I was terribly ashamed. As soon as I could free myself I called to my companions, 'Come away, my dear friends, this is no proper place for us,' and I took them with me home. We would not stop for the refreshments which were being served and where wine was being poured. The Khedive calls himself a good Moslem. He says he never drinks wine and leads a respectable life, but this entertainment of his was not respectable, and he himself was there, and they tell me that the ladies of his household are allowed by him to look from behind a screen at all these abominations." Such was Hammouda's naive account of his adventure. "My dear fellow," I said, "you do not understand that this is our work of civilizing the East, wait another twenty years and you will see all the Cadi's of Egypt with your brother the Mufti among them, dancing with ladies even more naked than these, and who knows, going with their own heads bare," "I can understand everything," he said, "except this, that the husbands of these ladies were there, actually there, in the dancing room and did not send them home."

—Wilfrid Scawen Blunt

Germans in Turkey (1914–18)

But who was this man in uniform? Fair, his blue eyes were somehow different from the blue of the Eastern eye; there was something hard, metallic, about him, his face, his movements. But Salahaddin Bey was pushing her gently toward the man.

"General Liman von Sanders Pasha—Her Highness Sherifa Musbah!" The man clicked his heels and bowed; then he smiled, sat down and picking up Musbah, placed her on his knees—such hard, bony knees, she thought—and began to show her some pictures in a book. They were becoming quite friendly when Salahaddin Bey returned to take Musbah away.

"She is very fair. So different from Oriental children," the General remarked.

A faint smile came and went on Salahaddin's face. "Her mother is English," he replied.

Musbah felt the man suddenly freeze. A click of the heels, a bow, and then he turned away. She was beginning to learn what racial hate meant.

—Princess Musbah Haidar

English Women and Men (1918)

"The English women, I am told," she said, "are frightened to know that they have a part to their bodies which men like! They are horrified, and even disgusted—not like us Eastern women who are proud to think that our men desire us. An Englishman is starved of all passion, that is why the poor things are always taking exercise."

—Princess Musbah Haidar

A Turkish View of Freedom and Eccentricity (1933)

When Abdulhak Hamit was counselor in the Ottoman Embassy in London, he received an order one day from the palace. Some enemies of the sultan had published a journal in Paris, where, at the sultan's request, the French government had suppressed it. They had moved to London and started printing the same paper. Abdulhak Hamit was instructed to request the English government to show the same courtesy as that of France.

The official at the Foreign Office to whom he applied listened at great length to the Ottoman counselor and then replied, briefly, "Impossible."

"But . . . the French did it for us."

"Maybe," said the Foreign Office official. "The French have a republic, but we have freedom."

During the Great War, some English newspapers began to publish anti-war articles. The government considered the matter carefully. There was no way of imposing censorship, so it prohibited the export of this kind of newspaper from the British Isles. At that time, Jaurès's body had already rotted; Caillaux faced the guillotine.*

Because in 1915, freedom was a hundred years old in France, seven hundred years old in England. . . .

While I was in Paris, I was discussing with a friend the different conceptions of freedom of the two countries. My friend repeated the remark of Chateaubriand: "The French are not for freedom, they are for equality."

Surely, part of the speeches given in Hyde Park would not be permitted by the police in Paris. But in the whole of England you will not find a taxi driver swearing at his customer or a waiter cutting his customer's throat.

A Frenchman who was traveling in Italy got tired of not being able to open his mouth and say anything for weeks on end. Whenever the name Mussolini came to the tip of his tongue, somebody jogged his elbow. When his trip was over, as soon as the train crossed the frontier, he got out of the carriage at the first French station and yelled at the top of his lungs, "Down with the Republic!"

A Frenchman, unless he can demonstrate his freedom by some gesture or word, even when harmful to his country, begins to wonder whether this right has been abrogated.

Because freedom in England is not an adornment but a reality, the Englishman knows that he does not need to talk about it. . . .

[The British Prime Minister Ramsay] MacDonald has come [to the World Economic Conference], gone up to the podium, sat down and struck the table with his gavel. The Siamese delegate who is in front of me does not even raise his head. . . .

---

* Jean Jaurès and Joseph Caillaux were French politicians who adopted pacifist positions and opposed France's entry into World War I. Jaurès was murdered by a fanatic in 1914; Caillaux was accused of providing intelligence to the Germans and imprisoned.

The distinctive feature of postwar conferences is that international problems have been transferred from closed rooms to open halls. In 1914, the representative of the Siamese emperor would have had great difficulty in getting to see the British prime minister. Now a mere secretary can chat with him. You should have seen how the delegates from Africa and Asia, in the early stages, crept stealthily to the meetings by side and back doors, frightened and disbelieving.

They were like a child who approaches a cheap toy, at first frightened and trembling, and then, realizing that it is inanimate, hits it angrily. Now, in the same way, the Siamese shows all his molar teeth in a broad grin, not because he understands, likes or disapproves, but simply to laugh and to convince himself that he can laugh.

[In England] foreigners are not masters, as in India, nor shoddy merchandise to be exploited, as in France. Here they are really parasites. As in France, so also in England, every foreigner struggles to assimilate—to become English, to put on English airs. But this is the place where it is most difficult to get away with it.

In the bird's-eye view of a foreigner, England, like life, consists of pleasant dreams.

Returning, I understand why throughout the nineteenth century, there was such an envious longing for England. The best Frenchman was the one who most resembled an Englishman. Likewise a good Belgian, a choice Russian or Italian. Oh, to be mistaken for an Englishman! The worst and most primitive puppets appeared in Cairo and Pera.*

It can be said that the English have adopted nothing from other nations. But there is a strange contradiction: they have taken their dances and their jazz from the blacks. . . .

What! Aren't you going to the Guildhall?
No. . . .
Quite apart from their dress, it's worth coming to London just to see everyone drinking from the same cup at the lord mayor's table.

I said that English eccentricity is something that makes you afraid to laugh. Face to face, one sitting, one standing, drinking wine from the same cup, wearing a white wig on your head—don't you find this funny?

But you can't laugh, because it is English. The fez of a Tunisian may strike you as funny, but the wig of an Englishman makes you regret that you can't put one on yourself. . . .

---

* The suburb of Istanbul where most of the Europeans live.

Yes, there was also an Ottoman eccentricity. We knew the last tales of the opulent ways of an old empire. An Ottoman whose mansion is burning places a chair before the fire and drinks coffee. When his steward rushes toward the fire to save his jewel box, he stops him from plunging into danger. Today his grandchild would perpetrate some insurance fraud. . . . The concept of the comic and the logical is not missing in England, but it applies only to the poor.

—Falıh Rıfkı Atay

An Egyptian View of Western Civilization (1933)

I admire Gandhi and spiritual leaders like him; I admire every idea that seeks to cleanse humanity from the mire. But I prefer without hesitation a civilization like that of Greece or its stepdaughter, the civilization of Europe after it had freed itself from the yoke of the Middle Ages. This is a civilization midway between spirituality and materialism, a civilization that calls for the unhobbling of the human mind so that it may think without constraint; it encourages philosophy and the study of nature in all its phases and aspects. It is a civilization that stands for beauty and the cult of beauty; it strives for social equality and opens the path of knowledge to the individual in society, enabling him to become an active element in the building of the world while sharing in its progress and enjoying the benefits of this progress, instead of being a dry stone on which the social structure is raised to elevate the privileged few—those who inhabit this structure and who alone enjoy its coolness in the summer and its warmth in winter.

I do not claim that European civilization has reached the heights proclaimed by philosophers and reformers, for alas, these have no weapon but ideas and freedom of thought, while practical men seize on the results of their talents and divert them to their own purposes.

Take, for example, the idea of colonization. From the point of view of pure thought, its purpose is to raise primitive peoples to the level of civilization and allow these peoples to join in the magnificent pageant of humanity advancing for the general good and under the protection of permanent peace. And then see what was done by those clever rogues who covered themselves with its veil and wrapped themselves in its flag and then went out to kill and loot in the name of civilization. No, indeed, I do not say that European civilization has attained the lofty ideal proclaimed by philosophers and reformers, but I greatly admire one manifestation of this civilization: freedom of thought, the permanent self-repairing device of civilization. . . .

In Europe, the individual went out to seek out for truth and beauty until he found the tree of knowledge and ate its fruit. He came to know good and evil and set forth what he had learned in the encyclopedia; his eyes perceived the tyranny of rulers and the remnants of religious bigotry; he denounced regimes by the tongues of Montesquieu and Rousseau and Voltaire and rose up to destroy the Bastille with the hands of the people. He proclaimed the end of arbitrary monarchy with the tongue of Danton and the Jacobins. He strove through the ages, through the mind of his scientists, toward the mastering of nature by the power of steam and electricity and magnetism and radiation. . . . I repeat: whatever the errors it may have committed, the great merit of this civilization is that it possesses an instrument of self-repair, which is freedom of thought.

—Ḥusayn Fawzī

Plagued by the West (1961)

During the nineteenth century, Muslims became increasingly aware of the culture as well as the political, military and commercial power of Europe. Some responded eagerly, learning a European language, reading and translating European books, sometimes even adopting European dress and social usages. Others responded negatively and condemned these alien and infidel innovations. In Arabic-speaking countries, this Westernizing movement was sometimes called tafarnuj, *pretending to be Frankish. In Iran, it was known as* gharbzadegi, *which has variously been translated as* westosis, westitis *and* westoxication. *Like the Frenchified fops in English, German and other European literatures in the period of French cultural ascendancy, the imitator of European ways became a figure of fun in Arabic, Persian and Turkish literature. Sometimes the attack was directed against any and every form of Western influence or borrowing; more often it was concerned with the mindless imitation of everything Western, good, bad and indifferent alike. The following excerpts are drawn from one of the more famous Persian tracts denouncing cultural Westernization.*

An Ass in a Lion's Skin, or a Paper Tiger?

A west-stricken man who is a member of the ruling establishment of the country has no place to stand. He is like a dust particle floating in space, or a straw floating on water. He has severed his ties with the essence of society, culture, and custom. He is not a bond between antiquity and modernity.

He is not a dividing line between the old and the new. He is something unrelated to the past and someone with no understanding of the future. He is
not a point on a line, but an imaginary point on a plane or in space—just like
that dust particle. Of course, you are probably asking: then, how has he
risen to a position of leadership among the people? He has done so through
the pre-determined decree of the machine and the prerequisites of politics
which cannot but conform to the politics of the great nations. In this part of
the world, especially in oil-rich countries, it is customary for that which is
lighter to float to the surface. The wave of events in this type of oil depository only brings the chaff to the surface. It does not have enough power to
touch the bottom of the sea and extract the gems lying there. We in our
west-stricken state with all of its concomitant problems are dealing with
lightweight drifters who float on the wave of events. The ordinary man on
the street is not at fault here; his voice is not heard, his record is clean. He
will go in any direction you point him; that is, he will assume any shape you
train him to. And if you really want to know the truth, this is because the
common man has no voice in determining his own destiny; that is, in order
to determine his destiny, we do not ask him what he thinks or consult with
him. Instead we ask and consult with foreign consultants and advisors; our
situation is this desperate! We are thus plagued by west-stricken leaders
who at times have even gotten an education and traveled to Europe and
America, but if only we were dealing exclusively with the foreign-traveled
and educated in our ruling establishment. But this is not so. As I see it, and
without going into details, it has become customary to have in a position of
power only the "lumpen" from every class or group, the "rejected" elements, the good-for-nothing, the irresolute in countries in this part of the
world, as an unavoidable result. The most disreputable merchants direct
the Bazaar and the Chamber of Commerce. The most useless educators are
the heads of the educational establishment. The most bankrupt of our
money-lenders are our bankers. The most impotent and corrupt individuals
are representatives in parliament. And the most misguided people are the
leaders of the nation. As I said before, disregard the exceptions. The general
rule in these parts is to give authority to the rootless and the spineless; not
to mention the mean and the vile. . . .

Generally the west-stricken man does not have a specialty. He is jack of
all trades and master of none. But since he has studied a bit, read a book or
two, and, perhaps, has gone to school, he knows how to speak convinc-
ingly in any gathering and draw attention to himself. Perhaps he once had
an area of expertise, but after he realized that in this country one cannot get
a piece of the pie with only one area of expertise, he had to dabble in other
areas. Just like one's grandmother, who because of her age and years of

experience knows a little about everything (of course only about old-womanish types of things), the west-stricken man also has a little information on everything (of course, only those things that are good for television, for the committees on education and seminars, for large-circulation newspapers, and for speeches to be given at the club).

The west-stricken man has no personality. He is a creature lacking in originality. He, his house, and his speech are colorless, representative of everything and everybody. Not "cosmopolitan." Never! Rather he is a nowhere man, not a home anywhere. He is an amalgam of individuals without personality and personality without specificity. Since he has no self-reliance, he puts on an act. Although he is a master of politesse and charm, he never trusts those with whom he speaks. And, since mistrust is a watchword of our times, he never reveals his true feelings. The only thing which might give him away and is visible is his fear. Whereas in the West the individual's personality is sacrificed to the requirements of specialization, in Iran the west-stricken man has neither personality nor specialty. Only fear. Fear of tomorrow. Fear of dismissal. Fear of anonymity and oblivion. Fear that he will be discovered for what he is, a blockhead. . . .

—Jalāl Āl-e Aḥmad (translated by Paul Sprachman)

Working Women: A View from Afghanistan (1998)

Men in the West have made women an object of their lusts and desires. They have used them [as] they pleased. When these slaves-of-their-desires had to go to work, to offices and factories, they drafted the women along with them also. Women were made to work in offices, restaurants, shops and factories for the gratification of [male] desires. In this way did the Western man destroy the personality, position and identity of a woman. . . .

The women of the West are laboring under a double burden. One, she is torn by anxiety as to who will look after her in case she remains unmarried. . . . She is thus forced to wander from door to door in search of security. Even in the matter of dress she is exploited. Men wear trousers which cover their ankles, while women are forced to wear skirts with their legs bare in every kind of weather. In the scantiest of dresses, merely a sleeveless blouse and miniskirt, the Western woman can be seen roaming in shops, airports, stations, etc. She is a target for unscrupulous men who satisfy their lust with them—wherever, whenever they please. . . . She has become no less than a bitch, chased by a dozen dogs in heat. If these are the rights of the Western women, then the West is welcome to them.

—www.taleban.com

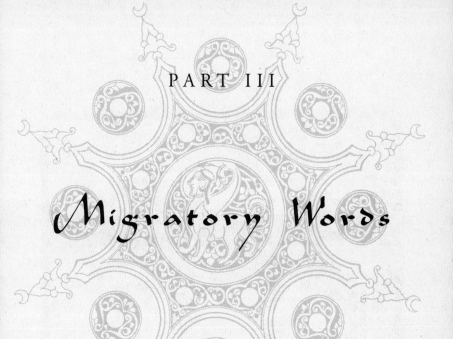

PART III

Migratory Words

What do you read, my lord?
Words, words, words.
—SHAKESPEARE

Handwriting in the shape of a lion by the calligrapher Shāh Mahmūd Nīsābūrī, 1426.

Introduction

English is a magpie of a language, collecting bright and shiny new words from all over the world, wherever English speakers have traveled and trafficked, studied and taught or fought, and bringing them home to adorn its nest. In this, English is quite different from, for example, French, whose authorized custodians are offended by the presence of immigrant words, declare them illegal, and seek to extrude them and replace them with native equivalents. Perhaps this quality of English goes back to our linguistic double heritage, Germanic and Romance— or rather, quadruple, since the Germanic element comes in both Anglo-Saxon and Scandinavian forms, while the Romance element comes both direct from Latin and mediated through Norman French. Thus English speakers can chose among royal, regal, kingly and queenly, big and great and gross and grand, where most other languages have to make do with just one word.

Among Middle Eastern languages, Turkish and Persian are rather like English in this respect. Persian draws heavily on Arabic; Turkish draws heavily on both Persian and Arabic and also shows a considerable openness toward words coming from the West. Arabic, like French, prefers bespoke native words to ready-to-wear imports—that is, in the formal literary language. Colloquial Arabic dialects are less fastidious and use many words of European and latterly also of American origin.

Not a few of the shiny words in the magpie's nest come from the Middle East. They were brought at different times, from different sources, and often served different purposes. Some derive from the Eastern experiences of the Greeks and Romans; others came with Christianity and derive from Hebrew and Aramaic through the Greek, then Latin and then English versions of the Bible. The Old Testament is almost all in Hebrew with some passages in Aramaic; the New Testament is in Greek but with elements of Middle Eastern origin. And in the original Hebrew Bible, as in the Greek and Latin classics, there are still deeper lexical strata dating from Babylon, Sumeria and pharaonic Egypt.

Most of our Hebrew borrowings have a religious connotation and are becoming archaic as old-fashioned religion comes to play a smaller part in modern life. They include such words as cherubim and seraphim, leviathan and behemoth, mammon and manna, hosannah and hallelujah, selah and amen, shibboleth and shekel and the like. Another little-used borrowing is *kabbala,* literally "receiving," a medieval term for Jewish mystical writings. In compensation, modern Hebrew has revived *shekel* and has given us *kibbutz* and *likud,* at opposite ends of the political spectrum.

Some biblical terms are still in common use: sabbath and sabbatical, from a Hebrew verb meaning "to rest"; messiah and messianic, from a Hebrew participle meaning "anointed" (the Greek equivalent is *khristos,* from *khriein,* "to anoint"); abbot and abbey, from a Hebrew or Aramaic word meaning "father"; and a word that has recently acquired a new significance, Satan, both directly from the Old Testament Hebrew and, markedly different, via the New Testament Greek *Satanas.* The Hebrew name of Satan may be related to a verb meaning "to oppose" or "to obstruct," but his parentage is uncertain. The same word also appears in Arabic in the form *shaytān.* Ancient borrowings preserved in the Bible and the classics give us such words as paradise from Persia, pharaoh from Egypt, and dragoman (interpreter), derived via Turkish, Arabic and biblical Aramaic from Assyrian *ragamu,* "to speak," and *rigmu,* "word." Even our common word "sack" probably goes back via Latin and Greek terms for packing material to an Assyrian original.

Also from ancient Assyria, imported via Aramaic, Persian, Greek and Latin, comes "naphtha," a word of portent for the Middle East and for its dealings with the outside world. More obviously—almost emblematically—Middle Eastern is "camel," probably from Hebrew or Phoenician, traveling by the same route via Latin *camelus* and Greek *kamelos.* This quintessential regional beast is known by variants of this name in Arabic and other Semitic languages.

A smaller animal, commonly associated with the region or at least one part of it, gives us a different set of words, this time with a connotation of joy and celebration. The ram's horn, one of the earliest wind instruments, has been used since remote antiquity to proclaim the advent of solemn occasions. Known as the *shofar,* it is still used in synagogues to announce both the coming of the new year and the ending of the fast of Kippur. Another ancient Hebrew word for the ram's horn, *yovel,* is mentioned in Leviticus 25:8–15. It is associated with the sabbath of sabbaths, celebrated every fifty years as a time of emancipation and restoration. In the form "jubilee," it retains the meaning of a fiftieth anniversary. In the form "jubilation," it has a wider meaning of exultant rejoicing.

The flow of Middle Eastern words into Western languages is not confined to scriptural and classical channels. During the Middle Ages, many more lines of communication were opened between Western Christendom and the lands of Islam in the Middle East, North Africa and, for a while, parts of southwestern Europe. The Arabs invaded Spain at the beginning of the eighth century; they were not finally defeated until 1492. The Muslim domination in Spain, Portugal and, more briefly, Sicily made a major contribution to the development of Western science and philosophy, through the translation into Latin of the Arabic versions of Greek philosophic and scientific works, enriched by the commentaries, additions and original writings of Arab and Persian scholars. Many stars are still known by the names that Arab astronomers gave them, like Fomalhaut, "the mouth of the fish"; mathematicians and chemists still use words of Middle Eastern origin like algebra, algorithm, alembic, alkali, azimuth, borax, natron and perhaps also elixir.

The Christian reconquest of Sicily and the Iberian Peninsula closed the channels through which these terms had flowed; later changes in the balance of scientific power between Christendom and Islam reversed the direction of the flow. But in the meantime, new channels were being opened. The Crusades, the attempt by western Europe to recover the lost lands of Eastern Christendom conquered by Islam in the seventh century, achieved some initial successes and ended in total failure, but the long struggle opened many lines of communication, commercial and political as well as military. And as the Crusades drew to an end, a new Muslim attack, this time under Turkish, not Arab, leadership, brought the power of Islam from Asia Minor to the Balkan Peninsula and twice, in 1529 and 1683, as far as the walls of Vienna. The Muslim retreat was followed by the great European counterattack, which brought the Russians, the French, the Dutch and the British into the Islamic lands of Asia and Africa and began the establishment of European empires in much of the Muslim world.

These interchanges brought into the languages of Christendom an immense vocabulary of Middle Eastern words, most of them Arabic, some of them Persian and Turkish. Some of them, in the earlier strata, are scientific and philosophical, reflecting the phase when Europeans were the pupils of masters who lived in such Muslim cities as Toledo in Spain and Syracuse in Sicily. Many are commercial, reflecting the rapidly growing trade between the rival civilizations even while they were in military confrontation.

Some reflect commercial and financial techniques and procedures, like "tariff," "check" and the French *douane,* from Arabic, originally Persian, *dīwān.* Many more are the names of commodities: foodstuffs, such as sugar and candy, oranges and lemons, julep and caviar, artichoke, aubergine, syrup, coffee, saffron, sherbet, tamarind; textiles like cotton, damask, muslin, gauze, mohair, satin, taffeta; flowers like tulip, jasmine and lilac; weapons, like the scimitar, from the Persian *shamshir,* and yatagan. There are other military terms. Some are medieval, like "admiral," from Arabic *amīr al-baḥr,* "commander of the sea," and "arsenal," from Arabic *dār al-ṣinā'a,* "house of crafts"; some are Ottoman, like "uhlan" and "Janissary"; others come from the later stages of European expansion into Islamic lands, such as "lascar," from Persian *lashkar* and/or Arabic *al-'askar,* probably ultimately from Latin *exercitus,* "army"; British Indian "sepoy" and French North African "spahi"—both from Persian *sipāhī,* a cavalryman; "Zouave" (from *Zawāwa,* a North African Berber tribe). Some are animals, either native to the Middle East or coming from remoter lands but first made known to Europeans through Arab intermediaries. They include the albatross, the gazelle, the giraffe, the jackal and the jerboa.

For many of these words, from algebra to zero, from abbot to zenith, their Middle Eastern origin is hidden and unknown. There are many others, however, whose Middle Eastern origin is obvious and whose primary meaning derives from their Middle Eastern connotation. Such, for example, are words specifically connected with the places and personnel of the Muslim religion, such as mosque, minaret and muezzin; of the Muslim law, such as mufti or qadi; or of Muslim beliefs, such as *jihād* and its reward, the houri. Some of these, like sultan and caliph, shah and shahanshah, shaykh and amir, pasha and bey, denote Middle Eastern rulers or lesser dignitaries. Some, like bazaar and caravan, reflect the movement of Middle Eastern trade; others, like turban, caftan, fez and burnoose, items of Middle Eastern clothing. A few, like baksheesh and chicanery, derive from the seamier side of Middle Eastern life.

Sometimes there are both visible and hidden derivatives of the same Middle Eastern term. Our word "turban" obviously comes from the region where this article of headgear is worn—in fact, from the Persian *tulband,* via Turkish. It is less obvious that the name "tulip" is derived from this Perso-Turkish word and that the flower is so called because of its resemblance to a turban.

Sometimes words are not so much borrowed as exchanged. Thus, while "customs" and "customshouse" are designated in several Western languages—e.g., French *douane*—by derivatives of the Arabic/Persian *dīwān,* the term commonly used in the Middle East is *gumruk,* which comes from the Latin *commercium,* via the Byzantine Greek *kommerkion.* Similarly, while our word "alcohol" comes from Arabic, jars of raw alcohol in Arab countries are often labeled *shirto,* from the Latin *spiritus.*

There are a number of words for which an Arabic, Persian or other Middle Eastern origin has been suggested with greater or lesser plausibility. Some may be dismissed out of hand. The sheriff, whether of Robin Hood's Nottingham or of the American West, has nothing whatever to do with the Arabic *sharīf,* which has the general meaning of "noble" and the specific

meaning of a descendant of the Prophet Muhammad. "Sheriff" comes from
the Middle English "shire reeve," the "reeve"—steward, bailiff, or overseer—of the "shire," that is, county. More plausible is the derivation of "al-
manac" from [al-]manākh, but the connection with manākh, a halting place
or way station on a caravan route, is unconvincing. A more probable etymology is the late Greek almenikhiaká, described by the fourth-century
Church father Eusebius as containing "the names of the Lords of the Ascen-
dant and their properties." A suggested derivation of "balcony" from Persian
bālākhāna—bālā, "high," khāna, "house"—is even less plausible. "Balcony" is attested in English in the early seventeenth century and is much
more likely to be related to the word "baulk," in the sense of a beam in a
structure. Another suggested derivative of bālākhāna is the Russian bala-
gan, meaning a show booth at a fair, with an extended connotation of confusion and buffoonery.

The following is a small sample of words of Middle Eastern origin. Some
of them are explicitly and obviously Middle Eastern in their meaning and
connotation. Others may come as a surprise.

Alcove: This comes via French and Spanish from the Arabic qubba, a
dome or dome-shaped edifice, with the definite article al. At some stage, it
acquired the meaning of a vaulted or arched recess.

Amber: This appears to come directly from the Arabic 'anbar, which,
however, means not amber but ambergris, a waxlike ash-colored secretion
from the intestines of the sperm whale, sometimes found floating in tropical
seas. It is used in perfumery and was in earlier times used in cookery. Later
the word was erroneously used in European languages, though not in Arabic, for the translucent yellow fossil resin found principally in the Baltic region. This latter was known to the ancient Greeks and Romans as elektron
and electrum and to the Arabs, both ancient and modern, as kahrabā'. In
the early seventeenth century, Sir Thomas Browne, Sir Isaac Newton and
other scientists sought a name for the attraction of light bodies by friction.
They chose the classical name of amber in which this property was first observed, and called it "electricity." Sometime later, when Arabic writers
sought an Arabic equivalent for this term, they resorted to loan translation
and gave to kahrabā' its modern Arabic meaning of electricity. Meanwhile,
in English and most other Western languages, the yellow resin that first revealed these electrical qualities is still known by the Arabic word for "ambergris."

Aryan: a name originally imported to Europe to designate a family of languages and then misappropriated and misused to promote a racist ideology
and pseudoscience. The Aryans were the kindred peoples who settled in

Iran and India. The name Iran (earlier forms Ērān and Ēryān) records their memory and derives from a genitive plural form, "[the land] of the Aryans," i.e., "the noble." The kindred peoples of Iran and India thus have the oldest and best-authenticated claim to the use of this name. In 1936 Dr. H. Schacht, economics minister of the Third Reich, visited Iran and informed the Iranians that as "pure Aryans" they were not subject to the provisions of the Nuremburg race laws. It was at this time of increasing Nazi influence that Reza Shah decreed that the name "Iran" must henceforth be used in all languages, replacing Persia and its equivalents.

Assassin: Derived from the Arabic *ḥashīshī,* "hashish taker." Here a complete change of meaning has occurred, since the Arabic term carries no connotation of murder, while the assassin of Western usage, though clearly guilty of murder, is innocent on the lesser narcotics charge. The link between the two is a radical Islamic sect that flourished in the Middle Ages. Founded in Iran in the eleventh century, it was extended to Syria, where its activities and, more particularly, the form of armed struggle that it practiced brought it to the attention of the Crusaders. There are various theories about why they were called *ḥashīshī* by their Muslim neighbors. From the context it is clear that this was a term of abuse—probably a comment on their behavior rather than a description of their practices, the implication being that they behaved in a strange and demented way, like hashish addicts. The earliest Western mentions of the name refer exclusively to the medieval Muslim sectaries. The modern generalized use of the term clearly derives from the Crusaders' impressions of their activities.

Baksheesh: From *bakhshīsh,* a Persian word meaning "gift," used by Turks and Arabs as well as Persians to describe any kind of gift, tip or bribe, from the beggar's alms and the porter's gratuity to the pasha's *douceur.*

Candy: See *sugar.*

Carafe: A French loanword in English, itself deriving from Italian *caraffa,* probably from Spanish *garrafa,* a decanter or water bottle. All these words go back to the Arabic verb *gharafa,* which means "to scoop [or spoon or ladle] food or water."

Caravan: This comes from the Persian *kärvän,* which occurs in early inscriptions and texts with the meaning of a group of travelers with their riding and pack animals and their goods, organized in a kind of convoy for protection against attack by bandits or other predators. The caravan carried supplies of food and, if necessary, water and traveled along fixed and known routes, passing through oases where the caravan could, so to speak, refuel. In most of the Middle East, the caravan usually consisted of camels, but horses, mules and donkeys were also used. Wheeled vehicles were, until modern times, extremely rare. From Persian this word passed into virtually all the languages of Europe. The later use of "caravan" in the sense of a covered dwelling on wheels is attested in English in the seventeenth century but appears to have no Middle Eastern antecedents.

A *caravanserai* was an inn or lodging for caravans where merchants, pilgrims, couriers and other travelers could stay overnight. The second part of the name derives from a Persian word meaning "house" or "palace" (see *seraglio*).

Cassock: This word has at various times denoted a soldier's or rider's cloak, a long loose coat or gown, and, in modern times, principally a long and usually black tunic worn by the clergy. In this sense it reached English from French *casaque* (compare Italian *casacca*). The word appears to derive from the western Turkish *kazak* or eastern Turkish *kuzzak*, a nomad, vagabond or adventurer, from a verb meaning "to wander from place to place." The word was brought to Europe by the Turkish-speaking nomads of the steppe. "Cossack," imported via Russian, derives from the same root.

Caviar: This name, along with the delicacy that it denotes, reached Europe via Turkey from Iran. The name appears to be of Iranian origin and is probably connected with a Persian word meaning "egg" and, in modern usage, "testes." It appears among imports to Europe from the Middle East as early as the fifteenth century and may well have been known before that. For Shakespeare it served as a metaphor for elitist taste : "The play, I remember, pleased not the million; 'twas caviar to the general" (Hamlet, II, 2, 465). Bartolomeo Scappi, personal cook to Pope Pius V, mentions it in his manual of gastronomy, first published in Venice in 1570. He writes, "Caviar is made from sturgeon's eggs and is brought from Alexandria and from places on the Black Sea by merchants who pack it . . . in kegs. It is served on hot toasted slices of bread with an eggplant sauce and capsicum."

Check: This word has many meanings: an order to pay money; a pattern on cloth; a call in chess; a minor rebuff or repulse; a control or verification of accuracy, especially of figures; a token of identification. Several of these meanings are remotely interrelated; most of them are ultimately derived from two Persian words.

One of these words is the Persian *chak* or *chek,* which also appears in the Arabic *ṣakk.* Its meanings, according to the classical dictionaries, include a "written acknowledgment of a debt, a written statement of a commercial transaction, purchase or sale, transfer, bargain, contract or the like, a written order for the payment of subsistence money, or of a stipend, salary, pension, or allowance." The use of checks to transfer money was already common practice in the Islamic world in the Middle Ages. In the forms *cheque* and its equivalents, it occurs in most European languages. The German term *Wechsel,* "exchange" or "bill of exchange," may also be of Middle Eastern origin, from the Arabic *waṣl,* which, among other things, means a voucher or receipt.

For two reasons, it seems unlikely that the Western word "check" is derived, as has often been stated, from the Arabic *ṣakk.* The first is that the European word departs considerably from the Arabic form but is much closer to the older Persian word from which the Arabic is derived. The second is that, unlike most of the commercial and financial terms that came with the Mediterranean trade, it does not appear in the Middle Ages, nor does it first occur in the languages of Mediterranean Europe. The Western word "check" is first attested in the late eighteenth century; it first appears in English, from which it seems to have spread to other European languages, reaching most of them only in the nineteenth century. All this makes it very likely that the word was encountered and borrowed in its Persian form, either through the British presence in India or through trade with the Ottoman Empire, where this, along with many other Persian terms, was in common use.

The chess terms "check" and "checkmate" come from a different source, by a different route. The game of chess, probably of Indian origin, came to Europe from the Middle East, where it is already attested in early medieval Persia. "Checkmate" derives clearly and directly from *Shāh māt. Shāh* clearly means "king"; *māt* is less obvious but probably comes from the third person singular past form of the Arabic verb "to die." *Shāh māt* would thus mean "The king is dead." The same game gives us such words as "check" and "checker," relating to the pattern of the chessboard. The British term "exchequer" for the government department concerned with income and expenditure also derived its name from the checkered tablecloth on which, in early times, government accountants did their work with counters.

Chicane, and ***chicanery:*** These words come from *chawgan,* a common word in Persian and several other languages for the game of polo and also for the polo stick. From Iran, the game and the word traveled to Byzantium, where it was known as *tzykanion,* whence the French *chicane.* From this it came to be used, first in the military and then in a larger figurative sense, to convey the idea of taking advantage, however petty or captious, of any accident or opportunity that the game might offer. According to Karl Lokotsch, author of the classical dictionary of European words of Oriental origin (Heidelberg, 1927), the French meaning "trick, hoax, pettifoggery, sharp practice is actually untranslatable [into German] as it denotes an essentially

French characteristic." The word also occurs in a French architectural term, *porte en chicane,* in English known as a "bent entrance." This consisted of two defensive walls with the door entrances not aligned, thus forcing anyone entering the building to walk or ride through the first entrance, then go some distance sideways before reaching the second entrance. The purpose of this arrangement was to break an enemy charge and stop any attacker from advancing through both lines of defense at one time. This useful device, widely used in the Middle Ages, appears to have been forgotten in modern times.

Crimson: From Middle English *crimesin* or *cremesin,* with equivalent forms in French, Spanish, Italian and other European languages. All appear to derive from the Arabic *qirmizī,* which denotes a deep red dye made from the dried bodies of an insect called *qirmiz.* This name, which is of Persian origin, is probably connected with the Persian *kirm* worm, possibly, as has been suggested, in the form *kirm-ī zībā,* beautiful worm. The name of the insect appears in English as early as the seventeenth century in the form "kermes." The dye, it is said, was made from the pregnant female. Another red dye, cochineal, is made from a related species native to Central America.

Divan: From *dīwān,* an Arabic word from the Persian *dīvān.* This word seems to have been first used by Muslims of the public registers of fighters and pensioners maintained in the early days of the Arab conquests. Later, it was extended to government departments generally. According to a popular but early etymology, the name derived from the Persian *dīvāne,* meaning, roughly, "crazy," that is, possessed by a *div,* and was first uttered by one of the ancient shahs of Iran as a comment on a noisy government department he visited. A more likely etymology derives it from an ancient Iranian verb, *dipi,* "to write." *Daftar,* a register or codex, and *dabīr,* a scribe, are from the same root.

In the Ottoman Empire, the imperial divan was a state council presided over in earlier times by the sultan, in later times by the grand vizier; it brought together all the high military, judicial and religious dignitaries of the empire. The term "divan" was also used more generally of the audience held by such a dignitary. *Dīwān* also designates the collected poems of an Arabic, Persian or Turkish poet.

This word reached Europe in several forms and by several routes. The most common English usage, denoting an article of furniture, presumably derives from the halls furnished with couches and cushions in which Western visitors were received in audience by Turkish dignitaries (see also *ottoman*). The bureaucratic and fiscal meaning is reflected in the term for customshouse and customs duty in a number of languages: French *douane,*

Italian *dogana,* Spanish *aduana,* all derived from *dīwān.* The poetic meaning was adopted by Goethe in his *West-Östliche Diwan.*

Gala: In the sense of festive attire, occurs in the same form in French, Italian and Spanish. All of these derive from the Arabic *khil'a,* the name of a special kind of brocaded garment conferred by a ruler on one whom he wished to honor.

Harem: From Ottoman Turkish *ḥarem.* As commonly used in Western languages, this word denotes the women's quarters of an old-style Turkish or other Muslim house. The word conjures up a vision of gorgeously but scantily clad odalisques (see below), guarded by eunuchs and taking turns to service their husband/master/owner. The meaning of the word and the reality it denotes are somewhat different. The term derives from an Arabic root with the basic meaning of "forbid" and with a connotation of awe and inviolability. The commonest derivative is *ḥarām,* "unlawful, sacrosanct, taboo," as opposed to *ḥalāl,* "permitted." Others include *iḥrām,* the state of ritual consecration of a pilgrim in Mecca; *Muḥarram,* the name of the first month of the Muslim year, during which warfare was forbidden in ancient Arabia; *ḥaram,* a sacred enclosure, such as the holy places in Mecca, Medina and Jerusalem; and *ḥarīm,* the closed inner part of a house, including the women's quarters. It is from the last of these that the Turkish word *ḥarem* is derived. The vowels should be pronounced approximately as in "bar them." There is no affinity either of sound or of meaning between *harem* and *harum-scarum.*

Hashish: From *hashīsh,* a classical Arabic noun variously used to denote hay and other dry herbage used as fodder, herbs cultivated or collected for medicinal purposes and weeds that should be removed. It was also used specifically, though by no means exclusively, of cannabis, or Indian hemp. It was apparently this herb or weed that most attracted the attention of European visitors and gave the word its exclusive meaning in European languages. (For another derivative from the same root, see *assassin.*)

Hazard: This word, which reached English from French, is obviously connected with the Spanish *azar,* defined in modern dictionaries as "unforeseen disaster; accident; disappointment; loosing card or throw at dice; impediment; hazard, chance; cushion sides of a billiard pocket." It is usually ascribed to an Arabic origin, though there is some doubt as to which. One suggestion connects it with *zahr,* which in modern Arabic means "dice." It has not, however, as yet been attested in medieval texts in this sense. Other suggestions are *ḥazz,* meaning "luck" or "fortune," and the verb *ḥazara,* "to estimate or appraise."

Lute: The initial *L* is a vestige of the Arabic article, and the name of this musical instrument derives from *al-'ūd*. The word originally had the general sense of "wood, stick, cane, reed or stalk" and was specialized as the name of a stringed musical instrument.

Magazine: From the Arabic *makhāzin,* the plural of *makhzan,* a storehouse or depository. Like many other such loanwords, this occurs in many western European languages and presumably arrived via the Mediterranean trade. The early meaning of the term in European languages was much the same as in Arabic. Later it was used in English—at first as a metaphor, then as a common term—to denote a periodical publication, presumably presented as a "storehouse" of information and entertainment.

Odalisque: A concubine, from the Turkish *odalık,* a derivative of *oda,* a room.

Orange: Perhaps via French, from the Spanish *naranja.* This is derived from the Arabic *nāranj,* which in turn comes from the Persian *nārang.* This denoted a small bitter fruit with attractive flowers used for ornamental, cosmetic and some culinary purposes. The sweet edible orange, long familiar in India and China, was introduced to the Middle East by Portuguese merchants at the beginning of the sixteenth century. This fruit, which in the West is called by the Perso-Arabic name "orange," in the Middle East is denoted by the Arabic, Persian and Turkish forms of the name "Portugal."

Ottoman, also ***Osmanli:***   From Osman (or Othman), the founder of the dynasty that gave the Turkish empire its name. The use of the word to denote the cushioned seat of a sofa presumably derives from the observations and experiences of European visitors to the Ottoman court. Like "divan" in the sense of a piece of furniture, it has no precedent in Ottoman usage.

Pajama (British spelling *pyjama*):   One of a number of words brought to England from India. This name came to English from Urdu and like many Urdu terms was originally Persian. It comes from *pāy,* meaning "foot," and *jāma,* meaning "garment." It originally denoted loose trousers tied around the waist. Later it was extended to include a jacket and restricted to mean garments used for sleep.

Paradise: From the old Persian *pairidaēza,* an enclosure or enclosed area. Already in antiquity, the Persian custom of enclosing, cultivating and maintaining parks and gardens attracted the attention of both the Greeks and the Israelites. Both borrowed the Persian word to describe this otherwise unknown innovation. Xenophon, probably the earliest Greek writer to describe gardens, uses the term *paradaisos,* obviously derived from the Persian. In the Hebrew Bible, the same word appears in the form *pardes* (Song of Songs 4:13; Ecclesiastes 2:5; Nehemiah 2:8). In the Authorized Version, *pardes* is translated as "orchard" in the first two instances and—surprisingly—as "forest" in the third. In some other translations of the Old Testament, *pardes* is rendered by the Greek *paradaisos* and its various Western derivatives. The same term appears in Arabic, probably via Aramaic, in the form *firdaws,* whence the name of the poet Firdawsī, the "Paradisiac." The use of an enclosed and cultivated garden as a metaphor for the delights of Heaven goes back to remote antiquity.

Seraglio: From the Persian *sarāy,* meaning a palace and hence, by extension, the seat of government. The European usage of this word limits the word to the women's quarter of the palace. This has no basis in Middle Eastern usage but appears to derive from the prurient curiosity and fevered imagination of European visitors barely able to conceal their envy.

Sugar and **candy:**   The word "sugar" and its equivalents in other western European languages almost certainly derive from the Arabic *sukkar,* which itself comes from the Persian *shäkär.* The Greek word *sakkharon,* whence "saccharine" and the names for sugar in Russian and other eastern European languages, may come either directly from Persian or from a cognate Indian word.

"Candy" is an Arabic adjectival form, *qandī,* from the Persian *qand,* (crystallized) sugar. Sugar was introduced to Iran from India, and both Persian words, *shäkär* and *qand,* may derive from cognate Indian originals. Sugar was introduced to Europe from the Middle East and remained a major Middle Eastern export to Europe until the eighteenth century, when colonial sugar, transplanted to the new European overseas possessions, came to dominate even Middle Eastern markets.

Zero: From Arabic *ṣifr,* meaning, among several other things, empty, void or vacant and hence, in arithmetical notation, the dot or circle used to indicate naught. The word "cipher" is derived from the same Arabic term. The replacement of the clumsy numbering of the Greeks and Romans by positional decimal notation with a sign for zero was perhaps the most important mathematical innovation of the Middle Ages. These numbers, which originally came from India, were taken to Europe by the Arabs and were therefore known to Europeans as "Arabic numerals."

PART IV

Travelers

> . . . the misled and lonely traveller.
> —MILTON

The Dome of the Rock in Jerusalem, sometimes incorrectly called the Mosque of Omar; painting by David Roberts, 1839.

Introduction

Since Roman times, there has been an unending stream of visitors from Europe and later from further west to the lands of the Middle East. They were impelled by a number of motives. One of them, for long the most compelling, was religion. For both Christians and Jews, the holiest places of their faith were in biblical Judea, which the Romans renamed Palestine. Under Roman rule, both Christians and Jews were subject to alien authority. With the conversion of the Emperor Constantine and therefore of the Roman Empire to Christianity, Christians, provided they belonged to an approved church, could go freely, while Jews were worse off than before.

In the seventh century, the advent of Islam and the advance of Muslim power brought a major change, and Palestine, along with the rest of the Levant and the whole of North Africa, passed from Christian to Muslim control. Now Christians, like Jews, could visit their holy places only subject to the consent and under the authority of an alien faith. For Jews, who offered no competition and no threat, this was manageable. For Christians, representatives of a rival world power, the pilgrimage to Christian holy places under Muslim rule was both a hardship and a challenge.

These old Christian lands had become Muslim through the jihād—the holy war of the faith—and in time the Christians responded with a holy war of their own, the Crusade, the purpose of which was to recover the lost holy places of Christendom from their Muslim masters and return them to Christian rule. The Crusades lasted for several centuries and, for a while, resulted in the establishment of Christian principalities along the Levant coast. They ended in total and final failure.

Along with the pilgrim and the Crusader, both inspired by religion, came a third traveler, in the long run more important than either: the merchant, of whom more later.

The Turks, who by the thirteenth century finally succeeded in evicting the Crusaders, continued their advance into Europe, where, under the leadership of the Ottoman dynasty, they established a mighty empire whose armies twice reached as far as Vienna. Though Muslim rule in Spain was ended in 1492, Muslims continued the naval jihād against European Christendom in the Mediterranean and beyond. Great numbers of European captives, male and female, were still offered for sale in the slave markets of the Islamic world—no longer brought as merchandise by unscrupulous fellow countrymen but taken as booty of war by the Ottoman armies in southeastern Europe or by the Barbary Corsairs in the sea-lanes and along the coastlines of the West. Most of these slaves were eventually converted to Islam and merged into the general population. But some escaped or were ransomed and returned to their countries of origin; some of them left accounts of their adventures and experiences while in captivity.

The eighteenth century brought a new kind of traveler: the gentleman—and sometimes even the lady—performing the grand tour. Normally this was limited to western and southern Europe, but increasing numbers extended their travels to the lands of the Ottoman sultan, in which it was now deemed reasonably safe for Europeans to travel. Some of the most intriguing travel records come from such travelers.

The Crusades were over and almost forgotten, but the religious traveler reappeared in a new form: the missionary. Converting Muslims to Christianity was, in principle, impossible. Apostasy is a crime punishable in Muslim law by death—both for the apostate and for his seducer. But Muslim authorities had no objection to Christians changing their allegiance from one church to another, and during the religious wars in Europe that followed the Reformation, both Catholics and Protestants had an interest in winning recruits among the many independent churches of the East that in principle belonged to neither the one camp nor the other. First Catholic and later Protestant missions became active among the Eastern Christians, and left considerable records of their activities.

As noted in the previous chapter, Muslims had little incentive to visit the West. They did, however, travel to the more hospitable lands beyond their eastern and southern frontiers, and—more important—within the vast realms of Islam. For Christians and Jews, pilgrimage to Jerusalem was meritorious but optional; for Muslims, pilgrimage to Mecca, at least once in a lifetime, was one of the five basic obligations of the faith. The pilgrimage, often linked with a variety of other purposes, gave rise to a rich literature. The most famous of these pilgrims was Ibn Baṭṭūṭa, a native of Morocco, who is sometimes referred to as the Traveler of Islam. Some of his exploits in Turkey, Iran and India are recorded in the pages that follow.

Another—and, for a brief interlude, a major—group of travelers consisted of those who went in the service of their governments. At first these were mostly diplomats, supplemented as is normal by spies. These will be discussed in the next chapter. With the rapid expansion of European imperial power in the nineteenth and twentieth centuries, both direct and indirect, great numbers of other Europeans, principally Englishmen, Frenchmen and Russians, began to play an active and sometimes a dominant role in Middle Eastern affairs. They too left some record of their activities and experiences.

Finally, one other group of Western visitors to the Middle East deserves a mention: the scholars. Already in the Middle Ages, small numbers of intrepid Westerners found their way to the great capitals of the Islamic world in order to learn Arabic and, through the medium of Arabic books and lectures, to gain some knowledge of philosophy and science, in which the Islamic world was then far more advanced.

By the end of the Middle Ages, the balance of exchange between the two worlds, in knowledge and ideas as well as in commodities and services, was shifting to the advantage of the West. The age of the great discoveries—of the world by the explorers, of scholarship and science by the exponents of the new learning—swiftly and inexorably moved Europe ahead in almost every significant field of knowledge, and European students no longer needed to travel to the Middle East to study the sciences. If anything, the reverse was true, though it took some time before Middle Easterners realized this and acted on that realization.

But the students and the scholars still came—no longer learning Arabic as an instrument to acquire other sciences but for the sake of Arabic itself, as a key to the riches of Islamic civilization in all its aspects. As Hellenists studied the civilization of Greece, as Romanists studied the civilization of Rome, so these used the same philological and historical methods to study the civilizations of the Orient. They came to be known as "Orientalists."

To some critics, the Orientalists are the deadliest of all the plagues the West has visited on the East, combining the worst features of the missionary, the Crusader, and the imperialist. Others have taken a more benign view and drawn attention to their immense contribution to the recovery and documentation of Arabic, Persian and Turkish cultures. A contribution uniquely theirs was the recovery of lost civilizations—Babylon, Persepolis, Pharaonic Egypt—through the decipherment of ancient and forgotten languages. For better or for worse, the Orientalists and their various successors have also contributed to the literature of travel, and although their productions in this area are perhaps less significant than those of others, they nevertheless deserve a place in this sequence.

Until comparatively modern times Middle Eastern visitors to Europe were few in number and sparing in their comments; excerpts from their writings will be found in Chapter 2. Middle Eastern Muslims were far more willing to travel south and east, to Africa and Asia, where they found a more tolerant environment and greater opportunities both to engage in commerce and to spread their faith. In time, by the normal combination of conquest, colonization and conversion, they were able to build up vast new Muslim communities, for whom Arabic was both a scriptural and a classical language.

The literature of travel is remarkably uneven in quality, and some travelers did indeed devote much effort to denouncing the foolishness of their predecessors and contemporaries. But sometimes, because they needed to explain to a Western reader things that would have been self-evident to a Middle Eastern reader, they provide information not readily available elsewhere. Perhaps their greatest value is as a source for the history not of realities, but of perceptions.

On Travel (1876)

It is not everyone who knows how to travel; nor is it everyone who knows how to love, to feel, and to understand. It is not everyone who can see beneath the surface of things, and read the significance of the changing background and the novel scenes that meet his gaze, any more than it is given to everyone to interpret the inner meaning of a Beethoven sonata, or a picture by da Vinci or Veronese, or the Venus of Arles, or the Passion of Bianca Capello.

—Count Gobineau (translated by J. Lewis May)

On Travelers (1717)

Your whole Letter is full of mistakes from one end to 'tother. I see you have taken your Ideas of Turkey from that worthy author Dumont, who has writ with equal ignorance and confidence. 'Tis a particular pleasure to me here to read the voyages to the Levant, which are generally so far remov'd from Truth and so full of Absurditys I am very well diverted with 'em. They never fail giving you an Account of the Women, which 'tis certain they never saw, and talking very wisely of the Genius of the Men, into whose Company they are never admitted, and very often describe Mosques, which they dare not peep into. The Turks are very proud, and will not converse with a Stranger they are not assur'd is considerable in his own Country. I speak of the Men of Distinction, for as to the Ordinary Fellows, you may imagine what Ideas their Conversations can give of the general Genius of the people. . . .

Since my Last I have stay'd quietly at Constantinople, a city that I ought in Conscience to give Your Ladyship a right Notion of, Since I know You can have none but what is Partial and mistaken from the writings of Travellers. 'Tis certain there are many people that pass years here in Pera* without having ever seen it, and yet they all pretend to describe it.

—Lady Mary Wortley Montagu

---

* The European name of a suburb of Istanbul where most of the diplomats and other Europeans lived (see Melville's warning on p. 160).

Hints to Travelers in the East (1847)

The following observations may be of use to those about to visit Egypt and Syria, as the state of affairs in these countries is hourly changing, and the latest intelligence is always of some value. . . .

The first class boats cost from £16 to £35 a month, including the pay of the twelve or fourteen sailors, who find themselves in every article of food, dress &c. If you take an Arab boat, it is far better to engage her by the job, stipulating to be allowed to remain wherever you please at a certain rate per day extra. This course avoids much delay and annoyance, caused by the devices of the Arabs to prolong the journey when taken by time. . . .

Your comfort during your stay in the East will depend mainly on your dragoman. These men offer themselves to you at Malta in swarms, but I am inclined to think that an Egyptian is preferable in his own country. It is well to engage your dragoman only on the recommendation of some European on whom you can rely. A Maltese dragoman charges a dollar a day: an Egyptian half that sum. You require two servants exclusive of the crew, one to cook, the other to attend you on your expeditions. . . .

The best route to Syria is through the desert by Suez and Mount Sinai, to Petra and Hebron. Our consul is the only person to be depended upon for making arrangements with the Bedouin to conduct you through the desert. The journey as far as Hebron or Jerusalem is performed on dromedaries; thenceforward on horses. Besides the interest of this route, you avoid a fortnight's quarantine, which you would have to undergo at Beyrout, in sailing thither from an Egyptian port. . . .

If you purpose only to visit Egypt, books are almost the only necessary you need take from England. Guns and wire cartridges for the various wildfowl; rifles and iron bullets for wild boars and crocodiles will suggest themselves to the sportsman. A camera lucida is of great use in taking a view of the complicated details of Egyptian architecture in a short time. Powder, books, and stationery are the three great essentials for the Egyptian traveller; they are scarcely to be procured after leaving Malta.

The traveller who proposes to visit Syria should in the first place endeavour to procure the Sultan's firman, which will be sent from Constantinople to meet him at Cairo, Jerusalem, or Beyrout. An English saddle and holsters, spurs and pistols, are indispensable. A small strong canteen is the only other English article of much importance. I am inclined to think that with regard to dress there is nothing like the turban of the country, a blouse of coloured camlet, (not green, which sometimes provokes indignation, as the sacred colour of the Moslem) a pair of loose doe-skin pantaloons, and half or Hessian boots, of tan leather, (black attracts the sun, and can't well be cleaned) will make the most convenient and comfortable costume.

The most convenient commissariat consists of macaroni, rice, and preserved meats, which should be taken from England in small packages. They are to be had, however, at Alexandria and Beyrout. Wine, porter, and liqueurs should be bought at Malta; the latter, particularly maraschino, are greatly prized by the Turkish governors, &c., and is the most popular present, except gunpowder. This, if good, is the most valuable present you can make, either to Oriental or to European.

A small medicine-chest is useful; but for all practical purposes, some calomel, quinine, ipecacuanha, Seidlitz powders, sticking-plaster, and a lancet, are sufficient. It would be well to have a measurement of the quantities for each dose made by some medical man who has visited the East, as the effect of medicine upon the system varies considerably with the climate. The principal use of remedies is for the people among whom you travel: temperance and your mode of life almost preclude illness, except the fevers of the country, from yourself; common caution will guard against these, and in most cases the severe but delightful action of a Turkish bath will remove any unpleasant sensation caused by suppressed perspiration, which is the chief if not the only danger of the climate.

The following articles are useful in Egypt:—Levinge's apparatus for keeping off vermin. Saddle, holsters, cloak-straps, spurs. Hammer, gimlets, nails, screws, thermometer, and compass. Fishing-rods, and strong tackle for the Nile. Gun, shot, powder, caps, strong fishing-tackle, wire cartridges. Sale's Koran, Arabic grammar, Assad-y Kayat's Vocabulary, and all sorts of books. Pencils, paper, all stationery, and lamps. Mackintosh beds are a great luxury, and are always clean. Cartridges for pistols, and wooden ramrod fixed in holsters to keep in the charge. Porter, potatoes, and Irish salt butter, from England. Sherry, from Gibraltar. Wine and liqueurs, macaroni, and ship biscuit; coarse check shirts, and duck trowsers, from Malta. . . .

With respect to money, letters of credit are preferable to any other mode. The bankers at Malta and Alexandria manage so as to lay a heavy deduction on circular notes. You receive for the latter about 96 per cent from the bankers. For bills cashed by merchants, you receive from 104 to 105½ per cent. About £50 a month cover all the expenses that the traveller, unless very luxurious, can require in the East; for two or more travelling together, I should think the expense was nearly half the above.

It is well to make your dragoman your purse-bearer; make him strictly accountable to you, but never pay with your own hands. Insist on the most profound respect; preserve your temper and nonchalance as your best title to influence and security. Never join in a row; let your people fight it out: if you must act, do so firmly, boldly, and fearlessly of consequences: there *are* no consequences that can concern a right-minded Frank. It is too frequently the habit among our countrymen to dress ludicrously or meanly. This is a great mistake, and militates much against the wearer. In the East, dress is naturally looked upon as a test of the wearer's quality, and he cannot be surprised if he is treated accordingly.

The English traveller should always remember that he is considered by the Orientals as a representative of his country; and that, according to his liberality, courage, and temper, impressions are formed of the nature [*sic:* probably an error for "nation"] he belongs to, from which the East is now expecting great things. The people of the West are known to the people of Egypt and Syria only as *Frangee,* or Franks, and *Ingeleez,* or English, and I think I may venture to say that they make a wide difference in favour of the latter, which it behoves every British traveller to maintain.

—Eliot Warburton

Salute to the Orient (1936)

Salute to the Orient! Given at Port Said presumably, where the statue of M. de Lesseps points to the Suez Canal with one hand and waves in the other a heavy bunch of large stone sausages. "Me voici!" he gesticulates, adding "Le voilà" as an afterthought. Voilà Egypt and Africa to the right, Syria and Asia to the left, while in front of M. de Lesseps is the sausages' outcome, the narrow trough that he has contrived across the sands to the Red Sea. It leads rather too far, that trough, to the mouths of the Indus and the Ganges, unmanageable streams. Nearer Port Said lie trouble and interest enough, skies that are not quite tropic, religions that are just comprehensible, people who grade into the unknown steeply, yet who sometimes recall European friends.

Prayers to be offered up after saluting the Orient. Numerous prayers.

May I never resemble M. de Lesseps in the first place; may no achievement upon an imposing scale be mine, no statistics, philanthropy, co-ordination or uplift. Good deeds, but scattered deeds, that shall be remembered for a few years only, like a wayside tomb. Oh, deliver my soul from efficiency! When obstacles cease to occur in my plans, when I always get the utmost out of Orientals, it will be the surest proof that I have lost the East.—A prayer against impropriety may follow—against hashish, almées, odalisques, the cancan;

coupled with a prayer against propriety, which is more difficult to frame. Beware of impeccable introductions. Seek not that which is best in native society, for it leads to mutual log-rolling, not to the best. "Sons of the Desert, I too am a gentleman. All hail!" This will not do at all.—Then there is the prayer against cynicism which if a man forget he shall be damned, shall not even notice the sunlight in time, or that the sea is dark blue and the sky light blue, or that there are kites in Cairo and none in Alexandria. So when the old residents say to me, as they will, "There is no such country as the Orient, there is only Dagoland": I must reply to them: "you may be right, but I must gain my own disillusionment, not adopt yours; you know much, I nothing, yet I cannot learn from you." Oh, reject the bitter tradition of mistrust that is served to the newcomer with his first cocktail, reject the little hints that the Club provides, so helpful in detail, so harmful in bulk! In India the tradition has lasted too long, the bitterness is irremediable, the hints have usurped the whole of speech. But in this nearer East there is still hope. Cynicism has not yet won, and I may help to defeat it. There's a nobler literature anyhow; Kinglake, Morier, Doughty, Blunt, Lucie Duff-Gordon discovered more than Dagoland: they found gravity and mirth here, also health, friendship, peace. . . .

The above prayers are all negative, dangers to avoid, fears to overcome. They are clinched by a prayer which is positive and which seems their contradiction: a prayer for dignity and impressiveness. The perfect traveller whom we are building up is a charming creature, with every advantage of heart and head, but he is diffident, and diffidence will not succeed in the East. Unless I have a touch of the regal about me, a glint of outward armour, my exquisite qualities will be wasted, my tact and insight ignored. The East is a bit of a snob, in fact. It does require its sympathizers to seem great as well as to be good, and I must do my best to oblige it in this little matter; so may I be mistaken for a king!

Moreover, it is desirable to be young. But this, alas! cannot be phrased as a prayer. "God," says a cruel Egyptian proverb, "has given earrings to those who have no ears," and few elderly travellers have escaped this irony of Allah's. They have letters of introduction and facilities, but not ears in any useful sense, and the jewels that they bring back are "I am much struck with the alterations in Bethlehem—not to say improvements, since my previous visit in 1885," or "representative institutions should be introduced into the Oasis of Siwa," or "after an interesting conversation with the Mufti, in which Henry acted as interpreter, Lucy and I proceeded to inspect the so-called tomb of Potiphar's wife." Elderly travellers don't write *Eothen*. It is hard to be generous and direct after thirty, even when the desire to be so remains, and even in England. And it is harder in the East. Prejudices or ideals (they amount to the same under a vertical sun) will arise in the mind and distort the horizon and slop pieces of sky into the sand. Only in youth or through memories of youth, only in the joyous light of the morning, can the lines of the Oriental landscape be seen, and the salutation accomplished.

—E. M. Forster

Looking the Other Way

Travelers from the Middle East mostly ventured into Africa and explored their own Orient, in China, India and the islands. Of the two following excerpts the first comes from an anonymous Arabic account of India and China, probably written in the early ninth century; in the second, a tenth-century author describes an adventure—or rather, misadventure—in Africa.

India and China

The Chinese and the Indians kill the animals they want to eat. They do not slaughter them but hit them on the head until they die. The Indians and the Chinese do not wash themselves after sexual intercourse, and the Chinese, after stool, only wipe themselves with paper. The Indians wash every day before breakfast and then eat. The Indians do not come to their wives during their periods but expel them from their houses in aversion. The Chinese come to their wives during their periods and do not expel them. The Indians use toothpicks, and no one among them eats without using a toothpick and washing himself. The Chinese do not do this.

India is twice as big as China and has more kings, but China is more populous. Neither the Chinese nor the Indians have date palms, but they have other trees and fruits which we have not. In India they have no grapes, and in China they have few; other fruits are numerous among them, and there are very many pomegranates in India.

The Chinese have no science, but the basis of their cult comes from India; they believe that the Indians gave them their Buddhas and that they are the people of religion. In both countries they believe in reincarnation and differ only in the details of their religion.

There is medicine and philosophy in India, and the Chinese also have medicine. Their medicine consists chiefly of cauterization [acupuncture?]. They have knowledge of astronomy, but the Indians have more. I know of no one on either side who is a Muslim or who speaks Arabic.

The Indians have few horses; the Chinese have more. The Chinese have no elephants and do not allow them in their country, regarding them as ill omens. . . .

The Chinese are better-looking than the Indians and more closely resemble the Arabs in dress and in the animals which they ride. In their appearance and in their ceremonies they resemble the Arabs. They wear coats [qabā] and belts, while the Indians wear two pieces of cloth, and both men and women adorn themselves with gold bangles and precious stones.

—*Akhbār al-Ṣīn wa'l-Hind*

An African Adventure (922–23)

Ismā'īlūya and several sailors told me that he had sailed from 'Umān on board his ship bound for Qanbaluh in the year 310 [922–23 C.E.], but the ship was carried off course by a violent wind and taken to Sufāla in the land of the Zanj [East Africa]. "When I had examined the place," said the ship's captain, "I realized that we had come to the land of the man-eating Zanj and that to land in this place was certain death. We therefore made our ablution, repented of our sins to Almighty God, and recited the prayer for the dead for one another. Canoes surrounded us and led us to an anchorage, where we entered, cast anchor, and went ashore with these people. They took us to their king. We found a young man, handsome for a Zanji and well built. He asked us about ourselves, and we told him that our destination was his country. 'You lie,' he said, 'you were bound for Qanbaluh and not here. The storm caught you and carried you to our country.' 'It is so,' we said, 'but we spoke as we did only in order to please you.' 'Unload your goods,' he said, 'and carry on your trade. You have nothing to fear.' We therefore opened our bales and did very good business. He imposed no tax on us, in kind or in cash, and when we gave him some presents, he gave us presents of equal or greater value.

"We stayed in his country for several months, and when it was time to go, we asked his permission, which he gave us. We therefore loaded our goods and wound up our business, and when we decided to leave, we informed him. Rising from his throne, he walked with us as far as the shore with a group of his companions and his slaves, embarked on a canoe, and came aboard our ship with us. He came on board with seven of his chief slaves. When they were on board ship, I said to myself, 'This king would be worth 30 dinars at auction at 'Umān and his seven slaves 160 dinars. They are wearing clothes worth 20 dinars, which would bring us at least 3,000 dirhams—and this would do us no harm at all.' So I shouted to the sailors,

and they hoisted the sail and raised the anchors while he was still expressing his friendship and goodwill and inviting us to return and promising to
treat us well when we did so.

"When the sails were hoisted and he saw that we were on our way, his
face changed. 'You are leaving,' he said, 'I bid you farewell,' and he rose to
go back to his canoe. But we cut the cable joining us to the canoe, and we
said to him, 'You will stay with us and we will take you to our country and
reward you for your kindness to us and repay you for what you have done
for us.' 'Good people,' he cried. 'When you came to me I could, as my people desired, have let them eat you and take your goods, as they did to
others. But I treated you well; I took nothing from you and even came to bid
you farewell on your ship as a mark of esteem from me to you. Therefore
give me my due and take me home.' We paid no attention to what he said
and took no notice of him. The wind was strong, and before very long his
country disappeared from sight, and by nightfall we were in the open sea.
The king and his companions were put with the other slaves, about two
hundred head, and we treated him in the same way as the other slaves. He
kept aloof and neither answered nor spoke to us. He ignored us as if he did
not know us, nor we him. When we got to 'Umān, we sold him and his companions along with the other slaves.

"In the year 31, we again left 'Umān bound for Qanbaluh, and the wind
carried us away to Sufāla in the land of the Zanj, and without telling any lies,
we arrived at the very same place. As soon as the people saw us, they came
out and their canoes surrounded us. This time we really were convinced
that we were lost, and we none of us said a word to one another, so great
was our fear. We made our ablution, recited the prayer for the dead, and
bade each other farewell.

"They came, seized us, brought us to the dwelling of their king and led
us in—and there was the very same king, seated on his throne as if we had
left him but a moment before. When we saw him, we fell prostrate and our
strength left us, so that we could not move ourselves to stand up. 'You are
my friends,' he said, 'no doubt about it.' None of us could speak, and all our
limbs trembled. 'Look up,' he said. 'I give you my pledge of safety for your
persons and your property.' Some of us looked up; others could not,
through weakness and shame. But he spoke to us in a friendly way until we
all raised our heads. We did not look at him, in our shame and fear.

"When, thanks to his promise of safety, we had recovered our composure, he said to us, 'Betrayers! I treated you as I did, and you repaid me by
treating me as you did!' 'Despise us, O King,' we cried, 'and forgive us.' 'I
have already forgiven you,' he replied. 'Carry on your trade as you did that
time; there is nothing to stop you.'

"Our joy was such that we could not believe what we heard, and we thought that this was a trick to get our goods ashore. We brought them ashore, and we offered him a present of great value, but he refused it, and said, 'I have not enough regard for you to accept a present from you, nor do I wish to render my own possessions unlawful by taking anything from you, for all that you possess is tainted.'

"We therefore carried on our trade, and when it was time to go, we asked his permission to load the ship, which he gave us. When we had decided to set sail I said, 'O King, we have decided to sail.' And he replied, 'Go under the protection of God.' 'O King,' I said. 'You have treated us better than we could ever repay, and we betrayed and wronged you. But how did you manage to escape and return home?'

" 'When you had sold me in 'Umān,' he said, 'the man who bought me took me to a town called Basra' (which he described). 'There I learned prayer, fasting, and also a little of the Qur'ān. Then my master sold me to another who took me to the city of the king of the Arabs, which is called Baghdad' (then he described Baghdad), 'where I learned to speak correct Arabic, learned the Qur'ān, and prayed with everybody in the mosques. I saw the caliph, who is called al-Muqtadir [reigned 908–32]. I stayed in Baghdad for a whole year and part of the next year. Then some people came from Khurāsān, mounted on camels. Seeing their great number, I asked who they were and why they had come, and they said they were on their way to Mecca. I then asked, "What is this Mecca?" And they said, "In it is the holy house of God, to which people go on pilgrimage," and they told me about this house. I said to myself, "I must follow these people to this house" and I told my master what I had heard, but I saw that he wished neither to go himself nor to let me go. I therefore pretended to think no more of it until the people had left, and when they did so I followed them and accompanied a group of travelers whom I served all the way. I ate with them, and they gave me two garments which I wore as the ritual dress of a pilgrim. They instructed me in the rites of the pilgrimage, and Almighty God helped me to complete my pilgrimage.

" 'Fearing to return to Baghdad, where my master would catch me and put me to death, I left with another caravan bound for Egypt. On the way I served some people, who took me with them and gave me a share in their provisions as far as Egypt.

" 'When I reached Egypt and saw this sea of sweet water which they call the Nile, I asked whence it came and they told me that its source lay in the land of the Zanj. "And in what part?" I asked. "In a part of Egypt," they said, "which is called Aswān, on the border of the land of the black people." So I followed the bank of the Nile, going from place to place, begging from people, and they fed me. Such was my way.

" 'Then I came among some black people who turned against me. They put me in chains and burdened me, along with other slaves, with more than

I had the strength to bear. So I fled and fell into the hands of others who seized me and sold me. I fled again, and so I went on, from the time I left Egypt until I reached a certain place in the land of the Zanj.

" 'There I disguised and hid myself, for from the time when I left Egypt, in spite of all my terrifying experiences, I was never so much afraid as when I found myself now near to my own country. In my own country, I thought, another king would have gained the kingship and would be sitting in my place. The soldiers would obey him, and it would be hard to wrest the kingship from him. If I showed myself or if anyone got to know of me, I would be taken to him and he would put me to death, or else some loyal supporter would make bold to cut off my head and use it to show his loyalty.

" 'I was frightened beyond endurance. I began to hide by day and hurry by night in the direction of my country, until I reached the seashore. There I took passage in disguise on a ship to such and such a place. Then I embarked again for another place, and the ship landed me at night on the shore of my own country. I made inquiries of an old woman. "Is your present reigning king just?" I asked. "By God, my son," she answered, "we have no king other than Almighty God." And she told me everything that had happened to their king. I expressed my astonishment as if I knew nothing about it and as if I were not myself that king. Then she said, "The people of the kingdom agreed among themselves that they would not have any king after him until they knew what had happened to him and until they despaired of his life, for their diviners had informed them that he was alive and well in the land of the Arabs."

" 'The next morning I came to this my town and entered this my palace and found my family just as I had left them, except they were full of sadness, as were also my subjects. I told them my story, and they marveled and rejoiced and joined with me in entering the religion of Islam. I became their king again one month before your arrival and am now full of joy and happiness that God has blessed me and my subjects with Islam and true faith and with the knowledge of prayer, fasting, and pilgrimage, of what is permitted and what is forbidden. I have thus attained what was never before attained by anyone in the land of the Zanj. Therefore I forgive you, since you were the cause of my coming to the true religion. There is only one other matter which weighs on me, and I ask God to release me from the sin.' I asked him what it was, and he said, 'My master. I left Baghdad for the pilgrimage without his permission or his consent, and I did not return to him. If I could find a reliable man, I would send him the price which he paid for me and ask him to accord me my liberty. If you had been honest and trustworthy men, I would have paid you my purchase price and asked you to remit it to him, and I would have given him ten times more as a gift in return for the patience which he showed me. But you are men of treachery and cunning.'

"We bade him farewell, and he said, 'Go. And if you come again, I will treat you in the same way and even more generously. Tell the Muslims to come to us, for now we are their brothers, Muslims as they are. As for accompanying you on board, I prefer not.' We bade him farewell and left."

—Buzurg ibn Shahriyār

The Traveler of Islam (Fourteenth Century)

This title is sometimes given to Ibn Baṭṭūṭa, certainly the most famous traveler of the Middle Ages. Starting from his native Morocco, he traveled extensively in Africa, through the Middle East, to India, Southeast Asia and China. The record of his travels is a major source—sometimes the only source—of information on many of the countries through which he passed.

In Turkey

The traveler discovers a new and strange conveyance: a four-wheeled cart.

These people call a waggon *araba*. They are waggons with four large wheels, some of them drawn by two horses, and some drawn by more than two, and they are drawn also by oxen and camels, according to the weight or lightness of the waggon. The man who services the waggon rides on one of the horses that draw it, which has a saddle on it, and carries in his hand a whip with which he urges them to go and a large stick by which he brings them back to the right direction when they turn aside from it. There is placed upon the waggon a kind of cupola made of wooden laths tied together with thin strips of hide; this is light to carry, and covered with felt or blanket-cloth, and in it there are grilled windows. The person who is inside the tent can see [other] persons without their seeing him, and he can employ himself in it as he likes, sleeping or eating or reading or writing, while he is still journeying. Those of the waggons that carry the baggage, the provisions and the chests of eatables are covered with a sort of tent much as we have described, with a lock on it. When I decided to make the journey, I prepared for my own conveyance a waggon covered with felt, taking with me in it a slave girl of mine, another small waggon for my associate 'Afīf al-Dīn al-Tūzarī, and for the rest of my companions a large waggon drawn by three camels one of which was ridden by the conductor of the waggon.

In Iran

The author describes the gardens and other delights of Isfahan.

We travelled on for the whole of this day between orchards and streams and fine villages with many pigeon-towers, and after the time of the 'aṣr prayer we reached the city of Iṣfahān, also called Iṣpahān, in Persian 'Irāq. The city of Iṣfahān is one of the largest and fairest of cities, but it is now in ruins for the greater part, as the result of the feud there between the Sunnīs and the Rāfiḍīs, which continues to rage between them still to the present day, so that they never cease to fight. It is rich in fruits, among them being apricots of unrivalled quality which they call *qamar al-dīn;* the people there dry these apricots, and preserve them, and their kernels when broken open disclose a sweet almond. Others of its products are quinces that are un-equalled for goodness of taste and size, delicious grapes, and the wonderful watermelons whose like is not to be found in the world, except for the water-melons of Bukhārā and Khawārizm. Their rind is green, and the inside is red; they are preserved as dried figs are preserved in the Maghrib, and are ex-ceedingly sweet. When anyone is not used to eating these fruit, they relax him on his first experience of them—and so indeed it happened to me when I ate them at Iṣfahān.

The people of Iṣfahān have fine figures and clear white skins tinged with red; their dominant qualities are bravery and pugnacity, together with gen-erosity and a strong spirit of rivalry between them in procuring [luxurious] viands. Some curious stories are told of this last trait in them. Sometimes one of them will invite his friend and will say to him, 'Come along with me for a meal of *nān* and *mās* [māst]—that is, bread and curdled milk in their lan-guage; then, when his friend goes along with him, he sets before him all sorts of wonderful dishes, with the aim of outdoing him by this [display]. The members of each craft appoint one of their own number as headman over them, whom they call the *kilū,* and so do the leading citizens from out-side the ranks of the craftsmen. One company [for example] will be com-posed of young bachelors. These companies try to outdo one another and invite one another to banquets, displaying all the resources at their disposal and making a great show in regard to the dishes and everything else. I was told that one company of them invited another, and cooked their viands with lighted candles, then the second company returned the invitation and cooked their viands with silk.

In India

In the course of his travels Ibn Baṭṭūṭa married and divorced many wives and acquired and disposed, by gift or sale, of many concubines.

There had arrived at that time some captives taken from the infidels and the vizier sent me ten girls from among them. I gave the man who brought them one of them—he was not at all pleased with that—and my companions took three young ones amongst them; as for the rest I do not know what happened to them. Female captives there are very cheap because they are dirty and do not know civilized ways. Even the educated ones are cheap, so that no one there needs to buy captives. The infidels in the land of India inhabit a territory which is not geographically separated from that of the Muslims, and their lands are contiguous, but though the Muslims have the upper hand over them yet the infidels maintain themselves in inaccessible mountains and rugged places, and they have forests of reeds, and as their reeds are not hollow but of large growth and are interlaced with one another, fire makes no impression on them and they are of great strength. The infidels live in these forests which are for them as good as city walls, and inside them they have their cattle and grain and supplies of water collected from the rains, so that they cannot be overcome except by strong armies of men who go into these forests and cut down those reeds with instruments made for the purpose.

—Ibn Baṭṭūṭa (translated by H. A. R. Gibb)

Quarantine

"Quarantine," from the Italian quarantina, *originally denoted the period of forty days that goods and passengers from the Levant were required to spend in isolation in the port of entry, to ensure that they did not bring the plague. These isolation centers were known by the Italian name* lazaretto, *sometimes anglicized as "lazaret," from the biblical figure of Lazarus. The earliest measures of this kind seem to have been taken by Venice, at the time of the Black Death (1348). The first lazaret was founded in Venice in 1403, on a small island near the city. Other Italian, French and Spanish ports adopted the same practice, as did a number of other countries. The delays and inconveniences of strictly enforced quarantine regulations greatly impeded travel and communication between the Middle Eastern and European worlds until relatively modern times.*

The danger of contagion, and the need for protection against it, were already understood by medieval Arab science, as two excerpts from fourteenth-century writers demonstrate. Both were translated by Max Meyerhof in The Legacy of Islam.

Contagion (Fourteenth Century)

The existence of contagion is established by experience, study, and the evidence of the senses, by trustworthy reports on transmission by garments, vessels, ear-rings; by the spread of it by persons from one house, by infection of a healthy sea-port by an arrival from an infected land . . . by the immunity of isolated individuals and . . . nomadic Beduin tribes of Africa. . . . It must be a principle that a proof taken from the Traditions has to undergo modification when in manifest contradiction with the evidence of the perception of the senses.

—Ibn al-Khaṭīb (translated by Max Meyerhof)

Symptoms (1369)

The result of my long experience is that if a person comes into contact with a patient, he is immediately attacked by the disease with the same symptoms. If the first patient expectorated blood, the second will do so. . . . If the first developed buboes, they will appear on the other in the same places. If the first had an ulcer, the second will get the same; and the second patient likewise transmits the disease.

—Ibn Khātima (translated by Max Meyerhof)

Prayer (1348)

I witnessed at the time of the Great Plague at Damascus in the latter part of the month of Second Rabī' of the year 49 [July 1348], a remarkable instance of the veneration of the people of Damascus for this mosque. Arghūn-Shāh, king of the amīrs and the Sultan's viceroy, ordered a crier to proclaim through Damascus that the people should fast for three days and that no one should cook in the bazaar during the daytime anything to be eaten (for most of the people there eat no food but what has been prepared in the bazaar). So the people fasted for three successive days, the last of which was a Thursday. At the end of this period the amīrs, sharīfs, qāḍīs, doctors of the Law, and all other classes of the people in their several degrees, assembled in the Great Mosque, until it was filled to overflowing with them, and spent the Thursday night there in prayers and liturgies and supplications. Then, after performing the dawn prayer [on the Friday morning], they all went out together on foot carrying Qur'āns in their hands—the amīrs too barefooted. The entire population of the city joined in the exodus, male and female, small and large; the Jews went out with their book of the Law and the Christians with their Gospel, their women and children with them; the whole concourse of them in tears and humble supplications, imploring the favour of God through His Books and His Prophets. They made their way to the Mosque of the Footprints and remained there in supplication and invocation until near midday, then returned to the city and held the Friday service. God Most High lightened their affliction; the number of deaths in a single day reached a maximum of two thousand, whereas the number rose in Cairo and Old Cairo to twenty-four thousand in a day.

—Ibn Baṭṭūṭa (translated by H. A. R. Gibb)

Departure from Europe:
Crossing the Sava River (1835)

At Semlin I still was encompassed by the scenes and the sounds of familiar life; the din of a busy world still vexed and cheered me; the unveiled faces of women still shone in the light of day. Yet, whenever I chose to look southward, I saw the Ottoman's fortress—austere, and darkly impending high over the vale of the Danube—historic Belgrade. I had come as it were to the end of this wheel-going Europe, and now my eyes would see the Splendour and Havoc of the East.

The two frontier towns are less than a gunshot apart, yet their people hold no communion. The Hungarian on the North, and the Turk and the Servian on the Southern side of the Save, are as much asunder as though there were fifty broad provinces that lay in the path between them. Of the men that bustled around me in the streets of Semlin, there was not, perhaps, one who had ever gone down to look upon the stranger race dwelling under the walls of that opposite castle. It is the Plague, and the dread of the Plague, that divide the one people from the other. All coming and going stands forbidden by the terrors of the yellow flag. If you dare to break the laws of the quarantine, you will be tried with military haste; the court will scream out your sentence to you from a tribunal some fifty yards off; the priest, instead of gently whispering to you the sweet hopes of religion, will console you at duelling distance, and after that you will find yourself carefully shot, and carelessly buried in the ground of the Lazaretto.

When all was in order for our departure, we walked down to the precincts of the Quarantine Establishment, and here awaited us the "compromised"*

---

* A "compromised" person is one who has been in contact with people or things supposed to be capable of conveying infection. As a general rule the whole Ottoman Empire lies constantly under this terrible ban. The "yellow flag" is the ensign of the Quarantine Establishment. [Footnote in source]

officer of the Austrian Government, whose duty it is to superintend the passage of the frontier, and who for that purpose lives in a state of perpetual excommunication. The boats with their "compromised" rowers were also in readiness.

After coming in contact with any creature or thing belonging to the Ottoman Empire, it would be impossible for us to return to the Austrian territory without undergoing an imprisonment of fourteen days in the Lazaretto. We felt therefore that before we committed ourselves, it was important to take care that none of the arrangements necessary for the journey had been forgotten; and in our anxiety to avoid such a misfortune we managed the work of departure from Semlin with nearly as much solemnity as if we had been departing this life. Some obliging persons from whom we had received civilities during our short stay in the place came down to say their farewell at the river's side; and now, as we stood with them at the distance of three or four yards from the "compromised" officer, they asked if we were perfectly certain that we had wound up all our affairs in Christendom, and whether we had no parting requests to make. We repeated the caution to our servants, and took anxious thought lest by any possibility we might be cut off from some cherished object of affection: were they quite sure that nothing had been forgotten—that there was no fragrant dressing-case with its gold-compelling letters of credit from which we might be parting for ever? No, every one of our treasures lay safely stowed in the boat, and we—we were ready to follow. Now therefore we shook hands with our Semlin friends, and they immediately retreated for three or four paces, so as to leave us in the centre of a space between them and the "compromised" officer. The latter then advanced, and asking once more if we had done with the civilized world, held forth his hand. I met it with mine and there was an end to Christendom for many a day to come.

—A. W. Kinglake

Western Travelers

A Pilgrim (867)

Now I will tell you how the Christians keep God's law both at Jerusalem and in Egypt. The Christians and Pagans have there such a peace between them, that if I should go a journey, and in the journey my camel or ass which carries my baggage should die, and I should leave everything there without a guard, and go to the next town to get another, on my return I should find all

my property untouched. The law of public safety is there such, that if they
find in a city, or on the sea, or on the road, any man journeying by night or
by day, without a letter, or some mark of a king or prince of that land, he is
immediately thrown into prison, till the time he can give a good account
whether he be a spy or not.

—Bernard the Wise (translated by Thomas Wright)

The Misadventures of an Italian Pilgrim (1384)

We reached Cairo and Babylon, which is almost the same thing, on October
11, and there that interpreter, to whom we have been entrusted in Alexandria, led us to the grand interpreter of the Sultan, who is in charge of all the
interpreters of the Sultan. This man had us put in a house, ourselves and our
things. To this house we went by a canal that leaves the Nile, and this house
is about three hundred miles inland. . . .

On the following morning [November 3] we broke camp before dawn,
on our way to the land of promise, and at daybreak as usual. At about the
ninth hour our interpreter left us, saying to the cameleers: Go ahead, I shall
overtake you. It looked bad to us, and we thought that he wished to deceive
us, so I told him that this did not seem to me to be good behaviour. So he
replied: Do not doubt, you have the safe-conduct of the Sultan and that of
the lord of the Arabs, and have them on you, and you are only one day and
a half from the city of Gaza, where there is law and there is also a king representing the Sultan. In fact he left us but overtook us late in the evening.
During the night we saw fires in the desert, which so far we had not seen,
and in the evening we were short of water. The next morning we left and
halted for a little about the third hour, and we found traces but not a lot of
horses' hoofs. A little farther on, on a hill, there came from the rear a company on foot and on horse, armed after their fashion, and among them there
was one who had in hand an iron mace. At once I said to our interpreter:
You have betrayed us; and I had my servant, Antonio da Pescia, give me my
sword and gauntlets. And our interpreter said: Don't be afraid, because he is
the official of the Arabs, who want to see your safe-conduct. And this they
asked when they reached us; so I had it produced, for it was in one of my
bags, in which were also my silver cups and some spoons and other delicate
things. At once they wanted to commence to plunder, but I made defence,
and meanwhile they put some of the baggage on the ground and beat the
camels, which scattered here and there.

Yet where I was, the interpreter and he with the iron mace remained
while I said to the interpreter, I know for certain that this day I must die for
the love of Christ, but you will die first, for the traitor that you are. He of the

mace had alighted and another held his horse. And the interpreter told him
I know not what, save that he prayed me to put back the sword in its sheath.
I said to them that we were companions and that what belonged to one,
would be for the other. Meanwhile some companions who had lost their
things, gave, saving the truth, XXII ducats to have them back; and having
taken that money, they fled with some things of our companions; but of
mine and my retinue, they took nothing, and so the others could have done
since all, save one, were younger than I.

—Lionardo Frescobaldi
(translated by Theophilus Bellorini and Eugene Hoade)

A Rabbi on the Road (1481)

From the balsam garden to Gaza and also close up to Jerusalem it is all
desert, and every man must carry on his beast two sacks, one of biscuits and
the other of straw and fodder, also water skins, for there you cannot find
sweet water, but only salt. You must also take with you lemons because of
the insects which I wrote about above, and you must go in a big caravan because of the robbers who frequent the desert, and you must go slowly for
two reasons; the one because in the desert there is much dust and sand and
the horses sink in it up to their knees and go with difficulty, and secondly
because the dust rises and gets into a man's mouth and makes his throat dry
and kills him with thirst, and if he drinks of the hot brackish water he is trou-
bled worse than before. Moreover, a man who does not know Arabic must
dress like a Turk in order that he may not be taken for a Jew or Frank, else
even a Jubilee would not set him free from paying much money to the cof-
fre, that is, taxes; but you must wear a white cover on your head like the
Turks and Moslems do, and there is great danger, lest, God forbid, anyone
of the caravan should tell that you are a Jew or Frank; and if you have escaped all these you will always find people lying in wait on the road who
are hidden in sand up to their necks, two or three days without food or
drink, who put a stone in front of them, and they can see other people but
the others cannot see them, and when they see a caravan rather smaller and
weaker than their own they go out and call their fellows and ride on their
horses swift as leopards, with bamboo lances topped with iron in their
hands, which are very hard. They also carry a pirate's mace in their hands
and bucklers made of parchment and pitch, and they ride naked with only
a shirt upon them, without trousers or shoes or spurs, and they come upon
the caravans suddenly and take everything, even the clothes and horses,
and sometimes they kill them; but generally they rob but do not kill them,
therefore it is good to be in a caravan of Turks who are all good bowmen,

Abū Zayd meets two merchants on camels, an episode from the adventures of Abū Zayd, the witty vagabond hero of a classic work by the Arab author al-Ḥarīrī of Basra. From an illustrated manuscript, probably Iraq, mid-thirteenth century.

and the robbers fear them because they are naked and cannot shoot, and two Turks could put ten Ishmaelites to flight. And if you escape them there is another great danger from corsairs. These are all foreigners who come in *Schioppette* (sloops) and are armed, and they are good fighters and wear Turkish clothes. When you come to the custom houses if you do a single thing not according to their usage they will at once understand that you are not a Turk or an Ishmaelite, and they are always on the watch, and if you ask me what their manner is and what to do it is necessary that when you reach those places you must immediately take your shoes off and sit on the ground and bend your legs under you and never let your legs appear or stand upon them at all, but you must eat on the ground, and if crumbs fall from the bread pick them up, but do not eat the bread until you have put it on your head, and you must give to the people around you a little of all you eat, even if they are not eating with you; and you must never take any of your clothes off, but you must sleep in them at night, and if they pass you anything to eat you must stretch forth your hand to take it with a bow, and, when you go to relieve yourself, take care not to lift up any of your clothes and keep close to the ground. You must never go to the house of anybody with shoes and never speak to anybody except seated with your legs bent beneath you, and even if you have only one loaf of bread and one cup of wine and a man comes and takes it and eats and drinks you must let him do so, for even if they take from Kings there is no redress and nothing to do. . . . It is also their custom to give no fodder to donkeys and nothing to drink, only all the caravan together, for it is by their law a great sin that the other horses or small donkeys should see one of them eat, because that would hurt those that are not eating, and that is cruelty to animals; and, therefore, every man must be careful not to transgress their customs lest, God forbid, they find out that he is a Jew or Frank, and unlucky is he that falls into this trap.

—Rabbi Meshullam da Volterra (translated by Elkan Nathan Adler)

Time and Space in Sixteenth-Century Turkey (1554)

In a letter written in 1554, Ogier Ghiselin de Busbecq, imperial ambassador to the Ottoman sultan, describes a problem he encountered on his journey to the Turkish capital.

There remained one annoyance, which was almost worse than a lack of wine, namely, that our sleep used to be interrupted in a most distressing manner. We often had to rise early, sometimes even before it was light, in order to arrive in good time at more convenient halting-places. The result was that our Turkish guides were sometimes deceived by the brightness of the moon and waked us with a loud clamour soon after midnight; for the Turks have no hours to mark the time, just as they have no milestones to mark distances. They have, it is true, a class of men called *talismans,* attached to the service of their mosques, who make use of water-clocks. When they judge from these that dawn is at hand, they raise a shout from a high tower erected for the purpose, in order to exhort and invite men to say their prayers. They repeat the performance half-way between sunrise and midday, again at midday, and half-way between midday and sunset, and finally at sunset, uttering, in a tremulous voice, shrill but not unpleasing cries, which are audible at a greater distance than one would imagine possible. Thus the Turkish day is divided into four periods, which are longer or shorter, according to the time of year; but at night there is nothing to mark the time. Our guides, as I have said, misled by the brightness of the moon, would give the signal for packing-up long before sunrise. We would then hastily get up, so that we might not be late or be blamed for any untoward incident that might occur; our baggage would be collected, my bed and the tents hurled into the carriage, our horses harnessed, and we ourselves girt up and ready awaiting the signal for departure. Meanwhile the Turks, having realized their mistake, had returned to their beds and their slumbers. . . . I dealt with this annoyance by forbidding the Turks to disturb me in future, and undertaking to wake the party at the proper time, if they would warn me overnight of the hour at which we must start. I explained to them that I had clocks which never failed me, and would arrange matters, taking the responsibility of letting them sleep on; they could, I said, safely trust me to get up. They assented, but were still not quite at their ease; they arrived in the early morning, and, waking my valet, begged him to go and ask me "what the fingers of my timepiece said." He did this, and then indicated as best he could whether a long or a short time remained before the sun would rise. When they had tested us once or twice and found that they were not deceived, they relied on us henceforward and expressed their admiration of the trustworthiness of our clocks. Thus we could enjoy our sleep undisturbed by their clamour.

—Ogier Ghiselin de Busbecq (translated by E. S. Forster)

A Spiritual Exercise (1523)

Although that year many pilgrims for Jerusalem had come, the majority of them had returned to their homelands on account of the new situation that had arisen as a result of the capture of Rhodes. Still, there were thirteen on the pilgrim ship, which left first, and eight or nine remained for the Governors' ship. As this was on the point of leaving, a serious feverish illness came over our pilgrim. After it had given him a rough time for a few days, it left him. The ship was due to depart on the day he had taken a purgative; the people in the house asked the doctor if he would be able to get on the ship for Jerusalem, and the doctor replied that certainly he could get on the ship if what he wanted was to be buried there. But he did get on the ship, and left that day. And he vomited so much that he was greatly relieved and really began to make a recovery.

On that ship there was some open dirty and obscene behaviour, which he would severely criticize. The Spaniards who were travelling on it were warning him not to do this, because the crew were talking of leaving him behind on some island. But Our Lord willed that they arrived quickly at Cyprus, where, having left that ship, they went overland to another port called Las Salinas, thirty miles away, and they boarded the pilgrim ship. Onto this ship too he brought nothing with which to feed himself beyond the hope he was placing in God, just as he had done on the other. Throughout this time Our Lord often appeared to him, which gave him great consolation and energy. Moreover, it seemed to him he repeatedly saw a large round object, apparently of gold: this began to appear to him after, having left Cyprus, they arrived at Jaffa. . . .

As they were making their way to Jerusalem on their donkeys, following custom, two miles before arriving at Jerusalem, a Spaniard named Diego Manes, apparently a nobleman, said to all the pilgrims, with much devotion, that, since they were shortly to arrive at the place from where the holy city could be seen, it would be good were all to prepare their minds and hearts and to travel in silence. This being agreeable to all, each one began to recollect himself. And a little before arriving at the place from which the city could be seen, they dismounted, because they saw the friars with the cross waiting for them. And on seeing the city the pilgrim had great consolation; moreover, from what the others were saying it was something they all had, with a joy that did not seem purely natural. And he always felt the same devotion during the visits to the holy places.

—Saint Ignatius Loyola (translated by Joseph A. Munitz)

On his return from this pilgrimage, after a period of study in Paris, Ignatius Loyola founded the Society of Jesus, popularly known as the Jesuits. He was canonized, along with Teresa of Avila, in 1622.

Letter from a Jesuit Missionary (1700)

Ballafore, in the Kingdom of Bengal

Reverend Father,

I have received the Letters you was so good as to send me. I will not tell you the Pleasure I felt, when these kind Testimonies of your Friendship came to my Hands. 'Tis a greater Satisfaction to us Travellers than you can imagine, to find, in such far distant Countries, that our Friends have not forgot us; but on the contrary, that they, whilst we are combating, lift up their Hands to Heaven, and assist us with their Prayers. I can assure you, I have had great Occasion for them since I left you, and have been exposed to imminent Dangers.

I came into India by Order of my Superiors. I will own that I was not displeased to leave Persia, I being desirous of engaging in another Mission,
imagining it to be more laborious, and more exposed to Sufferings. I met
with what I sought for sooner than I expected. In the Voyage I was taken by
the Arabs, and imprisoned for refusing to embrace the Mohammedan Religion. Those Infidels could not discover who we (Father Beauvollier my
Companion, and myself) were; tho' they did all that lay in their Power for
that Purpose, and still thought that we were born in Constantinople. What
misled them on this Occasion was, our reading Books in the Turkish and
Persian Languages. We did not endeavour to undeceive 'em, till one of 'em
insisted upon our professing their abominable Religion; upon which we declared aloud, that we were Christians, but at the same time concealed our
native country. We then inveighed against their Impostor Mohammed,
which exasperated them to such a Degree, that they seized our Ship, tho' it
belonged to Moors; and carrying us on Shore threw us into Prison. They
took my Companion and myself several times before the Magistrates, to se-
duce us, if possible; but finding that, by God's Mercy, we were always firm
and resolute, they at last grew weary of persecuting us; and thereupon sent
an Express to the Governor, to know in what Manner they should dispose
of us. Orders were sent to set us at Liberty, provided we were not Franks, or
Europeans, which these People hardly suspected, as we always spoke the
Turkish language; and as Father Beauvollier read none but Arabic Books,
and myself others writ in Persian. Thus God did not think us worthy of suffering Death on this Occasion, for the Glory of his holy Name; so that we escaped, after having been imprisoned, and otherwise ill treated.

—Father Martin

Testimony of Two English Slaves (Seventeenth Century)

*In the first half of the seventeenth century Muslim corsairs, mainly from
North Africa, preyed on Christian shipping and occasionally raided the
coasts in search of captives. In 1625 they raided Lundy, in 1631 Baltimore
(in Ireland), and in 1640 Penzance. In 1627 they sailed as far as Iceland,
where they were able to collect some four hundred captives for sale in the
slave market of Algiers.*

The Bashaw had the overseeing of all prisoners . . . who were presented
unto him at their first coming into the harbour; and so he chose one out of
every eight, for a present or a fee to himself. The rest were rated by the captains and so sent to the market . . . where, as men sell hackneys in England,
we were tossed up and down to see who would give us the most; many

came to behold us; sometimes taking us by the hand, sometimes turning us round about, sometimes feeling our brawns and naked arms; and so beholding our prices written in our breasts they bargained for us accordingly; and at last we were all sold.

—Anonymous

Their first policy is to look in the captives' mouths and a good, strong entire set of grinders will advance the price considerably . . . for they know that they who have no teeth, cannot eat, cannot work. . . . The next process is to feel their limbs, as whether there be any fracture, or dislocation in the bones; anything analogical to spavin, or ring-bone, for they will bring down the market wonderfully. . . . Age is also considerable . . . they go by general conjectures from the beard, face, or hair. . . . But they are very curious in examining the hands; for if they be callous and brawny, they will shrewdly guess that the captives have been inured to labour; if delicate and tender, they will suspect some gentleman or merchant, and then the hopes of good price of redemption makes him saleable.

—W. Okeley

On the Habits and Character of the Inhabitants of Syria (1782–85)

Volney was a French scholar who traveled extensively in Syria and Egypt in the 1780s. His account of his journey, published in 1787, had a considerable impact, and was used by Napoléon Bonaparte during his Egyptian campaign.

When the European arrives in Syria, or in general anywhere in the East, what strikes him most in the external aspect of the inhabitants is the almost total opposition of their manners and customs to our own. One might even say that premeditated design took pleasure in establishing a host of contrasts between the men of Asia and those of Europe. We wear short and tight clothes; they wear them long and spacious. We let our hair grow and shave our beards; they let their beards grow and shave their heads. Among us to bare the head is a mark of respect; among them a bare head is sign of folly. We salute bowing; they salute upright. We pass our life standing, they seated. They sit and eat on the ground; we raise ourselves on chairs. In sum, even in matters of language, they write in a way that is the reverse of ours, and most of our masculine nouns are feminine for them. For the generality of travelers, these contrasts are merely strange; but for philosophers it could be interesting to inquire whence comes this diversity of customs among men who have the same needs and among peoples who seem to have a common origin.

An equally remarkable characteristic is the religious aspect that dominates alike the faces, the speech, and the gestures of the inhabitants of Turkey. In the streets one sees only hands holding rosaries, one hears only emphatic utterances of *"Ya Allah"*—"O God," *"Allahu Akbar"*—"God is greatest," *"Allah ta 'ala"*—"God all highest!" At every moment the ear is struck by a profound sigh or a noisy eructation which follows the reciting of one of the ninety-nine names of God such as *"Ya ghānī!"*—"Source of riches!" *"Yā subḥan!"*—"Most praised!" *"Ya mastour!"*—"O Hidden One!" If one sells bread in the streets, one does not shout, "Bread," one shouts, *"Allah Kerim"*—"God is generous." If one sells water, it is *"Allah jawād"*—"God is bountiful" and likewise for other supplies. For greeting, one says "God preserve you"; for thanks, "God protect you." In a word, it is God in all and everywhere. "Are these men so devout?" the reader will ask. Yes, without being any the better for it. Why is this? It is that . . . this zeal, because of the diversity of cults, is only a spirit of jealousy, of contradiction. It is because for the Christians a profession of faith is an act of bravado, of independence; and for the Muslims, an act of power and of superiority; thus this devoutness, born of pride and accompanied by profound ignorance, is nothing but fanatical superstition that gives rise to a thousand disorders.

There is another outward characteristic of Easterners that draws the attention of an observer. It is their grave and phlegmatic air in everything that they do or say. In place of the open and merry face that one bears or affects among us, they have a face that is serious, austere or melancholy. They rarely smile, and our French sprightliness looks to them like an attack of frenzy. If they speak, it is without eagerness, without gesture, without passion. They listen without interrupting; they keep silent for whole days, and they make no effort to keep the conversation going. If they walk, they do so sedately and to accomplish some business, and they understand nothing of our turbulence and our walks up and down. Always seated, they spend entire days dreaming, cross-legged, pipe in the mouth, almost without changing position. One might say that movement is painful and that, like the Indians, they regard inaction as one of the elements of happiness.

In general, the people of the East are quick on the uptake, fluent of speech, with ardent and sustained passions and good sense in the things that they know. They have a particular taste for morality, and their proverbs prove that they know how to combine sharp observation and deep thought with pungent expression. Their dealings with others are at first cold, but habit makes them soft and attractive. This is the impression they leave, so that most of the travelers and traders who have had dealings with them agree in finding in these people a more humane and more generous character, a more noble and polite simplicity, and something more delicate and more open in the spirit of their manners than among the people of our own country.

—Volney

A Philosopher at Sea (1785)

Wednesday Nov. 9th.

On board a Turkish Caïk from Smyrna to Constantinople. E. of the Island of Metelin . . .

You will be curious to learn the situation of us poor Christians among these votaries of Mahomet. Our Vessel upon the largest computation is but 80 tons: upon the smallest not more than 60. . . . Our crew consists of 15 men besides the Captain: we have 24 passengers on the deck, all Turks; besides 18 young Negresses (slaves) under the hatches. Bugs, lice and fleas, of each a moderate provision: Maggots about twice the length of a meat maggot, out of number. The catching of these last as they crawl over the wainscoat, our cloaths, our persons and our provisions, forms no small part of our necessary occupation. Mr. Schnieder and Mr. Griffiths have a small cabbin between them at the head: with a kind of oblong box big enough to hold Mr. Schnieder's servant on one side of it. At the stern we have a larger Cabbin for Mr. H. the two ladies and myself: with two such boxes one on each side. This Cabbin which is a hole about 11 foot wide, 8 deep and 4 foot 2 or 4 inches high serves as a common-room for the whole half dozen of us and as a Bedchamber for the Ladies: the 2 boxes serve Mr. H. and me for bed chambers. A stratum of boxes serves me as a bedstead: on that I lay the mattress belonging to my cot. I squeeze in through a square hole just big enough to receive my body: it requires no small exertion to turn my head one way and my feet the other so as to lay myself at full length: this task accomplished there may be at the outside from 6 to 8 or so inches between my head as I lie and the tester of my bed or the ceiling of my bedchamber, call it which you please. As to the dining room to account for the heighth of it, you must consider that the passengers for whose use it was calculated sit with their legs folded in under them like Taylors, and know no such things as chairs. Being a bran-new ship and this her first voyage the Cabbin looked neat at first when decked out with a [hand]some carpet, and another spread double over it by way [of a] sopha: but this tempting appearance was much changed when upon taking possession of it we found the carpets taken up and the greatest part of the space filled up by the multifarious assemblage of boxes, hampers, bags, sacks and baskets that were necessary for the containing of our provisions, together with such parts of our baggage as are in most immediate use. Our provisions are mostly cold: but the Captain allows us the occasional use of his kitchen, upon our giving him a solemn promise not to introduce into his ship an atom of any thing that could come under the denomination of pork.

—Jeremy Bentham

A French General in Egypt (1798)

Egypt is part of Africa. Placed at the center of the ancient continent, between the Mediterranean and the Indian Ocean, it is the natural entrepôt for the commerce of the Indies. It is a vast oasis surrounded on every side by the desert and the sea . . . bounded in the north by the Mediterranean, in the west by the Libyan Desert, in the south by the Nubian Desert, in the east by the Red Sea and the Isthmus of Suez, which separates it from Syria. Egypt has no need to defend its frontiers by a system of strong points: the desert serves in their place: Egypt can only be attacked by the sea or through the Isthmus of Suez.

It rarely rains in Egypt, more on the coast than in Cairo, more in Cairo than in Upper Egypt. In 1798, it rained once in Cairo, for half an hour . . .

Egypt is one of the most beautiful, the most productive and the most interesting countries in the world; it is the cradle of the arts and the sciences. There one can see the greatest and the most ancient monuments created by the hand of man. If we had the key to the hieroglyphs with which they are covered, we would learn many things that are unknown to us concerning the early ages of society.

—Napoléon Bonaparte

A Swiss Pilgrim in Medina (1814)

The Medinans generally are of a less cheerful and lively disposition than the Mekkans. They display more gravity and austerity in their manners, but much less than the northern Turks. They outwardly appear more religious than their southern neighbours. They are much more rigid in the observance of their sacred rites, and public decorum is much more observed at Medina than at Mekka: the morals, however, of the inhabitants appear to be much upon the same level with those of the Mekkans; all means are adopted to cheat the hadjys. The vices which disgrace the Mekkans are also prevalent here; and their religious austerity has not been able to exclude the use of intoxicating liquors. These are prepared by the negroes, as well as

date-wine, which is made by pouring water over dates, and leaving it to ferment. On the whole, I believe the Medinans to be as worthless as the
Mekkans, and greater hypocrites. They, however, wish to approach nearer
to the northern Turkish character; and, for that reason, abandon the few
good qualities for which the Mekkans may be commended. In giving this
general character of the Medinans, I do not found it merely on the short experience I had of them in their own town, but upon information acquired
from many individuals, natives of Medina, whom I met in every part of the
Hedjaz. . . .

In their own houses, the people of Medina are said to live poorly, with
regard to food; but their houses are well furnished, and their expense in
dress is very considerable. Slaves are not so numerous here as at Mekka;
many, however, from Abyssinia are found here, and some females are settled, as married women. The women of the cultivators, and of the inhabitants of the suburbs, serve in the families of the town's-people, as
domestics, principally to grind corn in the hand-mills. The Medina women
behave with great decency, and have the general reputation of being much
more virtuous than those of Mekka and Djidda.

—John Lewis Burckhardt

Kinglake's Travels (1835)

*A. W. Kinglake devoted many years to the preparation of his detailed and
carefully documented history of the Crimean War, a work greatly appreciated at the time. He is, however, chiefly remembered for a little travel book
called* Eothen, *a Greek word meaning "toward the dawn." It contains a
record, at once perceptive and entertaining, of a journey to the Middle
East undertaken while he was still a student. It remains a classic of travel
literature.*

Portrait of a Governor

The Governor [of Suez] was a thorough Oriental, and until a comparatively
recent period had shared in the old Mohammedan feeling of contempt for
Europeans. It happened, however, one day that an English gun-brig had appeared off Suez, and sent her boats ashore to take in fresh water. Now fresh
water at Suez is a somewhat scarce and precious commodity; it is kept in
tanks, and the largest of these is at some distance from the place. Under
these circumstances the request for fresh water was refused, or at all events
was not complied with. The captain of the brig was a simple-minded man,

with a strongish will, and he at once declared that if his casks were not filled in three hours, he would destroy the whole place. "A great people indeed!" said the Governor—"a wonderful people, the English!" He instantly caused every cask to be filled to the brim from his own tank, and ever afterwards entertained for our countrymen a high degree of affection and respect.

Slave Market in Cairo

Slavery was gradually reduced during the nineteenth century and finally abolished in the twentieth. The slave markets that remained in many Middle Eastern cities aroused both honest indignation and prurient curiosity among Western travelers.

In the open slave-market I saw about fifty girls exposed for sale, but all of them black or "invisible" brown. A slave-agent took me to some rooms in the upper story of the building, and also into several obscure houses in the neighbourhood, with a view to show me some white women. The owners raised various objections to the display of their ware, and well they might, for I had not the least notion of purchasing. Some refused on account of the illegality of selling to unbelievers, and others declared that all transactions of this sort were completely out of the question as long as the Plague was raging. I only succeeded in seeing one white slave who was for sale, but on this treasure the owner affected to set an immense value, and raised my expectations to a high pitch by saying that the girl was Circassian and was "fair as the full Moon." There was a good deal of delay, but at last I was led into a long dreary room, and there, after marching timidly forward for a few paces, I descried at the farther end that mass of white linen which indicates an Eastern woman. She was bid to uncover her face, and I presently saw that, though very far from being goodlooking, according to my notion of beauty, she had not been inaptly described by the man who compared her to the full Moon, for her large face was perfectly round and perfectly white. Though very young she was nevertheless extremely fat. She gave me the idea of having been got up for sale—of having been fattened, and whitened by medicines or by some peculiar diet. I was firmly determined not to see any more of her than the face. She was perhaps disgusted at this my virtuous resolve, as well as with my personal appearance; perhaps she saw my distaste and disappointment; perhaps she wished to gain favour with her owner by showing her attachment to his faith. At all events she holloed out very lustily and very decidedly that "she would not be bought by the Infidel."

—A. W. Kinglake

Damascus (1835)

Until about a year or two years before the time of my going there, Damascus had kept up so much of the old bigot zeal against Christians, or rather against Europeans, that no one dressed as a Frank could have dared to show himself in the streets; but the firmness and temper of Mr. Farran, who hoisted his flag in the city as Consul-General for the district, had soon put an end to all intolerance of Englishmen. Damascus was safer than Oxford.

—A. W. Kinglake

Damascus (1845)

I thought Damascus was a great improvement upon Cairo, in every respect. It is much more thoroughly Oriental in its appearance, in its mysteries, in the look and character of its inhabitants. The spirit of the Arabian Nights is still quite alive in these, its native streets; and not only do you hear their fantastic tales repeated to rapt audiences in the coffee-houses, but you see them hourly exemplified in living scenes. In most countries, it is undignified and dangerous to speak a language imperfectly; but, in the East, where everything goes by contraries, it is one of the marks of high breeding and superiority. The lordly Turk never condescends to give himself any trouble about the Arab's language, and therefore his words, like those of other fashionables, are few, and well listened to. Such a peculiarity not only assists one in society, but also enables the traveller to wear the Turkish dress undiscovered: this is by far the handsomest, most comfortable, and best adapted to the climate and the habits of life; besides which it enables the wearer to mingle unobserved and unavoided in the places whence he can derive most amusement.

—Eliot Warburton

Persian Jews (1846–55)

Among the Persian Jews are some who are very rich, and this wealth is the source of so many dangers, that they are obliged to conceal their treasures like crimes.—I comprise their oppressions under the following heads:

1)   Throughout Persia the Jews are obliged to live in a part of the town separated from the other inhabitants; for they are considered as unclean creatures, who bring contamination with their intercourse and presence.

2)   They have no right to carry on trade in stuff goods.

3)   Even in the streets of their own quarter of the town they are not allowed to keep any open shop.—They may only sell there spices and drugs, or carry on the trade of a jeweller, in which they have attained great perfection.

4)   Under the pretext of their being unclean, they are treated with the greatest severity, and should they enter a street inhabited by Mussulmans, they are pelted by the boys and mob with stones and dirt.

5)   For the same reason they are forbidden to go out when it rains; for it is said the rain would wash dirt off them, which would sully the feet of the Mussulmans.

6)   If a Jew is recognised as such in the streets, he is subjected to the greatest insults. The passers by spit in his face, and sometimes beat him so unmercifully, that he falls to the ground, and is obliged to be carried home.

7)   If a Persian kills a Jew, and the family of the deceased can bring forward two Mussulmans as witnesses to the fact, the murderer is punished by a fine of 12 tumauns (600 piastres); but if two such witnesses cannot be produced, the crime remains unpunished, even though it has been publicly committed, and is well known.

8)   The flesh of the animals slaughtered according to Hebrew custom, but as Trefe [not kosher] declared, must not be sold to any Mussulmans. The slaughterers are compelled to bury the meat, for even the Christians do not venture to buy it, fearing the mockery and insult of the Persians.

9)   If a Jew enters a shop to buy anything, he is forbidden to inspect the goods, but must stand at a respectful distance and ask the price. Should his hand incautiously touch the goods, he must take them at any price the seller chooses to ask for them.

10)   Sometimes the Persians intrude into the dwellings of the Jews and take possession of whatever pleases them. Should the owner make the least opposition in defence of his property, he incurs the danger of atoning for it with his life.

11)   Upon the least dispute between a Jew and a Persian, the former is immediately dragged before the Achund, and, if the complainant can bring forward two witnesses, the Jew is condemned to pay a heavy fine. If he is too poor to pay this penalty in money, he must pay it in his person. He is stripped to the waist, bound to a stake, and receives forty blows with a stick. Should the sufferer utter the least cry of pain during this proceeding, the blows already given are not counted, and the punishment is begun afresh.

12)   In the same manner the Jewish children, when they get into a quarrel with those of the Mussulmans, are immediately led before the Achund, and punished with blows.

13)   A Jew who travels in Persia is taxed in every inn and every cara-

vanserai he enters. If he hesitates to satisfy any demands that may happen to be made on him, they fall upon him, and maltreat him until he yields to their terms.

14)   If, as already mentioned, a Jew shows himself in the street during the three days of the Katel (feast of mourning for the death of the Persian founder of the religion of Ali) he is sure to be murdered.

15)   Daily and hourly new suspicions are raised against the Jews, in order to obtain excuses for fresh extortions; the desire of gain is always the chief incitement to fanaticism.

These points give a clear insight into the wretched condition in which the Jews languish in a country where, not so very long since, a woman of their people was wife of the ruler, and one of her brethren was first minister. The only compensation which they find for these persecutions, insults, and oppressions, is the great confidence which is reposed in them in commercial matters. Their integrity in trade is recognised by the Persians to such a degree that a Jew, who fails, finds refuge with the Achund against all prosecutions, and thus gains time to settle with his creditors.

The Jewish doctors are likewise much sought after, and exercise great influence over the first people of the kingdom, which they nobly turn to the advantage of their oppressed brethren. Thus are fulfilled the sublime words of the scriptures when it is written: "And yet for all that, when they be in the land of their enemies, I will not cast them away, neither will I abhor them, to destroy them utterly, and to break my covenant with them: for I am the Lord their God." (Leviticus XXVI. 44).

The Christians in Persia are nearly as much oppressed as the Jews. Some time since they addressed themselves to the Pope with a prayer for protection, but this appeal was of no avail.

—J. J. Benjamin II

Travel Notebook
Qusseyr, on the Red Sea Coast of Egypt (1850)

Saturday, 18 May

We get up at first dawn—there are four slave ships moored on the beach—slaves who have landed walk along, led by two men, in bands of fifteen to twenty—when I mount my camel, Hadj Ismail jumps up to give me a handshake—(the man on the ground, stretching his arm to give a handshake or to offer something to the man mounted on his camel, is one of the most beautiful Eastern gestures—especially at departure, there is in this something solemn and gravely sad)—the inhabitants of Kéneh are not yet up—at their doors, the dancing girls, covered with gold piastres, sweep their thresholds with palm branches or smoke the morning chibouk. . . .

The ground, full of movement, is pebbly—the road is dry—we are in the midst of the desert—our camel drivers sing, and their song ends with a whistling, throaty modulation to arouse the dromedaries—on the sand one can see, in parallel, several tracks that twist and turn in accord—these are the tracks of caravans—each track was made by the walking of a camel—sometimes there are fifteen to twenty paths—the wider the road the more parallel tracks—from place to place, about every two or three leagues (but quite irregularly), large patches of yellow sand that looks as if it had been polished with a lacquer of burnt siena—these are the places where the camels stop to make water—it is hot—to our right a whirlwind of *khamsin* advances, coming from the side of the Nile at which we can still barely see a few palm trees along its bank—the whirlwind grows and advances on us—it is like an immense vertical cloud that, long before it envelops us, overhangs our heads, while its base, to the right, is still far from us—it is reddish brown—and pale red—we are right in it—a caravan passes us by—the men enveloped in kaffiyehs (the women very veiled) leaning on the necks of their dromedaries—they pass right by us—we say nothing to each other—like phantoms in the clouds—I feel something like a feeling of terror and furious admiration running up and down my backbone—I sneer nervously—I must have been very pale, and I enjoyed unheard-of delight—it seemed to me, while the caravan was passing, that the camels were not touching the ground, that they were breasting forward with a movement like a ship, supported from within, and raised high above the soil, as if they were walking in a cloud, belly high.

From time to time we met other caravans—on the horizon, first a long, wide line, barely distinguishable from the line of the horizon—then this black line rises above the other, and soon we see little points on it—the little points rise—they are the heads of camels walking in front—a regular balancing all along the line—seen foreshortened, these heads look like the heads of ostriches.

—Gustave Flaubert

A Pilgrim Arrives in Mecca (1853)

Richard Burton's account of his pilgrimage, disguised as a Muslim, to the holy places of Mecca and Medina is one of the most famous of Western travel books about the East. In the follwing passage he describes his arrival, shortly after dawn, before the Ka'abah.

There at last it lay, the bourn of my long and weary Pilgrimage, realising the plans and hopes of many and many a year. The mirage medium of Fancy invested the huge catafalque and its gloomy pall with peculiar charms. There were no giant fragments of hoar antiquity as in Egypt, no remains of graceful and harmonious beauty as in Greece and Italy, no barbarous gorgeousness as in the buildings of India; yet the view was strange, unique—and how few have looked upon the celebrated shrine! I may truly say that, of all the worshippers who clung weeping to the curtain, or who pressed their beating hearts to the stone, none felt for the moment a deeper emotion than did the Haji from the far-north. It was as if the poetical legends of the Arab spoke truth, and that the waving wings of angels, not the sweet breeze of morning, were agitating and swelling the black covering of the shrine. But, to confess humbling truth, theirs was the high feeling of religious enthusiasm, mine was the ecstasy of gratified pride.

—Sir Richard Burton

Missionaries (1856)

Wrote in this diary (Jerusalem) to day. In the afternoon called upon Mr. and Mrs. Saunders, outside the wall, the American Missionary.—Dismal story of their experiments. Might as well attempt to convert bricks into bride-cake as the Orientals into Christians. It is against the will of God that the East should be Christianized.

—Herman Melville

An Innocent Abroad: The Travels of Mark Twain (1867)

Oriental Splendor

This seaport of Smyrna, our first notable acquaintance in Asia, is a closely packed city of one hundred and thirty thousand inhabitants, and, like Constantinople, it has no outskirts. It is as closely packed at its outer edges as it is in the centre, and then the habitations leave suddenly off and the plain beyond seems houseless. It is just like any other Oriental city. That is to say, its Moslem houses are heavy and dark, and as comfortless as so many tombs; its streets are crooked, rudely and roughly paved, and as narrow as an ordinary staircase; the streets uniformly carry a man to any other place than the one he wants to go to, and surprise him by landing him in the most unexpected localities; business is chiefly carried on in great covered bazaars, celled like a honeycomb with innumerable shops no larger than a common closet, and the whole hive cut up into a maze of alleys about wide enough to accommodate a laden camel, and well calculated to confuse a stranger and eventually lose him; every where there is dirt, every where there are fleas, every where there are lean, broken-hearted dogs; every alley is thronged with people; wherever you look, your eye rests upon a wild masquerade of extravagant costumes; the workshops are all open to the streets, and the workmen visible; all manner of sounds assail the ear, and over them all rings out the muezzin's cry from some tall minaret, calling the faithful vagabonds to prayer; and superior to the call to prayer, the noises in the streets, the interest of the costumes—superior to every thing, and claiming the bulk of attention first, last, and all the time—is a combination of Mohammedan stenches, to which the smell of even a Chinese quarter would be as pleasant as the roasting odors of the fatted calf to the nostrils of the returning Prodigal. Such is Oriental luxury—such is Oriental splendor!

Respect for Relics

We brought not a relic from Ephesus! After gathering up fragments of sculptured marbles and breaking ornaments from the interior work of the Mosques; and after bringing them at a cost of infinite trouble and fatigue, five miles on muleback to the railway depot, a government officer compelled all who had such things to disgorge! He had an order from Constantinople to *look out for our party,* and see that we carried nothing off. It was a wise, a just, and a well-deserved rebuke, but it created a sensation. I never resist a temptation to plunder a stranger's premises without feeling insufferably vain about it. This time I felt proud beyond expression. I was serene in the midst of the scoldings that were heaped upon the Ottoman government for its affront offered to a pleasuring party of entirely respectable gentlemen and ladies. I said, "We that have free souls, it touches us not." The shoe not only pinched our party, but it pinched hard; a principal sufferer discovered that the imperial order was inclosed in an envelop bearing the seal of the British Embassy at Constantinople, and therefore must have been inspired by the representative of the Queen. This was bad—very bad. Coming solely from the Ottomans, it might have signified only Ottoman hatred of Christians, and a vulgar ignorance as to genteel methods of expressing it; but coming from the Christianized, educated, politic British legation, it simply intimated that we were a sort of gentlemen and ladies who would bear watching! So the party regarded it, and were incensed accordingly. The truth doubtless was, that the same precautions would have been taken against *any* travelers, because the English Company who have acquired the right to excavate Ephesus, and have paid a great sum for that right, need to be protected, and deserve to be. They can not afford to run the risk of having their hospitality abused by travelers, especially since travelers are such notorious scorners of honest behavior.

Damascus the Eternal

Though another claims the name, old Damascus is by right the Eternal City.

We reached the city gates just at sundown. They do say that one can get into any walled city of Syria, after night, for bucksheesh, except Damascus. But Damascus, with its four thousand years of respectability in the world, has many old fogy notions. There are no street lamps there, and the law compels all who go abroad at night to carry lanterns, just as was the case in old days, when heroes and heroines of the Arabian Nights walked the streets of Damascus, or flew away toward Bagdad on enchanted carpets.

It was fairly dark a few minutes after we got within the wall, and we rode long distances through wonderfully crooked streets, eight to ten feet wide, and shut in on either side by the high mud-walls of the gardens. At last we got to where lanterns could be seen flitting about here and there, and knew we were in the midst of the curious old city. In a little narrow street, crowded with our pack-mules and with a swarm of uncouth Arabs, we alighted, and through a kind of a hole in the wall entered the hotel. We stood in a great flagged court, with flowers and citron trees about us, and a huge tank in the centre that was receiving the waters of many pipes. We crossed the court and entered the rooms prepared to receive four of us. In a large marble-paved recess between the two rooms was a tank of clear, cool water, which was kept running over all the time by the streams that were pouring into it from half a dozen pipes. Nothing, in this scorching, desolate land could look so refreshing as this pure water flashing in the lamp-light; nothing could look so beautiful, nothing could sound so delicious as this mimic rain to ears long unaccustomed to sounds of such a nature. . . .

I do not know, but I think they used that tank between the rooms to draw drinking water from; that did not occur to me, however, until I had dipped my baking head far down into its cool depths. I thought of it then, and superb as the bath was, I was sorry I had taken it, and was about to go and explain to the landlord. But a finely curled and scented poodle dog frisked up and nipped the calf of my leg just then, and before I had time to think, I had soused him to the bottom of the tank, and when I saw a servant coming with a pitcher I went off and left the pup trying to climb out and not succeeding very well. Satisfied revenge was all I needed to make me perfectly happy, and when I walked in to supper that first night in Damascus I was in that condition. We lay on those divans a long time, after supper, smoking narghilies and long-stemmed chibouks, and talking about the dreadful ride of the day, and I knew then what I had sometimes known before—that it is worth while to get tired out, because one so enjoys resting afterward.

Palestine

Palestine sits in sackcloth and ashes. Over it broods the spell of a curse that has withered its fields and fettered its energies. Where Sodom and Gomorrah reared their domes and towers, that solemn sea now floods the plain, in whose bitter waters no living thing exists—over whose waveless surface the blistering air hangs motionless and dead—about whose borders nothing grows but weeds, and scattering tufts of cane, and that treacherous fruit that promises refreshment to parching lips, but turns to ashes at the touch. Nazareth is forlorn; about that ford of Jordan where the hosts of Israel entered the Promised Land with songs of rejoicing, one finds only a squalid camp of fantastic Bedouins of the desert; Jericho the accursed, lies a moldering ruin, to-day, even as Joshua's miracle left it more than three thousand years ago; Bethlehem and Bethany, in their poverty and their humiliation, have nothing about them now to remind one that they once knew the high honor of the Saviour's presence; the hallowed spot where the shepherds watched their flocks by night, and where the angels sang Peace on earth, good will to men, is untenanted by any living creature, and unblessed by any feature that is pleasant to the eye. Renowned Jerusalem itself, the stateliest name in history, has lost all its ancient grandeur, and is become a pauper village; the riches of Solomon are no longer there to compel the admiration of visiting Oriental queens; the wonderful temple which was the pride and the glory of Israel, is gone, and the Ottoman crescent is lifted above the spot where, on that most memorable day in the annals of the world, they reared the Holy Cross. The noted Sea of Galilee, where Roman fleets once rode at anchor and the disciples of the Saviour sailed in their ships, was long ago deserted by the devotees of war and commerce, and its borders are a silent wilderness; Capernaum is a shapeless ruin; Magdala is the home of beggared Arabs; Bethsaida and Chorazin have vanished from the earth, and the "desert places" round about them where thousands of men once listened to the Saviour's voice and ate the miraculous bread, sleep in the hush of a solitude that is inhabited only by birds of prey and skulking foxes.

Palestine is desolate and unlovely. And why should it be otherwise? Can the *curse* of the Deity beautify a land?

Palestine is no more of this work-day world. It is sacred to poetry and tradition—it is dream-land.

—Mark Twain

Jerusalem (1877)

Facing all these branches of the Christian family, like Ishmael against his brothers, the Jewish tribe, rancorous and closed, vegetates in its wretchedness, despite some establishments due to the generosity of their rich co-religionists in Europe. Can I again describe, without repeating myself, their implacable faith, their stubborn and vain hope, the mystery of their cult, of their existence, and of their abasement? Ignored and despised despite their numbers, pinned in a stifling quarter and in obscure synagogues, driven out of all the places made holy by the Bible, the Gospel or the Koran, the children of Israel cherish, more than all the others, pretensions for the future and the conviction of a national renaissance. They arrive from every corner of Europe, as strange as I have tried to depict them, with the instinctive regularity of migrating birds, to add their own tombs to those of their ancestors. A figure gives some idea of their numerical importance, so little in accord with their religious and political importance which is zero: of all the population of Jerusalem, which amounts to about twenty-six thousand souls, the Jews constitute more than half, fourteen thousand souls.

The rest breaks down as follows: Christians, seven thousand or eight thousand, Muslims, four thousand or five thousand. Most of the latter are desert bedouins or Arab townsfolk; the remainder consists of the Turks, officials and soldiers.

—Eugène-Melchun, Vicomte de Vogué

Fraternizing with Orientals (1894–96)

My sneaking wish to fraternise with Orientals, when I avowed it after hesitations, appeared good to him. And then I made acquaintance with a clever dragoman and one of the most famous jokers in all Syria, who happened to be lodging at my little hostelry, with nothing in the world to do but stare about him. He helped me to throw off the European and plunge into the native way of living. . . . We . . . frequented Turkish baths; ate native meals and slept in native houses—following the customs of the people of the land in all respects. And I was amazed at the immense relief I found in such a life. In all my previous years I had not seen happy people. These were happy. Poor they might be, but they had no dream of wealth; the very thought of competition was unknown to them, and rivalry was still a matter of the horse and spear. Wages and rent were troubles they had never heard of. Class distinctions, as we understand them, were not. Everybody talked to everybody. With inequality they had a true fraternity. People complained that they were badly governed, which merely meant that they were left to their devices save on great occasions. A Government which touches every individual and interferes with him to some extent in daily life, though much esteemed by Europeans, seems intolerable to the Oriental. I had a vision of the tortured peoples of the earth impelled by their own misery to desolate the happy peoples, a vision which grew clearer in the after years. But in that easy-going Eastern life there is a power of resistance, as everybody knows who tries to change it, which may yet defeat the hosts of joyless drudgery. . . .

In short, I ran completely wild for months, in a manner unbecoming to an Englishman; and when at length, upon a pressing invitation, I turned up in Jerusalem, and used my introductions, it was in semi-native garb and with a love for Arabs which, I was made to understand, was hardly decent. My native friends were objects of suspicion. I was told that they were undesirable, and, when I stood up for them, was soon put down by the retort that I was very young. I could not obviously claim as much experience as my mature advisors, whose frequent warnings to me to distrust the people of the country thus acquired the force of moral precepts, which it is the secret joy of youth to disobey.

—Marmaduke Pickthall

In Praise of Gardens (1894)

The East is full of secrets—no one understands their value better than the Oriental; and because she is full of secrets she is full of entrancing surprises. Many fine things there are upon the surface: brilliance of colour, spendour of light, solemn loneliness, clamorous activity; these are only the patterns upon the curtain which floats for ever before the recesses of Eastern life: its essential charm is of more subtle quality. As it listeth, it comes and goes; it flashes upon you through the open doorway of some blank, windowless house you pass in the street, from under the lifted veil of the beggar woman who lays her hand on your bridle, from the dark, contemptuous eyes of a child; then the East sweeps aside her curtains, flashes a facet of her jewels into your dazzled eyes, and disappears again with a mocking little laugh at your bewilderment; then for a moment it seems to you that you are looking her in the face, but while you are wondering whether she be angel or devil, she is gone.

She will not stay—she preferes the unexpected; she will keep her secrets and her tantalizing charm with them, and when you think you have caught at last some of her illusive grace, she will send you back to shrouded figures and blank house-fronts.

You must be content to wait, and perhaps some day, when you find her walking in her gardens in the cool of the evening, she will take a whim to stop and speak to you and you will go away fascinated by her courteous words and her exquisite hospitality.

For it is in her gardens that she is most herself—they share her charm, they are as unexpected as she. Conceive on every side such a landscape as the dead world will exhibit when it whirls naked and deserted through the starry interspace—a grey and featureless plain, over which the dust-clouds rise and fall, build themselves into mighty columns, and sink back again among the stones at the bidding of hot and fitful winds; prickly low-growing plants for all vegetation, leafless, with a foliage of thorns; white patches of salt, on which the sunlight glitters; a fringe of barren mountains on the horizon. . . . Yet in this desolation lurks the mocking beauty of the East. A little water and the desert breaks into flower, bowers of cool shade spring up in the midst of dust and glare, radiant stretches of soft colour gleam in that grey expanse. Your heart leaps as you pass through the gateway in the mud wall; so sharp is the contrast, that you may stand with one foot in an arid wilderness and the other in a shadowy, flowery paradise. Under the broad thick leaves of the plane-trees tiny streams murmur, fountains splash with a sweet fresh sound, white-rose bushes drop their fragrant petals into tanks, lying deep and still like patches of concentrated shadow. The indescribable charm of a Persian garden is keenly present to the Persians themselves—the 'strip of herbage strown, which just divides the desert from the sown,' an endlessly beautiful parable. Their poets sing the praise of gardens in exquisite verses, and call their books by their names. I fear the Muses have wandered more often in Sa'di's Garden of Roses than in the somewhat pretentious pleasure-ground which our Elizabethan writer prepared for them. . . .

As we sat on the deep step of the windowsill, a door opened softly, and a long-robed Persian entered. He carried in his hand a twanging stringed instrument, with which he established himself at the further side of the fountain, and began to play weird, tuneless melodies on its feeble strings—an endless, wailing minor. Evening fell, and the dusk gathered in the glittering room, the fountain bubbled lower and sank into silence, the wind blew the sweet smell of roses in to us where we sat—and still the Persian played, while in the garden the nightingales called to one another with soft thrilling notes.

—Gertrude Bell

On Punctuality (1947)

I have made and I still make the most sincere efforts, during my travels in the East, to arrive late at the appointments which they were kind enough to give me and the time of which was always carefully discussed and finally agreed. I must admit that these virtuous attempts remain unsuccessful.

Wise and experienced men . . . sometimes said to me: "Here the sky is too blue, the sun too hot. Why hurry? Why do injury to the sweetness of living? Here, everybody is late. The only thing is to join them. He who arrives at the appointed hour risks wasting his time, and that, after all, is not funny. Therefore, not too much precision. Strict exactitude has minor advantages, but is very inconvenient. It lacks suppleness, it lacks fantasy, it lacks pleasantness, even dignity."

These fine arguments ought to have convinced me. I confess with shame that they did not succeed. When I see the time that they have been kind enough to give me approaching, I cannot prevent myself from getting started. At least, if one could just apply a well-defined corrective coefficient, I would have a timetable to keep to, and I could make the necessary calculation more or less correctly. But is it a calculation? One should rather speak of an amiable caprice with unforeseeable effects. Therefore, as I see myself, in general and at least in this respect, lacking in humor and even invention, I keep to my old habits and I present myself, perhaps somewhat simplemindedly, at the time which I was told was the right one.

—Georges Duhamel

Facing History in Jerusalem (1975)

This morning's paper reports that nine men were found dead in an Argentine ditch, blindfolded and shot through the head; that South Moluccans seized a Dutch train and murdered some of the passengers. Scores of people are killed in the streets of Beirut every day; terrorists take hostages in London and explode bombs in Belfast. As an American, I can decide on any given day whether or not I wish to think of these abominations. I need not consider them. I can simply refuse to open the morning paper. In Israel, one has no such choice. There the violent total is added up every day. And nothing can be omitted. The Jerusalemite hooked by world politics cannot forget Gerald Ford and China, Ronald Reagan and California; he is obliged to know that Harold Wilson has just asserted in a speech that England is still a force to be reckoned with. He cannot afford to overlook the latest changes in the strategy of the French Communist Party nor the crises in Portugal and Angola; he must remember the mental character of the Muslim world, the Jews of the Diaspora. Israelis must, in fact, bear in mind four thousand years of Jewish history. The world has been thrown into their arms and they are required to perform an incredible balancing act. Another way of putting it: no people has to work so hard on so many levels as this one. In less than thirty years the Israelis have produced a modern country—doorknobs and hinges, plumbing fixtures, electrical supplies, chamber music, airplanes, teacups. It is both a garrison state and a cultivated society, both Spartan and Athenian. It tries to do everything, to understand everything, to make provision for everything. All resources, all faculties are strained. Unremitting thought about the world situation parallels the defense effort. These people are actively, individually involved in universal history. I don't see how they can bear it.

—Saul Bellow

A Journey to the Islamic Revolution (1981)

On the outskirts of the city [Tehran], in what looked like waste ground, I saw a low khaki-coloured tent, a queue of men and veiled women, and some semi-uniformed men. I thought of refugees from the countryside, dole queues. But then—seeing another tent and another queue in front of an unfinished apartment block—I remembered it was the day of an election, the second test of the people's will since the revolution. The first had been a referendum; the people had voted then for an Islamic republic. The election was for an "Assembly of Experts," who would work out an Islamic constitution. Khomeini had advised that priests should be elected.

Experts were necessary, because an Islamic constitution couldn't simply be adopted. No such thing existed or had ever existed. An Islamic constitution was something that had to be put together, and it had to be something of which the Prophet would have approved. The trouble there was that the Prophet, creating his seventh-century Arabian state, guided always by divine revelation, had very much ruled as his own man. That was where the priests came in. They might not have ideas about a constitution—a constitution was, after all, a concept from outside the Muslim world; but, with their knowledge of the Koran and the doings of the Prophet, the priests would know what was un-Islamic. . . .

One of the English-language magazines I bought was published from the holy city of Qom. It was *The Message of Peace* and, as its title warned, it was full of rage.

It raged about the Shah; about the "devils" of the West and the evils of Western technology; it even raged about poor old Mr. Desai, the Indian prime minister, who banned alcohol (good, from the Muslim point of view) but drank urine (from the Muslim point of view, deplorable). But it wasn't for its rages that I bought the magazine, or the speeches of Khomeini, or for the biographies of the Shia Imams. I bought *The Message of Peace* for an article on Islamic urban planning.

Could there be such a thing? Apparently; and, more, it was badly needed. Islam was a complete way of life; it didn't separate the worldly from the spiritual. Hence it was necessary, in addition to avoiding materialist industrial excess, to plan for "a theocentric society." In this society women also had to be sheltered. Problems! But the very existence of these problems proved the need for sensible Islamic planning. And a solution was possible. . . .

Technology was evil. E. F. Schumacher of *Small Is Beautiful* had said so: *The Message of Peace* quoted him a lot, lashing the West with its own words. But technology surrounded us in Tehran, and some of it had been so Islamized or put to such good Islamic use that its foreign origin seemed of no account.

The hotel taxi driver could be helped through the evening traffic jams by the Koranic readings on his car radio; and when we got back to the hotel there would be mullahs on television. Certain modern goods and tools—cars, radios, televisions—were necessary; their possession was part of a proper Islamic pride. But these things were considered neutral; they were not associated with any particular faith or civilization; they were thought of as the stock of some great universal bazaar.

Money alone bought these things. And money, in Iran, had become the true gift of God, the reward for virtue. Whether Tehran worked or not, seventy million dollars went every day to the country's external accounts, to be drawn off as required: foreign currencies, secured by foreign laws and institutions, to keep the Islamic revolution going.

—V. S. Naipaul

Interview with Qaddafi (1986)

By an American Correspondent

As I stepped off the bus in my high heels, I sank into a freshly plowed barley field. At the far end of the field I could dimly make out a tent, and as I squinted against the noonday sun, I saw a tractor speeding toward me. When it pulled up, the driver commanded, "Hop in." It was Qaddafi.

"Are you alone?" he said, grinning at me.

"I suppose so, Colonel," I replied idiotically, gesturing limply at the empty field and returning the grin.

"Good. Then we shall talk and try out the tractor."

Qaddafi laughed as he noticed my mud-covered shoes, one of which had lost its heel. His shoes, of course, had no mud on them. In dry, drab Libya, Qaddafi's wardrobe was more colorful than anything else in sight.

Dapper as ever, he was wearing a jumpsuit, a salmon-colored turban, black knee-high riding boots, matching black gloves, and his omnipresent sunglasses. But he did not know much about driving a tractor. The vehicle lurched violently as the leader ground the gears and cut an erratic path across the field, mangling the young plants. Qaddafi's mind was on weightier things.

"This farm is one of many projects that will help Libya become self-sufficient in food. We need to be independent in all things," he lectured. "The people are lazy; they don't want to work. It is a problem of all petroleum societies."

Qaddafi had pretended to try to solve the problem by expelling some eighty thousand foreign Arab workers—the Egyptians, Moroccans, and Tunisians who kept Libya running. The expulsions, I knew, were not, as he maintained, the result of his quest for self-reliance but of a shortage of foreign currency now that oil prices had fallen. On a trip the previous year, I had visited the main state supermarket in Tripoli and found neither fresh vegetables nor meat, no toilet paper, matches, detergent, or soap. The only commodities in ample supply were 10-pound bags of Cuban sugar, boxes of tea from China, canned tomatoes from Cyprus, salt, and dented cans of insect spray. I had bought the repellent and, to cheer up my hotel room, one of the dozens of potbellied teddy bears on display—a big hit with the country's four thousand Russian military "advisers" and their families. The only other well-stocked item was hundreds of pairs of men's huge tennis shoes, all size 45, stamped "Jamahiriya." The word, which was Qaddafi's neologism for Libya and translates roughly as "gathering of the masses," was stamped on each pair of soles. The shoes, I later learned, had been made in Asia.

This was a difficult period for the Jamahiriya, Qaddafi declared, theatrically sweeping back his turban's tail with one hand and steering the tractor with the other. But he was not intimidated by Washington. Reagan was "a monster, a bully." . . .

He would not be cowed, Qaddafi declared. American retaliation against Libya would lead to "World War III." "Suicide missions" would be launched against America and Israel. "Our aircraft bombers are fedayeen [freedom fighters] who can reach anyplace. We will act inside American streets if we are attacked."

But I should not feel threatened, Qaddafi said, placing his gloved hand on mine. Americans in Libya—and in 1986 there were between fifteen hundred (the State Department's estimate) and three thousand of them (according to a diplomat in Tripoli)—were "welcome." "You will never be harmed," he purred.

As the colonel spoke, I noticed that a busload of correspondents had arrived and were now racing across the field toward our tractor. Alarmed by the throng of camera-wielding reporters charging Qaddafi's vehicle, dozens of khaki-clad bodyguards and soldiers had leaped onto their own tractors and were trying to cut them off, heading straight toward us at top speed from the right. To our left was a huge irrigation ditch that Qaddafi's tractor was veering toward. We were close to a collision.

"Which way shall I go?" Qaddafi asked playfully.

"A la tule!" I yelled, Egyptian slang meaning "straight ahead." "Straight!" I said again as Qaddafi, probably to scare me, made a sharp right turn toward the oncoming tractor fleet whose drivers seemed no more adept than their leader. "For God's sake, Colonel, go straight! Qaddafi always goes straight!"

Qaddafi roared with laughter and corrected his course. "Tell Reagan that!" he shouted as the tractor screeched to a halt. "Tell America I always go straight!"

—Judith Miller

PART V

Diplomats

An ambassador is an honest man sent to lie
abroad for the good of his country.
—Sir Henry Wotton (1604)

Sultan Süleyman the Magnificent receiving Stephen Zapolya, the prince of Transyl-vania, 1566.

Introduction

A wicked messenger falleth into mischief," says the Book of Proverbs 13:17, "but a faithful ambassador is health." Already in the earliest books of the Hebrew Bible there are numerous references to the sending of messengers by Moses, Joshua, Samuel and by the judges and kings of Israel, to their various neighbors. The word commonly used in the Hebrew text in these early references is *mal'akh*, "messenger," which was later specialized to mean "angel," the messenger of God. The Greek word *angelos*, originally "messenger" or "envoy," underwent a similar semantic change, and both Hebrew and Greek found other words to designate those who were sent as envoys of worldly rulers.

The practice was already well established when the earliest books of the Hebrew Bible were first committed to writing. Rulers communicated with other rulers by means of such envoys on a variety of topics: the ransoming or exchange of prisoners, the avoidance or ending of war and, increasingly important with the growing sophistication of the economy, the establishment and supervision of commercial relations. The Roman and Persian emperors sent and exchanged such embassies, sometimes with each other, sometimes with remoter rulers in distant lands. The caliphs and sultans and shahs of Islam conducted their diplomacy in much the same way.

It was the normal practice, in antiquity and in the Islamic states, to send an ambassador to a foreign ruler when there was something to say, and to bring him home when he had said it. This eminently sensible practice was maintained for many centuries. It gave rise to a number of reports which were surely of interest and value to those who sent the ambassador and are still of interest and value to the historian today. An excerpt from a Turkish author of the period depicts the arrival of an Indian envoy in Istanbul and the choice of an Ottoman ambassador to travel with him to India.

The conduct of diplomatic relations through resident permanent missions—consulates, legations and embassies—began with the expansion of European—more particularly Italian—commerce in the Middle East during and after the Crusades. The Crusader princes allowed European merchants to establish quarters in the coastal cities, giving them a considerable degree of autonomy in their own affairs. After the Muslim reconquest, this practice was not only maintained by Muslim rulers, it was extended to other cities and strengthened by the granting of what was in effect an extraterritorial status to these communities. This was not, as in later centuries, a concession reluctantly conceded under foreign pressure. It was rather an extension to resident foreigners of the system by which non-Muslim religious communities under Muslim rule enjoyed a large measure of communal autonomy. Each community had its recognized head: a patriarch, a bishop, a rabbi or the like. Each foreign community was similarly expected to have a representative chief, responsible for the maintenance of order within his own community and for the conduct of relations with the dominant power. The title they chose was that of the chief magistrates of ancient Rome: consul. In time, the representational functions of the consul came to overshadow all the others.

One of the most important of these Italian representatives was the senior Venetian official in Constantinople. In 1082 C.E. the emperor Alexios Comnenos granted a chrysobull, a gold-sealed diploma, to the Venetians, allowing them complete exemption from Byzantine taxes and duties and assigning them their own quarter within the city. The chief Venetian officer in the city, known as the *bailo,* literally "bailiff," was appointed by the doge and council in Venice and exercised the dual function of head of the Venetian colony in the Byzantine capital and envoy of the Venetian republic to the emperor. Under later emperors the Venetian position grew stronger; the Turkish conquest in 1453 did not end it. The Venetian-Turkish peace treaty of 1451 expressed Venice's acceptance of the new situation and the sultan's acceptance of the need for good relations with Venice. Venice's great rival, Genoa, had already signed its own commercial treaty with the Ottomans in 1352.

Where the Italian city republics led, other European countries followed, and before long permanent resident embassies were established in Ottoman Istanbul by the rulers of France, England, Spain, the Netherlands, Austria, Poland and other countries. Many of these diplomats—heads of mission as well as members of their staffs—wrote and published books about their experiences and their observations. Notable among these were Sir Paul Rycaut, who was in Istanbul from 1660 to 1677, most of the time as secretary to the English ambassador, and Sir James Porter, who was there as ambassador from 1746 to 1762.

Much more can be found in the unpublished documents which still survive in the archives of most of the countries that sent them. In the British Public Record Office, Foreign Office Series 78, dealing with relations between Britain and Turkey from 1780 to 1905, comprises 5,490 volumes; Foreign Office Series 60, dealing with relations with Persia from 1807 to 1905, 734 volumes. In addition, there were of course many volumes of correspondence with British consuls in various cities, as well as separate files on special topics such as the suppression of the slave trade (2,276 volumes from 1816 to 1892).

In the twentieth century, with the vast improvement in the means of communication, the bulk is correspondingly greater and presents the historian with a task of daunting immensity.

For many centuries the Ottomans and other Middle Eastern rulers, while accepting a steadily increasing number of resident foreign missions in their capitals, felt no need to reciprocate. They saw these foreign diplomats not as one side of an exchange but rather as guests of the ruler, almost—in a sense—petitioners.

By the end of the eighteenth century Middle Eastern rulers, increasingly aware of the growing disparity in power between East and West, decided, one after another, that the time had come for a change. The pioneer was the Ottoman sultan Selim III, who resolved, as part of a larger program of modernizing reforms, to appoint resident missions in Europe. A first embassy was established in London in 1793 and was followed by others in the major European capitals. The shah of Persia, the only remaining fully independent ruler in the Middle East, followed some years later. In the course of the twentieth century, as the list of independent rulers grew longer and longer, so too did the procession of diplomats proceeding to and from Middle Eastern capitals.

Since European visitors to the Middle East—diplomats and soldiers, traders and pilgrims alike—were usually equally ignorant of Middle Eastern languages, interpreters were essential to all forms of communication between the Christian and Muslim worlds.

Who were these interpreters? Their profession goes back to remote antiquity and is attested both in the scriptures and in the Greek and Roman classics. The Jews attached great importance to the translation of the scriptures into the various vernaculars spoken by Jews, and there are many references in rabbinic literature to both oral and written translations into Aramaic, Greek and other languages. Translators and interpreters were also used in judicial hearings before the Sanhedrin. Imperial rulers, both ancient and modern, did not normally pay much attention to the languages of their subjects but expected those subjects to learn the language of their masters.

The Romans made extensive use of interpreters in dealings with both their subjects and their neighbors. The Byzantine emperors maintained a staff of professional interpreters who served both in embassies abroad and in dealings with foreign embassies to Constantinople. The title of grand or chief interpreter (*Megas hermêneutês*) first appears in the twelfth century and was maintained thereafter both by the Byzantine emperors and, with a similar function and a Turkish title, by their Ottoman successors.

The word in rabbinic texts for "translation" is *targum,* and the translator is called *turguman.* The word *dragoman,* probably of Assyrian origin, appears in a number of languages and was used of the official translators employed by Middle Eastern governments and by Western embassies accredited to those governments. Some of those dragomans were recruited among those whom the Christians called renegades and the Muslims called *muhtadī,* literally "one who has found the true path." A number of these entered the Ottoman service and acquired a sufficient knowledge of Turkish to perform this task. Later, the dragomans employed by the Ottoman government were recruited from among the Greek subject population, and especially from among a small group of patrician Greek families of Istanbul. Their department, forming part of the office of the grand vizier, was responsible for the day-to-day conduct of foreign relations. Its head had the title of chief dragoman of the Porte. This arrangement, which lasted for several centuries, ended abruptly in 1821 when, as a result of the Greek War of Independence, the last Greek chief dragoman, Stavraki Aristarchi, was dismissed and executed. Thereafter, this post was entrusted to a Muslim. At first finding qualified Muslims was no easy matter, and it took a little while before the Turks and eventually other Middle Eastern Muslims awoke to a new and painful reality in which they had to learn the barbarous idioms of the previously despised infidels.

Foreign diplomats accredited to the Ottoman, Persian and later other Middle Eastern governments rarely felt the desire or found the opportunity to learn the languages of these countries. Instead, they relied on dragomans. At first these were recruited mainly among the non-Muslim subjects of the state: Greeks, Armenians and occasionally Jews and Arab Christians. Later, they came to be recruited almost exclusively from among the long-established resident European population of Middle Eastern towns and especially seaports. They were of mixed, predominantly Italian origin, mostly Catholic by religion, multilingual and multicultural. They were known among Europeans as Levantines, to distinguish them from "genuine" Europeans coming from Europe. The Turks called them "sweetwater Franks," with the same purpose. Members of the same family, sometimes indeed the same individual, might work at different times for different foreign powers. Inevitably, these too adaptable purveyors of words came to be regarded with suspicion and even hostility by the diplomats with whom they worked and the foreign ministries who employed them. In time most European governments decided that it was no longer safe to rely on such representatives and began to train young diplomats of their own country for this task. A British Foreign Office memorandum of January 18, 1838, explains: "A Turkish Minister is known to fear, because he cannot trust, any Dragoman . . . and at the present time a British Minister in Constantinople cannot be said to have any certain means of ascertaining what are the real sentiments of a Turkish Minister."

Since then, considerable progress has been made in the teaching and study of Middle Eastern languages among Westerners. But serious problems of communication and understanding remain, and they would have been incomparably worse had it not been for the far greater development of the teaching and study of Western languages in the Middle East.

The following excerpts begin with some passages from ancient and medieval texts dealing with diplomacy and interpreting relevant bureaucratic procedures. The remaining texts, from inside and outside the region and the profession, illustrate the development of continuous diplomatic relations between Middle Eastern powers and the outside world.

Rules Concerning Ambassadors

From an Arabic Manual of Statecraft (Ninth Century)

It is the king's duty to choose an ambassador who is sound in body and in mind, eloquent and articulate, quick and effective in repartee, able to convey both the letter and spirit of the king's message. He must be sincere in his way of speaking, inclined neither to ambition nor to vice, and loyal to the task entrusted to him. The king should submit his ambassador to a long test before appointing him ambassador.

How to Test an Ambassador

When the kings of Persia decided to choose one of their subjects as ambassador to a foreign king, they would first test him by sending him as emissary to some dignitary or personage of the king's inner circle, having previously dispatched a spy with orders to observe his mission and to write down what he said. When the emissary returned from his mission, the spy brought the written record of his utterances and answers. The king then compared them with the emissary's report. If they tallied verbally or at least in meaning, the king knew that he could count on his integrity and sincerity. He would then send him as ambassador to an enemy and send a spy after him to remember his words, write them down and bring them back to the king. If the ambassador's report tallied with that of the spy, and if the king saw that he had faithfully reported the enemy's words, adding nothing because of their hostility, he would then appoint him ambassador to foreign sovereigns and put his trust in him. After these tests, his reports were considered reliable.

Ardashir I, the son of Babak, said, "How much blood has been unlawfully shed because of ambassadors! How many armies have been slaughtered, troops routed, women violated, riches looted and covenants broken because of the treachery and falsehood of ambassadors!"

—Al-Jāḥiẓ (attributed)

From a Persian Manual of Statecraft (Eleventh Century)

When ambassadors come from foreign countries nobody is aware of their movements until they actually arrive at the city gates; nobody gives any information [that they are coming] and nobody makes any preparation for them; and they will surely attribute this to our negligence and indifference. So officers at the frontiers must be told that whenever anyone approaches their stations they should at once despatch a rider and find out who it is who is coming, how many men there are with him, mounted and unmounted, how much baggage and equipment he has, and what is his business. A trustworthy person must be appointed to accompany them and conduct them to the nearest big city; there he will hand them over to another agent who will likewise go with them to the next city (and district), and so on until they reach the court. Whenever they arrive at a place where there is cultivation, it must be a standing order that officers, tax-collectors and assignees should give them hospitality and entertain them well so that they depart satisfied. When they return, the same procedure is to be followed. Whatever treatment is given to an ambassador, whether good or bad, it is as if it were done to the very king who sent him; and kings have always shewn the greatest respect to one another and treated envoys well, for by this their own dignity has been enhanced. And if at any time there has been disagreement or enmity between kings, and if ambassadors have still come and gone as occasion requires, and discharged their missions according to their instructions, never have they been molested or treated with less than usual courtesy. Such a thing would be disgraceful. . . .

It should also be realized that when kings send ambassadors to one another their purpose is not merely the message or the letter which they communicate openly, but secretly they have a hundred other points and objects in view. In fact they want to know about the state of roads, mountain passes, rivers and grazing grounds, to see whether an army can pass or not; where fodder is available and where not; who are the officers in every place; what is the size of that king's army and how well it is armed and equipped; what is the standard of his table and his company; what is the organization and etiquette of his court and audience-hall; does he play polo and hunt; what are his qualities and manners, his designs and intentions, his appearance and bearing; is he cruel or just, old or young; is his country flourishing or decaying; are his troops contented or not; are the peasants rich or poor; is he avaricious or generous; is he alert or negligent in affairs; is his wazir competent or the reverse, of good faith and high principles or of impure faith and bad principles; are his generals experienced and battletried or not; are his boon-companions polite and worthy; what are his likes and dislikes; in his cups is he jovial and good-natured or not; is he strict in religious matters and does he shew magnanimity and mercy or is he careless; does he incline more to jesting or to gravity; and does he prefer boys or women. So that, if at any time they want to win over that king, or oppose his designs or criticize his faults, being informed of all his affairs they can think out their plan of campaign, and being aware of all the circumstances, they can take effective action. . . .

For an embassy a man is required who has served kings, who is bold in speaking but does not say too much, who has travelled widely, who has a portion of every branch of learning, who is retentive of memory and far-seeing, who is tall and handsome, and if he is old and wise, that is better. If a boon-companion is sent as an envoy he will be more reliable; and if a man is sent who is brave and manly, skilled in arms and horsemanship, and renowned as a warrior, it will be extremely good, for he will shew the world that our men are like him; and if an ambassador be a man of noble family that will be good too, for they will have respect for his ancestry. Very often kings have sent envoys bearing gifts of money, valuables or weapons and shewn themselves weak and submissive; after giving this illusion they have followed up by preparing their forces, sending picked men in to the attack and defeating the enemy. The conduct and good sense of an ambassador are a guide to the conduct of his king.

—Niẓām al-Mulk (translated by Hubert Darke)

How to Write a Letter to Europe

From an early-fifteenth-century Egyptian guide for officials.

Addressing the Pope

He is the Patriarch of the Melkites, who occupies for them the position of Caliph. The author of the *Tathqif* [an earlier manual of bureaucratic proce-dure], surprisingly, sees him as the equivalent of the Khan among the Tatars. But the Khan is rather in the position of their great King, while the Pope is nothing of the kind but is in charge of religious matters, even to the point of deciding of what is permitted and what is forbidden. . . . He is called the Pope, which means the father of fathers. . . .

The form of address to be used in writing to him is:

May Almighty God increase the splendor of his Exalted Presence, the mighty, holy, spiritual, humble, active Pope of Rome, Mighty One of the Christian Sect, Supreme One of the Community of Jesus, Enthroner of the Kings of Christendom, Keeper of the Bridges and Canals*, Refuge of Pa-triarchs and Bishops and Priests and Monks, Reciter of the Gospel, who tells his people what is forbidden and what is permitted, the Friend of Kings and Sultans and Preachers. . . .

---

* Presumably an echo of the title Pontifex Maximus.

The King of the Romans, the Ruler of Constantinople

He should be addressed as follows:

May God increase the Splendor of his exalted and noble presence, the venerable, magnanimous and mighty King, the Courageous Lion, the valiant, high-born, noble, glorious Paleologos . . . Ruler of the Greek States, Embracer of the coast-lands, Heir of the ancient Caesars, Reviver of the teachings of the Philosophers and the Sages, learned in the precepts of his religion, just in his Dominions, Strengthener of the Nazarene Faith, Supporter of Christianity, Peerless among the kings of the followers of Jesus, Giver of thrones and scepters, Protector of Seas and Straits, Last of the Kings of the Greeks, King of the Syrian Kings, Buttress of the Sons of Baptism, Favored of the Pope of Rome, most trustworthy of friends, Friend of the Muslims, Model of Kings and Sultans. This is followed by the name of the Emperor.

Correspondence with the Ruler of Venice

We have received the letter of the High, Mighty, brave, revered and Honorable Doge, Marco Cornaro [Doge from 1365 to 1367], Pride of the Christian Community, Splendor of the Sect of the Cross, Doge of Venice and Dalmatia . . . Support of the Religion of the Followers of Baptism, Friend of Kings and Sultans and preachers. . . .

To the Ruler of Rhodes

This is an island facing the shores of the land of Rum. Its inhabitants are pirates. If they triumph over a Muslim, they rob him, let him live, and sell or keep him as a slave. If they take a Frank, they rob him and then kill him. The protocol used in addressing him is similar to that of others, but he is not called "Friend of the Pope of Rome." Some other titles are also shortened since he is of lower rank.

To the Queen of Naples

Her name is Joan, and toward the end of 773 [1371 c.e.] she was addressed as follows:

This missive is addressed to the Queen. . . . Most exalted, glorious and mighty Princess, Learned in her Faith, Just in her Kingdom, Great One of the Christian Religion, Supporter of the Nation of Jesus, Protectress of the Frontiers, Friend of Kings and Sultans. This is followed by an invocation, including her titles. When the kingdom is governed by a male, he should be addressed with the same titles but using the masculine form, or with loftier titles, in view of the superiority of men over women.

—Al-Qalqashandī

Reception and Negotiation

An Offer of Marriage and Friendship, Apparently Unrequited, from a Frankish Queen (Baghdad, 905–6)

Bertha, daughter of al-Awtari [Lothar], queen of Franja and its dependencies, sent a present to [the caliph] al-Muktafi billah by 'Ali the eunuch, one of the eunuchs of Ziyadatallah ibn al-Aghlab, in the year 293, consisting of . . . [gifts]

'Ali the eunuch brought the present and letter of the queen of Franja to al-Muktafi billah, and also a further message not included in the letter lest anyone other than the caliph become aware of it. The letter was on white silk, in a writing resembling the Greek writing, but straighter. The message was a request to al-Muktafi for marriage and for his friendship. . . .

Abu 'Abdallah Muhammad b. 'Abdallah al-Isfahani, the secretary of Abu Layla al-Harith b. 'Abd al-Aziz said, 'I was in the camp with al-Muktafi billah . . . and the authorities looked for someone to translate the letter, and there was in the clothes' storehouse, with Bishr the eunuch, a Frank who was able to read the writing of that people. The eunuch brought him into the caliph's presence, and he read the letter and translated it into Greek writing. Then Ishaq b. Hunayn was brought, and he translated it from Greek into Arabic.

—Al-Awḥadī (translated by M. Hamidullah)

A Letter from the Ottoman Grand Vizier Siyavush Pasha to Queen Elizabeth of England (1583)

In 1575 two London merchants, on their own initiative and at their own expense, sent agents to Turkey and obtained a safe conduct from the Sultan Murad III for one of their colleagues, a merchant called William Harborne, to have free access to the Ottoman lands. Despite efforts by the French and Venetian representatives to prevent this English encroachment on what they regarded as their own preserve, this new enterprise prospered. In 1580, in an exchange of letters between the sultan and Queen Elizabeth, the private commercial arrangement was expanded into a formal agreement between the two monarchs. In 1583 Harborne, still a merchant concerned primarily with commercial matters but now also accredited by the queen as her envoy, arrived in Istanbul. This letter from the grand vizier records his arrival and acceptance.

Model of the revered ladies of the Christian community, pattern of the virtuous matrons of the Sect of Jesus, who draws the trains of majesty and reverence, mistress of the tokens of grandeur and glory, Queen of England, Elizabeth, may her end be happy.*

After offering prayers fitting and appropriate to friendship, suitable and concordant with love and affection, what have we to say is this: Your letter of friendly content has just reached your well-wisher; with the perfection of friendship your great and esteemed envoy was sent with presents to the Court, the Nest of Power, of His Majesty our mighty and felicitous Padishah, God, may He be exalted, glorify his helpers. He has made expression of friendship and sincerity and has made known his devotion and fidelity. Your envoy, like those of the French and the other kings, will be present and ever tended and honored at the Court of Felicity, supervising and completing the interests and undertakings that concern you and your desire and purposes. When the graciously granted imperial charter, that none may interfere or oppose while your merchants and other men come in peace and security to the God-guarded realms, conduct their trade and engage in their affairs and commerce, reaches you, you will find it in accordance with your desires. Furthermore, it being your wish that the peace and good order that give rise to gain and prosperity shall be observed on both sides and shall not be violated in any way whatever until the Day of Resurrection, but shall remain firmly established, you have asked us to send and confirm the noble commands concerning these matters to the amirs and governors and other rulers and persons in the God-guarded realms.

In this matter, all that was written and made clear in your letter and all that your envoy has reported and explained has been submitted and reported, in its entirety, great and small, to the Footstool of the Imperial Throne of Felicity, and his noble cognizance has encompassed and comprehended it utterly. Consequently, the Sublime Court of our Felicitous Padishah—God, may He be exalted, glorify his helpers and strengthen his power—is open in grace and benevolence, his host, enkindled with felicity, is ready and prepared, as recompense for those who offer submission. It is

---

* A form of greeting commonly used when addressing non-Muslim rulers. It expresses a hope for eventual conversion to Islam.

an ancient, pleasing and illustrious custom from the times of our noble fathers and mighty forebears, may God illuminate their evidences, till today, never to reject or refuse those who offer either loyalty or submission. Your envoy too will be cared for and protected, tended and esteemed with limitless benevolence of diverse kinds, and, like the envoys of the kings of France and Venice and Vienna and other kings who offer homage and friendship at the Sublime Court, will abide at the Court of Felicity and attend to those interests which concern you. The imperial and felicitous license has been issued that he may supervise the important business and other affairs of your men who come and go. Please merciful God, no one will interfere or oppose the condition of compact and security and the bonds of peace and pledge that exist between us. It is necessary that when our friendship-encompassed letter arrives together with the magnanimous imperial missive, you too will be firm-footed on the path of submission and obedience, constant on the highway of friendship and devotion, ever in loyalty and amity with a sincere conscience and a pure mind, to the Court, the Emblem of Justice, of His Majesty, our mighty, felicitous, magnanimous, honoured Padishah, God, may He be exalted, glorify his helpers and strengthen his power. Let not your men omit to come and go, and do you not omit to inform us regularly of the news of your illustrious health and of the events and circumstances of that much-esteemed land. Make it known to your men and the rest of your merchants and traders that they can come to the God-guarded realms of the Padishah with their goods in safety and security, conduct their trade and commerce at leisure and in tranquillity. Do not be deficient in friendship. What more need be said that is not known?

Written at the end of Rabi al-Akhir of the year 991 [August 1573] in the residence of Constantinople the God-guarded.

—Translated from the text in the Public Record Office, London, State Papers 102/61/5

An Organ for the Sultan (1599)

In 1599 the English Levant Company decided to send an organ as a gift to the sultan of Turkey. The delivery and installation of the organ were entrusted to its maker, Thomas Dallam. His account of his adventures includes the following description of his briefing by the ambassador on the eve of his presentation at court.

The Ambassador's speech unto me in Love after he had given me my charge;—

"You are come hither with a present from our gracious Queen, not to an ordinary prince or king, but to a mighty monarch of the world, but better had it been for you if it had been sent to any Christian prince, for then you should have been sure to have received for your pains a great reward; but you must consider what he is unto whom you have brought this rich present, a monarch but an infidel, and the grand Enemy to all Christians. What we or any other Christians can bring unto him he doth think that we do it in duty or in fear of him, or in hope of some great favor we expect at his hands. It was never known that upon the receiving of any present he gave any reward unto any Christian, and therefore you must look for nothing at his hands. You would think that for your long and wearisome voyage, with danger of life, that you were worthy to have a little sight of him; but that you must not look for neither; for you see what great preparing we made and have been about ever since your coming, for the credit of our country, and for a Delivering of this present and my embassage, the which, by God's help, tomorrow must be performed. We call it kissing of the Grand Signor's hand; but when I come to his gates I shall be taken off my horse and searched, and led betwixt two men holding my hands down close to my sides, and so led into the presence of the Grand Signor, and I must kiss his knee or his hanging sleeve. Having delivered my letters unto the Kapiji [chamberlain], I shall be presently led away, going backwards as long as I can see him, and in pain of my head I must not turn my back upon him, and therefore you must not look to have a sight of him. I thought good to tell you this, because you shall not hereafter blame me, or say that I might have told you so much; let not your work be anything the more carelessly looked unto, and at your coming home our merchants shall give you thanks, if it gives the Grand Signor content this one day. I care not if it be none after the next, if it do not please him at the first sight, and perform not those things which it is told him that it can do, he will cause it to be pulled down that he may trample it under his feet. And then we shall have no suit granted, but all our charge will be lost."

After I had given my Lord thanks for this friendly speech, though small comfort in it, I told him that this much I understood by our merchants before my coming out of London, and that he needed not to doubt that there should be any fault either in me or my work. . . .

The next morning being the 25 I went to the Seraglio. . . . The Grand Signor, being seated in his Chair of state, commanded silence. All being quiet, and no noise at all, the present began to salute the Grand Signor; for when I left it I did allow a quarter of an hour for his coming thither. First the clock struck 22; then the chime of 16 bells went off, and played a song of 4 parts. That being done, two personages which stood upon two corners of the second storey, holding two silver trumpets in their hands, did lift them

The Ottoman grand vizier receiving a European ambassador, early eighteenth century.

to their heads, and sounded a tantarra. Then the music went off, and the organ played a song of 5 parts twice over. . . . Then the Grand Signor asked him if he did know any man that could play on it. He said no, but he that came with it could, and he is here without the door. Fetch him hither, quoth the Grand Signor, and let me see how he doth it. Then the Kapiji opened that door which I went out at, for I stood near unto it. He came and took me by the hand, smiling upon me; but I bid my dragoman ask him what I should do, or whither I should go. He answered that it was the Grand Signor's pleasure that I should let him see me play on the organ. So I went with him. When I came within the door, that which I did see was very wonderful unto me. . . . I stood there playing such things as I could until the clock struck, and then I bowed my head as low as I could, and went from him with my back towards him. As I was taking off my cloak, the Kapiji came unto me and bid me stand still and let my cloak lie; when I had stood a little while, the Kapiji bid me go and cover the keys of the organ; then I went close to the Grand Signor again, and bowed myself, and then I went backwards towards my cloak. When the Company saw me do so they seemed to be glad, and laughed. Then I saw the Grand Signor put his hand behind him full of gold, which the Kapiji received, and brought me forty and five pieces of gold called sequins, and then I was put out again where I came in, being not a little joyful of my good success.

Having got out of the Seraglio, I made all the speed I could to that gate where the ambassador went in, for he and all his Company stood all these two hours expecting the Grand Signor's coming to another place where he should deliver his embassage and Letters. . . .

The last of September I was sent for again to the Seraglio to set some things in good order again, which they had altered, and these two aje-moglans [pages] which kept that house made me very kindly welcome, and asked me that I would be contented to stay with them always, and I should not want anything, but have all the content that I could desire. I replied to them that I had a wife and children in England, who did expect my return. Then they asked me how long I had been married, and how many children I had. Though indeed I had neither wife nor children, yet to excuse myself I made them that answer.

Then they told me that if I would stay the Grand Signor would give me two wives, either two of his Concubines or else two virgins of the best I could choose myself, in city or country.

The same night, as my Lord was at supper, I told him what talk we had in the Seraglio, and what they did offer me to stay there, and he bid me that by no means I should flatly deny them anything, but be as merry with them as I could, and tell them that if it did please my Lord that I should stay, I should be the better contented to stay; by that means they will not go about to stay you by force, and you may find a time the better to go away when you please.

—Thomas Dallam

The Appointment of an Ottoman Ambassador to India (1653)

The Ottoman sultan Mehmed IV, having received an ambassador sent by the Mogul emperor Shah-Jahan I, appointed an ambassador of his own to return the compliment.

On 23d Rejeb he [the Indian ambassador] came to the divan and presented his gifts. They included three valuable presents, of an estimated combined value of 300,000 piastres—a turban crest with a diamond bigger than the sultan's, a sword and a dagger. Since the ambassador was one of the ulema, the vizier, the mufti, the kadi-askers and other high dignitaries all gave receptions in his honor, at which learned and worthy men, masters of the arts of conversation, were present and entertained the ambassador with scholarly discussion and witty repartee. These receptions were held in world-adorning palaces and in heart-delighting waterside pavilions, so as to show him the strange and wondrous sights of Istanbul. Indeed, it has never been heard that an ambassador has been received with so much attention and deference. After the ambassador had been treated with full honors, a letter of reply was written to the Emperor of India. An emerald-hilted dagger, twenty beautiful slave-girls and a finely caparisoned horse, whose trappings were estimated to be worth ninety purses, were given as gifts to the Emperor, while the ambassador was given six thousand pieces of gold, a fur robe and a caparisoned horse.

A meeting was held to choose an ambassador to accompany him back to India. According to ancient custom it would have been proper to send a man of experience from among the ulema or scribes, or else a man of eloquence from among the scholars and literati. In fact, however, these necessary qualifications were disregarded. Zulfikar Aga, the brother of Salih Pasha, asked for this embassy, saying, "I need no expenses. I will pay for it out of my own pocket." Deeming this arrangement both advantageous and suitable—on the principle that a cheap hire makes a suitable companion—they appointed this ignorant Bosniak as ambassador.

His Majesty the sultan, having heard of the excellence of the Indian ambassador and of his brilliant conversation . . . said, "Let a learned and able man be appointed as ambassador, for ambassadors are the honor of kings." The vizier and the mufti held council on whom to appoint. Certain learned men were put forward, whereupon someone said, "if you appoint a man of culture and discernment, then besides his travel expenses he will require a personal allowance and will pester and burden us with claims and demands for attention."

With this in mind, they decided on Zulfikar Aga and said to him, "Call on the ambassador . . . give him a fine reception, be friendly and sociable, but in company keep silent. Don't feel that you have to talk, and then commit some gross error." This is how they instructed him. This ass then set out with indescribable pomp to call on the ambassador, inform him of his own appointment, and invite him to a reception. The late Manoglu says that of the literary set he invited no one, of the poets only Jevri Chelebi, and of the wits of Kadizade's following, Ebu Ahmed-oglu. These two men were friends of his, confidants and intimates; they were to entertain the ambassador, and also to use their skill to cover up his own blunders, if he made any.

Zulfikar Aga gave a fine reception, where, among other dishes, he had ordered two or three dishes made from cabbage, which he regarded as the greatest of delicacies. The ambassador came and sat down, and in due course, after many social solecisms, dinner was served. When the cabbage was brought, Zulfikar turned to the ambassador and asked, "Are there any cabbages in India?" The ambassador replied, "Cold plants of no special quality are very rarely cultivated in temperate climates."

Zulfikar, not understanding what the ambassador had said, went on, "Sir, this is a useful thing. It strengthens a man's spirits."

The ambassador smiled, and remarked, "There is no doubt that it is a cause of wind, but apart from this verbal affinity I do not know of any connection with spirits."

Zulfikar understood neither the sense of the ambassador's words nor the reason for his smile. Stupidly imitating him, he also uttered a guffaw and said, "Sir, your joke is very good, but it is a fact that the Albanians are clever because they eat pluck [*chiger*] while the Bosniaks are strong and brave because they eat cabbage."

The ambassador, somewhat put out, retorted, "According to that principle you have laid down, the Albanians ought to be plucky [*chigerdar*] and the Bosniaks windy."

Jevri and Ebu Ahmed, who understood the point of his remarks, were bursting with involuntary laughter but were ashamed to do so over the food. Forcing back their laughter, they could not even eat.

The tables were cleared, and the reception came to an end. When the ambassador was about to go, Zulfikar said to him, "Please God, we shall enjoy our journey in the company of your excellency." To which the ambassador replied, "Yes, on the way we shall observe some very strange things and be diverted by them; may almighty God in any case keep us safe and sound." He then arose, remarking, "Praise be to God, who created an ox in the form of a man! It is a fine companion whose company we shall enjoy."—and went to his place.

The party having dispersed, Zulfikar detained Jevri and Ebu Ahmed-oglu, and said to them, "Didn't I talk properly to that pander? They brag about their cinnamon and cloves, but if we didn't buy their goods who would? Let us also take pride in the products of our country. He talked to me in fancy language, but I talked back well enough in plain Turkish."

Since, as he was a wealthy man and an ambassador designate, it was not proper to put him to shame, and since equally he lacked the capacity to be taught or made to understand, they found no way but to remain silent. . . .

Ebu Ahmed-oglu gave an account of the affair to Manoglu, who was a friend of his. "Looking at it impartially," he asked, "at a time when ulema and scribes and men of letters are available, is it proper to send such common fellows on embassies just because of their money? Are such scandals compatible with the preservation of the honor and reputation of the Empire?"

—Na'ima

The Manner of Reception of Foreign
Ambassadors Among the Turks, and the Esteem
They Have of Them (1667)

Sir Paul Rycaut was the son of a Flemish banker established in London. He
first went to Turkey in 1661, accompanying the ambassador, Lord Win-
chilsea, and remained there, with occasional brief absences on leave, for
eighteen years, the last twelve as consul at Izmir. His most important work
was The History of the Present State of the Ottoman Empire. *He also wrote*
continuations of the General History of the Turks, *by Richard Knolles, pub-*
lished in 1603.

Embassadours in this Country have need both of courage and circumspec-
tion, wisdom to dissemble with honour, and discreet patience, seemingly to
take no notice of Affronts and Contempts, from which this uncivilized people cannot temperate their Tongues, even when they would seem to put on
the most courteous deportment and respect towards Christians. The *French*
Embassadour, *Monsieur la Haye,* sent once to advise the great Vizier *Ku-*
perlee, that his Master had taken the strong City of *Arras* from the *Spaniard,*
and had obtained other Victories in *Flanders,* supposing that the *Turk*
would outwardly have evidenced some signs of joy, and return an answer
of congratulation; but the reply the Vizier gave, was no other than this,
"What matters it to me whether the Dog worries the Hog, or the Hog the
Dog, so my Masters head be but safe?" intimating that he had no other esteem of Christians, than as Savages or Beasts; and with no other answer than
this, due to an officious Courtship towards a *Turk,* the Messenger returned.
There is no doubt, but of all those means, wherewith Kingdoms and States
are supported, there are two more principal and chief of all others: The one
is the substantial and real strength and force of the Prince, which consists in
his Armies and interest; and the other is the honour and reputation he gains
abroad, which hath sometimes proved of that Authority and consequence,
as to make the State of the weaker Prince to appear more considerable; or at
least, equal to the greater forces of the other. This reputation is principally
maintained by a prudent manner of negotiation, and depends on the discretion of the Representative. . . .

An Embassadour in this Court ought to be circumspect and careful to
avoid the occasion of having his honour blemished, or of incurring the least
violation of his person; for afterward, as one baffled in his reputation, he becomes scorned, loses his power and interest, and all esteem of his worth
and wisdom; for having endured one affront, their insolence soon presumes
farther to trespass on his patience. . . . To reply according to the Pride and

Ignorance of a *Turk,* is properly to blow up fire into a flame; to support with submission and a pusillanimous spirit, his affronts and indignities, by negotiating faintly or coldly, is to add fuel and wood to the burning piles; but solid reason and discourse, accompanied with cheerful expressions, vivacity and courage in argument, is the only manner of dealing and treating with the *Turks.* That which is called good nature or flexible disposition, is of little use to a publick Minister in his treaty with *Turks:* a punctual adherence to former customs and examples even to obstinacy, is the best and safest rule, for the concession of one point serves to embolden them to demand another, and then a third.

—Sir Paul Rycaut

The Dangers of Interpreting (1667)

A principal matter, which a publick Minister ought to look to, is to provide himself of spirited, eloquent and intelligent Interpreters; spirited, I say, because many times the presence is great they appear before, and the looks big and soure of a barbarous Tyrant; and it hath been known, that the Embassadour hath been forced to interpose his own Person between the fury of the Vizier and his Interpreter, whose offence was only a delivery of the words of his Master; some of whom have notwithstanding been imprisoned, or executed for this cause.

—Sir Paul Rycaut

An Orientalist's View (Eighteenth Century)

It has generally happened, that the persons who have resided among the Turks, and who, from their skill in the Eastern dialects, have been best qualified to present us with an exact account of that nation, were either confined to a low sphere of life, or engaged in views of interest, and but little addicted to polite letters or philosophy; while they, who, from their exalted stations and refined taste for literature, have had both the opportunity and inclination of penetrating into the secrets of Turkish policy, were totally ignorant of the language used at Constantinople, and consequently were destitute of the sole means by which they might learn, with any degree of certainty, the sentiments and prejudices of so singular a people. . . . As to the generality of interpreters, we cannot expect from men of their condition any depth of reasoning, or acuteness of observation; if mere words are all they profess, mere words must be all they can pretend to know.

—Sir William Jones

Advice on Negotiations (1768)

Sir James Porter was appointed ambassador to Turkey in 1746, possibly because his brother had married the daughter of one of the most prominent merchants of the Levant Company. He remained in Istanbul for fifteen years and was recalled at his own request. Apart from a brief mission in Brussels, 1763–1765, he devoted the remainder of his life to scientific and literary pursuits. His Observations on the Religion, Law, Government, and Manners of the Turks *was published, in a second revised edition, in 1771.*

Upon such occasions as this, when the mind is not to be worked upon by facts and conviction, and all expedients prove ineffectual, the foreign minister has no other resource but to arm himself with patience, to endeavour to be as coolly firm as they are hot and passionate, to collect all his fortitude, and determine to bear the very worst effects of rage and disappointment. The Turks are persuaded that all events are in his disposal; but whatever his instructions may be, or however things may fall out, he must by all means avoid the most trifling and remote concession. He will be sure to hear many threats and menaces even from his own dragoman, as also insinuations of personal danger; let him then consider himself as Socrates in Plato, happy in adhering to duty and virtue, and carry with him in his own mind that conscious satisfaction, that it will not fail to prove its own reward.

Such perplexing and difficult conjunctures occur but seldom, especially in political affairs: in commercial, there are means to stem the torrent of their wrath by the soothing palliative of a golden unction; this never fails of success.

Let commercial treaties with them be ever so clear and explicit, they will still wrangle, dispute, and wrest them to their own meaning, which they will maintain to be a necessary explanation; when such treaties and capitulations have been at different times renewed, and subsequent advantages granted, it is then they will cavil, confound, and distinguish; they will never agree that the last more favourable article destroys the preceding, but insist that it is at their option to chuse either; nay, they will comment away with red ink on the side of black, till they reduce facts to a sort of metaphysical jargon. . . .

The Turks are exasperated or calm, and their treatment of the minister is more or less severe, according to the behaviour of his court, or as the events of war turn out to their advantage. Their treatment of him is bad at the best, and if the war lasts seven years, he must submit to his fate, and bear the horrors of a rigorous imprisonment. As ministers at every court avail themselves of the favourable moment to raise their master's and their own personal value, such a circumstance as that of war is what a neutral ambassador should seize. The method of proceeding among the Turks is always to conclude a peace by means of a mediation; a mediator they must have, and will most probably shew the most favour to that minister, on whom they think they can most depend. If it should be their fate to be unsuccessful, it will not be in their option to chuse; they then will constantly keep their eye on him, whom they know to have the most credit by friendship, alliance, or otherwise with their enemy. A minister so circumstanced may therefore assume something more, and ask favours which he could not flatter himself with hopes of obtaining at another time: at such a juncture the Turks will not fail to cultivate his friendship, and be cautious how they refuse him any thing he applies for.

—Sir James Porter

Interpreting Treaties (1768)

All negotiations with the Turks must necessarily be carried on in writing. The Vizir never grants an audience, without being previously informed of the general purport of the memorial. This method of treating in writing is dangerous; for, if they send you papers in their own tongue, as I have already observed in a former chapter, they take care to make use of such expressions, as they may afterwards interpret in a sense of their own; synonymous terms abound in their language, and the construction of most of them is precarious. A deep knowledge of the roots of the Arabian and Persian tongues is requisite to render a person perfectly master of theirs; very few of the interpreters employed in the service of the Christian powers are sufficiently versed in these languages: in affairs of importance it is therefore found necessary to have the original Turkish paper accompanied with an Italian translation of their own, however barbarous it may be, though they can write that language tolerably well; the sense will thus be ascertained, and if the minister understands the Italian, which he should by no means be ignorant of, he knows on what ground he stands; otherwise time may discover some capital errors in the substance of his negotiation. It is surprising to see how expert the Turks are at taking this critical advantage: I have known them dispute whole weeks about the wording of political treaties, and a single term has often given rise to the debate.

—Sir James Porter

Thoughts on Book Learning and Intelligence, Credulity and Pedantry (1768)

Many, I fear, will take it for granted, that the knowledge of books is super-fluous, and that the communicating of such intelligence as they pick up at court, will be their chief employment. It must, indeed, be acknowledged that great affairs present themselves only at certain periods; matters of importance do not every day occur: but even this seemingly trivial affair of writing such news as he may be occasionally informed of, becomes, if rightly considered, of much importance; for it will be found that it requires the knowledge of past alliances, connections, and interests of courts, which can be acquired only by reading their history, or such authentic records of past facts as may be entirely depended upon; whence we may combine with their present situations, the probability, truth, or falsehood of the reports we hear or such as are confidently told us for truth.

We must be upon our guard against credulity and distrust of every relator of political intelligence; for courts have sometimes the skill to impose on the foreign minister, by means of artful intelligencers, so that he may be tempted either to alarm, or lull in profound security his own court, according as they happen to have in view the gaining of some present or temporary point. Repeated mistakes of this kind, or sometimes one of importance, by which his court is misled, will cause him to be considered as light and futile, and, of consequence, as a man not fit to be employed in important transactions.

But, however useful or necessary such information from books may be to the statesman, it must be hoarded up like a treasure, and produced only in case of an absolute necessity. Pedantry and an affection of learning are most likely to be considered by men of good understanding as vain parade and ostentation, and, of consequence, produce contempt; besides, they may even pique and mortify the vanity of an ignorant man, who being sensible of his own defects, will look upon them as insults, and resent them accordingly.

—Sir James Porter

A Turkish Ambassador in Spain (1787)

A senior Ottoman official and man of letters, Vasif Efendi later held the post of imperial historiographer.

Barcelona, because of its size, is held by a large garrison commanded by one of the most distinguished generals in the army. This high officer, followed by all the military authorities of the province, came to welcome me on the disembarkation quay and, after having presented his apologies in the most courteous manner, conducted me to the lazaretto. During the whole of our stay in this establishment, the surrounding palisade was beset by an inquisitive crowd who greeted us from afar. Our dress was a new spectacle for them and seemed to cause them deep astonishment. On the twenty-seventh day of our quarantine, when the doctors had subjected every man to a detailed examination, we left in grand procession. Although the lazaretto was only a quarter of an hour's march from the city, we took almost five hours to cover the distance, so great were the crowds that had come to watch our passage. . . .

The commanding general in Valencia . . . was instructed by the king to receive us. He informed us that he would like to offer us dinner and asked us to send our cooks ahead. We accepted his invitation, and we took leave of him after the meal. As I had given the general in Barcelona a richly adorned purse, I felt obliged to make a similar gift to the commandant in Valencia. In return, he sent me two bottles of olive oil. From this alone, one may judge the petty and niggardly character of the Spaniards. . . .

The lodgings placed at my disposal in La Granja were barely sufficient to accommodate the members of the mission and the presents we had brought. However, not wishing to raise further difficulties, I turned a blind eye to this inconvenience. I then learned that they were proposing to give me the reception customary for a simple minister of the second class. The ambassadors of the other powers to the Court of Spain and in particular the Russian ambassador tried hard, however wounding this European custom might be, to make me accept it and overcome my stubbornness. They tried in effect, in a long discussion, to convince me of the need to submit to this treatment. To this I replied that my title was indeed that of a minister of second class but that I could not be treated in the same way as other envoys of this rank; that my mission, having as its purpose to consolidate a newly established alliance, was an extraordinary mission; that I myself enjoyed a very high rank at the Sublime Porte; that, finally, every government had its own distinctive ceremonial. This reply revived the discussion but, thanks be to God, I got what I was asking, and it was agreed that I would be accorded the treatment of ambassador extraordinary. The Court of Spain kept its word to me and gave me such exceptional honors that the other ambassadors were annoyed and could not hide their envy. . . .

The haughty character of the Spaniards and their ignorance of the usages of the imperial [Ottoman] government caused them to treat me on a footing of equality with the envoys of other powers. The chancellor and the master of ceremonies, an Armenian born in Jerusalem and a man of unequaled perversity, called on me one day in the company of the first dragoman and raised the question of the presents which I was to offer to the princes and princesses of the blood, to the first minister, to the viceroy of the Indies, and to all the grandees of the court, according to their ranks. They listed the presents their ambassador had offered to the Sublime Porte and asked me to reciprocate.

To this I replied, "When my government sends an ambassador to an emperor or to a king, that ambassador presents gifts to no one other than the sovereign. This is an established, well-known custom about which you may ask the foreign ambassadors resident in Madrid. It is not for me to depart from it. The envoys of other powers do indeed offer gifts to the officials of the Porte, but there is no precedent for this custom being followed by our own envoys. In any case, if the latter sometimes conform, it is of their own free will and out of their own natural generosity and not in performance of some diplomatic requirement." To all the reasons I expounded to them, to the references and even reproaches I addressed to them, they responded with so many untenable and irrelevant arguments that it was impossible for me to convince them. Finally they told me that if I persisted in my refusal, I would not get a second audience with the king and that the gifts I had brought for him would be returned to me. "Very well," I said, "give orders to arrange for my immediate departure." "You will have a reply within one or two hours," they said, and left.

However, the representatives of powers friendly to the Porte warned me that I could not hope to overcome the arrogant and presumptuous character of the Spaniards and that I should try to make known to the king what had happened at this discussion. The king, warned by well-intentioned third parties, began by expressing his regret at the line taken by these two officials, and especially at their threat not to allow me a second audience, but he added, "Although the custom of offering gifts to others besides the sovereign has not been adopted by Ottoman diplomacy, nevertheless the ambassador of the Porte would do me a great personal favor if he would be kind enough to distribute some curiosities coming from Constantinople."

This approach allowed me to abandon my resistance, and I sent the following items purchased by me in Constantinople: The crown prince received a saber with a gold-encrusted pommel, a gilded musket mounted in silver, five Indian shawls with gold-embroidered flowers, two turbans, a piece of ermine, a dagger with a diamond-covered hilt and some perfume. To the princess, his wife, I offered a dagger, a musket and a saber plus a sumptuous and complete bath outfit. To the first minister, a dagger similar to the one I had offered to the crown prince. Finally, the chancellors, the colonel of the royal bodyguard, a highly esteemed personage at the court, the first dragoman, the officials whose duty it was to introduce the ambassadors, received different souvenirs from me. Not only did neither the king nor the court offer me any gifts equivalent to my own, but the value of the rations accorded to me did not suffice to cover my expenses. It will be difficult to convey any idea of the poverty and dearth that afflict Spain. The three sheep we ate every day cost twelve piastres each. The fine oil, two piastres. A cartload of firewood, forty piastres, though I concede that the cart was very large. A chicken, forty paras, and so forth. . . .

While I was in Madrid, gifts addressed to the king by the bey [of Algiers] arrived. They consisted of three horses, two lions and some ostriches. Also, to show his disdain for his neighbors, the bey, instead of sending these gifts in charge of one of his officers, just handed them over to the Spanish consul in Algiers, who had himself come to present them to his government. Nor is that all. It was agreed that the bey would ransom the hundred-odd Algerian prisoners who remained in Spanish hands. When the time came to carry out this agreement, he replied, "These prisoners are rogues and cowards of no concern to me; otherwise they would not have allowed themselves to be captured."

—Vasif Efendi

Petition from a Dragoman
(c. 1767)

Aidé, also spelled Áida and Ayda, was the name of a Christian family of Aleppo who worked as dragomans for the British Levant Company in that city in the eighteenth century. Later the name also appears among the "language students" of the British embassy in Istanbul. George Aidé was appointed acting first dragoman in Aleppo in 1747 and continued his work until his death in September 1778. According to the Levant Company records, he was twice jailed by the authorities. The first time was in 1747, when he was arrested by order of the pasha in connection with a dispute arising from the merchant caravan to Baghdad. His release was secured by the British ambassador. In 1767 he was involved in a dispute between the Janissaries and the sharifs of Aleppo, on the side of the latter. As a result, he was imprisoned in the Citadel for a time. He was again released, apparently by the intervention of the British ambassador or consul. While in prison, he drafted a petition to the aga of the Janissaries, a copy of which is preserved in the Public Record Office in London (S.P. 102/62). The document is undated but appears to date from George Aidé's second imprisonment. A translation follows.

Having bowed my head in submission and rubbed my slavish brow in utter humility and humbleness and complete abjection and supplication to the beneficent dust beneath the feet of my mighty, gracious, condescending, compassionate, merciful, benefactor, my most generous and open-handed master and Sultan, I pray that the peerless and almighty Provider of Remedies may bless your lofty person, the extremity of benefit, protect my bene-factor from the vicissitudes and afflictions of time, prolong his days of his life, his might and his splendor, and perpetuate the shadow of his pity and mercy upon this slave. Amen.

The petition of your ancient slave to the might of the dust of the conde-scending residence is this: your enduring bondsman has spent thirty years in the service of your Highness, the manifester of generosity and nobility. As your Highness well knows, I have, in the days of my benefactor's might, presumed as far as I was able to perform, carry out and discharge my duties with loyalty and rectitude, for all and especially those who needed it in their business and affairs and the conduct of their interests and business. After all this, because of a slander and calumny, of which I was the victim, my inter-pretership which is the source of my livelihood was withdrawn, I was im-prisoned in the citadel of Aleppo and subjected to grievous affliction. I have no resort and refuge but my gracious and benevolent master. Your mercy and condescension have been previously granted to me, and your humble slave has heard that you have addressed excellent and merciful words to one of the slaves of the Lofty Lintel [i.e., the Ottoman government in Istan-bul]. At your order and ferman, I await your grace. Your slave, without crime or offence, and purely because of slander and calumny, has been humbled and humiliated and my impotent person is in the extremity of dis-tress. Consequently, I have sent a sealed petition concerning my dejected condition to your distinguished stirrup, the refuge of might, the center of mercy, the benefactor of the world, His Excellency, my glorious, puissant, mighty, powerful benefactor and master, for the imperial and majestic stir-rup [of the sultan]. Since I in my humble person have no refuge unless my master vouchsafes his condescension and mercy, let orders be given that my case be properly investigated and examined by the people of Aleppo, great and small, Muslims and others, and when it becomes known to the Eternal Dynasty that I have been oppressed and wronged, then I cannot conceive that, in the days of might of His Excellency my glorious and puis-sant master, imperial license will be given for such wrong and oppression to be wrought against any person. Since His Excellency my condescending master is my sole resort, prayer and hope for the investigation of the slan-derers in my case, the establishment of their identity and the freeing of this slave from the misfortune that has befallen him, I have dared to write a hum-ble petition to bring the matter to his gracious attention. Please Almighty God, when you condescend to give a gracious glance at this, since my mas-ter has deigned to help and succour other persons who had not the long-standing position of this slave, it is the sole wish and desire of this slave that you will save him from this catastrophe and grant him aid and succour. Fur-ther, it is possible that you request a properly authenticated attestation from all the people of the city of this slave's good character, innocence and wrongful condemnation. But if the merciful Sublime Porte, from its lofty consideration, refuses this . . . then let it be known to your Highness that I await your mercy and condescension with humility and patience, and in that case it is for my mighty, gracious and merciful benefactor, my most generous master and sultan, to command and be generous as he may please.

—The slave
George Aidé

In God's Almighty name

Petition to the mighty dust beneath the feet of my mighty, gracious, merciful, bounteous, compassionate benefactor, most generous master and sultan, now aga of the Janissaries of the lofty Court at the Sublime Porte.

The Dragoman System in the Levant: A Foreign Office Memorandum

By Mr. Murray, January 1838

The evils of the present Dragoman System in the Levant are so obvious and undoubted, that the Question has repeatedly been asked, what Plan can be devised for providing an effectual Remedy?

Without entering into the nature of those evils, which are too well understood to require to be here explained, it may merely be necessary to observe that the objects of any remedy must be to provide the services of British subjects, upon whom entire trust and reliance may be placed, in lieu of Foreigners, upon whom no reliance whatever can be placed, not only from the fact of their being Foreigners, and therefore alien to British feelings and interests, but from the more important circumstance of their being part of a united Body, such as the whole set of Dragomans employed by various Foreign Powers in the East are known to be.

The main question, then, appears to resolve itself into the following queries:

1. How can the efficient services of British subjects be best provided?
2. What class of men should be employed?
3. What system should be adopted for ensuring a succession of individuals competent to the discharge of the important duties of interpreters to HM Embassy in the Levant? . . .

It will be seen that Col. Campbell suggests—as the only means of effectively succeeding in making Englishmen thoroughly acquainted with Eastern languages, so as to render them fit for what is wanted from them—that several young Gentlemen should be sent out to Turkey. Being there placed under the charge of the Consuls, for the purpose of studying the languages and habits of the country, they could be usefully employed in the Consulates. . . .

In considering what Class of Men should be employed, we must look to what they have to do. The ultimate object is to place them in situations of the most confidential nature in the Embassy, where they will be the medium of communication between the Ambassadors and the Porte: The value of their services in these situations will therefore depend upon their integrity and intelligence, and upon the confidence reposed in them by the Turkish Authorities. A Turkish Minister is known to fear, because he can not trust any Dragoman—not even his own; and at the present time a British Minister of Constantinople cannot be said to have any certain means of ascertaining what are the real sentiments of a Turkish Minister, or in what degree his reported sentiments vary from the truth.

If we change the character of this medium of communication with the Turks, and make him instead of a mere *Interpreter,* an ostensible and important Member of the Embassy and of this Diplomatic Service, there can be no doubt that his footing, and the footing of the Embassies at the Porte, will be of a different kind from what it has hitherto been. Indeed the nature of the Duties of such a Functionary appear to require that he should hold Rank and Station in the Embassy and in the Service; and when the Turkish Minister finds himself in communication with persons holding such Rank and Station, his Pride will be flattered, and he will appreciate the pains that have been taken to hold safe intercourse with him.

From these considerations it appears that the class of Men to be employed, must be Gentlemen of Talent and Education, carefully selected as persons who may hereafter be promoted according to their merits, to those higher situations in the Diplomatic or Consular Service which they may be competent to fill.

In answer to the third question "What system should be adopted for ensuring a succession of individuals competent to discharge the important Duties of interpreters to their Embassy in the Levant, and also with reference to the previous observations, it is submitted that the Constitution of the Embassy at Constantinople might be hereafter changed, so that its subordinate Members and the Candidates for Employment in it may be permitted to look forward to Honours as well as to salary.

Without such Stimulus to exertion it is scarcely possible to exert oneself. The study of Eastern Languages, Manners, and Habits, appears rarely to have been undertaken for pleasure, and yet a perfect knowledge of all is requisite for the object in view. Of course such knowledge can only be gained *in* Turkey, and thence it is apparent most Students should be sent out. If Distinctions be held out as the reward of well directed Talent and application, abundant efforts will doubtless be made to gain such Distinctions; and there would be no difficulty in selecting from amongst the Students Persons qualified for the highest offices. . . .

This would render the Consular Service in the Levant more efficient and useful in every way. British influence amongst the Natives would doubtless be greatly increased; An opportunity would be afforded of judiciously encouraging the use of objects of British Production, and, independently of Political Advantages, commercial intercourse might in this way be considerably promoted.

—The Public Record Office, London

Embassy Etiquette and an Audience with the Sultan
(1824–27)

Impressions of a traveling physician.

One would expect that, where there are so many foreign ambassadors and Europeans attached to them, there would be much pleasant society; but it would be a vain expectation. The diplomatic people of Pera constitute the court, and the miserable Levantine droguemen the nobility; they actually are deemed such, and the airs they give themselves are quite ridiculous.

I flattered myself I should get an immense deal of information on Turkish subjects at the French ambassador's, where I had the honour of dining; but the "jeunes de langues," the young diplomatists, had other topics to discuss: the etiquette of embassies was their eternal theme; they thought of nothing but etiquette, they dreamed of nothing but etiquette, they talked of nothing but etiquette. I never was so nauseated in my life. I was invited to the English "chargé d'affaires;" "Here," I said, "at least there will be some rational conversation, a respite from the horrors of *etiquette;*" but I reckoned without my host; the oriental secretary was disputing a point of etiquette with the secretary of the French embassy, the moment I entered. The whole soul of the English employé seemed wrapped up in the subject of the debate, and nothing but etiquette rung on my tympanum from the beginning to the end of the entertainment. I was heartily sickened of diplomatic slang: and have had, ever since, a sort of instinctive horror of the nobility of Pera and of *etiquette*.

Nothing can exceed the ambition of the people of the embassy to attend the ambassador, in their laced coats, at his audience with the Sultan; and nothing can equal the absurdity of that ceremony except its humiliation. The French have the priority in all public audiences. The ambassador proceeds with his credentials to the *Porte,* passes through a large square thronged with soldiers, then through a garden where it is arranged the soldiers should, at that time, receive their *pilaw,* to astonish the infidels with the vastness of the Sultan's bounty. He next enters the *divan,* where a principal officer sits in great state on a splendid sofa, with a *cadilesker* on either side. Some cause here undergoes a mock trial, to prove to the unbelievers that his Imperial Highness is just, as well as generous; a number of money bags, containing paras (the fourth of farthings), are pompously displayed for the payment of the troops, to show the *giaours* the inexhaustible wealth of the *Grand Seignior.* The officer in waiting now writes a letter to the Sultan, stating that "a giaour, an ambassador, comes to throw himself at his Highness's feet;" and to this the Sultan graciously replies, "Feed and clothe the infidel, and let him come." The infidel is accordingly fed, gets a good dinner; and, during it, the Sultan is peeping through a lattice at his guests, where his person is hardly visible. The infidel is next clothed with a *caftan,* as are also a portion of his followers, who proceed to the audience chamber, where the arms of the ambassador are laid hold of by two assistants, and thus pinioned, he is led before the Sultan, and his body as much bowed as the force of the officers holding him admits of. The Sultan sits on a bed-shaped throne, ornamented with black velvet and precious stones; his dress has nothing peculiar to his station, but the diamond aigrette and feather in his turban, and the diamond girdle round his loins. The ambassador having bowed, remains covered, and makes his speech in French; the drogueman translates it; and then the principal officer of the Sultan replies, and this reply is again given in French to the ambassador. During the ceremony, the Sultan hardly deigns to look at the ambassador, or even to notice him on his retiring. The infidels are then forced out of the presence, with their faces to the throne. At the outer gate a richly-caparisoned horse is presented to the ambassador; and the trappings, which are principally of silver, are, some time after, sold to an *Armenian,* who sells them again to the *Porte* for a future present. I saw the French ambassador's present thus disposed of. Such is the degradation which we suffer our ambassadors to undergo, being even stripped of their swords before they are admitted to the presence of the haughty Sultan.

—R. R. Madden

A Lesson in Pride (1833)

Adolphus Slade was a British naval officer who traveled extensively in the Ottoman lands in the 1830s and was lent by the British admiralty as an advisor to the Ottoman navy during and after the Crimean War.

Pride is necessary to ensure respect from the Osmanley [Ottoman], who ascribes even common politeness to submission. It is not uncommon with him, in order to ascertain the quality of a stranger, to drop something, as a handkerchief; if the stranger neglect it he is set down as a person of distinction, who is accustomed to be served, not to serve others; if he pick it up, which is very natural, the contrary is inferred. It is one unpleasantness of being acquainted with Osmanleys, that you must, for your own sake, disregard good breeding in many points. For example, a bey or an aga pays you a visit; you rise to receive him; he attributes the movement to the innate respect of a Christian for a Mussulman. You may go into his room fifty times without receiving the same compliment, though he will pay it to a Mussulman of similar rank. The Frank, in short, in his intercourse with Osmanleys, should never abate one iota of his due as a gentleman; if he do, he is soon regarded in a menial light.

—Adolphus Slade

Levantine Manners

By a Levantine is meant a Frank who has totally abandoned his native country, and fixed himself in Turkey for good. He cannot be mistaken. He is a compound of the Turk, the Greek, and the Frank: disfigured by the moustache of the first, the long hair of the second, the whiskers and dress of the third; not the dress usually worn in Europe, but a mixture of fashions for the preceding half century; no wonder that the easterns think it unbecoming. He talks many languages—none well: he is servile with Moslems, pert with Christians—your humble servant abroad, a tyrant at home.

—Adolphus Slade

Reception and Reform (1867)

With Sultan Abdul Medjid's reign [1839–1861] commenced the intermittent sway of European ambassadors at Constantinople. Their position alone showed the significance of the change, effected within a few years, in the relations of Turkey with Christendom. Under the old régime, an ambassador had been tolerated rather than recognized in the capital of the successor of the caliphs. His presentation at court to deliver his credentials was a comedy. . . . He was regarded during his sojourn in Turkey as an accredited spy; and as such, on a declaration of war with his sovereign, was sent to the Seven Towers. In his rare interviews with the Grand Vizir, he sat lower than that functionary, and his dragoman, wearing a *calpak,* knelt at his highness's feet.

An ambassador, under the new régime, has had nothing to complain of on the score of etiquette; he has no longer been stuffed with *moalebbi* and *pilaf*, nor sprinkled with rosewater. He has stood, with sword by his side and cocked hat in his hand, face to face with the Sultan; he has lounged on the same sofa with the Grand Vizir; and his dragoman has smoked amicably with the Reis Efendi, thenceforwards ycleped minister for foreign affairs. The mission of ambassadors under the new régime was ostensibly to encourage or observe Turkey in the new path traced for her by fate. Some of them came out with theories ready cut and dried for her regeneration, and moulded facts to suit; others came with objects in reference to her, and wove theories to justify them. Either process was easy; for Levantines have the art to divine the bias of a man's mind, and the tact to adapt their conversation to it. An influential man in the East, be he Christian or Moslem, may give what shape he likes to the passing cloud—a camel, a weasel, or a whale; he will always find a Polonius ready to echo him. Thence, in part arises the difficulty of a diplomatist at Constantinople losing a wrong scent. Socially isolated, in a country devoid of periodical literature, he has not opportunities, as in other lands, to correct or confirm his views by friendly intercourse with natives of various callings and opinions. Remarks incidentally dropped in familiar conversation over a chibouque, throw light on doubtful points, suggest further inquiry, and sometimes vexatiously upset a pet theory based on misapprehension or hasty generalization. He has no intercourse with the ruling race, excepting ministers of state, conversing with those ignorant of a western language through an interpreter, when words are weighed and sentences measured; nor with the rayas, beyond a select few who thrive upon their footing at embassies. The dinners of the minister of foreign affairs, at which diplomatists and state dignitaries mingle, give him no insight into national manners; for the table is Parisian, the conversation vapid, and the Faithful drink as though the prophet had enjoined, not forbidden, indulgence in wine. At his dinners, given in return, the guests, leaving prejudices with their slippers at the door, discourse politely with unveiled ladies, and, blandly declining ham in conjunction with turkey, see merit in punch *à la Romaine*.

—Adolphus Slade

An English View of an American
Consul-General (1844)

After this community of holy men, the most important perhaps is the American Convent, a Protestant congregation of Independents chiefly, who deliver tracts, propose to make converts, have meetings of their own, and also

swell the little congregation that attends the Anglican service. I have mentioned our fellow-traveller, the Consul-General for Syria of the United
States. He was a tradesman, who had made a considerable fortune, and
lived at a country-house in comfortable retirement. But his opinion is, that
the prophecies of Scripture are about to be accomplished; that the day of
the return of the Jews is at hand, and the glorification of the restored
Jerusalem. He is to witness this—he and a favourite dove with which he
travels; and he forsook home and comfortable country-house, in order to
make this journey. He has no other knowledge of Syria but what he derives
from the prophecy; and this (as he takes the office gratis) has been considered a sufficient reason for his appointment by the United States Government. As soon as he arrived, he sent and demanded an interview with the
Pasha; explained to him his interpretation of the Apocalypse, in which he
has discovered that the Five Powers and America are about to intervene in
Syrian affairs, and the infallible return of the Jews to Palestine. The news
must have astonished the Lieutenant of the Sublime Porte; and since the
days of the Kingdom of Munster, under his Anabaptist Majesty, John of Ley-
den, I doubt whether any Government has received or appointed so queer
an ambassador. The kind, worthy, simple man took me to his temporary
consulate-house at the American Missionary Establishment; and, under pretence of treating me to white wine, expounded his ideas; talked of futurity
as he would about an article in *The Times;* and had no more doubt of seeing
a divine kingdom established in Jerusalem than you that there would be a
levée next spring at St. James's. The little room in which we sat was padded
with missionary tracts, but I heard of scarce any converts—not more than
are made by our own Episcopal establishment.

—William Makepeace Thackeray

Advice to a Vice Consul, from a Friend (1837)

Letter to Richard Wood, British vice consul in Syria.

My dear Wood,

I was very pleased to find a letter from you awaiting me on my return
from the North of Europe whither I have been taking a short excursion. . . .
If you have kept a Journal (which I know you have) of your Travels & could
put [them] into form you might make 7 or 800£ by it, but book making is
quite a knack as your stories must be dressed to suit the appetite of the reading public who will gourmandise a few stories or anecdotes well told, but
will close a Book at the second Page which contained perhaps valuable information appearing in a dry form.

—Captain William Lyon

And a Warning from an American Visitor (1856)

Pera, the headquarters of embassadors, and where also an unreformed diplomacy is carried on by swindlers, gamblers, cheats. No place in the world fuller of knaves.

—Herman Melville

Modern Diplomacy

A Persian Mission to England (1838–39)

In 1838 Muḥammad Shāh sent an envoy on a special mission to England, France and Austria.

While we were in Paris, I tried to get a book which would contain a description of the countries of the inhabited world and their true condition, so as to quote extracts from it on each country in these pages. When we were leaving Paris for Iran, M. Jouannin, interpreter to the French government, brought in, as a present, a geography book that described the whole world. . . . I had a provisional translation made by Mr. Jebra'il, a Christian who was first interpreter to our mission. . . .

In fact, since the Europeans always want to inform themselves about the true situation of all the countries in the world, they have for a long time been sending expert persons to all parts to note and record the situation and have assembled this information in this geography book. . . . If H.M. the Shahanshah . . . would order the translation of this book into the Persian language, it would be of lasting value for the realm of Iran and for all the peoples of Islam.

On Board Ship—On the Way to England

Four English girls came on board, very intelligent but very ugly. Surely they had been unable to find suitors in their own country; they had therefore found themselves obliged to go abroad and had traveled around for a long time in the hope of finding husbands, but had failed in their purpose and were now returning home.

The London and Croydon Railway, 1839

The railway and the steam train, which, in Europe, were invented and built in England, provide a very efficient mode of travel. During our stay in London, the director of the railway, which was six parasangs long and had then just been built, invited the ajudan-bashi, saying that thirty-two English notables had formed a society and built this railway line. He said that on that day crowds of Englishmen would gather at points on the line, at its beginning and at its end, to see the show and wait for the steam engine to get under way. In response to this invitation from the director, the ajudan-bashi and I went then at the appointed time. The line extended for six parasangs beyond the suburbs of London. The director asked us, saying, "Since you are Persian noblemen, we would be very honored if you would go first into the new coach." In view of his prayers and insistence, we left our coach, walked a few steps, and entered the train.

About thirty thousand or forty thousand men and women were assembled there. As soon as they saw us, they began to shout and cry out in astonishment and seemed to be about to surround us. But the ajudan-bashi saluted them politely, and they responded by taking off their caps, so all went well. But a little carelessness would have been enough to make it go badly. In fact, they for their part were not wrong, since our appearance, in clothing and otherwise, must have seemed very strange to their eyes—especially my beard, which has few equals in the whole of Europe.

[The journey took thirty-two minutes and ended with a great reception.]
—Embassy of Ḥusayn Khan Muqaddam Ajudanbashi
(account written by his secretary 'Abd al-Fattāḥ Khan Garmrūdī)

The Shah in Europe (1873)

Nāṣir al-Dīn Shah of Persia was not the first Muslim monarch to visit western Europe; he was preceded a few years earlier by Sultan 'Abd al-'Aziz of Turkey. He was, however, the first royal Muslim visitor to produce a record of his adventures and impressions, for the enlightenment of his subjects.

London

We were invited this evening to the house of the Lord Mayor,—the Governor of the old city of London, for an evening party and supper. . . . We passed along in front of imposing public buildings, magnificent shops, and open squares, and so came to the gate of the City (Temple Bar), i.e., of the old town of London, over which the Lord Mayor is Governor, though he has no authority over the other townships and parishes; i.e., the remainder of the town has no Governor, but each parish has a council (vestry), and if any (grave) event happen, it is referred to the head policeman, i.e., the head patrol-man, of the parish, and he refers to the Home Secretary. The police of this town is eight thousand strong, all handsome young men, in a particular dress. The citizens set great estimation on the police; whoever behaves disrespectfully to the police, is adjudged worthy of death.

Well; we arrived at the door of the Lord Mayor's house, ascended some steps, and there was a hall, where were assembled the Heirs-Apparent of England and Russia, their wives, all the Corps Diplomatique, our princes and others, the princes, the lady-princesses; ladies of distinction, the magnates, and the English Ministers. We shook hands with each of the Heirs-Apparent, and saluted. This is a Government building in which the Governor of London resides. It is called the Guildhall. Once a year, at the discretion and choice of the citizens, this Governor is changed. The members of the local administration wear a remarkable costume, large sable caps, gowns and robes lined with sable, &c., carrying in one hand a long thin stick, and in the other a small sword in the ancient fashion. They walked in front of us. . . .

Manchester

The city of Manchester, by reason of its exceeding number of manufactories, has its houses, doors and walls, black as coal. So much so, that the complexions, visages, and dresses of the people are all black. The whole of the ladies of that place at most times wear black clothing, because, no sooner do they put on white or coloured dresses, than lo! they are suddenly black.

The Governor, magnates, and nobles of the city, with the magistrates of the environs, were at the station waiting. We mounted a carriage and drove to the Government House, where there was a large hall. On the top of a flight of steps they had placed a chair, on which we took our seat. The Governor made a speech; and we gave a detailed reply, enunciatory of our friendship with the Government of England, and of the pleasure and gratification we had experienced from the fact that, from the first of our arrival on the soil of England, the greatest regard had been shown us by the Sovereign and the nation. Lārānsūn Sahib interpreted this in English. Every one approved.

We then went to another room, where breakfast was laid out. We ate a little; and then, mounting a carriage, we drove to see a manufactory of cotton yarn. We drove down a very long street, both sides of which were densely crowded with people. They so shouted their hurrahs that one's ears were nearly deafened. They showed a very great desire to see us.

We arrived at the manufactory, which was of five stories, in each of which one kind of work was carried on. For the most part, women were em-

ployed at the work, and made the yarns and other things. On the ground-
floor they wove cotton cloths, which, when taken to another place, were
colored as chintzes, and are carried to all parts of the world. The lower
workroom was exceedingly interesting, and was as spacious as a large public square. Certainly there were about two thousand looms there for weav-
ing, and at each loom four women were occupied. I walked past the whole.
Suddenly the manufactory was (as it were) overthrown by voices. Maidens,
matrons, and men sang a pretty song. After the singing was over we went
forth, mounted our carriage, and drove to the station, whence we started on
our return to Trentham. . . .

Paris

M. Cremieux, one of the French national deputies, and a Jew, who was always in opposition to Napoleon III, and is a marvellous orator, came to an
audience. He is an old man, and very short. He still speaks in the Assembly,
and is in opposition to the Government.

The celebrated Rothschild, a Jew also, who is exceedingly rich, came to
an audience, and we conversed with him. He greatly advocated the cause of
the Jews, mentioned the Jews of Persia, and claimed tranquillity for them. I
said to him: "I have heard that you, brothers, possess a thousand crores of
money. I consider the best thing to do would be that you should pay fifty
crores to some large or small State, and buy a territory in which you could
collect all the Jews of the whole world, you becoming their chiefs, and leading them on their way in peace, so that you should no longer be thus scattered and dispersed." We laughed heartily, and he made no reply. I gave
him an assurance that I do protect every alien nationality that is in Persia.

—*The Diary of H.M. the Shah of Persia During His Tour Through
Europe in A.D. 1873* (translated by J. W. Redhouse)

Letters from Persia (1925)

*Harold Nicolson was born in 1886, in the Legation Compound in Tehran, where
his father was secretary. He himself joined the foreign service in World War I and
in due course was posted to the British legation in Tehran, where he met Reza
Shah Pahlavi, who had come to power by the coup d'état of February 1921. The
following excerpts are taken from letters to his wife, Vita Sackville-West.*

An Audience with the Foreign Minister; December 3, 1925

This morning early I dressed in my tail-coat and was taken by Percy [Lo-
raine, the British minister in Tehran] to see the Foreign Minister. The Foreign

Office is rather a jolly old building with a courtyard and a fountain and the most heavenly picture running right across the top of the staircase. A life-size (or over-life-size) fresco of a Foreign Ambassador being received by Fath Ali-Shah.

Then we went into a little room with a wallpaper of yellow chrysanthe-mums and red damask curtains. And there were little red arm-chairs with tockles [lamps] and cigarettes: they brought us tea. The minister is a copper-coloured man, or rather bronze-coloured, and after a long discussion about my nativity, we settled down to business, which meant just silence and sighs. I see that this is no place for impiness and that I must realise that what took 5 minutes at home must take two hours here. So we smoked and drank tea and talked at very distant intervals about the weather, and then the M.F.A. [Minister of Foreign Affairs] fished in his frock coat and brought out a tiny bit of paper which the interpreter translated and which was all about a river I had never heard of and the iniquitous treatment accorded to that river by the Government of Iraq. And so by easy flatulent stages one passed on to more serious business.

Reza Shah Pahlavi; Tehran, December 10, 1925

In the afternoon I went to see Reza Khan. He lives in a little white villa in a garden. We went in by the street door, as the garden-door was crowded with guards and lancers. We were shown into a little white room with a huge fire and atrocious Louis XVI furniture. The room gave on to a sort of balcony or loggia and we hadn't been there long before the windows were darkened by an immense figure passing in front of them. The end-windows opened and he came in. He was in Khaki uniform with a peaked Khaki hat—slashed at the corners. He hadn't shaved very well and glowered out of the corner of his eye at us. He was quite alone. He is about six-foot-three and inclined to corpulence. He has fat red hands like Gerry [Wellesley]. He has bad teeth, fine eyes and chin, and a determined nose. A clipped greyish moustache. But he looked cross and tired and dirty. Then he sat down.

I told him of the interest he aroused in England and how we hoped he would make a nice good kind Shah. He was pleased by these assertions, and relaxed. He gave us cigarettes and cakes and tea. Suddenly he took his hat off—disclosing a tiny little shaven head like a Russian Cossack. He looked more of a scallywag than ever. But then gradually he began to talk quite calmly about becoming Shah, and his arrangements for his corona-tion, and how cross everyone was, and how he had felt his collar too tight at the opening ceremony, and how Farman Farma had been photographed sitting on the steps. And then he laughed a sort of non-commissioned officer laugh—and asked me how old I was. He wouldn't believe it when I told him and said evidently I had had no troubles in love or politics. I thought of my darling digging away over there at our mud-pie. Then he laughed a great deal—and for the rest of the interview was simple and jolly and with a certain force and dignity. But I am not so sure about him. I haven't seen enough Persians yet to compare him with. Anyhow he was very cordial and told me to come and see him as often as I liked when he was Shah. He adores Percy—and Percy is rather pleased with himself (and with justice) at having backed a winner from the start—and *such* a winner.

—Harold Nicolson

Politics in Syria Under the French Mandate (1934)

The British consul in Damascus describes how the Syrians resisted French attempts to replace the League of Nations Mandate with an unequal treaty. His somewhat acerbic comments on both the Syrians and the French evoke a friendly rebuke from his chief.

From: Gilbert MacKereth
To: Foreign Office, November 7, 1934

So long as the nationalists and, with them, the bulk of the population persisted, as they have done, in their intention not to be willingly bound by the terms of a treaty, which they believe would entangle them forever in the web of a French Army, the final suspension, based on precedent, of parliamentary sittings was a foregone conclusion. It had become abundantly clear that the only use the mandatory power had for a Syrian parliament was for it to give binding legal sanction to the treaty signed on November 16, 1933. Yet the seeming clumsiness of the French moves, apparently designed to persuade the deputies to vote for its ratification on the re-opening of the session, has been so flagrant that a doubt naturally arises concerning the sincerity of their efforts. Motives and facts have to-day become so distorted that any calm and reasonable discussion on the subject between the French and Syrians is well nigh impossible. In any case, they require a touch to correct them gentler than that with which Mr. de Martel [the French high commissioner] appears to be endowed. There is little doubt that had parliament reassembled with the treaty still on the agenda the representatives of the Syrian people, elected under French guidance in 1932, would have again rejected it, perhaps even more violently than on the first occasion. The position is thus farcical and in its bare reality engenders little esteem for the mandatory authorities.

The French attitude to the treaty obligations contained in Article 22 of the Covenant in respect to Syria appears to grow more confused at each successive raising of the question. The effrontery and disingenuousness of the answers of Mr. de Caix to the question put to him at the twenty-fifth session of the Permanent Mandates Commission of the League of Nations on June 4th, 5th, and 6th last on the subjects of the Franco-Syrian Treaty and the "Composition of the Syrian Cabinet and the Attitude of Parliament thereto" appear, examined in Syria, so palpable that, as they escaped derision by the members of the Mandates Commission, it is not easy to avoid the conviction that the Commission was itself bent on saving its face. It perhaps shirked a confession of its own complete and spineless ineptitude, fearing that the criticism it must have felt tempted to make would be flung contemptuously back at it.

It is not my desire to express views about the suitability of leaving the Syrians free to decide upon the form of government best fitting their needs, nor do I wish to pronounce upon their ability to govern themselves. These questions, though frequently asked, are fatuous in the absence of accepted standards of political consciousness and of government. It might, for instance, be thought by some a warp of intelligence to argue that as the government of Albania, for example, would probably fail to govern the United States of America under N.R.A. rules, so was it incapable of governing Albania well enough to please, as far as any government pleases the governed, the Albanians. Yet France and the League of Nations go some way in this direction in their sophistry about Syria. The result degrades Europeans in general and puts diplomacy back into the shifty age of intrigue, dependent upon the fabrication of half-truths.

That France intends to cling to what has come to her need astonish nobody. That the *Covenant* of the League of Nations should be pharisaically interpreted is no longer strange, especially when it is applied to the "weak and beggarly elements" once "communities formerly belonging to the Turkish Empire." It is immaterial now to consider whether it may or may not be to the eventual profit of the Syrians that France should resettle herself firmly in the Syrian saddle. It is, nevertheless, a pity that European civilization should, to gain its ends, need to stoop so low. It ought, therefore, to cause no surprise that the Syrians hoard their hate of the mandatory power. Had they only the physical courage they would to-day echo meaningly the words of Lord Hussey: "The world will never mend till we fight for it." But this part of the world had long since ceased to bear martyrs, otherwise the path of the Syrian mandate would have been strewn already with the bodies of French functionaries, innocent victims of popular discontent. As it is, the nationalists, to gain a cherished independence, piously pretend to eschew violence in a preference for "constitutional means." Their constitution being unconstitutionally flouted, they seek consolation in their flatulent manifestos.

A Reply from the Head of the Eastern Department

From: G. W. Rendel, Foreign Office, December 4, 1934
To: Gilbert MacKereth

My dear MacKereth:

I was very interested in your despatch No. 60 (2538/1/3) of November 7th regarding the indefinite suspension of the Syrian Parliament, but I wonder if you will forgive me if I give you a word of entirely private and friendly warning about the manner in which you make one or two of your points?

From this and one or two other recent despatches of yours some of us here have—possibly quite wrongly—derived the impression that you feel a good deal of contempt not only for the so-called mandatory system, but for the whole French administration in Syria and perhaps also for the Syrians themselves. I do not for one moment dispute that this may be more than justified. These things are, however, to a certain extent comparative. There are unfortunately a great number of old systems of government, and of contemptible, corrupt, inefficient and generally despicable administrations about. There are very few systems or nations that are wholly admirable; and having lived a good deal in the Levant myself, I can well understand the feelings with which certain aspects of Syrian "politics" do not inspire you. But as I say, these things are comparative, and most of this can be taken for granted. If this aspect of the local atmosphere is too much or too constantly insisted upon one is very apt to defeat one's own object. I think, therefore, if you will forgive my saying so, that your appreciation of the situation might "cut rather more ice" here if you were to assume that we are fully akin to this aspect of the business, and were to concentrate a little more on trying to pick out the facts or features which, when all this has been taken for granted, still may have some real or at least wider political importance.

There are two other small points where I think perhaps a word of friendly advice may not be out of place. The first is that here in the Foreign Office pressure of work from all sides, particularly with the higher officials, is so great, that the virtue which is most keenly appreciated in any document is brevity and conciseness. It has often happened to me to be unable to submit even to an Assistant Undersecretary of State, far less to the Secretary of State himself, an otherwise entirely admirable report on quite an important subject, simply because I knew that owing to its length, there would be not even the smallest possibility of its being read. The result is that it often happens that a report of one or two pages on a less important subject will go through to higher quarters, while one of five or more cannot go any higher.

The other point is the question of style. I feel sure you realize that reports of general interest are often given a wide circulation here, and that many of them are printed. But it is very necessary in writing a report likely to be given such a circulation, to bear one's audience in mind. Humour or sarcasm admirably fitted for domestic consumption of a particular department of the Foreign Office, may produce quite the wrong reaction in other places. There is a type of wit which, if delicately and tactfully used in just the right place, will win a despatch a very good reception from everyone. But sarcasm, particularly of a rather Meridithian tinge, or facetiousness of any kind at all, will generally do more harm than good, and it is wise in one's own interest to use it rather sparingly.

I hope you will forgive me for a rather straying outside my sphere in offering these few words of personal and genuinely friendly warning. I well remember how welcome something of the kind would have been to me personally when I was abroad before I had any experience of the inside working of the Office, and hope you will accept this in the same spirit.

—G. W. Rendel

Diplomacy and War: The Siege of Baghdad (1941)

In April 1941 Rashīd 'Alī ousted the regent and established a pro-Axis regime in Iraq. It was overthrown by British and royalist forces and the monarchy restored. Rashīd 'Alī fled to Berlin. Somerset de Chair fought in and later wrote about this campaign.

[Lord] Reading came to me. "Why do our troops not go into Baghdad?" he asked. "Already there may be looting. I know. There will be many people killed if our troops do not enter."

This was my own view and the ways of the Foreign Office were beyond my comprehension. From the hour of the Cease Fire their word had prevailed. Having fought our way, step by step, to the threshold of the city, we must now cool our heels outside. It would, apparently, be lowering to the dignity of our ally, the Regent, if he were seen to be supported on arrival by British bayonets. It was apparently believed in Whitehall to be beyond the imagination of the wily Baghdadis to see that his return was brought about by the victory of British arms. "Were there not Iraqi troops enough in the city, now loyal of course to the new Government, to keep order?"

So we waited and, as darkness settled like a mantle over the domes and minarets across the river, the shooting began. We did not hear it, but to the Brigadier's ears, sleeping in the white colonial house of the British Embassy, came the growing crescendo of rifle and machine-gun fire. Baghdad was given up to the looters. All who dared to defend their own belongings were killed; while eight miles to the west waited the eager British force which could have prevented all this. Ah, yes, but the prestige of our Regent would have suffered!

It was argued afterwards in the Chancery of Baghdad that the Iraqis would have gone on fighting rather than agree to an armistice on the basis of our immediate entry. Again, it was argued that our arrival would have precipitated street fighting with the brigade which we had pushed back into the town. Yet why, I asked, if they crumpled up on the outskirts, should they have stiffened in the middle?

Diplomacy is the continuation of war by other means, but it should not begin too soon.

—Somerset de Chair

An American Diplomat in Baghdad (1944)

All day we were barricaded in the legation (where the temperature never fell below 90°) by the much fiercer heat outside. We might look out the windows (as one looks out the windows in zero weather in the north) and see the burning dusty wind tearing at the eucalyptus trees and the flat, bleached country enveloped in the colorless sunshine of the desert; a sunshine with no nuances, no shades, no shadows—a sunshine which does not even brown the skin, but only strikes and penetrates and dissolves with its unbending hostile power. Into this inferno of heat only "mad dogs and Englishmen," as Noel Coward used to sing, could dream of venturing. At night, it cooled off considerably, and we slept in reasonable comfort on the roof. But by that time the real mad dogs and the jackals had come in from the desert, and it was not safe to walk in the outlying district where the legation was situated. The only tolerable time of day, when it would have been possible to break out of the prison walls, was the early morning.

The dryness of the heat was nerve-racking. One had to keep drinking water from morning to night; and even then the kidneys had a tendency to cease working entirely.

In general, it was possible to keep healthy only by a very strict and scientifically conceived discipline and routine of private life.

So much for the handicaps; what of the possibilities of service in Baghdad? A country in which man's selfishness and stupidity have ruined almost all natural productivity, where vegetation can survive only along the banks of the great rivers which traverse its deserts, where climate has become unfavorable to human health and vigor.

A population unhygienic in its habits, sorely weakened and debilitated by disease, inclined to all manner of religious bigotry and fanaticism, condemned by the tenets of the most widespread faith to keep a full half of the population—namely, the feminine half—confined and excluded from the productive efforts of society by a system of indefinite house arrest, deeply affected—and bound to be affected—by the psychological habits of pastoral life, which have ever been at variance with the agricultural and industrial civilization.

This people has now come just enough into contact with Western life so that its upper class has a thirst for many things which can be obtained only in the West. Suspicious and resentful of the British, they would be glad to obtain these things from us. They would be glad to use us as a foil for the British, as an escape from the restraints which the British place upon them.

If we give them these things, we can perhaps enjoy a momentary favor on the part of those interested in receiving them. But to the extent that we give them, we weaken British influence, and we acquire—whether we wish it or not—responsibility for the actions of the native politicians. If they then begin to do things which are not in our interests, which affect the world situation in ways unfavorable to our security, and if the British are unable to restrain them, we then have ourselves at least in part to blame and it is up to us to take the appropriate measures.

Are we willing to bear this responsibility? I know—and every realistic American knows—that we are not. Our government is technically incapable of conceiving and promulgating a long-term consistent policy toward areas remote from its own territory. Our actions in the field of foreign affairs are the convulsive reactions of politicians to an internal political life dominated by vocal minorities.

Those few Americans who remember something of the pioneer life of their own country will find it hard to view these deserts without a pang of interest and excitement at the possibilities for reclamation and economic development. If trees once grew here, could they not grow again? If rains once fell, could they not again be attracted from the inexhaustible resources of nature? Could not climate be altered, disease eradicated?

If they are seeking an escape from reality, such Americans may even pursue these dreams and enter upon the long and stony road which could lead to their fruition. But if they are willing to recall the sad state of soil conservation in their own country, the vast amount of social improvement to be accomplished at home, and the inevitable limitations on the efficacy of our type of democracy in the field of foreign affairs—then they will restrain their excitement at the silent, expectant possibilities in the Middle Eastern deserts, and will return, like disappointed but dutiful children, to the sad deficiencies and problems of their native land.

On June 28 I continued my journey to Tehran and was surprised to find myself already—in an atmosphere at least—halfway back in Russia.

—George F. Kennan

The Mad Hatter's Tea Party (Jordan, 1948)

On Saturday, May 15, 1948, Britain's Mandate for Palestine formally came to an end. Jordan, previously part of the Mandated territory, became independent in March 1946 and Sir Alec Kirkbride, a civil servant of the Mandatory government, became the first British minister to the Jordanian kingdom.

In the autumn of 1948 the fighting in and around Jerusalem between the Arab and Israeli armies appeared to have reached a crisis, for the Arabs. . . .

The danger to Jerusalem was acute and King Abdullah of Jordan was directly concerned both because the city was part of the sector for which his army was responsible and because he was titular Commander in Chief of the Arab forces . . . in view of the seriousness of the situation, he summoned a meeting at Amman of heads of the Arab Governments which had sent forces into Palestine. Nokrashi Pasha came from Egypt; Jamil Mardam represented his country, Syria; Riad es Solh was Prime Minister of the Lebanon; Fadhel Jamali came from Iraq and Tewfiq Abul Huda was Prime Minister of Jordan and the host.

The initial meeting with the traditional cups of over-sweet tea, took place under the chairmanship of King Abdullah, not, he explained, in his capacity as king but as the Commander in Chief who could give an authoritative account of the military position. He drew a pretty gloomy picture and wound up by asking the meeting to consider urgently ways of reinforcing or of removing the pressure on the forces in Jerusalem. The visitors, with one exception, hastened to produce the usual clichés about the sacred task to the successful conclusion of which no Arab would hesitate to sacrifice his life and future, etc. The exception was the Egyptian Prime Minister, who sat in a grumpy silence which became so pointed that King Abdullah felt obliged to ask him if he was not feeling well. Nokrashi Pasha replied shortly that he was perfectly well, thank you, but had come to the meeting to listen and not to talk. King Abdullah, whose tempter had a low flashpoint, then said that the Pasha would doubtless have plenty to listen to shortly but that before he, King Abdullah, withdrew to allow the Prime Ministers to get on with their task, he wished to say that, in his opinion, the action of the Egyptian Government in seizing at Suez a consignment of 25-pounder ammunition which was destined for Jordan for which the Arab Legion was in desperate need, was not the sort of treatment which one expected normally from an ally: it was possible, however, that the seizure had been made without Nokrashi Pasha's knowledge and he was confident that the ammunition would now be restored to its owners. He then withdrew. (The ammunition in question was, incidentally, neither restored nor paid for.)

The Jordan Prime Minister then proposed that the first item should be to consider ways and means of assisting the Arab forces in Jerusalem. He asked the Egyptian delegation whether it would not be possible for their forces, who were within a few miles of Jerusalem, to the south, to stage an attack so as to draw off some of the pressure on the Arab Legion. He remarked that, as far as he was aware, the Egyptian troops were not engaged in any active fighting at the time and were much stronger numerically than the Arab Legion. The Egyptian Military Adviser looked horrified and said hastily, "Good God no, we cannot attack; the Jews might attack us in turn!"

The Iraqi Minister asked, sweetly, "whether being attacked and attacking was not an inevitable and normal part of the activities of an army engaged in warfare." The Egyptian Military Adviser looked sulky and muttered something about technical problems with which a civilian would not be familiar. When others attempted to press for action by the Egyptian forces, Nokrashi Pasha weighed in with a long speech about his devotion to the common cause which, none the less, had to be subject to his duty to his own beloved country and people. The upshot being that the Egyptian Army was not going to do anything which might draw upon it the attention of the Israeli forces.

Jamil Mardam then rose to his feet and said dramatically, "Gentlemen, I have an important announcement to make. We Syrians cannot stand by and see the city, holy to both Moslems and Christians, fall into the hands of the Zionists. Therefore, despite the practical difficulties and the material sacrifices involved, we are prepared to send immediately a whole infantry division to fight on the battlements of Jerusalem!" Loud cheers and applause broke round the table, although everyone there knew perfectly well that the only infantry division possessed by Syria which was capable of taking the field was already fully committed in the fighting in Galilee. The representative of the Arab Legion could not bring himself to express any doubts in the face of all this enthusiasm, but did ask when the first Syrian troops might be expected to reach Jerusalem. The Syrian Prime Minister beamed and said, "In a matter of a few days, my dear, if God wills."

Jerusalem was then dismissed as saved and the talk turned to more pleasant matters such as the final offensive which was to sweep the Jews into the sea and how the Jewish property would be divided between the Arab Governments which had sent armies, the descendants of those who laid down their lives for the sacred cause or those who were incapacitated through wounds. Someone broached the subject of what would be the political future of a reconquered Arab Palestine, but as all the other Arab countries were bitterly opposed to Palestine becoming part of King Abdullah's domain, the question was hastily smothered in a fog of platitudes. Mercifully, at this point, someone said that the members could stuff themselves with rice and mutton and the happy feeling of leaving their work well done.

The Syrian infantry division never, of course, materialized. The Egyptian Army stayed where it was until, shortly afterwards, it was attacked by the Israelis with disastrous results to the Arab cause: King Abdullah continued to be a Commander in Chief from whom no one accepted orders. The Arab Press wrote with pride and pleasure of the historical meeting at which the leaders of the sister Arab countries reaffirmed their unshakable determination to carry on the struggle against the aggressors, regardless of the sacrifices involved, and took decisions of wide importance, the effects of which would be evident shortly and lead to the victory on which all had set their hearts.

It was lucky perhaps that, about this time, the Israelis apparently decided that they could not afford the heavy casualties which their attacks on Jerusalem were causing to their army and diverted their offensive to other parts of the front. So all was well, after all, except for the fact that the better half of Arab Palestine had been lost.

—Sir Alec Kirkbride

Mosadeq: Portrait of a Prime Minister (Tehran, 1951)

From the first moment I saw him a few months later Mosadeq became for me the character Lob in James Barrie's play *Dear Brutus*. He was small and frail with not a shred of hair on his billiard-ball head; a thin face protruded into a long beak of a nose flanked by two bright, shoe-button eyes. His whole manner and appearance was birdlike, marked by quick, nervous movements as he seemed to jump about on a perch. His pixie quality showed in instantaneous transformations. Waiting at Union Station in Washington, I watched a bent old man hobble down the platform supporting himself with a stick and an arm through his son's. Spotting me at the gate, he dropped the stick, broke away from his party, and came skipping along ahead of the others to greet us.

He had, I discovered later, a delightfully childlike way of sitting in a chair with his legs tucked under him, making him more of a Lob character than ever, with many and changing moods. I remember him sitting with the President and me after lunch in Blair House, his legs under him, when he dropped a mood of gay animation and, suddenly looking old and pathetic, leaned toward the President.

"Mr. President," he said, "I am speaking for a very poor country—a country all desert—just sand, a few camels, a few sheep . . ."

"Yes," I interrupted, "and with your oil, rather like Texas!" He burst into a delighted laugh, and the whole act broke up, finished. It was a gambit that had not worked. No one was more amused than he. He then went to work on the President for financial aid to fight the British imperialists. But the President was having none of it. Our aid, he said, was not for that purpose. Iran had resources aplenty and we were ready to help them with sensible accommodation in their development.

Another of Mosadeq's marked characteristics was his distrust of his own countrymen; he would never talk with any of them present. At this same luncheon there were many guests, including the Iranian Ambassador. Mosadeq waited until they had gone and the doors were closed, leaving the three of us and Colonel Walters, our interpreter, for our private talk. Seeing that the Ambassador had been shut out, I intervened to retrieve this mistake, only to find it was no mistake at all. Averell Harriman discovered in Iran that Mosadeq would talk freely only alone and with an American interpreter— never an Iranian. Nitze and McGhee learned it in New York. When they wanted to get the whole Oil Commission into a meeting, Mosadeq de- murred. "It's no use," he said. "You can't convince *them*." In a service often trying I found compensation, indeed joy, in the qualities of friendly col- leagues, of hostile combatants, and sometimes of neutral freebooters like Mosadeq. Only bores were insufferable.

Mosadeq's self-defeating quality was that he never paused to see that the passions he excited to support him restricted his freedom of choice and left only extreme solutions possible. We were, perhaps, slow in realizing that he was essentially a rich, reactionary, feudal-minding Persian inspired by a fa- natical hatred of the British and a desire to expel them and all their works from the country regardless of the cost. He was a great actor and a great gambler. Speaking in the Majlis, he would rant, weep real tears, and fall in a faint at his climactic moment. He told us once that nationalization would cost Iran nothing, since any damages which Anglo-Iranian could prove would be exceeded by Iranian counterclaims.* This unique character truly sowed the wind and reaped the whirlwind.

—Dean Acheson

---

* The British-controlled Anglo-Iranian Oil Company was nationalized by Dr. Mosadeq's gov- ernment shortly after he siezed power in 1950. That government was overthrown, and the Shah restored, with significant help from the CIA.

President Nasser and King Hussein: Impressions of a Secretary of State (1969)

It was never clear how Nasser thought Nixon could brave domestic opposition, Israeli refusals, and Soviet aloofness to support the maximum goals of a country that refused diplomatic relations with us and whose foreign policy remained fundamentally unfriendly. Nasser, in effect, sought to deal with us by blackmail but had nothing to threaten us with. When later in the year the Administration put forward precise plans on both the Egyptian and Jordanian borders along lines previously declared acceptable by Nasser, he refused either to accept them or to resume relations. He gloried in his radicalism, which he thought essential to his pan-Arab ambitions, and for this he must have felt compelled to remain in perpetual confrontation with us in the Middle East and the Third World, even at the cost of jeopardizing our willingness to move in his direction. . . .

Hussein was one of the most attractive political leaders I have met. The little King—as he was affectionately called by our officials—stoutly defended the Arab cause even when his Arab brethren failed to reciprocate his loyalty. Once I knew him reasonably well I could measure his irritation at what he considered insensitivity or bureaucratic pedantry by the heightening of his legendary courtesy; his use of the honorific "sir" would multiply while he assumed a glacial demeanor. (He, an hereditary monarch, called me "sir" even when I was a mere Presidential Assistant.)

He was as gallant as he was polite. Once he piloted my wife Nancy and me in his helicopter on a hair-raising ride at treetop level. To get him to fly higher, Nancy said innocently that she did not know helicopters could fly so low. The King assured her that they could fly lower still, making the rest of the trip almost on the deck. Had he exploited the opportunity he could have obtained my agreement to any political demand by promising to fly higher.

—Henry Kissinger

PART VI

Women

. . . any port from which we can sail to a Mahometan country, where men are protected from women.
—G. Bernard Shaw

Femme Turcque allant par la ville.

A Turkish woman walking through town, from Nicolas Nicolay, The Navigations, Peregrinations, and Voyages Made into Turkey, *1567.*

Introduction

Travelers to a foreign land, especially to an alien and exotic society, naturally give special attention to those features that are most different from home, and therefore most repulsive or enticing or—on occasion—both. By this measure, one of the most crucial differences between Western and Muslim society was the position of women. The laws of Christendom, in all sects and churches, prohibit polygamy and concubinage and place difficulties in the way of divorce. The laws of Islam allow a man four wives, as many concubines as he can afford and divorce virtually on demand. The social consequences of this difference attracted the attention of almost every traveler, both from West to East and from East to West, who left a record. Their comments reflect a range of responses, from shock to wonderment and—very rarely—approval.

Travel writers, especially on titillating topics, may not always be strictly factual. European visitors to Islamic lands, as Lady Mary Wortley Montagu noted, describe encounters with ladies whom they never met and visits to harems which they never entered. Some of them speak with ill-concealed and ill-informed envy of what they imagine to be the rights and privileges of a Muslim husband and master of the house. Muslim visitors to Europe speak with astonishment, sometimes indeed with horror, of the immodesty and forwardness of Western women, of the incredible freedom and absurd deference accorded to them, and of the lack of manly jealousy of European males, even in Spain, confronted with the immorality and promiscuity in which their womenfolk indulge. But some, from both sides, look a little deeper.

Muslim travel literature about the West until fairly modern times is exclusively male. Muslim women did not travel abroad alone. Those who accompanied their husbands or their owners on such trips lacked both the opportunity to observe and the education to record their observations. Visitors from the West, in contrast, included a number of women, some traveling with their husbands and enjoying the normal measure of freedom accorded to European wives; others—profoundly shocking to a Muslim—traveling independently on their own.

Western women in the East could do what no male—other than an occasional physician—could do; move freely in the harems and converse, albeit through an interpreter, with their inmates. These women writers present a more shaded and in general a more positive picture of a woman's life in the East. Several of them note a point which eluded the observation of most male visitors: the property rights accorded to women under Muslim law, far better than any enjoyed by Western women until comparatively modern times.

One Muslim visitor to the West in the late eighteenth century notes—with chagrin—another advantage enjoyed by Muslim women over their Western sisters. Western husbands, he observes, have better control over their women than their Muslim counterparts. For one thing, they can send them off to work to earn their own keep or more; for another, since their wives are unveiled and recognizable at sight, they can know where they are going and what they are doing at any time of the day. Western wives are thus much easier to observe and control than their Muslim sisters, who, hidden by the veil and the shawl, can get up to all kinds of mischief under the pretense of visiting women friends.

The absence of West-bound women travelers is part of a larger Middle Eastern pattern. In Middle Eastern history as related and in literature as transmitted, women are for the most part invisible and silent. True, there are some exceptions. From time to time, some rare combination of circumstances may permit a talented woman to play a political role. That role, however well she plays it, is invariably condemned by traditional historians. There are some women poets and mystics, seen as minor figures and known only by fragments of their work. Some few women, like the biblical matriarchs, are even venerated. Such are the daughter and some of the wives of the Prophet, as well as a few others who achieved renown for learning, piety or mystical insights. All these are rare and atypical. There are no Middle Eastern literary equivalents of Jane Austen or Madame de Staël, no royal counterparts of Queen Elizabeth of England or the empress Catherine of Russia. It was not until the late nineteenth century that, as part of the process of Westernization, some few Middle Eastern women became teachers, writers, intellectual leaders and eventually even politicians.

Traditional Islamic society was in principal egalitarian, insisting on the legal and religious equality, despite any differences of birth, rank, wealth and status, of all free male Muslims. Those who lacked any one of these three qualities—not free, not male, or not Muslim—were not extruded from society but were subjected to legal and therefore social disabilities, amounting to a status of legally enforced inferiority.

Of the three—the slave, the woman and the non-Muslim—the woman was obviously in one significant respect the worst placed. The slave could be freed by his master; the unbeliever could become a Muslim by his own choice. Only the woman was doomed forever to remain what she was—or so it seemed at the time.

The rise and spread of Western power and influence in the Middle East brought significant changes in all three inferiorities. The Christian powers were naturally concerned to secure equal rights for the Christian subjects of Muslim states, and exercised their not inconsiderable influence to that end. In general, they were successful, and with a few exceptions Christian citizens of predominantly Muslim countries in principle enjoy the same legal and constitutional rights as their compatriots. Chattel slavery has also been abolished by law, in most countries in practice as well as in theory, among peoples to whom this ancient institution was no longer morally and socially acceptable.

The equalization of women proved a much more difficult task, and the outcome of the struggle to achieve it is still far from clear. The European powers, which used their influence and even their armed forces to secure the abolition of slavery and the emancipation of Christians, showed no interest in ending the subjection of women.

There is little evidence that either the Ottoman reformers or their European mentors were much concerned about the status of Muslim women. Even the imperial powers, in this as in most other respects, pursued cautious conservative policies in the territories they ruled and took care to avoid any changes which would mobilize Muslim opinion against them and bring them no advantage. In some areas of intensive colonization, such as French North Africa and Soviet Central Asia, a small class of educated Muslims, culturally assimilated to their imperial masters, followed their practice also in the treatment of women. But these were in every sense limited and marginal. In the heartlands of Islam, such progress as was made in women's rights was due entirely to internal forces and to the unaided efforts of Muslim women and men. Their efforts, and the limited successes they achieved, are among the principal grievances of the so-called Islamic fundamentalists.

The issue of slavery, apart from a few pockets of survival and perhaps even recrudescence, is for most of the region dead. The issue of the unbelievers is, for the time being, in abeyance. The question of the status of women—what it should be, how it should be defined—remains a burning issue, with some men supporting the cause of feminism and many women supporting the fundamentalists. This issue has become an important, perhaps indeed the major, theme in the still undecided struggle between fundamentalists and modernizers, on the nature of the state, the law and society among the peoples of Islam.

The following excerpts begin with differing translations of a verse from the Qur'ān. The remainder fall into three groups. The first consists of views by Middle Eastern authors of their own and of foreign women; the second of European perceptions of the position of women in the Middle East. The concluding section contains four love poems, one each from Arabic, Persian, Hebrew and Turkish, and a quatrain by a Turkish lady.

Interpreting Scriptures

Men and Women: A Qur'ānic Verse

Chapter Four, Verse 34, of the Qur'ān deals with the relationship between men and women, and more particularly between husbands and wives. The Arabic text has been variously interpreted in a number of different translations into English, most of them, though not all, by Muslims. It will be noted that some of the translators have added interpretative words in parentheses; some have added explanatory notes. While they differ in interpretation and emphasis, all but one agree on the general purport of the Arabic words. The one exception is the translation of Ahmed Ali published in 1987, in which the Arabic verb daraba, *with the normal meaning of "to hit," "to strike" or "to beat," is rendered in an entirely different way.*

George Sale (1734)

Men shall have the pre-eminence above women, because of those *advantages* wherein GOD hath caused the one of them to excel the other, and for that which they expend of their substance *in maintaining their wives.* The honest women *are* obedient, careful in the absence *of their husbands,* for that GOD preserveth *them, by committing them to the care and protection of the men.* But those, whose perverseness ye shall be apprehensive of, rebuke; and remove them into separate apartments, and chastise them. But if they shall be obedient unto you, seek not an occasion of *quarrel* against them.

Mirza Abu'l-Fadl (1912)

Men are stand [*sic*] above women, for that God has graced the one of them above the other, and for that they spend of their wealth. So the virtuous women are devoted, careful in secret, for that God watches. But those whose perverseness ye fear, admonish them, and leave them into beds apart, and beat them; but if they obey you, then seek not against them a way.

Al-Haj Hafiz Ghulam Sarwar (1920)

Men are protectors over women, on account of that by means of which God has made some of them eminent above the others, and on account of what they spend out of their belongings; So that the good women are devout, guarding that, in the absence (of their husbands), what God has guarded and there are women whose disobedience you may be afraid of, then teach them, and (next) leave them alone in their beds. If then they obey you, then do not seek a way against them.

Abdullah Yusuf Ali (1934)

Men are the protectors and maintainers of women, because God has given the one more (strength) than the other, and because they support them from their means. Therefore the righteous women are devoutly obedient, and guard in (the husband's) absence what God would have them guard.

As to those women on whose part ye fear disloyalty and ill-conduct, admonish them (first), (next), refuse to share their beds, (and last) beat them (lightly); but if they return to obedience, seek not against them means (of annoyance).

Richard Bell (1937)

The men are overseers over the women by reason of what Allah hath bestowed in bounty upon one more than another, and of the property which they have contributed; upright women are therefore submissive, guarding what is hidden in return for Allah's guarding (them); those on whose part ye fear refractoriness, admonish, avoid in bed, and beat; if they then obey you, seek no (further) way against them.

Arthur J. Arberry (1955)

Men are the managers of the affairs of women for that God has preferred in bounty one of them over another, and for that they have expended of their property. Righteous women are therefore obedient, guarding the secret for God's guarding. And those you fear may be rebellious admonish; banish them to their couches, and beat them. If they then obey you, look not for any way against them.

Muhammad Asad (1980)

MEN SHALL take full care of women with the bounties which God has bestowed more abundantly on the former than on the latter, and with what they may spend out of their possessions. And the righteous women are the truly devout ones, who guard the intimacy which God has [ordained to be] guarded.

And as for those women whose ill-will you have reason to fear, admonish them [first]; then leave them alone in bed; then beat them; and if thereupon they pay you heed, do not seek to harm them.

Muhammad Zafrulla Khan (1981)

Men are appointed guardians over women, because of that in respect of which Allah has made some of them excel others, and because the men spend of their wealth. So virtuous women are obedient and safeguard, with Allah's help, matters the knowledge of which is shared by them with their husbands. Admonish those of them on whose part you apprehend disobedience, and leave them alone in their beds and chastise them. Then if they obey you, seek no pretext against them.

Maulana Abdul Majid Daryabadi (1981)

Men are overseers over women, by reason of that wherewith Allah has made one of them excel over another, and by reason of what they spend of their riches. So the righteous women are obedient *and* watchers in their *husbands'* absence by *the aid and* protection of Allah. And those *wives* whose refractoriness you fear, admonish them and avoid them in their beds and beat them; but if they obey you, do not seek a way against them.

T. B. Irving (1985)

Men are the ones who should support women since God has given some persons advantages over others, and because they should spend their wealth [on them]. Honorable women are steadfast, guarding the Unseen just as God has it guarded. Admonish those women whose surliness you fear, and leave them alone in their beds, and [even] beat them [if necessary]. If they obey you, do not seek any way [to proceed] against them.

Ahmed Ali (1987)

Men are the guardians of women as God has favoured some with more than others, and because they spend of their wealth (to provide for them). So women who are virtuous are obedient to God and guard the hidden as God has guarded it. As for women you fear are averse, talk to them suasively; then leave them alone in bed (without molesting them) and go to bed with them (when they are willing).* If they open out to you, do not seek an excuse for blaming them.

---

* To justify this rendering, Dr. Ahmed Ali offers examples of the use of the verb *daraba*, normally "to strike" or "to beat," as a euphemism for "to have sexual intercourse," as well as the more usual Arabic *waṭi'a*, literally, "to trample." Such euphemisms are common—e.g., the biblical use of "know" and farmyard English "cover" in this sense. Classical Arabic, a language used over a vast area for a very long period, has many.

A mystic preaching to a mixed congregation, Iran, sixteenth century.

Middle Eastern Views

Aphorisms (Eleventh Century)

A teacher was teaching girls how to write. A sage passed by and said, "This teacher is teaching wickedness to the wicked."

An intelligent woman was asked, "What are the virtues of women?" "And what," she rejoined "are the faults of men?" "Niggardliness and cowardice," they answered. "These," she said, "are among the virtues of women."

A sage wished (that) his short wife (might have been) tall. People asked him, "Why did not you marry a wife of full stature?" "A woman is an evil thing," he answered, "and the less (there is) of an evil thing the better."

—Al-Ghazālī (translated by F. R. C. Bagley)

A Consumer's Guide (Eleventh Century)

From a handbook for buyers of slaves by a Christian physician in Baghdad

The Turkish women combine beauty and whiteness and grace. Their faces tend to look sullen, but their eyes, though small, are sweet. They have a smooth brownness and their stature is between medium and short. There are very few tall ones among them. The beautiful ones are extremely beautiful and the ugly ones exceptional. They are treasure houses for children, gold mines for generation. It very rarely happens that their children are ugly or badly formed. They are clean and refined. . . . Bad breath is hardly ever found among them, nor any with large buttocks, but they have some nasty characteristics and are of little loyalty.

The women of Daylam [in northern Iran] are both outwardly and inherently beautiful, but they have the worst characters of all and the coarsest natures. They can endure hardship like the women of Tabaristan in every respect.

The women of the Alans [a people of the northern Caucasus] are reddish-white and well-fleshed. The cold humor predominates in their temperaments. They are better suited for service than for pleasure since they have good characters in that they are trustworthy and honest and are both reliant and compliant. Also, they are far from licentious.

The Greek women are blond, with straight hair and blue eyes. As slaves they are obedient, adaptable, serviceable, well meaning, loyal, trustworthy and reliable. They are good as treasurers because they are meticulous and not very generous. Sometimes they are skilled in some fine handicraft.

The Armenians would be beautiful were it not for their peculiarly ugly feet, though they are well built, energetic and strong. Chastity is rare or absent among them and thievery widespread. Avarice is very rare among them, but they are coarse in nature and speech. Cleanliness is not in their language. They are slaves for hard work and service. . . . This race is untrustworthy even when they are contented, not to speak of when they are angry. Their women are useless for pleasure. In fine, the Armenians are the worst of the whites as the Zanj are the worst of the blacks. And how much do they resemble one another in the strength of their bodies, their great wickedness, and their coarse natures!

—Ibn Buṭlān

Two Tales (Fourteenth-Century Egypt)

When 'Ā'isha the daughter of Ṭalḥa was given in marriage to Muṣ'ab, he said, "By God, this night I shall kill her with passion." He took her once and then fell asleep and did not awaken till dawn, when she shook him and said, "Wake up, killer."

Ash'ab heard Ḥubbā the woman of Medina say, "O please God, do not let me die until you have forgiven me for my sins!" Ash'ab said to her: "Wicked woman! You are not asking God for forgiveness, you are asking Him for immortality."

—Al-Nuwayrī

On Beauty (Fifteenth Century)

Wise men have set forth certain things that add beauty to a woman. Blackness is desirable in four places: eyes, eyebrows, eyelashes and hair. Whiteness in four: teeth, skin, hair-parting and the whites of the eyes. Redness in four: tongue, lips, cheeks and buttocks. Roundness in four: face, head, knees and heels. Length in four: stature, eyebrows, throat and hair. Fragrance in four: mouth, nose, armpit and pudenda. Breadth in four: brow, breast, eyes, thighs. Narrowness in four: ears, nostrils, navel and pudenda. Smallness in four: palms, mouth, breasts and legs. . . .

One of the ancient Arabs said, "The best of women is the tallest when she stands, the strongest when she sleeps, the most truthful when she speaks; she is magnanimous in anger and smiles when amused and excels in what she does. She stays in her house and obeys her husband; she is proud of her people and modest of herself."

—Jalāl al-Dīn al-Suyūṭī

An Egyptian View of Marriageability
(Seventeenth Century)

The wise have set forth ten qualities that render a woman unsuitable for marriage: that she is short, short-haired, meager of body, sharp-tongued, barren, stubborn, spendthrift, light-fingered, bedizened when she goes out, or is divorced.

When Pharaoh and his army and his nobles were drowned in the sea, no one remained in Egypt but the common people and the peasants, who then took as their wives the women of the nobility. Then the women ruled over the men, who were inferior to them. Thus began the domination of women over men, which has continued until our time.

—Aḥmad al-Qalyūbī

A Traveler's Tale from Vienna (1665)

In this country I saw an extraordinary spectacle. Whenever the emperor meets a woman in the street, if he is riding, he brings his horse to a standstill and lets her pass. If the emperor is on foot and meets a woman, he stands in a posture of politeness. The woman greets the emperor, who then takes his hat off his head to show respect for the woman. After the woman has passed, the emperor continues on his way. It is indeed an extraordinary spectacle. In this country and in general in the lands of the unbelievers, women have the main say. They are honored and respected out of love for Mother Mary.

—Evliya Çelebi

French Influences (Cairo, 1800–1801)

The Events of the Year 1215 [May 1800–May 1801]

In 1798 an expeditionary force from the French republic, commanded by General Napoléon Bonaparte, invaded and occupied Egypt. An Egyptian history of the time gives a detailed account of the occupation and its impact.

Another problem [caused by the French occupation] was the coquetry of women. Most of them went out of doors without modesty or shame. When the French arrived in Cairo, some of them with their wives, they went out in the streets with their women. These ladies had their faces uncovered, wore kilts, colored shawls, and embroidered cashmere head scarves that fell onto their shoulders. Thus attired, they rode on horses and donkeys without help, roaring with laughter and joking with the men who hired these animals and with riffraff in the streets. So one saw low-class women mixing with the French because of their liberality and their liking for the female sex.

This promiscuity was at first restrained by a certain shame and fear of scandal. They took precautions to hide it. But after the last revolt in Cairo and the fighting in the town of Bulaq, the French engaged in all kinds of destruction and raids. They took the women and the girls who pleased them, kept them by force, and dressed them up like their own women, whom they forced them to imitate in every respect. Most of these women gave up the veil completely, and those who had been carried off were seen to mingle with the women of ill repute.

While the people of Cairo were overwhelmed with disdain, abasement and the despoiling and looting of wealth by the French and their servants, the French displayed their strong appetite for women and their indulgence for women and their whims. These men had no self-restraint to hold back their lust for the other sex, even if they were rejected with scorn or struck with slippers by these women, who had given up all modesty and respect. . . .

Many Frenchmen asked for the daughters of notables in marriage, and these agreed in the desire for access to power or getting gifts. In the marriage contract the Frenchman made a show of Islam and pronounced the Islamic creed. This was no problem since he had no religion of his own which he might fear to violate. . . .

In the neighborhoods, Muslim women were seen dressed in French style, going out with the neighborhood officials for inspections and the like. . . . Sometimes a woman would go alone or with some female companions . . . making decisions, commanding and forbidding. At the time of the Nile flood, when ships could move freely on the canal, women gave free rein to this coquetry. They associated with the French, who took them on boat parties. Then there was dancing, singing, drinking by day and by night to the light of torches or candles, with these ladies wearing splendid clothes with gems and jewelry. All this to the sound of musical instruments. The sailors went on joking and clowning, exchanging responses at the tops of their voice to the rhythm of the oars, in stupid and vulgar improvisations, as if hashish had gone to their heads and was ruling their minds. So they were shouting, beating the drum, dancing, playing the flute, calling each other, imitating the sounds of the French language, and inserting French words in their songs. As for the Negresses, as soon as they became aware that the general purpose was the total freedom of women, they ran in crowds after these men, whether married or single. They jumped over walls, climbed through windows and told the soldiers where their masters hid their money.

—Al-Jabartī

Frenchwomen, and a Note on Ballroom Dancing (1826–31)

Comments from an Egyptian Visitor to Paris

Men among them are the slaves of women and subject to their commands whether they be beautiful or not. One of them said . . . women among the people of the East are like household possessions while among the Franks they are like spoiled children. The Franks harbor no evil thoughts about their women, even though the transgressions of these women are very numerous. . . .

Among their bad qualities is the lack of virtue of many of their women as above stated and the lack of manly jealousy of their men on occasions which would arouse manly jealousy among the Muslims as, for example, in association and intimacy and dalliance. . . . Fornication among them is a secondary rather than a major sin, especially in the case of the unmarried. . . .

The Frenchwomen excel in beauty and grace and conversation and courtesy. They always display themselves in their adornments and mingle with men at places of entertainment. . . .

A ball always includes both men and women, and there are great lights and chairs on which to sit. These are mostly for women to sit on, and no man may sit until all the women are seated. If a woman comes in and there is no vacant chair, then one of the men stands up and seats her. No woman stands up to seat her. Women are always treated at these gatherings with more consideration than men.

Dancing among them is considered an art . . . and is practised by every-one . . . as pertaining to the man of elegance and the gentleman and is not immoral in that it never goes beyond the bounds of decency. . . .

In Egypt, the dance is practiced only by women in order to excite desire. In Paris, on the contrary, the dance is simply a kind of jumping around with-out even a whiff of immorality.

Each man invites a woman so that he may dance with her, and when the dance is finished another man invites her for a second dance, and so on. There is a special kind of dance in which the man puts his arm around the waist of the person with whom he is dancing and usually grasps her with his hand. In general to touch a woman anywhere in the upper part of the body is not considered an offense among these Christians. The more a man excels in speaking to women and flattering them, the more he is regarded as well bred.

—Shaykh Rifā'a Rāfi'al-Ṭahṭāwī

The Need to Educate Women (1867)

From an article published by a young Ottoman reformer in an Istanbul newspaper.

Our women are now seen as serving no useful purpose to mankind other than having children; they are considered simply as serving for pleasure, like musical instruments or jewels. But they constitute half and perhaps more than half of our species. Preventing them from contributing to the sus-tenance and improvement of others by means of their efforts infringes the basic rules of public cooperation to such a degree that our national society is stricken like a human body that is paralyzed on one side. Yet women are not inferior to men in their intellectual and physical capacities. In ancient times women shared in all men's activities, including even war. In the coun-tryside, women still share in the work of agriculture and trade. . . . The rea-son why women among us are thus deprived is the perception that they are totally ignorant and know nothing of right and duty, benefit and harm. Many evil consequences result from this position of women, the first that it leads to a bad upbringing for their children.

—Namık Kemal

The Koltuk Ceremony (Early Twentieth Century)

In these modern days, when couples know each other before marriage, the *Koltuk* has no meaning. But in the days when women veiled, the *Koltuk* was the climax to a Turkish wedding.

The bride, escorted by her mother, her mother-in-law and her aunt, would be conducted to the entrance hall, where all the ladies of the Harem crowded round them; others taking up their position on either side of the staircase, and all along the corridors to the *salon,* where the bridal throne had been placed.

In the event of the wedding being an Imperial one, the bridegroom would be led to the entrance hall by the *Kızlar Aghası,* the Sultan's chief eunuch, a most important personage and much respected. There the bridegroom would greet his mother and his mother-in-law by kissing their hands. The two would then produce the bride, her features still hidden from his gaze by her veil. This was or should have been the first time that the two had met. The groom then either salaamed the bride, or, if he was bolder, kissed her hand. This accomplished, the *Kızlar Aghası* placed the bride's hand in that of the bridegroom and led the two up the staircase, through the lines of spectators and along the corridors to the *salon.*

As the newly married couple moved slowly forward, the older ladies who were the chief relatives threw new coins which had been especially minted for the occasion over the bride and bridegroom. There would then ensue a frantic scramble to pick up as many of the coins as possible; these being considered most lucky.

It was indeed an ordeal for the man. To walk through a lane of laughing and giggling women, whose remarks were often to the point, with a complete stranger on one's arm, a wife whose face had not yet been seen, a voice still unheard. To walk with dignity under such circumstances, when the women of the Harem for once, on this occasion only, did not veil their faces at the approach of a man, might well daunt the boldest husband. The veil was useless, as it was rare for any husband to look up; for he had to walk through a shower of coins, under a cascade of jokes, blessings, exclamations on his looks, his clothes, his bearing, up those stairs—sometimes they were a long flight—through the corridors to the comparative haven of the *salon,* where no one dared to follow. At last the door would be closed on the noise and laughter outside.

But here, perhaps, a greater nerve was needed. Having seated the lady upon the bridal throne, the husband had to sweep aside the veil and look upon the face of his wife for the first time—a nervous moment—full of tension. And if that face displeased—? The man had of course the right to end the marriage there and then; but few ever had the moral courage.

It was not considered etiquette for the bridegroom to stay with his bride for more than a few minutes, during which he had to open the veil and give her a jewel. Then, bidding her *au revoir,* the husband would retire. The doors would burst open letting in the ladies of the Harem in a rush to congratulate the bride.

—Princess Musbah Haidar

Lessons and Learning (Cairo, Early Twentieth Century)

My brothers and I and our two companions began our daily lessons early in the morning and finished at noon. We took up various subjects with tutors who came to the house under the supervision of Said Agha. I was devoted to my studies and became completely absorbed at lesson time.

Of all the subjects, Arabic was my favourite. One day when I asked the teacher why I was unable to read the Koran without making a mistake he said, "Because you have not learned the rules of grammar." I pressed him, "Will I be able to read perfectly once I have done so?" When he said yes I asked him to teach me. The next day, when he arrived carrying an Arabic grammar under his arm, Said Agha demanded arrogantly, "What is that?" to which he responded, "The book Mistress Nur al-Huda has requested in order to learn grammar." The eunuch contemptuously ordered, "Take back your book *Sayyidna Shaikh*. The young lady has no need of grammar as she will not become a judge!" I became depressed and began to neglect my studies, hating being a girl because it kept me from the education I sought. Later, being a female became a barrier between me and the freedom for which I yearned. The memory and anguish of this remain sharp to this day.

—Huda Shaarawi (translated by Margot Badran)

In Praise of Women

From a speech delivered in Izmir on January 31, 1923.

The Creator created mankind in two sexes, each needing and needed by the other. There are various theories about Adam and Eve and how they were created. I will not discuss them, but will concern myself with what happened later. Of this we must be sure, that everything we see on the face of the earth is the work of women. Thus, at a time when we all cherished absurd fantasies about the sultan, these were the results of misapprehensions transmitted to us by our mothers. If a society contents itself with modernizing only one of the sexes, it will be weakened by more than half. A nation that seeks progress and civilization must of necessity accept this point as basic. But lack of success of our own society is the result of our negligent and flawed treatment of women. . . . If in a society one limb is active while another is inert, that society is paralyzed. . . . Therefore, just as knowledge and science are necessary for our society, so to the same degree must they be acquired by both our men and our women. It is known that, as in every stage, so also in social life, there is a division of labor. While in this general division of tasks women will carry out those that are specific to them, at the same time they will share in the common effort needed for the comfort and happiness of our society. Household tasks are the smallest and least important of the tasks of women.

—Mustafa Kemal Atatürk

European Views

A Wedding (1384)

We shall speak of the Saracen women, of their customs when they marry. The evening before many porters go to the house of the new wife, and according to his means the husband sends to the house; one carries a bedstead, one basins and jugs of Damascus which are really the most beautiful in the world; one carries linens, one carries trunks very beautiful in their way, according to the means of the bride. The porters go laden with chattels, and the wife waits to get married at night by the light of torches and accompanied by many women. Before the wife gets married all the relatives and neighbours are in the bride's house, and, in short, the women undress her: she cries, and they make her turn around. And there are there women who can paint and they paint all her front, that is the body, the breast, the ribs, the legs and the arms, and they paint greyhounds and kids, birds, trees and foliage; and so they put on very fine colours, according to the design so is the colour, so that each thing has sense. This done, they redress her and put on her seven dresses one over the other according to the means and the grandeur of the husband. All the said dresses are of white cloth, and of cotton, and really they have cottons which are of the fine things of the world to see, all clear and delicate and shining so that in truth they appear to be silk cloths, so that there are some of them which cost two gold besants for a braccio of our measure; a besant is worth one and a quarter gold florins. Then they go in the evening with the bride; and when the bride reaches the husband's house, she draws from her side a scimitar, and she takes it by the point and gives it to her husband, then she pulls off the sheath and gives it to the husband. Then at the end of the salon there are from six to eight mattresses one on the other, and all this bed is covered with a silk cloth. Then this bride is made to sit on this bed and at her side is placed a very fine Damascene basin, and the women who wish to dance they dance one at a time and not more, and she who wishes to dance first goes to the bride and makes a gift of what she can, either a gold besant or a ring, and attaches it to the bride's head with something to hold it firm. And when she has made her gift, she begins to dance, and the bride takes the gift from her head and puts it in the basin aside her, and she that is dancing through the salon makes the latest movements in the world; she jumps high, and then almost sits, and then she rises and lifts her dresses, that is a side hem; and so they lift now one hem, then another, placing it on their head, and so they make the finest movements in the world and the most dexterous. And in so lifting the dress, they cannot show anything of immodesty, for they have all breeches down to their boots: and when she has danced, another moves and does in like manner, and so they all; and the bride is there, and according to him to whom she will be related, she will collect the value of hundreds of gold besants.

—Simone Sigoli (translated by Theophilus Bellorini
and Eugene Hoade)

A Peek at the Harem (Istanbul, 1599)

Thomas Dallam, an English organ maker, was sent by the Turkish Levant Company to deliver an organ to the Sultan and demonstrate its use. His description of that event can be found on page 138.

The 12th, being Friday, I was sent for to the Court, and also the Sunday and Monday following to no other end but to show me the Grand Signor's Privy Chambers, his gold and silver, his chairs of estate; and he that showed me them would have me to sit down in one of them, and then to draw that sword out of the sheath with which the Grand Signor doth crown his king.

When he had showed me many other things which I wondered at, then crossing through a little square court paved with marble, he pointed me to go to a grate in a wall, but made me a sign that he might not go there himself. When I came to the grate the wall was very thick, and grated on both the sides with iron very strongly; but through that grate I did see thirty of the Grand Signor's Concubines that were playing with a ball in another court. At the first sight of them I thought they had been young men, but when I saw the hair of their heads hang down on their backs, plaited together with a tassle of small pearls hanging in the lower end of it, and by other plain tokens, I did know them to be women, and very pretty ones indeed.

They wore upon their heads nothing but a little cap of cloth of gold, which did but cover the crown of their head; no bands about their necks, not anything but fair chains of pearl and a jewel hanging on their breast, and jewels in their ears; their coats were like a soldier's mandilion, some of red satin and some of blue, and some of other colors, and girded like a lace of contrary colors; they wore britches of scamatie, a fine cloth made of cotton wool, as white as snow and as fine as lane; for I could discern the skin of their thighs through it. These britches came down to their midleg; some of them did wear fine cordovan buskins, and some had their legs naked, with a gold ring on the small of her leg; on her foot a velvet slipper four or five inches high. I stood so long looking upon them that he which had showed me all this kindness began to be very angry with me. He made a wry mouth, and stamped with his foot to make me give over looking; the which I was very loath to do, for that sight did please me wondrous well.

—Thomas Dallam

In Praise of Polygamy and Concubinage (1656)

In one of the earliest English books on Ottoman government, Francis Osborn sets out to explain Turkish power and success. He finds much to admire in their system, notably the subordination of ecclesiastical to political author-ity. And that is not all. After commending the austere way of life of the Turks, in such matters as drink, dwellings and furnishings, Osborn continues:

Neither is this people apt to follow the European vanities of Horse-races, Hunting, Hawking, and amorous Entertainments: Their plurality of Women quenching with more security in regard of Health, and less Charge, the thirst of change ordinarily attending the tedious cohabitation with one. . . . [The same arguments apply, with even greater force, to monarchs.]

The Grand Segnior . . . seeks not to match his Daughters out of his own Territories, esteeming no blood royal, but what runs in his own veines, and his that is to succeed him: Neither is he lycorish after the choice of the Issue of Kings for his own Bed, finding the same content in the embraces of a Sub-ject or a Slave, that a more bewitched Imagination apprehends in those of a Princesse: Nor doth his modesty abuse him, but acquits him from the dan-ger of having a Spie in his Bosome, or a coëquall in his Counsells; giving him leave to put to death or exchange his Wives upon occasion, without the feare of any other frown but that of Heaven; amongst whose joyes (accord-ing to his Creed) is Change of Women, and all Carnall Delights.

And by the division he makes of his Love among many Wives, he ren-ders the Government less factious: The Distaffe having been found no friend to the Scepter, opening often a back door to Innovation; apparent in Christians, who marrying the daughters of more potent Princes than them-selves, are so farre over-awed by them, as to make them partners in their most secret designes, else they are able to distresse them through the strength of their own friends. Thus a Prince comes to have an Enemy in his bosome, and such an one as he dares not question, for feare of a shower at home, and a storme from abroad. . . .

The birth of the first Son gives the title of Sultana to a slave, the highest honor or employment a woman can be borne to: and what might abundantly content them also in Europe, where they are made the Arbitrators of the Royall Line.

—Francis Osborn

Women's Quarters (Istanbul, c. 1667)

And since I have brought my Reader into the quarters of these Eunuchs, which are the Black guard of the sequestered Ladies of the Seraglio, he may chance to take it unkindly, should I leave him at the door, and not introduce him into those Apartments, where the Grand Signor's Mistresses are lodged: And though I ingeniously confess my acquaintance there (as all other my conversation with Women in Turkey) is but strange and unfamiliar; yet not to be guilty of this discourtesy, I shall to the best of my information write a short account of these Captivated Ladies, how they are treated, immured, educated and prepared for the great achievements of the Sultans affection; and as in other stories the Knight consumes himself with combats, watching, and penance to acquire the love of one fair Damsel; here an Army of Virgins make it the only study and business of their life to obtain the single nod of invitation to the Bed of their great Master.

The Reader then must know that this Assembly of fair Women (for it is probable there is no other in the Seraglio) are commonly prizes of the Sword, taken at Sea and at Land, as far fetched as the Turk commands, or the wandering Tartar makes his excursions, composed almost of as many Nations as there are Countries of the world; none of which are esteemed worthy of this Preferment, unless beautiful and undoubted Virgins.

As the Pages before mentioned are divided into two Chambers, so likewise are these Maids into two Odaes [Turkish *oda,* a room], where they are to work, sow, and embroider, and are therefore lodged on *Safawes,* every one with her bed apart, between every five of which is a *Kadun* or grave Matron laid to oversee and hear what actions or discourse passes either immodest or indecent. Besides this School they have their Chambers for Music and Dancing, for acquiring a handsome air in their carriage and comportment, to which they are most diligent and intent, as that which opens the door of the *Sultans* affections, and introduces them into Preferment and Esteem.

Out of these the Queen Mother chooses her Court, and orderly draws from the Schools such as she marks out for the most beauteous, facetious,

Chief Black Eunuch of the Ottoman Palace, from Paul Rycaut, The History of the Present State of the Ottoman Empire, *1675.*

or most corresponding with the harmony of her own disposition, and prefers them to a near attendance on her Person, or to other Offices of her Court. These are always richly attired and adorned with all sorts of precious stones, fit to receive the address and amours of the *Sultan:* over them is placed the *Kadun Kahia* or Mother of the Maids, who is careful to correct any immodest or light behavior amongst them, and instructs them in all the Rules and Orders of the Court. . . .

The Daughters that are born from the Grand Signor, are oftentimes at four or five years of Age wedded to some great *Pasha* or *Beglerbeg* with all the Pomp and solemnities of Marriage, who from that time hath care of her Education; to provide a Palace for her Court, and to maintain her with that state and honor as becomes the dignity of a Daughter to a *Sultan*.

—Sir Paul Rycaut

Tales of an English Lady (1717–18)

Lady Mary Wortley Montagu was the wife of the British ambassador in Istanbul. She spent just over one year in Turkey, during which time she had a baby, learned some Turkish and corresponded with Alexander Pope about Turkish poetry. Her letters, describing the places she visited, the Turks she met and their public and private lives, were published in 1763, the year after her death.

I was invited to dine with the Grand Vizier's Lady and twas with a great deal of pleasure I prepar'd my selfe for an Entertainment which was never given before to any Christian. I thought I should very little satisfy her Curiosity (which I did not doubt was a considerable Motive to the Invitation) by going in a Dress she was us'd to see, and therefore dress'd my selfe in the Court habit of Vienna, which is much more Magnificent than ours. However, I chose to go incognito to avoid any disputes about Ceremony, and went in a Turkish coach only attended by my Woman that held up my Train and the Greek Lady who was my interpretress. I was met at the Court door by her black Eunuch, who help'd me out of the Coach with great Respect and conducted me through several rooms where her She Slaves, finely dress'd, were rang'd on each side. In the innermost, I found the Lady sitting on her Sofa in a Sable vest. She advanc'd to meet me and presented me halfe a dozen of her freinds [*sic*] with great Civillity. She seem'd a very good Woman, near 50 year old. I was surpriz'd to observe so little Magnificence in her House, the furniture being all very moderate, and except the Habits and Number of her Slaves nothing about her that appear'd expensive. She guess'd at my thoughts and told me that she was no longer of an Age to spend either her time or Money in Superfluitys, that her whole exigence was in charity and her Employment praying to God. There was no Affectation in this Speech; both she and her Husband are entirely given up to Devotion. He never looks upon any other Woman, and what is much more extrodinary touches no bribes notwithstanding the Example of all his Predecessors. He is so scrupulous in this point, he would not accept Mr. W[ortley]'s present till he had been assur'd over and over twas a settle'd perquisite of his place at the Entrance of every Ambassador. . . .

I am well acquainted with a Christian Woman of Quality who made it her choice to live with a Turkish Husband, and is a very agreable sensible Lady. Her story is so extrodinary I cannot forbear relateing it, but I promise you it shall be in as few words as I can possibly express it. She is a Spaniard and was at Naples with her family when that Kingdom was part of the Spanish Dominion. Coming from thence in a Feloucca, accompany'd by her Brother, they were attack'd by the Turkish Admiral, boarded and taken; and now, how shall I modestly tell you the rest of her Adventure? The same Accident happen'd to her that happen'd to the fair Lucretia so many Years before her, but she was too good a Christian to kill her selfe as that heathenish Roman did. The Admiral was so much charm'd with the Beauty and long-suffering of the Fair Captive that as his first complement he gave immediate Liberty to her Brother and attendants, who made haste to Spain and in a few months sent the sum of £4,000 sterling as a Ransom for his sister. The Turk took the Money, which he presented to her, and told her she was at Liberty, but the Lady very discreetly weigh'd the different treatment she was likely to find in her native Country. Her Catholic Relations, as the kindest thing they could do for her in her present Circumstances, would certainly confine her to a Nunnery for the rest of her Days. Her Infidel Lover was very handsome, very tender, fond of her, and lavish'd at her feet all the Turkish Magnificence. She answer'd him very resolutely that her Liberty was not so precious to her as her Honnour, that he could no way restore that but by marrying her. She desir'd him to accept the Ransom as her Portion and give her the satisfaction of knowing no Man could boast of her favours without being her Husband. The Admiral was transported at this kind offer and sent back the Money to her Relations, saying he was too happy in her Possession. He marry'd her and never took any other wife, and (as she says her selfe) she never had any reason to repent the choice she made. He left her some years after one of the richest widows in Constantinople, but there is no remaining honnourably a single woman, and that consideration has oblig'd her to marry the present Capitan Bassa (i.e., Admiral), his Successor. . . .

—Lady Mary Wortley Montagu

On the Domestic Life of the Inhabitants of Syria and Why There Is so Little to Envy (1782–85)

A . . . source of gaiety among us is the free communication between the sexes that takes place above all in France. The effect is that, in a more or less vague hope, men seek the goodwill of women and do the things that might procure it. Such is the spirit or such the education of women that in their eyes the first merit is to amuse them; and certainly of all the ways of accomplishing this, the first is sprightliness and gaiety. It is thus that we have formed a habit of badinage, of complaisance and of frivolity, which has become the distinctive character of our nation in Europe. In Asia, on the contrary, women are rigorously secluded from the company of men. Always shut up at home, they communicate only with a husband, a father, a brother or at most a first cousin; carefully veiled in the streets, they hardly dare speak to a man, even on business. All must be strangers to them: it would be indecent to look at them, and one must let them pass with averted eyes, as if they were something contagious. That is almost how it is seen by Easterners, who have a general feeling of scorn for the female sex. What, one might ask, is the cause of this? That of everything else, legislation and government. . . .

What people tell of the domestic life of husbands who have several wives does not incline one to envy their fate, nor does it give a lofty idea of this part of the Islamic legislation. The house is the theater of a continuous civil war. Endlessly, there are quarrels between wife and wife, complaints of wives to the husband. The four titular wives complain that slave girls are given preference over them and the slave girls that they are delivered to the jealousy of their mistresses. If a woman gets a jewel, a favor, permission to go to the bath, all the others want the same, and become allies in a common cause. To keep the peace, the polygamist is obliged to rule as a despot; and as such he can find only the sentiments of slaves, the appearance of attachment and the reality of hatred. In vain does each of these women protest to him that she loves him more than the others; in vain do they hurry when he comes in to present him his pipe and his slippers, to prepare his dinner, to serve him his coffee; in vain when he stretches languidly on his carpet do they chase away the flies that bother him; all these cares, all these caresses have as their sole purpose to procure an addition to the sum of their jewels and appointments, so that if he divorces them, they can tempt another husband or find a resource in the objects which are their sole property. They are truly courtesans, who think only of despoiling their lover before he leaves them; and this lover, long since deprived of desires, obsessed with complaisance, overwhelmed with the boredom of satiety, does not enjoy, as one might have thought, an enviable fate.

—Volney

A Physician Visits the Harem, with Notes on Certain Feminine Concerns (1824)

Dr. Richard Robert Madden traveled extensively in the Middle East in 1824–27. His work as a physician gave him unique access.

The state of female society in Turkey, and of the condition of the sex generally, I am solely indebted to my profession for knowing any thing of correctly. The Turks have long been accustomed to choose their wives from
the fairest women of Georgia and Circassia, and, latterly, of Greece; as
beauty is the only quality sought after, it may be imagined that lovelier
women are nowhere to be found, and more beauteous children nowhere to
be seen. On my first visit to a *harem* the women were generally veiled, and
the pulse was even to be felt through the medium of a piece of gauze; but,
subsequently, my fair patients submitted to inspection with a good grace,
and, in the absence of the husband, even laughed and jested in my presence. Some, who called me "dog" at the first interview, and did every thing
but spit upon me, became familiarized with the presence of an infidel, and
made me presents of embroidered handkerchiefs and purses. They asked
me the most ridiculous questions about the women of my country, "if they
were let to go abroad without a eunuch; if they could love men who wore
hats; if we drowned them often; if they went to the bath every week; if they
sullied or washed their elbows; if I was married, and how many wives I
had;" and sometimes the husband was even present at the conversation and
condescended to laugh with pity, when he heard that English ladies walked
unveiled, and that it was unusual to have more than one at a time for a wife;
but what seemed to create the greatest horror of all, was the disuse of those
lower garments, which are indispensable to Turkish ladies.

They never seemed to feel they suffered any constraint; they appeared
gay and happy; they embroidered, played a rude sort of spinet, and sang in-
terminable songs; but whether the music of their voices, or of the spinet,
was most appalling to a Christian ear, it would be difficult to say. They certainly are the loveliest women in the world, so far as the beauty of the face
is regarded: but their persons are so little indebted to dress for the preservation of shape, that I very much question the correctness of Lady Mary Wortley Montagu's remark on the *peculiar* attraction of the Turkish form. Their
beauty is particularly delicate, and the paleness of their features is delightfully contrasted with their raven locks, and with eyes as soft and black as the
gazelle's. The larger the latter are, the better; and the more arched the eyebrow, either by art or nature, the more captivating the charmer; but the bath,
though it smooth the skin, and soften the complexion, in course of time
prejudices their beauty. In short, while they do reign, they are irresistible; in
their own figurative language, their "eyes are full of sleep, and their hearts
are full of passion." Where personal charms are all that make a woman valuable, it is to be supposed that every care is taken to heighten them: cosmetics are used in abundance; they tinge their eyelids with a metallic powder,
which the Turks call *surme,* and the Egyptians *kohol.* They smear a little
ebony rod with this, apply it to the eyelids, which they bring in contact, and

squeezing the rod between them, a small black line is left to the edge of either lid, which adds greatly to the beauty of the long eyelashes, and, by its relievo, to the brilliancy of the eye. The *surme* is used to extend the arch of the eyebrow, not to elevate it; for the Turkish women well know, that the beauty of the eye, in most instances, depends on its elongation. They also embue their nails and finger tops with the juice of *henna,* and fine ladies even extend its application to the toes. The vulgar frequently rouge; but I have seldom seen fashionable women use paint, except on their lips. Various amulets are worn on the neck. The *Sheik* of the districts sells charms by wholesale; one is to make a lady fat, another fruitful; one is to keep off the evil eye, which is always to be apprehended, when a stranger extols the size or beauty of their children; another to keep the *shitan,* or devil out of the house. A triangular paper, surmounted with an amber bead, is seldom omitted, to preserve the lustre of their eyes; and a little leather bag, with the dust of a dried mummy, like "parmaceti, is a sovereign remedy for an inward bruise." But when amulets fail to make a lady fertile, or to increase her size to the requisite degree of magnitude and beauty, she then has recourse either to the Turkish barber, or the Frank physician.

I have been teased to death for fattening filtres, and fertilizing potions; I have heard serious disputes between the slender and the robust, the barren and the prolific: it is not to be wondered at, for a woman has no honour or respect until she prove a mother; and a young wife has little chance of eclipsing the competitors for her husband's favour, till she is "beautifully fat." Notwithstanding the size of these women, they are graceful in their movements, easy, and even elegant in their manners; and, strange as it may appear, I often thought there was as much elegance of attitude displayed in the splendid arm of a Turkish beauty, holding her rich *chibouque,* and seated on her Persian carpet, as in the finest form of an European belle, bending over her harp, or moving in the mystic circle of the waltz. The female apparel is superb, and certainly becoming: there is a profusion of gaudy colours, but well disposed; and the head is constantly decked with all the fair one's diamonds and pearls. . . .

I can now look on a greasy finger with as much complacency as a silver fork, and drink soup with a wooden spoon out of a tureen that supplies perhaps a dozen. . . .

On Marriage, Baths, Indiscretion and Divorce

Polygamy in Turkey is limited to a certain number, namely, four; no one can take a greater number of wives, but the society of as many slaves as a man can purchase is tolerated; and the children by such slaves are equally legitimate with those born in wedlock, upon performing a public act of manumission before the Cadi. Marriage is a civil institution, and is effected by the appearance of the suitor, with the next male relative of the bride, before the magistrate; the happy man avows his affection for a girl he never saw, makes a settlement on her according to his circumstances (for a Turkish lady brings nothing but her beauty for a dower), and having owned her for his lawful wife, the match is registered, and the marriage is of course made (as all marriages are) in Heaven. The happy man invites all his male friends and those of his wife (whom he has not yet seen) to his house, and treats them with music, vocal and instrumental, sherbet, and coffee. The bride, in the mean time, receives admirable lectures from all the neighbouring matrons, on the power of her husband, and the submission he expects. She is taken to the bath with great pomp, where she undergoes the process of ablution, anointing, and perfuming; and is, at last, conveyed to her husband's house, under a gaudy canopy, dressed in her richest garb, and covered all over with a veil which scarcely transmits her blushes to the spectators; a troop of cavaliers are in attendance, a buffoon and a band of music form part of the procession. She is received at the door of the husband by his father or himself, and is immediately conveyed to the women's apartments, where she remains, whilst her lord and his guests are banqueting without.

I will not enter into the merits of the state of female society in the East; I believe the customs of every country are generally adapted to its climate and its circumstances. Restraints may be requisite in oriental climates, for aught I know; and women may deem themselves, under such restraints, the best treated women in the world.

The confinement to the walls of the harem is neither so close nor so irksome as most people imagine. The women visit one another frequently, and once a week they revel in the bath, which is the terrestrial Paradise, the Italian opera, in Turkey, of a Mahometan lady; they pass the entire day there; breakfast, and sup in the outer apartment, and are as happy as possible; they have plenty of "looking-glasses," and lots of "sugarplums." Lady M. W. Montagu's description of the bath would be excellent, if it were correct; but her ladyship has certainly overlooked the features of her beauties too much, and has exhibited truth, though in "puris naturalibus," in too *attractive forms*.

Here, whatever intrigue is practised, is usually carried on through the medium of female emissaries; but I believe it to be less than in any large city in Christendom: the penalty of the crime is death. The detection of a single imprudent act, every woman knows, leads to a short consultation with the cadi, and that summary process to the Bosphorus, an eunuch and a sack. The ladies are, therefore, extremely circumspect.

There are three different kinds of divorce, each differing in the importance of its nature. A woman can only have one plea for demanding a divorce; the man has several, and finds little difficulty in separating from a loathed or injured wife.

When the woman sues for separate maintenance, she pleads the ill treatment of the husband, or his particular neglect on the day called *Gium a guin* [literally, coition day]; or, if the charge be more serious, or more scandalous, she simply substantiates it by taking off her slipper, and presenting the sole to the cadi.

When the husband sues for divorce on the ground of his wife's adultery, a similar meeting of the parties taking place before the judge, he takes "the oath of bitterness," which consists in imprecations on his head, if he have brought forward a false accusation. The wife is desired to take a somewhat similar oath, calling maledictions on her head, if she be guilty of the charge. If she refuse to take the oath, the divorce is granted; but if she take it, the case must be disposed of after the hearing of witnesses on both sides.

After divorces have been granted more than once, and the parties are again reconciled, it is wisely ordained, to prevent their future separations, that, in the event of their again disuniting, they cannot come together until the woman be married to another man, and spend one night under his roof; the former husband may then get her divorced from her new lord; and if his good nature can get over the *horns* of the dilemma, he takes his gentle partner back to bed and board. The tale of throwing a handkerchief to the fair competitors for their master's favour, is an idle invention. I believe caprice very rarely predominates; and that, in well regulated harems, every lady has an allotted share of her lord's affection.

—R. R. Madden

The Price of a Slave (Istanbul, 1824)

I had an opportunity . . . of seeing the horrid place where human beings are bought and sold like cattle, the women inspected by every scoundrel who wears a turban, and submitted to the scrutiny of every dealer who frequents the market. Franks are not suffered to visit this *bazaar*; but now and then, when an opulent slave merchant falls sick, a Christian *hakkim,* or doctor, gains admittance. In this way I was brought in to see a plague patient, whose couch was the bench of a public coffeehouse; twenty or thirty people were smoking with great composure by his side; and when I pointed out the hopeless condition of the unfortunate patient, they only "drank another pipe," (to use their own language), and exclaimed "there was but one God, *Allah wakbar.*" The patient died the following morning; and the ensuing week I had three cases more of plague in the same house.

The slave *bazaar* is a large quadrangular courtyard, with a shed running along a range of narrow cells on the ground floor, and a gallery above, which surrounds the building: on the second stage, the chambers are reserved for the Greeks and Georgians; below are the black women of Darfur and Sennaar, and the copper-coloured beauties of Abyssinia: the latter are remarkable for the symmetry of their features, and the elegance of their forms: they commonly sell for one hundred and fifty dollars (£30); while the black women seldom bring more than eighty dollars (£16).

The poor Greek women were huddled together; I saw seven or eight in one cell, stretched on the floor, some dressed in the vestiges of former finery, some half naked; some of them were from Scio, others from Ipsara; they had nothing in common but despair! All of them looked pale and sickly; and appeared to be pining after the homes they were never to see again, and the friends they were to meet no more! Sickness and sorrow had impaired their looks; but still they were spectres of beauty: and the melancholy stillness of their cells was sadly contrasted with the roars of merriment which proceeded from the dungeons of the negro women. No scene of human wretchedness can equal this: the girl who might have adorned her native village, whose innocence might have been the solace of an anxious mother, and whose beauty might have been the theme of many a tongue, was here subjected to the gaze of every licentious soldier, who chose to examine her features, or her form, on the pretence of being a buyer. I saw one poor girl of about fifteen, brought forth to exhibit her gait and figure to an old Turk, whose glances manifested the motive for her purchase: he twisted her elbows, he pulled her ankles, he felt her ears, examined her mouth, and then her neck; and all this while the slave merchant was extolling her shape and features, protesting she was only turned of thirteen, that she neither snored nor started in her sleep, and that, in every respect, she was warranted.

I loitered about the bazaar till I saw this bargain brought to a conclusion; the girl was bought for two hundred and eighty dollars, about 55l. sterling. The separation of this young creature from her companions in wretchedness was a new scene of distress; she was as pale as death, and hardly seemed conscious of her situation, while all the other girls were weeping around her, and taking their last farewell. Her new master laughed at the sad parting, and pushed her before him to the outer gate; but there she stopped for a moment, and entreated permission to go back for the remnant of her Greek attire, which, I dare say, she prized more than any thing in the world, for probably it was all on earth that remained to her of what she brought from that home which she had left for ever. The old Moslem accompanied her back; and in a few minutes I saw her returning to the gate with a little bundle under her arm, trembling from head to foot, and weeping bitterly.

It was a sad sight; and a man who thinks highly of human nature, and loves mankind, should never cross the threshold of the slave *bazaar*. I left the unhallowed spot where the Moslem deals in the flesh and blood of his fellow creatures, and where the atrocious sacrifice of beauty and of innocence is offered up on the altar of slavery, to the Turkish demon of concupiscence.

—R. R. Madden

The Second Wife (Cairo, 1833–35)

When there are two or more wives belonging to one man, the first (that is, the one first married,) generally enjoys the highest rank; and is called "the great lady." Hence it often happens that, when a man who has already one wife wishes to marry another girl or woman, the father of the latter, or the female herself who is sought in marriage, will not consent to the union unless the first wife be previously divorced. The women, of course, do not approve of a man's marrying more than one wife. Most men of wealth, or of moderate circumstances, and even many men of the lower orders, if they have two or more wives, have, for each, a separate house. The wife has, or can oblige her husband to give her a particular description of lodging, which is either a separate house, or a suite of apartments (consisting of a room in which to sleep and pass the day, a kitchen, and a latrina,) that are, or may be made, separate and shut out from any other apartments in the same house. A fellow-wife is called "durrah." The quarrels of durrahs are often talked of: for it may be naturally inferred, that, when two wives share the affection and attentions of the same man, they are not always on terms of amity with each other; and the same is generally the case with a wife and a concubine-slave living in the same house, and in similar circumstances. If the chief lady be barren, and an inferior (either wife or slave) bear a child to her husband or master, it commonly results that the latter woman becomes a favourite of the man, and that the chief wife or mistress is "despised in her eyes," as Abraham's wife was in the eyes of Hagar on the same account. It therefore not very unfrequently happens that the first wife loses her rank and privileges; another becomes the chief lady, and, being the favourite of her husband, is treated by her rival or rivals, and by all the members and visiters of the hareem, with the same degree of outward respect which the first wife previously enjoyed: but sometimes the poisoned cup is employed to remove her. A preference given to a second wife is often the cause of the first's being registered as "náshizeh [a shrew]," either on her husband's or her own application at the Mahkemeh [tribunal]. Yet many instances are known of neglected wives behaving with exemplary and unfeigned submission to the husband, in such cases, and with amiable good nature towards the favourite.

—Edward Lane

Thoughts on Polygamy (1849–50)

Polygamy strikes at the root of everything in woman—she is not a wife— she is not a mother;—and in these Oriental countries, what is a woman, if she is not that? In all other countries she has something else to fall back upon. The Roman Catholic woman has a religion—the Protestant has an intellect; in the early Christian, in the old Egyptian time, women had a vocation, a profession, provided for them in their religion, independent of their wifedom; here, she is nothing but the servant of a man. No, I do assure you, the female elephant, the female eagle, has a higher idea of what she was put into the world to do, than the human female has here.

—Florence Nightingale

The Superior Sex (1858)

[Ottoman women] are far before the men in intelligence, far less prejudiced, and far more willing to know and adopt wiser and better ways.

—Emilia Hornby

Women in Muslim Law (Turkey, c. 1900)

The Turkish nation—soldiers, peasants, merchants, and the learned professions—never touch alcohol. Against the moral value of this abstinence may be set off the position assigned to women; but any just criticism of Mohammed's legislation on this subject and its results must not lose sight of two points. Firstly, Mohammed did not invent the seclusion and subjection of women. He accepted, with some improvements, the current Arabian ideas on the subject. The system of the harem is in its origin not Moslim, but simply Oriental. The only reproach that can be made against the Prophet is that on which I have already dilated—namely, that by too definite legislation he rendered subsequent development and reform impossible. Secondly, those who talk of the degradation of Mohammedan women would do well to remember that in Mohammedan countries prostitution and illegitimacy are almost unknown. It is true that only the length of his purse and the temper of his lawful wives (both of them very effective restraints) limit the unions which a Moslim may contract with slaves, but the offspring of such unions are legitimate children, and inherit share and share alike with the children born in wedlock. A Moslim woman is never free, but, on the other hand, it is almost impossible to imagine any circumstances in which she would be cast on the world without a protector. A certain solidarity characterises, not only family relations, but all Moslim society. There are no paupers; giving alms is not a mere theoretical obligation, but an essential religious duty really discharged. It may be replied that there are many beggars. There are, and the spectacle is very unpleasant; but, from the beggars' point of view, could they, given their misfortunes, have a better life? If one has twisted limbs or any incurable malady, including laziness, is it not more healthy, interesting, and lucrative, to sit begging at street corners than to be the inmate of a charitable institution? One thing is certain—Moslim beggars never starve.

—Odysseus (Sir Charles Eliot)

Behind the Veil (Egypt, 1923)

Women . . . are present in a vague sort of way in the fields and railway stations. But what is going on inside that lump of dusty black cloth, that carriage whose shutters suggest that a commercial traveller lurks cocooned, that other part of the house? We have much information, from the Arabian Nights onward, but it arrives in so literary a condition that to me it never seems very real, and the Harem presents itself less as a mystery than an emptiness. It seems the more unreal because the tiny glimpses I have had of domestic arrangements in those parts were the least according to recipe, and nothing that I have read has illuminated them. No doubt they were exceptional; one spends one's life among exceptions. But these other gentlemen, who write with such profusion and aplomb—what exactly were their glimpses? Those European ladies with heavy faces who enter the Harem to dispense morality and quinine—to what extent are they capable of reporting what they hear? When one visits a show interior, such as that of the House of Gamal-ud-din at Cairo, and sees the pretty little shelves, and peeps through the lattices into the street, one feels that the bird is indeed flown, and that by no possibility can its plumage or song be reconstructed. The abolition of slavery and the growth of industrialism are weakening the Harem system, so the problem may not be important practically. But the

imagination abhors a void, and when the East is easiest it will suddenly reflect, "But this is only half, and I cannot even remember that there is another half," and will be humiliated.

—E. M. Forster

Four Classical Love Poems

Arabic

She said, "Do not loiter by our house,
    my father is a jealous man."
I said, "I shall snatch you from him,
    my sword is sharp and keen."
She said, "The castle is between us."
    I said, "I shall climb over it."
She said, "The sea lies between us."
    I said, "I am a skilful swimmer."
She said, "Seven brothers stand about me."
    I said, "I am mighty and invincible."
She said, "God is above us."
    I said, "My Lord is merciful and forgiving."
She said, "You have out-argued me,
    come when the evening company sleeps
And fall on me as the dew falls
    by night, when none forbids or interferes."

—Waddāḥ al-Yaman (seventh century)

Persian

Though my heart bleeds with pain of parting,
Pain I endure for you is more joy than pain.
Each night I ponder, and I say: "O God,
If such is parting from her, how will union be?"

I do not dye my hair black because
I want to seem young and commit more sins,
but because people dye their clothes black in mourning.
I have dyed my hair black, mourning my old age.

When you see me dead, my lips forever closed
And see this passion-racked form empty of life,
You can sit by my bedside and say, so charmingly,
It was I who killed you, and now I am sorry.

—Rūdagī (tenth century)

Hebrew

Ofra washes her clothes in the waters
Of my tears
And spreads them to dry in the sun
Of her radiance
With my two eyes, she needs no spring
With her beauty—no sun.

—Yehuda Halevi (twelfth century)

Turkish

My love has tired me of my life—will she not tire of cruelty?
My sigh has set the spheres on fire—will not the candle of my passion
*   burn?*

On those who faint and fail for her, my love bestows a healing drug
Why does she give none to me; does she not think that I am sick?

I hid my pain from her. They said tell it to your love.
And if I tell that faithless one—I do not know, will she believe, or will
*   she not?*

In the night of separation, my soul burns, my eye weeps blood
My cries awaken; does my black fate never wake?

Against the rose of your cheek red tears stream from my eye
Dear love, this is the time of roses, will not these flowing waters cloud?

It was not I who turned to you but you who drove my sense away
When the fool who blames me sees you, will he not be put to shame?

Fuzuli is a crazy lover and a byword among folk
Ask then what kind of love is this—of such a love does he not tire?

—Fuzuli (sixteenth century)

Last Word from a Turkish Lady

Woman, they say, is deficient in sense
so they ought to pardon her every word.
But one female who knows what to do
is better than a thousand males who don't.

—Mihri Hatun (fifteenth century)

PART VII

Government

The four pillars of government . . . are religion,
justice, counsel, and treasure.
—FRANCIS BACON

The Prime Vizier

The Ottoman grand vizier, from Paul Rycaut, The History of the
Present State of the Ottoman Empire, *1675.*

Introduction

In the Middle East, as in other parts of the world, men arose who made themselves rulers over others, founded kingdoms, promulgated or enforced laws and, exercising one of the basic prerogatives of sovereignty, made war.

The formation of states in the Middle East began in remote antiquity, probably earlier than anywhere else in the world. The irrigated river valley economies of Egypt and Mesopotamia required some measure of central organization: technicians to construct and maintain the dikes and canals, administrators to supervise their work and control the distribution of the precious water. The invention of writing, with the resulting possibility of storing, accumulating and transmitting information, added a new dimension to the exercise of power and permitted—perhaps even required—the creation of bureaucracy. Around the ruler, his administrators and his enforcers, a new phenomenon emerged: the city.

Enforcers served the king in two ways: by maintaining his authority over his subjects and by defending or extending it in conflicts with neighboring rulers. With the growing sophistication on the one hand of political organization, on the other of weaponry, what began as tribal feuding developed into interstate warfare.

Middle Easterners, again like other people elsewhere, found ways of involving their religions both in their politics and in their wars. Usually the cult, and its authorized exponents the priests, served to buttress kingship and to lend divine sanction to the king's justice. Sometimes, however, religious arguments and leaders served the opposite purpose—not to uphold but to challenge and sometimes even overthrow the existing authority.

Both aspects of religion are exemplified in the Old Testament. Political leadership among the children of Israel, according to the biblical record, began with Moses and his immediate successors and was transmitted first to the judges and then after them to the anointed kings. The kings of Israel, unlike most other rulers, had a resident opposition: the prophets, who invoked the same religious authority to rebuke and on occasion to remove an erring monarch. After the fall of the ancient Jewish kingdoms and the establishment of foreign imperial rule over the Jews, rabbinic writings reflect a more cautious attitude to authority.

Christianity, which arose while the Jews were under Roman domination, followed a delicate line between religious and political authority, until, with the conversion of Constantine, it was able to take over the Roman Empire itself.

The Prophet Muhammad was, so to speak, his own Constantine, and his career exemplified both rebellion and authority. In Mecca he was a rebel against the ruling authority; in Medina he himself was the ruling authority. The traditions of the Prophet, and the biographical passages in the Qur'ān itself, reflect both aspects, and provide texts which can be—and have been—cited both to defend a government and to condemn and subvert it.

Middle Eastern societies, especially since the advent of Islam, have devoted great attention to the problems of government, law and opposition. A major part of the resulting literature comes from jurists, concerned with formulating and interpreting the political implications of revelation and Holy Law. Much of it emanates from the bureaucratic classes, reflecting their ethos and describing their professional skills and functions.

Evidence on the actual functioning of government and opposition may be found in documents which survive in considerable numbers from the Middle Ages and in the form of massive archives for the modern period. Descriptions are provided in a variety of sources: historians and other writers from within the region, visitors from abroad and principally from the West. These latter acquire a special importance during the period of Westernization or, more precisely, modernization under Western influence. This process and the resulting changes also evoked many significant comments from both reformers and reactionaries. The chapter concludes with a number of passages, from internal and external sources, on the progress and setbacks of reform and on the revolutionary movements in Turkey and Iran.

The Theory and Practice of Government

Wisdom of the Rabbis

Advice to Judges (First Century B.C.E.)

Shimon ben Shatakh said: Be very thorough in investigating witnesses, and be careful with your words, lest through them they learn how to lie.

Shemaya said: Love work and hate lordship, and don't seek acquaintance with the authorities.

Beware of the authorities, for they bring no one near them save for their own needs and purposes. They appear as friends when they are satisfied, but they help no man in his hour of need.

—*Pirqē Avot*

From the Qur'ān

Obey God, obey His Prophet, and obey those in authority over you (4:59).

But fear God and obey me, and do not obey the orders of the wanton who work evil in the land and do no good (26:150–52).

Sayings Attributed to the Prophet

I charge the caliph after me to fear God, and I commend the community of the Muslims to him, to respect the great among them and have pity on the small, to honor the learned among them, not to strike them and humiliate them, not to oppress them and drive them to unbelief, not to close his doors to them and allow the strong to devour the weak.

Hear and obey, even if a shaggy-headed black slave is appointed over you.

Whosoever shall try to divide my community, strike off his head.

If allegiance is sworn to two caliphs, kill the other.

He who sees in his ruler something he disapproves should be patient, for if anyone separates himself from the community, even by a span, and dies, he dies the death of a pagan.

Obey your rulers, whatever happens. If their commands accord with the revelation I brought you, they will be rewarded for it, and you will be rewarded for obeying them; if their commands are not in accord with what I brought you, they are answerable and you are absolved.

If you have rulers over you who ordain prayer and the alms tax and the Holy War for God, then God forbids you to revile them and allows you to pray behind them.

If anyone comes out against my community when they are united and seeks to divide them, kill him, whoever he may be.

Do not revile the sultan, for he is God's shadow on God's earth.

Obedience is the duty of the Muslim man, whether he like it or not, as long as he is not ordered to commit a sin. If he is ordered to commit a sin, he does not have to obey.

Do not obey a creature against his Creator.

The nearer a man is to government, the further he is from God; the more followers he has, the more devils; the greater his wealth, the more exacting his reckoning.

He who commends a sultan in what God condemns has left the religion of God.

The Severity of Ziyād (Seventh Century)

Ziyād was an illegitimate half brother of the caliph Muʿāwiya, whence his title Ibn Abīh, literally "son of his father." He became famous for the strictness and effectiveness with which he maintained order in the rebellious province of Iraq. His severity became legendary. The following account, though based on earlier sources, dates from the beginning of the nineteenth century.

When Muʿāwiya appointed Ziyād ibn Abīh as governor of Iraq, that country was full of robbery and violence. As soon as he was appointed, Ziyād entered the mosque. He mounted the pulpit and he said to the congregation, "By God, if any man comes out of his house after the evening meal his blood is on his head. Let this be known both by the present and the absent." Then he sent a herald to announce this order in all the towns for three days.

On the fourth day Ziyād went out at the end of the first watch to wander about in the town. He met a shepherd with his flock. Ziyād said to him, "What are you doing here?" The shepherd said, "I have come to the town and I have not found any lodging, therefore I slept where I was. Tomorrow morning, please God, I shall sell my sheep." Ziyād said to him, "I know that you speak truth. But if I let you be, I fear lest the thing will become known and people will say that Ziyād speaks but does not act, and then my policy will be destroyed and fear of me will disappear. Paradise is therefore better for you." So he cut off his head.

That same night Ziyād killed with the sword 5,500 men and hung their skulls on the gates of his palace. Fear of him seized everybody. On the fifth night he went out to walk in the town. He met 300 men and killed them all with the sword and hung their skulls. From that time onward no man dared to go out of his house after the evening meal.

On Friday, he went up to the pulpit of the mosque and said, "Let no man lock his shop by night. If anything is stolen, I will pay."

They did as he said. After a few days, a goldsmith came and said, "Four hundred dinars were stolen from my shop." Ziyād said to him, "Swear that you speak truth." The man swore. Ziyād weighed out four hundred dinars to him and ordered him to keep the matter secret.

On Friday Ziyād stood up and preached in the mosque to the congregation. "From a certain goldsmith's shop," he said, "four hundred dinars were stolen. Now all of you stand here. If you return his money to him, it will be better, but if not, then I swear that no man of you will leave this mosque alive. You will all be killed." At once they sought out the man suspected of the theft and placed him before Ziyād. The thief returned what he had stolen and was taken out and hanged.

On another occasion Ziyād asked, "Which is the wildest place in Basra where there is no security?" They replied, "The quarter of the Banū Azd." Then he gave orders to place a valuable silk cloak at the crossroads there. It lay there for several days and no one touched it.

—Shaykh Muḥammad ibn Aḥmad al-Yamanī

Cutting Bureaucracy (Eighth Century)

[An official] wrote to the caliph 'Umar ibn 'Abd al-'Azīz [717–720] asking for papyrus. 'Umar replied, "Sharpen your pen and write less. It will be more swiftly understood." The caliph also wrote to another official, who had written asking for papyrus and complaining that he had very little of it, "Cut your pen fine and your words short, and make do with what papyrus you have."

—Al-Jahshiyārī

A Letter to Secretaries (Eighth Century)

May God protect you, O you who practice the art of writing, and may He guard you and help you and guide you. For Almighty God has divided mankind, after the prophets and apostles, may God bless and save them all, and after the honored kings, into classes, these being in fact equal, and has disposed them among different kinds of crafts and sorts of endeavor, by which they gain their livelihood and earn their keep. He put you secretaries in the most distinguished positions, men of culture and virtue, of knowledge and discernment. By your means the excellences of the caliphate are well ordered, and its affairs uprightly maintained. By your counsel God fits government to the people, and the land prospers. The king cannot do without you, nor can any competent person be found, save among you. You are, therefore, for kings the ears with which they hear, the eyes with which they see, the tongues with which they speak, the hands with which they strike. May God let you profit from the merit of the craft which he has assigned to you, and may He not withdraw from you the grace which He has vouchsafed to you.

—Al-Jahshiyārī

Maxims on Statecraft (Seventh–Ninth Centuries)

A selection of sayings attributed to various Persian kings and Muslim caliphs, from the chapter on government in a classical Arabic work of literary scholarship.

Al-Ḥasan used to say: Islam assigns four things to government: dispensing justice, booty, the Friday prayer, and the Holy War.

The Prophet said: God has his guards. His guards in heaven are the angels, and His guards on earth are the keepers of the *dīwān* [administrative records and office].

They used to say: Government and religion are two brothers; neither can stand without the other.

Chosroes said: Do not stay in a country which lacks these five things: a strong rule, a just judge, a fixed market, a wise physician, and a flowing river.

They used to say: Obedience to the government is of four kinds: through desire, fear, love, or religion.

When Anūshirwān appointed a man to a position of authority, he ordered the scribe to leave four lines blank in the brevet of appointment so that he might write something in his own hand. And when the brevet was brought to him, he wrote, "Govern the best of the people by love; mingle desire and fear for the common people; and govern the lowest by terror."

'Umar ibn al-Khaṭṭāb said: No one is fit to govern, save he who is mild without weakness and strong without harshness.

Mu'āwiya said: I do not use my sword where my whip will do; I do not use my whip where my tongue will do. If there were no more than a hair between me and the people, it would not be broken." He was asked, "How so?" and he answered, "If they stretch it I let go, and if they let go I stretch it."

Walīd asked 'Abd al-Malik, "Father, what is statecraft?" He answered, "To win the respect and sincere affection of the upper classes; to bind the hearts of the common people by just dealing; to be patient with the lapses of your underlings."

A certain king described his statecraft thus: "I was never in jest when I promised or threatened or commanded or forbade; I never punished in anger; I employed men for reward, which I fixed according to their effort, not my caprice; in their hearts I stored respect untainted with hate and love untainted with disrespect; I provided food for all but avoided a glut."

Al-Manṣūr said in audience to his commanders, "That Bedouin was right who said, 'Starve your dog and he will follow you.' " Then Abu'l-Abbās al-Ṭūsī rose and said, "O Commander of the Faithful, I fear lest someone else tempt him with a morsel, and he follow him and leave you."

—Ibn Qutayba

Advice on Government (Ninth–Tenth Centuries)

Some sayings ascribed to Ibn al-Furāt, a vizier of the caliphs in Baghdad.

The basis of government is trickery; if it succeeds and endures, it becomes policy.

It is better to keep the affairs of government moving on the wrong path than to stand still on the right one.

If you have business with the vizier and can settle it with the archivist of the *dīwān* or with the privy secretary, do so and do not bring it to the vizier himself.

—Hilāl al-Ṣābi'

The Democratic City (Tenth Century)

*Abū Naṣr al-Fārābī, a central Asian Turk who wrote in Arabic, was one of
the founders of the medieval Islamic school of philosophy. His book on the
"virtuous city" owes much to Aristotle, by then available in Arabic translation, but contains much that is new and original.*

The democratic city is that in which every one of the inhabitants has complete
personal independence, and does whatever he pleases. The inhabitants are
equal, and it is their custom that no man has any privilege over any other man
in any respect whatsoever. The inhabitants are free and do as they please. No
one among them can have any authority over others, nor can any outsider,
unless he acts in such a way as to increase their freedom. There arise among
them many kinds of morals and many interests and many desires, and they
delight in countless things. The inhabitants are of many groups, both similar
and dissimilar, too numerous to be counted. In this city those who in all other
kinds of city are separated, the humble and the noble, are joined together.
Public functions of all kinds are assigned in the way we have already described. Those of the population who do not possess what the rulers possess
have power over their so-called rulers; those who rule them do so only by the
will of the ruled, depending on the caprice of the ruled. . . .

   The honored ones are those who bring the city to freedom and to whatever they crave and desire, and who protect freedom from the contradictions
of their various wishes and against enemies who attack them, confining their
own desires to what is necessary and no more. Such a one is honored, accorded precedence, and obeyed among them.

—Al-Fārābī

Three Views of Kingship

*Poets played an important part in traditional Islamic government, as eulo-
gists, satirists, and more generally as practitioners of public relations for the
monarchs they served. The following represent three relatively independent
views of government, from two tenth-century Persian poets and one Turkish
poet from the thirteenth century.*

> *She said to me: this is God's paradise, not a garden*
> *I said: this is a garden, blissful as God's paradise*
> *but that one is unseen, this one is seen*

that is credit, this cash
that is hidden, this revealed
that earned by prayer, this by eulogy
that is God's grace, this the king's bounty.

—Rūdagī

There are two things with which men gain a kingdom,
one steel blue and one of saffron colour.
One is gold, stamped with the king's name,
the other iron, tempered in the Yemen.
Whoever aspires to kingship
must have an urge from heaven,
an eloquent tongue, a liberal hand,
a heart both vengeful and loving.
For kingship is a quarry that cannot be caught
by a soaring eagle or raging lion.
Only two things can make it captive:
a well-forged blade, and mined and minted gold.
Seize it with the sword,
chain it, if you can, with good coins.
Whoever has sword, money and luck
needs neither lofty stature nor royal pedigree,
but only wisdom, munificence and courage
for heaven to grant him the gift of sovereignty.

—Daqīqī

To keep the realm needs many soldiers, horse and foot;
To keep these soldiers needs much money.
To get this money, the people must be rich;
For people to be rich, laws must be just.
If one of these is left undone, all four are undone;
If these four are undone, kingship unravels.

—Yūsuf

A Bureaucratic Parody (Eleventh Century)

A story about a prince of Aleppo, whose governor in Antioch had a stupid secretary.

Two Muslim galleys were lost at sea with all hands, and the secretary reported this, on behalf of his master, to the prince. He wrote, "In the name of

Allah the Merciful and the Compassionate. Be it known to the Prince—God strengthen him—that two galleys, I mean two ships, foundered, that is sank, because of the turbulence of the seas, that is, the force of the waves, and all within them expired, that is, perished." The prince of Aleppo replied to his lieutenant, "Your letter has come, that is, arrived, and we understood it, that is to say, we read it. Chastise your clerk, that is, hit him, and replace him, that is, get rid of him, since he is dim-witted, that is, stupid. Farewell, that is to say, the letter is finished."

—Ghars al-Niʿma al-Ṣābiʿ

On Taxation and Its Effects (Eleventh–Twelfth Centuries)

From a treatise by a Spanish Arab author on the duties and responsibilities of kingship.

Jaʿfar ibn Yaḥyā said, "The land tax [*kharāj*] is the tent pole of the realm. How great it becomes by justice, how mean by oppression!"

The quickest way to the ruin of the country, the disuse of the cultivated land, the destruction of the subjects, and the cessation of the land tax is by tyranny and extortion. A ruler who burdens his taxpayers until they cannot cultivate the land is like one who cuts off his own flesh and eats it when he is hungry. He grows stronger in one part and weaker in another, and the pain and weakness he brings on himself are greater than the pang of hunger he remedies. He who taxes his subjects beyond their capacity is like one who coats his roof with earth from the foundations of his house. He who makes a habit of cutting the tent pole will weaken it and bring down the tent. If the cultivators become weak, they cannot cultivate the land, and they leave it. Then the land is ruined, cultivation is weakened, and the tax diminishes. This leads to the weakening of the army, and when the army is weakened, enemies covet the realm.

O King, be more glad at what remains in your subjects' hands than at what you take from them. In prosperity nothing will diminish; in ruin nothing will remain. Protecting what is slight produces might. The bungler has no money; the successful does not suffer poverty.

It is related that al-Maʾmūn lay sleepless one night and summoned a courtier to tell him a story. He said, "O Commander of the Faithful! There was an owl in Basra and an owl in Mosul, and the Mosul owl asked the Basra owl to give her daughter in marriage to her son. The Basra owl replied, 'I will not give my daughter to your son unless you settle on her a marriage portion of a hundred ruined farms.' To this the Mosul owl replied, 'I can't do it now, but if our governor, may God keep him safe, stays another year, I shall do this for you.' " Al-Ma'mūn was roused and sat to hear grievances, dealt equitably with the people, and investigated the actions of the governors.

—Al-Ṭurṭūshī

Decline and Fall

Showing that empires, like individuals, have their natural term of life

As a rule an empire does not last more than three generations—reckoning a generation as the middle life of an individual. . . . The first maintains its nomadic character, its rude and savage way of life; inured to hardships, brave, fierce, and sharing renown with each other, the tribesmen preserve their solidarity in full vigour: their swords are kept sharp, their attack is feared, and their neighbours vanquished. With the second generation comes a change. Possessing dominion and affluence, they turn from nomadic to settled life, and from hardship to ease and plenty. The authority, instead of being shared by all, is appropriated by one, while the rest, too spiritless to make an effort to regain it, abandon the glory of ambition for the shame of subjection. Their solidarity is weakened in some degree; yet one may notice that notwithstanding the indignity to which they submit, they retain much of what they have known and witnessed in the former generation—the feelings of fierceness and pride, the desire for honour, and the resolution to defend themselves and repulse their foes. These qualities they cannot lose entirely, though a part be gone. They hope to become again such men as their fathers were, or they fancy that the old virtues still survive amongst them.

In the third generation the wandering life and rough manners of the desert are forgotten, as though they had never been. At this stage men no longer take delight in glory and patriotism, since all have learned to bow under the might of a sovereign and are so addicted to luxurious pleasures that they have become a burden on the state; for they require protection like the women and young boys. Their national spirit is wholly extinguished; they have no stomach for resistance, defence, or attack. Nevertheless they impose on the people by their [military] appearance and uniform, their horsemanship, and the address with which they manoeuvre. It is but a false show: they are in general greater cowards than the most helpless women, and will give way at the first assault. The monarch in those days must needs rely on the bravery of others, enrol many of the clients [freedmen], and recruit soldiers capable, to some extent, of guarding the empire, until God proclaims the hour of its destruction and it falls with everything that it upholds. Thus do empires age and decay in the course of three generations.

—Ibn Khaldūn (translated by R. A. Nicholson)

A Connoisseur's View of Kingship (1532)

All the Turkish monarchy is governed by one ruler, the others are his servants, and dividing his kingdom into "sangiacates" [Turkish *sanjak,* "flag": an administrative district in the Ottoman Empire]," he sends to them various administrators, and changes or recalls them at his pleasure. But the King of France is surrounded by a large number of ancient nobles, recognised as such by their subjects, and loved by them; they have their prerogatives, which the king cannot deprive them of without danger to himself. Whoever now considers these two states will see that it would be difficult to acquire the state of the Turk; but having conquered it, it would be very easy to hold it.

—Niccolò Machiavelli, (translated by Luigi Ricci, 1903)

Another View, Some Time Later (1786)

The French ambassador in Constantinople reports:

Here things are not as in France, where the king is sole master. He has to persuade the ulema, the men of law, the holders of high offices, and those who no longer hold them.

—Count de Choiseul-Gouffier

An Ottoman Official Offers Advice and a Warning to the Sultan (1630)

First, let it be known to His Imperial Majesty that the origin of the good order of kingship and community and the cause of the stability of the foundations of the faith and the dynasty are a firm grasp of the strong cord of the Muhammadan law. For the rest, let the imperial attention and favor be given to the men of religion, who with care and knowledge attend to the affairs of the subjects entrusted to the emperor of God, and to the soldiers who give up their lives in the Holy War. Let him show favor to the worthy men of every class, and contempt for the unworthy. . . .

In fine, the like of the present oppression and maltreatment of the poor peasantry has never existed at any time, in any clime or in the realm of any monarch. If in the lands of Islam one atom of injustice is done to any individual, then on the Day of Judgment not officials but kings will be asked for a reckoning, and it will be no answer for them to say to the Lord of the World, "I delegated this duty" . . . the world can go on with irreligion, but not with injustice.

—Koçu Bey

Crime and Punishment

Requisites of a Judge
(Early Twelfth Century)

The qadi, may Almighty God help him, must be eloquent in his speech, incisive in his commands, just in his verdicts, respected by the people, the ruler and the public, and familiar with God's commandments. For these are the scales of justice which God established on Earth to succor the oppressed against the oppressor, to defend the weak against the strong, and to see that the punishments prescribed by God are enforced in accordance with established rules.

He should not allow himself to be influenced and should avoid easy familiarity with the jurists or the helpers, for harm can come to him from them . . . he should take care that none of them should show familiarity with him in word or deed, for this would lower him and diminish his orders and worsen his position. His judgment could be changed by someone's word or deed and the people would despise him. This would disturb the state of religion and disrupt the good order of this world and the next. The qadi should not jest with anyone of his entourage or indeed with anyone else, for this would destroy his prestige so that his decisions would be contested, his orders rejected, and he would be at the mercy of the envious. It is also necessary that he should be steadfast in all his affairs. He should neither speak nor act in haste but only after reflection and examination, considering the effect on his fate in the hereafter. He should not spend much time in idleness nor be eager for repose, for this would be held against him. Rather should he be active, zealous, dedicated to the service of God as if he were engaged in a holy war or a pilgrimage. . . .

The qadi should in himself be merciful, clement, kindly and compassionate to the Muslims; he should be both magnanimous and learned . . . for he is a model and their kindly father.

—Ibn 'Abdūn

Justice in Damascus (1384)

When we left Damascus, we met near Sardana several Saracens of low ex-
traction, who had tied a dead man across a camel's back, and behind came
another camel on which was another live man tied in the same way; this latter had killed the former, and was led to the officers who represent the Sultan in Damascus. When we came back those of us who wished to go and
see justice administered could go without let. Justice is done in a great pi-
azza, which is beside the castle of the Sultan within Damascus. They placed
this man naked on a camel as if astride, tied to certain planks made like a
cross, and on this he was hanged with his arms so high that he was almost
entirely suspended. Then came the executioner with a big naked scimitar
and picked a little at the body, and quickly with the scimitar he gave him a
stroke above the navel which cut him through; the arms with the upper part
remained hanging on high, the thighs and the remnant of the body remained on the camel, save the bowels which went to the ground.

—Lionardo Frescobaldi (translated by Theophilus Bellorini
and Eugene Hoade)

Ottoman Advice on Trust and Fear
(Mid–Seventeenth Century)

If the fear of punishment were to pass away from people's hearts, the evildoers would become more numerous and more arrogant. The right thing is
that there should be fear among the bad and trust among the good people.
Permanent fear and permanent trust are both harmful. While the people are
between fear and hope, let the sultanate be well ordered and let the sultan
be generous.

—Huseyn Hezarfenn

An English Merchant Reviews
Methods of Execution (1600)

I think not good heare (as I have said before) to note their cruelty in sundry
sorts of executions; yet some I cannot let pass. Their usual punishment for
adulterous women is binding in a sack and so throw them into the sea.
Seven I have seen so used one morning, in the time that the eunuch Hassan
Bassa governed Constantinople, when the Great Turk was at the wars. But
for such cruelty and other actions the Queen Mother got his head at her

son's return. The commonest death for men is guanchinge [impaling]; which is to be stripped into their linen breeches, with their hands and feet bound all four together at their backs, and so drawn up with a rope by a pulley upon the gallows and let fall upon a great iron hook fastened to a lower crossbar of the gallows, most commonly lighting upon their flank and so through their thigh. There they hang, sometimes taking a day or two together. But if they be gaunched through the belly and back then are they dead in two or three hours. Thus they use their common thieves at Constantinople. In Cairo and other parts they stake them, a most cruel death, yet speedy or lingering, as they list to execute. But hanging by the neck they use in a favor to any offender who merited death; yet sometimes cutting down for dogs to eat. They strangle with a bowstring their brethren, pashas, and other great men; but for their religious men, false judges, their law is to pashe [crush] them all to pieces in a stone mortar with wooden mallets; and for their false witnesses, they are set upon an ass, with their faces towards the tail, which they hold in their hands, and the innards of a bullock poured upon and bound about them, and so ride they through the city. And for any found drunk in the time of their Ramazan, which is a fast they have one whole month in the year, their law is to melt a ladle full of lead and pour it down their throats. Their manner of fast is [not] to eat nor drink any thing, neither water or other, until they see a star appear in the evening; and then they may begin and eat till morning. Any thief officer belonging to their artillery is bound to the mouth of a brass piece and so shot into the sea; thus I saw one used at Tophane. And alike in my time a ajemoglan [page], found drunk in their fast, was used as I have reported. I did see upon the gaunch Ussine Bassa [Huseyn Pasha], the traitor that first rose in Asia; but he, for a more cruelty, had upon each shoulderbone a muscle taken out, in presence of the bench of viziers, the Great Turk also looking out at a lattice over their heads. By reason of that torment he died presently upon the gaunch, being led from the Seraglio half a mile or more before he was put thereon.

—John Sanderson

Turkish Justice (1650)

The main points wherein Turkish justice differs from that of other Nations are three: it is more Severe, Speedy and Arbitrary: They hold the foundations of all *Empire* to consist in exact obedience, and that in exemplary severitie; which is undenyable in all the world, but more notable in their State, made up of severall People different in *Bloud, Sect,* and *Interesse,* one from another, nor linkt in affection, or any common engagement toward the publique good, other than what mere terrour puts upon them; a sweet hand were ineffectual upon such a subject . . . therefore the Turkish justice curbes and executes, without either remorse or respect . . . they have no fixt law, and therewith flourishing, they pretend to judge by the Alcoran. . . . The Alcoran is no Book of particular law cases, wherefore they pretend its study does not informe the Judge literally, but by way of illumination.

—Sir Henry Blount

Summary Justice in Syria (1782–85)

As the image of the sultan, the pasha is the chief of all the police in his governorship, and this title also includes criminal justice. He has the most absolute right of life and death; he exercises it without formality and without appeal. Wherever he encounters a crime, he has the culprit seized; then the hangmen who accompany him either strangle him or cut off his head on the spot; sometimes he does not disdain to perform this function himself. Three days before my arrival in Tyre, Jezzar had disemboweled a mason with the blow of an ax. Sometimes the pasha prowls in disguise; and woe to anyone who is caught at fault! Since he cannot perform this duty everywhere, he sends in his place an officer who is called the wali; this wali performs the functions of our watch patrol. Like them, he prowls by night and by day; he looks out for sedition, he arrests thieves; like the pasha, he judges and sentences without appeal. The culprit lowers his head, the hangman strikes, the head falls and the body is carried away in a leather sack. This officer has a crowd of spies who are almost all scoundrels, and by their means he knows everything that happens. In view of this it is not surprising that cities like Cairo, Aleppo and Damascus are safer than Genoa, Rome or Naples; but at what a price in abuses is this safety bought! And how many innocents must pay with their lives for the partiality of the wali and of his agents!

The wali also polices the merchants, that is to say, he supervises weights and measures; on this point they are extremely strict. For the least false weight in bread or meat or molasses or sweets, they give fifty strokes with a stick or sometimes even the death penalty. Examples are common in the big cities. Yet there is no country where more is sold with false weights. The merchants keep a watch for the passing of the wali and of the muhtasib. As soon as they appear on horseback, everything is swiftly hidden away and other weights are produced. Sometimes the shopkeepers make deals with the servants who march in front of the two officers, and for a consideration they are sure of impunity.

For the rest, the functions of the wali in no way involve those useful or agreeable purposes which are the merit of the police among us. They have no care either for the cleanliness or the health of the cities. In Syria as in Egypt there are no paved ways, no sweeping and no sprinkling. The roads are narrow and twisting and almost always encumbered with garbage. Above all, one is shocked to see a pack of hideous dogs that belong to nobody. They form a kind of independent republic that lives on the charity of the public. They are cantoned by families and neighborhoods, and if any one of them goes outside his limits, dogfights ensue which vex the passerby. The Turks who so readily shed the blood of men do not kill them; they just avoid contact with them as unclean. They claim that they make the cities safe by night; but the wali and the gates by which each street is shut off do it better. They add that these dogs eat carrion, and in this they are helped by a pack of jackals hidden in the gardens and among the garbage and the tombs. One must not seek in their cities promenades or plantations. In such a country, life seems neither safe nor pleasant, but that is also the effect of the absolute power of the sultan.

—Volney

Comments of a Military Adviser (1785)

Defeat in the battlefield—a new experience for the Ottomans—demonstrated the need to reform the military, and, for this purpose, to learn from the previously despised European enemy. From the eighteenth century onward, first the Turkish and then other Middle Eastern governments employed European and later American officers as advisers, to help reorganize and modernize their armed forces. One of the most influential of these advisers was the Baron de Tott, a French engineering officer of Hungarian origin. His memoirs, published in 1785, throw light on many aspects of public life, including civil and criminal justice.

Civil Justice

Everything must be adjudicated according to the deposition of the witnesses. This is the first law of the legislator of the Arabs. One cannot, therefore, present oneself before a court unless the plaintiff and the defendant are equally provided with them; there is therefore no trial without false witnesses. The skill of the judge consists of divining by careful interrogations to which of the two parties he must grant the rights to affirm, and this first judgement decides the case. If one party denies it, the other is admitted to prove it; so that, summoned to justice by a man whom I have never seen, to pay him a sum which I never owed him, I could be obliged to pay it to him by the deposition of two Turkish witnesses who would attest my debt. What defense would be left to me? It would be to admit that I owed it but to assure him that I had paid it. If the cadi has not been won over, he will allot me witnesses, and I shall soon find some of them myself, and it will not cost me more than a modest reward for people who will take the trouble to commit perjury for me and a due of 10 percent for the judge who will have caused me to win my case.

It is always the winner who pays the expenses; the fear of losing the money that one has does not curb the desire to get hold of the money of others; and the penalties prescribed for suborners of witnesses or the false witnesses themselves are rarely pronounced; the judge whose domain they fructify owes them some consideration.

A Turk wanted to rob his neighbor of a field which he possessed very legitimately. This Turk began by securing a sufficient number of witnesses ready to depose that the field had been sold to him by the proprietor; then he found the judge and sent him a payment of five hundred piastres, engaging him to authorize his usurpation. This action in itself proved the iniquity of his claim. It aroused the anger of the cadi, which, however, he dissimulated. He listened to the two sides, and when the legitimate possessor could offer only his insufficient title of possession, the judge said, "Then you have no witnesses? Well then, I have five hundred who will testify in your favor." He then showed the bag which had been sent to him to corrupt him and drove out the corruptor.

This episode, which does honor to the integrity of the judge, does not, however, do so to the law; it is still the same, and not all cadis resemble the one that I have cited.

In complicated cases, the parties in addition to the witnesses take the precaution of arming themselves with a fetwa from a mufti. But since these are given only on the basis of the petition presented, each party can easily obtain a fetwa favorable to his side.

One does not finish an affair with a formal judgment in one's favor. Nothing is certain but the costs that have to be paid. If the opposing party produces a new incident, one must plead again, and again pay costs.

A precious advantage of the civil law among the Turks would surely be the right it gives to each individual to plead his own cause in person; but what remains of this advantage in a country where judgment is arbitrary? . . .

Criminal Justice

They never fight duels but murder each other, and it is thus that they settle quarrels in which there is no accommodation. The offended person publicly sharpens his knife or prepares firearms: some friends try to calm him, others excite and encourage him to murder; but no measures are taken to prevent the crime that these preparations announce. Drunkenness must, however, precede the crime. Wine is needed to give a Turk the degree of courage that he needs to serve his anger. Having reached this point, he leaves the tavern, and after that the offender has no hope of salvation but the clumsiness of the offended. If the murder is completed, and if the guard, armed only with batons, sets out in pursuit of the murderer, then one sees him give remarkable proofs of courage; he defends himself like a lion; one would say that the crime has raised his soul; and if he succumbs, the threats of his friends soon convince the kinsman of the deceased to accept an accommodation which leaves the culprit to enjoy the high consideration that this event ensures him.

It is therefore only some Turkish mercenaries, some Christians or some Jews who provide examples of public punishment for any murders they might commit. In such a case, the culprit is led to the Porte and receives his sentence; no formalities accompany his torture; and I have seen them walking through the crowds which are normally in the streets chatting with the one who is to execute them. Criminals normally have only their hands tied, and the hangman holds them by the belt. This is the moment to negotiate with the kinsfolk of the deceased and to work for the accommodation of which I have just spoken. People have assured me that there have been bargains of this kind which failed only through the avarice of the culprit. This seems devoid of all probability, but if it could be true, it would be no doubt, because under despotism, money is everything and life counts for little.

The custom of despising Christians and honoring Muslims has established the practice of placing the severed head of a true believer on his arm, bent for this purpose, and that of an infidel on his behind.

—Baron de Tott

The Bastinado (Nubia, 1850)

We discuss the bastinado with the governor. When they want to put a man to death, four or five blows are enough—they break his back and his neck—when they just want to punish the condemned, they strike him on the buttocks—four or five hundred strokes are normal—that is enough to make him sick for five or six months—he must wait until the flesh falls, the Effendi said to us with a laugh—more commonly, in Nubia, the bastinado is administered on the soles of the feet—the Nubians greatly fear this torture because afterward they cannot walk.

—Gustave Flaubert

Disobedience and the Rules of Roguery
in Cairo (1844)

A short time since, one of his Highness's grandsons, whom I shall call Bluebeard Pasha (lest a revelation of the name of the said Pasha might interrupt
our good relations with his country)—one of the young Pashas being rather
backward in his education, and anxious to learn mathematics, and the elegant deportment of civilised life, sent to England for a tutor. I have heard he
was a Cambridge man, and had learned both algebra and politeness under
the Reverend Doctor Whizzle, of ——— College.

One day when Mr. MacWhirter, B.A., was walking in Shoubra Gardens,
with his Highness the young Bluebeard Pasha, inducting him into the usages of polished society, and favouring him with reminiscences of Trumpington, there came up a poor fellah, who flung himself at the feet of young
Bluebeard, and calling for justice in a loud and pathetic voice, and holding
out a petition, besought his Highness to cast a gracious eye upon the same,
and see that his slave had justice done him.

Bluebeard Pasha was so deeply engaged and interested by his respected
tutor's conversation, that he told the poor fellah to go to the deuce, and resumed the discourse which his ill-timed outcry for justice had interrupted.
But the unlucky wight of a fellah was pushed by his evil destiny, and
thought he would make yet another application. So he took a short cut
down one of the garden lanes, and as the Prince and the Reverend Mr.
MacWhirter, his tutor, came along once more engaged in pleasant disquisi-
tion, behold the fellah was once more in their way, kneeling at the August
Bluebeard's feet, yelling out for justice as before, and thrusting his petition
into the Royal face.

When the Prince's conversation was thus interrupted a second time, his
Royal patience and clemency were at end. "Man," said he, "once before I
bade thee not to pester me with thy clamour, and lo! you have disobeyed
me,—take the consequences of disobedience to a Prince, and thy blood be
upon thine own head." So saying, he drew out a pistol and blew out the
brains of that fellah, so that he never bawled out for justice any more.

The Reverend Mr. MacWhirter was astonished at this sudden mode of
proceeding: "Gracious Prince," said he, "we do not shoot an undergraduate
at Cambridge even for walking over a college grass-plot.—Let me suggest to
your Royal Highness that this method of ridding yourself of a poor devil's
importunities is such as we should consider abrupt and almost cruel in Europe. Let me beg you to moderate your Royal impetuosity for the future;
and, as your Highness's tutor, entreat you to be a little less prodigal of your
powder and shot."

"O Mollah!" said his Highness, here interrupting his governor's affec-
tionate appeal,—"you are good to talk about Trumpington and the Pons
Asinorum, but if you interfere with the course of justice in any way, or prevent me from shooting any dog of an Arab who snarls at my heels, I have another pistol; and, by the beard of the Prophet! A bullet for you too." So
saying he pulled out the weapon, with such a terrific and significant glance
at the Reverend Mr. MacWhirter, that that gentleman wished himself back in
his Combination Room again; and is by this time, let us hope, safely housed
there.

Another facetious anecdote, the last of those I had from a well-informed
gentleman residing at Cairo, whose name (as many copies of this book that
is to be will be in the circulating libraries there) I cannot, for obvious reasons, mention. The revenues of the country come into the august treasury
through the means of farmers, to whom the districts are let out, and who are
personally answerable for their quota of the taxation. This practice involves
an intolerable deal of tyranny and extortion on the part of those engaged to
levy the taxes, and creates a corresponding duplicity among the fellahs,
who are not only wretchedly poor among themselves, but whose object is
to appear still more poor, and guard their money from their rapacious overseers. Thus the Orient is much maligned; but everybody cheats there: that is
a melancholy fact. The Pasha robs and cheats the merchants; knows that the
overseer robs him, and bides his time, until he makes him disgorge by the
application of the tremendous bastinado; the overseer robs and squeezes
the labourer; and the poverty-stricken devil cheats and robs in return; and
so the government moves in a happy cycle of roguery.

—William Makepeace Thackeray

Aspects of Reform

*The Napoleonic wars demonstrated beyond all doubt the vast disparity, in
sophistication and effectiveness, between European and Middle Eastern
armies. A growing awareness of this disparity, and of the potential threat
that it contained, led in the early nineteenth century to a new wave of reforms. First in Egypt, then in Turkey, later in Iran, rulers attempted to modernize their armed forces, their administration and—indirectly and for the
most part unintentionally—their societies. The following comments on the
reform process are selected from a large number by both foreign and domestic observers.*

Despotism, Democracy and Human Rights:
Reflections of an English Conservative (1832)

Civilization, forced, is as inimical to a people's happiness as is a constitution abruptly presented. That deprives them of their liberties; this of their judgment: the shackles of the former are felt, before the corresponding silken bands are fitted to disguise the iron; the condescension of the latter is abused before its beauty is respected: the one sharpens the sword of state; the other puts clubs in the hands of the mob. For the former hypothesis look at Russia; for the latter observe France.

When a nation, comparatively barbarous, copies the finished experience of a highly civilized state, without going through the intermediate stages of advancement, the few are strengthened against the many, the powerful armed against the weak. The sovereign, who before found his power (despotic in name) circumscribed, because with all the will, he had not the real art of oppressing, by the aid of science finds himself a giant—his mace exchanged for a sword. In scanning over the riches of civilization, spread out before him for acceptance, he contemptuously rejects those calculated to benefit his people, and chooses the modern scientific governing machine, result of ages of experiments, with its patent screws for extracting blood and treasure,—conscription and taxation. He hires foreign engineers to work it, and waits the promised result—absolute power. His subjects, who before had a thousand modes of avoiding his tyranny, have not now a loop-hole to escape by: the operations of the uncorroding engine meet them at every turn, and, to increase their despair, its movement accelerates with use, and winds closer their chains. A people thus taken by surprise, and thrown off their guard, will be centuries before they acquire sufficient knowledge—every beam of which is carefully hid from them by the clouds of despotism—to compare their situation with that of their neighbours—(who, although ruled by the same means, have advantages to counterbalance its weight)—to assert human rights, and to dare to say "we are men." In the mean time, they are dispersed, or collected, or worked, as cattle; suffered to perish of disease, or starve, as things of no import compelled to march like puppets from zone to zone, for the caprice of one man—to slaughter and be slaughtered for his pleasure; and if any one, using his reason, pronounce such proceedings against the eternal fitness of things, he is denounced as revolutionary, an enemy of order, little short of mad, and unfit to live. Such are the fruits which civilization, so called, has produced in one country. Newspapers act as oil to the engine, are, under such auspices, the direst enemies of freedom and rational reform, simply because they dare only espouse one side of a question, the side which suits the powers that are. Even supposing, which is not probable, the editors to have any thing dearer at heart than their own profits, they dare not expose corruption in the heads of departments, and therefore, as a *juste milieu* is seldom the part of a newspaper, they applaud their measures, however tyrannical, the more particularly if they receive money for so doing. It is a long time in any state before the press acquires sufficient respectability, as well as independence, to expose abuses; until that time it only serves to abet them. . . .

It is curious to observe the similarity of advantages which are enjoyed by nations in opposite spheres of knowledge, and separated by perfectly distinct manners and religion. Hitherto the Osmanley has enjoyed by custom some of the dearest privileges of freemen, for which Christian nations have so long struggled. He paid nothing to the government beyond a moderate land-tax, although liable, it is true, to extortions, which might be classed with assessed taxes. He paid no tithes, the vacouf sufficing for the maintenance of the ministers of Islamism. He travelled where he pleased without passports; no custom-house officer intruded his eyes and dirty fingers among his baggage; no police watched his motions, or listened for his words. His house was sacred. His sons were never taken from his side to be soldiers, unless war called them. His views of ambition were not restricted by the barriers of birth and wealth; from the lowest origin he might aspire without presumption to the rank of pasha; if he could read, to that of grand vizir; and this consciousness, instilled and supported, by numberless precedents, ennobled his mind, and enabled him to enter on the duties of high office without embarrassment. Is not this the advantage so prized by free nations? Did not the exclusion of the people from posts of honour tend to the French revolution?

—Adolphus Slade

Politics Here and There (1849–50)

European politics are disgusting, disheartening, or distressing—here there are no politics at all, only hareem intrigues, and deep, grinding, brutalizing misery. Let no one live in the East, who can find a corner in the ugliest, coldest hole in Europe.

—Florence Nightingale

Reform and Emancipation

A Turkish View (1856)

The Imperial Rescript of 1856 was a major step in the process of Ottoman reform. Among other changes it proclaimed, specifically and categorically, the complete equality of all Ottoman subjects irrespective of religion. Welcomed abroad, the rescript had a mixed reception at home, even among those it sought to benefit.

In accordance with this ferman [decree], Muslim and non-Muslim subjects were to be made equal in all rights. This had a very adverse effect on the Muslims. Previously, one of the four points adopted as the basis for peace agreements had been that certain privileges were accorded to Christians on condition that these did not infringe the sovereign authority of the government. Now the question of specific privileges lost its significance; in the whole range of government, the non-Muslims were forthwith to be deemed the equals of the Muslims. Many Muslims began to grumble, "Today we have lost our sacred national rights, won by the blood of our fathers and forefathers. At a time when the Islamic *millet* was the ruling *millet,* it was deprived of this sacred right. This is a day of weeping and mourning for the people of Islam."

As for the non-Muslims, this day, when they left the status of *rayah* and gained equality with the ruling *millet,* was a day of rejoicing. But the patriarchs and other spiritual leaders were displeased, because their appointments were incorporated in the ferman. Another point was that whereas in former times, in the Ottoman state, the communities were ranked, with the Muslims first, then the Greeks, then the Armenians, then the Jews, now all of them were put on the same level. Some Greeks objected to this, saying, "The government has put us together with the Jews. We were content with the supremacy of Islam."

As a result of all this, just as the weather was overcast when the ferman was read in the audience chamber, so the faces of most of those present were grim. Only on the faces of a few of our Frenchified gentry dressed in the garb of Islam could expressions of joy be seen. Some notorious characters of this type were seen and heard to say, "If the non-Muslims are spread among the Muslims, neighborhoods will become mixed, the price of our properties will rise, and civilized amenities will expand." On this account they expressed satisfaction.

—Jevdet Pasha

An English View (1867)

[Sultan Mahmud II] tranquillized their fears, and justified their hopes, by his tanzimat [reforms] proclaimed four months after his accession. This famous proclamation, conceived in a spirit of clemency and tolerance, inaugurated a new era for Turkey. The direct power of death by decapitation was taken from scores of vizirs; the indirect power of death by vexation, from hundreds of inferior station. Oriental ductility was severely tested. An ensanguined nation was ordered to be gentle, and the order was obeyed. Pashas used to rule with the sabre were required to rule by exhortation. Mudirs and agas, wont to admonish rayas with the stick, were enjoined to be civil to them. The exhaustion of the nation, after twenty years of unparalleled suffering, favoured the experiment: anything for quiet was the universal aspiration. The Ottomans, with the instincts of a dominant race, adapted themselves to altered circumstances; they leant upon their prestige, and it did not fail them. Fatalists, they were not sorry to see their Sultan cease, of his own accord, to be the direct instrument of fate in regard to them.

—Adolphus Slade

Two Comments from a Turkish Liberal

The Ottomans Compared with the French (1868)

[The Ottomans] could very well be governed under a more liberal constitution than that of France. . . . Since the French are of a very fiery disposition, they are always inclined to change. The basis of their actions is reason, but under the impulsion of one specious sophism they spoil the result of a thousand sound deductions. . . . Since the great republic, they have established thirty or forty different forms of government. . . . The Ottoman people, on the other hand, thanks to their innate gravity and calm, are in no danger of running to extremes. . . . In the course of six centuries we have made hundreds of revolts; in all of them the men who governed were changed, but the form of government remained.

The Functions of the State (1872)

There must be no doubt that the government is neither the father nor the teacher, neither the guardian nor the tutor of the people. If it renders service to the education of the individual, the prosperity of the realm, the advancement of mankind, the progress of civilization, it will contribute significantly to the welfare of itself, of its people, and indeed of all the world. . . . But even if it confines itself to its primary duty, which is the maintenance of justice, can you complain? Have we any right to require it to serve us as nursemaid?

—Namik Kemal

An Ottoman View of Ottoman Officials (1872)

If we are still deficient as regards judicial officials, we are even more deficient as regards executive officials and are growing daily more so. It is an urgent necessity to expand the *mülkiye* [civil service] school in accordance with the time and situation, to rearrange the program of studies correspondingly, to employ its graduates progressively in important posts, and thus to train competent administrative officials. Our immediate obligation is to choose and employ those who are already fairly experienced and thus put the state administration on the right path. If we give up finding jobs for men and instead make it our policy to find men for jobs, then it is certain that within a short time officials capable of administering the country will emerge. . . .

The servants of the state should be superior to the mass of the people in ability and competence. But if there is no recompense, outstanding persons among the population will have no inclination to enter the service of the state and will choose other professions, leaving only mediocrities to carry on

"Consultative menagerie," January 1885. A parody of clerks in the legal bureau of the Ottoman foreign office by Yussuf Bey, an Ottoman diplomat. The chief custodians and interpreters of government treaties are represented as a parrot, a duck and a monkey. From an album of satirical drawings by an Ottoman official.

the business of the state. These, lacking all prestige in the eyes of the people, will be quite unable to administer men who are in fact their superiors.

—Jevdet Pasha

Persons and Institutions: a British View (1878)

In any scheme of reform, I believe your attention will be far more usefully directed to persons than to paper institutions. Good officers, well selected for a length of time, will create suitable traditions of administration which will gradually harden into institutions, and, made this way, reformed institutions will regenerate a people. But if they are merely written in a pretentious law, they will have no other effect but to disturb the few traditions that are left and to give perpetual subject-matter for diplomatic wrangling.

—Lord Salisbury to Sir Henry Layard, June 25, 1878

Education: a Memorandum to the Sultan (1880)

In order to remedy this situation, first and foremost a serious and powerful effort must be made to improve public education. As long as public education is not disseminated, there will be no leaders capable of directing the internal and external affairs of the empire soundly, no judges who can administer the public laws justly, no commanders who can run the army efficiently and no finance officers who can show how to manage and increase the sources of revenue in accordance with economic principles. None of the institutions and operations that serve public prosperity and well-being can be brought into existence as long as education is not disseminated. . . .

—Said Pasha

Encounter with Freedom (1878)

In front of the central gate [of the Paris Exposition] one encounters a statue of freedom; she has a staff in her hand and is seated on a chair. Her appearance and manner convey this meaning to spectators: "O worthy visitors! When you look upon this fascinating display of human progress, do not forget that all these perfections are the work of freedom. It is under the protection of freedom that peoples and nations attain happiness. Without freedom, there can be no security; without security, no endeavour; without endeavour, no prosperity; without prosperity, no happiness!"

—Sadullah Pasha

A Young Turk's View of Old Turk Government (1897)

Our sovereign and our government do not want the light to enter our country: they want all the people to remain in ignorance, on the dunghill of misery and wretchedness; no torch of awakening may blaze in the hearts of our compatriots. What the government wants is for the people to remain like beasts, submissive as sheep, fawning and servile as dogs. Let them hear no word of any honest lofty new idea. Instead, let them languish under the whips of ignorant gendarmes, under the aggressions of shameless, boorish, oppressive officials.

—Abdullah Jevdet

Imperial Sidelights

Britain in Egypt (1883)

It has indeed been asserted by the illustrious statesman whose loss England and France equally deplore that order in Egypt can only continue to exist under the combined discipline of a couple of foreign schoolmasters and the domestic "courbash." This theory seems to be supported by a consensus of foreign opinion in this country. According to this view, the Egyptian people are condemned as for ever incapable of managing their own affairs, the only administration considered possible being that of an irresponsible centralized bureaucracy. I would press upon Her Majesty's Government a more generous policy—a policy as is implied by the creation within certain prudent limits, of representative institutions, of municipal and communal self-government, and of a political existence untrammelled by external importunity, though aided, indeed, as it must be for a time, by sympathetic advice and assistance. Indeed, no middle course is possible. The Valley of the Nile could not be administered with any prospect of success from London. An attempt upon our part to engage in such an undertaking would at once render us objects of hatred and suspicion to its inhabitants. Cairo would become a focus of foreign intrigue and conspiracy against us, and we should soon find ourselves forced either to abandon our pretension under discreditable conditions, or to embark upon the experiment of a complete acquisition of the country. If, however, we content ourselves with a more moderate role, and make the Egyptians comprehend that instead of desiring to impose upon them an indirect but arbitrary rule, we are sincerely desirous of enabling them to govern themselves, under the uncompromising aegis of our friendship, they will not fail to understand that while, on the one hand, we are the European nation most vitally interested in their peace and well-being, on the other, we are the least inclined of any to allow the influence which the progress of events has required us to exercise to degenerate into an irritating and exasperating display of authority, which would be fatal to those interests of patriotism and freedom which it has been our boast to foster in every country where we have set our foot.

—Lord Dufferin to Lord Granville

The Leisure of a [British] Egyptian Official (1921)

The trials of a civil servant during the British occupation.

When I arrive back at my office I find my outer office crowded with a growling mob of officials, waiting to see me. Before I can attend to them however, there are between twenty and thirty letters to sign. You have to read through those prepared by Egyptian subordinates with some care, as, apart from their playful habit of inserting matter to suit their own ends, they are apt, through their limited knowledge of foreign languages, to make you say things which give an impression to your correspondent that you have become insane. For example, here is a letter about removing a wreck from the entrance to Alexandria Harbour, in which I am made to say to the Director-General of Ports and Lights that we approve of his employing dynamite "to puff up the bones of the dead ship," and another to the Controller of Government Lands in which I solemnly enjoin him to prevent trespassers from entering on a certain piece of Government land, "whensoever, howsoever, and whatsoever it is," which might well confuse him.

Having disposed of these, I begin to interview the waiting officials in turn. This is the hardest bit of the day's work. It consists in giving decisions or rulings on points submitted to you, and giving them, if possible, on the spot, as a delay is often very inconvenient to all concerned. As the rulings are, within limits, practically absolute, a faulty decision may give rise to a lot of trouble. One has to combine rapid decision with careful work, and to turn one's mind frequently on to a new subject, which is very tiring.

The native officials are far too fond of referring questions to superior authority, partly because they are timid, and partly because they have no sense of proportionate importance. This is due to the undeveloped state of their intelligence, and to the tradition of bad government which makes them live, like all whose tenure of position or livelihood is precarious, in the present. The immediate effect, not the ultimate result, is what they care about.

Their anxiety, too, to be on the winning or popular side is almost pathetic. I recently asked a high official of the Accounts Department for some

figures connected with a certain subject. He immediately asked me what I
wanted to prove: I told him, and the figures he produced were absolutely
convincing and quite fallacious.

—Lord Edward Cecil

Trouble in Palestine (1920–22)

The earliest recognition I received in Europe of the realities of the British officer's position in Palestine was from the lips of Mr. Lloyd George. I had first
met him during the Peace Conference, and he was good enough to invite me
to breakfast with him alone at 10 Downing Street. Greeting me sternly, he remarked that complaints of me were reaching him from Jews and Arabs alike.
I answered that this was all too probable, imagining for a moment from his
tone that he was leading up to my resignation. "Well," he said as we sat down,
"If either one side stops complaining, you'll be dismissed." A principle which
should hearten All Ranks in the Palestine Service for some decades to come.

—Ronald Storrs

Glubb Pasha on Arab Prospects (1941)

*General Sir John Glubb was an outstanding figure among British military
advisors in Arab states. He was made a pasha by King 'Abdollah for his services to the Jordanian army.*

Glubb's views on the Arab peoples were particularly interesting. "We have
given them self-government for which they are totally unsuited. They veer
naturally towards dictatorship. Democratic institutions are promptly twisted
into an engine of intrigue—thus the same bunch crop up after each coup
in a different guise, until disposed of by assassination. The same thing used
to happen in the South American Republics at one time, so perhaps the
falling off in the number of political assassinations and revolutions there
augurs well for the eventual stabilization of Government in the Arab
lands." . . . Glubb's views on military missions to Arab peoples were even
more trenchant. "All we do is to send people to teach them how to fight
against us, without any attempt to select men who understand the Arabs to
whom they are sent. In future, military missions to Arabs ought to be selected for their understanding of the people they have to deal with rather
than their military capacity."

—Somerset de Chair

Intellectuals and the State

Dependence (1978)

The dependence of intellectuals on power is an old custom in our region. As in the Middle Ages, modern Arab thought inspires despots only when it is entirely under their control. . . . The sultan gives orders and the mullahs give their blessings. The amir makes the law and the qadi judges accordingly. This civility is not only the result of external pressures; it has interiorized itself in the faith and in opinion. Therefore it gives rise to a feeling of impotence, a lack of will or of intellectual initiative, as well as a lack of any original commentary on reality independent of the order installed by the dictator.

—Ḥasan Ḥanafī

Words Versus Deeds (1986)

The alienation of the Arab people from their governments is frightening in degree and in potential consequences. The cynicism with which the Arab media are viewed is a clear sign of this. People in the Arab world expect their media neither to tell them the truth nor to stand up for their rights. They have no illusions: the media exist to serve the interests of the man who is in power—no more, no less. That does not mean the Arabs are badly informed. Word-of-mouth is the true medium of the Arab people and rumours are its daily headlines. The Arabs are adept at analysing rumours—this one clearly put about by the government, that one probably circulated by the opposition—and then sifting truth from lies. From the established media, however, they expect only lies.

This loss of faith in the media reflects loss of confidence in the regimes which control them. How can the man in the street have faith in a newspaper which told him yesterday that the Camp David Treaty was an act of treason but which today tells him that Egypt must return to the Arab fold with that treaty intact? If yesterday he was asked to believe that those calling for rapprochement with the United States were traitors and CIA agents, why today should he believe that those who criticise American policies are Soviet agents? The same absurdities run through his daily life. How can he believe that the Arabs are boycotting Israel when he sees Israeli manufactured goods on open sale in every market? How can he take seriously the proclaimed Arab policy of liberating Jerusalem when he sees that the head of the Islamic Committee charged with that strategy hosts an international conference—this was in May 1984—in which 35 Israelis took part, eight of them members of the Knesset which sits in Jerusalem? How, finally, can he have the slightest belief in slogans about the struggle against Israel being a pan-Arab responsibility when he watched the Israelis invade Lebanon while the bulk of the Arab world stood idly by?

—General Saad el-Shazly

Reflections of an Egyptian Statesman (1997)

When I returned home, I found many bouquets of flowers and hundreds of congratulatory telegrams. The telephone rang incessantly. In Egypt, from pharaonic times to the present, the tradition is one of al-Hakem, the ruler. One is the ruler or one is nothing. Therefore, the highest position to which one can aspire is in the service of the ruler. To be a minister in the cabinet, as I had become, was to possess far greater prestige than an artist, scholar, or man of wealth. In the developing countries there are only two kinds of real power: political power and religious power.

—Boutros Boutros-Ghali

Revolution

The spread of new ideas was greatly helped by the Russo-Japanese war of 1904–5 and its consequences. The Japanese victory sent a wave of exultation through the Middle East. Like other regions governed or threatened by the expansion of the European imperial powers, Middle Easterners saw with delight the defeat of one of these powers, Russia, by a small upstart Asian nation. There were some who drew a further inference—that Russia was the only European imperial power that had not adopted constitutional government, while Japan was the only Asian power that had done so. The lesson of this contrast was driven home by the Russian revolutionary upheavals of 1905, which seemed to confirm the proposition that constitutional and parliamentary government makes a nation healthy, wealthy and strong. In December 1905 the first Middle Eastern protest against incompetent despotism linked with foreign interests occurred in Iran, where the Shah was obliged to yield to popular demands and convene a national assembly, which drew up a liberal constitution. In 1908 in the Ottoman lands the revolutionary movement known as the Young Turks forced the Sultan Abdul Hamid to re-

*store the aborted constitution of 1876 and reduce his own role to that of a
constitutional monarch.*

*The two following passages give contemporary impressions, one by a
British visitor, the other by an Irish journalist, of the revolutionary out-
breaks in Iran and in Turkey. They are followed by three poems by a Turkish poet, written at the time of the Young Turk Revolution. They vividly
illustrate the hope and disillusionment that have accompanied so many
subsequent revolutionary movements in the region.*

Tehran, August 1906

*E. G. Browne, an Orientalist at Cambridge University and a strong sup-
porter of the Persian cause, cites the account of an eyewitness (whom he
does not name) to the Persian Constitutional Revolution.*

"I do not know whether you are aware of the great events which have been
taking place in Tehran. The English papers practically ignore the 'Land of
the Lion and the Sun,' and the Persian news is generally relegated to small,
out-of-the-way paragraphs. I feel sure that these events will interest you,
and am therefore writing this letter to give you some description of what has
happened.

"About a month ago [in July 1906] it was rumored that a number of people
intended to take *bast* [sanctuary] at the British Legation in town. . . . I went
down and found some forty and odd merchants and *mullás* in the Legation
garden. . . . On the following day their numbers increased largely. . . . I stayed
there three weeks, and it was certainly a unique experience. The number of
bastis increased by leaps and bounds, until the *bázárs* were all closed, and
some 12,000 refugees were encamped in the Legation. It was a most curious
sight, and I am sure would have delighted you. . . . Imagine the Legation Garden with tents in every available place, and crammed with thousands of all
classes, merchants, *'ulamá,* members of all the guilds, etc., sitting there day
after day with stubborn patience, determined not to leave the shelter of the
British flag until their demands were satisfied. They policed themselves in a
most remarkable manner, and, considering their numbers, gave little trouble.
Their kitchens and feeding arrangements were a model of order. They ex-
temporized a rough kitchen behind the guardroom, and every day a circle of
enormous cauldrons was to be seen cooking the meals of this vast multitude.
The meals were served by guilds, and each meal took three hours to serve.

"Perhaps the scene was most picturesque at night. Nearly every tent used
to have a *rawza-khwán,* and it was really an admirable tableau, these tents

with their circles of listeners and the *rawza-khwán* at one end, relating the old, old stories of Hasan and Husayn. At the tragic parts, the audience would weep in that extraordinary Persian manner, and beat their heads in sign of grief. I used to stroll round the tents every evening to witness this curious sight. I really believe that in those three weeks I learned more Persian than during all the months I have been in Persia. Every day the leaders of the people used to pay me visits and ask for news or advice. In spite of the heat and the putrid air from the garden, I was really quite sorry when it was over.

"I will try to put before you briefly the essential points of this popular uprising. Under the late *Atábak,* Aynu'd-Dawla*, the country has been going to rack and ruin. The Persians can stand a great deal of misgovernment, but even they could no longer support the tyranny and mismanagement of this Minister. Moreover the Russian Revolution has had a most astounding effect here. Events in Russia have been watched with great attention, and a new spirit would seem to have come over the people. They are tired of their rulers, and, taking example of Russia, have come to think that it is possible to have another and better form of government. The discontent culminated in December [1905], when the whole body of the *'ulamá* left the town and took *bast* at Sháh 'Abdu'l-Azím, as a protest against the Government. After a six weeks' stay they were induced to return on being promised . . . Courts of Justice. Needless to say, the Atábak had no intention of carrying out his promises. Contrary to expectation, Muharram [February 25–March 26, 1906] passed quietly, and there was comparative calm until the middle of June, when the people, seeing that none of the Sháh's promises were being carried out, became restless, and finally, at the beginning of July, serious riots took place. The *bázárs* were closed, and some 5,000 of the people took refuge in the Masjid-i-Jum'a. The Atábak surrounded the Mosque with troops, thus cutting off their supplies and forcing them to come out. A fight took place outside the Mosque, and two Sayyids, Qur'án in hand, were killed. The soldiers, however, chiefly owing to the high pay given them during the riots, proved unexpectedly loyal, and the resistance collapsed. The ringleaders and several important *mujahids* were expelled from the town, and all seemed quiet again. But it was only the lull before the storm. Finding that they were unable to oppose armed resistance to the Government, the people decided to take *bast* in the British Legation, and this proved a very successful method of attaining their ends. The Sháh sent several envoys down to the Legation with *dast-khatts* [autograph letters], but the people refused to receive them. Finally, the Sháh was compelled to dismiss the Atábak, and the *Mushíru' d-Dawla* became *Sadr-i-*

---

* Chief minister from September 1903 to July 1906. Atábak (from Turkish *Atabeg*) was a military title.

A'zam. He, at any rate, is not an obstinate old fool like his predecessor, and, seeing how dangerous the situation had become, induced the Sháh to make large concessions. After endless discussion, the people at last accepted a Royal *dast-khatt,* granting them a Parliament to be composed of all classes, Princes, Qájárs, Nobles, landed proprietors, merchants, tradesmen, etc. Blood-money was promised to the relatives of the murdered Sayyids; the exiled *mullás* have been asked to return, and will be brought back in triumph, and the Courts of Justice are to be established.

"The question every one is now asking is, 'Are we witnessing the Dawn of Liberty in Persia, or the beginning of a sorry farce?' I think it unlikely that the people will have any real power in this Parliament. The Government will be sure to pack it so that it may but endorse the views of the Court. But I believe that in the end the people will win. They are, of course, absolutely ignorant of the principles of government, with the exception, perhaps, of a few of their chiefs. When I was in the Tehran Legation, they used to come and asked me how our constitution was worked, and would show a *naïveté* which was almost pathetic. They see clearly the object in view, but they are very hazy as to the means of attaining it. Undoubtedly it will be many years before this Parliament can become really effective. But many of the chiefs, amongst whom is a celebrated Bábí, have really a very clear conception of what is needed. If only they will remain united, and not let the Government sow dissensions amongst them, they should carry the day. *Qui vivra verra!*

"It seems to me that a change must be coming over the East. The victory of Japan has, it would appear, had a remarkable influence all over the East. Even here in Persia it has not been without effect. . . . From the little study I have devoted to the question, it almost seems to me that the East is stirring in its sleep. In China there is a marked movement against the foreigners, and a tendency towards the ideal of 'China for the Chinese.' In Persia, owing to its proximity to Russia, the awakening would appear to take the form of a movement towards democratic reform. In Egypt and North Africa it is signalized by a remarkable increase of fanaticism, coupled with the spread of the Pan-Islamic movement. The simultaneousness of these symptoms of unrest is too remarkable to be attributed solely to coincidence. Who knows? Perhaps the East is really awakening from its secular slumber, and we are about to witness the rising of these patient millions against the exploitation of an unscrupulous West.

"One remarkable feature of this revolution here—for it is surely worthy to be called a revolution—is that the priesthood have found themselves on the side of progress and freedom. This, I should think, is almost unexampled in the world's history. If the reforms which the people, with their help, have fought for become a reality, nearly all their power will be gone. The causes of this remarkable phenomenon are not without their explanation, and are very interesting, but the subject is a lengthy one, and I feel that I have already transgressed all reasonable limits as regards prolixity . . ."

—As cited by E. G. Browne

Istanbul, 1908

From a Western newspaper correspondent's contemporary description of the opening of Parliament, for the first time in thirty years, shortly before the fall of Sultan Abd-ul-Hamid.

The scene presented by the great Square of S. Sophia at noon on December 17, 1908, was unforgettable. To give an idea of the density of the crowd I need only say that the dogs—the famous dogs of Constantinople—had temporarily disappeared, there being in that tightly wedged mass of solid humanity no room for a pin, much less for a dog. The spaces in front of the ancient church—the Augusteum, the Hippodrome, and all the surrounding *meidan* whose ancient names carry one so far back into the centuries—were a sea of bright red fezzes, with a sprinkling of the white or green turbans of ecclesiastics, and through this sea ran like breakwaters long lines of fixed bayonets, while a brilliant sun glistened on the gorgeous uniforms of the Household troops.

Here and there were phalanxes of young, beardless faces, the faces of Turkish, Greek, Armenian, Jewish and Persian schoolboys, of military students, clerical students, law students, all sorts of students, marshaled in military order under their respective teachers. On the left of the Parliament House were the Albanian soldiers of the Guard in their white uniforms, on the right were the Syrian Zouaves in their green turbans. In close proximity were the men from Salonica, the famous khaki-clad soldiers of the 3rd Corps whose action in July 1908 gave freedom to Turkey. These pillars of the Constitution were evidently ready for any emergency, as I noticed that each man carried not only a beltful of cartridges round his body but also scores of additional cartridges stowed away in three little pockets arranged, one above the other, in the front of each coatsleeve. The Sultan might be murdered or deposed (his deposition was not impossible in case he refused to open the Parliament in person), there might be a reactionary coup d'état, or a mutiny among the Palace Guards, but, come what might, these Macedonians were ready for it. They foresaw everything.

But who could have foreseen that, in less than four months, these champions of Young Turkey, corrupted by the Sultan's gold, would themselves have headed a reactionary mutiny in front of this very Parliament House, and would have carried with them in their downfall the whole of the 1st

Army Corps whose soldiers make such a brave show in the streets of the capital to-day?

Despite the fact that the festival was supposed to mark the triumph of the democracy over despotism, I must say that the soldiers sometimes treated their masters, the people, with scant ceremony; for whenever the order was given to drive back the crowd, the military ran like mad bulls or New York policemen at the nearest civilians, whom they mercilessly belabored with their fists and with the butts of their muskets. Then there would be a feeble, swaying movement in the first few ranks of sightseers, but nothing short of machine-guns could dislodge the main body.

The populace was, however, not quite a herd of dumb, driven cattle. It knew something of politics, it seemed, else why that loud cheering for the men from Salonica and for Sir Gerard Lowther, the British ambassador? Why that ominous silence when the Marquis Pallavicini, the Austrian ambassador, drove past?

From the heart of the crowd came smothered, high-pitched shouts of "Iradé! Iradé!" (official proclamation). They came from cute newsboys who were selling slips of paper which were anything but official and on which were printed appeals to the deputies to begin their legislative labors by punishing the criminals of the old *régime* "who drank the people's blood for thirty years." Even under the nose of the Sultan the crowd afterwards sang and the military bands played the "Song of Liberty" wherein "the old tyranny," "the thirty years of shame," and, in biblical phrase, "the Days of the Oppression" were freely alluded to. Many of the crowd gave vent to their feelings in a less praiseworthy way by discharging their revolvers in the air, for since the restriction on the sale of arms has been abolished, an enormous trade has been done here in revolvers. . . .

Eleven o'clock! The processions of deputies, of notables, of ecclesiastics, of foreign ambassadors, begin to converge on Parliament House. Their progress is slow, for the streets are crammed with a variegated crowd of Turks, Greeks, Armenians, Albanians, mariners from the Isles, shepherds from Asia Minor, Arabs from the Holy Cities and the mysterious Peninsula, Montenegrins, Bulgarians, Mongols, Turkomans, Tartars, Kirghiz, Aryans, Kurds, Kutzovalaks, Jews, Gypsies, Caucasians, Druses, Maronites and representatives of all the other races which make up this most composite empire. The pressure is so great that the smaller and weaker members of the crowd are squeezed in underneath the wheels of the carriages and the legs of the horses, but, luckily, they are in no danger there as the carriages cannot move at anything but a snail's pace and as complete stops are frequent and lengthy. Sometimes these stops are due to amusingly unexpected causes. In one case a flock of sheep crossing the main street blocked for ten minutes the way of a squadron of cavalry just after the bugler had given the

signal to advance, and it was not until the shepherd boy had put in his appearance with the last of the stragglers that the lancers and the dozen ambassadors whom they escorted were able to continue their course. . . .

The interior of the Chamber looked at first less picturesque than I had
expected, for the deputies were mostly youngish, business-like men, clad in
the conventional black of Europe and only distinguished from the legisla-
tors of other lands by their red fezzes, while the hall itself was so redolent of
our most advanced civilization that I was in continual fear lest the jerry-built
balcony whereon a place had been found for me would collapse. The opening of the first Duma, a ceremony which I also attended, seemed to me to be
a more impressive sight owing to the contrast between the sheep-skins of
the *muzhiks* on the one hand and the splendor of the Winter Palace on the
other. But this, after all, is no mean assembly. It contains representatives
from Jerusalem, Bagdad and Mecca, from the races which have given us the
Talmud, the Bible and the Koran, from the tribes which founded Judaism,
Christianity and Islam. . . .

A figure seemed to cross the sunlight, the silence of death fell on the
crowded room: Abd-ul-Hamid had entered.

To do justice to this dramatic appearance of the mysterious chief of
Islam, I should have been born a Turk or an Armenian and then I would
have been awe-stricken, perhaps, by the memories of this Presence, by the
recollection of the Sultans whose flags floated on three continents and four
seas, who ruled from the Adriatic to the Persian Gulf, from the Carpathians
to the Nile, and for whom prayers were offered up in thirty kingdoms. Not
having been born an Armenian or a Turk I could only see a tottering old
man, bent, ashy-faced, weary, and with a way of shuffling instead of walking which made him look ten years older than he really was. He wore his in-
separable dark grey military overcoat, edged with red and provided with
heavy epaulettes, but both his overcoat and his fez seemed too large for him
and very much out of place. In fact, Shylock's gabardine is the only dress
that would suit Abd-ul-Hamid to perfection.

The vaster the scale on which a criminal acts, the more presentable and
even heroic he appears and perhaps feels. But in the case of Abd-ul-
Hamid, this rule did not certainly hold good, for he looked like some obscene and treacherous beast of prey that, after having hidden in the bowels
of the earth for years, is finally trapped, caged and brought forth, blinking
and reluctant, into the blessed sunlight, while, afar off, the people shudder
at the Horror.

The Padishah's manner corresponded to his appearance, being common and undignified. On the present occasion he entered by mistake the
empty box reserved for the heir-apparent (whom the Cabinet had probably
advised to absent himself from the function in view of the fact that the Sul-

tan might be assassinated on his way through the streets), and as Ghalib Pasha, the Master of Ceremonies, tried to explain matters to him, he exhibited for a moment the pathetic hesitancy of a very old man whose hearing is not good and whose mental apparatus is rusty. But finally he shuffled feebly into the central box and stood there looking down on the crowded hall, leaning with both hands—a favorite attitude of his—on his sword-hilt, and occasionally shifting in an awkward and ungraceful way from one foot to the other.

It was a supreme historical moment, but the chief actor cannot be said to have cut an imposing figure. The autocrat was now, for the first time, facing his masters. He seemed rather to be facing his judges. He looked like a murderer whose judge is putting on the black cap rather than a ruler blessing his people. The young Tzar is a far less powerful and intricate personality than the Sultan, but at the opening of the first Duma he bore himself correctly and committed no *gaucheries*. At the opening of *his* Duma, Abd-ul-Hamid looked, on the contrary, like a man who expected corpses to rise from the grave and denounce him. Dazed, horror-stricken almost, the aged Sultan glared blankly downwards as if he saw something supernatural, unseen by all else. His eyes wandered slowly around the hall while everybody waited, standing, in painful suspense. At last his glance rested on some familiar face—there were not very many of them in that hall—and he brought his white-gloved hand to his lips and then to his forehead in sign of salutation. Again an awkward pause, while the Padishah was trying to discover another familiar face, and finally—having probably failed in the attempt—he half turned towards Ghalib Pasha, who stood with two Generals at the entrance to the Imperial box, and irritably motioned him to approach. What was going to happen? I craned my neck forward in expectation, but it seemed that the Sultan had accidentally dropped one of his white gloves and that he merely wished the Master of Ceremonies to pick it up for him.

—Francis McCullagh

Three Poems of Revolution

Reactions of a Turkish poet before, during and after the Young Turk Revolution of 1908.

1898

Once more a stubborn mist has swathed your horizons . . .
A dusty, fearsome darkness, which the eye
Takes care not to pierce, for it is afraid.

But for you this deep, dark veil is right and fitting,
This veiling becomes you well, O scene of evil deeds. . . .
Yes, veil yourself, O tragedy, veil yourself, O city;
Veil yourself and sleep forever, whore of the world!

1908

Now we are far from that accursed night,
The night of calamity has joined the nights of oblivion,
Our eyes have opened to a radiant morning.
Between you, O world of renewal, and that ill-omened night
There is no kinship; you are noble and great.
There is no mist or shade about your face, only splendor and majesty,
A bursting brightness like the dawning sun.

1912

This dainty spread, gentlemen,
waiting to be devoured,
trembling before your presence,
is this nation's life:
this nation in suffering,
this nation in the throes of death—
But have no fear, and don't hold back:
just eat and gorge and gobble.
   Eat, gentlemen, eat; this tasty feast is yours:
    stuff yourselves until you gag and burst . . .
Though the banquet may be heavy,
so much food, hard to digest,
never mind—enjoy the splendor
and the sweetness of revenge.
For your gracious condescension,
see, this table waits and hopes,
and displays these bloody morsels:
brain, head, liver, all for you.
   Eat, gentlemen, eat; this tempting feast is yours:
    stuff yourselves until you gag and burst.
This poor land of ours is giving
all it has, and all its wealth;
gives its life and gives its body,
gives its hope and gives its dream,
giving up its peace of mind,

giving up its heart's desire—
Gulp it all, and do not worry
what is lawful, what is not.
   Eat, gentlemen, eat; this tempting feast is yours:
   stuff yourselves until you gag and burst.
This harvest time draws to an end:
grab what you can while there's still time.
The crackling hearth you hear today
tomorrow will be dead and cold.
Today your stomachs are still strong—
today, while the soup is still hot,
snatch and grab from every pot,
and gorge and gag.
   Eat, gentlemen, eat; this tempting feast is yours:
   stuff yourselves until you gag and burst.

—Tevfik Fikret

Atatürk on the State of the Union

Of the many movements and seizures of power that have claimed the name revolution in the Middle East in the twentieth century, two were of particular importance: the Kemalist Revolution in Turkey and the Khomeinist Revolution in Iran, the one seeking to establish a secular democracy, the other an Islamic theocracy. Each of these was based on a diagnosis of the ills of society, and a prescription for their cure. Both had had impact far beyond the territories which they controlled, and probably represent the two most likely alternative futures for the peoples of the Middle East, Christians and Jews and well as Muslims.

The following passages, the first consisting of excerpts from speeches by Mustafa Kemal Atatürk, the other from a message to the nation by the Ayatollah Khomeini, represent these two different revolutionary concepts through the words of their founders and leaders.

Fantasy and Reality (1921)

Every one of our compatriots and coreligionists may nourish a high ideal in his mind; he is free to do so, and no one will interfere. But the government of the Grand National Assembly of Turkey has a firm, positive, material policy, and that, gentlemen, is directed to the preservation of life and independence . . . within defined national frontiers. The Grand National Assembly and government of Turkey, in the name of the nation they represent, are very modest, very far from fantasies, and completely realistic. . . .

We are not men who run after great fantasies and present a fraudulent appearance of doing things which in fact we cannot do. By looking as though we were doing great and fantastic things, without actually doing them, we have brought the hatred, rancour, and malice of the whole world on this country and this people. We did not serve pan-Islamism. We said that we had and we would, but we didn't, and our enemies said: "Let us kill them at once before they do!" We did not serve pan-Turanianism. We said that we could and we would, and again they said: "Let us kill them!" There you have the whole problem. . . . Rather than run after ideas which we did not and could not realise and thus increase the number of our enemies and the pressure upon us, let us return to our natural, legitimate limits. And let us know our limits. We are a nation desiring life and independence. For that and that alone may we give our lives.

The People's Government (1921)

If we must define our government sociologically, we would call it "people's government" . . . We are toiling people, poor people, who work to save their lives and independence. Let us know what we are! We are people who work and who must work to be saved and to live. For this every one of us has the right and the authority, but only by working do we acquire that right. There is no room, and no right, in our society for men who want to lie on their backs and live without working. Populism is a social principle that seeks to rest the social order on its work and its law. We are men who follow a principle that entitles us, in order to preserve this right and to safeguard our independence, to struggle as a whole nation against the imperialism that seeks to crush and the capitalism that seeks to swallow our very nationhood . . . that is the basis on which our government rests, a clear sociological basis. . . . But what can we do if we don't resemble democracy, we don't resemble socialism, we don't resemble anything? We should be proud of defying comparison! Because we resemble ourselves!

Sword and Plough (1923)

My friends, those who conquer by the sword are doomed to be overcome by those who conquer with the plough, and finally to give place to them. That is what happened to the Ottoman Empire. . . . The arm that wields the sword grows weary and in the end puts it back in the scabbard, where perhaps it is doomed to rust and moulder; but the arm that holds the plough grows daily stronger, and in growing stronger becomes yet more the master and owner of the soil. . . .

Civilization Is One (1924)

Countries may vary, but civilization is one and for a nation to progress, it must take part in this one civilization. The decline of the Ottomans began when, proud of their triumphs over the West, they cut their ties with the European nations. This was a mistake which we will not repeat.

Old Laws and New (1925)

At the opening of a law school in Ankara University.

When I speak to you of legal foundations, of the laws required by our new needs, I am not merely referring to the dictum that "every revolution must have its own special sanctions." While restraining myself from useless recriminations, I must at the same time observe, with the deepest regret, how the efforts made by the Turkish nation for at least three centuries to profit from the means and benefits of modern civilization have been frustrated by such painful and grievous obstacles.

The negative and overwhelming force that has condemned our nation to decay, that has ultimately broken and defeated the men of initiative and drive whom our fecund nation has in no period failed to produce, is the law that has hitherto been in your hands, the law and its faithful followers. . . .

Think of the Turkish victory of 1453, the capture of Istanbul, and its place in the course of world history. That same might and power, which in defiance of a whole world made Istanbul for ever the property of the Turkish community, was too weak to overcome the ill-omened resistance of the men of law and to receive in Turkey the printing press, which had been invented at about the same time. Three centuries of observation and hesitation were needed, of effort and energy expended for and against, before the old laws and their exponents would permit the entry of printing into our country. Do not think that I have chose a remote and ancient period, incapable of resuscitation, to illustrate the old law and the old lawyers. If I were to start giving you examples of the difficulties caused during our new revolutionary era, to me personally, by the old law and its exponents, I would run the risk of overburdening you. . . . All these events show that the greatest and at the same time the most insidious enemies of the revolutionaries are decayed laws and their decrepit upholders. . . .

It is our purpose to create completely new laws and thus to tear up the very foundations of the old legal systems. . . .

Shaykhs and Charlatans (1927)

Can a civilized nation tolerate a crowd of people who let themselves be led by the nose by sheikhs, dervishes and the like . . . and who entrust their faith and their lives to fortunetellers, magicians, witch-doctors, and writers of amulets?
—Mustafa Kemal Atatürk

New Year's Message (1980)

This message, delivered by Imam Khomeini in Tehran on the occasion of the Iranian New Year, on March 21, is in the nature of a comprehensive review of the problems and dangers faced by the new order in Iran a full year after the revolution.

God Almighty has willed—and all thanks are due to Him—that this noble nation be delivered from the oppression and crimes inflicted on it by a tyrannical government and from the domination of the oppressive powers, especially America, the global plunderer, and that the flag of Islamic justice wave over our beloved land. It is our duty to stand firm against the superpowers, as we are indeed able to do, on condition that the intellectuals stop following and imitating either the West and the East, and adhere instead to the straight path of Islam and the nation. We are at war with international communism no less than we are struggling against the global plunderers of the West, headed by America, Zionism and Israel.

Dear friends! Be fully aware that the danger represented by the communist powers is no less than that of America; the danger that America poses is so great that if you commit the smallest oversight, you will be destroyed. Both superpowers are intent on destroying the oppressed nations of the world, and it is our duty to defend those nations.

We must strive to export our Revolution throughout the world, and must abandon all idea of not doing so, for not only does Islam refuse to recognize any difference between Muslim countries, it is the champion of all oppressed people. Moreover, all the powers are intent on destroying us, and if we remain surrounded in a closed circle, we shall certainly be defeated. We must make plain our stance toward the powers and the superpowers and demonstrate to them that despite the arduous problems that burden us, our attitude to the world is dictated by our beliefs.

Beloved youths, it is in you that I place my hopes. With the Qur'ān in one hand and a gun in the other, defend your dignity and honor so well that your adversaries will be unable even to think of conspiring against you. At the same time, be so compassionate toward your friends that you will not hesitate to sacrifice everything you possess for their sake. Know well that the world today belongs to the oppressed, and sooner or later they will triumph. They will inherit the earth and build the government of God.

Once again, I declare my support for all movements and groups that are fighting to gain liberation from the superpowers of the left and the right. I declare my support for the people of Occupied Palestine and Lebanon. I vehemently condemn once more the savage occupation of Afghanistan by the aggressive plunderers of the East, and I hope that the noble Muslim people of Afghanistan will achieve victory and true independence as soon as possible, and be delivered from the clutches of the so-called champions of the working class. . . .

I see that satanic counterrevolutionary conspiracies, aiming at promoting the interests of the East and the West, are on the rise; it is the God-given human and national duty of both the government and the people to frustrate those conspiracies with all the powers at their command. I wish to draw particular attention to several points.

1.   This is the year in which security must return to Iran so that our noble people can pursue their lives in utter tranquillity. I declare once again my complete support for the honorable Iranian army. I stress that the army of the Islamic Republic must fully observe military discipline and regulations. It is the duty of the president of the Republic, whom I have appointed commander-in-chief of the armed forces, to admonish severely all those, irrespective of rank, who foment disorder in the army, incite strikes, neglect their duties, ignore military discipline and regulations, or disobey military commands. If they are proven to have committed any of these offenses, they should be immediately expelled from the army and prosecuted.

I can no longer tolerate any form of disorder in the army. Anyone who incites disorder in the army will immediately be denounced to the people as a counterrevolutionary, so that the nation may settle its accounts with any remaining vestiges of the criminal shah's army.

Dear brothers in the army, you who turned your backs on the vile shah and his plundering agents and joined the ranks of the people, today is the day for serving the nation, for serving Iran! With ceaseless efforts, devote yourselves to the task of defending this land against the enemies of Islam and Iran.

2.   I declare once again my support for the Corps of Revolutionary Guards. I wish to impress upon them and their commanders that the slight-

est laxity in the fulfillment of their duties is a punishable offense. If they act (God forbid) in such a way as to disturb the order of the corps, they will immediately be expelled, and what I have said concerning the army applies equally to them. Revolutionary sons of mine, take heed that your conduct toward each other be inspired by affection and Islamic ethics.

3. The police and gendarmerie must also observe discipline. I have been informed that a remarkable laziness prevails in the police stations. The past record of the police is not good; they should therefore do their utmost to establish harmonious relations with the people, maintaining order throughout the country and regarding themselves as an integral part of society. A basic reorganization of the gendarmerie and police is envisaged for the future. In the meantime, the security forces must regard themselves as being at the service of Islam and the Muslims. . . .

4. The Revolutionary Courts throughout Iran must be a model of the implementation of God's laws. They must try not to deviate in the slightest from the ordinances of God Almighty; observing the utmost caution, they must display revolutionary patience in fulfilling the judicial tasks entrusted to them. The courts do not have the right to maintain their own armed forces, and they must act in accordance with the constitution. An Islamic judicial system will gradually assume the responsibilities now fulfilled by the Revolutionary Courts, and in the meantime, judges must do their best to prevent all irregularities. If any judge (God forbid) deviates from the commands of God, he will immediately be exposed to the people and punished.

5. It is the duty of the government to provide the workers and laborers with all they need for productive labor. For their part, the workers should be aware that strikes and slowdowns not only tend to strengthen the superpowers in their hostility to the Revolution, but also tend to transform into despair the hopes now placed in us by the oppressed of the world, who have risen in revolt in both Muslim and non-Muslim countries. As soon as the people learn that a strike is taking place at a factory in their town, they should proceed there immediately and investigate, identifying and exposing to the people all counterrevolutionary forces. There is no reason for the noble people of Iran to pay wages to a handful of godless individuals. . . .

6. I do not know why the government has failed to proceed with its suspended plans for promoting the welfare of the people. It must immediately implement existing plans and adopt new ones in order to remedy the economic situation in our country.

7. Everyone must obey governmental authorities in government offices, and stern action is to be taken against those who fail to do so. Anyone who wishes to create a disturbance in any government office must immediately be expelled and denounced to the people. I am amazed at the failure

of the government to appreciate the power of the people. The people are able to settle their accounts with counterrevolutionaries themselves and to disgrace them.

8. Confiscation of the property of miscreants by unauthorized individuals or courts lacking the proper competence is to be severely condemned. All confiscations must take place in accordance with the *shari'a* and after a warrant has been obtained from a prosecutor or judge. . . .

9. Land must be distributed according to the criteria of the *shari'a,* and only the competent courts have the right to sequester land after due investigation. No one else has the right to encroach on anyone's land or orchards. . . . Anyone who acts in defiance of Islamic and legal criteria will be subject to severe prosecution. . . .

10. The Housing Foundation and the Mustazafan Foundation must each submit a report balance sheet of their activity as soon as possible to acquaint the people with their revolutionary operations. . . .

11. A fundamental revolution must take place in all the universities across the country, so that professors with links to the East or the West may be purged, and the university may provide a healthy atmosphere for cultivation of the Islamic sciences. The evil form of instruction imposed by the previous regime must be stopped, because all the miseries of society during the reign of that father and that son were ultimately caused by such evil instruction. If a proper method of education had been followed in the universities, we would never have had a class of university-educated intellectuals choose to engage in factionalism and dispute, in total isolation from the people and at a time of intense crisis for the country; they overlooked the sufferings of the people so completely that it was as if they were living abroad. All of our backwardness has been due to the failure of most university-educated intellectuals to acquire correct knowledge of Iranian Islamic society, and unfortunately, this is still the case. Most of the blows our society has sustained have been inflicted on it precisely by these university-educated intellectuals, who, with their inflated notions of themselves, speak in a manner only their fellow so-called intellectuals can understand; if the people at large cannot understand them, too bad! Because the people do not even exist in the eyes of these intellectuals; only they themselves exist. The evil form of instruction practiced in the universities during the time of the shah educated intellectuals in such a way that they paid no regard to the oppressed and exploited people, and unfortunately, they still fail to do so.

Committed, responsible intellectuals! Abandon your factionalism and separation and show some concern for the people, for the salvation of this heroic population that has offered so many martyrs. Rid yourselves of the "isms" of the East and the West; stand on your own feet and stop relying on foreigners.

The students of the religious sciences as well as the university students must take care that their studies are entirely based on Islamic foundations. They must abandon the slogans of deviant groups and replace all incorrect forms of thought with the true Islam that we cherish. Let both groups of students be aware that Islam is an autonomous, rich school of thought that has no need of borrowings from any other school. Furthermore, let everyone be aware that to adopt a syncretic ideology is a great act of treason toward Islam and the Muslims, the bitter fruits of which will become apparent in the years ahead. Unfortunately, we see that because of a failure to understand certain aspects of Islam correctly and precisely, these aspects have been mixed with elements taken from Marxism, so that a melange has come into being that is totally incompatible with the progressive laws of Islam.

Beloved students, do not follow the wrong path of university intellectuals who have no commitment to the people! Do not separate yourself from the people!

12.   Another matter is that of the press and the mass communications media. Once again, I request the press throughout the country to collaborate, to write freely whatever they wish, but not to engage in conspiracies. I have said repeatedly that the press must be independent and free, but unfortunately, I see some newspapers engaged on a course designed to serve the evil aims of the right and the left in Iran. In all countries, the press plays a fundamental role in creating an atmosphere that is either healthy or unhealthy. It is to be hoped that in Iran, the press will enter the service of God and the people.

Radio and television must also be free and independent, and they must broadcast all forms of criticism with complete impartiality, so that we do not again witness the kind of radio and television we had under the deposed shah. Radio and television must be purged of all pro-shah and deviant elements. . . .

Finally, at the beginning of this new year, I seek God's mercy for the martyrs of the Islamic Revolution, and express my gratitude for the sacrifices they made. I also offer my congratulations to those they left behind, the mothers and fathers who reared those lion-hearted women and men. I also offer congratulations to those who were crippled or wounded when they were in the vanguard of our people's movement for the establishment of an Islamic republic. Our Islamic Revolution is indeed indebted to the sacrifices made by these valiant people. The people and I will never forget their courage and we will always cherish their memory.

I pray to God Almighty that He grant dignity and greatness to Islam and the Muslims.

Peace be upon you, and also the mercy and blessings of God.

—Imam Khomeini (translated by Hamid Algar)

Turkey and Iran Look at Each Other

The first of the following excerpts comes from the memoirs of a Turkish diplomat who was his country's ambassador in Tehran during the Iranian Revolution. After an extensive discussion, he summarizes the causes and consequences of the Revolution. The second passage cites Turkish press reports of an incident in December 1996, when Hashimi Rafsanjani, then president of Iran, went to Turkey on a state visit at the invitation of Necmettin Erbakan, then leader of the Islamist party and prime minister of Turkey.

The Causes and Consequences of the Revolution in Iran: A Turkish View (1998)

CAUSES

1.   The important role played by religion at all times in Iran—the distinctive character of Shi'ism, and, linked with this, the institution of *taqlīd* [submission to the authority of a religious leader].

2.   The attempt of the Pahlavi dynasty to achieve a process of westernization without recourse to the principle of separation between state and religion.

3.   The inability of the people to get their share of the opportunities created by the sudden rise in oil prices.

4.   The spread of the irregularities affecting the country even to the shah's family.

5.   The migration from the villages to the cities caused by the neglect of agriculture, and the resulting unemployment.

6.   The effort of the West to remedy the shock caused to the world economy by the oil crisis by trying to close the gap in the current balance, and the resulting impression, in Iran, of being exploited.

7.   The secret help given to the revolution by the Soviet Union, much disturbed by the American military presence in Iran.

CONSEQUENCES

1.   The American political, military and economic presence in Iran has been eradicated, and this situation has, for nineteen years, created a void in the region that is difficult to compensate.

2.   The Soviet Union, seeking to exploit this, attempted to occupy Afghanistan, and before long itself dissolved because of the quagmire into which it had fallen.

3.   Its successor the Russian Federation, when it has strengthened its central administration and freed itself from Western economic tutelage, may

be expected to make common cause with Iran and make its weight felt in the region.

4.   The dissolution of the CENTO alliance has brought new projects to the Middle East agenda. The new dimensions achieved through the Turkish-Egyptian rapprochement and the Turkish-Israeli relationship are the first positive results.

5.   The fundamentalist conception of religion brought by the Iranian revolution, and the reactions against attempts to export it to other Muslim countries, may lead to new groupings in the Islamic world.

6.   Among such groupings, the growing trend toward integration in international relations may launch a similar trend in the Middle East.

7.   In our region, dominated by historically transmitted hatreds, lasting peace can be based only on a four-sided balance. The four pillars of this balance are Turkey, Israel, Egypt and Iran.

8.   In the time of the shah, the obstacle to the establishment of such a four-sided cooperation was the PLO, the protégé of the Iranian revolutionaries, and its leader Arafat. Today it is Iran's protégés who embody the strongest opposition to Arafat's peace initiatives.

9.   Two points must not be overlooked. A: Fundamentalism exists in every religion, and terrorist activities occur in every part of the world. It does no service to anybody to present these as coterminous with the Muslim lands. B: As long as the Muslim-Christian divide and the double standard in international relations continue, it will not be possible to remove the current instability in the Middle East and in the Caucasian and Central Asian lands that are linked to it.

—Turgut Tülümen

Ankara: An Iranian View

President Rafsanjani was accompanied by his daughter Faezeh Rafsanjani, president of the Iranian Olympic Committee and minister of sports. Asked by Turkish journalists what she thought of Ankara, she said that it reminded her of Tehran in the last years of the shah.

—*Turkish Press,* December 20, 1996

PART VIII

War

"A war is just when it is necessary."
—Niccolò Machiavelli

Sultan Mehmed IV, illustration from Happelius, Die Kurze Beschreibung der Gantzen Turckey, *1688.*

Introduction

S ince early times the Middle East has been the scene of many wars—within states, between states and, perhaps most important of all, with the outside world. The terms "jihād" and "crusade" have commonly been used to denote the long struggle between Islam and Christendom, two religions that—unlike most others—claim exclusive possession of God's final and complete revelation to mankind. For those who hold such beliefs, any previous religion is at best incomplete, any subsequent religion necessarily false.

Jihād is an Arabic word commonly translated "holy war" but literally meaning "striving," as in the Qur'ānic phase "striving in the path of God." Some Muslims—an increasing number in modern times—interpret jihād in a spiritual and moral sense. The classical authorities, citing Qur'ān, tradition and commentaries, usually discuss jihād in terms of warfare. Virtually every juristic treatise on Islamic law has a section on jihād which sets forth the laws of warfare in considerable detail.

According to Sharī'a law, war may legitimately be waged against four kinds of enemies: infidels, apostates, rebels and bandits. Only the first two count as jihād. Those who are killed in a jihād are called martyrs, with all the rights and privileges pertaining thereto. He who commits suicide, according to a well-known saying of the Prophet, earns eternal damnation, his punishment to consist of the unending repetition of the act by which he killed himself. Opinions differ on whether a suicide bomber earns the reward of martyrdom or the punishment of suicide. Those who choose this path may be sacrificing not just life but eternity.

The Christian Crusade was a response and in a sense an imitation of the jihād—an attempt to recover by holy war what had been lost by holy war. The Christians succeeded in reconquering the Iberian Peninsula and Sicily from the Moors, Russia from the Tatars, the Balkans from the Turks. They failed to hold Palestine or the Levant; they failed again, on a grander scale and at a slower pace, in the attempt to pursue the defeated Moors, Turks and Tatars into Africa and Asia and impose Christian imperial rule in the Islamic world. By the end of the twentieth century the masters of the four great European empires that had ruled the Muslim lands—the British, French, Dutch and finally, the Russians—went home.

Like "crusade," the word "jihād" is often used figuratively nowadays, to denote a peaceful campaign for some good cause. Unlike "crusade," however, it is still sometimes used in the Middle East and elsewhere in its original sense.

The jihād against infidels was waged against non-Muslim peoples beyond the frontiers of Islam; the jihād against apostates was often invoked by rebels, who accused their rulers of the capital crime of apostasy and thus justified their rebellion.

There have been many such rebel movements in the Islamic world, from the earliest to the most recent times. Of the four caliphs who succeeded the Prophet as heads of the community, three were murdered, one by a disgruntled slave, the other two by pious killers who believed that they were carrying out God's will. Of the many opposition movements that argued and acted in this sense, the most famous—though by no means the most important—are the medieval Assassins who flourished in Iran and in Syria during the Crusades period. Their name, along with lurid descriptions of their activities, was brought back to Europe by the crusaders and has entered the vocabulary of most European languages.

In any form of warfare, whether domestic or international, espionage plays an important part. Clearly, a secret service which isn't secret doesn't serve, and successful spies leave little or no record of their successes to inform and guide the historian. Some texts, however, survive, indicating how espionage was perceived and how it was practiced.

The following excerpts deal with war and peace, power and dominion, espionage and terror.

War and Peace

Scriptures

Now go and smite Amalek, and utterly destroy all that they have, and spare them not.

—I Samuel 15:3

They shall beat their swords into plowshares, and their spears into pruning-hooks: nation shall not lift up sword against nation, neither shall they learn war anymore.

—Isaiah 2:4

Blessed are the peacemakers, for they shall be called the children of God. Blessed are they which are persecuted for righteousness' sake: for theirs is the Kingdom of Heaven.

—Matthew 5:9

Think not that I am come to send peace on earth: I came not to send peace, but a sword. For I am come to set a man at variance against his father, and the daughter against her mother, and the daughter-in-law against her mother-in-law. . . . And he that taketh not his cross, and followeth after me, is not worthy of me. He that findeth his life shall lose it: and he that loseth his life for my sake will find it.

—Matthew 10:34–6

To those who fight in God's cause, who barter this life for the sake of the Hereafter . . . who are killed or victorious, we shall give an immense reward.

—Qur'ān 4:74

Fight on the path of God against those who fight against you but do not transgress, for God does not love transgressors. And kill them wherever you catch them, and drive them out from whence they drove you out, for discord* is worse than killing. . . . That is the punishment of the unbelievers. But if they

---

*The Arabic word *fitna,* here translated as "discord," also has a connotation of temptation and sedition.

desist, God is forgiving and merciful. Fight them until there is no more discord, and the religion is of God.

—Qur'ān 2:190–193

Fight against those who do not believe in God or in the Last Day, and do not forbid what God and His Prophet have forbidden, and who do not follow the true religion, of those who were given the Book, until they pay the polltax, directly, they being humbled.

—Qur'ān 9:29

If they incline to peace, then incline likewise, and put your trust in God.

—Qur'ān 8:61

Sayings Attributed to the Prophet

Jihād is incumbent upon you with every amir, whether he be godly or wicked and even if he commit major sins.

Paradise is under the shadow of swords.

The unbeliever and the one who kills him will never meet in Hell.

A day and a night of fighting on the frontier is better than a month of fasting and prayer.

Fight against the polytheists with your property, your persons and your tongues.

If a campaigner by sea is seasick, he has the reward of a martyr; if drowned, of two martyrs.

Learn to shoot, for what lies between the two marks is one of the gardens of Paradise.

Warfare is deception.

Go in the name of God and in God and in the religion of the Prophet of God! Do not kill the very old, the infant, the child or the woman. Bring all the booty, holding back no part of it. Maintain order and do good, for God loves those who do good.

Expel the Jews and the Christians from the Arabian Peninsula.

Accept advice to treat prisoners well.

He who flees is not one of us.

On Suicide

The Prophet said: Whoever kills himself with a blade will be tormented with that blade in the fires of Hell.

The Prophet also said: He who strangles himself will strangle himself in Hell, and he who stabs himself will stab himself in Hell. . . . He who throws himself off a mountain and kills himself will throw himself downward into the fires of Hell for ever and ever. He who drinks poison and kills himself will carry his poison in his hand and drink it in Hell for ever and ever. He who kills himself with steel will take it in his hand to Hell and plunge it in his belly for ever and ever. . . . Whoever kills himself in any way will be tormented in that way in Hell. . . . Whoever kills himself in any way in this world will be tormented with it on the day of resurrection.

God said [of a wounded man who killed himself with his knife]: My servant preempted me in taking his life. Therefore I forbid him Paradise.

Abū Bakr on the Rules of War

Abū Bakr was the first caliph after the death of the Prophet. During his reign the Arab armies began the conquest of vast territories in Asia and Africa.

O people! I charge you with ten rules; learn them well!

Do not betray, or misappropriate any part of the booty; do not practice treachery or mutilation. Do not kill a young child, an old man or a woman. Do not uproot or burn palms or cut down fruitful trees. Do not slaughter a sheep or a cow or a camel, except for food. You will meet people who have set themselves apart in hermitages; leave them to accomplish the purpose for which they have done this. You will come upon people who will bring you dishes with various kinds of foods. If you partake of them, pronounce God's name over what you eat. You will meet people who have shaved the crown of their heads, leaving a band of hair around it. Strike them with the sword.

Go, in God's name, and may God protect you from sword and pestilence.

—As cited by Al-Ṭabarī

St. Augustine on the Desire for Peace (413)

Saint Augustine began The City of God *three years after the sacking of Rome.*

That even the fierceness of war and all the disquietude of men make towards
this one end of peace, which every nature desires

Whoever gives even moderate attention to human affairs and to our common nature, will recognise that if there is no man who does not wish to be
joyful, neither is there any one who does not wish to have peace. For even
they who make war desire nothing but victory—desire, that is to say, to attain to peace with glory. For what else is victory than the conquest of those
who resist us? and when this is done there is peace. It is therefore with the
desire for peace that wars are waged, even by those who take pleasure in
exercising their warlike nature in command and battle. And hence it is obvious that peace is the end sought for by war. For every man seeks peace
by waging war, but no man seeks war by making peace. For even they
who intentionally interrupt the peace in which they are living have no hatred of peace, but only wish it changed into a peace that suits them better.
They do not, therefore, wish to have no peace, but only one more to their
mind.

—Saint Augustine
(translated by Marcus Dodds)

Two Views on the Origins of the Crusades

As Seen by Niccolò Machiavelli (1525)

Urban II, who was hated in Rome, had come to the pontificate. And as it appeared to him that because of the disunities in Italy he could be secure, he
turned to a generous enterprise, went away to France with all the clergy,
and in Auvergne gathered up many peoples to whom he made a speech
against the infidels [at Clermont in 1095]. This speech so inflamed their spirits that they decided to make a campaign in Asia against the Saracens. This
campaign along with all the others like it were later called the Crusades because all those who went on them had their arms and clothing marked with
a red cross. The princes of this enterprise were Godfrey, Eustace, and Baldwin of Bouillon, counts of Boulogne, and one Peter the Hermit, celebrated
for his holiness and prudence. Many kings and many peoples participated
in it with money, and many private individuals fought without any pay—so
great a power did religion have then on the spirits of men, moved by the example of those who were the heads of it. This enterprise was glorious in the
beginning because all Asia Minor, Syria, and a part of Egypt came under the
power of the Christians; and through it the Order of the Knights of

Jerusalem was born, which still rules today and holds the island of Rhodes,* the single remaining obstacle to the power of the Mohammedans. Also born of it was the Order of the Templars, which shortly after disappeared on account of their bad customs. There followed at various times various unforeseen events in which many nations and particular men were celebrated. The king of France and the king of England came to the aid of the enterprise, and the Pisan, the Venetian, and the Genoese peoples acquired very great reputation there; they fought with varying fortune until the times of the Saracen Saladin. His virtue and the discords of the Christians in the end took from them all the glory they had acquired in the beginning, and after ninety years the Christians were driven out of the place they had successfully recovered with such honor.

—Niccolò Machiavelli
(trans. by Laura F. Banfield and Harvey C. Mansfield, Jr.)

As Seen by Ibn al-Athīr (Thirteenth Century)

Contemporary Arab historians describe in some detail the arrival of the Crusaders in Syria-Palestine, their activities and their departure. The words "Crusade" and "Crusader" do not, however, occur, and the historians show little or no interest in whence or why these invaders came. Ibn al-Athīr—by common consent one of the greatest Arabic historians of the Middle Ages— offers a rare exception. Though his curiosity about these invaders is greater than that of his colleagues, his disrespect is no less.

The first appearance of the power and strength of the Franks and their attack on the lands of Islam and their capture of some of them occurred in the year 478 [1085], when they captured Toledo and other cities in Andalusia, as already explained above. Then in the year 484 [1091] they attacked and took possession of the island of Sicily, as I have also described. They even reached as far as the coast of North Africa, where they seized some places. These were recaptured from them, but they then took possession of some others, as you will see. In the year 490 [1097] they attacked the land of Syria. The reason for this attack was that their king Baldwin† gathered together a large Frankish host. He was a kinsman of Roger the Frank, who had con-

---

* This passage was presumably written before 1522, when Rhodes was taken by the Turks.

† Ibn al-Athir was no doubt misled by the subsequent appearance of no less than five Baldwins among the Latin kings of Jerusalem. Baldwin I was crowned king in 1100. A brother of the more famous Godfrey of Bouillon, he did indeed take part in the first Crusade, but at that stage was neither king nor leader.

quered Sicily. Baldwin sent a message to Roger in which he said: "I have assembled a mighty host. I will come to you, and from your land I will attack and conquer Africa, so that I shall be your neighbor." Then Roger summoned his companions and sought their counsel on this, and they said: "By the truth of the Gospels, this is excellent for us and for them, and all the land will become Christian." Then Roger raised his leg and emitted a mighty fart and said: "By my troth, this is better than your words." They asked him how so, and he said: "If they come to me I shall have to provide vast supplies and ships to carry them to Africa, and some of my own soldiers to reinforce them. And if they do conquer the land it will be theirs. The provisions from Sicily will go to them, and I shall lose the money which I collected every year on the harvest in Sicily. And if they do not succeed they will come back to my lands and cause much trouble, and Tamīm [the Muslim ruler of Tunisia] will say: 'You have deceived me and broken our agreement, and that will be the end of good relations and business dealings between us.' North Africa will remain where it is, and it will be ours when we have the strength to take it." So he summoned Baldwin's envoy and said to him: "If it is your desire to make holy war against the Muslims it would be better for you to conquer Jerusalem and rescue it from their hands. This would be bring you great glory. As for Africa, there are pacts and agreements between me and its peoples." So they made their preparations and went out against Syria.

—Ibn al-Athīr

Terrorists in the Holy Land

Crusader Encounters with the Assassins
(Twelfth–Thirteenth Centuries)

Among the most remarkable stories that the Crusaders brought back from the East was that of an extremist Muslim religious sect known as the Assassins. The subsequent meaning of this word derives from their form of struggle, what is nowadays called terrorism. Founded in Iran, the sect established a base in Syria, where their chief was locally known as Shaykh al-Jabal, usually translated Elder or Old Man of the Mountain. Contrary to popular belief, their main target was not the Crusaders, among whom they had few victims and even found some friends. Their attack was primarily directed against the ruling kings and princes of Islam.

There is in the province of Tyre, otherwise called Phoenicia, and in the neighbourhood of the bishopric of Antarades, a people who possess ten strong castles, with their towns and dependencies, and with a strength of 60,000 souls or more, according to what I have often heard. This people has the custom of giving themselves a master and choosing a chief who rules, not by hereditary right, but solely by virtue of merit. He is called the Elder, to the exclusion of any other title which might indicate a dignity. The bond of submission and obedience that binds the people to this Chief is so strong, that there is no task so arduous, difficult or dangerous that any one of them would not undertake to perform it with the greatest zeal, as soon as the Master has commanded it. If for example there be a prince who is hateful or dangerous to this people, the Chief gives a dagger to one or more of his followers, and at once whoever receives the command departs, without considering the consequences of the event nor whether he would be able to escape, and goes, in his burning zeal for the accomplishment of his mission, to run and weary himself as long as may be necessary, until chance gives him the opportunity to carry out his orders and fulfill the wishes of his Master. Our people, as well as the Saracens, call them Assissini, and I have not been able to find out the origin of this name.

—William of Tyre (translated by Emily Atwater Babcock and
A. C. Krey)

Murder and Paradise (1192)

After these days Conrad, king of Jerusalem, was killed . . . two of [the Elder's] men . . . killed him. I shall now relate things about this elder which appear ridiculous but which are attested to me by the evidence of reliable witnesses. This elder has by his witchcraft so bemused the men of his country that they neither worship nor believe in any God but himself. Likewise, he entices them in a strange manner, with such hopes and with promises of such pleasures with eternal enjoyment, that they prefer rather to die than to live. Many of them even, when standing on a high wall, will jump off at his nod or command, and, shattering their skulls, die a miserable death. The most blessed, so he affirms, are those who shed the blood of men and in revenge for such deeds themselves suffer death. When therefore any of them have chosen to die in this way, by murdering someone by craft and then themselves dying so blessedly in revenge for him, he himself hands them knives which are, so to speak, consecrated to this affair, and then intoxicates them with such a potion that they are plunged into ecstasy and oblivion, displays to them by his magic certain fantastic dreams, full of pleasures and delights, or rather of trumpery, and promises them eternal possession of these things in reward for such deeds. This man . . . sent two of his sect . . . to kill him. As soon as he was killed, they themselves were killed, but I do not know whether they were indeed deified.

—Arnold of Lübeck

A Social Call on the Assassins (1198)

The Lord of the Hassessis heard that Count Henry [of Champagne] was in Armenia, and he sent to ask of him that on his return from Armenia he should pass his way, and he would be grateful, for he desired greatly to see him. The Count replied that he would go willingly, and he did so. When the Lord of the Hassessis knew that the Count was coming, he went to meet him and received him very joyously, and with great honour, and led him through his land and his castles. One day he came before a castle, on which there was a high tower, and at each loophole were two men all dressed in white. The Lord of the Hassessis said to him: "Sire, your men would not do for you what mine would do for me." "Sire," replied the Count, "That may well be." The Lord of the Hassessis shouted, and two of the men who were at the loophole threw themselves down and broke their necks. The Count marvelled greatly, and said that indeed he had no man who would do this for him. He said to the Count: "Sire, if you wish I will make all those whom you see up there leap into the valley." The Count replied: "By no means." And when the Count had sojourned as long as he desired in the land of the Old Man, he took his leave. The Lord of the Hassessis gave him great store of his jewels and escorted him out of his land, and on parting said to him, that for the honour he had done him by coming to his lands, he assured him of his permanent good will. And if there was any man who had done him an injury, he should let him know, and he would have him killed. Thereupon they parted.

—Anonymous continuator of William of Tyre

Plus Ça Change (1250)

The Old Man of the Mountain, the King of the Assassins, sent assassin emissaries to France, with orders to kill Louis the King of France. But when they had gone, God changed his heart, and put into him thoughts of peace and not of killing. He therefore sent other emissaries as quickly as possible after the first ones, warning King Louis to guard himself from those, on account of which the King thereupon had his person well guarded by men always carrying copper cudgels. The new emissaries diligently sought out the first ones and having discovered them, brought them to King Louis. Seeing these things, the King, rejoicing, honored both groups with gifts, and, as a token of peace and friendship, sent them to their king with most precious gifts and presents.

—Guillaume de Nangis

The Proper Use of Spies

The Spies of Moses

And the Lord spake unto Moses, saying,

Send thou men, that they may search the land of Canaan, which I give unto the children of Israel: of every tribe of their fathers shall ye send a man, every one a ruler among them.

And Moses by the commandment of the LORD sent them from the wilderness of Paran: all those men *were* heads of the children of Israel . . .

And Moses sent them to spy out the land of Canaan, and said unto them, Get you up this *way* southward, and go up into the mountain:

And see the land, what it *is*; and the people that dwelleth therein, whether they *be* strong or weak, few or many;

And what the land *is* that they dwell in, whether it *be* good or bad; and what cities *they be* that they dwell in, whether in tents, or in strong holds;

And what the land *is*, whether it *be* fat or lean, whether there be wood therein, or not. And be ye of good courage, and bring of the fruit of the land. Now the time *was* the time of the firstripe grapes.

So they went up, and searched the land from the wilderness of Zin unto Rehob, as men come to Hamath.

—Numbers 13:1–3, 17–21

The Qur'ān on Privacy

Enter houses through the proper doors (2:189).

O you who believe! Do not enter other people's houses until you have greeted and asked leave of those who live in them (24:27).

O you who believe! Avoid too much suspicion, for suspicion is often a sin. Do not spy on each other nor speak evil behind each other's backs (49:12).

Catching Spies and How to Deal with Them:
Two Legal Views (Eighth Century)

You have asked, O Commander of the Faithful, about a man of the people of war who goes out of his country and seeks to enter the House of Islam and crosses one of the frontier posts of the Muslims, either by the road or otherwise. He is taken and says, "I have come out and I seek to go into the lands of Islam and I ask for a safe conduct for myself, my wife and my children." Or else he says, "I am an envoy." Shall he be believed or not, and what action should be taken in his case?

Abū Yūsuf said: If this man of the enemy seeks to pass our frontier post concealing himself from them, he shall not be believed and his statement shall not be accepted, but if he does not conceal himself from them he shall be believed and his statement accepted. If he says, "I am an envoy of the king, who sent me to the king of the Arabs, and this is his letter that I have with me, and the mounts and effects and slaves that I have with me are a gift to him," then he shall be believed and his statement accepted, provided that the matter is known, and that what he has with him is such as might really be, as he says, a present from the king to the king of the Arabs. Then no difficulty or impediment is placed before him, and the arms, slaves and money he has with him, except that if he has any private possessions of his own with him that he is bringing for trade, he must pay a tithe on them when he passes the customs collector. No tithe is collected from an envoy sent by the king of the Greeks nor from one to whom safe conduct has already been given, except on what they bring by way of merchandise. Their other effects are free from tithe.

If this enemy says on arrest, "I left my country and came here to adopt Islam," this is not to be believed, and he is booty for the Muslims unless he really accepts Islam. Concerning him the Muslims have a choice. If they wish they may kill him, and if they wish they may enslave him. If, when he is brought forward for decapitation, he says, "I believe in your religion and I testify that there is no God but God and I testify that Muḥammad is the Prophet of God," his conversion saves his life. His property remains booty, but he is not killed. . . .

You have asked, O Commander of the Faithful, concerning captured spies, who may be Dhimmīs, enemies or Muslims. If they are enemies or Dhimmīs subject to poll-tax, whether Jews or Christians or Magians, have them beheaded. If they are known Muslims, punish them severely and keep them in prison a long time, until they show penitence.

Abū Yūsuf said, It is proper for the caliph to establish frontier posts at those places where the roads enter the lands of the polytheists, and to inspect all merchants who pass them. If anyone carries arms, they shall be confiscated and he shall be sent back. Whoever brings slaves shall be sent back. If one has letters with him, his letters shall be read, and if any letters contain reports on the affairs of the Muslims, their bearer shall be arrested and sent to the Imam, who will decide what to do.

—Abū Yūsuf Ya‘qūb

If the Muslims find a man who claims to be a Muslim acting as a spy for the polytheists against the Muslims and writing reports on their secrets to them, and he confesses this voluntarily, he shall not be killed, but the caliph shall punish him suitably. Likewise, if a *dhimmī* [protected non-Muslim subject] does this, he shall be punished severely and put in prison, but shall not thereby forfeit his status as a *dhimmī*. Nor shall a *musta'min* [a holder of an *amān,* or safe-conduct] among us who does this, but he shall be suitably punished for everything.

But if, when he asked for the *amān,* the Muslims said to him, "We give you *amān* on condition that you do not spy on the Muslims for the polytheists" or "We give you *amān,* on condition that it ceases to be valid if you report on the secrets of the Muslims to the people of war," then the case is dealt with accordingly, and there is no objection to killing him. And if the imam decides to crucify him as an example to others, there is no objection to that. If he decides to treat him as booty [i.e., enslave him], that also is permissible, as with other prisoners. But it is better to kill him as an example to others.

If it is a woman instead of a man, there is no objection to killing her either, but it is preferable not to crucify her.

If they catch a youth under age in these circumstances, he shall be made booty and shall not be killed.

An old man who cannot fight but is of sound mind is in the same position as a woman.

If the *musta'min* denies that he has done this, and says, "The letter that they found on me was one I found on the way and picked up," then the Muslims may not kill him without proof. If they threaten him with shackles or beatings or imprisonment until he confesses that he is a spy, then this confession is null and void. He can be convicted as a spy only by his own voluntary confession or by the testimonies of two public witnesses. In this matter, the testimony of *dhimmi*s or enemy subjects may be accepted against him.

If the imam finds, on a Muslim or a *dhimmi* or a *musta'min,* a letter in his handwriting, and known as such, addressed to the king of the people of war, informing him, he shall not beat him in this case; but he shall imprison him for the protection of the Muslims until his affair is made clear. If it is not made clear, he shall be released and deported to the House of War, and the imam shall not allow him to reside after this in the House of Islam for a single day.

—Al-Shaybānī

A Pilgrim's Progress (721–27)

Willibald's party had now increased to eight in number, and they became an object of suspicion to the Saracens, who, seeing that they were strangers, seized them and threw them into prison, because they know not of what country they were and supposed them to be spies.

—Willibald (translated by Thomas Wright)

Advice to Kings on How to Use Spies

Iraq (Ninth Century)

The king must distinguish between his friends and his enemies, by seeking to know their secrets and even their most trivial actions, to such a degree that if possible, he should find out where and how each of them spends the night and the siesta.

The people will not respect the king in their hearts, even if both jinn and men worship him and the kings of the nations seek his friendship, unless he is more diligent in looking after his subjects and in knowing their inmost thoughts than the mother of an only child watching his every action and inaction.

—Al-Jāḥiẓ (attributed)

Iran (Eleventh Century)

Spies must always go to all parts, disguised as merchants, travelers, Sufis, medicine-sellers, or beggars and report on all that they hear, so that nothing may remain hidden and so that if anything happens it may be dealt with in time. For it has often happened that governors, fief holders, officers, and commanders have plotted mutiny and rebellion and intended mischief against the king, but a spy came and informed the king, who at once mounted his horse and set out, took them by surprise, captured them, and brought their plans to nothing. Likewise if a foreign king and army were preparing to invade the country, he did his work and they were repelled.

Spies also reported news, good and bad, about the subjects, and kings attended to them.

—Niẓām al-Mulk (translated by Hubert Darke)

Egypt (Fourteenth–Fifteenth Centuries)

[Espionage] is an important part of the basis of kingship and a pillar of the kingdom. The head of Chancery is the pivot of espionage, and it is his task to run it and to choose and assign its men. He must be very careful concerning spies, even more than in the matter of couriers and envoys, for envoys are sent to both friends and enemies, while spies are only sent to enemies. . . .

Certain conditions are laid down concerning a spy.

1.   That it should be possible to trust both his advice and his truthfulness, since the reports of one who is suspect are useless even when he speaks truth. . . .

2.   That he should be a man of sound instincts and good judgment, so that he may attain knowledge of the enemy through both intelligence and intuition. . . .

3.   That he should be shrewd and resourceful and capable of deceit. . . .

4.   That he should be well informed concerning the routes and lands to which he is sent, not needing to ask questions about them and about their people, since such questions might give him away.

5.   That he should know the language of the country to which he is sent. . . .

6.   That he should have the endurance to stand whatever may be inflicted on him.

—Al-Qalqashandī

USA (1997)

Western women can often loosen the lips, if not gain the confidence, of even devout Muslim males more quickly than Western men. Journalists . . . women not scared to project their femininity in the company of Muslim men, can gain impressive access in Iran and throughout the Muslim world. Talent aside, that access is in part due to their sex. They would very likely not be allowed as deep inside a Muslim man's mind as an equally talented male observer, but they'd get through the heavily guarded front gate more quickly than even the most intrepid, clever, or duplicitous male colleague.

I'd always thought women case officers should be used against Muslim volunteers, men who would offer their services at U.S. embassies and consulates abroad. . . .

A Western woman can turn a Muslim man topsy-turvy by her walk, hair, dress, and lips, while doing virtually nothing. The sensual stimulation can cause him to believe his words with a dreamworld woman don't really count. Perhaps for the first time in his life, he can tell the truth without penalty. What a woman case officer lacks in authority—and no woman, no matter how strong or ugly, can command the physical authority of any man in a Muslim's eyes—she makes up for through disorienting allure.

I never thought this female magic had a long life: the more contact between a Muslim and a Western female, the more the rules returned. And even if an American woman case officer did her best to act like a man, a sense of embarrassment would still start to replace the thrill in a protracted nonsexual relationship with an all-powerful Western woman. But as a general rule, if an Islamic fundamentalist walked into a U.S. embassy, I'd rather have a five-foot-ten Arabic-speaking blond debrief him than one of the Near East Division's ex-military khaki-clad Arabists.

—Edward Shirley

Ottoman Advances and Retreat

The Battle of Lepanto (1571)

In 1571 a Spanish fleet, with papal and Venetian contingents, won a major naval victory over the Turks near the entrance of the Gulf of Corinth, known at that time as the Gulf of Lepanto. The victory gave rise to a wave of exultation all over Christendom, and in Turkish annals is known simply as sıngın—*the rout. In fact, it made very little difference to the real balance of power in southeastern Europe and the Mediterranean. The Turkish armies remained dominant on land; the Turkish fleets were swiftly rebuilt. When the sultan expressed concern about the cost, his grand vizier replied: "The might of our empire is such that if we wished to equip the entire fleet with silver anchors, silken rigging and satin sails, we could do it."*

The following consists of selections from a celebratory poem composed by the king of Scotland, probably in 1585, and excerpts from two Turkish imperial orders.

I sing a wondrous worke of God,
I sing his mercies great,
I sing his justice heere-withall
Powr'ed from his holy seat.
To wit a cruell Martiall warre,
A bloodie battell bolde,
Long doubtsome fight, with slaughter huge
And wounded manifold.
Which fought was in Lepantoes gulfe
Betwixt the baptiz'd race,
And circumsised Turband Turkes
Rencountring in that place. . . .

Then Ali-Basha visied all
With bolde and manly face
Whose tongue did utter courage more
Then had alluring grace:
He did recount amongst the rest
What victorie Turks obtained
On catife Christians, and how long
The Ottomans race had raigned.
He told them als, how long themselves
Had ever victours bene. . . .

The clinkes of swords, the rattle of Pikes,
The whirre of arrows light,
The howles of hurt, the Captaines cryes
In vaine do what they might,
The cracks of Gallies broken and bruzd,
Of Gunns the rumbling beire
Resounded so, that though the Lord
Had thundered none could heare.
The Sea was vernished red with blood,
And fishes poysond all,
As Iehova by Moses rod
In Aegipt made befall.
This cruell fight continued thus
Uncertaine all the while,
For Fortune oft on either side,
Did frowne and after smile. . . .

In end, when they with blood abroad
Had bought their meeting deare,
The victorie first on Spanish side
Began for to appeare:
For even the Spanish Prince himselfe
Did hazard at the last,
Accompanied with boldest men,
Who followed on him fast,
By force to winne the Turquish decks,
The which he did obtaine,
And entered in their Galley syne
But did not long remaine:
For Ali-Basha proov'd so well
With his assisters brave,
That backward faster than they came
Their valiant foes they drave,
That glad they were to scape themselves,
And leave behind anew
Of valiant fellowes carcases,
Whom thus their enemies slew
The Generall boldned then with spite,
And vernisht red with shame
Did rather chuse to leese his life
Then tine his spreading fame:. . . .

Praise him with Trumpet, Piphre, and drumme,
With Lutes, and Organes fine,
With viols, Gitterns, Cistiers als
And sweetest voices syne:
Sing praise, sing praise both younge and olde,
Sing praises one and al,
To him who hath redeemd us now,
From cruell Pagans thrall.

—James VI of Scotland, later James I of England

Turkish Orders After Lepanto (1571)

4 Jumada II 979 A.H. [October 24, 1571]. Order to the Vizier Ahmed Pasha:

Ali, now governor-general of Algiers, sent a letter on 18 Jumada I to our Sublime Porte. He informed us that the imperial fleet encountered the fleet of the wretched infidels, and that the will of God turned away.

8 Jumada II order to Pertev Pasha*:

A battle can be won or lost. It was destined to happen this way according to God's will.

—Ottoman Imperial Firmans

The Struggle for the Heart of Europe

In 1529 the Ottoman armies advancing through southeastern Europe reached Vienna and laid siege to the Austrian capital, inaugurating a century and a half of stalemate in Hungary and the Yugoslav lands. It ended with the second Turkish siege of Vienna in 1683, this time a crushing defeat. The first of the following two passages, by an Ottoman historian, describes border warfare between the Austrian and Ottoman empires; the second, by an English writer, enumerates the spoils of war taken by the Austrians and their allies from the Turks.

Skirmishes in Bosnia and Croatia (1592–93)

Mustafa Páshá, when he was commander in the Sanjak of Kilis, was in the habit of committing depredations on the frontiers of the infidels' dominions; and this also provoked the Germans and Croatians to cross their respective boundaries, and to commit atrocities against the Osmanlis. The Beglergeg of Bosnia, Hasan Páshá, entered the country of the Croatians, as we have already observed, and erected two fortresses there, which he named Novograde. On one or two occasions he succeeded in defeating the infidels, and thus acquired some considerable degree of glory. When he communicated this intelligence to the Ottoman court, he stated at the same time, that if the enemy should assemble in greater numbers in future, the Bosnian troops alone would not be able to cope with them, and therefore requested that the troops of Romeili [Rumeli, i.e. land of Rum: the Ottoman name for the European provinces of the Empire] might be sent to his aid. The former grand vezír, Síávúsh Páshá, conferred on a relative of his own, Kirli Hasan Páshá, the government of Romeili, and appointed him to afford the aid which Hasan Páshá deemed necessary. When Kirli Hasan Páshá, with his Romeilian troops, reached the Sanjak of Serim, he learned that Sinán Páshá had been created grand vezír. It is necessary to observe here, however, that when Sinán Páshá was formerly grand vezír, the váli of Bosnia, Hasan Páshá, gave him his house in Constantinople, but the Páshá refused to give

---

* Commander of the Ottoman naval forces.

The Battle of Mohacs, August 29–30, 1526: the decisive Ottoman victory over the Hungarians that opened the struggle for the heart of Europe. It would end with the second Turkish siege of Vienna a century and a half later. From the Suleymanname of Arifi, 1558.

it back when he was deposed. The circumstance of Hasan's seeking back his house offended Sinán Páshá and put him into a complete rage.

About the end of the Ramazan of this year Kirli Hasan Páshá was translated to the vezírship of Temisvar, and his son, Mohammed Páshá, was made governor of Romeili in his father's stead.

Hasan Páshá, proud of the succours he had reason to anticipate, and in addition to his eruptions for the last two years, in violation of the existing treaty of peace, went and besieged a fortress called Siska, in the enemy's country. The infernal infidels, in consequence of this infringement of the peace by Hasan Páshá, collected an immense army, the command of which was given to the accursed wretch, Zerín Oghlí, ruler of Katpaz. With this mighty army, furnished with all sorts of apparatus of war, he marched to the frontiers of Bosnia.

Hasan Páshá, in the mean time, becoming hopeless as to the aid which had been promised him, and not suspecting that the enemy was on his march to attack him, threw two bridges over the Kupa, near Yení Hisár, and marched over into Croatia. Hearing of the movements of the enemy, he hastened to prepare to give them battle, although he had only about ten thousand Bosnians under his command. Being a very brave and fearless man, he acquired very great glory by his skill in military tactics on this occasion.

The enemy having asked assistance from Maximilian, brother of the Emperor of Austria, received a large augmentation of forces, raised by the great princes of Germany, and thus became much more formidable. This vast multitude, many of whom were covered with steel, resembled the raging waves of the sea. The brave and veteran Páshá resolved on encountering the enemy, and commanded Ghází Khója Mimí Beg, father of Serkhúsh Ibrahim Páshá, celebrated in war, to cross the river and reconnoitre the enemy. He did so; and when he returned, he assured Hasan Páshá that it would be altogether ruinous to give battle to so superior a force as the enemy possessed. When Ibrahim delivered this disheartening report Hasan happened to be playing at chess, and, after hearing him patiently to the end of his tale, said, with a stern voice, "Curse you, you despicable wretch! to be afraid of numbers: out of my sight!" and immediately mounted his horse, passed his troops across the bridges he had before erected, and prepared for the conflict, which was not long in commencing. The infidels gained, at the very commencement, an evident advantage; which Zerín Oghlí no sooner perceived that he gave orders for a general assault, which proved fatal to the Osmanlis. The Páshá of Kilis, Sultán Zádeh Mustafa Páshá, mentioned above, perished. The troops of Izvernick were routed: those of Usk fell into confusion and were repulsed; but the veteran troops of Novo, well skilled in the use of muskets, maintained their ground for a while, slew a great number of the opposing káfirs; but the son of Zerín, by an artful manœuvre, succeeded in driving them back, and cut them to pieces. The Moslems were now obliged to retreat to their bridges, when a most terrible conflict ensued, in which the Khója Ghází Mimí Beg perished. The brave Hasan Páshá himself also met with his fate, having fallen into the river with one of the bridges, which had been cut to prevent the pursuit of the enemy. Such was the result of this terrible day. Though Hasan had acted throughout with the utmost skill, and had fought with unequaled bravery; though his military prudence had never forsaken him, yet such was the immense superiority of the enemy's forces, augmented besides by forty thousand Germans, that it does not appear surprising that the Moslems were defeated. Eight thousand Moslems fell or were drowned. The nephew of Rustem Páshá, Mohammad Beg, and three other Sanjak princes, perished along with Hasan Páshá in the river at the falling of the bridge. The victorious infidels retired from the field of battle in triumph.

When intelligence of this unfortunate day reached the court of Constantinople, the ocean-like zeal of the emperor was stirred up within him, and at once led him to determine to prosecute the war with vigour and without delay.

—Naima (translated by George Fraser)

Spoils of War (1683)

After the defeat and withdrawal of the Turkish army besieging Vienna.

The Emperor . . . surveyed the Batteries, Trenches and Approaches of the Enemy, and saw the Stores of Ammunition and Provisions which they had left behind them . . . the List and Account of which were as followeth:

Six thousand five Hundred Tents, four Thousand five Hundred Barrels of Powder, six Thousand weight of Lead, 20,000 Granado Shells, eight Thousand Hand-granadoes, 11,000 Shovels and Pickaxes, one Thousand six Hundred weight of Match, two Thousand five Hundred Fire-balls, 52 Hundred weight of Pitch, eleven Hundred weight of Oyl of Petrolium and of Tar, and five Hundred Thousand of Lincet-oyl, Ninety-five Hundred of Salt-peter, five Thousand on Hundred Pieces of coarse Linnen, two Hundred Thousand Hair Sacks for carrying Earth and Sand, eight one Hundred weight of Barrs of Iron and Horse-shoes, an Hundred Ladles for melting Pitch, two Hundred weight of Pack-thread, and Thongs made of Camels Hides, two Thousand Halberts, four Hundred Scythes and Scycles, five Hundred and sixty Barrels of Guns for use of the Janisaries, Fifty two Sacks of Cotton and Cotton-yarn, one Thousand five Hundred Woolsacks empty, two Thousand Plates of Iron for covering Targets, an Hundred and twenty three Hundred weight of Greese and Tallow, two Hundred thirty Power-horns, two Thousand six Hundred Raggs for Powder; four pair of Smith's Bellows for a Forge, twenty one instruments, or Engines for raising Carts when overturned, eight Thousand Carts for carrying Ammunition and Pro-visions, all empty, one Thousand great Bombs, eighteen Thousand Cannon-bullets, great and small, an Hundred and ten Pieces of Cannon of all sorts, as Culverin, Demiculverin, demy and whole Cannon, Sakers, etc. thirteen Mortar-pieces, mounted for shooting Bombs, six great Anvils, diverse Sacks for use of the Ordnance, and many Ladders made of Cords. All which, as we have said, were carried into Vienna, and laid up amongst the Stores of the Arsenal.

—Sir Paul Rycaut

Modernizing the Ottoman Army: A European View (1757)

They will probably persist in their errors for some time, and submit to be re-peatedly defeated for years, before they will be reconciled to such a change;

so reluctant are all nations, whether it proceeds from self-love, laziness, or folly, to relinquish old customs: even good institutions make their progress but slowly amongst us, for we are grown so incorrigible in our prejudices, that such, whose utility is confirmed by the whole world, are, notwithstanding, frequently rejected by us; and then, to vindicate our exceptions upon every such occasion, we only say *'tis contrary to custom.* . . .

. . . The Turks are now an instance of the same; for it is neither in courage, numbers nor riches, but in discipline and order, that they are defective.

—Count Maurice de Saxe

General Bonaparte in Egypt (1798–1801)

In 1798 a French expeditionary force, commanded by General Napoléon Bonaparte, invaded Egypt, then governed by the Mamluks under Ottoman suzerainty. They defeated both the Mamluks and the Ottomans but in 1801 were forced to leave by a British naval squadron commanded by Admiral Horatio Nelson. The first of the following passages comes from Napoléon's recollections, dictated during his exile in St. Helena; the second is the eyewitness account of an Egyptian historian of the time.

Why Egypt?

Several campaign plans were discussed for the year 1798. There was talk of a landing in England, with punts sailing from Calais under the protection of a combined operation of French and Spanish squadrons. But the preparations would have cost a hundred million, and the disordered financial situation left no hope of this. Anyway, an invasion of England would have required the main French forces; this would have been premature, given the disturbed situation still prevailing on the continent.

The government adopted the plan of keeping 150,000 men encamped on the channel coast, threatening England with imminent invasion but in fact ready to move to the Rhine if necessary, while two small armies, of 30,000 men each, would take the offensive. One would be embarked on the Brest squadron and make a landing in Ireland, where 100,000 insurgents awaited them; the other would operate in the East, crossing the Mediterranean which was controlled by the Toulon squadron. The British establishments in India would be shaken by this. Tippoo Sahib, the Mahrattas, the Sikhs were just waiting for a signal. Napoléon was seen as necessary to the army of the East. Egypt, Syria, Arabia, Iraq were waiting for a man.

The Turkish government had fallen into decrepitude. The results of this expedition might be as vast as the luck and genius of the chief who would direct it.

Napoléon Addresses the Troops, May 9, 1798, Toulon

Soldiers, you are one of the wings of the army against England. . . . The
Roman legions, whom you have imitated but not yet equalled, fought
Carthage on this same sea and on the plains of Zama. . . . Europe has its eyes
on you . . . you have great destinies to fulfill!

After the occupation of Cairo comes a threat, a promise and an entreaty.

[General] Berthier posted a proclamation in the city in French, Arabic and
Turkish, and distributed many copies: "Kadis, Shaykhs, Ulema, Imams,
Chorbajis, people of Egypt! For long enough the Beys have insulted
Egypt; the time has come to punish them. God, on Whom all depends,
has said: The reign of the Mamluks has ended. You will be told that I
come to destroy the religion of Islam: answer that I love the Prophet and
the Qur'ān, that I come to restore your rights to you. Throughout the centuries, we have been the friends of the great sultan. Thrice happy those
who join us! Happy those who stay neutral. They will have the time to get
to know us. Misfortune to the fools who take arms against us! They will
perish.

—Napoléon Bonaparte

The French in Cairo:
A Contemporary Egyptian View (1799–1801)

Friday, 15 Shawwāl 1213 [March 22, 1799]

Auxiliary policemen went around the markets, the baths and the cafés, forbidding the people to say bad things about the French. They said, "Let all
those who believe in God and the Prophet and the Last Day desist and re-
nounce all remarks that could arouse hatred." If, they said, the commandant
was told by one of his informants that someone had made hostile remarks,
he would order them to give him the bastinado or even to put him to death.
But people did not stop talking. Some may even have been arrested for this,
beaten and put to death. . . .

Monday, 22 Jumāda II 1215 [November 17, 1800]

A man came to the council to ask for help for his family on behalf of his son, whom a French guard had arrested and thrown into jail. This man was an oil merchant. What happened is this: A woman had come asking to buy butter. The merchant replied that he did not sell butter. The woman insisted to the point of annoying the merchant and said to him, "You have butter, but you are keeping it for the Ottomans!" She said this by way of a joke, and the merchant responded, "Just so, to spite you and the French." This remark was repeated by a boy who was with her, and the merchant was brought to the prefect, who had him questioned and jailed. The father of the merchant pleaded and said he was afraid that they would kill him. The French inspector replied, "No, we do not kill for a witticism. Rest assured, the French do not commit such injustices." The following day this man was put to death with four others, for what offense it is not known.

17 Dhu'l-Hijja 1215 [May 1, 1801]

The French react to the news that the Ottoman forces, with British support, have reentered Egypt. Four months later, the French evacuated their troops.

A meeting was held of the treasurer, the inspector, [various named officials and Egyptian merchants] and the interpreter. The treasurer Estève spoke and the interpreter translated: "Commanding General Menou sends you his greetings and warm congratulations. These events will pass, please God, and all will turn out well. The people of Egypt will find their happiness. Many of the English have died. The survivors are stricken with ophthalmia and dysentery. Some of them even surrendered to the French, driven by hunger and thirst. You should know that the French were not forced to evacuate Rosetta but did so for a precise purpose. The same is true of Damietta. The enemy, seeking to occupy the whole country, was obliged to scatter his forces, and this enabled us to wipe them out. We hereby inform you that a ship from France has arrived at Alexandria, bringing us the news that a comprehensive peace has been agreed with the Coalition except for the English. They have not made peace. Their aim is to foment war and trouble in order to seize people's property. You should also know that the shaykhs detained at the Citadel and their companions are in good shape. The sole purpose of placing them under arrest was to prevent sedition and to avoid danger to them. French law provides for such measures. It cannot be opposed. To oppose it is like opposing the Qur'ān.

We have learned that the Ottoman sultan has written to instruct his troops not to attack the French, and to return. Some shameless ones rejected this order and disobeyed the sultan, continuing the war without his approval.

Some of those attending the meeting responded, "There is only one objective: peace and quiet. In our view the French are at present better than the English, since we know their ways and we know that the English have joined the Ottomans only for their own selfish interests. They are manipulating the Ottomans and deceiving them, bringing them into a dangerous situation. Then they will abandon them as they have done on other occasions."

The treasurer resumed, "The French hate falsehood. It is not known among them. You may therefore trust all the news that they bring you." One of those present added, "Only hashish smokers lie, and the French do not smoke hashish."

The treasurer Estève continued, "If the people of Cairo let themselves go and misbehave, they will be punished more severely than last year. You should know that the French will never give up Egypt. They will not leave it, since the country is now theirs and is under their rule. Even if destiny decides that they be defeated in Cairo, they will leave for upper Egypt and come back again from there. Do not think that the soldiers are only a few in number. They are of one heart, and reunited they will become great."

The conversation thus continued with remarks as false as they were futile, and those present responded accordingly.

—Al-Jabartī

The Outbreak of the Crimean War: A Contemporary Marxist View (1854)

London, March 24, 1854

War has at length been declared. The Royal Message was read yesterday in both Houses of Parliament—by Lord Aberdeen in the Lords, and by Lord J. Russell in the Commons. It describes the measures about to be taken as "active steps to oppose the encroachment of Russia upon Turkey." Tomorrow *The London Gazette* will publish the official notification of war, and on Friday the address in reply to the message will become the subject of the Parliamentary debate.

Simultaneously with the English declaration, Louis Napoléon communicated a similar message to his Senate and *Corps Législatif*.

The declaration of war against Russia could no longer be delayed after Captain Blackwood, the bearer of the Anglo-French *ultimatissimum* to the Czar, returned on Saturday last with the answer that Russia would give to that paper no answer at all. The Mission of Captain Blackwood, however, has not been altogether a gratuitous one. It had afforded to Russia the month of March, that most dangerous epoch of the year to Russian arms.

The publication of the secret correspondence between the Czar and the English Government, instead of provoking a burst of public indignation against the latter, has—*incredible dictu*—been the signal for the Press, both weekly and daily, to congratulate England on the possession of so truly national a Ministry. I understand, however, that a meeting will be called together for the purpose of opening the eyes of a blinded British public to the real conduct of the Government. It is to be held on Thursday next in the Music Hall, Store Street, and Lord Ponsonby, Mr. Layard, Mr. Urquhart, etc., are expected to take part in the proceedings. . . .

We are informed that on the 12th inst., a treaty of triple alliance was signed between France, England, and Turkey, but that, notwithstanding the personal application of the Sultan to the Grand Mufti, the latter supported by the corps of the Ulemas, refused to issue his *fetva* sanctioning the stipulation about the changes in the situation of the Christians in Turkey, as being in contradiction to the precepts of the Koran. This intelligence must be looked upon as being most important, as it caused Lord Derby to make the following observation:

"I will only express my earnest anxiety that the Government will state whether there is any truth in the report that has been circulating during the last few days, that in this convention entered between England, France and Turkey, there are articles which will be of a nature to establish a protectorate on our part as objectionable at least, as that which, on the part of Russia, we have protested against."

The Times of to-day, while declaring that the policy of the Government is directly opposed to that of Lord Derby, adds: "We should deeply regret if the bigotry of the Mufti or Ulemas succeeded in opposing any serious resistance to policy."

In order to understand both the nature of the relations between the Turkish Government and the spiritual authorities of Turkey, and the difficulties in which the former is at present involved with respect to the question of a protectorate over the Christian subjects of the Porte, that question which ostensibly lies at the bottom of all the actual complications in the East, it is necessary to cast a retrospective glance at its past history and development.

The Koran and the Mussulman legislation emanating from it reduce the geography and ethnography of the various peoples to the simple and convenient distinction of two nations and of two countries; those of the Faithful and of the Infidels. The Infidel is *"harby,"* i.e., the enemy. Islamism proscribes the nation of the Infidels, constituting a state of permanent hostility between the Mussulman and the unbeliever. In that sense the corsair ships of the Berber States were the holy fleet of Islam. How, then, is the existence of Christian subjects of the Porte to be reconciled with the Koran?

"If a town," says the Mussulman legislation, "surrenders by capitulation, and its habitants consent to become rayahs, that is, subjects of a Mussulman prince without abandoning their creed, they have to pay the *kharatch* (capitation tax), when they obtain a truce with the faithful, and it is not permitted any more to confiscate their estates than to take away their houses. . . .

Constantinople having surrendered by capitulation, as in like manner the greater portion of European Turkey, the Christians there enjoy the privileges of living as *rayahs,* under the Turkish Government. This privilege they have, exclusively by virtue of their agreeing to accept the Mussulman protection. It is, therefore, owing to this circumstance alone that the Christians submit to be governed by the Mussulmans, according to Mussulman law, that the Patriarch of Constantinople, their spiritual chief, is at the same time their political representative, and their Chief Justice. Wherever, in the Ottoman Empire, we find an agglomeration of Greek *rayahs,* the Archbishops and Bishops are by law members of the Municipal Councils, and, under the direction of the Patriarch, rule over the repartition of the taxes imposed upon the Greeks. The Patriarch is responsible to the Porte as to the conduct of his co-religionists. . . .

As the Koran treats all foreigners as foes, nobody will dare to present himself in a Mussulman country without having taken his precautions. The first European merchants, therefore, who risked the chances of commerce with such a people, contrived to secure themselves an exceptional treatment and privileges originally personal but afterwards extended to their whole nation. Hence the origin of capitulations. Capitulations are imperial diplomas, letters of privilege, granted by the Porte to different European nations, and authorizing their subjects to freely enter Mohammedan countries, and there to pursue in tranquility their affairs, and to practice their worship. They differ from treaties in this essential point, that they are not reciprocal acts, contradictorily debated between the contracting parties, and accepted by them on the condition of mutual advantages and concessions. On the contrary, the capitulations are one-sided concessions on the part of the Government granting them, in consequence of which they may be revoked at its pleasure. The Porte, has, indeed, at different times nullified the privileges granted to one nation by extending them to others, or repealed them altogether by refusing to continue their application. This precarious character of the capitulations made them an eternal source of dispute, of complaints on the part of Ambassadors, and of a prodigious exchange of contradictory notes and firmans revived at the commencement of every new reign.

It was from these capitulations that arose the right of a *protectorate* of foreign Powers, not over the Christian subjects of the Porte—the rayahs—but over their co-religionists visiting Turkey, or residing there as foreigners. The first Power that obtained such a protectorate was France. The capitulations between France and the Ottoman Porte made in 1535 under Suliman the Great and Francis I; in 1604 under Ahmet I and Henry IV; and in 1673 under Mustapha II and Louis XIV, were renewed, confirmed, recapitulated, and augmented in the compilation of 1740, called "ancient and recent capitulations and treaties between the Court of France and the Ottoman Porte, renewed and augmented in the year A.D. 1740 and 1153 of the Hedgra, translated (the first official translation sanctioned by the Porte) at Constantinople by M. Devel, Secretary Interpreter of the King, and his first Dragoman at the Ottoman Porte." Art. 32 of this agreement constitutes the right of France to a protectorate over all monasteries professing the French religion, to whatever nation they may belong, and over the Frank visitors to the Holy Places.

Russia was the first power that, in 1774, inserted the capitulation, imitated after the example of France, into a treaty, the Treaty of Kainardji. Thus, in 1802, Napoléon thought fit to make the existence and maintenance of the capitulation the subject of an article of treaty, and to give it the character of synallagmatic contract. . . .

Parts of the Holy Places and of the Church of the Holy Sepulchre are possessed by the Latins, the Greeks, the Armenians, the Abyssinians, the Syrians, and the Copts. Between these diverse pretendants there originated a conflict. The sovereigns of Europe, who saw in this religious quarrel a question of their respective influence in the Orient, addressed themselves in the first instance to the masters of the soil, to fanatic and greedy pashas, who abused their position. The Ottoman Porte and its agents adopting a most troublesome *système de bascule,* gave judgment in turn favorable to the Latins, Greeks, and Armenians, asking and receiving gold from all hands, and laughing at each of them. Hardly had the Turks granted a firman, acknowledging the right of the Latins to the possession of a contested place, when the Armenians presented themselves with a heavier purse, and instantly obtained a contradictory firman. The same tactics with respect to the Greeks, who knew, besides, as officially recorded in different firmans of the

Porte and "hudjets" (judgments) of its agents, how to procure false and apocryphal titles. On other occasions the decision of the Sultan's Government were frustrated by the cupidity and ill-will of the pashas and subaltern agents in Syria. Then it became necessary to resume negotiations, to appoint fresh commissaries, and to make new sacrifices of money. What the Porte formerly did from pecuniary considerations, in our days it has done from fear, with a view to obtain protection and favour. Having done justice to the reclamations of France and the Latins, it hastened to grant the same conditions to Russia and the Greeks, thus attempting to escape from a storm which it felt powerless to encounter. There is no sanctuary, no chapel, no stone of the Church of the Holy Sepulchre, that has been left unturned for the purpose of constituting a quarrel between the different Christian communities.

Around the Holy Sepulchre we find an assemblage of all the various sects of Christianity, behind the religious pretensions of whom are concealed as many political and national rivalries.

Jerusalem and the Holy Places are inhabited by nations professing different religions: the Latins, the Greeks, the Armenians, Copts, Abyssinians, and Syrians. There are 2,000 Greeks, 1,000 Latins, 350 Armenians, 100 Copts, 20 Syrians, and 20 Abyssinians—3,490. In the Ottoman Empire we find 13,730,000 Greeks, 2,400,000 Armenians, and 900,000 Latins. Each of these is again sub-divided. The Greek Church, of which I treated above, the one acknowledging the Patriarch of Constantinople, essentially differs from the Greco-Russian, whose chief spiritual authority is the Czar, and from the Hellenes, for whom the King and the Synod of Athens are the chief authorities. Similarly, the Latins are sub-divided into the Roman Catholics, United Greeks, and Maronites; and the Armenians into Gregorian and Latin Armenians—the same distinction holding good with the Copts and Abyssinians. The three prevailing religious nationalities at the Holy Places are the Greeks, the Latins, and the Armenians. The Latin Church may be said to represent principally Latin races; the Greek Church, Slav, Turko-Slav, and Hellenic races; and the other Churches, Asiatic and African races.

Imagine all these conflicting peoples beleaguering the Holy Sepulchre, the battle conducted by the monks, and the ostensible object of their rivalry being a star from the grotto of Bethlehem, a tapestry, a key of a sanctuary, and altar, a shrine, a chair, a cushion—any ridiculous precedence!

In order to understand such a monastical crusade, it is indispensable to consider, firstly, the manner of their living, and secondly, the mode of their habitation. . . .

Besides their monasteries and sanctuaries, the Christian nations possess at Jerusalem small habitations or cells, annexed to the Church of the Holy Sepulchre, and occupied by the monks who have to watch day and night that holy abode. At certain periods these monks are relieved in their duty by their brethren. These cells have but one door, opening into the interior of the Temple, while the monk guardians receive their food from without, through some wicket. The doors of the church are closed, and guarded by Turks, who do not open them except for money, and close them according to their caprice or cupidity.

The quarrels between Churchmen are the most venomous, said Mazarin. Now fancy these churchmen, who not only have to live upon but live in, these sanctuaries together!

To finish the picture, be it remembered that the fathers of the Latin Church, almost exclusively composed of Romans, Sardinians, Neapolitans, Spaniards, and Austrians, are all of them jealous of the French Protectorate, and would like to substitute that of Austria, Sardinia, or Naples, the kings of the two latter countries both assuming the title of King of Jerusalem, and that the sedentary population of Jerusalem numbers about 15,300 souls, of whom 4,000 are Mussulman and 8,000 Jews. The Mussulman, forming about a fourth part of the whole, and consisting of Turks, Arabs, and Moors, are, of course, the masters in every respect, as they are in no way affected by the weakness of their Government at Constantinople. Nothing equals the misery and the suffering of the Jews at Jerusalem, inhabiting the most filthy quarter of the town, called *hareth-el-yahoud,* in the quarter of dirt, between the Zion and the Moriah, where their synagogues are situated—the constant objects of Mussulman oppression and intolerance, insulted by the Greeks, persecuted by the Latins, and living only upon the scanty alms transmitted by their European brethren. . . .

To make these Jews more miserable, England and Prussia appointed, in 1840, an Anglican bishop at Jerusalem, whose avowed object is their conversion. He was dreadfully thrashed in 1845, and sneered at alike by Jews, Christians and Turks. He may, in fact, be stated to have been the first and only cause of a union between all the religions at Jerusalem.

It will now be understood that the common worship of the Christians at the Holy Places resolves itself into a continuance of desperate Irish rows between the diverse sections of the faithful; that, on the other hand, these sacred rows merely conceal a profane battle, not only of nations but of races; and that the protectorate of the holy Places, which appears ridiculous to the Occident, but all important to the Orientals, is one of the phases of the Oriental question incessantly reproduced, constantly sniffled, but never solved.

—Karl Marx, New York *Daily Tribune,* April 15, 1854

Balance of Power in Central Asia:
A View from London (1873–74)

12 June 1873

Talk about the Shah's visit: Lord Lawrence says from what he knows of orientals, he does not believe in any result following from their seeing European civilisation: it merely puzzles them: it is odd and new and that is all. . . .

17 December 1874

I have been seriously considering the question whether or not it will be expedient to protest against the advance of the Russians to the line of the Atrek, which the Persian govt desires. My decision is against it, for various reasons. The protest will be useless; nothing can come of it unless we were prepared to back up our words by acts, which in such a matter we are not; the Persians are not to be trusted as allies, any prospect of momentary advantage, or a bribe offered to their statesmen, would induce them to throw us over while we were engaged in fighting their battles: and on the question of right it is not easy to say that the Russians may not be justified in occupying a desert tract, inhabited only by wandering tribes, who own no allegiance, and live by plunder. The Persian territory is neither attacked nor threatened: and we are in no way pledged to protect the independence of nomad Turcoman hordes.

—Lord Derby

The First World War and the Arab Rising

In 1914 the Ottoman Empire, the last of the greatest Islamic monarchies, was still a major power, and fought as such, on several fronts, against the might of both the Russian and British empires. Egypt, though technically under Ottoman suzerainty, had for some time been under British occupation. After the failure of an Ottoman military attempt to end that occupation and restore Egypt to Ottoman rule, the British counterattacked and

*were able, with assistance from Arab rebels against Ottoman rule, to con-
quer Palestine and most of Syria. The following excerpts are principally
concerned with the Syrian campaign and the Arab rising. The first two reflect a German and a Turkish point of view—the general commanding the
German military mission to Turkey, and the commander of the Ottoman
forces in Syria. The remainder deal with the enigmatic figure of T. E.
Lawrence, containing excerpts from his own writings, and two later comments on him, chosen from among a great number. One is by an Arab historian, the other by an Englishman.*

The War in Syria:
Impressions of a German General (1918)

About May 10th I was confidentially informed that the Turkish government
intended to confer on me the internal political power in Syria.

It is proper here to cast a glance at the inner political conditions of Syria,
as otherwise it is unintelligible why the Turkish government contemplated
this step which was contrary to all of their previous principles.

The interior situation must be characterized as completely hopeless. An
orderly and reliable civil administration was a prerequisite for effective influence on the population.

Maladministration of centuries, the corruption of high and low officials
(with a few exceptions) and the total lack of discipline of the Turkish gendarmerie had brought about a state of general dissatisfaction.

The poor inhabitants, no matter of what religion, were exposed to any
license and spoliation, which were increased under wartime conditions.
This people, living in an ancient civilization and which had laid down its demands in the fifteen articles of the Beirut reform program, enjoyed fewer
rights during the war than ever.

How was an orderly administration of justice possible in a country
where not even the judges understood Arabic, the local language!

Among the mixed population of Syrians, in which the Semitic elements
predominate, there is a good deal of pure Arabic stock.

The real Syrian is a shrewd trader and an enterprising merchant. The
Christian Syrian as a rule represents the wholesale business, the Mohammedan the retail trade. The development of commerce and industry, instead of being favored and fostered by the government, was at the mercy of
the intrigues of Turkish officials unless they were bribed.

It is not surprising that by far the greater part of the people longed for orderly conditions regulated by law, such as were possible only under the protection of some European power since no Turkish promise had ever been kept. The differences between Syrians and Turks are perhaps best characterized by the Syrian adage: "Wherever a Turk sets his foot, there the earth becomes unproductive for a century."

Of course, I declined the offer of the government, transmiteed to me through Enver,* in no uncertain way, claiming that my military duties required every minute of my time. . . .

In the second half of August I was informed by Djemal Pasha, commander of the Fourth Army, that Sheríf Faisal was willing to take over the Jordan front of the Fourth Army with his troops, provided he received definite guarantees from the Turkish government that an Arabian state would be formed; that according to the statements of Faisal a great British attack was in preparation in the coast district, and that in this case the troops of the Fourth Army would become available to reenforce the front between the sea and the Jordan. Through General Kiazim, my Turkish chief of the general staff, I instructed General Djemal Pasha to open negotiations to that effect. In the same way I requested Enver to give the desired guarantees.

Neither from Enver nor from Djemal did I ever receive information, or a reply, concerning this matter. I am therefore unable to judge of the sincerity or of the scope of Faisal's offer. From the report of my Turkish chief I gained the impression that the Turks distrusted the offer and considered it merely a trick to put our Jordan positions into the hands of the Arabs, while the British main attack took place in the coast sector, or between the sea and the Jordan.

—Otto Liman von Sanders

The War in Syria: Calculations of the Ottoman Commander (1916–18)

At this time my greatest desire was to do anything and everything to prevent the revolutionary tendencies displayed by Sherif Hussein from developing and to persuade him to send an auxiliary force to Palestine under the command of one of his sons. With that end in view I conferred continuously with Sherif Faisal and conducted a very intimate correspondence with Sherif Hussein. As will be seen later . . . I had no success in spite of all my efforts, and at length, on January 2, 1916, I was faced with the fact of Sherif Hussein's rebellion.

---

* Enver Pasha, the Ottoman minister of war.

As I have already said, the policy I desired to see pursued in Syria was a policy of clemency and tolerance. I left no stone unturned to create unity of views and sentiments in all the Arab countries. . . .

As I knew that one of the most effective ways of pleasing the Arabs was to avoid requisitioning anything from them and pay for what we wanted cash down, the first order I issued on my arrival was that nothing should be taken by way of requisition from the civil population of Syria and Palestine in the 4th Army area. Prompt cash was to be paid for everything of any description whatever—food, equipment or clothing. In view of the injustice and inequality in insisting that everything must be paid for in Syria and Palestine, while food and other articles were simply requisitioned in other parts of the Empire, I recommended the Government at home to adopt the same course. . . .

As the stretch of coast between Beirut and Syria lies on no great highway, neither officers nor administrative officials were in the habit of visiting it. I myself had never thought of making a journey to that region. Thus the revolutionaries could work there quite undisturbed, and after thoroughly preparing and poisoning public opinion, they could have been assisted by a hostile force, landed at night, and have occupied the mountainous district in the interior and put in a state of defence against attack from north, east, and west.

As a matter of fact, while Abdul Kerim el Halil and Riza Bey el Sulk were fomenting disorder several not unimportant attempts on Tyre and Sidon were made by the enemy's vessels employed in watching the coast. From time to time and for no apparent reason men were landed from these ships to destroy the telegraph lines, but each time they were driven back to their ships by our gendarmes. The discovery of these traitorous activities showed the aim and purpose of the enemy's operations, and henceforth I, of course, considered it would be simply fatuous on my part to place any further trust in the reformers. I decided to take ruthless action against the traitors.

—Djemal Pasha

Lawrence Before and After

Handling Hejaz Arabs: From a Confidential British Manual (1917)

The following notes have been expressed in commandment form for clarity and to save words. They are, however, only my personal conclusions, arrived at gradually while I worked in the Hejaz and now put on paper as stalking horses for beginners in the Arab armies. They are meant to apply only to Bedu; townspeople or Syrians require totally different treatment. They are of course not suitable to any other person's need, or applicable unchanged in any particular situation. Handling Hejaz Arabs is an art, not a science, with exceptions and no obvious rules. At the same time we have a great chance there; the Sherif trusts us, and has given us the position (towards his Government) which the Germans wanted to win in Turkey. If we are tactful, we can at once retain his goodwill and carry out our job, but to succeed we have got to put into it all the interest and skill we possess.

1.   Go easy for the first few weeks. A bad start is difficult to atone for, and the Arabs form their judgments on externals that we ignore. When you have reached the inner circle in a tribe, you can do as you please with yourself and them.

2.   Learn all you can about your Ashraf* and Bedu. Get to know their families, clans and tribes, friends and enemies, wells, hills and roads. Do all this by listening and by indirect inquiry. Do not ask questions. Get to speak their dialect of Arabic, not yours. Until you can understand their allusions, avoid getting deep into conversation, or you will drop bricks. Be a little stiff at first.

3.   In matters of business deal only with the commander of the army, column, or part in which you serve. Never give orders to anyone at all, and reserve your directions of advice for the C.O., however great the temptation (for efficiency's sake) of dealing direct with his underlings. Your place is advisory, and your advice is due to the commander alone. Let him see that this is your conception of your duty, and that his is to be the sole executive of your joint plans.

4.   Win and keep the confidence of your leader. Strengthen his prestige at your expense before others when you can. Never refuse or quash schemes he may put forward; but ensure that they are put forward in the first instance privately to you. Always approve them, and after praise modify them insensibly, causing the suggestions to come from him, until they are in accord with your own opinion. When you attain this point, hold him to it, keep a tight grip of his ideas, and push him forward as firmly as possibly, but secretly, so that no one but himself (and he not too clearly) is aware of your pressure. . . .

11.   The foreigner and Christian is not a popular person in Arabia. However friendly and informal the treatment of yourself may be, remember always that your foundations are very sandy ones. Wave a Sherif in front of you like a banner and hide your own mind and person. If you succeed, you

---

* Plural of Sherif.

will have hundreds of miles of country and thousands of men under your orders, and for this it is worth bartering the outward show.

12. Cling tight to your sense of humour. You will need it every day. A dry irony is the most useful type, and repartee of a personal and not too broad character will double your influence with the chiefs. Reproof, if wrapped up in some smiling form, will carry further and last longer than the most violent speech. The power of mimicry or parody is valuable, but use it sparingly, for wit is more dignified than humour. Do not cause a laugh at a Sherif except among Sherifs. . . .

18. Disguise is not advisable. Except in special areas, let it be clearly known that you are a British officer and a Christian. At the same time, if you can wear Arab kit when with the tribes, you will acquire their trust and intimacy to a degree impossible in uniform. It is, however, dangerous and difficult. They make no special allowances for you when you dress like them. Breaches of etiquette not charged against a foreigner are not condoned to you in Arab clothes. You will be like an actor in a foreign theatre, playing a part day and night for months, without rest, and for an anxious stake. Complete success, which is when the Arabs forget your strangeness and speak naturally before you, counting you as one of themselves, is perhaps only attainable in character: while half-success (all that most of us will strive for; the other costs too much) is easier to win in British things, and you yourself will last longer, physically and mentally, in the comfort that they mean. Also then the Turks will not hang you, when you are caught.

—T. E. Lawrence

Reflections After the War (1921–22)

In these pages the history is not of the Arab movement, but of me in it. It is a narrative of daily life, mean happenings, little people. Here are no lessons for the world, no disclosures to shock peoples. It is filled with trivial things, partly that no one mistake for history the bones from which some day a man may make history, and partly for the pleasure it gave me to recall the fellowship of the revolt. We were fond together, because of the sweep of the open places, the taste of wide winds, the sunlight, and the hopes in which we worked. The morning freshness of the world-to-be intoxicated us. We were wrought up with ideas inexpressible and vaporous, but to be fought for. We lived many lives in those whirling campaigns, never sparing ourselves: yet when we achieved and the new world dawned, the old men came out again and took our victory to re-make in the likeness of the former world they knew. Youth could win, but had not learned to keep: and was pitiably weak against age. We stammered that we had worked for a new heaven and a new earth, and they thanked us kindly and made their peace.

All men dream: but not equally. Those who dream by night in the dusty recesses of their mind wake in the day to find that it was vanity; but the dreamers of the day are dangerous men, for they may act their dream with open eyes, to make it possible. This I did. I meant to make a new nation, to restore a lost influence, to give twenty millions of Semites the foundation on which to build an inspired dream-palace of their national thoughts. So high an aim called out the inherent nobility of their minds, and made them play a generous part in events: but when we won, it was charged against me that the British petrol royalties in Mesopotamia were become dubious, and French colonial policy ruined in the Levant.

I am afraid that I hope so. We pay for these things too much in honour and in innocent lives. I went up the Tigris with one hundred Devon Territorials, young, clean, delightful fellows, full of the power of happiness and of making women and children glad. By them one saw vividly how great it was to be their kin, and English. And we were casting them by thousands into the fire to the worst of deaths, not to win the war but that the corn and rice and oil of Mesopotamia might be ours. The one need was to defeat our enemies (Turkey among them), and this was at last done in the wisdom of Allenby with less than four hundred killed, by turning to our use the hands of the oppressed in Turkey. I am proudest of my thirty fights in that I did not have any of our own blood shed. All our subject provinces to me were not worth one dead Englishman. . . .

For my work on the Arab front I had determined to accept nothing. The cabinet raised the Arabs to fight for us by definite promises of self-government afterwards. Arabs believe in persons, not in institutions. They saw in me a free agent of the British government, and demanded from me an endorsement of its written promises. So I had to join the conspiracy, and, for what my word was worth, assured the men of their reward. In our two years' partnership under fire they grew accustomed to believing me and to think my Government, like myself, sincere. In this hope they performed some fine things, but, of course, instead of being proud of what we did together, I was continually and bitterly ashamed.

It was evident from the beginning that if we won the war these promises would be dead paper, and had I been an honest adviser of the Arabs I would have advised them to go home and not risk their lives fighting for such stuff: but I salved myself with the hope that, by leading these Arabs madly in the final victory I would establish them, with arms in their hands, in a position so assured (if not dominant) that expediency would counsel to the Great Powers a fair settlement of their claims. In other words, I presumed (seeing no other leader with the will and power) that I would survive the campaigns, and be able to defeat not merely the Turks on the battlefield,

but my own country and its allies in the council-chamber. It was an immodest presumption: it is not yet clear if I succeeded: but it is clear that I had no
shadow of leave to engage the Arabs, unknowing, in such hazard. I risked
the fraud, on my conviction that Arab help was necessary to our cheap and
speedy victory in the East, and that better we win and break our word than
lose. . . .

Some of the evil of my tale may have been inherent in our circumstances.
For years we have lived anyhow with one another in the naked desert,
under the indifferent heaven. By day the hot sun fermented us; and we were
dizzied by the beating wind. At night we were stained with dew, and
shamed into pettiness by the innumerable silences of the stars. We were a
self-centered army without parade or gesture, devoted to freedom, the
second of man's creeds, a purpose so ravenous that it devoured all our
strength, a hope so transcendent that our earlier ambitions faded in its glare.

—T. E. Lawrence

Lawrence and Clemenceau at the Versailles Peace Conference (1919)

Observations of a member of the British Delegation

At Paris in 1919, the French had been finding Lawrence's activities increasingly annoying. Lawrence had the ability to do any new thing that might be
required of him by his mission, which was to promote the Arab cause. His
impromptu translation of his English speech for the Council of Ten was a
case in point. Among other things, he had proved an adept at organizing
press conferences and inducing the newspapers to put things in the way he
wanted. Finally, Clemenceau complained of Lawrence to the British delegation, and the British were embarrassed. Though Lawrence was technically a
member of the Hâshimî delegation—as he signalled by wearing Arab, not
British, military uniform—the British Government could not credibly dis-
claim responsibility for him. Moreover, they themselves had already gone to
the limit of prudence in provoking the French on their own account. They
had, for instance, already pocketed the Mosul district, which, according to
the war-time agreements between the Allied Powers, had been one of those
Arab territories whose "independence" was to be under French, not British,
control. In diplomacy, possession is nine-tenths of the law, and, after the
conclusion of the Turco-British armistice, a British force had raced across

the armistice line in Iraq to Mosul while the French high commissioner designate for Mosul had been kept waiting at Basra. Eventually, Clemenceau had resigned himself to renouncing Mosul, but he could not be expected to stand much more. After all, he was "the Tiger." Accordingly, the British delegation made a show of washing their hands of Lawrence when Clemenceau announced that he was proposing to send for that young man and give him a talking-to. Lawrence's countrymen at Paris knew Lawrence well enough by now to feel sure that, even in the Tiger's jaws, he would be able to take care of himself.

The command from Clemenceau arrived, Lawrence obeyed it, and the engagement was soon over. "You know, Colonel Lawrence," said Clemenceau as his opening gambit, "you know that France has been interested in Syria ever since the Crusades." "Yes," Lawrence answered, "but the Syrians won the Crusades, and they have never forgotten that."

—Arnold J. Toynbee

The Lawrence Legend: An Arab View (1969)

Many books have been published about Lawrence, bringing him great fame in the Western world. Some of these books were translated into other languages, but although the whole Lawrence story was connected with the Arab lands and with the Arabs, we have not found any Arab author who wrote about Lawrence or offered a defense to the accusations against the Arabs raised in these writings. The only exceptions are two books published by Professer Suleymān Mūsā, one of them in Arabic and the other in English. In these he revealed the truth about Lawrence and refuted what was said by him and written about him.

The American journalist Lowell Thomas was the first who worked to spread Lawrence's fame and the first to write a book about him, entitled *With Lawrence in Arabia.* In this he depicts Lawrence as an amir among the Arabs, leading them and distributing gold among them and acting as if he were an absolute ruler, working wonders and marvels. . . .

All the writers who wrote about Lawrence drew their basic positions from what Lowell Thomas wrote about him, in the manner of fairy tales. . . .

Lawrence became famous, and his fame filled the world, but he built this fame on lies and deceit and fantasies and claims to the deeds of others. But every building which is erected on flawed foundations will collapse, and this is what happened to Lawrence. . . . He tricked the Arabs, but history tricked him and revealed his falsity.

—Ṣubḥī al-'Umarī

Mustafa Kemal, Later Surnamed Atatürk, and the Turkish War of Independence (1929)

As first lord of the Admiralty, Churchill was responsible for launching the ill-fated attack on Gallipoli in 1915. Here he surveys the hero of that rout, at the start of his campaign of 1919.

On June 9 in the little town of Kharas near Amasia, Mustapha Kemal publicly expounded his plans for the salvation of Turkey. All the half raked-out fires of Pan-Turkism began to glow again. That Greeks should conquer Turks was not a decree of Fate which any Turk would recognise. Loaded with follies, stained with crimes, rotted with misgovernment, shattered by battle, worn down by long disastrous wars, his Empire falling to pieces around him, the Turk was still alive. In his breast was beating the heart of a race that had challenged the world, and for centuries had contended victoriously against all comers. In his hands was once again the equipment of a modern army, and at his head a Captain, who with all that is learned of him, ranks with the four or five outstanding figures of the cataclysm. In the tapestried and gilded chambers of Paris were assembled the law-givers of the world. In Constantinople, under the guns of the Allied Fleets there functioned a puppet Government of Turkey. But among the stern hills and valleys of "the Turkish Homelands" in Anatolia, there dwelt that company of poor men . . . who would not see it settled so; and at their bivouac fires at this moment sat in the rags of a refugee the august Spirit of Fair Play.

—Winston S. Churchill

The Second World War and After

The Middle East was profoundly affected in many ways by the Second World War. The most important of the military engagements was the struggle in North Africa, between the Italians and later the Germans on one side, and the British and Commonwealth forces on the other. The following passages contain a French, an Italian, an Egyptian and a British view of the situation.

De Gaulle in Cairo (1941)

Towards the complexities of the Middle East I flew with simple ideas. I knew that, in a welter of intricate factors, a vital game was being played there. We therefore had to be in it. I knew that, for the Allies, the key was the Suez Canal, whose loss would lay Asia Minor and Egypt open to the Axis, but whose retention would, on the contrary, make it possible one day to act from the east westwards upon Tunisia, Italy, and the South of France. That meant that everything commanded us to be present at the battles of which the Canal was the stake. I knew that between Tripoli and Baghdad, passing through Cairo, Jerusalem, and Damascus, and between Alexandria and Nairobi, passing through Jidda, Khartoum, and Jibuti, political, racial, and religious passions and ambitions were being sharpened and drawn tenser under the excitement of the war, that France's positions there were sapped and coveted, and that there was, on any hypothesis, no chance of her keeping any of them if, for the first time in history, she remained passive when everything was in the melting pot. My duty, then, was to act, there as elsewhere, in place of those who were not doing so. . . .

Cairo, where I landed on April 1, was where the heart of the war was beating—but a shaky heart. The situation of the British and their allies there was indeed clearly unstable, not only because of military events, but also since they were on soil undermined by political currents, in the midst of populations who were watching, without taking part in, the battle between Western nations and were ready, whatever happened, to profit from the spoils of the vanquished.

These conditions gave a most complex character to the conduct of the war in the Middle East. General Wavell, the British commander-in-chief, by good fortune very highly gifted both with judgment and with coolness, moved in the midst of multiple contingencies, many of which had only an indirect relation to strategy. Besides, this strategy itself was as uneasy as could be. At the beginning of April, Wavell was carrying on a battle on three fronts painfully supplied over immensely long lines of communications.

In Libya, after handsome successes which had brought the British to the threshold of Tripolitania, it had been necessary to withdraw. Cyrenaica, except Tobruk, was about to be lost. The command, for all its value, the troops, for all their courage, had not yet finished their apprenticeship in this desert struggle, so mobile and rapid over vast spaces without cover, so exhausting with the chronic thirst and fever, under the fiery sun, in the sand, among the flies. Rommel was busy reversing fortune at the very moment when the London government was ordering Wavell to strip his battle corps by sending an important fraction of his forces to Greece. On the Hellenic front things were not going well either. It is true that the victories in Eritrea and Abyssinia brought some consolation. But alarming signs were making their appearance in the Arab countries. Iraq was growing restless. Egypt remained enigmatic. On the subject of Syria the Germans were opening disquieting dealings with Vichy. In Palestine the latent conflict between Arabs and Jews made many precautions necessary.

—Charles de Gaulle (translated by Richard Howard)

Ciano's Diary (1939–43)

Of the vast documentation on the Second World War, few accounts can compare with the diaries of Count Galeazzo Ciano in the frankness, honesty and clarity with which he reflects on the successive phases of the war. Count Ciano was an Italian statesman and fascist leader who married Mussolini's daughter in 1930 and served as foreign minister from 1936 to 1943. He was later arrested by the Germans and executed for treason by the fascist authorities in northern Italy. After his execution, his widow smuggled his diary out of Italy into Switzerland, where it was published.

May 30, 1940.   The decision has been taken. The die is cast. To-day Mussolini gave me the communication he has sent to Hitler about our entry into the war. The date chosen is June 5th, unless Hitler himself considers it convenient to postpone it for some days. . . .

August 27, 1940.   Mussolini . . . is entirely occupied with the plan of the attack on Egypt, and says that [Marshal Wilhelm] Keitel also thinks that the taking of Cairo is more important than the taking of London. Keitel has not said this to me. The attack is to take place on September 6th. . . .

September 9, 1940.   The drive against Egypt has suffered a new delay. Graziani* is doing his best to approach his objective, and is preparing to begin action on the 12th. Never has a military operation been undertaken so much against the will of the commanders. . . .

September 14, 1940.   The attack on Egypt has begun. At the moment the British are withdrawing without fighting. They wish to draw us away from our base and lengthen our lines of communication. The Duce, whose good humour has returned, considers the arrival at Mersa Matruh as a great vic-

---

* Rodolfo Graziani, 1882–1955, Italian soldier and colonial administrator. He was appointed chief of staff of the Italian army in 1939 and governor of Libya in 1940.

tory, especially since it permits our Air Force to attack Alexandria by day, with fighter escort. . . .

September 30, 1940.   I confer with the Duce. I find him in good humour and very happy that Italy could score in Egypt a success which affords her the glory she has sought in vain for three centuries. . . .

December 1, 1941.   . . . The Libyan situation has stabilized somewhat, but the British are receiving reinforcements. Cavallero* defines it as difficult but logical. God only knows what he means. Experience tells me that when generals entrench themselves behind unintelligible jargon it means that there is a fly in the ointment. . . .

I have protested to the Nuncio about the publication in the Osservatore Romano of some photographs showing that our prisoners in Egypt are having a great time—football, concerts, gaiety. Mussolini is concerned about it. "It is a known fact," he says, "that they are inclined to let themselves be taken prisoners. If they see that their comrades are having such a good time over there, who can hold them back?" . . .

May 20, 1942.   The B.B.C. gives us to understand that Rommel's preparations for his coming offensive in Libya have not escaped their notice. . . .

June 2, 1942.   The offensive in Libya has not yet taken a definite turn. On the whole, the Duce is optimistic, but at High Command Headquarters they are a little less so.

June 3, 1942.   Optimism prevails at the Palazzo Venezia on the progress of operations in Libya. The Duce talks to-day about the imminent siege of Tobruk and about the possibility of carrying the action as far as Mersa Matruh. If these are roses . . . they will bloom. . . .

June 21, 1942.   Tobruk has fallen and the British have left twenty-five thousand prisoners in our hands. This is a great success for us and opens the way for new developments. On the other hand, I learned from a conversation with [Naval Commander] Bigliardi that the results of our aerial-naval battle were a great deal more modest than had been announced. The merchant ships were, in fact, hit, and many were sunk, but the British naval losses were limited to a cruiser probably sunk and a destroyer sunk. . . .

---

* General Count Ugo Cavallero, appointed chief of the general staff of the Italian forces in December 1940.

June 24, 1942. In Libya, Rommel's action is progressing at full speed. The rosiest forecasts can now be made. . . .

June 26, 1942. Mussolini is pleased over the progress of operations in Libya but angry that the battle is identified with Rommel, thus appearing more and more as a German rather than an Italian victory. Also Rommel's promotion to Field Marshal, "which Hitler evidently made to accentuate the German character of the battle," causes the Duce much pain. Naturally, he takes it out on Graziani, "who has always been seventy feet underground in a Roman tomb at Cyrene, while Rommel knows how to lead his troops with the personal example of the general who lives in his tank." For the moment Mussolini does not make forecasts but hopes that "before fifteen days are over we can establish our commissariat in Alexandria" . . .

June 29, 1942. Mussolini has left for Libya. . . .

July 2, 1942. Mussolini telegraphs, giving instructions to get in touch with the Germans about the question of the future political government of Egypt. Rommel is to be the military commander, and an Italian is to be civilian delegate. I am asked to suggest a name. I suggest Mazzolini, who was our last Minister at Cairo. . . .

July 3, 1942. Hitler answers that he agrees so far as Rommel is concerned, but he is postponing his answer about the Italian delegate, also about German representation. At any rate, he does not consider the question "urgent." He is not wrong, because a sudden and not unforeseen British resistance compels us to mark time before El Alamein. At the G.H.Q. in Rome they are very optimistic, and convinced that the lull is altogether temporary. . . .

July 6, 1942. I have returned to Rome. There is a vague concern in the air because of the lull before El Alamein. It is feared that after the impact of the initial attack is spent Rommel cannot advance farther, and whoever stops in the desert is truly lost. It is enough to think that every drop of water must come from Mersa Matruh, over almost two hundred kilometres of road under bombardment by enemy aircraft. It is reported to me that in military circles there is violent indignation against the Germans because of their behaviour in Libya. They have grabbed all the booty. They have thrust their claws everywhere, placed German guards over the booty, and woe to anyone who comes near. The only one who has succeeded in getting plenty for himself, naturally, is Cavallero, and he has sent the goods to Italy by plane. This information is correct. It was given to me by Colonel Casero, the head of the air bureau. There is no question about it, Cavallero may not be a great strategist, but when it is a question of grabbing, he can cheat even the Germans. . . .

August 31, 1942.   Yesterday evening at eight o'clock Rommel attacked in Libya. He has chosen the day and the hour well, at a time when no one was expecting the attack and whisky had begun to appear on the English tables. Mussolini expresses no opinion, but is substantially optimistic. Cavallero, who had shown no signs of life for a long time, telephones to give me news of the operation. As usual he wavers between "yes" and "no." He does not wish to compromise himself, but intends to remain sufficiently near to gather the fruits of victory, if there are any. Churchill, according to what the Turkish Ambassador has telegraphed to his Government, has said that if Rommel had not attacked in two weeks he would have taken the initiative in the operations. He believes that the British forces are sufficient for any eventuality, but wishes to adopt a phrase used by Stalin: "Anything is possible, since war is war."

November 3, 1942.   A new and more violent British attack renders our Libyan situation very dangerous. Our forces are wearing out and supplies are arriving in minute quantities. We really seem to be condemned to fight wars overseas. . . .

November 5, 1942.   The Libyan front collapses. . . .

November 6, 1942.   The Libyan retreat is assuming more and more the character of a rout. . . .

November 12, 1942.   Rommel continues to withdraw from Libya at breakneck speed.

—Count Galeazzo Ciano (translator unknown)

Rommel at El-Alamein: An Egyptian View (1942)

El-Alamein was the site of a major battle, the first decisive Allied victory over the Axis forces. In this excerpt, a future president of Egypt reviews the situation as it affects his country.

Rommel had arrived in Libya with the German Panzer divisions. The general feeling in Egypt was against the British and, naturally, in favor of their enemies. The British knew this. In February 1942 they asked King Farouk to request el-Nahas, as leader of the parliamentary majority, to form a new government in the hope of winning over the Egyptian public opinion. When the king said no, Lord Killearn, the British ambassador, ordered British tanks to besiege the Royal Palace in Abidin. On February 4 an ultimatum was issued to the king, either to accept the British demand or to abdicate. Under that threat, the king summoned el-Nahas and asked him to form a new government.

February 4, 1942, is a date our generation cannot forget. It was on that day that Mustafa el-Nahas Pasha lost our respect. How could he agree to be imposed upon his people, literally at gunpoint, by the colonizing power? Officers assembled in Cairo and marched out to Abidin Palace to salute the king, and he came out to return their salute. We were not of course happy with King Farouk, but then he represented Egyptian sovereignty which had also been violated. The incident was humiliating alike to Egypt, army, and people. So when we heard, a few days after the Abidin Palace siege, that Lord Killearn had issued another ultimatum to the king in connection with an incident at Cairo airport which had hurt Britain's pride, we—the Free Officers—decided to take up positions around the Royal Palace and engage the British if their tanks besieged it again. I borrowed Zakaria Mohieddin's car (he was the only one of us who had a private car) and kept driving around the palace all night watching for anything unusual. But nothing happened, and I returned the car in the morning to its owner.

The general feeling against the British mounted every day. In the summer Field Marshal Rommel destroyed the British Eighth Army and reached El Alamein, 65 miles from Alexandria. Then the Egyptians gave vent to their emotions. They demonstrated in the streets, chanting slogans like "Advance Rommel!" as they saw in a British defeat the only way of getting their enemy out of the country. The British panicked and began to burn their official documents and papers, evacuating British subjects and supporters to the Sudan. With El Alamein falling into his hands, the way into Egypt lay wide before Rommel. There was no doubt at all that he would continue to advance to Alexandria, and thence to Cairo; it was only, we thought, a question of time, and a very short time too. The rumor was that Egypt would be given to Italy, and that Mussolini had actually prepared a white horse which he would ride into Cairo, just as they used to do in the days of the Roman Empire.

I called a meeting with my friends in the Free Officers' Organization. Something had to be done, I said, as we couldn't let Rommel invade Egypt unresisted. It was agreed that one of us would be sent to El Alamein to tell Rommel we were honest Egyptians who had an organization within the army; that, "like you," we were fighting against the British; that we were prepared to recruit an entire army to fight "on your side," and to provide him with photographs showing the lines and positions of the British forces in Egypt; and that we would take it upon ourselves not to let one British soldier leave Cairo, in return for granting Egypt complete independence so that she would not be given to Italy or fall under German domination, and so that no one whatsoever would interfere in her affairs, internal or external.

—Anwar el-Sadat (translator unknown)

An Anglo-French Interlude in Syria (1945)

In the uneasy interlude between the German surrender and the Tripartite Conference in Berlin General de Gaulle was also determined to assert the position of France both in Syria, where he ran counter to the policy we had consistently pursued of Syrian independence, and in Italy, where he affronted the United States. . . .

The liberation of France led to a serious crisis in the Levant. It had been evident for some time that a new treaty would be needed to define French rights in this area, and on my way home from Yalta I had met the President of Syria in Cairo and urged him to make a peaceful settlement with France. The Levant States had been unwilling to start negotiations, but we had persuaded them to do so and conversations had begun. The French delegate, General Beynet, went to Paris for instructions, and his proposals were awaited with anxiety and excitement throughout Syria. Delay occurred; no proposals arrived; and then news spread that French reinforcements were on their way. On May 4 I had sent a friendly message to de Gaulle explaining that we had no ambitions of any kind in the Levant States and would withdraw all our troops from Syria and the Lebanon as soon as the new treaty was concluded and in operation, but I also mentioned that we had to keep our war communications throughout the Middle East free from disturbance and interruption. We represented to him that the arrival of reinforcements, however small, was bound to be looked upon as a means of pressure, and might have serious consequences. This advice was not accepted, and on May 17 French troops landed at Beirut.

An explosion followed. The Syrian and Lebanese Governments broke off negotiations and said that now the war was over the Allies would be asked to evacuate all foreign troops. Anti-French strikes and demonstrations began. Eight people were killed and twenty-five injured in Aleppo. The Syrian Chamber of Deputies ordered conscription. A Foreign Office announcement of May 26 regretting the arrival of French reinforcements drew a reply from Paris next day that the disturbances were artificially provoked and that many more British troops had also been moved in without protest by the Syrians or the Lebanese and without agreement by the French. We had in fact appealed to the Syrian government on May 25 to keep control of the situation, but on the 28th they told us that events were too much for them and they could no longer be responsible for internal order. French shelling had begun in Homs and Hama; French armoured cars were patrolling the streets of Damascus and Aleppo; French aircraft were flying low over the mosques during the hour of prayer, and machine-guns were mounted on the roofs of buildings.

At about seven o'clock in the evening of May 29 fierce fighting began in Damascus between French troops and Syrians, and continued for several hours into the night. French artillery opened fire, with serious loss of life and damage to property, and French troops occupied the Syrian Parliament buildings. Shelling continued on and off till the morning of May 31, and about two thousand people were killed and injured.

The Government of Homs had already appealed to the British Ninth Army to arrange a truce. It was now impossible for us to stand aside, and on May 31 General Sir Bernard Paget, Commander-in-Chief Middle East, was told to restore order. He communicated our request to the French commander, and the latter, on instructions from Paris, proclaimed the "Cease fire." I sent the following message to General de Gaulle:

Prime Minister to General de Gaulle (Paris)

31 May 45

In view of the grave situation which has arisen between your troops and the Levant States, and the severe fighting which has broken out, we have with profound regret ordered the Commander-in-Chief Middle East to intervene to prevent the further effusion of blood in the interests of the security of the whole Middle East, which involves communications for the war against Japan. In order to avoid collision between British and French forces, we request you immediately to order the French troops to cease fire and to withdraw to their barracks.

Once firing has ceased and order has been restored we shall be prepared to begin tripartite discussions in London.

By an error in transmission, and with no intentional discourtesy, this message was read to the House of Commons by Mr. Eden about three-quarters of an hour before it reached the General. He felt obliged to issue a public reply in Paris on June 1, saying in effect that the French troops had been attacked by the Syrians, but had everywhere gained control, and that the French Government had themselves ordered a "Cease fire" on May 31.

A vehement protest reached me from the President of the Syrian Republic. But the action we had already taken proved effective. I was most anxious not to vex the French more than was inevitable, and I understood de Gaulle's view and mood about a cause for which he felt passionately. But he also struck a statesmanlike note. "We feel," he said, "not the slightest rancour or anger towards the British. France and myself have the highest regard and affection for them. But there are opposing interests, and these must be reconciled. There are too many common interests at stake. There must be peace."

I was in accord with this view, and when I gave an account of these regrettable incidents to the House of Commons on June 5 I said it was a case of "the less said the better."

Prime Minister to General Paget

3 June 45

As soon as you are master of the situation you should show full consideration to the French. We are very intimately linked with France in Europe, and your greatest triumph will be to produce a peace without rancour. Pray ask for advice on any point you may need, apart from military operations.

In view of reports that French soldiers have been killed, pray take the utmost pains to protect them.

And to the Syrian President, whom I deemed a sensible and competent man:

Prime Minister to President of Syria

3 June 45

Now that we have come to your aid I hope you will not make our task harder by fury and exaggeration. The French have got to have fair treatment as well as you, and we British, who do not covet anything that you possess, expect from you that moderation and helpfulness which are due to our disinterested exertions.

Our intervention was immediately effective.

On June 4 Mr. Shone, our Minister at Damascus, delivered my message to the Syrian President, who took it well and sent the following reply:

President of Syria to Prime Minister

4 June 45

I sent my message of May 31 to Your Excellency under stress of bombardment and of deep emotion at the sufferings which the Syrian people were undergoing, and which I assure you were no exaggeration. Your Excellency will since have received my message of June 1 expressing the gratitude of the Syrian people for the intervention of the British Government, and I and my Government have assured His Majesty's Minister and the Commander-in-Chief that our one desire is to co-operate with the British authorities in their task of restoring order and security in Syria. Your Excellency can be sure that this co-operation with the British authorities will soon have its good results.

"The President," said Mr. Shone, "who was ill in bed when he sent his message of May 31, is now up again and seems fully composed. He is in full accord with you and deeply grateful. As regards fair treatment for the French, he said they could have their schools (if any Syrians still wanted to go to them) and their commercial interests, but neither the Syrian Government nor the Chamber nor the people could ever give them any privilege in this county after what had happened."

General Paget handled the situation with much discretion. All passed off smoothly, and this difficult and untoward Syrian episode came to an end.

—Winston S. Churchill

Declaration of a Jihad (1998)

On February 23, 1998, Al Quds al-Arabi, *an Arabic newspaper published in London, printed in full the text of a "Declaration of the World Islamic Front for Jihad against the Jews and the Crusaders," faxed to them under the signatures of Usāma bin Lādin, the Saudi blamed by the United States for masterminding the August bombing of its embassies in East Africa, and the leaders of militant Islamist groups in Egypt, Pakistan and Bangladesh. The statement reveals a version of history that most Westerners will find unfamiliar. Bin Lādin's grievances are not quite what many would expect. For Muslims, the holy land par excellence is Arabia—Mecca, where the Prophet was born; Medina, where he established the first Muslim state; and the Hijaz, whose people were the first to rally to the new faith and become its standard-bearers. For Muslims, no piece of land once added to the realm of Islam can ever be finally renounced, but none compares in significance with Arabia and Iraq. Of these two, Arabia is by far the most important.*

Since God laid down the Arabian peninsula, created its deserts, and surrounded it with its seas, no calamity has ever befallen it like these Crusader hosts that have spread in it like locusts, crowding its soil, eating its fruits, and destroying its verdure; and this at a time when the nations contend against the Muslims like diners jostling around a bowl of food. . . .

First—for more than seven years the United States is occupying the lands of Islam in the holiest of its territories, Arabia, plundering its riches, overwhelming its rulers, humiliating its people, threatening its neighbors, and using its bases in the peninsula to fight against the neighboring Islamic peoples. . . .

Second—Despite the immense destruction of the Iraqi people at the hands of the Crusader-Jewish alliance and in spite of the appalling number of dead, exceeding a million, the Americans nevertheless, in spite of all this, are trying once more to repeat this dreadful slaughter. It seems that the long blockade following after a fierce war, the dismemberment and the destruction are not enough for them. So they come again today to destroy what remains of this people and to humiliate their Muslim neighbors.

Third—While the purposes of the Americans in these wars are religious and economic, they also serve the petty state of the Jews, to divert attention from their occupation of Jerusalem and their killing of Muslims in it.

There is no better proof of all this than their eagerness to destroy Iraq, the strongest of the neighboring Arab states, and their attempt to dismember all the states of the region, such as Iraq and Saudi Arabia and Egypt and Sudan, into petty states, whose division and weakness would ensure the survival of Israel and the continuation of the calamitous Crusader occupation of the lands of Arabia. . . .

By God's leave we call on every Muslim who believes in God and hopes for reward to obey God's command to kill the Americans and plunder their possessions wherever he finds them and wherever he can. Likewise we call on the Muslim ulema and leaders and youth and soldiers to launch attacks against the armies of the American devils and against those who are allied with them from among the helpers of Satan.

—Usāma bin Lādin

The Poetry of War, and of War Weariness

The first two poems, by an eleventh-century Hebrew poet and a twentieth-century Palestinian, reflect the disillusionment of both.

War begins like a pretty girl
with whom every man wants to flirt
and ends like an ugly old woman
whose visitors suffer and weep.

—Samuel Ha-Nagid

When I am killed one of these days
The killer will find in my pocket
Tickets for travel

One to peace
One to the fields and the rain
One
To the conscience of mankind.
Please don't waste the tickets
My dear killer
Please use them and travel.

—Sāmiḥ al-Qāsim

The following poems by two Turkish poets reflect different eras and different moods. The first, written during the First World War, honors the Turkish dead at the great battle of Gallipoli. The second and third, by a poet who died young and whose main work was written in the 1940s, reflect national and international disillusionment.

Gallipoli (1916)

Soldier, you who have fallen for this earth
Your fathers may well lean down from heaven to kiss your brow.
You are great, for your blood saves the True Faith
Only the heroes of Badr* are your equals in glory.
Who can dig a grave that will not be too narrow for you?
If I say, "Let us enshrine you in history," it will not contain you
That book cannot hold your time of troubles
Only eternity can embrace you.
If I were to set up the Kaʻba as your headstone
If I could seize the revelation in my soul and write it as epitaph
If I could take the firmament with all its stars
And lay it as pall over your bloody coffin
And make a ceiling of purple clouds for your open tomb
And hang the seven lamps of the Pleiades
If, as you lie swathed in blood under this chandelier
I could detain the moonlight by your side
To stay till dawn as guardian of your tomb
If I could charge your chandelier with morning light
And wrap the silken sunset about your wounds—
Still I could not say, "I have done something for your memory . . ."

—Mehmet Akif Ersoy

---

*One of the battles of the Prophet.

Epitaph

> They put his rifle back in the stores
> they gave his clothes to another one
> now there are no more bread crumbs in his kit bag
> no lip marks on his water bottle.
> Such a wind, that he himself went
> and not even his name remained as a memory.
> Only this verse remained
> traced by his hand in the hearth at the coffee-house
> "Death is God's decree.
> If only there were no parting."

—Orhan Veli Kanık

For the Fatherland

> What have we not done for this our fatherland!
> Some of us have died;
> Some of us have made speeches.

—Orhan Veli Kanık

PART IX

Commerce and Trafficking

There are few ways in which a man can be more
innocently employed than in getting money.
—Dr. Johnson (1775)

Slave market in Yemen. From the Maqāmāt *of al-Ḥarīrī, illustrated by al-Wāsiṭī, Baghdad, 1237.*

Introduction

Since remote antiquity, the merchant has been a familiar figure in the Middle East. His import and export business, and the ships and caravans by which he conducted them, are mentioned in many ancient writings and, most familiarly, in the Hebrew Bible. Joseph was found and sold by "Midianite merchant men" (Genesis 37:28). King Solomon had a fleet of ships which, every three years, brought him "gold, and silver, ivory, and apes, and peacocks" (1 Kings 10:22). The celebrated description of "a virtuous woman" and good wife notes, "She is like the merchants' ships, she bringeth her food from afar" (Proverbs 31:14). The Muslim historiographic tradition presents the Prophet himself as a merchant and records many traditions in praise of the upright and honest trader. While interest is forbidden by Muslim law, profit is lawful, and trade is respected and encouraged.

In the intervals between the jihâds, Crusades and other wars between Islam and Christendom, and often while the wars were still in progress, the main form of communication between the two worlds was commerce. In premodern times, Middle Eastern trade was principally with East, Southeast and South Asia, where countries of high civilization and advanced economies offered a wide range of goods. There were also some imports from tropical Africa, notably gold, ivory and slaves. Middle Eastern travelers and traders tell interesting stories of these distant lands.

In the early centuries, when Europe, and especially western Europe, was a semibarbarous land beyond the frontiers of the civilized world, Europeans had little enough to offer by way of merchandise. The sources mention furs from the north, amber from the Baltic lands, fine wool from the famous sheep of England and scarlet-dyed cloth.

Far more important than any of these were two products which brought substantial and immediate gain to the merchants—and long-term ruin to many of their countrymen: slaves and weapons. European slaves were appreciated in the Islamic lands, particularly the east European Slavs, from whom our word "slave" is derived. These were the European slaves par excellence. Western European slaves were also provided, by means of the maritime jihad waged by the Barbary corsairs against European coasts and shipping. From medieval Spain through North Africa to the Ottoman lands, European slaves, both male and female, commanded good prices.

So too did European weapons. From early times, Europeans displayed a special skill, even by comparison with the more advanced societies to the south and to the east of them, in the devising and manufacture of weapons of war. They also displayed a unique willingness to sell them, even to their enemies. Protests by rival powers and even by the Church had little or no effect.

With the money earned from this traffic, European merchants bought a wide range of commodities for which there was a ready market at home. These included textiles, for both clothing and furnishings; sugar, coffee, pepper and spices, some from the Middle East, most imported through the Middle East from the more distant lands of Asia and Africa; and a great variety of exotic fruits and other foodstuffs.

The European colonization of America and the expansion of European colonial activity to parts of Asia and Africa vastly increased the range of commodities which Europeans could sell and the amount of money with which they could buy. Trade between the two areas expanded enormously, and the terms of trade changed greatly, to the Western advantage. A simple example—a cup of coffee—vividly illustrates this change. First sugar, then coffee came to Europe from the Middle East and for long figured prominently among European imports from that region. By the eighteenth century European powers were growing both coffee and sugar in their tropical colonies and exporting them to the Middle East. Even textiles, once a staple of Middle Eastern export, were now imported from India. The development of new industrial techniques and new commercial and financial methods increased and consolidated this Western advantage.

The following selection of texts comes from both Western and Middle Eastern sources, from traders, observers and, occasionally, opponents of trade.

Early Islamic Views

Sayings Attributed to the Prophet

The best of gain is from honorable trade and from a man's work with his own hands.

To seek lawful gain is the duty of every Muslim.

To seek lawful gain is Holy War.

The honest, truthful Muslim merchant will stand with the martyrs on the Day of Judgment.

If a man works for his aged parents, that is in the path of God; if he works for his young children, that is in the path of God; if he works for himself, to be free of want, that too, is in the path of God.

I commend the merchants to you, for they are the couriers of the horizons and God's trusted servants on earth.

The devils come to the markets early in the morning with their flags; they arrive with the first to arrive, and they leave with the last to leave.

The most worthy of earnings are those of the merchants who, if they are spoken to, do not lie; if they are trusted, do not betray; if they promise, do not fail; if they buy, do not condemn; if they sell, do not extol; if they owe, do not delay; and if they are owed, do not press.

If God permitted the inhabitants of Paradise to trade, they would deal in cloth and perfume.

If there were trade in Heaven, they would sell cloth, and if there were trade in Hell, they would sell food. Whoever sells for forty days, mercy is plucked out of his heart.

He who brings supplies to our market is like a warrior in the Holy War for God. He who hoards and corners supplies in our market is like a heretic deviating from the Book of God.

It is God who fixes prices.

Dearness and cheapness are two of God's soldiers. One is called greed, and the other is called fear. If God desires dearness, He puts greed in the hearts of the merchants, who become greedy and hoard their wares. If God desires cheapness, He puts fear in the hearts of the merchants, and they release what is in their hands.

When God is angry with a people [*umma*], He makes their prices high, their markets sluggish, their misdeeds many, and their rulers very oppressive, whereupon their rich do not thrive, their sultan does not remit, their poor do not pray.

A Clear Look at Trade (Ninth Century)

You have inquired, may God favor you, concerning the commodities that are prized in all countries, such as high-quality products, precious objects and costly jewels, so that my answer may serve as an aid to those taught by experience and as a help to those trained in sundry trades and pursuits. I have therefore called it "A Clear Look." May God grant me success.

Certain men of experience among the ancients were of the opinion that whatever article is present is cheap because of its presence; it becomes dear because of its absence, when a need for it is felt.

The Byzantines say: If one of you cannot make a living in a country, let him move to another country.

The Indians say: Whatever becomes plentiful becomes cheap, except for good sense, which gains in value as it increases in quantity.

The Persians say: If you do not make a profit in a trade, leave it for another. If one of you does not make a living in a country, let him exchange it.

The Persians say: He who makes a profit in any market is he who sells that for which money is spent there.

The Arabs say: If you see a man whom fortune favors, then cling to him, for he attracts wealth.

A rich man was asked, "How did your wealth accumulate?" He replied, "I never sold on credit; I never refused a profit, however small; I never acquired a dirham without using it in another deal."

—Al-Jāḥiz (attributed)

Trafficking with the Enemy

Saladin Defends Constructive Engagement (1174)

Sultan Saladin sent an envoy to the caliph saying: the Venetians, the Pisans, the Genoese and all these people sometimes come as attackers doing great harm . . . and sometimes come as envoys. Now all of them compete to bring to our country their weapons of war and struggle and ingratiate themselves with us by bringing their choice products. . . . Dealings have been established and a truce arranged with all of them, to our advantage and to their disadvantage.

—Abū Shāma

An Egyptian Ruler Condemns It (1288)

Al-Najīb, the secretary of Bekjiri, one of the finance officers of the realm, denounced the vizier al-Shujā'ī. He reported certain matters concerning him to the sultan [Qala'un of Egypt] and accused him in the sultan's presence. Among other things, he said that he had sold a quantity of weapons, including lances, which were in the royal stores, to the Franks. Al-Shujā'ī did not deny this but answered, "I sold them with great satisfaction and manifest advantage. The satisfaction was that I sold them antiquated and damaged weapons of little use for which I received a price many times their value. The advantage was that the Franks should know that we sell weapons out of contempt for them and disdain for their cause and lack of concern about them." The sultan was inclined to accept this, but al-Najīb said, "You wretch! What you have hidden is more important than what you have stated. Your story is something that you thought up in the hope that it would be accepted as an answer, but as for the Franks and other enemies, they do not see the sale of weapons to them as you have pretended. Instead, they spread the story among themselves and pass it around among our various enemies that the sovereign of Egypt is in such dire need that he sells weapons to his enemies." The sultan could not tolerate this. He became very angry with al-Shujā'ī and dismissed him from his position on Thursday, the second day of the month of Rabī' al-Awwal, and ordered him to pay an immense quantity of gold. The sultan forbade him to sell any of his horses or weapons or equipment but required him to pay the fine in gold.

—Al-Maqrīzī

Contraband of War: A Papal Bull of 1527

We excommunicate and anathematize all those who take to the Saracens, Turks and other enemies of the Christian name horses, weapons, iron, iron wire, tin, copper, bandaraspata, brass, sulfur, saltpeter and all things suitable for the making of artillery and all kinds of instruments, weapons and machines . . . as also ropes and wooden articles required for naval warfare, with which they will attack the Christians.

—Bull of Pope Clement VII

The Turkish Trade (1606–7)

The wares that the Englishe sende into Turkie are tinne, leade, gunpowder, muskettes, swoordes, copper, kersies, broadeclothe, conniskinnes, brimstone, cordages, cables, steele, & caveare.

Some of these are laudable & good wares, other abhominable & naughte, & bringeth mutche sclaunder to our nation & religion, whyche is powder & other munition for warre & shyppinge broughte by the Englishe in greate abundans thither, & by noe other nation els. . . .

The Englishe keepe 3 open shoppes of armes & munition in Constantinople. The gayne is verye greate that the merchants made in the Turkie trade, for all Englishe commodityes are solde there at a most hyghe rate.

Gunpowder is solde for 23 & 24 chikinoes the hundred; in Englande it costeth but 3 pounde. Tinne in Constantinople beareth the same price. Muskettes are solde for 5 or 6 chikinos the peyce; in Englande they buy the ordinary ones of 2 markes, the best for 18 shillinges. Copper & swoordes are not inferior to these, nor anye other commoditye that is brought from Englande.

—Sir Thomas Sherley

Business as Usual

Trade in Damascus (1522)

As described by a Jewish traveler from Italy.

Damascus is a great city, twice the size of Bologna. It is surrounded by very strong walls and fortifications, and by a moat. There is also a very strong citadel. There are many beautiful markets, and those where business is conducted are covered on top. Damascus has a large population and much commerce. All kinds of crafts and wares may be found there, more than in Venice. In particular, the manufacture and commerce in silk are extensive.

Women also earn much money, and in general, anyone who is willing to work hard in commerce can keep his family in plenty, even if he has little capital, since there is profit in everything. Some set up clothes shops with only a hundred ducats. The Venetian merchants give them clothes to sell at a fixed price, anything above it being for themselves. Some, with their help, set up a haberdashery or a perfumery. Others take things from shops and peddle them in the city, for every day the buying and selling and the crowd are greater than at the great fairs of Italy. Any one who has a little capital and is reliable can get credit from both the Muslims and the Venetians, and can earn money in whatever he applies himself to. The wealthy acquire large stocks when things are cheap and store them until prices rise. There are some who lend money to the Venetians, and get at least two percent per month, and more in times of scarcity. Some give pledges, and to some money may be lent without pledges, as to the Samaritans. One can also lend at a fixed rate of eighteen percent or at least fifteen percent through the Karaite known as Mu'allim Sedaqa and through other reliable persons. The wise man has eyes in his head.

—Moshe Bassola of Ancona

A Business Letter (June 3, 1586)

English merchants appeared in the Mediterranean during the fifteenth century and began to trade in the Ottoman dominions during the sixteenth century. In 1581, after long negotiations, a group of English merchants with interests in the Middle East formed the Levant Company, sometimes also known as the Turkey Company. With a charter from the queen, the company enjoyed a monopoly of trade between England and the Ottoman dominions. The Levant Company was instrumental in establishing diplomatic relations between the two countries. The English—later the British— Embassy in Constantinople and the consulates in provincial cities were financed and maintained by the company until the Napoleonic Wars, when the embassy was finally taken over by the crown. In its heyday, the company maintained a number of trading posts in various cities of the Ottoman Empire, manned by members and employees of the company. These posts were known as factories, those who ran them as factors.

Since the writing of our last we have received letters from Constantinople of the 7th March, wherein they writ us that the bill of exchange that James Tomson took up of 10,000 d[ucat]s should go back again protested, for that they could not agree upon the discharge thereof at Constantinople; whereof we are very sorry, because of our credit, which we have been all this time procuring to get and now, when we have got it, to overthrow it again, surely it doth much grieve us. Whether they had just cause so to do or no, we know not; but it being done, it is not to be remedied. The money we doubt but they will send us, for they had the sum ready, as they do write us. Now for our sales there, if you find them not good, you may make the less haste to sell but to a good reckoning, for that we will not send again afore November or December next, and then we will send but a small quantity of goods, to say 2 or 3,000li. at the most. For this perilous [time?] we will not bear so great adventure, but will retire home our stock as fast as we can; praying you to give over all Baghdad and Balsera [Basra] and let us stay ourselves only upon Homflet [?Hama] and Aleppo. And for the Cyprus wool, you may buy it of some of the Colchester factors, though you give the more for it, for avoiding further trouble in that place; referring the same to your discretion. And we would have you to buy as much indigo as you can, being fine and good, and price [as] reasonable as you can. Also as many nutmegs as you can. But for maces, they be so ill colored that we find them an ill commodity. Also of galls buy us 500 bags at the least, for here commeth no sumacko, by reason of the troubles in Spain, and therefore galls have the better vent; so that we can trust they will yield 3li. the c[wt.]; so that at ds. [ducats] 20 per quintal you need not to fear to buy quantity of them. For raw silk, for so much that the price is higher, we have small dispatch thereof; therefore we had rather have other commodities. Also for botans [pieces of linen], blue and white, though you send us none we can be contented, for we have store in our hands which we cannot sell; they be so dear. For cotton yarn, we would have you send us 60 bags at the least; whereof some 20 or 30 bags may be of the biggest [i.e., coarsest] you can get, and the other [of the] finest you can get; for the great sort serveth for candles and the smallest for fustian. For conserves send none but only green ginger. For other commodities according to your discretion. The prices of wares herewith we send you. For those at Alexandria, if you think pepper be good cheap there, you shall do well to send them some commodity and money to provide some quantity thereof; but write them to buy us no more cassia fistula, ginger, gum Arabic, nor lacquers nor conserves, for those things we cannot sell for that they cost.

[Appended List]: Pepper, the ld. [i.e., lb.] 3s.; cloves, the ld. 5s.; maces, large, ld. 6s. 8d.; maces, small, ld. 5s.; nutmeg, case, ld. 5s.; ginger, large, ld. 10d.; wormsed, best, ld. 5s.; turmeric, ld. 9d.; longe pepper, ld. 4s. 6d.; galls, ld. 3s. 3; indico, ld. 6s. 6; raw silk, the ld. 20s.; cotton warn [i.e., yarn], the ld. 1s. 4d.; cotton wool, the ld. 1s. 2d.; aniseeds, 2li. 15s. the c[wt.]; synamond, large, ld. 6s.; middle synomond, ld. 4s.

—Letter from the Turkey Company to the Aleppo Factors

An Errant Vice Consul; Some Businessmen Complain
(August 4, 1596)

A letter addressed by a group of Levant merchants to the English vice consul, i.e., the representative of the Levant Company, in Aleppo.

We are assembled here together, as well little as great, with one unity of heart and mind, briefly to give you to understand that we will be no longer under your yoke and government; which indeed has been so far out of order that we have good cause to refuse you. You have not hitherto read unto us the statutes and orders of the Company, which you and we are faithfully to obey, but keep and lay them up, that we by no means see them. You unfaithfully and untruly deny and seem not to know them, nor how to govern us by them; and we are altogether ignorant of the laws we live under. Which hath wrought this effect in your bad nature, that your government is altogether out of order. Our Company commandeth that all things done by the consul or vice-consul for the time being be registered in the chancellery, and yearly a copy of all things past sent home in a book to the Company. You have neither chancellery nor ever kept register yourself of anything that passed; which doth argue you would not have your doings come to light. Is it not a shame that hitherto we have not had so much as a general book, to write in before you what goods the malem receiveth of everyone? Which how necessary a thing it is, let everyone judge. You contrary to the consul's orders heretofore, and contrary to the prescript order of the Company, will receive consulage into your own hands and we denying to pay, you like a tyrant your [*sic*] swear by Jesus and Justus (and oaths are as common with you as words almost, which is an unseemly thing in a government) that you will take our goods perforce. As for your justice done amongst our nation, you stand for a cipher, for we think few or none ever came to decide their controversies, as knowing you have hid the laws of the Company from us; and as touching the law of our country, alas! You are altogether ignorant. Lastly, your defense [of us?] against Turks we can in no case allow of; condemning your ability therein, both in the order of your proceedings, in the manner of your behavior, and your unorderly speaking or not speaking at all. And to your want therein you have taken a dragoman so simple of wit and ignorant in languages that what you speak amiss he makes it worse; whereby, when you come before a magistrate, you are a laughing stock to all the audience. Besides all this, which nearly toucheth ourselves, you are publicly a man defamed in all the city; the Turks calling you a Jew, and Jews say you are a Turk, and Christians reproach you by the name of both Turk and Jew. We could report diverse tricks of yours that doth in a manner merit the same, but will not, for brevity's sake. Thus we by you are all defamed likewise. For such reasons above said, and many more which are too long to repeat, we cannot nor will bear your government any longer. We speak this absolutely, for that we are to leave and to take you, being indeed no longer vice-consul, but as a person mansuld* per adviso. Here we might end; but as yet you being in place of vice-consul, we pray and desire you in good peace and friendship to resign the said office, and voice [i.e., vote] with us to the confirmation of another. . . . Now we rest for your answer, which we pray let be brief, negatively or affirmatively.

—Ralph Fitch and other Merchants of the Levant Company

Diplomatic Reports on English Trade in the Levant (Some Illegal) to the King of Spain

English trade in the Levant caused some concern to the Mediterranean Christian powers, as is attested by the reports of their envoys. Of the following documents, the first two were sent by the Spanish ambassador in London; the third by the Venetian ambassador in Istanbul, enclosing a consular report. All three, in English translation, were published in the British Calendar of State Papers. *The originals are in the Spanish and Venetian archives.*

28 Nov. 1568

This Queen [Elizabeth I] has received another letter from the Turk by way of France, which, in addition to many other offers, promises a favourable reception of Englishmen who come to his country, either by land or sea. . . . The Turks are also desirous of friendship with the English on account of the tin which has been sent thither for the last few years, and which is of the greatest value to them, as they cannot cast their guns without it, whilst the English make a tremendous profit on the article, by means of which alone they maintain the trade with the Levant. Five ships are ready to sail thither now, and I am told that, in one of them, they are sending nearly twenty thousand crowns worth of bar tin, without counting what the rest of them take. As this sending tin to the infidel is against the apostolic communion, and your Majesty has ordered that no such voyage shall be allowed to pass the Messina light, to the prejudice of God and Christianity, I advise the viceroy of Sicily of the sailing of these ships as I understand that they will touch at Palermo, where the tin can be confiscated.

---

* From the Turkish *ma'zul,* dismissed.

15 May 1580

In former letters I reported about the mission of an ambassador here from Denmark. . . .

The English also settled through the Muscovite with the Tartars on the banks of the Volga to allow the free passage of their merchandise down the river to the Caspian Sea; whilst the Persian, building large ships in Astrachan, should give them leave to trade and distribute the merchandise, through Media and Persia, in exchange for goods which reach the Persians by the rivers that run from the East Indies to the Caspian Sea. This privilege was granted to the English by the Persian.

Two years ago they opened up the trade, which they still continue, to the Levant, which is extremely profitable to them, as they take great quantities of tin and lead thither, which the Turk buys of them almost for its weight in gold, the tin being vitally necessary for the casting of guns and the lead for purposes of war. It is of double importance to the Turk now, in consequence of the excommunication pronounced "ipse facto" by the Pope upon any person who provides or sells to infidels such materials as these.

> —Bernardino de Mendoza (Spanish ambassador in London)

Ottaviano Bon, Venetian ambassador in Constantinople, to the Doge and Senate:

I enclose a letter from the Consul of Melos, containing many details about the English *berton* captured by privateers.

Pera, 14th March, 1606

To my most Excellent Lord and Honoured Master:—

Via Chios I have already written a full account of all that the ship "Vidalla" has done. I now add that on the 24th an Englishman arrived here in the Gulf of Melos. She was bound for Constantinople with a cargo as below. On the same day there arrived from a different quarter, in the harbour of Argientera, called Polognia, other two *bertons,* westerlings each one with a tartana and a felucca. . . . As soon as they cast anchor in the harbour of Polognia they were informed about the Englishman lying at Melos; they immediately set sail and came round to the Gulf of Melos, where the Englishman was at anchor. They captured the Englishman without any fighting, and put all the crew in prison. They then transshipped all the cargo and put it on board a Perastina, intending to take it to Malta. The cargo consisted to two hundred bales of kerseys and English woollens, seven hundred barrels of gunpowder, one thousand harquebuss barrels, five hundred mounted harquebusses [the harquebus was one of the earliest portable guns, supported on a tripod or rest], two thousand sword blades, a barrel full of ingots of fine gold (*moreli d'oro fino*) twenty thousand sequins, many great dollars (*tolori molti grossi*—?dobloons), and other things of high value. Further, there was found a note written in Turkish character on parchment, issued by the sultan's orders. There was a Jewish supercargo, but his name I do not know.

> Milos, 28th November, 1605. [O.S.]
> Your most humble servant,
> Januli Piperi

Advantages of Free Trade with the Ottoman Empire
(Mid–Seventeenth Century)

We cannot now but pity those Poor Borderers in Hungary, Styria, Croatia, and other parts subject to the Incursions of this cruel Enemy, since we know that in the last War, not three English Miles from Vienna, many poor people have been surprised, and fallen into the hands of the Tartar and Turk, and sold afterwards into perpetual Slavery. This Consideration ought to move us, who are barricaded and fortified by the Seas from the violence of our Enemies, to bless God we are born in so happy and so secure a Country, subject to no dangers but from ourselves, nor other miseries but what arise from our own freedom and too much felicity; we ought to consider it is a blessing, that we have never felt any smart of the Rod of this great Oppressor of Christianity, and yet have tasted of the good and benefit which hath proceeded from a free and open Trade and an amicable Correspondence and Friendship with this People; which having been maintained for the space of above eighty years, begun in the Reign of Queen Elizabeth of blessed memory, preserved by the Prudence and admirable Discretion of a series of worthy Ambassadors and daily improved both in Business and Reputation by the excellent Conduct and Direction of that Right Worshipful Company of the *Levant* Merchants, hath brought a most considerable benefit to this Kingdom, and gives employment and livelihood to many thousands of people in England; by which also His Majesty without any expense gains a very considerable increase of his Customs.

—Sir Paul Rycaut

Business Correspondence from Voltaire (1771)

A group of religious refugees from Geneva, most of them watchmakers, had settled in a village on Voltaire's estate at Ferney. As this correspondence shows, he made some effort to market their wares.

To Frederick II, King of Prussia: Ferney, 1st March, 1771

I shall always hate the Turks, the oppressors of Greece, although not long ago they asked me for some watches from my colony. What wretched barbarians! For seventy years they have been sent watches from Geneva, and they don't yet know how to make them; they don't even know how to set them.

Letter to the Comte de Saint-Priest, French Ambassador in Constantinople: Ferney, 17th June, 1771

I believe that Mr. Pinel will leave soon, carrying several watches which he ordered from these artists; I believe that this will be the first time that a little village in France trades with Turkey, Russia, Holland and Spain. . . . If his first attempt succeeds in Turkey, there is reason to hope that my village of clocks will succeed. They have already built several fairly large freestone houses, which are not common in our hamlets, and even, I am told, not very numerous in Istanbul. . . . Turkey could be a better outlet even than Paris, when peace will be made; for it must after all be made. The Christian princes have never reached agreement to send the Turks to the other side of the Bosporus, and they will probably stay there for a long time, despite the victorious arms of the Russians.

Letter to Catherine II, Empress of Russia: Ferney, 19th June, 1771

On the news of a forthcoming peace between Your Imperial Majesty and His Highness Mustafa, I renounced all my projects of war and destruction. . . .

I learned at this moment that my colony [of watchmakers] has just dispatched another enormous crate of watches. I severely scolded these poor artists; they take too much advantage of your bounty; emulation made them go too far. Instead of sending watches for three or four thousand rubles at the most, as I had expressly instructed them, they sent about eight thousand rubles worth. This is very indiscreet. I do not think that Your Majesty has any intention of giving that many watches to the Turks, though they like them very much. But here, madam, is what you could do. There are some very fine ones with your portrait, and none are dear. You could take about three or four thousand rubles worth to use as presents, made up of watches priced from about fifteen to about forty or fifty rubles. The rest could be left to your traders, who would make a great profit on them. . . .

If Your Majesty is satisfied with these deliveries and these prices, my manufacturers say that they will carry out whatever orders you place with them. . . . I would have preferred that you had sent some carillons for Santa Sophia or for the Mosque of Ahmed. But since this time you did not choose to take possession of the Bosporus, the grand turk and his grand vizier will be too honored to receive from you watches with your portrait, and to learn to respect you at every hour of the day.

—Voltaire

Trade in Baghdad (Mid–Nineteenth Century)

The importance and extent of the commerce of the town are universally known; enormous caravans, some more than 2000 camels strong, come and go daily in ceaseless change from and to all parts. I was told that twice a year a caravan of more than 6000 camels went to Damascus. The trade with India is completely in the hands of the Jews, who possess manufacturies in Calcutta, Bombay, Singapore, and even at Canton. The most important articles of trade in these countries are indigo, spices, silk stuffs, some kinds of rare fruits and dyes, which come from different provinces of China. From Persia come chiefly carpets, shawls, silk, tombako (a kind of tobacco), wines, almonds, &c. From the same country are also obtained precious stones, rubies, emeralds, and corals; and from the Island Rein in the Persian Gulf beautiful pearls are procured.

—J. J. Benjamin II

The Slave Trade

From the beginning of the nineteenth century, successive British governments made a determined effort to abolish slavery worldwide and were sometimes able to enlist the support of Middle Eastern rulers in this effort. The Ottoman sultan could not legally abolish slavery, which was sanctioned by the Holy Law, but he could join in suppressing the slave trade.

Letter from the Sultan to the Ottoman Governor of Baghdad (9 Safar 1263 A.H./January 27, 1847)

Whereas special agreements were made between the British government and certain rulers on the African continent, to prevent the transportation of black slaves from the said African continent to America and other places, it has been observed that certain merchant ships are still approaching the African coasts, stealing slaves, and transporting them elsewhere. Since, for this reason, it has not been possible to enforce the provisions of these agreements, the British government has requested that we help them in this and initiate the appropriate measures.

The treatment accorded to slaves who are stolen and transported to those parts is harsh and bereft of humanity and mercy, to a degree not comparable with the treatment of slaves coming to these parts. Since, for this reason it is in accordance with justice and compassion to prohibit the slave trade, henceforth it is totally prohibited for merchant ships flying the flag of my state to engage in this traffic of slaves. If any of them violate this prohibition, then with God's help they will be seized by our warships to be sent to those waters or by British warships cruising in those parts. The ships will be surrendered to the officers in our ports on the Gulf of Basra, and their captains will be arrested and punished.

—Ottoman Imperial Firman

Slavery and Diplomacy (1960)

From a speech delivered during a debate on slavery in Africa and Arabia, in the House of Lords, London, July 14, 1960.

Viscount MAUGHAM: My Lords, I must beg that indulgence which is bestowed by your Lordships on those addressing you for the first time. Recently I read an article which seemed to me relevant to the Question of my noble friend Lord Shackleton. It said:

"Among the calamities of war may be justly numbered the diminution of the love of truth, by the falsehoods which interest dictates, and credulity encourages. A peace will equally leave the warrior and relater of wars destitute of employment; and I know not whether more is to be dreaded from streets filled with soldiers accustomed to plunder, or from garrets filled with scribblers accustomed to lie."

The magazine was the *Idler,* dated November 11, 1758, and the author—as I expect your Lordships will have guessed—was Dr. Johnson. Times have changed since then, and I am glad to say that we no longer have anything to fear from the soldiers in our streets or, come to that, from the scribblers in our garrets. And I am all the more glad to say this because I was once a soldier and I am now most definitely a scribbler.

But the relevance of the quotation is this: in war and in cold war, truth is the first casualty, because both sides use propaganda. And propaganda is a boomerang which recoils upon the person who uses it. A Government puts out a distorted version of the truth and ends by accepting its own lies, and believing in them. The relevance of this to our present problem is this. Her Majesty's Government in general, and the Foreign Office in particular, have managed to convince themselves that slavery does not exist; and therefore, in the end, they have managed even to persuade the public that it is practically non-existent.

Why do the Foreign Office want to believe that slavery does not exist? Your Lordships have heard from the noble Lord, Lord Shackleton, that Saudi-Arabia is the greatest slave-buying area in the world; and there are over half a million slaves there to-day. The main oil company operating in Saudi-Arabia is the Arabian-American Oil Company—"Aramco"—and if it were known that children are enslaved in Saudi-Arabia this might be taken as a criticism of Aramco's general moral influence over the country. Moreover, Aramco wields considerable influence in Washington; and the Foreign Office do not want to embarrass the Government of Britain's largest ally.

A friend of mine was attached to the Trucial Oman levies who in the autumn of 1955 captured the Buraimi Oasis for the Saudi-Arabian forces. In one of the outlying villages in that uncertain frontier between Oman and Saudi-Arabia, he discovered children in fetters. There they were, in a corner of the marketplace, and there were shackles on their ankles. This story haunted me, and so I approached the Anti-Slavery Society in London; I met more officers from the Trucial Oman levies; I consulted travelers; and all the sources confirmed what we have already been told, that Saudi-Arabia is the main and largest market. And as the wealth has increased so, of course, the demand for slaves has risen, because a man is known by the number of slaves he has; it is a form of snobbery out there—like having a Cadillac. Whereas formerly an able-bodied man slave cost £50, he now cost £150. Whereas formerly an attractive girl cost £150, she now costs anything between £400 and £700.

There are two main slave routes into Saudi-Arabia. The first comes from West Africa. It goes from the High Volta through the Niger Provinces and the region of Timbuktu, across Africa to the Port of Suakin, and across the Red Sea, by dhow to Lith, a port south of Djedda. The other goes from Iraq and Persia and Baluchistan across the Gulf and then, by caravans of camels, across to Riyadh. The children taken on this route are generally children bought from poor parents in these countries, but quite often they have been kidnapped. What happens to these slaves after they have reached the slave markets? Arabists have told us time and time again that, in fact, the lot of a slave is really not all that bad; that, after all, he is valuable property, and so it is worth while looking after him and feeding and clothing him. Certainly when I crossed the frontier into Saudi-Arabia with Sir John Glubb in 1943 to visit the Emir Abdul Azziz el Sidari, at Kaf, I saw no sign of ill-treatment of the slaves there.

But, my Lords, conditions in Arabia have been changing and, as the noble Lord has said, the new wealth has undermined many of the ancient and respectable traditions. Western goods, Cadillacs and canned food, refrigerators and radios, and Western ideas (which also come in cans, in the form of films) have undermined the old sanction of Koranic law, and sanctions of morality have crumbled. Vice is unrestrained and the means to gratify unusual lusts can easily be procured with money. There are now sheikhs who can obtain sexual satisfaction only with very young children. Slaves are often horribly abused for pleasure or mutilated as a punishment, and the castration of young boys is practised. The operation is performed on boys between the ages of ten and fourteen, and the amputation is done radically, both the penis and the scrotum being cut away.

My Lords, the children in shackles in the Buraimi Oasis were destined for Riyadh. The boys might be castrated and the girls bought by any merchant who fancied them. One of the British representatives there, in the Buraimi Oasis, noticed caravans and lorries coming into a little village called Hamasso at night, and when he tried to visit the houses he was denied admittance. So he began to watch the departure of Saudi aeroplanes. I should say that the planes were all Dakotas and, with the exception of one pilot, all the air crews were American. Shortly before the take-off a lorry would drive on to the airstrip and the children would be literally pushed and herded into the plane. My friend (I am sorry to have to keep saying "my friend" but he does not want his name used) then spoke to one of the American pilots and asked him into his house for a drink. He said to him, "Do you realise that you are carrying children into captivity?" And the man answered, "When I took on this job I was told to keep my eyes shut and my ears shut as to what was going on around here. And that is the way it is going to be. Another seven years of flying for King Saud and I'll have earned enough money to retire for life."

This information, in point of fact, I happen to know, was reported to the Foreign Office. It was never used at the time of the Buraimi frontier dispute, nor since. Why? Because the Foreign Office do not want to embarrass a powerful Ally. Nor, I may say, is it only Foreign Office who do not want to embarrass a powerful Ally. When I tried to interest various editors in this matter, some of these steely-eyed despots were alarmed at the matter which they thought might be revealed by my inquiries. The very steel of their eyes grew tarnished at the prospect.   —Viscount Maugham

Slavery was abolished by decree in Saudi Arabia and Yemen in 1962.

The Business of Oil

The presence of petroleum in the Middle East has been known for a very long time. In antiquity, it maintained the sacred flame in Zoroastrian temples; in the Middle Ages, it was used by both Byzantine and Muslim rulers as an ingredient in the making of the so-called Greek fire, an explosive mixture placed in pots and used as a missile in siege and naval warfare. Its modern commercial use for fuel is conventionally dated from 1842, when the first drilling was made in Baku, which had been annexed by Russia in 1806. The commercial exploitation of petroleum in the West is dated from the opening of Drake's Well at Titusville, Pennsylvania, in 1859. The use of oil as a source of energy developed very rapidly in both Russia and America. In this report, the U.S. ambassador in Turkey considers the possibilities of petroleum in the Middle East.

Possibilities of Petroleum: an American Report (1887)

To enhance the American influence in the Ottoman empire requires something besides our American teachers and preachers. Trade is the forerunner of civilizing influences as well as its concomitant. Our trade with Turkey is insignificant. Our flag is never seen on the Bosporus, except upon our launch. Such trade as we have is the importation of petroleum and the exportation of rugs and carpets. The petroleum trade is of the largest amount and interest. From recent developments, it would seem as if the crust of the ultra-American earth was in competition with our own crust, in spouting its petroleum. . . .

Meanwhile, the world demands more light. The lamp holds out to burn in realms that never knew aught but natural illumination—a farthing dip or a little wick in a small vessel of grease. It demands cheap illumination, which means cheap transportation; and if the Orient can furnish her own oil, the day is not distant when the American article will have a limited territory for its market. . . .

To what uses, besides that of light, may not this element be dedicated! It is already taking the place of coal. Twelve barrels of oil in a tank on the tender ran a Pennsylvania locomotive 116 miles. The residuum of petroleum, as a substitute for coal, is just coming into use in America. In this we are copying the carriers of Baku. Three years ago, on the Russian railroads in Asia, oil was used as fuel; then, a year later, its residuum; then it fired up the

300 steamboats on the Caspian and the Volga. The use extended to Swedish and Egyptian railroads and factories, at a great saving.

The refineries of Baku and the factories of Odessa gave up English coal for the cheaper fuel. One ton of it was equal to two of coal. . . .

Petroleum is not by any means peculiar to our time or to America. It is as old as the earth, and its development antedates the "Cities of the Plain." That it should be found in Asia was not a surprise. . . .

There are many other evidences in the East of the existence of petroleum. . . .

What possibilities or probabilities there may be in the Orient for the production of petroleum are not yet fully ascertained. They are in the region of conjecture. . . . Here was once the garden of the world, which had in its circuit such cities as Aleppo, Antioch and Tarsus. It is surrounded by splendid mountain ranges. It produces wool, madder, gums, skins, berries and wheat. These seek, even over bad roads, by donkeys, camels and carts, exportation to the ports of Europe and Turkey. Nor is it marvelous that signs of petroleum should here exist.

—Samuel Cox

Striking Oil in Persia (1908)

From a letter to his father by a young political officer, later a major figure in British imperial policy.

Early on May 26th one of the two wells struck oil—at 1,200 feet. I was sleeping outside my tent close by and ran to the spot as soon as I heard the unaccustomed noise and shouting. It rose 50 feet or so above the top of the rig, smothering the drillers and their devoted Persian staffs who were nearly suffocated by the accompanying gas. I at once sent news to Bushire, via the Persian office at Shustar—to the annoyance of G. B. Reynolds [the chief engineer of the oil company] a month later when he found that his principals had first heard the news from the Foreign Office. It had not occurred to me that he would follow his usual routine and send a courier to Ahwaz or Mohammerah with telegrams to be dispatched thence. As I had no Telegraph Code I wired to Lorimer [Captain D. L. R. Lorimer of the Indian Political Department]: "See Psalm 104 verse 15 third sentence and Psalm 114 verse 8 second sentence."* This told him the news and in the circumstance was quite as effective as a cipher.

---

* "That he may bring out of the earth oil to make him a cheerful countenance"; "the flint stone into a springing well." [Footnote in original edition]

My comments to my father were brief:

"It is a great event: it remains to be seen whether the output will justify a pipe line to the coast, without which the field cannot be developed. It will provide all our ships east of Suez with fuel: it will strengthen British influence in these parts. It will make us less dependent on foreign-owned oilfields: it will be some reward to those who have ventured such great sums as have been spent. I hope it will mean some financial reward to the Engineers who have persevered so long, in spite of their wretched top-hatted directors in Glasgow, in this inhospitable climate. The only disadvantage is personal to myself—it will prolong my stay here!"

Reynolds' first concern was to save as much as possible of the oil that was running to waste. A great pit or reservoir was dug in the hard red clay about 200 yards from the well: the well was capped—no easy task—and the stream of oil diverted into the pit, whence it was carried by earth thereafter for use as fuel in the other drilling engines and for a score of other purposes for which wood had hitherto been used.

One well on this field, some years later, was producing 450,000 gallons a day, nearly twice as much as the Abadan refinery required in 1914. In fifteen years it produced nearly 7 million tons of oil. It was worthy of Reynolds.

Writing to my father later, I sketched briefly the historical aspect of the oil industry in this part of the world.

"This is really the home of the world's oil industry. Ur of the Chaldees, whence Abraham started his journey westwards, is known locally as Mughir-Umm Qir—the mother of pitch. Noah's ark, like local craft, was 'pitched within and without' and the tower of Babel (Bab-il the gate of God) was built with 'slime' [i.e. bitumen] for mortar. Herodotus mentions the practice and mentions the town of Hit whence all the bitumen used in Mesopotamia still comes. Layard constantly refers to its use in Nineveh and Babylon and there was a tradition here that the burning fiery furnace into which Shadrach, Meshach, and Abednego were cast was at Kirkuk where there is a lot of natural gas always alight, and Plutarch probably mentions this place in his Life of Alexander. It does not speak well for British business men who have been dominant here for half a century that they should have left this undeveloped for so long."

I wrote almost daily to my father and mother in order, as I put it, "to unwind my mind" every day before going to bed, and in my letters at this time are many references to India and domestic political issues. My father was inclined to take the orthodox Liberal view; I sympathized, but could not believe that Liberal institutions could be transplanted in Eastern countries.

—Arnold Wilson

Oil Comes to Kuwait (1937)

In a few years' time oil will have come to Kuwait and a jaunty imitation of the West may take the place of its desert refinement. The shadow is there already, no bigger than a man's hand—a modest brass-plate on a house on the seafront with the name of the Anglo-American K.O.C., Kuwait Oil Company. Small camps here and there are pitting the desert with holes inspired by geology. But the industrial age is not coming here with a rush, as elsewhere: its few representatives are pleasant people who—marooned away from their familiar atmosphere—are learning to deal kindly with a scale of values so different from their own. Their women do not stroll about in shorts and sleeveless among the veiled inhabitants; nor do their men shout abuse at servants unused to the unmannerliness of European speech. Time is everything—and luckily it takes eight months or so to drill an oil hole; and the first experiment has failed: by the time the next is made, the Company and Kuwait will have learnt to cherish each other's virtues: Civilization will come tempered, more like a Marriage and less like a Rape; and the poor little town—that looks to her untried bridegroom hopefully for all temporal blessings—may yet, with gentle treatment, keep her peculiar charm.

At present oil, like the aeroplane, gives a certain piquancy of contrast. One bumps for miles over scrub and sand and comes to a drilling machine alone in the desert under its aerial scaffolding. It brings to the surface the unviolated secrets of earth, spitting them out in grit and sand; and has a splendour about it of human courage, here where hitherto man's day has ever been as grass, "the wind passeth over it and is gone, and the place thereof shall know it no more."

The drilling machine too is an Idea, stronger than the elemental matter around it: it bites away serenely, regardless of landscape or climate, the cynosure of its human devotees: and as one looks at their ministering figures moving about it, actively adoring, feeding it with grease and water, one is reminded of that definition of the Englishman, which will do across the Atlantic just as well—"a self-made man who worships his creator."

But the pleasantest of all the things one can do in Kuwait is to treat it as its inhabitants do—as a town to be got outside of.

—Freya Stark

The Oilmen Come to Arabia (1984)

From a novel depicting events in an unnamed Persian Gulf state in the 1930s. Its author, Abdelrahman Munif, served as director of planning in

the Syrian Oil Company and later as director of crude oil marketing. He
was born in Jordan into a trading family of Saudi Arabian origin and was
stripped of his Saudi citizenship for political reasons.

He sensed that something terrible was about to happen. He did not know
what it was or when it would happen, and he took no comfort in the explanations offered him from all sides. The very sight of the foreigners and their
constant activity all day, the instruments they carried around, the bags of
sand and stones they had amassed after writing in their notebooks and
drawing symbols on them, the discussions that lasted from sundown until
after supper and the writing that followed, the damned questions they
asked about dialects, about tribes and their disputes, about religions and
sects, about the routes, the winds and the rainy seasons—all these caused
Miteb's fear to grow day by day that they meant harm to the wadi and the
people. The wadi's inhabitants, who at first viewed the three foreigners with
scorn and laughed when they saw them carrying bags of sand and rock,
grew more surprised when they discovered that the three knew a lot about
religion, the desert, the bedouin's life and the tribes. The profession of faith
they repeated whenever asked, and their scriptural citations, moved many
people of the wadi to wonder among themselves if these were jinn, because
people like them who knew all those things and spoke Arabic yet never
prayed were not Muslims and could not be normal humans.

Ibn Rashed, who had seemed a different person since the arrival of the
foreigners, showing them lavish attention and hospitality in the most
demonstrative way, as if he had been expecting them, or perhaps had prior
orders from the emir given by their guides—Ibn Rashed inwardly believed
that there was great gain to be had from these men. As a consequence, he
overdid everything, his speech and his actions, which was more than the
wadi could bear and more than the people could stand. If at first people
tended to feel arrogant, as if they enjoyed ease and prosperity in the wadi
and knew how to honor their guests, soon they were overtaken by doubt as
to whether they could keep it up: the foreigners had been there quite a
while and showed no signs of moving on. . . .

The emir began talking before Ibn Rashed spoke, as if he knew why
they had come and what it was they wanted. After general remarks about
hunting, the weather and Wadi al-Uyoun, he came to the point: "People of
Wadi al-Uyoun, you will be among the richest and happiest of all mankind,
as if God saw none but you."

He went on in a different tone: "You have been patient and endured
much. God is your witness, but you will be living as if in a dream. You will
talk about times past as if they belonged to some old legend."

He resumed his original tone: "And once blessings come, my friends—they have come."

Ibn Rashed had been preparing the words he had planned to speak, how he would begin and lead the discussion to the sensitive points. If he could not convince the emir, he at least wanted to create doubts in his mind. He wanted to persuade him to visit them—soon—to see for himself and verify everything they were telling him now. But when the emir began speaking, giving the conversation this direction, Ibn Rashed was disconcerted and did not know how to begin.

"As you know, Your Excellency," he ventured desperately, "money is not everything in this world. More important are honor, ethics and our traditions."

He wanted to continue in this vein, but the emir's ringing laugh changed the atmosphere once again and utterly confused the men. Ibn Rashed spoke in embarrassment. "Whatever we say, Your Excellency, the ear is not the eye. Hearing a tale is not the same as seeing and believing."

The emir shifted in his seat, decisively harsh lines drawn on his face. "If, Ibn Rashed, you speak of ethics, then know we are the most covetous of ethics, and if you want religion, religion is ours and no one's else's."

"But you should come and see everything for yourself."

"Don't be afraid. We want you to help them in every possible way. They have come from the ends of the earth to help us."

"God damn them," said Miteb al-Hathal angrily. "We don't want them and we don't want their help."

"But we do want their help," said the emir mockingly, looking at Miteb. "And if you don't—then know that the earth is wide."

"Yes, by God . . . the earth is wide."

"But Your Excellency, what do they want?" asked Ibn Rashed hastily, to calm the situation.

"They don't want anything," said the emir with the same sarcasm. "We invited them, and they have come to help us."

"What kind of help, Your Excellency?" Ibn Rashed asked innocently.

"Under our feet, Ibn Rashed, there are oceans of oil, oceans of gold," replied the emir. "Our friends have come to extract the oil and the gold."

Ibn Rashed looked at the emir and nodded in surprise and trust, then looked at the men to see the effect of the emir's words on them. He addressed the emir with the same innocence: "How did you know, Your Excellency?"

"How would we ever have known without their help?" replied the emir testily and self-confidently. "They told us, 'There are oceans of blessings under this soil,' and because they love blessings, because they are our friends, they agreed to come here and help us out."

"Is the gold in Wadi al-Uyoun, Your Excellency?"

"In Wadi al-Uyoun, and here, and in every part of this blessed land. When His Majesty liberated this land with the edge of his sword, fighting enemies and infidels, he knew what he was fighting for."

Miteb al-Hathal spoke coldly and firmly, "We're the ones who fought. With our own swords we took this land, inch by inch."

The emir appeared deeply angry at being challenged in that tone, but he ignored Miteb. "Since God bestowed grace upon us we must thank him, not create problems."

—Abdelrahman Munif (translated by Peter Theroux)

PART X

Arts and Sciences

Art and Science cannot exist but in minutely
organized Particulars.
—WILLIAM BLAKE

Firdawsī in a bathhouse receiving his pay for his great epic poem the Shāhnāma, *or* Book of Kings.

Introduction

$\mathcal{A}$n early-tenth-century Egyptian collection of edifying tales tells the story of a merchant who was shipwrecked on an island in the Indian Ocean and lost all his possessions. "There I was met by a crowd of people who took me before their king. He said to me, 'You have lost all that which was outside of you. Now what have you that is part of your very self?' I replied, 'I have writing and arithmetic.' The king said, 'What you have kept is better than what you have lost. I would like you to teach my son Arabic writing and arithmetic.' "

Letters and numbers are two of the most important inventions in human intellectual history. Systems of writing and numbering were developed in various parts of the world—in India, China, and pre-Columbian America as well as the Middle East. But all of them were slow, complex and cumbrous. Two major steps forward were the devising of the alphabet and of positional notation. Of these the first was invented in the Middle East; the second, of Indian origin, was adopted in the Arab world, incorporated into the body of mathematical theory, and transmitted to the Christian world, where it is still known as "Arabic numerals." Modern science is inconceivable without it.

The ancient civilizations of the Middle East, like those in other parts of the world, devised systems of writing: the ideographic characters of the Far East, the cuneiform script of Assyria and Babylon, the hieroglyphs of pharaonic Egypt. All of these represented whole words or, at the very least, syllables. To read, still more to write, required a knowledge of hundreds or even thousands of different characters. The idea of an alphabet, of reducing the whole range of sounds uttered in human speech to a few simple characters representing the basic sounds of which speech is composed, seemed to have originated in the Levant, among peoples speaking a Semitic language of the Canaanite branch. The best-known languages of this family are Phoenician and Hebrew. The Hebrew, Greek, Latin, Cyrillic and many other alphabets are derived from this first epoch-making invention.

Not only letters and numbers came from the Middle East but also some basic and by now universally accepted innovations in the measurement of time. The day, the month and the year are natural phenomena, but the hour, the week and the calendar are arbitrary choices. The hour and its subdivisions, the minute and the second, derive from Babylonian astronomy and mathematics; the seven-day week, ending in a day of rest, from the Hebrew scriptures; the calendar by which almost the whole world now dates events begins with the birth of Christ in Bethlehem.

Every civilization in every era has its own distinctive arts and letters, its own special contribution to the advancement of science. At the present time, the most widely accepted cultural tradition is that which originated in the early modern centuries in western Europe and has since embraced the whole world. Of its forerunners, by far the most influential was its immediate predecessor, the Islamic civilization of the Middle East—of all the premodern civilizations, in many ways the richest and the most diverse. Until then, virtually all civilizations—in China, India, Europe, the Americas—were limited to one region, one culture and usually one race. The Islamic culture of the Middle East was the first that was truly international, intercultural, interracial, in a sense, even intercontinental, and its contribution—both direct and indirect—to the modern world is immense. Without Indian numbers and Chinese paper, modern science and modern literature would have had a very restricted expansion. And Middle Eastern scientists, scholars, philosophers and artists added their own distinctive contribution to that already rich heritage.

In the development and transmission of the sciences, the scientists in the medieval Middle East—some Christian, some Jewish, most of them Muslim—were of crucial importance. Their heritage was the ancient knowledge of Egypt and Babylon. To this, the skill and diligence of translators enabled them to add a significant part of the otherwise lost sciences of Persia and Greece. The enterprise and curiosity of travelers further enriched this already rich heritage with new knowledge of the sciences and techniques of India and China, previously unknown to the Middle East.

The role of medieval Islamic science was not, however, purely one of collection and preservation. Scientists and—a new approach little known among the ancient Greeks—experimenters brought major advances in astronomy and cosmography, in physics and chemistry, in medicine and technology.

From the Middle East, this new knowledge eventually percolated to Europe and in time helped to illuminate the outer darkness of the lands beyond the northwest frontier of Islam. Arabic works, some original, some adapted from ancient Greek texts, were translated into Latin; European students went to study in the academies of what were then the Muslim cities of Spain and Sicily.

By the end of the Middle Ages, there was a dramatic change and in a sense a reversal of roles. In the Muslim world the spirit of independent inquiry was stifled and died; science was reduced to the endless repetition of approved formulae. In the West, in contrast, the scientific movement, already discernible in the late Middle Ages, advanced enormously in the era of the Renaissance, the Discoveries, the technological revolution, and the immense economic, social and intellectual changes that preceded, accompanied and followed them. Those who had been disciples now became teachers—and their former masters proved recalcitrant pupils. As one might expect, the products of alien and infidel science were most readily accepted in medicine and warfare, where they could make the difference between life and death, between victory and defeat. The acceptance of the underlying philosophy and sociopolitical systems that made these scientific achievements possible proved more difficult.

When a Middle Eastern sultan equipped his troops with muskets and cannon, imported or copied from Europe, his action might be called modernization, necessary for survival in the modern world. When he dressed his troops in European-style uniforms and accoutrements, this could be defended as useful for the efficient handling of European weapons. But when he provided them with a brass band led by an Italian bandmaster, this was clearly a cultural choice—not modernization but Westernization. The art of music is deeply rooted and widely appreciated in both Middle Eastern and Western civilizations. The encounter between the two may serve as a paradigm of the relations between two cognate but different cultures.

Three books, first committed to writing in the Middle East, are probably the most widely read in all human history: the Old Testament, the New Testament and the Qur'ān, which brought the Arabic language and script and the teachings enshrined in them to previously untouched regions and peoples in Asia, Africa and elsewhere.

The Middle Eastern textual contribution is not limited to sacred scriptures, important as these may be. But literature is another matter. Poetry and letters, especially when written in a remote and alien language and deriving from an unfamiliar culture, are difficult to appreciate. The medieval Arabs made or procured translations of ancient Greek works on philosophy and science. They showed no interest in poetry or drama or even history. The translation of European scientific works into Middle Eastern languages began in the sixteenth century; the translation of literature began very tentatively in the early nineteenth century. It did not become significant until the late nineteenth century, when the growing European world dominance made the study of Europe in all its aspects a necessity of survival.

The Europeans, in contrast, showed an early interest in Middle Eastern literature, and by the end of the eighteenth century a large body of Arabic,

Persian and Turkish prose and poetry was available in translation in many European languages.

Even in the Middle Ages, there are signs of literary influence. One piece of literature, regarded by the Arabs themselves as popular and rather trivial, achieved universal fame. This was the collection of tales known as *The Thousand and One Nights*. The frame story of this celebrated collection—itself perhaps related to the Book of Esther—was known in Europe at an early date. Elements of it appear in a novel by the Italian author Giovanni Sercambi (1347–1424) and, later, in Boccaccio's *Decameron*. It is likely that the story was first brought back in pieces by European travelers in the East. The full text was first translated into French in the early seventeenth century by a secretary to the French Embassy in Istanbul. It at once acquired and has ever since retained immense popularity and inspired a whole series of imitations by European writers.

A much more famous Italian masterpiece, Dante's *Divine Comedy,* is foreshadowed in a medieval Arabic work describing a visit to Heaven and Hell and some encounters there with deceased poets and others. The *Epistle of Forgiveness* of the Syrian poet Abu'l-'Alā al-Ma'arrī (973–1058) was probably not known to Dante, but it anticipated several of his themes. The Arab influence is clear and unequivocal in *Robinson Crusoe.* This English classic was written not long after the publication, in English translation, of an Arabic philosophical novel by Ibn Ṭufayl (died 1185), portraying the intellectual and spiritual development of a man living alone on a desert island. The translator was Simon Ockley, an English Arabist who in 1711 was appointed to the chair of Arabic at Cambridge University.

Scientific and philosophic works, many of which were translated into Latin in the Middle Ages, had a much greater impact but were by their very nature superseded by the scientific movement which they themselves had helped to provoke.

The following excerpts illustrate different aspects of scientific, medical and cultural life in the region. They include comments from Western observers of the Middle Eastern scene and Middle Eastern observers of Western science, music and letters. The section ends with some views, from inside and outside, of ancient Arabian poetry, which many Arabs regard as their chief glory, and some examples of Middle Eastern literature.

Choice of a Profession
(Thirteenth Century)

A tumbler scolded his son and said, "You do no work and you waste your life in idleness. How often must I tell you to practice somersaults and to learn how to dance on a rope and to make a dog jump through a hoop so that you can achieve something with your life? If you don't listen to me, I swear by God I shall abandon you to the *madrasa* [college], to learn their dead and useless science and to become a scholar so as to live in contempt and misery and adversity and never be able to earn a penny wherever you go."

—'Ubayd-i Zākānī

Science and Medicine

A Guide for Physicians
(Ninth–Tenth Centuries)

Since the science of medicine is very vast and the life of man too short to reach its end, therefore expert physicians must be distinguished and separated from the fools. They busy themselves constantly with the study of books and pore over them by night and day, and devote themselves to this above other men who do not join them in this work. . . .

If the knowledge and wisdom of a physician were seen and visible on his face and in his appearance, then most men would not err in recognizing them and in assessing the extent of their knowledge. But most of the common people do not look with discernment but judge physicians by their talk and chatter and self-praise, by their height and the size of their bellies and the length of their beards. Hence the saying "The fool looks to the outward appearance, the wise man to the heart."

If the physician comes from a far land and speaks in a strange and unintelligible language, the common people think him clever, gather around him, and seek his advice.

The physician does not work the cure. He does but prepare and clear the path for nature, the real healer. . . .

Since the object of the practice of medicine is the possible and not the necessary, and since death is ordained and inevitable, there can be no physician who is good and praiseworthy in the eyes of all men. . . .

There is less need of a physician to preserve health than to remove disease, though it is better for a man not to be sick than to be sick and recover. . . .

If you can feed the patient on food similar to his diet when in health, do so. Try also to feed him at his usual mealtimes. By this you will strengthen his nature.

The better you know and understand the temperament and characteristics of the patient when he is healthy, and the more you feel his pulse and examine his urine, the more easily will you cure him.

If you can carry out your treatment effectively with diet or with healing foods, then do not use drugs, for most of them are enemies and antagonists of nature, especially the purgatives.

If a man consults many physicians, then, unless they all visit him at once and reach a joint agreement, he endangers his life. For if each comes alone, the second will try to alter or add to the instructions of the first.

Try always in your treatment to use simple drugs, for it is easier for you to know their power than to know that of the compound drugs.

Do not despise any cure of which you hear, for often results may be achieved by simple means which you could not accomplish with a multiplicity of prescriptions and medicines.

Do not rely in your treatment on specifics, for most of them are foolishness and superstition.

Stop your mouth from uttering prophecies or pronouncing decrees. Let most of your remarks be conditional.

Do not let your mouth sin because of what happens to any other physician, for every man has his hour. Let your deeds alone praise you, and do not seek glory in the shame of a colleague.

Be most diligent in visiting and healing poor and needy patients, for there is no greater charity than this.

Reassure and encourage the patient with the prospect of recovery, even if you are not sure of it, for thus you will strengthen his nature.

Do not trust in apothecaries and in makers of compound drugs, for sometimes they give less because of the high price or use old and weakened ingredients and spoil your treatment. Therefore, make sparing use in your treatment of the compound drugs which they sell. . . .

If a patient does not follow your instructions, if his servants and his household do not attend speedily to your orders, and if they do not accord you proper respect, give up the case.

The more you charge for your work and the more costly is your treatment, the more will your work be respected by men. Only those for whom you work for nothing will think lightly of your skill.

Do not visit the patient too often nor sit with him too long unless the treatment of his disease requires it, for it is new faces that give pleasure.

—Isaac Israeli

A Syrian View of Crusader Medical Practice
(Twelfth Century)

The lord of Munaitira wrote to my uncle, asking him to send a physician to treat one of his companions who was sick. He sent him a [Syrian] Christian physician called Thābit. He had hardly been away for ten days when he returned, and we said to him, "How quickly you have healed the sick!" and he replied:

"They brought me two patients, a knight with an abscess on his leg and a woman afflicted with a mental disorder. I made the knight a poultice, and the abscess burst and he felt better. I put the woman on a diet and kept her humor moist. Then a Frankish physician came to them and said to them, 'This man knows nothing about how to treat them!' Then he said to the knight, 'Which do you prefer, to live with one leg, or to die with two?' and the knight said, 'To live with one leg.' Then he said, 'Bring me a strong knight and a sharp ax,' and they brought them. Meanwhile I stood by. Then he put the sick man's leg on a wooden block and said to the knight, 'Strike his leg with the ax, and cut it off with one blow!' Then, while I watched, he struck one blow, but the leg was not severed; then he struck a second blow, and the marrow of the leg spurted out, and the man died at once. The physician then turned to the woman, and said, 'This woman has a devil in her head who has fallen in love with her. Shave her hair off.' So they shaved her head, and she began once again to eat their usual diet, with garlic and mustard and the like. Her disorder got worse, and he said, 'The devil has entered her head.' Then he took a razor, incised a cross on her head, and pulled off the skin in the middle until the bone of the skull appeared; this he rubbed with salt, and the woman died immediately. Then I said to them, 'Have you any further need of me?' And they said no, and so I came home, having learned things about their medical practice which I did not know before."

—Usāma ibn Munqidh

A Hospital and Asylum in Baghdad (1165–73)

[The Caliph] built, on the other side of the river, on the banks of an arm of the Euphrates which there borders the city, a hospital consisting of blocks of

Preparing medicine from honey, from an Arabic manuscript of Dioscordes' De
Materia Medica, *Baghdad, 1224.*

houses and hospices for the sick poor who come to be healed. Here there are about sixty physicians' stores which are provided from the Caliph's house with drugs and whatever else may be required. Every sick man who comes is maintained at the Caliph's expense and is medically treated. Here is a building which is called Dar-al-Maristan, where they keep charge of the demented people who have become insane in the towns through the great heat in the summer, and they chain each of them in iron chains until their reason becomes restored to them in the winter-time. Whilst they abide there, they are provided with food from the house of the Caliph, and when their reason is restored they are dismissed and each one of them goes to his house and his home. Money is given to those that have stayed in the hospices on their return to their homes. Every month the officers of the Caliph inquire and investigate whether they have regained their reason, in which case they are discharged. All this the Caliph does out of charity to those that come to the city of Baghdad, whether they be sick or insane.

—Benjamin of Tudela (translated by Elkan Nathan Adler)

Physicians in Constantinople: Customs and Costumes (c. 1551)

In Turkie and principally at Constantinople, are found dyuers Phisitions professing the Art of physicke, and exercysing the practyse thereof, but a greater number of them Jewes then Turkes, amongest the which there are many that are skilfull in Theorica, and experimented in practise, and the reason wherefore in this Arte they doe commonly exceede all other nations, is the knowledge which they have in the language and letters, Greeke, Arabian, Chaldee and Hebrewe. In which languages as to them partly, peculiar, and originall, have written the principall Authours of physicke and naturall phylosophie and Astronomie, beying the sciences meete and necssarye for those that study phisick. Besides, the common Phisitions which the Turkes call Echim [Turkish *hekim*], the great Lord hath of his owne proper and ordinary, waged wyth great stipendes, and intertainments, whereof part are Turkes and parte Jewes. Hee which in the tyme that I was in Levant, had the first dignity and authority, amongest the order of Phisitions was of nation an Hebrew called Amon, of age about sixtie yeeres, a personage great of authorytye, and muche esteemed, as well for his goods, knowledge, and renowne, as for honour and portlinesse. They are moreover besides those aforesaide within the Sarail of the great Turk, ten common Phisitions, which for their salarie have every one of them tenne aspres a day, and meate and drinke, their charge being such that so soone as there falleth any sicke withing the Sarail, one of them goeth into the great Turk to aske licence to heale him, (for otherwise they dare not take him in hand) which having obtayned, he causeth the patient to bee brought into a place which within the Sarail is ordayned for sick folke, and is bound to visite him foure times a daye, untill such time as he have recovered his health: but if it chaunce the sicke to waxe dayly worse and worse: then all the other Phisitions are bound to come to his assistance: As for the apparrell of the phisitions of Turkie it doth not differ much from that of the comon people: but yet from that of the Jewish Phisitions, for insteede of a yealow Tulbant very reere like unto the Jewishe nation, they were a high topped cappe, died of redde scarlet.

—Nicolas Nicolay (translated by T. Washington the Younger)

The Perils of Printing: Advantages of a Turkish Education (1656)

The Turk finding Printing and Learning the chief fomentors of Divisions in Christendome, hath hitherto kept them out of his Territories. Yet, whilst we tire out our best time in tugging at the hard Text of a dry Book, or the study of strange Languages (which are but the Bindings of Learning, and do often cover lesse Knowledge than may be had in our own Ideom) they come more adapted into State-employments, and sooner furnished with clear Reason, drawn from the quicker Fountains of less-erring Experience; And were never yet found to be out-reached in Prudence, by the most politick and learned Princes in Europe. Nor can any think this strange, that considers what the custome of Universities requires at the hands of Students, viz. knowledge in the Arts so called, and a nimble mouthing of canting Termes, coyned by themselves, and so current in the commerce of no larger Understandings than their own, & such as are sworn to the same Principles: The vanity of which is in nothing more apparent than in this, that they can easier start ten Errors, than kill one; as is manifest in the Differences between us and Rome, concerning which, though in right reason we do, and cannot but agree in many things, yet the heat and rancour of the dispute is no whit abated.

All Sciences any waies resembling those we call Liberall, are taught no where but in the Seraglio, where the Grand Segnior hath the power to increase or diminish the number of their Professors, according as it suits his occasions: Able men resembling wanton Boyes, that, rather than be unemployed, will do mischief; None attaining to any perfection but what he hath use for: Idle Valor being the tool, as Learning & Knowledge are the operators of all Civill Dissentions. A course quite contrary to the ill husbandry of Europe, or more particularly England . . . For the parents of Schooleboyes not being able to advance them higher, all the rest is lost but Reading and

Writing, and they rendred, by seven or eight yeares lazy living, uncapable of the labour belonging to the more profitable Plough, and so become Serving-men, and Lawyers, and Justices Clerks; by the vertue of which professions they turne cunning Knaves, and cozen their Country: A charge circumcised in Turkey, by mixing the expensive Callings of Law and Divinity together, by which the Priests are so fully employed as no leisure is given to study Innovation in either profession, and consequently dries up the Fountaines of Rebellion.

—Francis Osborn

A Visit to the Observatory (1748)

The Ottoman ambassador visits the observatory in Vienna and gets an electric shock.

At the emperor's command we were invited to the observatory, to see some of the strange devices and wonderful objects kept there. We accepted the invitation a few days later and went to a seven- or eight-story building. On the top floor, with a pierced ceiling, we saw the astronomical instruments and the large and small telescopes for the sun, moon and stars.

One of the contrivances shown to us was as follows. There were two adjoining rooms. In one there was a wheel, and on that wheel were two large, spherical, crystal balls. To these were attached a hollow cylinder, narrower than a reed, from which a long chain ran into the other room. When the wheel was turned, a fiery wind ran along the chain into the other room, where it surged up from the ground and, if any man touched it, that wind struck his finger and jarred his whole body. What is still more wonderful is that if the man who touched it held another by the hand, and he another, and so formed a ring of twenty or thirty persons, each of them would feel the same shock in finger and body as the first one. We tried this ourselves. Since they did not give any intelligible reply to our questions, and since the whole thing is merely a plaything, we did not think it worthwhile to seek further information about it.

Another contrivance which they showed us consisted of two copper cups, each placed on a chair, about three ells apart. When a fire was lit in one of them, it produced such an effect on the other, despite the distance, that it exploded as if seven or eight muskets had been discharged.

The third contrivance consisted of small glass bottles, which we saw them strike against stone and wood without breaking them. Then they put fragments of flint in the bottles, whereupon these finger-thick bottles, which had withstood the impact of stone, dissolved like flour. When we asked the meaning of this, they said that when glass was cooled in cold water straight from the fire, it became like this. We ascribe this preposterous answer to their Frankish trickery.

Another contrivance consisted of a box with a mirror inside and two wooden handles outside. When the handles were turned, rolls of paper in the box were revealed in stages, each depicting various kinds of gardens, palaces and other fantasies painted on them.

After the display of these toys, a robe of honor was presented to the astronomer and money given to the servants of the Observatory.

—Mustafa Hatti Efendi

A View of Western Science (1947)

The educated men whom I saw in all the lands of Islam have long since abandoned any attitude of scorn toward European science. They do not like it, but they respect it. For the technician, for example, they have even a kind of admiration. But they are little attracted by the philosopher, whose method is after all the very basis of a technology. They know that technicians are necessary, that a country must either import technicians from abroad or, preferably, produce them. They are well aware that this engendering of technicians is a long-term business; some of them think that European science can be bought, like everything else. The idea that in order to produce an ample supply of technicians it is necessary to acquire the spirit of the method, that is to say, to accomplish radical reforms in the way of thinking—this idea disturbs them. But I nevertheless take the liberty of telling them that it is the only salvation.

—Georges Duhamel

Music

An Appreciation
(Early Tenth Century)

These are excerpts from the chapter on music in a classical Arabic the-saurus entitled Al-'Iqd al-Farīd *(The Precious Necklace).*

We do not wish this book of ours, after dealing with the different branches of polite literature, and wisdom, and curiosities, and proverbs, should be neglectful of this art which is the foraging ground of audition, and the pasturage of the soul, and the spring grass of the heart, and the arena of love, and the comfort of the dejected, and the companionship of the lonely, and the provision of the traveller, because of the important place of the beautiful voice in the heart and its dominating the entire soul.

Physicians assert that the beautiful voice moves in the body and flows in the veins. In consequence, the blood becomes pure through it, and the heart is at rest through it, and the soul is quickened through it, and the limbs are agitated, and the movements are brisk. And for that reason they disliked that the child should be put to sleep after crying unless it be danced and sung to.

Sometimes one apprehends the blessings of this world and the next through beautiful melodies. And a proof of that is that they induce generosities of character in performing kindness, and observing family ties, and defending one's honour, and overlooking faults. And sometimes man will weep over his sins through them, and the heart will be softened from its hardness, and man will remember the joys of the Kingdom [of Heaven], and image it in his mind.

Did Allāh ever create anything more striking to the heart and more impressive to the mind than the beautiful voice especially if it comes from a beautiful face.

—Ibn 'Abd Rabbihi (translated by Henry George Farmer)

Western Music (Tenth Century)

I have never heard worse singing than that of the people of Schleswig. It is a humming that comes out of their throats, like the barking of dogs, but more beastlike.

—Ibrāhīm ibn Ya'qūb

Turkish Chamber Music (1717)

Her fair Maids were rang'd below the Sofa to the number of 20, and put me in Mind of the pictures of the ancient Nymphs. I did not think all Nature could have furnish'd such a Scene of Beauty. She made them a sign to play and dance. 4 of them immediately begun to play some soft airs on Instruments between a Lute and a Guitarr, which they accompany'd with their voices while the others danc'd by turns. This Dance was very different from what I had seen before. Nothing could be more artfull or more proper to raise certain Ideas, the Tunes so soft, the motions so Languishing, accompany'd with pauses and dying Eyes, halfe falling back and then recovering themselves in so artfull a Manner that I am very possitive the coldest and most rigid Prude upon Earth could not have look'd upon them without thinking of something not to be spoke of. I suppose you may have read that the Turks have no Music but what is shocking to the Ears, but this account is from those who never heard any but what is play'd in the streets, and is just as reasonable as if a Foreigner should take his Ideas of the English Music from the bladder and string, and marrow bones and cleavers.

—Lady Mary Wortley Montagu

Paris Opera (1720)

There is in Paris a special kind of entertainment called opera, where wonders are shown. There was always a great crowd of people, for all the great lords go there. The regent goes often, and the king from time to time, so I decided to go too. . . . Each is seated according to his rank, and I was seated next to the king's seat, which was covered with red velvet. The regent came that day. I cannot say how many men and women there were. . . .

The place was superb; the staircases, the columns, the ceilings and the walls were all gilded. This gilding, and the brilliance of the cloth of gold that the ladies were wearing, as well as of the jewels with which they were covered, all in the light of hundreds of candles, created the most beautiful effect.

Opposite the spectators, in the place of the musicians, hung a brocaded curtain. When everyone was seated, the curtain was raised, and a palace appeared, with actors in theatrical costumes and about twenty angel-faced girls, with gold-laced dresses and skirts, that cast new radiance on the assembly. Then there was music, then a moment of dancing, and then the opera began.

—Mehmed Efendi

Musical Diplomacy in Spain: A Turkish Ambassador Reports (1787–89)

During meals . . . [the Spaniards] greatly admired the musicians and singers who accompanied our mission. At the king's command, all the grandees, one after another, invited us to dinner, and we suffered the tedium of their kind of music.

—Vasif Efendi

"If it Had Not Been for Lehar" (1916)

The winter of 1916 in Stamboul was enlivened by the visit of Lehar with an excellent company from Vienna. The leading actress, Milovitch, had a great success, and was fêted and admired by German officers and Turkish Beys.

The Harems buzzed with stories of the fabulous presents she was receiving from her many admirers. One well-known personage was reputed to have made a cover of hundred-pound notes as an offering, and had spread it over a divan where he wished to taste the charms of the fascinating creature.

"Allah! These Western women," they murmured. "It seems that these 'Marguerites' like to be paid before permitting a man to savour them! Had one heard how Talaat Pasha had had his face slapped by the *Giaour* [Christian] Milovitch?"

With many a laugh the story went the round of the harems. How Talaat had invited the fair enchantress to a banquet in her honour. Wine and champagne had flowed, and the lady had been most lavish in her smiles and caresses. The soup appeared—Talaat watched and waited. Would she now acknowledge him as her loved one? The glamorous lady was hungry—the soup was excellent. But she, alas, swallowed with large greedy gulps, when suddenly she spluttered and choked in a most unglamourous way. Talaat thumped her on the back and implored her not to let it go down the wrong way! Had he not dropped a huge diamond in her plate?

The lady spewed out the soup and the diamond, turned round on him and slapped his face. "Clumsy pig!" she had called him. An oaf, an imbecile. Why had he not given it in a bouquet or a box?

A slap was all the reward that Talaat had for trying to stage a modern version of Cleopatra's pearl.

—Princess Musbah Haidar

Arts and Letters

A Well-Turned Thought
(Ninth Century)

Poetry is the mine of knowledge of the Arabs, the book of their wisdom, the muster-roll of their history, the repository of their great days, the rampart protecting their heritage, the trench defending their glories, the truthful witness on the day of dispute, the final proof at the time of argument. Whoever among them can bring no verse to confirm his own nobility and the generous qualities and honored deeds which he claims for his forebears, his endeavors are lost though they be famous, effaced by the passage of time though they be mighty. But he who binds them with rhymed verses, knots them with scansion, and makes them famous through a rare line, a phrase grown proverbial, a well-turned thought, has made them eternal against time, preserved them from negation, averted the plot of the enemy, and lowered the eye of the envious.

—Ibn Qutayba

The Power of Poetry
(Mid–Twelfth Century)

Poetry is the art by which the poet arranges imaginary propositions and the deductions drawn from them, so as to show what is small as great and what is great as small, to present beauty in the guise of ugliness and ugliness in the form of beauty. Through the imagination, he stirs up the forces of anger and lust, so that by these imaginings moods may be exalted or depressed and mighty things accomplished in the order of the world.

—Niẓāmī-i Arūḍī of Samarkand

Lady Mary on Turkish Scholars (1717)

I had the advantage of lodging 3 weeks at Belgrade with a principal Effendi, that is to say, a Scholar. This set of men are equally capable of preferments in the Law or the Church, those 2 Sciences being cast into one, a Lawyer and a preist being the same word. They are the only men realy considerable in the Empire; all the profitable Employments and church revenues are in their hands. The Grand Signor, thô general Heir to his people, never presumes to touch their lands or money, which goes in an uninterrupted succession to their Children. 'Tis true they lose this privelege by accepting a place at Court or the Title of Bassa, but there are few examples of such fools amongst 'em. You may easily judge the power of these men who have engross'd all the Learning and allmost all the Wealth of the Empire. Tis they that are the real Authors, thô the Souldiers are the Actors of Revolution. They depos'd the late Sultan Mustapha, and their power is so well known 'tis the Emperor's interest to flatter them.

—Lady Mary Wortley Montagu

Ancient Arabian Poetry: Four Western Views

1966

It is impossible to imagine the prehistory of this literature, any more than its transition to the alphabet used in the time of Muhammad. As everywhere in the world, Arab civilization was born, before the emergence of prose, with a magnificent flourishing of lyrical poems which were declaimed, not written. These are skilled works, full of obscure terms, preserving a powerful rhythm. Our translations cannot render the incomparable wealth of vocabulary that is the mark of the great artists; they leave in the shadows the grave sonorities and the musical grace of the Arabic language. The charm of the cadence is broken, and the harmony of the vowels no longer appears; all that one achieves is banalities, redeemed in the original by the sumptuous finery of the language. Their authors are masters of all their technical devices: they are virtuosos who know all the resources of their language, its subtleties as well as its difficulties, of which it is stylish to make light. These are the indisputable poetic skills. These works are therefore not easily accessible without a commentary, even for native Arabic speakers; hence scholiasts have devoted themselves to their hearts' content to explain, in current, everyday language, the arabesques of a verbal game.

—Gaston Wiet

1951

Pre-Islamic poetry is the expression, one-sided and stylized but faithful in its one-sidedness, of primitive Arab society before Islam came to give it a new face and a dynamic faith. It reflects the harsh and rough life of nomadic tribes wandering in the deserts of northern and central Arabia. . . . The most prized virtues are prowess in war and liberality toward guests, the needy, and petitioners, in the hard daily struggle for existence against an inclement nature. The joys of life are the love that nomadic existence condemns to frequent partings and separations, the wine bought from foreign merchants, the game of *maisir,* which, with arrows used as lots, determines the division of the parts of a slaughtered animal, the hunt for ostriches, onagers, and wild cows, already perceived as an aristocratic and chivalrous sport.

—Francesco Gabrieli

1926

The most striking feature in Arabic literature is its unexpectedness. Over and over again, with scarcely a hint to give warning of what is coming, a new literary art emerges fully-fledged, often with a perfection never equalled by later exponents of the same art. Nowhere is this element of surprise more striking than in the first appearance of Arabic as a vehicle of literature. At one moment Arabia seems, in a literary sense, empty and dumb except for some votive or businesslike inscriptions in a variety of dialects. At the next, companies of poets spring up all over northern Arabia, reciting complex odes, *qaṣīdas,* in which a series of themes are elaborated with unsurpassed vigour, vividness of imagination, and precision of imagery, in an infinitely rich and highly articulated language, showing little or no traces of dialect, and cast into complex and flexible metrical schemes that rhyme throughout the poem.

—Sir Hamilton Gibb

1899

Whether the aesthetic pleasure . . . repays the immense effort that is required to achieve an understanding of ancient Arabian poetry seems questionable.

—Theodore Noeldeke

Precursors

The following excerpts are translated from two classics of medieval Arabic literature. The first and second come from an early eleventh-century work purporting to describe the adventures of a Syrian scholar named Ibn al-Qârih who was permitted to visit Heaven and Hell. The third comes from a twelfth-century philosophic tale, and tells of the gradual awakening of a child left alone on an uninhabited island.

Conversations in Heaven and Hell
with Pious Houris and a Pagan Poet
(Early Eleventh Century)

One of the houris laughing in her astonishment, he asked her what she was laughing at—to which she replied "I am laughing for joy at the grace of Allah! Do you know who I am, Ibn ul Qârih?"

"You are one of the houris of Paradise, whom Allah has created to reward the faithful" replied he. "His holy word says: As they were rubies and coral."

"I am like that by the blessing of Allâh the Most High! In the world I was known as Hamdûna, and I dwelt in the Iraqi quarter of Aleppo. My father owned a mill-stone, and I married a rag-picker, who divorced me on account of the stench from my breath, and I was one of the ugliest women in Aleppo. When I realised that, I took to asceticism in the world and devoted myself to prayer, living by my spinning, and that has brought me to what you see me now!"

Then said the other: "Do you know who I am, Ibn ul Qârih? I am Tawfiq the Black who served as secretary in the Bagdad Library in the time of Abû Mansûr Muhammad ibn Alî the librarian, and I used to fetch out the books for the copyists."

"There is no deity but Allâh!" exclaimed he. "You were black, and you have become whiter than camphor!"

"Are you surprised at that?" replied she, "when the poet says of a certain mortal: 'If a single spark from his whiteness were to fall on all the negroes, it would turn the black men into white.' " . . .

Conversation with Imru ul Qais (a Major Pre-Islamic Arabic Poet)

Ibn Qârih then enquired for Imru ul Qais ibn Hujr, "Abû Hind (Imru ul Qais)," said Ibn Qârih, "tell me about the doggerel attributed to you; is it true that the following verse is by you (reciting a verse repeated by certain people):

> *If passion plagues the lad*
> *Who goes to worse from bad,*
> *He loses half his strength,*
> *Till the passion drives him mad.*
> *And the lover declines at length."*

"By Allah," replied he, "I have never heard it. It is a style I do not affect. Slander is all too common, and I attribute this calumny to one of the post-Islamic poets, who did me injustice and injury. . . .

"Is such stuff as this attributed to me? Doggerel is the lowest form of poetry, and this metre is the weakest form of doggerel metre."

                    —Abu'l-'Alā' al-Ma'arrī (translated by G. Brackenbury)

Growing up on a Desert Island
(Twelfth Century)

Thus far had his observations brought him . . . when he was one and twenty years old. In which time he had made abundance of pretty contrivances. He made himself both clothes and shoes of the skins of such wild beasts as he had dissected. His thread was made of hair, and of the bark of the stalks of Althaea, mallows or any other plants, which afforded such strings as were fit for that purpose. He learned the making of these threads from the use he had made of the rushes before. He made awls of sharp thorns, and splinters of cane, sharpened with flints. He learned the art of building from the observations he made upon the swallows' nests. He built himself a store-house and a pantry, to lay up the remainder of his provision in: and made a door to it of canes twisted together, to prevent any of the beasts getting in during his absence. He took birds of prey and brought them up for hawking; and kept tame poultry for their eggs and chickens. He took the tips of the buffalo's horns and fastened them upon the strongest canes that he could get, and staves of the tree *al-zan* and others; and so, partly by the help of fire, and partly of sharp-edged stones, he so fitted them that they served him in-

stead of so many spears. He made him a shield of hides folded together. All
these pains he took to furnish himself with artificial weapons, because he
found himself destitute of natural ones.

Now, when he perceived that his hand supplied all these defects very
well, and that none of all the various kinds of wild beasts durst stand against
him, but ran away from him, and were too nimble for him, he began to con-
trive how to be even with them, and thought there would be no way so
proper as to choose out some of the strongest and swiftest beasts of the island, and bring them up tame, and feed them with proper food, till they
would let him back them, and then he might pursue the other kinds of wild
beasts. There were in that island both wild horses and asses; he chose of
both sorts such as seemed fittest for his purpose, and by exercise he made
them so gentle and tractable that he was complete master of his wishes. And
when he had made out of the skins of beasts such things as served him com-
petently well, instead of bridles and saddles, he could very easily then overtake such beasts as he could scarce ever have been able to have caught by
any other manner of way.

—Ibn Ṭufayl (translated by Simon Ockley)

Persian Quatrains

*Thanks to Edward FitzGerald's translation of the Quatrains (Rubaiyat) of
Omar Khayyám, this verse form has become familiar to readers of English
poetry. It was used by many other Persian poets.*

They said be patient, patience will bear fruit.
I suppose it will, but in another life.
I have spent my whole life being patient;
I'll need another life to reap the fruits.

—Daqīqī

If coming had been my choice, I would not have come.
If going were my choice, would I ever go?
Better this ruined abode had never seen me,
Not come, not stay, not go.

—Sanā'ī

In one hand the Qur'ān, in the other a wineglass,
sometimes keeping the rules, sometimes breaking them.

Here we are in this world, unripe and raw,
not outright heathens, not quite Muslims.

—Mujīr

The spring of youth has gone its dismal way,
   it gave me only pain the livelong day.
My life is blank like death, and all my song
   is but a dirge for lights melting away.

—Khāqānī

He who built the heavens and made the stars
and fashioned mind and soul and made mankind
tied all the strings of being in a knot,
then lost the thread of this cosmic tangle.

Lord, of your grace all that I hope is this—
keep the realm of my pleasure prosperous,
avert from me the calamity of chastity,
and keep far from me the doom of repentence.

—'Ubayd-i Zākānī

PART XI

Food and Drink

I drink to the general joy of the whole table.
—SHAKESPEARE

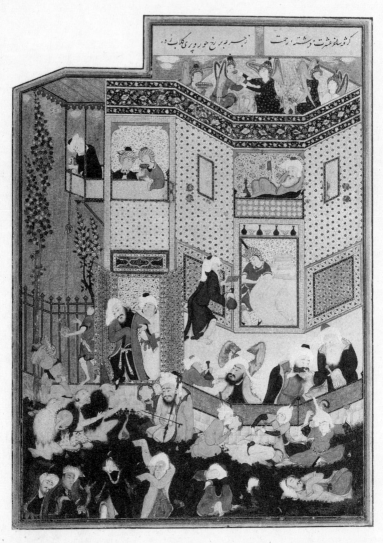

Worldly and otherworldly drunkenness from the Dīwān of the great Persian lyrical poet Ḥāfiẓ, c. 1527.

Introduction

ookery—that is, the art of preparing food to give pleasure as well as mere nourishment—is already attested in the ancient Middle East. What may well be the oldest recipe in the world survives in a cuneiform inscription from ancient Assyria. This is all the more remarkable, coming as it does from a time when writing required a rare skill and involved great toil, and when reading was the privileged mystery of a small group of initiates. There are texts dealing with the selection and combining of ingredients, the preparation and serving of dishes and the holding (with details) of feasts, for family, political and above all religious occasions.

The Jews were also interested in these matters and devote a surprising amount of attention in their religious and legal literature to the selection and combination of ingredients. Their primary concern is with what is lawful rather than what is tasty, but some interest in the latter appears in other texts.

Islam also has dietary laws, but they are less complex and less restrictive than those of the Jews. The Jews made dining almost a religious rite. The Friday-evening dinner to welcome the Sabbath is a family occasion, with both menu and ritual to match. For every meal there are blessings to be recited in gratitude for God's bounty: blessings on the fruit of the earth, the fruit of the tree, the fruit of the vine. There are special dinners for major festivals, the most noteworthy being the Seder, the prescribed sequence of prayer, food and drink that introduces the great Passover commemoration of the Israelites' exodus from Egypt. The Last Supper, it will be recalled, was a Seder.

Banquets could serve a political as well as a religious purpose. The Assyrian king Ashurnasirpal II, who ruled from 884 to 816 B.C.E., thought it worthwhile to include a description of a meal in a major inscription near the doorway to his throne room. The inscription lists the king's achievements, among them a celebratory banquet to inaugurate a new palace. The banquet lasted ten days, with food and drink for 69,574 invited guests, including—it may be noted—both men and women. The food served to these guests is specified and enumerated in great detail: so many head of cattle, calves, sheep, lambs, stags, gazelles, ducks, geese, doves and other birds, fish, eggs, bread, as well as vegetables, fruits, nuts, condiments and spices, all listed in great detail. The service also included ten thousand kegs of beer and ten thousand skins of wine.

The ancient Arabs had a diet of extreme simplicity, consisting basically of milk and dates, occasionally supplemented, when circumstances permitted, by some kind of meat. The Arab conquests of the seventh and eighth centuries brought greater sophistication in this as in so many other matters. A revealing anecdote from an early historian tells how the Arabian Bedouin first learned about rice from the conquered Persians. Classical Arabic literature preserves historical reports about what the ancient kings of Persia and Arabia ate and how their meals were prepared, as well as practical advice on how to prepare tasty dishes and how to serve them to the best advantage. Tax records and historical narratives based on them provide much information on the food supply, especially in discussions of taxes levied in kind.

Wine, with appropriate benedictions, figures prominently in Jewish rituals, notably in the evening feasts that introduce the Sabbath and the festivals. The use of wine was retained by Christianity but was rejected by Islam, which bans all intoxicating drinks. The intermittent enforcement and flouting of this ban form an interesting chapter in the social history of the Middle East.

The Greek word for wine, *oinos* (compare Latin *vinum* and its equivalents), and the Hebrew *yayin* are clearly related. Both probably derive from some earlier people who belonged to neither the Indo-European nor the Semitic families but who taught both of them how to ferment, prepare and drink wine. The brewing of beer from barley and other cereals is also attested in antiquity and continued into Islamic times. To fermentation and brewing, human ingenuity added distilling.

From early times, Middle Eastern peoples devised, made and used a wide variety of stoves, ovens and the like for heating their food, and of cook pots, bowls and dishes for preparing and serving it. Unlike their neighbors to the east and to the west, they used no implements for conveying the food from the dish to the mouth. Using neither chopsticks nor cutlery, they relied on the five fingers of the hand—the right hand only, since the left hand was reserved for unclean bodily functions. They did, however, develop an elaborate code of eating etiquette and table manners, respected by the great and the humble alike.

For those who observed the ban on alcohol, there was no lack of other drinks. Milk from various animals, both sweet and curdled; fruit juices, pure, spiced or mixed with water; all helped to slake the thirst and wash down food. The two hot drinks most widely consumed in the Middle East both came late and from outside: coffee from Africa, tea from China. Coffee, first cultivated and consumed in Ethiopia, was taken from there to Yemen and then through western Arabia to Egypt, the Levant and Turkey. Its use became general in the sixteenth century. The first descriptions of coffee and coffee drinking by Western travelers are mostly rather disdainful, but in time the habit spread. Tea is mentioned by Arab visitors to China at an early date and may have been introduced to Persia by the Mongols, but its use did not become general until centuries later, when it was reintroduced by European merchants.

The discovery of America brought a number of new commodities to Europe and eventually to the Middle East, where some of them became enormously popular. The potato and the tomato have become essential ingredients in Middle Eastern cuisine; chocolate also was well received. In the Middle East as in Europe, exotic products were given exotic—and often wrong—names. A strange American bird was called "turkey" in England, though it had nothing to do with the country of that name. The same bird, brought to the Middle East, is called *hindi,* that is, "Indian," in Turkish and is variously known as the "Greek cock" or Ethiopian cock" in Arabic. Maize, another American product, is called *mısır,* i.e., "Egypt," in Turkish and "Syrian sorghum" in Arabic. Perhaps the most widely used American import was tobacco, first introduced by English merchants at the beginning of the seventeenth century.

A seventeenth-century Turkish review of the annual parade of the guilds and crafts of Istanbul gives some idea of the scale of the food industry in a major city. The first section, led by the "chief of the farmers," is that of cultivators. These include gardeners, grafters and sellers of vegetables. The next group, led by the "chief of the bakers," includes the bakers (with special bakers employed in the bakehouses of the Janissaries), the salt makers, the cracker bakers, several different kinds of pastry cooks, followed by the water carriers, millers, flour merchants, purifiers of corn, sieve makers, bag makers, starch makers and biscuit bakers. Another group includes the "Egyptian merchants," importers of rice, coffee and sugar; the purveyors of rice, lentils, sugar and sweets, musk sherbets and coffee (these last are "three hundred men and shops, Greek and rich"). The next section consists of the butchers, slaughterers, beef butchers, Jewish butchers, sheep butchers and a number of others concerned with the care, slaughter and sale of animals for food. A large group are the milkmen, divided into purveyors of buffalo milk, sheep's milk, cheesemongers, cream merchants, butter merchants and yogurt sellers. The cooks in various groups form an important contingent, as do the sellers of various kinds of dried and salted meat. There are also the purveyors of liver, tripe and a kind of haggis, of vinegar, pickled fruits and vegetables, garlic and onions, all separately listed. An inter-

esting group are those who cook for the poor—2,000 men, with 555 shops.
There is also a separate guild of carvers: "At every cook shop there is found
at least one carver, who, after having set the dish before the guests, says
'Bismillah' ['In God's name'] eats two morsels, and then bids the guests eat."
There are roasters and stewers and preparers of saffron pilâv, stuffers [*dol-
maci*] of pumpkins, eggplants, vine leaves, onions, etc.; purveyors of mustard, almond cream, syrups and sherbets and other drinks. The snow and
ice merchants have a place near the vegetable market. The fish inspector is
responsible for various groups of fishermen, with separate listings for those
who fish with line, harpoon, pots, baskets and other devices, and various
different kinds of nets. In addition, there are the net makers who serve the
fishermen and the fish cooks whom the fishermen serve. The author of this
description notes that while some of these guilds have shops, which he enumerates, others sell and even prepare their wares in the streets. The general
habit of buying prepared food in the markets or in the streets is noted by
several European travelers to the Middle East.

This section begins with two sets of rules for eating, one from a medieval
Persian theologian, the other from a modern English handbook of etiquette
for travelers to the Middle East. The remainder offers a selection of extracts
from Western and Middle Eastern authorities dealing with various aspects of
the procurement, preparation and consumption of food and drink. It ends,
appropriately, with coffee and tobacco.

Rules

A Medieval Muslim Guide (Eleventh–Twelfth Centuries)

He [who eats] should begin with "In the name of God" and conclude with
"Praise be to God." It is even better if he says, "In the name of God" with
every bite so that gluttony does not distract him from naming Almighty God.
With the first bite, he should say, "In the name of God," with the second bite
"In the name of God, the Merciful," and with the third bite "In the name of
God, the Merciful and the Compassionate." He should say it aloud so as to
remind others.

He should eat with his right hand, begin with the salt and end with it. He
should take small bites and chew them well. He should not stretch out his
hand to take another mouthful until he has completely swallowed the first,
as this would show excessive haste in eating.

He should not find fault with any dish. It was the custom of the Prophet, may God bless and preserve him, not to complain of any dish. If he liked it, he ate it, and if not, he left it.

He should eat that which is near to him except for fruit, for which he is free to move his hand around. . . .

He should not eat from the belly of the bowl nor from the middle of the food; but he should eat from the roundness of the loaf except when there is only a little bread. He should break bread and not cut it with a knife. Nor should he cut meat, since it is forbidden. [The Prophet] said, "Tear it with your teeth." No bowl or other vessel should be placed on the bread, but only foodstuffs. The Prophet said, "Honor bread, which Almighty God sent down as a blessing from Heaven." He should not wipe his hand with bread. The Prophet said, "If any of you lets a mouthful drop, he should pick it up, remove any dirt on it and not leave it for the Devil."

He should not wipe his hand on the napkin until he has licked his fingers, since he does not know which part of his food is blessed. He should not blow on hot food, for that is forbidden. He should be patient until he can eat it. . . . He should not drink much while eating, unless he is choking on a mouthful or is really thirsty. That is recommended medically and strengthens the stomach.

As regards drinking, good manners require that he should take the jug with his right hand and say, "In the name of God" and drink in sips, not gulps. The Prophet said, "Sip the water but do not gulp it, since liver disease comes from gulping." He should drink neither standing nor lying, since the Prophet has forbidden drinking while standing. . . .

He should stop eating before being sated, lick his fingers and wipe them on the napkin. Then he should wash them and collect the crumbs. The Prophet said on this point, "He who eats what falls from the table lives in comfort and has healthy children." He should use toothpicks and not swallow everything that the toothpick pushes from between the teeth, but only what is collected from the teeth by the tongue. Whatever is brought out by the toothpick should be thrown away. After using the toothpicks, he should rinse his mouth. . . . He should lick the bowl and drink its liquid, since it is said, "Whoever licks the bowl and drinks the liquid has as great a merit as if he freed a slave." It is also said, "The breadcrumbs from the table are the dower of the lustrous-eyed houris."

Some Additional Rules Concerning Eating in Company

He should not begin to eat if he is in the company of someone who deserves precedence either for seniority in age or for greater merit. If he himself is the one who gives the lead and is followed, it would be proper for him not to keep people waiting too long if they have come together in order to eat.

They should not be silent during the meal, for that is the custom of the foreigners. But they should speak of suitable things and tell stories of pious men, eating, and other topics.

He should be attentive to his neighbor who shares the same bowl and not try to eat more than he does, for that is forbidden. . . . It is better for him to offer precedence to the other. He should not eat two dates at a time, unless the others do it or he has sought their permission. If his companion shows little alacrity or inclination to eat, he should urge him and say, "Eat" but should not do so more than three times, for that would be to harass and importune him. It was the custom of the Prophet, when he was spoken to on a matter three times, not to respond after the third. He would repeat what he said three times only, for more than that would not be good manners. It is also forbidden to induce people to eat by oaths. Ḥasan, the son of 'Alī, may God be content with both of them, said, "Food is too trivial for oaths."

He should not oblige his companion to say to him, "Eat." A man of culture said, "The best of eaters is he who does not oblige his friend to concern himself with him while eating and spares his friend the trouble of speaking."

He should do nothing which would disgust another person. He should not move his hand around in the bowl and should not bring his head too close to it when he puts a mouthful in his mouth. If he takes anything out of his mouth, he should turn his face away from the food and take it out with his left hand. He should not soak fat pieces in vinegar nor throw vinegar on the fat pieces, for his neighbors would dislike this. If he has bitten a piece of something with his teeth, he should not soak the remainder in the gravy or the vinegar. Further, he should not converse about matters that arouse disgust.

—Al-Ghazālī

A Modern Guide (1984)

Most formal entertaining nowadays is to some extent an adaptation of the old style and large official gatherings in Saudi Arabia and the Arabian Peninsula combine features of the old and new worlds, but everywhere now there are likely to be tables and chairs. Coffee is likely to be served in the Arabian style before the meal in a *majlis* or outer room. One will be then invited to the dining room with the word *"Tafaddal!"*—which really means "be pleased to" or "be good as to . . ." do something, for example, proceed to the table, start eating or precede another. There are few lunches or dinners given by hosts in the Arab world where there is a formal placement at tables, though sometimes seats are allocated at a high table, and possibly other prominent tables, for V.I.P.s. More often there is free seating at such functions for the majority.

The places at table are like to be set in European style with knives, forks, spoons and plates, but the dishes set out on the table will usually be traditional Arab ones, such as piled rice, a whole sheep or goat, some fish dish and a variety of side dishes. Though one's plate may well be heaped by one's host or neighbour with far more food than one can manage, it is not obligatory to eat it all, even if chided gently for lack of appetite with some phrase as "But you have not eaten." . . .

A very large formal gathering in Iraq, Jordan, Syria or parts of North Africa may take this form but elsewhere, for example, in Egypt, Sudan and Lebanon smaller dishes may be provided and the whole sheep or goat is less often displayed. . . .

Gestures and Actions

In some places parties, including lunches and dinners, are held sitting on the ground and it is regarded in the Middle East as a sign of pride and boorishness to point the soles of one's feet at any one. The fact that one may have done this without any comment being made does not mean that it has passed unnoticed. It is also very impolite not to rise if anyone, particularly someone senior, comes into a room or joins an assembly or meeting. Casual posture on some occasions may also attract unfavourable attention. It is a major faux pas, and almost certain to be misunderstood, if one beckons someone, underhand, in the manner usual in Britain, Europe and the U.S. Such a gesture has the same sort of connotations as the incorrect form of Churchill's famous wartime V sign. Much the same applies to the thumbs up sign. Beckoning in the Middle East has to be done by putting up the hand like a policeman halting traffic and then rolling all the fingers over together outward and overhand. Waving of the left hand in greeting is wrong. This, as with the handshake, must be done with the right hand.

Belching is never obligatory in the Arab world, but at a traditional Arab feast some guests will mark their appreciation by deep belches. . . .

The Arab tradition is to take off one's shoes or sandals when entering the house. This custom is less rigid nowadays, particularly when the entertaining is of a sophisticated nature or involves people other than Arabs; and it does not apply at all in the great cities of the Middle East. However, if the gathering is a small one—in the Arabian Peninsula—it is wise to watch what one's host or other guests do.

—Sir Donald Hawley

Middle Eastern Views

The Discovery of Rice (Seventh Century)

Some Persian pickets whom an Arab force surprised in the marshes took flight, leaving behind them two baskets, one containing dates and the other what they afterward learned to be unhusked rice. The Arab commander told his men, "Eat the dates, but leave this other thing, for it must be poison which the enemy has prepared for you." They therefore ate the dates and avoided the other basket. But while they were eating, one of their horses broke loose and started to eat the rice. They were about to slaughter the horse, so that they could eat it before its flesh was poisoned, but the horse's owner told them to wait and said that he would see to it in due course. The following morning, finding that the horse was still in excellent health, they lit a fire under the rice and burned off the husks, and their commander said, "Pronounce the name of Allah over it and eat." And they ate of it, and they found it a most tasty food.

—Ibn al-Faqīh

Tales of a Wine Bibber (Eighth Century)

One day, the poet Abū Nuwās was passing a school and he heard a boy ask the teacher, "What did Abū Nuwās mean in his verses

Pour me wine and tell me, this is wine!
Do not pour it in secret when you can pour it openly.

What is the purport of this?"

The teacher said, "I don't know." The boy said, "The poet wanted to complete the five senses. When he drinks wine, he enjoys the pleasures of sight, touch, smell and taste. This is the purport of his saying, 'Pour me wine.' But the pleasure of hearing was missing, and that's why he said, 'Tell me, this is wine,' so that he might find it in the sound of these words and thus complete the pleasures of all five senses."

Abū Nuwās said, "You have explained to me things in my poem which I myself neither understood nor intended."

A man was found with the appurtenances of wine in his possession and was brought before the prince. The prince said, "Punish him with the prescribed punishment [*ḥadd*] for the wine bibber." The man asked, "Why, O Prince?" to which the prince replied, "The instruments of drinking were found in your possession." The man said, "You should therefore also punish me with the punishment for the fornicator." The prince asked, "Why?" and the man said, "Because I also have in my possession the instrument of fornication." The prince laughed and ordered his release.

—Al-Qalyūbī

Warnings (Ninth Century)

Three things cause emaciation: drinking water on an empty stomach in the morning, going to sleep without making a bed and much talking in a loud voice.

It is said that four things are injurious to life and often kill: to go into the bath in gluttony, to have intercourse after repletion, to eat dried jerked meat and to drink cold water on an empty stomach in the morning. Some add: to have intercourse with an old woman.

—Ibn Qutayba

In Praise of Wine (Thirteenth Century)

One day Abū Nuwās was seen with a glass of wine in his hand, a bunch of grapes on his right and a dish of raisins on his left, and every time he drank from the glass he took a grape and a raisin. "What does this mean?" they asked him, and he replied, "This is the Father, the Son and the Holy Spirit."

—'Ubayd-i Zākānī

Watching People Eat: A Turk in Paris (1720)

Men and women began to come in crowds, some to pay me visits, others just out of curiosity. They overwhelmed me with ceremonies and compliments. What they most wanted was to see me eat. They came to announce the daughter or the wife of someone or other, requesting permission to be present at my dinner. Sometimes it happened that these were people whom I couldn't refuse and was therefore obliged to admit then. Since it was their fast time and they themselves could not eat, they surrounded the table and watched us. This unfamiliar behavior caused us some annoyance, but we endured it out of courtesy. It is a custom of the French to watch people eat. When for example the king takes his meal it is their custom to grant permission to those who want to watch him. What is even more strange, they go to watch how the king gets up in the morning and gets dressed.

—Mehmed Efendi

An Egyptian Shaykh Discovers the Restaurant (1826–31)

You should know that the food of the Parisians is wheat, mostly in small grains unless it is imported from foreign countries. They grind it in windmills and water mills and bake it in bakeries. The bread is sold in shops. Everyone has a daily ration which he buys from the baker. The purpose of this is to save time and money since everyone else is busy with his own special work from which the baking of bread at home would distract him.

The market inspector orders the bakers to keep a daily supply of bread sufficient for the city. Indeed, there is never a shortage of bread in Paris nor for that matter, of any other foodstuff.

Besides bread, the ordinary diet of the Parisians consists of meat, groceries, vegetables, dairy products, eggs, etc. The dishes are in general varied even among the poor. The slaughterhouses are placed on the outskirts of the city, not inside. This serves both to contain the filth and to prevent the damage which the beasts might do if they escaped. The method of slaughter is different. To kill a sheep, which is easier, they put the knife behind the throat, that is to say, between the throat and the neck, and cut it in the opposite way from ours. They slaughter calves in the same way. As to oxen, they hit them in the middle of the head with a poleax. The ox is stunned by the force of the blow, which they repeat several times. The ox is felled but is still twitching, and they then slaughter it in the same way as sheep. I sent my Egyptian servant to the slaughterhouse to slaughter the animals which I had bought, as usual. When he saw how they treated the oxen in this loathsome way, he came back giving praise and thanks to God for not having made him an ox in the land of the Franks. . . .

To make life easier for the people of Paris, there are certain eating places called "restaurants." There a man can find everything he finds at home or more. Sometimes what he orders is prepared and ready. In "restaurants," there are many fine rooms, with home conveniences. Some even include places to sleep, splendidly appointed. As well as food and drink, the restaurants supply a variety of fresh and candied fruit.

It is the habit of the French to eat on plates, resembling Persian and Chinese plates, never on copper dishes. Before each diner they place a fork, a knife and a spoon on the table. The fork and the spoon are of silver. They consider it a mark of cleanliness and good manners not to touch anything with the hand. Each person has a plate in front of him, a different plate for each dish. Likewise, each man has a glass in front of him, in which he pours his drink from a large bottle on the table. Then he drinks, and no one intrudes on another's glass.

The vessels containing drink are crystal and glass. On the table there are several small glass receptacles, of which one contains salt, another pepper, another mustard, etc.

In a word, their manners and customs at table are excellent. The meal begins with soup and ends with dessert and fruit. As drink, they usually take wine rather than water with their food. Usually, especially among the great, their drinking stops short of drunkenness, which they regard as a vice and a scandal. After the meal, they may drink a kind of brandy. Though they drink wine, they do not compose much poetry about it, nor do they have as many names for wine as do the Arabs. They enjoy the pleasure of the thing and do not imagine far-fetched conceits and metaphors. . . .

In Paris, they often drink tea after the meal, saying that it helps to digest the food. Some drink coffee with sugar. Most people make a practice of crumbling bread into their coffee, mixed with milk, and taking it in the morning. . . .

Despite their versatility in the preparation of food and sweetmeats, their dishes in general lack flavor, and there is no real sweetness in the fruits of this city, apart from peaches.

There are innumerable taverns, and there is not a street that is not full of them. Only dissolute people frequent them, the riffraff with their women. They make a lot of noise and come out shouting words that mean "Drink, bring drink." In spite of this, even when drunk, they do no damage.

One day, when I was walking in the street in Paris, a drunkard shouted, "Hey, Turk, hey Turk," and grabbed my garment. As we were near a shop where they sold sugar and suchlike, I went in with him, seated him on a chair and said to the proprietor, jokingly, "Would you give me some sugar or candied fruit for the value of this man?" "Here," replied the proprietor, "unlike your country, it is not permitted to traffic in human beings." To which I replied, "But this drunkard is not, in his present state, a human being." All this happened without the man, slumped in the chair, being aware of anything. I left him there and went my way.

—Shaykh Rifā'a Rāfi' al-Ṭahṭāwī

Western Views

Table Manners in Cairo (1384)

In the city there are very many cooks, who cook outside in the street, by night and by day, in great cauldrons of copper, the finest and good meats. And no citizen, however rich, cooks at home, and so do all in pagandom, and they even send to buy at these bazaars, as they call them. And often they set themselves to eat on the streets, where they spread a skin on the ground, and they place the viands in a basin in the centre, and they sit around on the ground with legs crossed or squatting. And when they have soiled the mouth, they lick it with the tongue as dogs, which they are.

—Lionardo Frescobaldi

Discovering the Banana in Alexandria (1384)

Alexandria . . . is a very attractive city and has very beautiful and spacious streets; and it trades in goods of every kind, and it abounds in victuals of all kinds, meat, fruits of the world's best, and especially very large pomegranates, which within are like the blood of a he-goat and are as sugar. And so with pears, apples, plums and other like fruits, very large water melons, yellow within and with pips between red and yellow, and truly the tongue of man could not recount their sweetness. Again there is a fruit on which our forefather Adam sinned, which fruit is called muse [Arabic *mawz*, "banana"]; and they are in colour like our cucumbers. It is true they are somewhat longer and a little thinner, and they are delicate to the taste, very soft, and the taste is so different from our fruits that he who gets used to eating the said fruit, enjoys it so much as to leave everything else. In this fruit is seen a very great wonder, for when you divide it in any way, either by its length or by its breadth, whichever way you cut it, the Crucifix is distinctly to be seen inside: and in proof our company did it several times. And by many these are called Paradise apples, and this must be the proper name.

—Simone Sigoli

Street Vendors in Damascus (1384)

There is always snow in Damascus; and in summer they put it on the fruit, so they are fresh when eaten, and so iced are they that it is a pleasure. In

Damascus, and in all the cities over there, all foods are sold on the street, as bread, water, cooked meat of every kind, and every kind of fruit, since the Saracens over there do no cooking at home and nothing in the necessities of life. But they send out for everything they want, and throughout the whole city there are in several places cooks, who cook a great deal of every kind of meat; and they make kitchen in everything, and they cook well and clean: and so they give to others any kind of meat or kitchen a man may wish, and the amount a man may wish, and so they go through the city selling the said things. And those who go about selling the said things carry a table on IV legs on their heads; and on it is a fire-place with a pan, all the while aboiling; and on it is the meat, a bowl, a small ladle, the water and the salt and everything necessary. And the Saracens set themselves down on benches on the street to eat; and he waits until he has eaten; and they drink mere water, or certain waters with dried grapes or prepared some other way, and they spend little on their food, on their kitchen, or on their dress.

—Giorgio Gucci

Dining in Turkey

Orders from the Sultan (1573–85)

Infidels may have their wine but should not try to corrupt the true believers.

23 Rabi 'I 981 [July 23, 1573]

Order to the kadi of Istanbul: In former times the infidels were forbidden to bring wine into the cities, and the collection of taxes from wine was forgone. The infidels, however, have by trickery brought in wine after all, and since no tax was collected the treasury suffered serious loss. This matter was referred to the chief mufti, the most learned of the ulemas of the time, who rules as follows: "It is lawful to collect the tithe at the half rate on wine brought by non-Muslim subjects of the Sultan, and at the full rate on wine brought by foreign infidels. It is, however, certainly not lawful publicly to import wine into cities where the Friday prayer is performed, nor is it lawful for them to sell publicly to one another the wine which they have bought secretly, still less to sell it to Muslims. When they sell wine to one another let them in no way make this public."

Acting in accordance with this noble fetva, a commissioner has been appointed to collect the tithe on wine, and an Imperial order to this effect has been issued. At the present time it has been made known to me that Jews and Christians in the God-guarded city of Istanbul, contrary to the noble fetva and to my imperial order, are publicly introducing wine and spirits in barrels, casks and skins and are holding feasts and playing music at their gatherings and parties. I have therefore decreed that, as soon as this order reaches you, you shall give clear and proper warning to the Jews and Christians, and also the gatekeepers of the God-guarded city, not to bring wine and spirits publicly into the city in barrels, casks or skins, not to sell to Muslims that which they bring secretly by night for their own use, and to keep their sales of wines among themselves secret; not to turn their houses into taverns, or sell wines and spirits publicly; not to perform music at their feasts.

An application from the butchers of Istanbul for a remission of taxes is rejected.

26 Ramazan 993 [September 21, 1585]

Order to the kadi of Istanbul: You have stated in a letter to us that the butchers of the God-guarded city have come to the court of the Holy Law, saying, "While the authorized price of mutton in the God-guarded city is one oke [400 dirhams] for three aspers, in accordance with an old law it must be sold to Janissaries at the rate of 150 dirhams for one asper. In 5½ months of the year 993, we have slaughtered 23,500 head of sheep and sold them to Janissaries at the prescribed price. Because of the resulting losses which we have suffered, we are now unable to pay the debt of 200,000 aspers which we owe to the cattle dealers." You have further stated that when they asked for a gracious remission of the butcher's tax due from them, Ilyas Chaush, the sheep commissioner, confirmed the truth of what they said.

In this matter my decree has been issued that the law must be observed. I have commanded that . . . whatever the ancient law may be, you must act in accordance with it and henceforth avoid anything contrary to it.

—Ottoman Imperial Orders

A Turkish Palace Feast, and its Disappointing Menu
(1582)

"The True description of the magnificall Triumphs and Pastimes, represented at Constantinople, at the solemnizing of the Circumcision of the Soldan Mahument, the sonne of Amurath, the thyrd of that name, in the yeare

*of our Lorde God 1582, in the Monethes of Mai and June," contained in a
letter written by Francis Billerbeg in Latin to "A Godly learned man of Germanie." This English translation was published in London shortly after,
probably in 1585.*

If you now ask me what and how many sorts of meats there were then
served at this feast: there was no other thing at all, but hens and mutton,
with some porridge and boiled broth, and such like things set upon the
table: but there you should not see venison, wildfowl, nor any kind of fish,
whatsoever, nor no dainty nor licquorish meat, all simply, and homely
dressed, if a man should compare them with ours here, and yet nevertheless, all the guests were well content with their fare, but they were ill served
with their drink, for they were served with no other, but water and sugar:
they be such people, as openly before anybody, they abstain altogether
from drinking of wine: but among themselves privately, all the wine in the
world would not satisfy, nor suffice them, such gluttons, and licquorish people they are: and thus do they feast themselves twice every day. And toward
the evening, they bring forth before the people (so desirous to see the Triumphs, and magnificencies, which pass day by day, to behold) into the
same Park aforesaid, being set down together there upon rushes, they bring
forth (I say) green cheese, bread, broth, and mutton, in a thousand platters,
and dishes every day: and as soon as the meat is brought, the tabers, and
trumpets sound out, at the first sound whereof, the people comes running
to this kitchen, fighting and scrambling for their supper, and for their meat,
as earnestly as if it were to run to make an assault: so that one snatcheth on
one side, and another on the other side, and that as one hath caught and
gotten, another is ready to pluck and tear again from him. . . . You should
see them run so on heaps after their vituals, as if they were dogs half starved
to death; yea, and a man might well call this a feast for dogs, for there was
nothing at all brought them to drink. The meats being taken away, Amu-
rathe cast down from his graffolds, of gold and silver by handfuls, with gob-
lets of gold and silver, very cunningly inwrought and made with pieces of
gold, and diverse sorts of money: behold now what a solemn feast this was.

—Francis Billerbeg

Lady Mary on Spices and Soop (1717)

She entertain'd me with all kind of Civillity till Dinner came in, which was
serv'd one Dish at a time, to a vast Number, all finely dress'd after their manner, which I do not think so bad as you have perhaps heard it represented.
I am a very good Judge of their eating, having liv'd 3 weeks in the house of

an Effendi at Belgrade who gave us very magnificent dinners dress'd by his own Cooks, which the first week pleas'd me extremely, but I own I then begun to grow weary of it and desir'd my own Cook might add a dish or 2 after our manner, but I attribute this to Custom. I am very much enclin'd to beleive an Indian that had never tasted of either would prefer their Cookery to ours. Their Sauces are very high, all the roast very much done. They use a great deal of rich Spice. The Soop is serv'd for the last dish, and they have at least as great Variety of ragoûts as we have. I was very sorry I could not eat of as many as the good Lady would have had me, who was very earnest in serving me of every thing. The Treat concluded with Coffee and perfumes which is a high mark of respect. 2 slaves kneeling cens'd my Hair, Cloaths, and handkercheif. After this Ceremony she commanded her Slaves to play and dance, which they did with their Guitars in their hands, and she excus'd to me their want of skill, saying she took no care to accomplish them in that art. I return'd her thanks and soon after took my leave.

—Lady Mary Wortley Montagu

Dinner-Dance in Istanbul (1785)

My application in collecting many words, and above all my eagerness to use them, enabled me within a short time to express myself passably well; I had already reached the point when I could dispense with an interpreter, when M. de Vergennes, wishing to give a feast assembling all the foreign ministers as well as all the Europeans established in Constantinople, ordered the necessary preparations. This news aroused the curiosity of several distinguished Turks, who asked if they could be present, and I undertook the more willingly to do the honors for them as I saw in this a new opportunity to practice their language.

I had recently got married, and the friendly relations between my father-in-law and one of the most important of these Turks added to the interest inspired in him by my zeal to improve my knowledge. He asked me when he arrived to point out Madame de Tott among the numerous women whom he saw; and soon, very attentive to her smallest movements, he followed her with his eyes and seemed uneasy if she escaped his attention for one instant in the crowd. . . . The questions of my Turkish guests were no less enjoyable than instructive for me.

A minuet opened the ball; they asked me who was the dancer? "It is the Swedish envoy." "What!" said the Turk with surprise—"the Swedish envoy;—the minister of a court allied to the Sublime Porte!—but this is not possible—you are mistaken; look, look more closely." "I am not mistaken," I said to him. "It is indeed he." The Turk, finally convinced, lowered his eyes, reflected, and was silent until the end of this minuet, which was then followed by another; a new question, to know who was the dancer. "It is the ambassador of Holland"—"Oh, for that one," the Turk said gravely, "that I will never believe." "I know," he continued, "how far the magnificence of an ambassador of France can stretch; and despite my surprise, I can carry this opinion far enough to conceive that he might be rich enough to hire a minister of second class to dance; but at what price could he obtain this service from an ambassador?" . . . I used all the Turkish words that I knew to make him understand that these ministers were the guests of the feast, that they were not hired performers, that they were dancing for their pleasure, that the ambassador of France would himself dance. It was hard to persuade him. However, an object which the Turk thought no doubt even more interesting soon occupied him entirely. "I no longer see your wife," he said to me—"Ahh! There she is—but someone is speaking to her! Go quickly to stop this conversation." "Why should I?" I asked. He then explained himself more clearly and I undertook to calm him when Madame de Tott, still talking, entered the gaming room and disappeared. The Turk then lost all countenance. He stood up and dragged me with him; I let him lead me, and the spectacle of several tables where women and men were arguing was certainly not that which his friendship desired for me.

Supper was served, and my friend, observing that the guests were distributed among different tables, wanted to leave. An anxiety of an even more serious kind seemed to agitate him. I urged him to stay to the end of the feast. "It's all over," he said to me, sharply. "They are starting to drink. Let us go, and if you believe me, take your wife and you go too." "I hear what you say," I said to him; "but be assured, all will pass more calmly than you think." I insisted and I managed to take them around the tables, and to persuade them to sit down at the places which had been assigned to them. Some glasses of liquor, giving them courage, completed the persuasion; they stayed until morning, and told me when leaving that if such a feast were given among them, it would not end without thirty murders.

—Baron de Tott

Dinner with the Kapudan Pasha (1829–31)

A British naval officer is guest of the head of the Ottoman fleet.

The ceremony being concluded, his excellency and myself prepared to sup, for which task the Black Sea air had given me a keen appetite. A small carpet was spread between two guns on the main deck outside his cabin. It was not skreened off. On it we sat down, cross-legged opposite to each other. Two agas—they were gentlemen of no less rank—knelt to us with ewers to wash our hands; then tied napkins round our necks, and placed between us a circular metal tray upon a low stool, provided with four saucers, containing as many kinds of conserves, slices of bread and of cake, salt, and a bowl of salad sauce, to be eaten at discretion. Our fingers were the operating instruments.

The first dish was a pile of red mullet. The pasha of course had the first help; being a bit of an epicure, he pawed every one individually before choosing. I took one whose tail only had come in contact with his forceps. The next dish was a fowl. The pasha steadied it with the thumb of his left hand, and with his right hand pulled off a wing. I tried the same manoeuvre on a leg; but, owing to delicacy in not making free use of both hands, failed in dislocating it. The pasha perceiving my awkwardness, motioned to an officer to assist me. I would fain have declined his services, but it was too late. The fellow took it up in his brawny hands, ripped off the joints with surprising dexterity, peeled the breast with his thumb-nail, tore it in thin slices, and, thus dissected, laid the bird before me with an air of superiority, saying, "Eat." I was very hungry, or I should not have been able. The third dish was lamb stewed with olives. On this I showed that I had fully profited by my late lesson, and, dreading the intrusion of another person's fingers on so slippery a subject, dug my own in with unblushing effrontery. I followed precisely the pasha's motions, scooping the olives out of the dish, with a piece of bread and my thumb, as adroitly as though I had never seen a fork. The attendants winked at each other, and my host's unmeaning eyes faintly radiated at the rapidity with which I adapted myself to existing circumstances. I never fully understood before the point of saying, "Do at Rome as Rome does." Various other meats followed, which I will not enumerate; they were all diminished by a similar process; suffice to say that they were excellent, the Turkish kitchen being in many points equal to the French kitchen, and in one article superior—the exquisiteness of lamb drest in Turkey far, very far, surpasses my feeble praise. About twelve dishes, of which, in compliment, I was obliged to eat more than my inclination prompted, rendered still more irksome by the absence of wine, had been shifted with great dispatch, and a pause ensuing, I began to breathe, thinking my repletory task over, when, to my utter dismay, a huge platter of pilaff, the standing last dish, was placed between us. Never having liked rice since I was at school, the sight of the pressed greasy mess before me was positively revolting. However there it was, and had I only been required to eat a pound of it, I might have esteemed myself happy. A much severer trial awaited me. The pasha immersing his fingers deep into it, drew forth a tolerable quantity, with which he amused himself some minutes, rolling it into a ball, while I stared, simply supposing that the delicate morsel, when it should have received the last touch, was destined for *his* throat. It was lucky that I did not foresee its right destination, or the bare thought would infallibly have made me forget myself, which would have grieved me before so many witnesses, not to mention the insult of the restitution. When fairly reduced to the substance of a rape-shot, the pasha stretched his lean hand over the tray; I involuntarily shrunk back; he stretched further, and inserted it—O nausea!—into my mouth. I swallowed it with an effort of despair, but know not what power of nerves kept it down. The attendants arched the brows of wonder: a capitan pasha bestow such an exceeding mark of distinction on a stranger! Had there been then a gazette in Stamboul the circumstance would have been published, at our return, as the most notable event of the cruize. I was delighted to find that the honour was too great to be repeated.

The appetizers which came on with the tray were removed, and replaced by a bowl of koshub, a sweet liquid, composed of various preserved fruits, perfumed with rose; two tortoise-shell spoons were in it. This was very good, especially as we were not reduced to lap it up with the palms of our hands, as I might have reasonably expected after what had passed. A glass of sherbet assisted our deglutition, and chibouques, with coffee, assured its efficacy: while enjoying the latter, an Albanian bagpipe, harsher, if possible, than a Scotch one, supplied the absence of conversation.

—Adolphus Slade

Coffee and Tobacco

A Turkish Cure for Melancholy (1621)

The Turks have a drink called Coffa (for they use no wine) so named of a berry as black as soot, and as bitter . . . which they sip still of, and sup as warm as they can suffer; they spend much time in those Coffa-houses, which are somewhat like our Ale-houses or Taverns, and there they sit chatting and drinking to drive away the time, and to be merry together, because they find by experience that kinde of drink so used helpeth digestion, and procureth alacrity.

—Robert Burton

Coffee and Tobacco in Istanbul (c. 1635)

As seen by an Ottoman historian who disliked both.

Until the year 962 [1555 C.E.], in the high, God-guarded capital city of Constantinople, as well as in the Ottoman lands generally, coffee and coffeehouses did not exist. About that year, a fellow called Hakam from Aleppo and a wag called Shems from Damascus came to the city; they each opened a large shop in the district called Tahtalkale, and began to purvey coffee. These shops became meeting places of a circle of pleasure seekers and idlers, and also of some wits from among the men of letters and literati, and they used to meet in groups of about twenty or thirty. Some read books and fine writings, some were busy with backgammon and chess, some brought new poems and talked of literature. Those who used to spend a good deal of money on giving dinners for the sake of convivial entertainment found that they could attain the joys of conviviality merely by spending an asper or two on coffee. It reached such a point that all kinds of unemployed officers, judges and professors, all seeking preferment, and corner sitters with nothing to do, proclaimed that there was no place like it for pleasure and relaxation, and filled it until there was no room to sit or stand. It became so famous that, besides the holders of high offices, even great men could not refrain from coming there. The imams and muezzins and pious hypocrites said, "People have become addicts of the coffeehouse; nobody comes to the mosques!" The ulema said: "It is a house of evil deeds; it is better to go to the wine tavern than there." The preachers in particular made great efforts to forbid it. The muftis, arguing that anything which is heated to the point of carbonization, that is, becomes charcoal, is unlawful, issued fetvas against it. In the time of Sultan Murad III, may God pardon him and have mercy on him, there were great interdictions and prohibitions, but certain persons made approaches to the chief of police and the captain of the watch about selling coffee from back doors in side alleys, in small and unobtrusive shops, and were allowed to do this. . . . After this time, it became so prevalent, that the ban was abandoned. The preachers and muftis now said that it does not get completely carbonized and to drink it is therefore lawful. Among the ulema, the shaykhs, the viziers, and the great, there was nobody left who did not drink it. It even reached such a point that the grand viziers built great coffeehouses as investments and began to rent them out at one or two gold pieces a day.

The Coming of the Fetid and Nauseating Smoke of Tobacco

The English infidels brought it in the year 1009 [A.D. 1600–1] and sold it as a remedy for certain diseases of humidity. Some companions from among the pleasure seekers and sensualists said, "Here is an occasion for pleasure," and they became addicted. Soon those who were not mere pleasure seekers also began to use it. Many even of the great ulemas and the mighty fell into this addiction. From the ceaseless smoking of the coffeehouse riffraff the coffeehouses were filled with blue smoke, to such a point that those who were in them could not see one another. In the markets and bazaars too their pipes never left their hands. Puff-puffing in one another's faces and eyes, they made the streets and markets stink. In its honor they composed silly verses and declaimed them without occasion.

Sometimes I had arguments with friends about it. I said: "Its abominable smell taints a man's beard and turban, the garment on his back and the room where it is used; sometimes it sets fire to carpets and felts and bedding and soils them from end to end with ash and cinders; after sleep its evil vapor rises to the brain; and, not content with this, its ceaseless use withholds men from toil and gain and keeps hands from work. In view of this and other similar harmful and abominable effects, what pleasure or profit can there be in it?"

To this the only answer they could give was "It is an amusement and, moreover, a pleasure of aesthetic taste." But there is no possibility of spiritual pleasure from this which could pertain to matters of aesthetic taste. This answer is no answer. It is pure pretension.

Apart from all this, it has several times been the cause of great fires in the high God-guarded city of Constantinople. Several hundred thousand people suffered from those fires. Only this much is conceded, that it is of use for the guarding of galley slaves, as the guards on the ships can to some extent ward off sleep by using it, and that, by guarding against humidity, it induces dryness. But it is not permissible, according to reason or tradition, to perpetuate such great damage for such small benefit. By the beginning of the year 1045 [A.D. 1635–36], its spread and fame were such that they could not be written or expressed.

May Almighty God add increase to the life and might and justice and equity of our sovereign emperor [Murad IV] (God strengthen his helpers), who has closed all the coffeehouses throughout the divinely guarded realms and caused suitable shops to be opened in their place and who has commanded that smoking be totally forbidden. By this means he has conferred such great boons and benefactions on the rich and poor alike, that if they thank him until the Day of Judgment, they will not properly discharge their debt of gratitude.

—Ibrahim Peçevi

The Sin of Smoking: Arabia (c. 1869)

'Abd-el-Kereem doubted not that he had a sincere scholar before him, nor would refuse his hand to a drowning man. So, putting on a profound air, and with a voice of first-class solemnity, he uttered his oracle, that "The first of the great sins is the giving divine honours to a creature."

*Jewish woman in Turkey smoking a chibouk, by G.
Rumpf, 1768.*

"Of course," I replied, "the enormity of such a sin is beyond all doubt.
But if this be the first, there must be second; what is it?"

"Drinking is shameful," in English, "smoking tobacco," was the unhesi-
tating answer.

"And murder, and adultery, and false witness?" I suggested.

"God is merciful and forgiving," rejoined my friend; that is, these are
merely little sins.

—William Gifford Palgrave

PART XII

Wit
and
Wisdom

. . . some work in which the most thorough
knowledge of human nature, the happiest delineation
of its varieties, the liveliest effusions of wit and
humor are conveyed to the world in the
best chosen language.
—JANE AUSTEN

Socrates and two students, from an Arabic manuscript of The Choicest Maxims and Best Sayings of al Mubashshir; *probably Syria, first half of the thirteenth century. An English translation of this work was the first book printed in England.*

Introduction

The ancient literatures of the Middle East offer a great deal of wisdom but not very much wit. In the words of the late Sabatino Moscati, "Humor, as our experience teaches, is rare in the ancient Orient; indeed, if these cultures produce any one direct and spontaneous impression, it is of their profound and almost gloomy seriousness" (*The Face of the Ancient Orient: A Panorama of Near Eastern Civilization in Pre-Classical Times,* New York, 1962, p. 192). Moscati allows some "exceptions to this general judgment" in Egypt, where "the peculiar geographical and political situation favors tranquillity of spirit, and the highly refined culture facilitates the further advance consisting in a readiness to smile." But there are few indications of such readiness in ancient literature. The Talmud indeed, in a number of places, explicitly condemns frivolous and lighthearted speech and conduct.

It is of course possible, even probable, that there is more wit than the modern reader can recognize or understand. Wit and humor depend very much on implied allusion to a frame of reference shared by the humorist and his audience. While some of this belongs to our common humanity, much of it is culture-bound, and with the passage of time and the change in cultures, the point has been lost and forgotten.

Wit as a weapon—sarcasm, satire, parody—was often used to discredit or ridicule beliefs, practices or manners that were seen as inappropriate. Elijah's taunting of the priests of Baal when their god failed to respond (1 Kings 18:27) is a classical example: "Elijah mocked them, and said, Cry aloud, for he is a god; either he is talking, or he is pursuing, or he is in a journey, or peradventure he sleepeth and must be awaked." More commonly, however, in the Bible mockery and ridicule are seen as evil—used by the wicked, suffered by the good.

The rabbis of the talmudic period, while disapproving of unseemly levity, do not disdain to make their points by using some of the devices of the humorist: puns and homonyms, deliberate mistranslations, even parodies of sacred texts. In the early centuries of the Islamic era, some Muslim writers show a similar willingness to use humor to make their point, even on sacred matters. In the later centuries a more rigorist attitude prevailed, and religion—though little else—was exempted from humorous treatment.

Two forms of humorous writing were especially favored in the classical Arabic tradition: parody and the pungent, pointed anecdote. Parody, depending for its effect on the reader's knowledge of the text or genre that is being parodied, is difficult to translate, and few parodies, however brilliant in the original, can survive the transition to another language, culture and time. The anecdote has fared much better, and some that are a thousand years old or more can still evoke immediate laughter.

Wisdom literature—the stringing together of a series of pithy aphorisms on loosely connected topics—is familiar to us from the biblical books of Proverbs and Ecclesiastes. There are many later collections of such aphorisms, written or compiled by Jewish, Christian and Muslim authors, in all the languages of the Middle East. A few samples follow.

Sayings of the Rabbis (First Century B.C.E.–Third Century C.E.)

Hillel [president of the Sanhedrin 30 B.C.E. to 10 C.E.] said: Don't separate yourself from the community, and don't trust in yourself until the day of your death, and don't judge another until you have been in his place. Don't say something incomprehensible, expecting it to be understood in the end, and don't say I shall study when I have time, for you may never have time. He also said: A boorish man does not fear sin and an ignorant man is not pious. The bashful do not learn and the pedant cannot teach, and not every successful trader grows wise. In a place where there is no man, try to be a man.

Akavya ben Mehallalel [second–third centuries C.E.] said: Pay attention to three things, and you will not fall into the way of sin. Know whence you come and whither you go and before whom you will be called to account. You come from a fetid drop and you go to a place of dust and worms and in the end you will give an account to the Almighty, blessed be He.

Ben Zoma [second century C.E.] said: Who is wise? He who learns from everyone. . . . Who is mighty? He who conquers his own passions. . . . Who is rich? He who is content with his portion. . . . Who is honored? He who honors mankind.

Shimon ben Elázar said: Do not soothe your friend when he is angry, and do not try to console him when his dead one is stretched out before him; do not question him while he is making a vow, and do not try to see him at the moment of his disgrace.

Elisha ben Abūya said: Learning as a child is like writing with ink on new papyrus. Learning in old age is like writing with ink on blotted papyrus.

Yose ben Judah from a village in Babylon said: He who learns from the young is like one who eats unripe grapes and drinks wine straight from the winepress. He who learns from the old is like one who eats ripe grapes and drinks old wine.

There are four measures of man. There is he who says, "What's mine is mine and what's yours is yours." This is a moderate middling measure. . . . He who says, "What's mine is yours and what's yours is mine" is an ignoramus.

He who says, "What's mine is yours and what's yours is yours" is pious, and he who says, "What's yours is mine and what's mine is mine" is wicked.

There are four measures of temper. Quick to anger and quick to be appeased, his gain equals his loss. Slow to anger and slow to be appeased, his loss equals his gain. Slow to anger and quick to be appeased is pious. Quick to anger and slow to be appeased is wicked.

There are four measures of pupils. Quick to learn and quick to forget, his gain is canceled by his loss. Slow to learn and slow to forget, his loss is canceled by his gain. Quick to learn and slow to forget, that is the good portion. Slow to learn and quick to forget, that is the bad portion.

—*Pirqē Avot*

A Saying Attributed to the Prophet

Lying is lawful only in three cases: when a man speaks to his wife, to soothe her; deceit in war; and a lie told to make peace among people.

Friends and Enemies

Ninth Century

The Prophet said, "The curse of God fall on the threefold sinner." They asked him, "O Prophet of God, who is a threefold sinner?" He answered, "He who denounces his friend to the ruler, thereby bringing destruction on himself, on his friend and on the ruler."

—Al-Mubarrad

Tenth Century

"If you see a fault in your brother and you hide it from him, then you betray him; if you tell it to anyone else, you slander him; if you confront him with it, you injure him." He was asked, "Then what should I do?" and he replied, "Convey it to him by hint and allusion as part of a general conversation."

He also said, "If you see a lapse in your brother, find seventy excuses for him. And if you do not find any, then blame yourself."

—Abū Ḥayyān al-Tawḥīdī

Eleventh Century

The measure of prudence and resolution is to know a friend from an enemy; the height of stupidity and weakness is not to know an enemy from a friend.

Do not surrender your enemy to oppression, nor oppress him yourself. In this respect treat enemy and friend alike. But be on your guard against him, and beware lest you befriend and advance him, for this is the act of a fool. He who befriends and advances friend and foe alike will only arouse distaste for his friendship and contempt for his enmity. He will earn the scorn of his enemy and facilitate his hostile designs; he will lose his friend, who will join the ranks of his enemies. . . .

Magnanimity is not to befriend the enemy but to spare them, and to remain on your guard against them.

—Ibn Ḥazm

Twelfth Century

Mus'id was asked: "Would you agree to have your faults enumerated?" He answered: "From one who wishes to counsel me, yes. From one who wishes to abuse me, no."

Be moderate in your love of your friend, lest one day he become your enemy. And be moderate in hating your enemy, lest one day he become your friend.

—Ibn Ḥamdūn

Beware of your enemy,
  and beware a thousand times of your friend;
For often a friend becomes an enemy
  and then he knows best how to harm you.

—Anonymous poet, cited by Ibn 'Abdūn

Early Fourteenth Century

Sufyān al-Thawrī said: "It is better for my enemy if I shoot an arrow at him rather than attack him with my tongue. Arrows may hit or miss, but the tongue never misses the target."

Injury with the tongue is worse than injury with a spear, and the wounds of words are heavier than the wounds of arrows.

A man of Medina was asked: "Won't you go out to fight against the enemy?" He answered: "I don't know them and they don't know me. How did we become enemies?"

—Al-Waṭwāṭ

Classical Arab Wit and Wisdom

Ibrāhīm ibn Sayāba wrote to a friend of his who had great wealth, a large income and much cash, requesting a gift or a loan of money. The man replied, "My children are many, my income small, my debts heavy, my wealth untrue." Ibrāhīm then wrote to him, "If you speak false, may God make it true. If what you say is a pretext, may God validate it."

Ibn Zubayr was denounced for his overlong sermon on the night of the festival of 'Arafa. He was astonished and he said, "I am standing and they are sitting. I am talking and they are silent. So what are they complaining about?"

Abū 'Ubayda said, "They asked an old man, 'What is left to you?' He said, 'Whoever is with me, goes ahead of me; whoever is behind me, catches up with me. I forget what is recent, I remember what is old; I doze in company and am wakeful when I am alone. When I stand, the ground comes up towards me, and when I sit down, it moves away from me.' "

Muwarriq al-'Ijlī [early eighth century] said, "I have been asking God for a boon for forty years. He has not granted it, but I have not despaired of it." He was asked, "What is it?" and he replied, "To mind my own business."

—Al-Jāḥiẓ (ninth century)

Salm ibn Qutayba asked Al-Sha'bī, "What does your soul desire?" He answered, "The most precious when it is missing, the most simple when it is present." Salm said to his servant, "Bring him water."

—Ibn Qutayba (ninth century)

Ḥātim passed by some men who were writing words of wisdom. He said to them, "There are three things such that if you have them, you will not succeed." They asked him, "What are they?" and he said, "Worry of yesterday, sorrow of today, fear of tomorrow."

Abū Ḥurayra [a companion of the Prophet] saw a man [whom he knew] with another and asked him, "Who is this with you?" The man answered, "My father." Abū Hurayra said, "Don't walk in front of him, and don't sit in his presence; don't call him by name, and don't expose him to insult [by anything you may do]."

—Abū Ḥayyān al-Tawḥīdī (eleventh century)

A ruler without justice is like a cloud without rain. A wise man without piety is like soil without plants. A youth without repentance is like a tree without fruit. A rich man without generosity is like a lock without a key. A poor man without patience is like a lamp without light. A woman without shame is like a dish without salt.

—Muḥammad ibn al-Walīd al-Ṭurṭūshī (twelfth century)

A prisoner was brought, with a group of other prisoners, to Ma'n ibn Zā'ida. He gave orders for them to be killed. The prisoner said, "O Ma'n! Will you kill thirsty prisoners?" Ma'n gave orders, and they were given drink. When they had drunk, the man asked, "O Ma'n! Will you kill your guests?" And he released them.

—Shihāb al-Dīn al-Nuwayrī (fourteenth century)

A man asked a slave, "Should I buy you?" The slave replied, "No." The man said, "Why not?" The slave replied, "How can you take me as a slave after you have taken me as an adviser?"

—Jalāl al-Dīn Suyūṭī (fifteenth century)

Dicts and Sayings
(ca. Eleventh Century)

The following excerpts are taken from a volume entitled The Dicts and Sayings of the Philosophers. *The English text, completed by one Stephen Scrope in 1450, was translated from a French book, itself a translation of a Latin version of a Spanish rendering of an Arabic original, consisting of a collection of aphorisms and anecdotes culled from the sages and writings of antiquity. Its author was Mubashshir ibn Fātik, an eleventh-century Egyptian scholar and writer, said to have been of Syrian origin. This collection is the only one of his many works that has survived. According to a late and unreliable source, when Mubashshir died, his wife, as an act of vengeance, had all his books thrown into the pool in their courtyard. It was, she said, for the sake of these books that he had neglected her. The popularity of this book is attested by its numerous manuscripts and citations. The Spanish translation, dropping the author's name, was made in about 1250, and served as a basis for other European versions. Scrope's English version, published by Caxton in 1477, was the first dated book printed in England. Three more editions followed before the end of the century.*

He that wille not be chastisid bi feire and soft wordis schulde be correctid bi foule and scharpe correccioun . . .

It is bettir to be stille than to speke to oon that is ignoraunt and to be aloone than to be in company and felawschip of eville peple . . .

It is bettir to a woman to be baraigne than to bere evil condicioned childre . . .

. . . Whenne a kinge may not Refreyne his evill couetises how maye he Reproue his seruauntis and whan he can not correct ne snybbe his owne seruauntis how may he Redresse his peple and tho that be ferre fro him A kinge than first must be lord of him silf and after that of other bi ordre . . . a verai king schuld not be suspecious for suspecion makeithe the peple to drawe fro him and also he schuld no suspecious peple haue in his house and in especial non accusrs contreuours ne reporters of wordis bihinde a mannes bakke for if the kinge suffre suche paciently he schall vnnethe haue in his hous sufficiaunt seruauntes ne good counsaillors . . .

. . . lif is schort & peyne is longe experience perillus & Iugement daungerus . . .

. . . The tunge of a discreete man is in his herte and the herte of a foole is in his tunge . . .

—Mubashshir ibn Fātik (translated by Stephen Scrope)

The Wisdom of Al-Watwāṭ (Thirteenth–Fourteenth Centuries)

Al-Watwāṭ was an Egyptian scholar and compiler of a well-known collection of anecdotes and aphorisms.

Rabī' ibn Khuthaym was asked, "Why do you never find fault with anybody?" He said, "I am not so fully satisfied with myself that I have leisure to seek out the defects of others."

Muḥammad ibn Wāsi' passed by a group of men. He asked about them and was told that they were pious men who had renounced the world. He asked, "Has the world enough value to make it worth renouncing?"

Shu'ayb al-'Ula'ī neither fasted nor prayed. He used to say, "Who am I to fast or pray? Let those who are proud and puffed up pray because they need to humble their pride. Let those who are sated fast, so that they may know the suffering of the hungry."

One of the sages of Persia said, "He who claims that he does not love money is a liar in my view, until he proves the truth of what he says. And if he does prove the truth of what he says, then he is a fool in my eyes."

They said to Bashshār ibn Burd, "So-and-so claims that he does not care whether he goes to battle against one or against a thousand." He answered, "He is right, since he runs away from one just as he runs away from a thousand."

A man was told, "If you encounter someone in the night, be brave and do not fear, for he is as much afraid of you as you are of him." He answered, "I am afraid that he would have heard this saying before I did."

They said to a hermit, "How great is your patience in solitude!" He replied, "I am the friend of God. When I wish Him to speak to me, I read his book, and when I wish to speak to Him, I pray."

When the qadi of Marv, Ibn Abī Maryam, wanted to find a bride for his son, he asked the advice of his Magian neighbor. The Magian said to him, "God be praised! People ask your advice, and you come and ask my advice?" The qadi answered, "You must give me your advice." The Magian said to him, "The emperor of Persia used to choose for money, the emperor of Rome used to choose for beauty, the Arabs used to choose for pedigree and Muḥammad your Prophet used to choose for religion. You choose whom you please."

—Al-Kutubī al-Watwāṭ

Thoughts from a Persian Satirist (Fourteenth Century)

Some Maxims

Dear friends, consider life as booty.

Don't postpone today's pleasure till tomorrow.

Use the moment, for life does not come round again.

Don't frequent the halls of kings, and bestow any gifts they give you on their doorkeepers.

Curse all those who frown and scowl and pucker their brows, who speak in deadly earnest, who are sour of face and shifty of temperament, misers and liars and defaulting debtors.

Fart in the beards of lords and great ones who are without decency.

As far as you can, speak no word of truth, so as not to get into trouble and not to cause needless pain to others.

Let your way of life consist of tomfoolery, pimping, begging, informing, bearing false witness, selling religion for worldly goods, and showing ingratitude for benefits received, so that thereby you may be esteemed among the great and enjoy a good life.

Don't set up house in a street where there are minarets, so that you may not be given headaches by the screaming of the muezzins.

Free yourselves from the bonds of name and reputation, so that you can live as free men.

Don't marry a preacher's daughter, so as not to beget donkeys.

Beware of the nurse's delight, the midwife's skill, the pregnant woman's tyranny, the cradle's noise, the father-in-law's greeting, the wife's importunity, and the child's clamor.

Let not the tools of eating and loving be idle at the same time.

Don't take your food and wine alone, for that is the way of qadis and of Jews.

Do not seek peace, joy or blessing in a house where there are two wives.

A just ruler, an unbribed qadi, an ascetic who speaks no hypocrisy, a pious chamberlain, an unsodomized courtier—do not seek them in this age.

Beat your wives hard, and when you have beaten them, love them hard so that they may fear and obey you. Let household authority be between fear and hope, so that sorrow may be changed into happiness.

Do not go on pilgrimage, lest zealotry overcome you, leaving you with neither faith nor decency.

When it is not necessary, do not jump into a well, so as not to injure your head and legs.

Some Definitions

From a Chapter on Government

The tax inspector—a thief.

The market inspector—a hellhound.

The general—a storehouse thief.

The night watch—one who robs by night and demands wages from the merchants by day.

The informer—the secretary of the Chancery.

From a Chapter on the Administration of Justice

The qadi—he whom everyone curses.

The qadi's deputy—he who has no faith.

The advocate—he who annuls truth.

The witness—he who never speaks truth.

The arbitrator—he who pleases neither God nor man.

The qadi's men—a band who sell their testimony for cash.

From a Chapter on Great Men and their Ways

Bragging and boasting—the working capital of the great.

Nothingness—their existence.

Emptiness—their civility.

Vanity and foolishness—their talk.

The simpleton—he who hopes for any good from them.

The nonexistent—their generosity.

The absent—their decency.

The phoenix—their justice and equity.

Cunning and deceit and hypocrisy and falsehood—the normal behavior of the great.

On the True Nature of Men and Women

A lady—a woman who has many lovers.

A matron—one who has few lovers.

A virtuous lady—one who is content with one lover.

A benefactor—one who makes love to an old woman.

A virgin—a girl who has not yet learned to make love.

Virginity—a reference without a referent.

—'Ubayd-i Zākānī

Servant Problems (Late Fourteenth Century)

Ibn Khaldūn is chiefly known for his immense contribution to historical and sociological thought rather than for witticisms and aphorisms. But the following passage, drawn from his prolegomena to the study of history, offers an attractive combination of wit and wisdom.

Really satisfactory and trustworthy servants are so rare as to be virtually nonexistent. Most servants fall into four categories and no more: those who are both competent and trustworthy; those who are neither; those who are competent but not trustworthy; and those who are trustworthy but incompetent.

As to the first category, few may hope to employ them since their competence and trustworthiness raise them above the need to accept wages from persons of low rank. Such are employed only by princes and others of high rank. As to the second category, no rational man would want to employ someone who is neither competent nor honest and who would injure his master in two different ways, harming him through his incompetence and betraying him by his dishonesty.

Since these two first categories are either unattainable or undesirable, there remain only the other two: honest and incompetent or competent and dishonest. Opinions differ on which is preferable. But the competent servant, even if he is dishonest, is better since one can take precautions against his dishonesty, while the incompetent servant, even if he is honest, does more harm than good.

—Ibn Khaldūn

Fuad Pasha (1815–69)

Fuad Pasha was five times foreign minister and twice grand vizier of the Ottoman Empire. His knowledge of French, acquired as a student, and his career first as an interpreter and then as a diplomat made him one of the first Ottoman statesmen with a mastery of a European language and a direct knowledge of Europe. As well as being one of the architects of the great Ot-

toman reforms of the nineteenth century, he was famed for his wit, stories of which have passed into Turkish folklore. The following are examples.

In 1867, Fuad Pasha, as foreign minister, accompanied Sultan Abdülaziz on a trip to Paris, London and Vienna. When the Emperor Napoléon III was told that the sultan had come to see him, he snapped, "Let him wait!" Then, remembering that Fuad Pasha knew French, he added hastily, "Please don't tell his Majesty the sultan what I just said!" Fuad Pasha, solicitous for the dignity of his master, replied, "Of course not—no more than I would tell Your Majesty what my master the sultan said."

In the course of one of his meetings in Europe, conversation among the diplomats and ministers turned to the question "Which is the strongest state in the world at the present time?" Some named England, others France, others Austria-Hungary, others Russia. Fuad Pasha said, "Gentlemen, you are all mistaken. The strongest state in the world today is the Ottoman Empire." Observing their expressions of polite disbelief, he added, "Don't think that I say this out of mere national pride. Just think—for centuries, you from outside, we from inside, we have all been trying to destroy it, and still it stands."

One evening in Istanbul, Fuad Pasha invited the foreign ambassadors and their wives to a reception in his palace. As often happened, arrangements were made for the ladies of the ambassadors to go on a conducted tour of the harem quarters. One of the ambassadors, perhaps unaware of the proprieties of Muslim domestic life, asked whether he could join the tour. To this Fuad Pasha replied, *"Monsieur l'ambassadeur, vous êtes accrédité à la Porte, mais pas au delà de la Porte."*

PART XIII

Prophecy

and

Retrospect

Rabbi Abdimi of Haifa said, "From the day the Temple was destroyed, prophecy was taken from prophets and given to the wise."

Rabbi Yohanan said, "From the day the Temple was destroyed, prophecy was taken from the prophets and given to fools and children."

—TALMUD, BABA BATRA

Aquarius, in an illustration from the Kitab al-Bulhan, *an Arabic tract on astrology, divination and prognostication; Baghdad, 1399.*

Introduction

The Middle East has traditionally been the home of the prophets, that is, all those who are revered as prophets in the three prophetic religions, Judaism, Christianity and Islam. The prophets revered by Jews and Christians all lived and died without exception in the little country which is holy to both religions and which has been known at different times by different names: Canaan, Israel, Judea, Palestine. Muslim tradition and scripture recognize some, though by no means all, of the biblical prophets and add a few others: Ṣāliḥ, Shuʿayb, Hūd and, most important of all, Muhammad. These all lived in the holy land of Islam: Arabia.

The followers of these different scriptures appear to agree that the mission of the prophets has come to an end and that there will be no more. The Islamic view is categorical: Muhammad was the last and greatest—the seal—of the prophets, and after him there will be no more. Any who claim prophethood are impostors. The Judeo-Christian position is less explicit, but no additional claims have been recognized.

During the Middle Ages the most common form of prophecy was the apocalyptic tract, foretelling the advent, struggles and final triumph of some messianic figure who would overcome the powers—and practitioners—of evil, and establish the kingdom of heaven on earth. The forces of evil and of good and the bringer of redemption are variously defined and identified in a succession of Jewish, Christian and Muslim apocalypses. Sometimes they express the frustration and aspirations of the dispossessed, or those who see themselves as such; sometimes they are propaganda designed to win support for a claimant to rule or a revolutionary sect or faction promising a better world. So far, all of them have failed—some quickly and simply, by being crushed in an unsuccessful bid for power; others in a slower and more complex way, by seizing power, and then showing themselves to be as bad as those whom they had supplanted or worse.

The older type of apocalyptic tract has almost died out, yet there must be something about the Middle Eastern air that continues to inspire men and women to predict the future—particularly though not exclusively the future in relation to the traditional home of the prophets. What follows is a selection of nineteenth- and twentieth-century prophecies that have from time to time been committed to writing. They are chosen from a much larger number. Some are from inside the region. Others are the work of visitors from elsewhere. Some of them are egregiously wrong; others show remarkable prescience.

Prophecy and Empire

The Ottoman Lands (1837)

So indifferent . . . are the authorities become . . . to Frank rights, so difficult is it to obtain redress for their arbitrary actions—so ready an excuse is forthcoming in our habitual shielding of a crime, that unless something be arranged, and a firm stand be made thereon, Turkey will soon become, I repeat it, too hot for anyone except Russian subjects, their protégés, and Americans.

—Adolphus Slade

The Dangers of Balkan Nationalism (1862)

From the Minister of Foreign Affairs, Constantinople, 18th September 1862, to the Ottoman Ambassador, Paris:

The existence of the Ottoman Empire, it is said, is important for the maintenance of the equilibrium of Europe. I believe it, and if one examines, thoroughly and without prejudice, the mind and condition of the members of the different nationalities that make up the population of Turkey, one will finally be convinced that only the Turks can hold them together and that, left to themselves, whether trying to impose the domination of one among them or trying to create between them something like a confederation, the result would be chaos and civil war in perpetuity. There is nothing in the East that could replace this old empire, which its enemies are pleased to call sick and of which impartial observers can only state the contrary. The hatred of the Bulgars and the Armenians for the Greeks, the condition of independent Greece, the result we have under our eyes of the autonomous administration in the principalities are so much proof in support of what I have just said.

Italy, which is inhabited by one race speaking the same language and professing the same religion, suffers so many difficulties in achieving its unification. For the moment, all that Italy has gained in its present state is anarchy and disorder. Think what would happen in Turkey if one gave free rein to all the different national aspirations that the revolutionaries, and with them certain governments, are trying to develop. It would take a century and torrents of blood to establish even a fairly stable state of affairs.

—Âli Pasha

New Zeal (1876)

Nations have revived. We may live to see a new outburst of force in the Arabs, who are being inspired with a new zeal. . . .

A new Persia with purified religion magnified itself in art and wisdom. So will a new Judaea, poised between East and West—a covenant of reconciliation.

—George Eliot

A Prophecy at the Turn of the Century

Diary entry, December 31, 1900

I bid good-bye to the old century, may it rest in peace as it has lived in war. Of the new century I prophesy nothing except that it will see the decline of the British Empire. Other worse empires will rise perhaps in its place, but I shall not live to see the day. It all seems a very little matter here in Egypt, with the Pyramids watching me as they watched Joseph, when, as a young man 4000 years ago, perhaps in this very garden, he walked and gazed at the sunset behind them, wondering about the future just as I did this evening. And so, poor wicked nineteenth century, farewell!

—Wilfrid Scawen Blunt

Intimations of War (1912–1914)

The first of the two following predictions is from a diary kept by one of the Young Turk leaders while serving in Libya against the Italians in 1912. He later became minister of war. The second is from a speech delivered by the British prime minister shortly after the outbreak of war in 1914.

Diary entry, October 4, 1912

At the moment everything in my fatherland is in flames. We are being attacked from every side. I often weigh the possibility of a world war. If Austria and Germany do not intervene to mediate, then very soon war will break out in the Balkans, and who knows what the consequences would be. . . .

A special embassy has arrived from the Grand Senussi Sidi Ahmad Sharif, bringing me greetings and gifts from the grand shaykh: two Negresses, ivory, etc. My God, what shall I do with these black ladies? He also sends me his own gun, which he has blessed.

—Enver Pasha

"The Death-Knell of Ottoman Dominion"

At length Mr. Asquith replied to the toast of "His Majesty's Ministers" for the seventh time in succession at this board. He first reviewed the new situation created by Turkey's appearance in the field. He showed how the Allies were compelled, in spite of their hopes and efforts and against their will, to recognize Turkey as an open enemy. It was the Ottoman Government which had drawn the sword, and which, he predicted, would perish by the sword. "It is they," the Prime Minister continued in impressive tones, "and not we who have rung the death-knell of Ottoman dominion, not only in Europe, but in Asia. The Turkish Empire has committed suicide and dug its grave with its own hand."

—The Prime Minister's Speech at the Guildhall Banquet, reported in *The Times,* London, November 10, 1914

A Turk in Hyde Park (1933)

Every time I come out of the conference chambers, I want to mount one of the soapboxes in Hyde Park. Indeed, if I only knew English, I would not be able to hold myself back. . . .

I, too, was the child of a great empire. We knew its last days as one comes to a dinner table where only the leavings remain. I don't know if you can imagine the map of this empire such as it still was in the time of our grandparents. Let me tell you what happened to us, in terms of your own present-day geography. We began our fighting retreat in Bombay and fought all the way back to London. Finally we made our last stand in Glasgow. Today our frontier is at Dover.

The Ottoman Empire was a hundred years old when England, which did not then include Scotland or Ireland, was a little country of three million inhabitants and London a town of forty thousand. Like Bulgaria, England sold sheep to the Europeans; like India, raw materials to the industrialized Flemings.

Because our empire was founded by conquerors, its dissolution was an epic. Because yours was organized by businessmen, you are conducting a business liquidation. As recently as 1918, General Milne was in Istanbul as virtual governor general of Turkey; in 1919 Sir Percy Cox in Tehran was virtual governor general of Persia; Japan was your fifth dominion. In the space of ten years, you had destroyed four empires by cracking them against one another like Easter eggs. But I saw that, at the conference in 1933, the Canadian delegate spoke over the head of Ramsay MacDonald. . . . [We Turks] returned to the soil of Anatolia, singing melancholy songs about Buda when we left the Danube, the Algerian march when we left North Africa, the Gaziler lament when we withdrew from the Arabian Seas. But for you, it is a downward graph that is driving you back to your island.

Because I was born and grew up amid the mood and the manners of an empire, I respond from afar with the sensitivity of a seismograph and feel in the mood and the manners of London the tremors of impending collapse.

—Falıh Rıfkı Atay

Prophecy and the Holy Land

Return to Judea (1843)

The Hebrew persecuted and down trodden in other regions takes up his abode among us with none to make him afraid. He may boast, as well as he can, of his descent from the Patriarchs of Old—of his wise men in council, and strong men in battle. He may even more turn his eye to Judea resting with confidence on the promise that is made him of his restoration to that holy land and he may worship the God of his fathers after the manner that that worship was conducted by Aaron and his successors in the priesthood, and the Aegis of the Government is over him to defend and protect him.

—President John Tyler

Jewish National Home: An Ottoman Prophecy (1917)

The German ambassador reports a conversation with the grand vizier.

That was the time of the Balfour declaration, and I too had discussed with Talaat Pasha the establishment of a Jewish home in Palestine. Talaat was ready to promise all I wanted, provided Palestine remained Turkish after the War, but he took every opportunity of saying: "I will gladly establish a national home for the Jews to please you, but mark my words, the Arabs will destroy the Jews."

—Count Bernstorff

Visions of Arab-Jewish Cooperation and Confrontation at Versailles (1919)

In 1919, during the Peace Conference in Paris, an attempt was made by T. E. Lawrence and Richard Meinertzhagen to bring the Zionist and Arab delegations together, and persuade them to cooperate. At first all went well, and good relations were established between the Zionist leader Dr. Weizmann and Prince Faisal. The following letter, addressed by the Prince to Felix Frankfurter, head of the Zionist delegation, illustrates the point. This honeymoon was of brief duration.

We Arabs, especially the educated among us, look with deepest sympathy on the Zionist movement. Our deputation here in Paris is fully acquainted with the proposals submitted yesterday by the Zionist Organization to the Peace Conference, and we regard them as moderate and proper. We will do our best, insofar as we are concerned, to help them through: we will wish the Jews a most hearty welcome home. With the chief of your movement, especially with Dr. Weizmann, we have had and continue to have the closest relations. He has been a great helper of our cause, and I hope the Arabs may soon be in a position to make the Jews some return for their kindness. We are working together for a reformed and revived Near East, and our two movements complete one another. The Jewish movement is national and not Imperialist, and there is room in Syria for both of us.

Indeed I think that neither can be a real success without the other.

People less informed and less responsible than our leaders and yours, ignoring the need for co-operation of the Arabs and Zionists, have been trying to exploit the local difficulties that must necessarily arise in Palestine in the early stages of our movements. Some of them have, I am afraid, misrepresented your aims to the Arab peasantry and our aims to the Jewish peasantry, with the result that interested parties have been able to make capital out of what they call our differences.

I wish to give you my firm conviction that these differences are not on questions of principle but on matters of detail such as must inevitably occur in every contact of neighbouring peoples, and are as easily adjusted by mutual goodwill. Indeed nearly all of them will disappear with further knowledge.

I look forward and my people with me look forward to a future in which we will help you and you will help us, so that the countries in which we are mutually interested may once again take their place in the community of civilized peoples of the world.

—Faysal ibn Ḥusayn (translated by R. Meinertzhagen)

Later in the same month Colonel Meinertzhagen wrote unofficially to Lloyd George, in London.

25.III.1919. *Paris   Personal*

My Dear Prime Minister,

You asked me yesterday to send you an unofficial letter on the subject of the sovereignty of Sinai. I regard this question as supremely important—not at the moment but in years to come. May I enter more fully into the question than I was able to do yesterday. . . .

In fifty years time both Jew and Arab will be obsessed with nationalism, the natural outcome of the President's self-determination. Nationalism prefers self-government, however dishonest and inefficient, to government by foreigners however efficient and beneficial. Nationalism moreover involves the freedom of the State but ignores the freedom of the individual; it is a sop to professional politicians and agitators, and may involve gross injustices to the people.

A National Home for the Jews must develop sooner or later into sovereignty; I understand that this natural evolution is envisaged by some members of H.M.G. [His Majesty's Government]. Arab nationalism will also develop into sovereignty from Mesopotamia to Morocco.

Jewish and Arab sovereignty must clash. The Jew, if his immigration programme succeeds, must expand and that can only be accomplished at the expense of the Arab who will do his utmost to check the growth and power of a Jewish Palestine. That means bloodshed. . .

(signed) R.M.
—Colonel Richard Meinertzhagen

Another Opinion (1920)

Two new elements of some interest have just set foot in Asia, coming rather as adventurers by sea—the Greeks in Smyrna, and the Jews in Palestine. Of the two efforts the Greek is frankly an armed occupation—a desire to hold a tit-bit of Asiatic Turkey, for reasons of trade and population, and from it to influence affairs in the interior. It appears to have no constructive possibilities as far as the New Asia is concerned. The Jewish experiment is in another class. It is a conscious effort, on the part of the least European people in Europe, to make head against the drift of the ages and return once more to the Orient from which they came. The colonists will take back with them to the land which they occupied for some centuries before the Christian era samples of all the knowledge and technique of Europe. They propose to settle down amongst the existing Arabic-speaking population of the country, a people of kindred origin, but far different social condition. They hope to adjust their mode of life to the climate of Palestine, and by the exercise of their skill and capital to make it as highly organised as a European state. The success of their scheme will involve inevitably the raising of the present Arab population to their own material level, only a little after themselves in point of time, and the consequences might be of the highest importance for the future of the Arab world. It might well prove a source of technical supply rendering them independent of industrial Europe, and in that case the new confederation might become a formidable element of world power. However, such a contingency will not be for the first or even for the second generation, but it must be borne in mind in any laying out of foundations of empire in Western Asia. These to a very large extent must stand or fall by the course of the Zionist effort, and by the course of events in Russia.

—T. E. Lawrence

"We Will Sweep Them into the Sea" (1948)

Recollection of the British Minister in Amman

The next caller of note at Amman was Abder Rahman Azzam [the Secretary General of the Arab League]. . . . We met on May 15th. After an exchange of insincere compliments, he told me about the abortive meeting at Jericho. He next asked me for an assurance that the British forces from Palestine, who were congregated in the north of Sinai, would not cut off the retreat of the Egyptian army formations if the latter advanced into Palestine. I felt able to reply that, in my view, any such move by our forces would be highly unlikely. He pressed me for a more categorical promise but he declined to take advantage of my offer to refer the matter to the Foreign Office.

After some more wavering, he stood up, struck a pose, and said, dramatically: "It is my duty to announce to you the intention of the Arab armies to march into Palestine tomorrow at midnight!" I retorted that the news did not surprise me. He went on to enumerate the approximate strengths of the various Arab armies available for the influx and, when I asked him for his estimate of the size of the Jewish forces, waved his hands and said: "It does not matter how many there are. We will sweep them into the sea!" He became quite peevish when I pointed out that, when one was considering a military problem, it was normal to take into account the courses which were open to the enemy as well as those open to one's self. It seemed to me that he was missing out the first part of the Jewish strength, but he dismissed as absurd my reply that common report placed it at about eighty thousand people. I put an end to the argument by remarking that it was difficult to talk sensibly if he, while admitting that he did not know the answer, refused to believe what I said to him. We parted on terms which were fairly correct but rather frigid. I never met him again.

—Sir Alec Kirkbride

War and Peace

The Future of King Hussein (1958)

In Jordan King Hussein faces a triple threat to his throne. The first will come when United States forces withdraw from Lebanon; the second when the West recognizes the Iraqi regime; and the third when the Soviets put on pressure at the summit for British withdrawal from Jordan. However much one may admire the courage of this lonely young king, it is difficult to avoid the conclusion that his days are numbered. A year ago he might have met great desire for change and secured his position by declaring himself president. But the time for such a stroke is past. Moreover, as the king admitted to me in Amman, the days are gone when he could look for help to King Saud whose ultra-cautious neutrality was shown by his refusal to allow oil for Jordan to be flown from Bahrein over Saudi Arabia. The best service Britain can now render Hussein seems to be, therefore, to offer to fly him to Cyprus when she withdraws her troops.

—Anthony Nutting

The Coming War (1967)

Observations of an Egyptian Journalist

I believe an armed clash between the United Arab Republic and Israel is inevitable. This armed clash could occur at any moment, at any place along the line of confrontation between the Egyptian forces and the enemy Israeli forces—on land, air or sea along the area extending from Gaza in the North to the Gulf of Aqabah at Sharm ash-Shaykh in the South. But why do I emphasise this in such a manner? There are many reasons, particularly the psychological factor and its effect on the balance of power in the Middle East. . . .

I am confident this means, and that is what I intend to say in the second observation of this inquiry, that the next move is up to Israel. Israel has to reply now. It has to deal a blow. We have to be ready for it, as I said, to minimise its effect as much as possible. Then it will be our turn to deal the second blow, which we will deliver with the utmost possible effectiveness.

In short, Egypt has exercised its power and achieved the objectives of this stage without resorting to arms so far. But Israel has no alternative but to use arms if it wants to exercise power. This means that the logic of the fearful confrontation now taking place between Egypt, which is fortified by the might of the masses of the Arab nation, and Israel, which is fortified by the illusion of American might, dictates that Egypt, after all it has now succeeded in achieving, must wait, even though it has to wait for a blow. This is necessitated also by the sound conduct of the battle, particularly from the international point of view. Let Israel begin. Let our second blow then be ready. Let it be a knockout.

—Ḥasanain Haykal (translator unknown)

Cairo: A Visitor Predicts Sadat (1969)

A picture that is often presented abroad is of Nasser as a moderate, holding back—with increasing difficulty—an infuriated Egyptian nation that is hell-bent for war. My own impression is the exact opposite—of a peaceable and weary people lashed and dragged by their leaders. The average Egyptian, young and old, is heartily sick of adventure and war. He asks nothing better than peace, even with Israel, on terms that are reasonable and honourable for Egypt. It is the régime which needs a state of war and a war-psychosis, with an endless series of incidents and crises, in order to maintain its rule over a reluctant country. Nasser himself is too heavily committed to pan-Arabism and the struggle against Israel to make peace even if he wants to—and the appearances are that he doesn't. . . . Nasser himself would prefer a state of war, short of actual war. . . . It is by no means unlikely that a régime might emerge after him, or even a successor in the same régime, which is much more likely, who would be able to take a different point of view. One should not underrate the possibilities of rapid change of mood and direction in Egyptian politics.

—Ibn el-Assal (pseudonym)

Lebanon's Future (1975)

The temporary breakdown of Muslim-Christian cooperation, complicated as it is by economic, social, and above all political factors extending beyond Lebanon's own frontiers, is in many respects the result of outside forces that have reason to resent, even fear Lebanon's historic example. To the conservative Muslim president of Libya, Mu'ammar Qaddafi, a Christian-dominated state in the midst of the Arab World is an embarrassment as acute as that of Israel, and certainly one more vulnerable to the kind of threats and pressures he is able to wield. For Israel itself, a successful Christian-Muslim experiment makes Lebanon the most dangerous of all enemies to Zionist survival, for it is a living example of the kind of society the Palestinians have lately advocated in place of the narrowly nationalistic and ethnically based state that is Israel today.

—Robert Brenton Betts

The Rising Tide of Discontent (1986)

There are about a thousand million Moslems in the world, of whom perhaps 15 per cent are Arabs. In the absence of any democracy, it is impossible to know in detail what those people think. Certainly no public-opinion survey would elicit the truth: too many people have learned the hard way not to speak frankly. Yet there is compelling evidence that a storm is brewing. Increasingly of recent years, the Moslem world has been torn by the violence of clandestine groups, as like-minded and determined people organise secretly for what is ever more clearly seen to be an inevitable clash between the oppressed and their oppressors. The Islamic revolution in Iran, the epidemic spread of fanatic Moslem organisations, the short but bloody occupation of the Grand Mosque in Mecca in December 1979, the assassination of Sadat, the Jihad organisation, the suicide attacks in Lebanon: in execution these may all have been isolated events, yet all are portents of the same cataclysm to come. They are the surface manifestations of deep discontents welling up with explosive force among the younger generation of Moslems.

A characteristic of this younger generation is its loss of faith in the present leadership. They look around, these younger people, and they see the yawning gulf between words and deeds. They hear honeyed words and they feel betrayed. As one of the greatest American presidents pointed out, you can fool all of the people some of the time, and some of the people all of the time, but you cannot fool all of the people all of the time. Across the Moslem world, people are waking from sleep and realising they have been fooled. How can leaders expect to retain allegiance when anyone may read of decisions taken, pledges given, resolutions solemnly passed, and then no action taken? How can leaders be trusted to defend Islam against its enemies without, when the principles and rules of Islam are so blatantly flouted within?

Viewing the Arab world today, an analyst must surely conclude that the tide of militant Islam is rising. A storm is brewing. There will be violence. The tragedy is that the violence will be Moslem pitted against Moslem. Can it be averted? Probably it is too late. Certainly the only hope of averting it lies in swift and far-reaching reforms in democracy, human rights, social justice, and foreign policy.

—General Saad El-Shazly

Saddam Hussein (1991)

Saddam Hussein does not forget and forgive. His foes brought him close to perdition and then let him off, being weak fools as he had always known, though their weakness and foolishness turned out differently than he had foreseen. He will strive to exact revenge as long as there is life in his body. He will smirk and conciliate and retreat and whine and apply for fairness and generosity. He will also make sure that within his home base it remains understood that he has not changed and will never change, with all the means he has shown in the past for making himself understood. And the day will come when he will hit—we do not know with what weapons, nor does he now know himself. And when he does hit he may by the grace of God miscalculate as he has miscalculated in the past. But even so the innocent will pay by the millions.

This must never be put out of mind: Saddam Hussein from now on lives for revenge. All else—Kurds, Saudis, chemical armaments, Western contacts, competent media—however important for present consideration, become traps, perhaps deadly traps, when not related to the main issue. If this sounds irrational or paranoid, it is no more or less so than he is, and it is he who is the measure.

—Uriel Dann

There Must Be Something

This poem, by a Turkish poet who died in 1950 at the age of thirty-six, expresses an attitude widely held among those who inhabit the Middle East and increasingly shared by those who study it.

> *Is the sea as beautiful as this every day?*
> *Does the sky look like this all the time?*
> *Are these furnishings, this window*
> *always as lovely as this?*
>
> *No*
> *by God, no*
> *There must be something behind this somewhere.*

—Orhan Veli Kanık

WHAT IS YOUR NAME, AND HOW DO YOU SPELL IT?

The vast majority of the countries and peoples of the Middle East write their languages in scripts other than the Latin; therefore, the form in which Middle Eastern names and terms reach us is not so much a spelling as a transcription—an attempt to transfer sounds from one kind of writing to another. Unfortunately there is great variation in the systems of transcription used and even greater variation in the ways that names and terms are pronounced.

In most of the region the Arabic script dominates. It is, of course, used in all the Arab countries; it is also used in Iran to write the Persian language and was until modern times also used to write Turkish and many other Islamic languages, in the former Russian Empire as well as in Central, South and Southeast Asia.

In modern times there have been significant changes. In Turkey, the Arabic script was formally abolished in 1928, and replaced by a modified version of the Latin script adapted to express Turkish sounds. In the Soviet-ruled Muslim territories of Transcaucasia and Central Asia, the alphabetic reform began even earlier. The Arabic script, previously in general use, was replaced first by a Latin script and then by a form of the Russian Cyrillic script. Since independence, some of these countries have been considering Latin scripts adapted from that used in Turkey. The other major change was the restoration and adoption of Hebrew, in the Hebrew script, as an official language, first in British-mandated Palestine and then in the state of Israel. The other ancient languages are for all practical purposes dead and have been replaced by the three major living languages of the region, Arabic, Persian and Turkish.

Of these by far the most widely used is Arabic. Like English and Spanish, Arabic is the language of many states and nations extending over a vast area. Even more than English and Spanish, it varies greatly in usage and in pronunciation from country to country and often even from district to district. The same words, names, and even letters will be pronounced differently by a Moroccan, a Libyan, an Egyptian, an Iraqi, not to speak of a Turk, a Persian or a Central Asian. They will be heard and transcribed differently by a Frenchman, an Italian, an Englishman, a German or a Russian. So an Arabic word meaning "river valley" was heard and written *wadi* by Englishmen in the Middle East and *oued* by Frenchmen in North Africa. It also survives, as a relic of Moorish rule, in a number of Spanish place-names beginning with *guad*. Two of the most famous Muslim names are variously written as "Muhammad," "Mohammad," "Mahommed," "Mohamed," "Mahomet," "Mehmet," and "Ahmad," "Achmad," "Ahmed," "Ahmet," "Akhmad." The holy book of Islam is named "Koran," "Kuran," "Qur'ān," and "Alcoran." These lists could easily be lengthened.

The "al" of Alcoran is the Arabic definite article *al*, usually written without a capital and joined to the following word by a hyphen, e.g., al-Hasan, al-Malik, al-'Alamain (or al-'Alamayn). Certain letters at the beginning of a word assimilate the "l" of the article, as for example, ar-Raḥmān for al-Raḥmān and an-Nāṣir for al-Nāṣir. This elision is sometimes followed, sometimes disregarded in transcription. Raḥmān ("Merciful") and Nāṣir ("Helper," i.e., to victory) both belong to the ninety-nine names of God. Preceded by 'Abd, "slave of," these divine names or attributes figure in many personal names, beginning with 'Abd Allah (also Abdallah, Abdullah, etc.), "slave of God." The name of Allah may be replaced by any of the other ninety-nine—as for example, 'Abd al-Karīm, "Slave of the Generous," 'Abd al-Majīd, "Slave of the Glorious," etc. Other compounds with Allah also figure as personal names, e.g., Hibat Allah, "Gift of God." Some names are compounded with Dīn, "religion," as for example, Nāṣir al-Dīn (or Nasruddin), "Helper of the religion," and Ṣalāḥ al-Dīn, "probity [or truth] of the religion," whence Saladin.

In most of the modern world a personal name has two basic components: a first or given name, in England usually known as a Christian name, irrespective of the religion of the holder, and a last name, also known as a family name or surname. The first is personal to the holder; the last is transmitted through the family, hitherto in the male line. In some countries, as for example Hungary and China, the order of given name and surname is reversed, but the principle is the same. Between the two, one or more middle names may be inserted, but the use and number of these are entirely optional.

This was not the pattern in the Islamic Middle East. In Turkey, a law of 1934 imposed on every Turkish citizen the obligation to adopt a surname, with effect from January 1, 1935. In Israel, the founding fathers brought with them the practices, and often the actual names, of their countries of origin. Elsewhere, more traditional patterns prevailed, though the Western practice of surnames is spreading rapidly.

A traditional Islamic name may be made up of the following components: (1) the personal name, (2) the *kunya,* a name compounded with *Abū,* "father of," or *Umm,* "mother of." The *kunya* might be real, referring to the offspring of the holder, or metaphorical, referring to some desirable quality. Another possible component was (3) the *nasab,* or pedigree, introduced by *ibn,* "son," or *bint,* "daughter," followed by the name of the father and as many generations as may be thought necessary. In Iran and Turkey, and in most of the Arab lands of the present time, *ibn* is no longer used in simple personal names. It may, however, be retained to refer to some distinguished ancestor or to a clan or tribal affiliation, e.g., Ibn Saud (correctly Suʿūd). The Persian suffix *zāda/zāde* and the Turkish suffix *oghlu/oglu* may serve the same purpose.

Two other possible components of a name are the *laqab* and the *nisba.* The first is an honorific or descriptive epithet, perhaps a nickname, sometimes even a title. Names ending in *dīn* were originally used in this category. A *nisba* is an adjective indicating the place of birth, origin or residence, the sect, tribe or family, occasionally the trade or profession of the holder. As in the West, these may be arbitrarily handed down from father to son, even though the original relevance has been lost.

In premodern times, a person may be known or a writer cited by any one of these components, or by a combination of any two or more. In the signatures at the end of the excerpts and in the following lists, I have placed them alphabetically according to the name most commonly used.

In the modern Arab world the usual practice is for a person to have two names, the first personal, the second normally that of his father. The latter may, however, also be the name of a grandparent or still remoter ancestor or a second personal name adopted by choice or given in the family, at school, in the army, and so on. The use of family names, in the past mainly confined to distinguished families, is now spreading rapidly, and the introduction of compulsory registration in many countries is accelerating the process.

In the Western world, except for monarchs, it is customary to refer to both historical and contemporary figures by their last names. In the Islamic Middle East there is no such consensus. Famous figures may become famous and be cited by any one or more of these components of their name. Poets are often known by a special poetic pen name unrelated to any of these. Such, for example, are the Persian poets Firdawsī, the "paradisiac," and Ḥāfiẓ, a title of one who has memorized the entire Qurʾān. In this book authors are quoted in the form most usually used in Middle Eastern literature.

CAST OF CHARACTERS

Abū Shāma (1203–68): Syrian historian. His history of Saladin and his time preserves valuable earlier narratives and documents.

Abū Ṭālib Khān, Mīrzā (1752–1806): Born in Lucknow, India, to a family of Perso-Turkish origin. Between 1799 and 1803 he traveled extensively in Europe and wrote a book, in Persian, describing his experiences. An English translation by Charles Stewart was published in 1814.

Abū Yūsuf Yaʿqūb al-Kūfī (d. 807): Iraqi jurist, one of the founders of the Hanafi school of jurisprudence.

Acheson, Dean Gooderham (1893–1971): U.S. secretary of state, 1949–52.

Āl-e Aḥmad, Jalāl (1923–69): Persian novelist and social critic. His book *Plagued by the West* was first submitted as a report to the Council of Educational Goals of Iran in 1961, and was published in 1962.

Âli Pasha (1815–71): Ottoman statesman. The son of a shopkeeper, he joined the imperial civil service at the age of fourteen and held a succession of administrative and diplomatic posts, including Vienna, St. Petersburg and London. He was later appointed foreign minister and grand vizier.

Altınay, Ahmet Refik (1881–1937): Turkish historian.

Ammianus Marcellinus (c. 330–400): Roman historian, born in Antioch. His history of the Roman Empire covered the years 96–378 C.E., but only the last few books, covering the years 353–78 C.E., survive. He devotes much attention to Syrian affairs.

Apuleius, Lucius (second century): Latin writer, born in Hippo, Algeria; author of *The Golden Ass*.

Arnold of Lübeck (d. 1213–14?): German priest and historian. His chronicle of the Slavs, covering the years 1171–1209, includes an account of the Crusades in that period.

Asim Efendi (c. 1755–1813): Ottoman official and historian. His history covers the years 1791–1808.

Asquith, Herbert (1852–1928): British prime minister, 1908–16.

Atatürk, Mustafa Kemal (1881–1938): Ottoman general who fought against the British at Gallipoli. The founder of modern Turkey, he was the first president of the Turkish Republic. Many of his speeches were collected and published in Ankara.

Atay, Falıh Rıfkı (1892–1971): Turkish journalist and author.

Augustine, Saint (d. 430): Bishop of Hippo (modern-day Bona) in North Africa and one of the most influential early Christian theologians. *The City of God* was begun as a defense of the Catholic Church shortly after the sack of Rome.

al-Awḥadī, Shihāb al-Dīn Aḥmad ibn ʻAbdallāh (1359–1409): Arab historian.

Azulai, David (1727–1806): A native of Jerusalem who traveled extensively to collect funds for rabbinical seminaries.

Bell, Gertrude (1868–1926): English archaeologist, traveler, diplomat and writer who played an important role in Middle Eastern politics.

Benjamin, J. J.: Eastern European Jewish traveler in the Middle East, 1846–55. He called himself Benjamin II, in allusion to the famous Benjamin of Tudela.

Benjamin of Tudela: Spanish Jewish traveler in the East, 1165–73.

Bentham, Jeremy (1748–1832): English jurist and political philosopher; visited the Middle East in 1785–86.

Bernard the Wise: French pilgrim to Jerusalem (c. 870).

Bernstorff, Johann Heinrich, Count (1862–1939): German diplomat.

Blount, Sir Henry (1602–82): English traveler in the Levant, 1634–36.

Blunt, Wilfrid Scawen (1840–1922): English traveler, writer and poet; traveled extensively in the Middle East.

Bonaparte, see Napoléon.

Boutros-Ghali, Boutros (1922–): Egyptian scholar and diplomat; secretary-general of the United Nations, 1992–96.

al-Bukhārī, Abū ʻAbdallāh Muḥammad ibn Ismāʻīl (810–70): Compiler of a standard collection of traditions of the Prophet.

Burckhardt, John Lewis (1784–1817): Swiss explorer and scholar; traveled in Egypt, Syria and Arabia, including Mecca and Medina.

Burton, Sir Richard Francis (1821–90): An English explorer, Arabic scholar, and writer. He joined the service of the East India Company in 1842 and mastered a number of languages, including Persian and Arabic. In 1853, disguised as a Muslim, he went on a pilgrimage to Mecca and Medina, which he described in his *Personal Narrative of a Pilgrimage*. In later years, during many travels in many countries, including a brief spell as British consul in Damascus, he found time to produce an English translation of *The Thousand and One Nights,* published from 1885 to 1888 in sixteen volumes.

Busbecq, Ogier Ghiselin de (1522–92): Illegitimate son of a Flemish nobleman. A diplomat in the service of the Holy Roman Empire, he carried out a number of important diplomatic missions. Between 1555 and 1562 he was imperial ambassador to the court of Süleyman the Magnificent in Istanbul. His four Turkish letters, first published in Antwerp in 1581, became a classic of Western literature about the Ottoman lands.

Buzurg ibn Shahriyār (tenth century): Persian ship's captain; author of an Arabic handbook about India.

Cecil, Lord Edward (1867–1918): British soldier and civil servant; served in Egypt for many years before and during World War I.

Chair, Somerset de (1911–95): British writer, soldier and politician. In 1940–41 he served in Palestine, Syria and Iraq. Wounded by Vichy French fire at Palmyra in 1941, he wrote *The Golden Carpet* while convalescing.

Chateaubriand, François de (1768–1848): French poet and novelist; traveled in Greece, Turkey, Palestine and Egypt in 1806–07. He published an account of his travels in 1811.

Choiseul-Gouffier, Marie-Gabriel, Comte de (1752–1817): Traveler, scholar and diplomat; served as French ambassador in Istanbul from 1784 to 1791.

Churchill, Winston Leonard Spencer (1874–1965): British statesman and historian; he dealt with the Middle East in both capacities. He was First Lord of the Admiralty from 1911 to 1915 and left after the debacle of the Dardanelles expedition, which he had sponsored. He was later prime minister from 1940 to 1945.

Ciano, Count Galeazzo (1903–44): Italian statesman and fascist leader. In 1930 he married Mussolini's daughter, and he served as foreign minister from 1936 to 1943. He was later arrested by the Germans and executed for treason by the fascist authorities in northern Italy. After his execution his widow smuggled his diary out of Italy into Switzerland.

Constantine, Porphyrogenitus (905–59): Byzantine emperor, 945–59; compiled a guide to the world situation in his time.

Cox, Samuel Sullivan (1824–89): American legislator and statesman; U.S. minister in Istanbul, 1885–86.

Dallam, Thomas: English organ maker; visited Turkey in 1599–1600.

Dann, Uriel (1922–91): Israeli historian.

Davānī, Jalāl al-Dīn (1427–1502/3): Persian philosopher. His best-known work is a treatise on ethics, economics and politics, consisting of an updated and popularized version of Naṣīr al-Dīn Ṭūsī's earlier work on the same subject. Davānī's book was translated and published in English in 1839 under the title *Practical Philosophy of the Muhammedan People*.

Derby, Edward Henry Stanley, Earl of (1826–93): British statesman.

Douglas, Norman (1868–1952): British diplomat, novelist and travel writer.

Dufferin, Frederick Temple, Marquess of (1826–1902): British diplomat; ambassador in Turkey in 1881–82, special envoy to Egypt in 1882–83.

Duhamel, Georges (1884–1966): French writer.

Eliot, George (pseudonym of Mary Ann Evans) (1817–90): English novelist. In her novel *Daniel Deronda* the hero explores his Jewish roots.

Enver Pasha (1881–1922): Young Turk revolutionary, soldier and statesman. In 1911 he resigned his post as Ottoman military attaché in Berlin to volunteer for service in the Italo-Turkish war in Libya, where he acquitted himself with distinction.

Ersoy, Mehmet Akif (1873–1936): Turkish poet.

Evliya Çelebi (1611–84): Ottoman Turkish author of a famous account of his travels, in ten volumes. A man of means, he traveled mostly as a private individual, occasionally in the retinue of some official. He visited Vienna as part of a Turkish embassy in 1665.

al-Fārābī, Abū Naṣr (d. c. 950): A Central Asian Turk whose works, written in Arabic, establish him as one of the major Muslim philosophers of the Middle Ages.

Fawzī, Ḥusayn (1900–1988): Egyptian scholar, scientist and man of letters.

Fayṣal ibn Ḥusayn (1883–1933): Prince of the Hejaz, later king of Iraq.

Fikret, Tevfik (1867–1915): Turkish poet.

Fitch, Ralph: Sixteenth-century English merchant in the Levant.

Flaubert, Gustave (1821–80): French novelist; traveled in Egypt in 1851.

Forbin, Louis-Auguste, Comte de (1777–1841): French traveler and writer; traveled in the Middle East in 1817–19.

Forster, E. M. (1879–1970): English novelist; served with the Red Cross in Egypt during World War I.

Frescobaldi, Lionardo di Niccolò: Florentine traveler in Egypt and the Holy Land, 1384.

Fuzuli (1480?–1556): Turkish poet.

Gabrieli, Francesco (1904–96): Italian scholar; specialist on Arabic literature.

Garmrūdī, 'Abd al-Fattāḥ Khan: Persian diplomat; part of a mission to London, 1839.

de Gaulle, Charles (1890–1970): French soldier and statesman, first president (1959–69) of the Fifth Republic. As leader of the London-based Free French Forces, he paid visits to the Middle East during World War II.

Ghars al-Ni'ma (eleventh century): Pen name of Muḥammad ibn Hilāl al-Ṣābi'; author of a collection of comic and curious anecdotes.

al-Ghassānī, Muḥammad ibn 'Abd al-Wahhāb, al-Wazīr (d. 1707): Moroccan ambassador in Spain, 1690–91.

al-Ghazāl, the gazelle, nickname of Yaḥyā ibn al-Ḥakam (d. 860): Spanish Arab poet and diplomat.

al-Ghazālī, Abū Ḥāmid Muḥammad (1059–1111): Theologian, jurist and mystic; author of many works in Arabic and some in Persian.

Gibb, Sir Hamilton (1895–1971): British scholar; specialist in Arab Islamic history and literature.

Gobineau, Joseph Arthur, Comte de (1816–82): French diplomat, traveler and writer, and a pioneer of modern racism.

Gucci, Giorgio: Italian pilgrim in 1384.

Guillaume de Nangis (d. 1300): French historian.

Haidar, Princess Musbah (1908–?): Daughter of the former grand sharif of Mecca and an English mother. Princess Haidar grew up in an Ottoman harem, which she describes in her memoir, written in English, with vivid detail.

Halet Efendi (1761–1822): Ottoman diplomat and statesman.

Halevi, Yehuda (c. 1080–1140): Hebrew poet and philosopher.

Ḥanafī, Ḥasan (1935–): Egyptian scholar and writer.

Ha-Nagid, Samuel (993–1056): Spanish Hebrew poet and statesman.

Hārūn ibn Yaḥyā (ninth century): An Arab prisoner of war in Rome. His account of his captivity is preserved in a citation by a later geographical writer, Ibn Rusteh.

Hatti Efendi, Mustafa: Ottoman ambassador in Vienna, 1748.

Hawley, Sir Donald: British diplomat; served in many Middle Eastern posts.

Haykal, Ḥasanain: Egyptian journalist and editor.

Hezarfenn, Huseyn (d. 1691?): Ottoman treasury official, historian and man of letters.

Hilāl al-Ṣābi' (d. 1056): Secretary to a vizier in Iraq; author of books on secretaries and viziers.

Hornby, Emilia: British traveler.

Ibn 'Abdūn (late eleventh–early twelfth centuries): Jurist in Seville.

Ibn al-Athīr, 'Izz al-Dīn (1160–1233): Arab historian, lived in Mosul, Iraq. His multivolume history, from the creation of the world to A.H. 628 (1231 C.E.), is an accepted masterpiece of Arabic historical writing.

Ibn Baṭṭūṭa (1304–1368 or 1377): Moroccan Arab traveler. His account of his wideranging travels between West Africa and East Asia is a major source of historical information and a classic of travel literature.

Ibn Buṭlān (d. 1066): Christian physician in Baghdad. His most important scientific work was on hygiene and macrobiotics. He is best known for his "Treatise on Buying Slaves," a consumer's guide.

Ibn Dihya (1159–1235): Spanish-Arab philologist born in Valencia. His writings preserve important earlier texts, including the story of al-Ghazāl.

Ibn al-Faqīh (ninth century): Persian geographer, born in Hamadān; author of a major geographic work in Arabic.

Ibn Ḥamdūn, Muḥammad ibn al-Ḥasan (1102–66): Government official and literary scholar in Baghdad; author of a highly esteemed collection of sayings and anecdotes.

Ibn Ḥazm, Abū Muḥammad ʿAlī (994–1064): Poet, scholar, moralist and theologian; one of the major writers of Spanish Arabic literature.

Ibn Khaldūn, ʿAbd al-Raḥmān (1332–1406): Born in Tunis, died in Cairo; the major historical and social thinker of the Middle Ages.

Ibn al-Khaṭīb (1313–75): Spanish Arab historian and essayist.

Ibn Khātima, Abū Jaʿfar Aḥmad ibn ʿAlī (fourteenth century): Statesman and historian in Muslim Granada.

Ibn Māja (824–87): Compiler of one of the standard collections of traditions (*ḥadīth*) concerning the actions and utterances of the Prophet.

Ibn Qutayba, Abū Muḥammad ʿAbdallāh ibn Muslim (828–89): Iraqi literary historian and anthologist.

Ibn Saʿīd (1214–74): Spanish Arab geographer.

Ibn Ṭufayl, Abū Bakr Muḥammad (d. 1185 or 1186): Spanish Arab philosopher.

Ibn Yaʿqūb, Ibrāhīm al-Isrāʾīlī al-Ṭurṭūshī (tenth century): A native of Tortosa, then under Arab Muslim rule, who traveled in Christian Europe on a diplomatic mission, probably from the caliph of Cordova to the emperor Otto. His soubriquet "al-Isrāʾīlī" indicates that he was Jewish or of Jewish descent. His account of his travels survives only in extracts cited by later writers.

al-Idrīsī, Abū ʿAbdallāh Muḥammad ibn Muḥammad (1100–65): Moroccan geographer; author of a major work on the geography of the known world.

Israeli, Isaac (d. c. 932): Jewish physician and medical writer in Hebrew and Arabic; born in Tunisia, died in Egypt.

al-Jabartī, ʿAbd al-Raḥmān (1753–1825): The major Arabic historian of his time. Wrote an eyewitness account of the French occupation of Egypt.

al-Jāḥiẓ, ʿAmr ibn Bahr (776–869): Of Basra; major Arabic essayist and prose writer.

al-Jahshiyārī, Abū ʿAbdallāh Muḥammad ibn ʿAbdūs (tenth century): Author of a work on wazirs and officials.

Jarvis, Claude Scudamore (1879–1953): British army officer, author of several books; served in the Middle East, principally in Egypt, in World War I and stayed until his retirement in 1936.

Jemāl Pasha, also written Djemal and Cemal (1872-1922): One of the Young Turk leaders, served as governor of Constantinople, as Ottoman naval minister, and, during the war years, commander of the Ottoman Fourth Army in Syria-Palestine. His memoirs were published shortly after his death in 1922.

Jevdet, Abdullah (1869–1932): Turkish writer, mainly of political and ideological works.

Jevdet Pasha (1850–1900): Ottoman historian and jurist.

Jones, Sir William (1746–94): British scholar; one of the pioneers of the modern study of Oriental languages and laws.

Juvenal (Decimus Junius Juvenalis) (first–second centuries): Roman satirist.

Kai Kāʾūs ibn Iskandar, Prince of Gurgān (1021–1098/9): Persian author of a famous book on statecraft.

Kanık, Orhan Veli (1914–50): Turkish poet.

Kemal, Namık (1840–88): Ottoman poet and writer; ideological leader of the Young Ottoman Reformers.

Kennan, George Frost (1904–): U.S. diplomat and historian.

Khomeini, Imam Ruhullah (1902–89): Iranian religious and political leader. Founder of the Islamic Republic of Iran, he held the position of Supreme Guide until his death.

Kinglake, Alexander William (1809–91): An English lawyer, traveler, and historian. He graduated from Cambridge in 1828, where he was a contemporary and friend of Tennyson and Thackeray. After leaving Cambridge, he studied law, and was called to the bar in 1837. In 1835, while still a student, he undertook an extensive journey through the Middle East, which he described in a little book called *Eothen*, published in 1844. In 1854 he went to the Crimea, and spent most of the rest of his life preparing and writing his life work, *The History of the Crimean War*.

Kirkbride, Sir Alec (1897–1978): British colonial official and diplomat; served in Arabia, Palestine, Jordan and Libya.

Kissinger, Henry Albert (1923–): German-born American historian and statesman, U.S. secretary of state, 1973–77.

Koçu Bey, Mustafa: Ottoman official; author of a famous memorandum presented to the sultan in 1630 in which he set forth his views on what was wrong with the empire and how to set it right.

Lane, Edward William (1801–76): English scholar and lexicographer; visited Egypt in 1825 and 1833–35.

Lawrence, Thomas Edward (1886–1935): English scholar and soldier, better known as Lawrence of Arabia.

Liman von Sanders, Otto Viktor Karl (1855–1929): German cavalry general. In 1913 he went to Turkey as head of the German military mission to reorganize the Ottoman army. In World War I he commanded the Turkish armies in the Gallipoli campaign, and in 1918 was given supreme command in Palestine. His memoirs were published in German in 1920, in English translation in 1927.

Loyola, Saint Ignatius (1491–1556): Wounded at the Siege of Pamplona in 1521, he underwent a sudden conversion and set off, once recovered, for Jerusalem in a pilgrimage filled with perils. On his return he studied in Paris and founded the Society of Jesus, popularly known as the Jesuits. He was canonized in 1622.

al-Maʿarrī, Abu'l-ʿAlā' (973–1058): Syrian Arab poet and prose writer.

Machiavelli, Niccolò (1469–1527): Italian statesman, historian and political philosopher.

MacKereth, Gilbert (1893–1962): British soldier and consular official; was consul in Damascus from 1933 until the outbreak of World War II.

Madden, Richard Robert (1798–1886): Irish physician and writer; traveled in the Middle East in 1824–27.

al-Maqrīzī, Taqī al-Dīn Aḥmad ibn ʿAlī (1363–1442): Egyptian historian and topographer; author of standard works in both fields.

Marx, Karl (1818–83): German historian and philosopher, best known as the theorist of modern socialism and communism. From London, where he settled in 1849, he contributed occasional articles to the *New York Tribune*.

al-Masʿūdī, Abu'l-Ḥasan ʿAlī ibn al-Ḥusayn (893–956): Historian and geographer. He traveled extensively and was one of the most important Arabic authors of the Middle Ages.

Mehmed Efendi (d. 1731): Ottoman diplomat; ambassador to Paris in 1720.

Meinertzhagen, Col. Richard (1878–1967): British officer; served in Palestine in World War I and was a member of the British delegation to the Paris peace talks. He was chief political officer in Syria and Palestine from 1919 to 1920 and military adviser to the Middle East Department of the Colonial Office from 1921 to 1924. His *Middle East Diary* covers the period 1917–56.

Melville, Herman (1819–91): American novelist. He traveled in the Middle East in 1856–57.

Mendoza, Bernardino de (sixteenth century): Spanish ambassador in London.

Meshullam ben Menahem da Volterra: Rabbi from Volterra, in Italy, who traveled in the East from June to October 1481 and wrote a book in Hebrew about his adventures.

al-Miknāsī, Muḥammad ibn 'Uthmān: Moroccan ambassador to Spain in 1779 and 1788.

Mihri Hatun (d. 1506): Turkish woman poet.

Miller, Judith: A *New York Times* correspondent and former Cairo bureau chief. Has written extensively on the Middle East.

Montagu, Lady Mary Wortley (1689–1762): Wife of the British ambassador in Turkey, 1716–18. Lady Mary spent just over one year in Turkey, during which time she had a baby, learned some Turkish and corresponded with Alexander Pope about Turkish poetry. Her letters, describing the places she visited, the Turks she met and their public and private lives, were published in 1763, the year after her death.

al-Mubarrad, Abu'l-'Abbās Muḥammad ibn Yazīd (826–900): Of Basra; writer on philology and literature.

Mubashshir ibn Fatik (eleventh century): Egyptian scholar and writer.

Munif, Abdelrahman (1933–   ): Arab novelist of Saudi Arabian origin, by training and profession an oil economist.

al-Muttaqī, 'Alā' al-Dīn 'Alī ibn Ḥusām al-Dīn al-Hindı (1480–1567/69): Compiler of a major collection of traditions of the Prophet.

al-Muqaddasī, Shams al-Dīn, (tenth century): Native of Jerusalem; author of one of the most informative works of travel and geography in Arabic.

Nadīm, 'Abdallāh (1843–96): Egyptian writer and orator.

Na'ima (1655–1716): Ottoman historian, born in Aleppo. His history, covering the years 1591–1660, includes earlier writings and documents.

Napoléon Bonaparte (1769–1821): Emperor of the French. As a young general in the service of the republic, he commanded an expedition to Egypt in 1798. After his deposition and exile in 1815, he dictated memoirs.

Nicolay, Nicolas: French traveler in the Ottoman lands, 1551.

Nicolson, Sir Harold (1886–1968): British scholar, historian and diplomat. Born in Tehran, he entered the Foreign Office in 1909 and served in various parts of the world.

Nightingale, Florence (1820–1910): English nurse, regarded as the founder of modern nursing. She worked in Egypt in 1840 and in Turkey during the Crimean War.

Niẓām al-Mulk (1018–92): Persian statesman in the service of the Seljuq sultans; author of a classic manual of statecraft.

Niẓāmī-i'Arūdī (twelfth century): Persian writer; chiefly known for his *Four Discourses*.

Noeldeke, Theodore (1836–1930): German Semitist and Arabist.

Nutting, Sir Anthony (1920–99): British politician and writer.

al-Nuwayrī, Shihāb al-Dīn Aḥmad ibn ʿAbd al-Wahhāb (1279–1333): Egyptian ency-
clopedist and historian.

Odysseus (pen name of Sir Charles Eliot) (1862–1931): British diplomat, served in
the Middle East in the last years of the nineteenth century.

Okeley, W.: English seaman captured and enslaved by Barbary corsairs, later freed.

Osborn, Francis (seventeenth century): English writer on the Turks.

Palgrave, William Gifford (1826–88): British traveler in Arabia in 1862–63.

Patton, George Smith, Jr. (1885–1945): U.S. general; commanded a corps in North
Africa during World War II.

Peçevi, Ibrahim (1574–c. 1649): Ottoman historian; a native of Pécs in Hungary.

Pickthall, Marmaduke W. (1875–1936): English travel writer and novelist; converted
to Islam.

Plutarch (46?–c. 120): Greek biographer; known above all for his *Parallel Lives*.

Porter, Sir James (1710–86): British ambassador in Turkey, 1746–62.

Prophet (sayings attributed to): Traditions concerning the actions and utterances of
the Prophet Muhammad are called *ḥadīth*. Hundreds of thousands of such ha-
diths were transmitted orally by the first generations of Muslims and later committed to writing in a number of collections. From an early date, Muslim scholars
and theologians developed a scientific study of such traditions, dividing them
into authentic, spurious, and shades of uncertainty between the two.

al-Qalqashandī, Abuʾl-ʿAbbās Aḥmad (1355–1418): Egyptian scholar and encyclope-
dist.

al-Qalyūbī, Aḥmad ibn Aḥmad (d. 1659): Egyptian medical author; compiled a collection of stories and pleasantries.

al-Qāsim, Sāmiḥ (1939–   ): Israeli Arab poet.

al-Qazwīnī, Zakariyyā ibn Muḥammad (c. 1203–83): Persian geographer and cosmographer.

Rashīd al-Dīn Faḍlallah (c. 1247–1318): Persian statesman and historian.

Rendel, Sir George William (1889–1979): British diplomat, head of the Eastern Department of the Foreign Office, 1930–38.

Resmi, Ahmed (1700–83): Ottoman ambassador to Vienna in 1757 and Berlin in
1763. His reports are cited at length in the Ottoman chronicle of Vasif Efendi.

Rūdagī, Abū ʿAbdallāh Jaʿfar (d. 940): Persian poet.

Rycaut, Sir Paul (1628–1700): British diplomat, traveler and author; served in Turkey
c. 1661–69.

el-Sadat, Anwar (1918–81): Egyptian soldier and politician. One of the group of
young officers who carried out the coup d'etat of 1952, he became vice president in 1969 and, on Nasser's death, succeeded him as president of Egypt.

Sadullah Pasha (1838–91): Ottoman liberal reformer; author of a much-cited ode,
"The Nineteenth Century."

Ṣāʿid ibn Aḥmad al-Andalusī (1029–70): Andalusian Arab jurist and writer; author of
The Categories of Nations.

Said Pasha (1838–1913): Ottoman grand vizier; author of a famous book of memoirs.

Salisbury, Robert Arthur, Marquess of (1830–1903): British statesman.

Sanderson, John (1560–1627): English merchant; traveled in the Middle East between 1584 and 1607.

Saxe, Count Maurice de (1696–1750): Marshal of France; writer on military matters.

Scott, Rochfort Charles (d. 1872): British army officer. His travels in Egypt began in
1833.

Seneca, Lucius Annaeus (d. 65 C.E.): Roman philosopher and dramatist; born in Spain. His book on superstition survives only in fragments and citations. The passage given in this book is taken from St. Augustine.

Shaarawi, Huda (1879–1947): The daughter of a wealthy landowner who became president of the Egyptian Chamber of Deputies, she was brought up in the harem. As an activist, writer and leader, she played a major role in the Egyptian, and more generally the Arab, feminist movement. Her memoirs were published in English translation in 1986.

al-Shaybānī, Muḥammad ibn al-Ḥasan (749–804): Iraqi jurist.

El-Shazly, Saad: Egyptian general, chief of staff of the Egyptian armed forces during the war of October 1973.

Sherley, Sir Thomas (d. 1625): English traveler in Turkey and Persia.

Shihāb, Ḥaydar Aḥmad (d. 1835): Lebanese amir and historian. Exiled by the Ottoman authorities, he spent his last years in Malta and wrote several important historical works.

Shirley, Edward: Pseudonym of a former CIA case officer who writes on Iran.

Sigoli, Simone: Florentine pilgrim, 1384.

Slade, Sir Adolphus (1802–77): British naval officer. He first went to Turkey in 1829 and traveled extensively in the Middle East during the 1830s. In 1849 he was lent by the British admiralty as an adviser to the Ottoman navy and stayed there for seventeen years.

Stark, Freya (1893–1993): British writer; author of numerous travel books about the Middle East.

Storrs, Ronald (1881–1955): British official; served in Egypt and Palestine in 1909–26.

al-Suyūṭī, Jalāl al-Dīn (1445–1505): Egyptian author of many works of history, religion, literature and other topics.

al-Tabarī, Abū Ja'far Muḥammad ibn Jarīr (839–923): The most important Arabic historian of the Middle Ages.

al-Ṭahṭāwī, Rifā'a Rāfi' (1801–73): Egyptian educator, scholar and writer. He went to Paris in 1826 as religious preceptor to a group of Egyptian students and stayed there until 1831. He wrote a book explaining the mysterious Occident to his Egyptian and other Arab readers.

al-Tawḥīdī, Abū Ḥayyān (d. 1023): Arab essayist, and a major literary figure of his time.

Thackeray, William Makepeace (1811–63): English novelist; traveled in the Middle East in 1844.

al-Tirmidhi, Abū 'Īsā Muḥammad (d. 892): Compiler of one of the standard collections of traditions of the Prophet.

Tocqueville, Alexis de (1805–59): French politician and political philosopher. He devoted much attention to the problems of Algeria, where he traveled extensively in 1841.

Tott, Baron François de (1733–93): Hungarian engineer officer in the French service; accompanied the French ambassador to Turkey in 1755. A witness of the Russo-Turkish War of 1768–74, he proposed necessary reforms in the Ottoman armed forces that he undertook between 1774 and 1776.

Toynbee, Arnold J. (1889–1975): English historian.

Tülümen, Turgut (1929–   ): Turkish diplomat; served as his country's ambassador in Tehran, 1978–80. His book *Recollections of the Iranian Revolution* was published in Turkish in 1998.

al-Ṭurṭūshī, Abū Bakr, called Ibn Abī Randaqa (1059–1130): Spanish-Arab writer, born in Tortosa. His best-known book deals with the duties of kings and the qualities to which they should aspire, both in peace and in war.

Ṭūsī, Naṣīr al-Dīn (1201–74): Persian scientist and politician; author of a celebrated manual of personal and public ethics. A later and more popular version of his book was produced by Jalāl al-Dīn Davānī.

Twain, Mark (pseudonym of Samuel Clemens) (1835–1910): American writer; traveled in the Middle East in 1867.

'Ubayd-i Zākānī (1300–71): Persian poet and author, notably of satirical works.

Usāma ibn Munqidh (1095–1188): Syrian country gentleman, courtier and man of letters; author of a famous autobiography.

Vasif Efendi (d. 1806): Ottoman diplomat and historian.

Vogué, Eugène-Melchior, Vicomte de (1848–1910): French diplomat in Constantinople, 1871–79; pilgrim to Jerusalem, 1872.

Volney (Constantin François Chasseboeuf) (1757–1820): Between 1783 and 1785, he traveled extensively in Syria and Egypt, and he published an account of his travels in 1787. After the French Revolution, he taught at the new École Normale. In 1791 he published his most famous book, *The Ruins,* containing his reflections on his experience of the East.

Waddāḥ ibn Ismā'īl, known as Waddāḥ al-Yaman (seventh–eighth centuries): Arabic poet, said to have been put to death by order of the caliph Walīd (705–15) because of his attentions to the Princess Umm al-Banīn.

Warburton, Bartholomew Elliott George, usually known as Eliot, (1810–52): Traveler and writer; traveled in the Middle East in 1843.

al-Waṭwāṭ, Muḥammad ibn Ibrāhīm al-Kutubī (1235–1318): Egyptian compiler of a collection of ancedotes.

Wiet, Gaston (1887–1971): French Orientalist.

William, Archbishop of Tyre (d. before 1185): Historian of the Latin Kingdom of Jerusalem.

Willibald, Saint: Anglo-Saxon pilgrim, 723–26.

Wilson, Sir Arnold (1884–1940): British soldier and imperial civil servant; spent much of his career in various parts of the Middle East.

al-Yamanī, Shaykh Aḥmad ibn Muḥammad (d. 1840): Yemeni author who lived in India. His *Nafḥat al-Yaman* was published in 1811. An English translation, *Breezes from Yemen,* appeared in Calcutta in 1907.

Young, Sir George (1872–1952): British diplomat and author; served in Turkey in 1901.

BIBLIOGRAPHY

Abū Shāma, Shihāb al-Dīn 'Abd al-Raḥmān ibn Ismā'īl. *Kitāb al-Rawḍatayn fī akhbār al-dawlatayn,* ed. M. Ḥilmī M. Aḥmad (Cairo, 1962).

Abū Ṭālib Khān, Mīrzā. *Masīr-i Ṭālibī yā Sefarnāma-i Mīrzā Abū Ṭālib Khān,* ed. H. Khadīv-Jam (Tehran, 1974); English translation, C. Stewart, *Travels of Mīrzā Abū Ṭālib Khān . . .* (London, 1814).

Abū Yūsuf Ya'qūb al-Kūfī. *Kitāb al-Kharāj* (Būlāq, A.H. 1302/1885 C.E.)

Acheson, Dean. *Present at the Creation: My Years in the State Department* (New York, 1987).

Adler, Elkan Nathan. *Jewish Travellers* (London, 1930).

Akhbār al-Ṣīn wa'l-Hind (*Relation de la Chine et de l'Inde*), ed. J. Sauvaget (Paris, 1948).

Âli Pasha, in *Tarih Dergisi,* 5, ed. Cavid Baysun, (September 1953).

Āl-e Aḥmad, Jalāl, *Plagued by the West,* trans. Paul Sprachman (New York, 1982).

Arnold of Lübeck. *Chronicon Slavorum,* in *Deutschlands Geschichtsquellen,* ed. W. Wattenbach (Stuttgart and Berlin, 1907).

Asim Efendi. *Tarih* (Istanbul, n.d.).

Atatürk, Kemal. *Atatürk'ün Söylev ve Demeçleri* (*Collected Speeches*) (Ankara, 1945–52).

———. Speech in *Milli Egitim Söylevleri,* vol. 1 (Ankara, n.d.).

———. *Nutuk* (Ankara, 1945–52).

Atay, Falıh Rıfkı. *Taymıs Kıyıları* (Ankara, 1934).

Augustine, Saint. *The City of God,* trans. Marcus Dods (New York, 1950).

al-Awḥadī, Shihāb al-Dīn Aḥmad ibn 'Abdallah. "Embassy of Queen Bertha to Caliph al-Muktafi Billah in Baghdad 293/906," ed. M. Hamidullah, *Journal of the Pakistan Historical Society,* 1 (1953).

Azulai, David. Translated in Elkan Nathan Adler, *Jewish Travellers.*

al-Bakrī, Abū 'Ubayd 'Abdallāh. *Jughrāfīya al-Andalus wa-Urūba,* ed. A. A. el-Haji (Beirut, 1968).

Bassola, Moshe. *A Pilgrimage to Palestine,* transcribed and published by Isaac Ben-Zevi (Jerusalem, 1938).

Bell, Gertrude. Letter, 1917, cited in Janet Wallach, *Desert Queen* (New York, 1996).

———. *Persian Pictures* (New York, 1928).

———. *Syria: The Desert and the Sown* (London, 1907).

Bellow, Saul. *To Jerusalem and Back* (New York, 1976).

Benjamin, J. J. II. *Eight Years in Asia and Africa from 1846 to 1855* (Hanover, 1859).

Benjamin of Tudela. Translated in E. N. Adler, *Jewish Travellers.*

Bentham, Jeremy. *Correspondence,* eds. Timothy L. Sprigge and Ian R. Christie (London, 1968–71).

Bernard the Wise. "The Travels of Bernard the Wise," in *Early Travels in Palestine,* ed. Thomas Wright (New York, 1968).

Bernstorff, Johann. *Memoirs of Count Bernstorff* (New York, 1936).

Betts, Robert Brenton. *Christians in the Arab East* (Atlanta, 1978).

Bible cited in the *King James Version.*

Bin Lādin, Usāma, in *Al-Quds al-'Arabī,* Feb. 23, 1988.

Blount, Sir Henry. *A Voyage into the Levant* (London, 1650).

Blunt, Wilfrid Scawen. *My Diaries: Being a Personal Narrative of Events, 1888–1914,* Part 2, 1900–1914 (London, n.d.).

Boutros-Ghali, Boutros. *Egypt's Road to Jerusalem: A Diplomat's Story of the Struggle for Peace in the Middle East* (New York, 1997).

Browne, Edward G. *The Persian Revolution of 1905–1909* (Washington, D.C., 1995).

al-Bukhārī, Abū 'Abdallāh Muḥammad ibn Ismā'īl. *Al-Ṣaḥīḥ,* ed. L. Krehl (Leiden, 1868).

Bulla Clementis VII (May 1527).

Burckhardt, John Lewis. *Travels in Arabia* (London, 1829).

Burton, Sir Richard. *Personal Narrative of a Pilgrimage to al-Madinah and Meccah* (London, 1853).

Busbecq, Ogier Ghiselin de. *The Turkish Letters of Ogier Ghiselin de Busbecq,* trans. Edward Seymour Forster (Oxford, 1927).

Buzurg ibn Shahriyār. *Kitāb 'Ajā'ib al-Hind,* ed. P. A. van der Lith (Leiden, 1883–86).

Canning, George. *The Letter-Journal of George Canning, 1793–1795,* ed. Peter Jupp (London, 1991).

Cecil, Lord Edward. *The Leisure of an Egyptian Official* (London, 1921).

Chair, Somerset de. *The Golden Carpet* (New York, 1945).

Chateaubriand, François de. *Itinéraire de Paris à Jérusalem,* ed. Georges Faugeron (Paris, 1964).

Choiseul-Gouffier, Marie-Gabriel, Comte de, cited in Léonce Pingaud, *Choiseul-Gouffier* (Paris, 1887).

Churchill, Winston S. *The World in Crisis 1918–1928: The Aftermath* (New York, 1929).

———. *The Second World War: Triumph and Tragedy* (Boston, 1953).

Ciano's Diary 1939–1943, ed. with an introduction by Malcolm Muggeridge, foreword by Sumner Wells (London, 1947).

Constantine, Porphyrogenitus. *De Administrando Imperio,* trans. R. J. H. Jenkins (Budapest, 1949).

Cox, Samuel S. *Diversions of a Diplomat in Turkey* (New York, 1887).

Dallam, Thomas. "The Diary of Master Thomas Dallam (1599–1600)." In *Early Voyages and Travels in the Levant,* ed. J. Theodore Bent (London, 1893).

Dann, Uriel. "Getting Even," *New Republic,* June 3, 1991.

Davānī, Jalāl al-Dīn. *Practical Philosophy of the Muhammadan People,* trans. W. F. Thompson (London, 1839).

Derby, Lord. *The Diaries of Edward Henry Stanley, 15th Earl of Derby (1826–1893) Between September 1869 and March 1878,* vol. IV, ed. John Vincent (London, 1994.)

Despatches from Damascus: Gilbert MacKereth and British Policy in the Levant, 1933–1939, eds. Michael G. Fry and Itamar Rabinovich (Tel Aviv, 1985).

Djemal Pasha. *Memoirs of a Turkish Statesman 1913–1919* (London, 1922).

Douglas, Norman. *Fountains in the Sand* (London, 1912).

Dufferin, Frederick Temple, Marquess of Lord Dufferin to Lord Granville, 1883, *Parliamentary Papers,* c. 3529 (Egypt, No. 6, 1883 LXXXIII).

Duhamel, Georges. *Consultation aux Pays d'Islam* (Paris, 1947).

Eliot, George. *Daniel Deronda* (London, 1876).

Engels, Fr. cit. in Marx, Karl, *q.v.,* article in *New York Daily Tribune,* April 15, 1854. Reprinted in *Karl Marx on Colonialism and Modernization, his Despatches and Other Writings on China, India, Mexico, the Middle East and North Africa,* edited with an Introduction by Shlomo Avineri, New York, 1968.

Enver Pasha, *Um Tripolis* (Munich, 1918).

Evliya Çelebi, *Seyahatnâme,* vol. 7 (Istanbul, A.H. 1314/1897 C.E.).

The Famous and Wonderful Recovery of a Ship of Bristol, called Exchange, *from Turkish Pirates of Algier.* Cited in D. D. Hebb, *Piracy.*

al-Fārābī, Abū Naṣr. *Kitāb al-Siyāsāt al-Madaniyya* (Hyderabad, A.H. 1346/1928 C.E.).

Fawzī, Ḥusayn. *Sindbād al-'Aṣrī* (Cairo, 1938).

Fayṣal ibn Ḥusayn. Cited in R. Meinertzhagen, *Middle East Diary.*

Fitch, Ralph, and other merchants of the Levant Company in Aleppo, letter to George Dorrington, vice consul in that city, August 4, 1596, published in *The Travels of John Sanderson in the Levant 1584–1602,* ed. Sir William Foster (London, 1931).

Flaubert, Gustave. *Voyage en Egypte,* ed. Pierre-Marc de Biasi (Paris, 1991).

Forbin, Louis-Auguste, Comte de. Cited in Choiseul-Gouffier, *Voyage Pittoresque dans l'Empire Ottoman,* 2d ed., vol. 4 (Paris, 1842).

Forster, E. M. *Abinger Harvest* (London, 1936).

Frescobaldi, Lionardo, Simone Sigoli, and Giorgio Gucci. *Visit to the Holy Places of Egypt, Sinai, Palestine and Syria in 1384,* trans. Fr. Theophilis Bellorini, O.F.M., and Fr. Eugene Hoade, O.F.M., with a preface and notes by Fr. Bellarmino Bagatti, O.F.M. (Jerusalem, 1948).

Gabrieli, Francesco. *Storia della letteratura araba* (Rome, 1951).

Garmrūdī, 'Abd al-Fattāḥ Khan. Embassy of Ḥusayn Khan Muqaddam Ajudanbashi, 1838–39. Account written by his secretary 'Abd al-Fattāḥ Khan Garmrūdī. Published by A. Bausani, "Un Manoscritto Persiano inedito sulla ambasceria di Husein Ḥān Moqaddam Āḡūdānbāšī in Europa negli anni 1254–1255 H. (1838–39 A.D.)," *Oriente Moderno* 33 (1953).

de Gaulle, Charles. *The Complete War Memoirs of Charles de Gaulle: The Call to Honor* (*vol. 1*), trans. Richard Howard (New York, 1955).

Ghars al-Ni'ma al-Ṣābi'. *Al-Hafawāt al-Nādira,* ed. Ṣāliḥ al-Ashtar (Damascus, 1967).

al-Ghazālī, Abū Ḥāmid Muḥammad. *Counsel for Kings,* trans. F. R. C. Bagley (London, 1964).

———. *Iḥyā' 'Ulūm al-Dīn,* Book 2, Part 1 (Cairo, n.d.).

al-Ghassānī. Muḥammad ibn 'Abd al-Wahhāb, al-Wazīr. *Riḥlat al-Wazīr fī Iftikāk al-Asīr,* ed. Alfredo Bustānī (Tangier, 1940).

Gibb, Sir Hamilton. *Arabic Literature,* 2d ed. (Oxford, 1963) (first ed. 1926).

Gobineau, Count. *Tales of Asia,* trans. J. Lewis May (London, 1947).

Gucci, Giorgio. See Frescobaldi, Lionardo.

Haidar, Princess Musbah. *Arabesque,* rev. ed. (London, 1968).

Halet Efendi. Cited in Enver Ziya Karal, *Halet Efendinin Paris Büyük Elçiligi 1802–6* (Istanbul, 1940).

Hamilton, Alexander. *The Federalist Papers* (New York, 1961).

Hanafī, Hasan. In *Dirāsāt 'Arabiyya* (Beirut, 1978).

Hārūn ibn Yahyā. Cited in Ibn Rusteh, 'Abū Alī Ahmad ibn 'Umar. *Kitāb al-A'lāq al-nafīsa*, ed. M. J. de Goeje, 2d ed. (Leiden, 1892).

Hatti Efendi, Mustafa. Embassy Report, in *Tarih-i 'Izzi* (Istanbul, A.H. 1199/1785 C.E.).

Hawley, Sir Donald, KCMG, MBE. *Debrett's Manners and Correct Form in the Middle East* (London, 1984).

Haykal, Hasanain. In *Al Ahrām*, May 26, 1967, translated in *The Israel-Arab Reader: A Documentary History of the Middle East Conflict*, ed. Walter Laqueur and Barry Rubin, rev. ed. (London, 1976).

Hebb, David Delison. *Piracy and the English Government, 1616–1642* (London, 1994).

Helffrich, Johann. *Kurtzer und Wahrhafftiger Bericht von der Reise aus Venedig nach Hierosalem . . .* (Leipzig, 1581).

Hezarfenn, Huseyn. *Hezarfen Hüseyin Efendi'nin Osmanlı Devlet teşkilatına dair mülahazaları*, ed. Robert Anhegger, *Türkiyat Mecmuası* 10, (Istanbul, 1951–53).

Hilāl al-Sābi'. *Kitāb al-Wuzarā'*, ed. H. F. Amedroz (Leiden, 1904).

Hornby, Emilia. *In and Around Stamboul* (Philadelphia, 1858).

Ibn 'Abd Rabbihi, *Music: The Priceless Jewel*, ed. and trans. Henry George Farmer (Bearsden, Scotland, 1942).

Ibn 'Abdūn. *Risāla fi'l-Qadā wa'l-hisba*, in *Documents Arabes Inédits* 1st series, *Trois Traités Hispaniques de Hisba*, ed. E. Lévi-Provençal (Cairo, 1955).

Ibn el-Assal (pseudonym). "Return to Cairo," *Encounter*, August 1969.

Ibn al-Athīr. *Al-Kāmil*, ed. C. J. Tornberg (Leiden-Upsala, 1851/1876), vol. 10, Cairo edition, vol. 8.

Ibn al-Faqīh. *Mukhtasar Kitāb al-Buldān*, ed. M. J. de Goeje (Leiden, 1885).

Ibn al-Khatīb. *On Plague*, cited by Max Meyerhof in *The Legacy of Islam*, ed. Sir Thomas Arnold and Alfred Guillaume (Oxford, 1931).

Ibn Battūta, *The Travels of Ibn Battūta*, vols. I, II, III, translated by H. A. R. Gibb, (London, 1958, 1962, 1971).

Ibn Butlān, Abu'l-Hasan al-Mukhtār ibn al-Hasan. *Risāla fi shirā al-raqīq*, ed. 'Abd al-Sālam Hārūn (Cairo, 1954).

Ibn Dihya, in A. Seippel, ed. *Rerum Normannicarum Fontes Arabici* (Oslo, 1896).

Ibn Hamdūn, Muhammad ibn al-Hasan. *Tadhkira* (Cairo, 1927).

Ibn Hazm, Abū Muhammad 'Alī. *Kitāb al-Akhlāq wa'l-Siyar*, ed. N. Tomiche (Beirut, 1961).

Ibn Khaldūn. *Al-Muqaddima*, ed. E. Quatremère (Paris, 1858) (reprinted Beirut, 1900). The passage on the Jews is given in the translation by Charles Issawi, *An Arab Philosophy of History*, 2d ed. (Princeton, 1987). The passage on empires is given in the translation by Reynold Nicholson, *Translations of Eastern Poetry and Prose* (Cambridge, 1922).

Ibn Khātima. Cited by Max Meyerhof in *The Legacy of Islam*, ed. Sir Thomas Arnold and Alfred Guillaume (Oxford, 1931).

Ibn Māja, Muhammad ibn Yazīd. *Sunan*, ed. Muhammad Fu'ād 'Abd al-Bāqī (Cairo, A.H. 1372/1952 C.E.).

Ibn Qutayba, Abū Muhammad 'Abdallāh ibn Muslim. *'Uyūn al-akhbār*, ed. Ahmad Zakī al-'Adawī (Cairo, A.H. 1343–8/1925–30 C.E.).

Ibn Saʿīd. *Kitāb Basṭ al-arḍ fiʾl-ṭūl waʾl-ʿarḍ,* ed. J. V. Gines (Tetuan, 1958).

Ibn Ṭufayl, Abu Bakr Muḥammad. *The Improvement of Human Reason, Exhibited in the Life of Hayy ibn Yakzan,* trans. Simon Ockley (London, 1708).

Ibn Yaʿqūb, Ibrāhīm al-Isrāʾīlī al-Ṭurṭūshī. Cited by al-Qazwīnī and al-Bakrī [*qq.v.*].

al-Idrīsī, Abū ʿAbdallāh Muḥammad ibn Muḥammad. *Opus Geographicum,* ed. A. Bombaci, U. Rizzitano, R. Rubinacci, and L. Veccia Vaglieri (Naples, 1970).

Israeli, Isaac. *Sefer Musar Rōfʾīm,* ed. David Kaufmann, in *Magazin für die Wissenschaft des Judenthums* (Berlin, 1884).

al-Jabartī, ʿAbd al-Raḥmān. *ʿAjāʾib al-Āthār* (Cairo, 1878).

al-Jāḥiẓ, ʿAmr ibn Baḥr. *Al-Bayān waʾl-tabyīn,* ed. ʿAbd al-Salām Muḥammad Hārūn (Cairo, A.H. 1380/1940 C.E.).

——— (attributed). *Al-Tabaṣṣur biʾl-tijāra,* ed. Ḥasan Ḥusnī ʿAbd al-Wahhāb (Cairo, 1935).

——— (attributed). *Kitāb al- Tāj* (Cairo, 1914).

al-Jahshiyārī, Abū ʿAbdallāh Muḥammad ibn ʿAbdūs. *Kitāb al-Wuzarāʾ waʾl-kuttāb,* ed. Muṣṭafā al-Saqqāʾ, Ibrāhīm al-Abyārī, and ʿAbd al-Ḥafiẓ Shalabī (Cairo, A.H. 1357/1938 C.E.).

James VI. *The Poems of James VI of Scotland,* 2 vols., ed. J. Craigie, vol. I (Edinburgh, 1955–58). (His Majesty's Poeticall Exercises at Vacant houres, Edinburgh, 1591)

Jarvis, C. S. *Desert and Delta* (London, 1938).

Jevdet, Abdullah. *Iki Emel* (Cairo, A.H. 1316/1898 C.E.).

Jevdet Pasha. *Tarih,* vol. 4 (Istanbul, A.H. 1301–9/1883–92 C.E.).

———. *Tezakir,* ed. Cavid Baysun (Ankara, 1953).

———. (Vakanüvis Cevdet Paşaʾnın-Evrakı) *Tarih-ı Osmani Encümeni Mecmuası,* no. 44 (A.H. 1333/1915 C.E.).

Jones, Sir William. *Works,* vol. 2 (London, 1807).

Kai Kāʾūs ibn Iskandar, Prince of Gurgān. *The Qābūs Nāma, a Mirror for Princes,* trans. Reuben Levy (London, 1951).

Kemal, Namık. Cited in Mehmed Kaplan, *Namık Kemal: Hayatı ve Eserleri* (Istanbul, 1948).

Kennan, George E. *Memoirs 1925–1950* (Boston, 1967).

Khomeini, Ayatollah. *Islam and Revolution,* trans. Hamid Algar (Berkeley, California, 1981).

Kinglake, A. W. *Eothen* (London, 1844).

Kirkbride, Sir Alec. *A Crackle of Thorns: Experiences in the Middle East* (London, 1956).

———. *From the Wings: Amman Memoirs 1947–1951* (London, 1976).

Kissinger, Henry. *White House Years* (Boston, 1979).

Koçu Bey, Mustafa. *Risale* (Istanbul, 1939).

Kutadgu-bilig, ed. Reşid Rahmeti Arat (Istanbul, 1947).

Lane, Edward William. *An Account of the Manners and Customs of the Modern Egyptians, Written in Egypt During the Years 1833, -34, and -35,* vol. 1 (London, 1871).

Lawrence, T. E. "The Changing East," published anonymously in *The Round Table,* September 1920; reprinted in T. E. Lawrence, *Oriental Assembly* (London, 1939).

———. *The Essential T. E. Lawrence,* ed. David Garnett (London, 1951).

———. *Seven Pillars of Wisdom,* privately printed 1926 (reprinted London, 1941).

Letter from the Ottoman Sultan to the Vizier Mehmed Nejib Pasha, Governor of

Baghdad, published by Hamdi Atamer, "Zenci Ticaretinin Yasaklanması," in *Belgelerle Türk Tarihi Dergisi 3* (1967).

The Letter of Tansar. Trans. Mary Boyce (Rome, 1968).

Letter from the Turkey Company to the Aleppo Factors, 3 June 1586, in *The Travels of John Sanderson in the Levant 1584–1602,* ed. Sir William Foster (London, 1931).

Liman von Sanders, Otto Viktor Karl. *Five Years in Turkey* (Annapolis, 1927).

Loyola, Saint Ignatius. *Personal Writings,* trans. Joseph A. Munitz (London, 1996).

al-Ma'arrī, Abu'l-'Alā'. *Risālat ul Ghufrān: A Divine Comedy,* trans. G. Brackenbury (Cairo, 1943).

McCullagh, Francis. *The Fall of Abd-ul-Hamid* (London, 1910).

Machiavelli, Niccolò. *The Prince,* trans. Luigi Ricci (London, 1903).

————. *Florentine Histories,* trans. Laura F. Banfield and Harvey C. Mansfield, Jr. (Princeton, 1988).

Madden, R. R. *Travels in Turkey, Egypt, Nubia and Palestine, 1824, 1825, 1826, & 1827,* 2d ed. (London, 1833).

al-Maqrīzī, Taqī al-Dīn Aḥmad ibn 'Alī. *Kitāb al-Sulūk li-ma'rifat duwal al-mulūk,* vol. 1, ed. M. M. Ziyāda and others (Cairo, 1934).

Marx, Karl. Article in *New York Daily Tribune,* April 15, 1854. Reprinted in *Karl Marx on Colonialism and Modernization, His Despatches and Other Writings on China, India, Mexico, The Middle East and North Africa,* ed. with an Introduction by Shlomo Avineri (New York, 1968).

al-Mas'ūdī, Abu'l-Ḥasan 'Alī ibn al-Ḥusayn. *Kitāb al-Tanbīh wa'l-ishrāf,* ed. 'Abdallāh Ismā'īl al-Sāwī (Cairo, A.H. 1357/1938 C.E.).

Viscount Maugham. *The Parliamentary Debates, Fifth Series—Volume CCXXV House of Lords Official Report,* 7th vol. of Session 1959–60, July 11, 1960–October 27, 1960 (London).

Mehmed Efendi. *Paris Sefaretnamesi* (Istanbul, A.H. 1306/1889 C.E.).

Meinertzhagen, Richard. *Middle East Diary* (London, 1959).

Melville, Herman. *Journal of a Visit to Europe and the Levant,* ed. Howard C. Horsford (Princeton, 1955).

Mendoza, Bernardino de. in *Calendar of State Papers* (translations of Spanish documents) vols. 2, 1568–1579 (London, 1894) and 3, 1580–1586 (London, 1896).

Meshullam ben Menahem da Volterra. Trans. in E. N. Adler, *Jewish Travellers.*

Meyerhof, Max. "Science and Medicine," in *The Legacy of Islam,* ed. Sir Thomas Arnold and Alfred Guillaume (Oxford, 1931).

al-Miknāsī, Muḥammad ibn 'Uthmān. *Al-Iksīr fī Fikāk al-Asīr,* ed. Muḥammad al-Fāsī (Rabat, 1965).

Miller, Judith. *God Has Ninety-nine Names: Reporting from a Militant Middle East* (New York, 1996).

Montagu, Lady Mary Wortley. *The Complete Letters, Vol. 1, 1708–1720,* ed. Robert Halsband (Oxford, 1965).

Al-Mubarrad, Abu'l-'Abbās Muḥammad ibn Yazīd. *Al-Kāmil,* vol. 2, ed. W. Wright (Leipzig, 1874).

Mubashshir ibn Fatik. *The Dicts and Sayings of the Philosophers,* trans. Stephen Scrope, London, 1477; ed. Margaret E. Schofield (Philadelphia, 1936).

Munif, Abdelrahman, *Cities of Salt,* trans. Peter Theroux (London, 1988).

al-Muqaddasī, Shams al-Dīn. *Descriptio Imperii Moslemici: Aḥsan al-Taqāsīm,* ed. M. J. de Goeje, 2d ed. (Leiden, 1906).

al-Muttaqī, 'Alā al-Dīn 'Alī ibn Ḥusām al-Dīn al-Hindi. *Kanz al-'Ummāl,* vols. 6, 7, 8 (Hyderabad, A.H. 1312/1894–95 C.E.).

Nadīm, 'Abdallāh. *Sulāfat al-Nadīm fī Muntakhabāt al-Sayyid 'Abdallāh Nadīm,* vol. 2 (Cairo, 1901).

Na'ima. *Tārīkh,* vol. 5 (Istanbul, A.H. 1283/1866 C.E.).

Naima. *Annals of the Turkish Empire from 1591 to 1659 of the Christian Era,* vol. 1, trans. Charles Fraser (London, 1832).

Naipaul, V. S. *Among the Believers: An Islamic Journey* (New York, 1981).

Namik Kemal. Article in *Tasvir-i Efkâr* (Istanbul, 1867).

Nangis, Guillaume de. *Annales du Regne de Saint Louis* (Paris, 1761).

Napoléon Bonaparte. *Campagnes d'Egypte et de Syrie,* ed. Henry Laurens (Paris, 1998).

Nicolay, Nicolas. *Les Navigations, peregrinatons et voyages, faicts en la Turguie* (Lyons, 1567). Trans. T. Washington the Younger (London, 1585).

Nicolson, Nigel, ed. *Vita and Harold: The Letters of Vita Sackville-West and Harold Nicolson* (New York, 1992).

Nightingale, Florence. *Letters from Egypt: A Journey on the Nile 1849–1850,* selected and introduced by Anthony Sattin (New York, 1987).

Niẓām al-Mulk. *The Book of Government or Rules for Kings,* trans. Hubert Darke (London, 1960).

Niẓāmī-i 'Arūḍī of Samarkand. *Chahār Maqāla,* ed. Mohammad Qazvīnī, rev. Mohammad Mo'īn (Tehran, 1964).

Noeldeke, Theodore. *Fünf Moallaqāt,* vol. 1 (Vienna, 1899).

Nutting, Anthony. "A Mid-East Settlement Is Imperative," *New York Herald Tribune,* July 31, 1958.

al-Nuwayrī, Shihāb al-Dīn Aḥmad ibn 'Abd al-Wahhāb. *Nihāyat al-Arab,* vol. 6 (Cairo, A.H. 1343/1925 C.E.).

Odysseus (Sir Charles Eliot). *Turkey in Europe* (London, 1900).

Okeley, W. *Eben-ezer; or a Small Monument of Great Mercy Appearing in the Miraculous Deliverance of W. Okeley [and others] from . . . Slavery.* Cited in D. D. Hebb, *Piracy and the English Government, 1616–1642* (London, 1994).

Osborn, Francis, *Political Reflections upon the Government of the Turks,* 3d. ed. (Oxford, 1662).

Ottoman Imperial Orders, published in Ahmet Refik, *Hicri onuncu asırda Istanbul hayatı* (Istanbul, 1933).

Palgrave, William Gifford. *A Year's Journey Through Central and Eastern Arabia* (London, 1869).

Patton, George S. *War As I Knew It* (New York, 1947).

Peçevi, Ibrahim. *Tarih* (Istanbul, A.H. 1283/1866 C.E.).

Pickthall, Marmaduke. *Oriental Encounters: Palestine and Syria (1894–5–6)* (London, 1918; new edition 1929).

Porter, Sir James. *Observations on the Religion, Law, Government, and Manners of the Turks,* 2d ed. revised by the author (London, 1771).

al-Qalqashandī, Abu'l-'Abbās Aḥmad. *Ṣubḥ al-A'shā,* vol. 8 (Cairo, 1915).

al-Qalyūbī, Aḥmad ibn Aḥmad. *Nawādir al-Shaykh* (Cairo, A.H. 1314/1896 C.E.).

al-Qazvīnī, Zakariyyā ibn Muḥammad. *Āthār al-bilād wa-akhbār al-'ibād* (Beirut, A.H. 1380/1960 C.E.).

Qur'ān versions cited in text.

Rashīd al-Dīn Faḍlallah. *Kitāb Tārīkh-i Ifranj,* ed. Karl Jahn (Leiden, 1951).

Resmi, Ahmed, in Vasif Efendi, *Tarih,* vol. 1 (Istanbul, A.H. 1218/1803 C.E.).

Rycaut, Paul. *The History of the Present State of the Ottoman Empire,* 4th ed. (London, 1675).

————. *The History of the Turks Beginning with the Year 1679* (London, 1700).

el-Sadat, Anwar. *In Search of Identity: An Autobiography* (New York, 1978).

Sadullah Pasha, "The Paris Exhibition," 1878, in Ebüzziya Tevfik, *Nümune-i Edebiyat-i Osmaniye,* 3d ed. (Istanbul, A.H. 1306/1889 C.E.).

Ṣā'id ibn Aḥmad al-Andalusī. *Kitāb Ṭabaqāt al-Umam* (Cairo, n.d.).

Said Pasha. *Hatirat,* vol. 1 (Istanbul, A.H. 1328/1889 C.E.).

Salisbury, Lord, to Sir Henry Layard (June 25, 1878).

Sanderson, John, *The Travels of John Sanderson in the Levant 1584–1602,* ed. Sir William Foster (London, 1931).

Saxe, Field-Marshal, Count Maurice de. *Reveries or Memoirs upon the Art of War* (London, 1757).

Sayings Attributed to the Prophet. Translations from the following collections: al-Bukhārī; al-Muttaqī; al-Tirmidhī; Ibn Māja.

Scott, C. Rochfort. *Rambles in Egypt and Candia,* 2 vols. (London, 1837).

Shaarawi, Huda. *Harem Years: The Memoirs of an Egyptian Feminist,* trans. Margot Badran (New York, 1987).

Shah of Persia. *The Diary of H.M. the Shah of Persia, During His Tour Through Europe in A.D. 1873,* trans. J. W. Redhouse (London, 1874).

al-Shaybānī, Muḥammad ibn al-Ḥasan. *Kitāb al-Siyar,* in Sarakhsī, *Sharḥ al-Siyar al-Kabīr,* vol. 4 (Hyderabad, A.H. 1335/1917 C.E.).

El-Shazly, General Saad. *The Arab Military Option* (San Francisco, 1986).

Sherley, Sir Thomas. "Discours of the Turkes," ed. Sir E. Denison Ross, *Camden Miscellany,* vol. 16 (London, Royal Historical Society, 1936).

Shihāb, Ḥaydar Aḥmad. *Ta'rīkh Aḥmad Bāshā al-Jazzār* (Beirut, 1955).

Shirley, Edward (pseudonym). *Know Thine Enemy: A Spy's Journey into Revolutionary Iran* (New York, 1997).

Sigoli, Simone. See Frescobaldi, Lionardo.

Slade, Adolphus. *Records of Travels in Turkey, Greece &c. and of a Cruise in the Black Sea, with the Capitan Pasha, in the Years 1829, 1830, and 1831* (London, 1833).

————. *Turkey and the Crimean War* (London, 1867).

Stark, Freya. *Baghdad Sketches* (London, 1937).

Storrs, Ronald. *Orientations* (London, 1937).

al-Suyūṭī, Jalāl al-Dīn. *Al-Kanz al-Madfūn* (Cairo, A.H. 1288/1871 C.E.).

————. *Al-Jāmi' al-Ṣaghīr,* vol. 2 (Cairo, A.H. 1323/1915 C.E.).

al-Ṭabarī, Abū Ja'far Muḥammad ibn Jarīr. *Ta'rīkh al-Rusul wa'l-mulūk,* ed. M. J. de Goeje and others (Leiden, 1879–1901).

al-Ṭahṭāwī, Rifā'a Rāfi'. *Takhlīṣ al-Ibrīz,* ed. Mahdī 'Allām, Aḥmad Aḥmad Badawī, and Anwar Lūqā (Cairo, 1958.)

al-Tawḥīdī, Abū Ḥayyān. *Kitāb al-Imtā' wa'l-Mu'ānasa,* ed. Aḥmad Amīn and Aḥmad al-Zayn (Cairo, 1939).

Thackeray, William Makepeace. *Eastern Sketches: A Journey from Cornhill to Cairo* (London, 1846).

al-Tirmidhī, Abū 'Īsā Muḥammad. *Al-Ṣaḥīḥ* (Cairo, A.H. 1292/1875 C.E.).

Tocqueville, Alexis de. *De la Démocratie en Amérique* (Paris, 1835).

Tott, Baron de. *Mémoires sur les Turcs et les Tartares* (Maestricht, 1785).

The Travels of John Sanderson in the Levant 1584–1602, ed. Sir William Foster (London, 1931).

Travels of the Jesuits into Various Parts of the World, trans. and ed. John Lockman (London, 1762). Based on Charles Le Gobien's *Lettres Edifiantes et Curieuses, écrites des missions étrangères par les missionaires de la compagnie de Jésus.*

"The True description of the magnificall Triumphs and Pastimes, represented at Constantinople, at the solemnizing of the Circumcision of the Soldan Mahument, the sonne of Amurath, the thyrd of that name, in the yeare of our Lorde God 1582, in the Monethes of Mai and June," contained in a letter written by Francis Billerbeg in Latin to "A Godly learned man of Germanie." An English translation was published in London shortly after, probably in 1585.

Tülümen, Turgut. *Iran Devrimi Hatıraları* (Istanbul, 1998).

al-Ṭurṭūshī, Abū Bakr Muḥammad ibn al-Walīd, called Ibn Abī Randaqa. *Sirāj al-mulūk* (Cairo, A.H. 1289/1872 C.E.).

Ṭūsī, Naṣīr al-Dīn. *The Nasirean Ethics,* trans. G. M. Wickens (London, 1964).

Twain, Mark. *Notebooks & Journals,* vol. 1, ed. Frederick Anderson, Michael B. Frank, and Kenneth M. Sanderson (London, 1975).

———. *The Mark Twain Papers,* ed. Walter Blair, Claude M. Simpson, and Henry Nash Smith; series ed. Frederick Anderson (Berkeley, 1967).

'Ubayd-i Zākānī. *Kulliyyāt,* ed. 'Abbās Iqbāl (Tehran, 1343 Persian solar/1964 C.E.).

Al-'Umarī, Ṣubḥi. *Lawrence Kamā 'araftuhu* (Beirut, 1969).

Usāma ibn Lādin. See Bin Lādin, Usāma.

Usāma ibn Munqidh. *Kitāb al-I'tibār,* ed. P. K. Hitti (Princeton, 1930).

Vasif Efendi. Embassy report in Jevdet, *Tarih,* vol. 4 (Istanbul, A.H. 1307–9/1889–92 C.E.).

———. *Tarih,* vol. 1 (Istanbul, A.H. 1218/1803 C.E.).

Vogué, Eugène-Melchior de. *Syrie, Palestine, Mont Athos: Voyage au Pays du Passé* (Paris, 1876).

Volney. *Voyage en Egypte et en Syrie,* ed. Jean Gaulmier (Paris/The Hague, 1959).

Voltaire. *Voltaire's Correspondence,* ed. Theodore Besterman, vols. 78, 79 (Geneva, 1962).

Warburton, Eliot. *The Crescent and the Cross; or, Romance and Realities of Eastern Travel,* vol. 1 (London, 1845).

Washington, George. 1774, cited in Lucretia Perry Osborn, *Washington Speaks for Himself* (New York, 1927).

al-Waṭwāṭ, Muḥammad ibn Ibrāhīm al-Kutubī. *Ghurar al-Khaṣā'iṣ al-Wāḍiḥa* (Cairo, A.H. 1344/1926 C.E.).

Wiet, Gaston. *Introduction à la littérature arabe* (Paris, 1966).

William, Archbishop of Tyre. *A History of Deeds Done Beyond the Sea,* trans. Emily Atwater Babcock and A. C. Krey (New York, 1943).

Willibald. "The Travels of Willibald," in *Early Travels in Palestine,* ed. Thomas Wright (New York, 1968.)

Wilson, Sir Arnold. *South-West Persia: A Political Officer's Diary 1907–1914* (London, 1942).

Wood, Richard. *The Early Correspondence of Richard Wood (1831–1841),* ed. A. B. Cunningham (London, 1966).

al-Yamanī, Shaykh Muḥammad ibn Aḥmad. *Nafḥat al-Yaman* (Cairo, A.H. 1324/1906 C.E.).

Young, George. *Egypt* (London, 1927).

WORKS OF UNKNOWN OR COLLECTIVE AUTHORSHIP

Akhbār al-Ṣīn wa'l-Hind (News of China and India) a work of unknown authorship written in 851 C.E.

Kutadgu-bilig (The Science of Happiness) a long poem in Central Asian Turkish, dedicated in 1269 C.E. to the ruler of Kashgar. The author's name is given simply as Yūsuf, born in Balasagun. Nothing else is known about him. The poem, of more than six thousand couplets, is narrative in form and tells the story of a king called Sunrise, his minister Full Moon, the latter's son Prudent and a wise man called Abstinent. Their dialogue contains much discussion of political, religious and ethical matters. As Abstinent is dying, he bequeaths his sole possessions: his staff to the king, his bowl to the minister.

The Letter of Tansar, a treatise on politics from pre-Islamic Persia, known only through an Arabic translation probably made in the eighth century C.E. The name Tansar may be a misreading for Tusar, said by some authorities to be an abbreviation of the name of the chief priest of the founder of the Sasanid dynasty, Ardashir (c. 224–240 B.C.E.).

Pirqē Avot (The Chapters of the Fathers), variously translated as the "Sayings," "Wisdom" or "Ethics" of the Fathers. A Hebrew collection of ethical and religious sayings and precepts, ascribed to rabbinic masters and dealing with both individual and social behavior. It was probably committed to writing in its present form in late Roman Palestine but preserves a much older oral tradition.

UNPUBLISHED SOURCES

Aidé, George. Petition translated from the Turkish document in the Public Record Office, London, State Papers 102/62.

Murray, Mr. Memorandum on the Dragoman System in the Levant, January 1838. Public Record Office, London, F.O. 366/569.

Siyavush Pasha, Letter to Queen Elizabeth. Translated from the Turkish document in the Public Record Office, London, State Papers 102/61/5.

INDEX

Page numbers in *italics* refer to illustrations.

'Abd al-'Aziz, Sultan, 161–63, 412
'Abd al-Malik, Caliph, 223
'Abd al-Raḥmān, Sultan, 27–28
Abdimi of Haifa, Rabbi, 413
Abdul Hamid, Sultan, 248–49, 252–55
Abdullah, King of Jordan, 171–73
Abidin Palace (Egypt), siege of (1942),
    315
Abū Bakr, Caliph, 273
Abu'l Fadl, Mirza, 183
Abul Huda, Tewfiq, 171–72
Abū Nuwās, 382–83
Abū Shāma, 328–29, 432
Abū Ṭālib Khān, Mīrzā, 25, 43–45, 432
Abū 'Ubayda, 404
Abū Yūsuf Ya'qūb al-Kūfī, 280–81, 432
Abū Zayd, 97
Acheson, Dean, 173–74, 432
adultery, 205–6, 230, 396
Afghanistan, 26, 57, 261, 265
Africa, sub-Saharan, x, 7–8, 10, 24, 77–78,
    84–89, 270, 273, 310, 325–26, 353
Ahmad Sharif, Sidi, 418
Ahmed-oglu, Ebu, 142–43
Ahmed Pasha, 286–87
Ahmet I, Sultan, 297
Aidé, George, 151–53
Akavya ben Mehallalel, Rabbi, 401
Albania, 18, 166, 393
Āl-e Aḥmad, Jalāl, 55–57
Aleppo, 10, 151, 225–26, 232, 316–17,
    332–34, 343, 369
Alexandria, 67, 81, 245, 293, 310, 312, 315,
    332, 386
Alexios Comnenos, Emperor, 128
Algeria, 151, 440
Ali, Abdullah Yusuf, 184
Ali, Ahmed, 183, 185
Âli Pasha, 285–86, 417, 432
Allenby, Viscount, 306
alphabets, 351, 429

amber, 31, 65, 325
Ammianus Marcellinus, 6, 432
Amon (physician), 359
amulets and charms, 204, 260
animals, 34–35, 62, 64–65, 84–85, 109,
    151, 233, 273, 368, 377, 384
Anūshirwān, King, 223
Apocalypse, 159, *414,* 415
apostasy, 76, 270
Apuleius, Lucius, 5, 435
Arabia, 303–8, 319, 345–48, 367, 377, 380,
    395–96, 415
    see also Mecca; Medina
Arabic language, xi–xiv, 26, 61–72, 77–78,
    101, 108, 147, 185*n*, 194, 269, 271*n*,
    301, 406, 429–31
    as language of religion, 6, 78, 194,
        353–54
    as language of science, 77, 351–53, 359
    as literary language, 78, 182, 211,
        353–54, 367–68
Arab-Jewish conflict, 18, 171–73, 246–48,
    311, 319–20, 420–25
Arab League, 423–24
Arab Legion, 171–72
Arabs, 6–12, 85, 116, 171–73, 209, 328,
    367–68, 426–27
    characteristics attributed to, 8–12,
        16–20, 102–8, 169–70, 246, 301, 408
    conquest by, x, 16, 63, 254, 273, 376
    independence sought by, 299–309, 418,
        422–23
Arafat, Yasser, 266
Aramaic, 61–62, 72, 129
Aramco (Arabian-American Oil Com-
    pany), 340
Arberry, Arthur J., 184
architecture, 65, 69, 80, 364
Ardashir I, King of Persia, 132
Arghūn-Shāh, Amīr, 92
Aristarchi, Stavraki, 130

Aristotle, 224
Armenian people, 18–19, 130, 156, 188, 240, 297–98, 417
armies, 16, 75–76, 128, 144, 243, 252, 258, 284, 287–94, 303–7, 310–16, 353
  discipline of, 16, 227, 261–62, 272, 291, 294
  payment of, 16, 225, 250, 306
Arnold of Lübeck, 277–78, 432
Aryans, 65–66
Asad, Muhammad, 184
Ashurnasirpal II, King of Assyria, 375–76
Asim, 41, 432
Asquith, Herbert Henry, 418–19, 432
assassination, 246, 253–54, 270, 276–79, 426
Assassins (sect), 66, 270, 276–79
Assyrian language, xiv, 62, 130, 351
Assyrian people, 375–76
astronomy, 63, 84, 352, 359, 361–62
Atatürk, Mustafa Kemal, 194–95, 257–60, 309, 432
Atay, Falıh Rıfkı, 51–54, 419–20, 432
Atif Efendi, 40
Augustine, Saint, 273–74, 433, 439
Austen, Jane, 12, 180, 397
Austria, 93–94, 128, 253, 287–90, 412, 418
Avot, Pirqē, 219, 401–2
al-Awḥadī, Shihāb al-Dīn Aḥmad ibn 'Abdallah, 136, 433
Aynu'd-Dawla, Atábak, 250
Azulai, David, 37–38, 433
Azzam, Abder Rahman, 423–24

Babylon, 77, 95, 344, 352
Babylonian language, xiv, 61, 351
Baghdad, 168–71, 187, 254, 310, 332, 338–39, 357–59
Bahrain, 424
Baldwin of Bouillon, Count, 274–76
Balfour Declaration (1917), 420–21
Balkans, 63, 269, 417–18
bananas, xi, 386
banking and finance, 81, 326, 331
Barbary pirates, see corsairs
Basra, 307, 332, 339
Bassola, Mosse, 330–31
bastinado, 235, 237, 292
bazaars, 56, 64, 112–13, 121, 206–8, 250, 330, 386–87, 395
beards, 34, 102, 161, 355, 395, 408
Beauvollier, Father, 101
Bedouins, 15, 16, 80, 92, 223, 376
begging, 87, 210, 282
Beirut, 80, 119, 303, 316
Belgrade, 93, 366–67, 389–90
Bell, Gertrude, 16, 433
Bell, Richard, 184
Bellow, Saul, 119–20
Benjamin, J. J., 108–10, 338, 432
Benjamin of Tudela, 357–59, 432

Ben Shatakh, Shimon, 219
Bentham, Jeremy, 104–5, 432
Ben Zoma, Rabbi, 401
Berber peoples, xiii, 296
Bernard the Wise, 94–95, 432
Bernstorff, Johann Heinrich, Count, 420–21, 432
Bertha, Queen of Franja, 136
Bethlehem, 115, 198
Betts, Robert Brenton, 426
Bible, 61–62, 254, 271
  see also New Testament; Old Testament
Billerbeg, Francis, 388–89
bin Lādin, Usāma, 319–20
Black Death, 91–93
Blount, Henry, 231–32, 432
Bluebeard Pasha (pseudonym), 236–37
Blunt, Wilfrid Scawen, 50–51, 83, 418, 432
Bocaccio, Giovanni, 354
Bon, Ottaviano, 335–36
Bonaparte, Napoléon, 42, 102, 105, 190, 291–92, 438
Book of Kings (Firdawsī), 350
Bosnia, 287–89
Boulogne, counts of, 274–76
Boutros-Ghali, Boutros, 248, 433
bravery, 8–10, 14, 16, 40, 82, 90, 97, 134, 227, 235, 277–78, 289, 309, 407
bribery, 66, 146, 229, 232, 234, 297–98, 300–301
British imperialism, 16–18, 24–25, 77, 82–84, 106–8, 123–24, 165–69, 244–46, 270, 293–95, 300–301, 306–8, 418
  linguistic effects of, 63–64, 68
  resistance to, 117, 170, 174, 244, 315–16, 419–20, 422
Browne, E. G., 249–52
Bulgaria, 417, 419
Buraimi Oasis, slaves in, 340–41
Burckhardt, John Lewis, 105–6, 436
bureaucracy, 49, 56, 166–67, 217–18, 221–22, 225–26, 242–46, 262–63, 297–98, 301, 409–10
Burton, Sir Richard, 111–12, 433
Burton, Robert, 393
Busbecq, Ogier Ghiselin de, 98–99, 433
Buzurg ibn Shahriyār, 85–89, 433
Byron, George Gordon, Lord, 4, 12
Byzantine Empire, 3–4, 7–9, 64, 68, 128–30, 135, 328, 342

cadi, see qadis
Caillaux, Joseph, 52
Cairo, 53, 80, 93, 95, 105, 107–8, 190–91, 210, 231–33, 236–37, 244, 292–94, 314–16, 386
calendars, 34, 70, 352
camels, 62, 110–11, 230, 338, 340
Camp David Agreement (1978), 247

capitation (poll) tax, 272, 280, 296
capitulations (privileges), 296–97
captives, 24–25, 91, 101–2, 201, 272, 312,
    405, 438
  conversion of, 85–88, 101, 280
  ransom of, 127, 151
caravans, 66–67, 96–98, 111, 151, 338, 340
Catherine II (the Great), Empress of Rus-
    sia, 180, 337–38
Catholics, Roman, 76, 99–100, 130, 201,
    209, 298, 360
Cavallero, Ugo, 312–14
Cecil, Lord Edward, 245–46, 433
censorship, 51–52, 264
Central Asia, xi, 10, 181, 266, 300
Central Intelligence Agency (CIA), 174n,
    247, 440
Chair, Somerset de, 168–69, 246, 433
charity, 87, 210, 359, 378
charms and amulets, 204, 260
Chateaubriand, François de, 12, 52, 433
Chaush, Ilyas, 388
Chelebi, Jevri, 142–43
chemistry, 63, 352
chess, 68, 289, 394
chibouk (pipe), 114, 204, 393, 396
children, 187, 198, 200, 204–5, 272–73,
    340–41, 366–67, 406, 409, 413
China, x, xi, 8, 17, 48, 71, 84–85, 251, 338,
    352, 377, 430
Choiseul-Gouffier, Marie-Gabriel, Comte
    de, 228, 434
Christendom, medieval, xii, 23–24, 27–35,
    48, 54, 61–63, 66–69, 75–76, 269–71
Christianity, 13, 15, 17–18, 48, 75–76, 93,
    103, 189, 218, 257, 266, 269–71, 352,
    360
  branches of, 18, 48, 76, 116, 296–99
  holy places of, 75, 115, 297–99
Churchill, Winston S., 309, 314, 316–19,
    381, 434
Ciano, Count Galeazzo, 311–14, 434
Cicero, Marcus Tullius, 3
Circassian people, 16, 107, 203
cities, 29, 37, 47, 112–14, 128, 217, 224,
    232–33, 265, 419
City of God, The (Augustine), 273–74, 433
Clemenceau, Georges, 307–8
Clement VII, Pope, 329–30
clothing, 29, 43–45, 50–51, 57, 108, 149,
    326, 331
  protective, 81, 111, 162
  symbolism of, 81–82, 96, 156–57, 227,
    274, 305, 307, 360
  Westernization of, 55, 190–91, 254, 353
  of women, 180, 190–91, 196–97, 200,
    203–5
coffee, x, 11, 205, 326, 377–78, 385, 390,
    393–94
colleges, see universities and colleges

colonialism, 54–57, 246, 293–94, 326
  see also imperialism, European
commerce and trade, x, 23–24, 32–33, 42,
    47, 63–64, 67–71, 72, 75, 121–22,
    323–48, 367, 377, 419
  in humans, see slavery
  international agreements on, 128,
    136–37, 146, 334–36
  Jews in, 108–10, 330–31, 336, 338
  with Ottoman empire, x, 42, 68, 128,
    136–37, 146, 296–97, 329–44
  promotion of, 49, 77–78, 127–28, 146,
    155, 330–32, 336–38, 342–43
  regulation of, 49, 127, 232, 237, 280–81,
    296–97, 329–30, 334–36, 384, 387
  revenues from, 325, 328–30, 334, 336,
    344
  wartime, x, 63, 75, 325–26, 328–30
  women in, 37–38, 331
communications, 25, 62–63, 217, 245, 247,
    343
  diplomatic, 128–36, 142–47, 154–55,
    417, 423–24
  military, 19–20, 303–5, 310–14, 317
  print, 44–47, 49, 259, 264, 360–61
communism, 260–61, 264
concubinage, 12, 71, 90–91, 141, 179,
    203–4, 208
Conrad of Montferrat, King of Jerusalem,
    277–78
conscription, 238–39, 316
conservation, 169–70, 226
Constantine I, Emperor, 75, 218, 437
Constantine X (Emperor Constantine Por-
    phyrogenitus), 3–4, 6
Constantinople, see Istanbul
Constantinople, Patriarch of, 296, 298
constitutional government, 14, 120, 238,
    248–49, 251, 262
consulates, 128–29, 153–55, 331–36
conversion, religious, 76–78, 87–89, 101,
    112, 137n, 181, 271–72, 280, 299
Copts, 297–98
Cornaro, Doge Marco, 135
corporal punishment, 109, 123–24,
    183–86, 281
corsairs, 76, 97–98, 101–2, 296, 326, 439
cosmetics, 45, 203–4
Cox, Sir Percy, 419–20
Cox, Samuel S., 18, 342–43, 434
credit, 81, 331–32, 404
crime, 76, 95–98, 109, 208, 230–37,
    382–83
Crimean War, 294–99, 437, 438
Croatia, 287–89, 336
cross-dressing, 187
Crusades, x, 23, 25–26, 32–34, 66, 75–76,
    269–70, 274–79, 308, 319, 357
  trade stimulated by, 32–33, 63, 75,
    127–28, 325, 328–30

curses, 187, 289, 402, 408
Cyrillic alphabet, 351, 429

Dallam, Thomas, 138–40, 196–97, 434
Damascus, 16, 92–93, 108, 114–15, 123,
      230, 232, 310, 317, 330–31, 338,
      386–87
dancing, 50–51, 53, 191–92, 195–96, 198,
      204, 363–64, 390–91
Dann, Uriel, 427, 434
Dante Alighieri, 354
Danton, Georges Jacques, 55
Daqīqī (poet), 225, 371
Darfur women, 207
Daryabadi, Maulana Abdul Majid, 185
Davānī, Jalāl al-Dīn, 10, 434
deception, 68–69, 134, 223, 237, 402, 410,
      427
Declaration of the Rights of Man (1789),
      40
Declaration of the World Islamic Front for
      Jihad (Bin Ladin), 319–20
Defoe, Daniel, 354
De Materia Medica (Dioscordes), 358
democracy, 224, 246, 251–54, 257–58,
      426–27
   see also government; republicanism
Derby, Edward Henry Stanley, Earl of,
      300, 434
despotism, 9–15, 49, 144–47, 202, 220–21,
      226–27, 233, 235–39, 246–48, 292–93,
      301–2, 328
dhimmī (protected non-Muslim), 280–82
Dicts and Sayings of the Philosophers, The
      (Scrope), 406–7
dietary laws, 5, 11, 23, 32, 35, 105, 273,
      375–76, 392–93
diplomacy, x, 18, 24–25, 27–29, 76–77,
      125–75, 236, 242, 243, 294–99, 307–8,
      331
   gift-giving in, 28–29, 85, 88–89, 134,
      139–42, 149–51, 156, 200, 278–80,
      337, 408
   intelligence gathering in, 76, 132–34,
      148, 280–82
   language of, 28–29, 127, 129–30,
      134–43, 146–47, 153–54, 157
   manners and customs in, 52–53, 69–70,
      138–45, 148–51, 155–58, 164, 168,
      175, 200, 304–5, 390–93
   recruitment and training for, 129–34,
      138–43, 145, 148, 153–55, 246, 283
   trade issues in, 128, 136–37, 146,
      334–36, 340, 342–43
disguise, 108, 111–12, 280–81, 305
Divine Comedy (Dante), 354
divorce, 90, 179, 189, 201, 205–6, 208–9
dīwān, 63, 69–70, 222–23, 374
Djemal Pasha, see Jemāl Pasha
Douglas, Norman, 17, 434

dragoman, see interpreters
drinking and drunkenness, 11, 45, 81,
      105–6, 209, 231, 235, 374, 376,
      382–83, 385, 391, 396
drugs, 47, 70, 109, 277–78, 294, 356
Dufferin, Frederick Temple, Marquess of,
      244–45, 434
Duhamel, Georges, 118–19, 362, 434
durrah (fellow-wife), 208–9
Dutch imperialism, 63, 270
dyes, 35, 69, 211, 325, 332, 338

East, idea of, xi–xii, 16, 48–49, 82–84,
      102–4, 108, 117–18, 237, 251
economics, 49, 122, 243, 262, 327–28
Eden, Sir Anthony, 317
education, 24–25, 34, 44, 48–49, 134, 148,
      241, 243–44, 352–55, 360–61, 370–71,
      401–2
   in foreign languages, 42–44, 108,
      130–31, 147, 153–55, 245, 283, 360
   religious, 48, 263–64
   of women, 179, 187, 192, 194, 198–99
Egypt, x, 8, 80–82, 87, 94–95, 175, 192,
      236–37, 251, 266, 320, 377, 399
   ancient, xii, 5–6, 16, 61–62, 77, 105, 189,
      209, 217, 351–52, 418
   in Arab-Israeli conflicts, 171–72, 423–25
   British administration of, 106–7, 244–48,
      300–301, 314–16, 418
   in Crusades, 274, 329
   French occupation of, 26, 105, 190–91,
      291–94, 436
   Westernization of, 26, 190–91, 237
   in world wars, 300–301, 310–16
Egyptian language, xiv, 61–62, 105
El Alamein, Battle of (1942), 313–16
Elijah, Prophet, 399
Eliot, Sir Charles (Odysseus) 209–10
Eliot, George (Mary Ann Evans), 418, 434
Elisha ben Abūya, Rabbi, 401
Elizabeth I, Queen of England, 136–39,
      180, 334, 336
eloquence, 8–10, 17, 29, 142, 225–26, 229,
      246, 401
embassies, permanent, 24–25, 27–29, 113,
      127–31, 153–55, 165–70, 319, 331,
      334–36
   see also envoys
Engels, Friedrich, 15
England, 25, 30–35, 50–55, 161–63, 249,
      275, 291–92, 299–319, 325, 360–61
   Arab uprising supported by, 300–301,
      303–8
   diplomatic relations of, 33, 128–29,
      136–41, 144–48, 153–58, 160–173,
      196, 294–95, 339–41, 412
   in international trade, 33, 68, 136–38,
      146, 151, 330, 331–34, 343–44, 377,
      394–95

England (*cont.*)
manners in, 43–44, 50–51, 162, 333, 345
political system of, 30, 33, 51–52, 162
in world wars, 300–301, 305–16, 419–20
see also British imperialism
English language, 61–72, 185*n*, 245, *398,* 429–30
Enver Pasha, 302, 418–19, 434
envoys, 24, 27–29, 127–28, 130–31, 132–34, 142, 148, 328–29, 390–91
treatment of, 132–34, 138–51, 155–58, 161, 164–65, 196–97, 280
see also embassies, permanent
Eothen (Kinglake), 83, 106, 437
Epistle of Forgiveness (al-Ma'arrī), 354
"Epitaph" (Kanık), 322
Erbakan, Necmettin, 265
Eritrea, 311
Ersoy, Mehmet Akif, 321, 437
Ethiopia, 7–8, 10, 106, 207, 297–98, 311, 377
eunuchs, 136, 193–94, 198–99, *199,* 203
Europe:
on Arab independence, 165–68, 305–8, 418
ascendancy of, x, 24–26, 34, 63–64, 77, 129, 181, 259, 326, 353, 360–62
emulation of, 55–57, 82, 170, 180, 190–91, 218, 233, 237, 263–64, 353
imperial expansion of, *see* imperialism, European
Middle Easterners in, 24–25, 27–29, 35–38, 50–52, 129, 148–51, 160–63, 189, 300, 361–62, 383–84, 412
Muslim geographers on, 29–35
political systems in, 49, 117, 162, 166, 228, 238, 241, 244–45
women in, 28–29, 37, 45, 57, 163, 179–80, 197–98, 201–4
Eustace of Bouillon, Count, 274
Evliya Çelebi, 25, 35–36, 189, 434
excommunication, 329–30, 335

Face of the Ancient Orient, The (Moscati), 399
factories, 49, 162–63
factors (agents), 331–32, 338
Faisal, Sherif, 302
al-Fārābī, Abū Naṣr, 224, 434
Far East, xii, 77–78, 326, 338, 351
Farouk, King of Egypt, 314–15
Farren (British consul), 108, 123
farting, 143, 276, 408
fasting, 231, 272, 407
Fawzī, Ḥusayn, 54–55, 434
Fayṣal ibn Ḥusayn, Prince, 421–22, 434
feasts and festivals, 90, 110, 190–92, 375–78, 388–93, 404
fermentation, 106, 376
fertility, 204, 208, 406
fetwa (decision), 234, 295, 387–88, 394

Fikret, Tevfik, 255–57, 434
finance and banking, 81, 326, 331
Firdawsī (poet), 72, *350,* 431
firmans (imperial orders), 80, 286–87, 297–98, 338–39
Fitch, Ralph, 333–34, 434
FitzGerald, Edward, 371
Flaubert, Gustave, 110–11, 235, 434
food and foodstuffs, 29, 81, 84, 90, 142–43, 205, 365, 375–96, 409
blessings over, 375, 378–79
preparation of, 32, 45, 67, 90, 356, 375–78, 384–93
trade in, 45, 63, 67, 71, 72, 326–27, 338, 384–87
Foreign Office, British, 128–29, 131, 165–68, 316, 340–41, 343, 423, 439
Forster, E. M., 82–84, 210–11, 434
"For the Fatherland" (Kanık), 322
France, 25–26, 32–34, 37–42, 45–47, 53, 91, 128, 136–38, 163, 275, 291, 294–95, 297, 310–11, 337, 412
manners in, 30, 34, 42, 45, 47, 52, 103, 191–92
political system of, 39–41, 51–52, 228, 238, 241
see also French imperialism
Francis I, King of France, 297
Frankfurter, Felix, 421–22
Franks, xi, 18–19, 30, 32–33, 96–98, 108, 130–31, 151–54, 157, 297, 357, 417
Frederick the Great, King of Prussia, 36–37, 337
freedom, 51–57, 116–17, 166, 179–81, 210, 224, 238–39, 243, 307, 336, 422
of expression, 45–46, 51–52, 238–39, 264, 293
religious, 48–49
of thought, 54–55, 352–53, 362, 426
Free Officers' Association, Egyptian, 315–16
French imperialism, 26, 77, 165–68, 270, 291–94, 306–8, 310, 316–19
cultural effects of, 63–64, 190–91
French language, 61, 64–66, 67–71, 406, 411–12
French Revolution, ix, 39–42, 55, 238–39
Frescobaldi, Lionardo, 95–96, 230, 386, 435
Fuad Pasha, 411–12
furniture, 69, 71, 156, 164, 191, 200, 326, 380
Fuzuli (poet), 212, 435

Gabrieli, Francesco, 367–68, 435
Gallipoli, Battle of (1915), 309, 321, 432, 437
games and sports, 68, 133, 196, 289, 368, 394
Gandhi, Mohandas K., 54

gardens, 71–72, 90, 117–18, 224–25, 236, 272

Garmrūdī, 'Abd al-Fattāḥ Khan, 160–61, 435

de Gaulle, Charles, 310–11, 316–18, 435

Gaza, 95

General History of the Turks (Knolles), 144

Genoa, 128, 232, 275, 328–29

Georgian women, 203, 207

German language, 68–69

Germany, Germans, 51, 66, 287–89, 301–2, 309–16, 418, 420–21, 434

Ghalib Pasha, 255

Ghars al-Ni'ma (Muḥammad ibn Hilāl al-Ṣābi'), 225–26, 435

al-Ghassānī, Muḥammad ibn 'Abd al-Wahhāb, al-Wazīr, 37, 435

al-Ghazāl (Yaḥyā ibn al-Ḥakam), 27–29, 435

al-Ghazālī, Abū Ḥāmid Muḥammad, 187, 378–80, 435

Gibb, Sir Hamilton, 368, 435

gift-giving, 33, 66, 81, 195–96, 203, 365, 418–19
  diplomatic, 28–29, 85, 88–89, 134, 139–42, 149–51, 156, 200, 278–80, 337, 408

Glubb, Sir John, 246, 340–41

Gobineau, Joseph Arthur, Comte de, 79, 435

Godfrey of Bouillon, Count, 274, 275n

Goethe, Johann Georg Wolfgang von, 70

gold, 33, 142, 325, 329, 336, 389

government, 30, 33, 49, 51–52, 117, 162, 166, 197–98, 217–66, 282–83
  constitutional, 14, 120, 238, 248–49, 251, 262
  despotic, 9–11, 13–15, 49, 144–47, 202, 220–21, 226–29, 233, 235–39, 246–48, 292–93, 301–2, 328
  fear in, 43, 221–23, 230–32
  literary commentary on, 123–24, 224–25, 255–57, 405–6, 409–10
  reform of, 157–58, 181, 192, 218, 228–29, 237–44, 250–52, 261–64, 303
  religious challenges to, 217–18, 251–52
  republican, 39–42, 49, 52, 238, 241, 244
  see also freedom; laws

Grand National Assembly, Turkish, 257–58

grand vizier, office of, *see* Porte

Graziani, Rodolfo, 311, 313

Greece, 310–11, 417, 422–23
  ancient, xi–xiii, 3, 24, 54, 71–72, 129, 224, 352, 353

Greek language, 61–62, 64–65, 71–72, 127, 129, 351, 359, 376

Greek Orthodox church, 18, 296, 298

Greek peoples, 7, 14, 18–19, 130, 188, 203, 207, 240, 297–98, 309, 417

Gucci, Giorgio, 386–87, 435

Guillaume de Nangis, 278–79, 435

ḥadīth (sayings of the Prophet), xv, 4, 6–7, 219–20, 222, 269, 272–73, 327–28, 379, 402, 433, 436, 439

Hafiz (poet), *374*, 431

Haidar, Princess Musbah, 51, 193, 365, 435

hairstyles, 34, 45, 53, 102, 157, 187, 273

Hakam (merchant), 394

Halet Efendi, 42, 435

Halevi, Yehuda, 212, 435

el Halil, Abdul Kerim, 303

Hama, Syria, 32, 317, 332

Hamilton, Alexander, 4, 15

Hamit, Abdulhak, 51–52

Hamoud Bey, 50–51

Ḥanafī, Ḥasan, 247, 435

Ha-Nagid, Samuel, 320, 435

Harborne, William, 136–37

harem, 70, 180, 193, 196–206, 209–11, 365, 412, 435

al-Harīrī of Basra, *97, 324*

Harriman, Averell, 174

Hārūn ibn Yaḥyā, 25, 29–30, 435

al-Ḥasan, Caliph, 222

hashish, 66, 82, 294

ḥashīshī, see Assassins

Hassan Pasha, 230–31, 287–89

Ḥātim, 405

Hatti Efendi, Mustafa, 361–62, 435

Hatun, Mihri, *see* Mihri Hatun

Hawley, Sir Donald, 380–81, 435

Haykal, Ḥasanain, 424–25, 435

Heaven, 72, 205, 222, 225, 271–73, 277–78, 327, 354, 363, 369, 378, 415

Hebrew Bible, *see* Old Testament

Hebrew language, xiii, 61–62, 127, 129, 182, 351, 359, 429

Hejaz, the, 303–5, 434

Hell, 272–73, 354, 369

Hellenes (Christian sect), 298

Henry IV, King of France, 297

Henry of Champagne, Count, 278

hermits, 273, 408

Herodotus, 344

Hezarfenn, Huseyn, 230, 435

hieroglyphs, 105, 351

Hilāl al-Ṣābi', 223, 435

historical consciousness, xiv–xv, 16, 49, 119–20, 148, 210, 295, 308, 353, 366

History of the Present State of the Ottoman Empire, The (Rycaut), 144, *199, 216*

Hitler, Adolf, 311, 313

holy war, *see* Crusades; *jihād*

Hornby, Emilia, 209, 435

houris, 369, 379

Hūd, Prophet, 415

Hugo, Victor, 12

Hume, David, 4, 14

humor, xv, 25, 30, 53–54, 168, 174, 229, 293, 383, 397–412
  satirical, 142–43, *242,* 305, 399–400
Hungary, 93–94, 287–88, *288,* 336, 430
Hurso (knight), 32–33
Huseyn Pasha, 231
Hussein, King of Jordan, 175, 424
Hussein, Saddam, 427
hygiene, 12, 19–20, 34, 43, 81, 84, 91, 104, 109, 169–70, 188, 203, 233, 376

Iberia, x–xi, 25, 63, 269
Ibn 'Abd al-'Azīz, 'Umar, 221
Ibn 'Abd Rabbihi, 363
Ibn 'Abdūn, 229, 403, 435
Ibn Abī Maryam, Qadi, 408
Ibn 'Alqama, Tammām, 29
Ibn el-Assal (pseudonym), 425–26
Ibn al-Athīr, 'Izz al-Dīn, 275–76, 435
Ibn Baṭṭūṭa, 76, 89–91, 435
Ibn Burd, Bashshār, 407
Ibn Buṭlān, 187–88, 435
Ibn Dihya, 29, 436
Ibn al-Faqīh, 8, 382, 436
Ibn al-Furāt, 223
Ibn al-Ḥakam, Yaḥyā (al-Ghazāl), 27–29
Ibn Ḥamdūn, Muḥammad ibn al-Ḥasan, 403, 436
Ibn Ḥazm, Abū Muḥammad 'Alī, 403, 436
Ibn Khaldūn, 'Abd al-Raḥmān, 9–10, 25, 34, 227, 411, 436
Ibn al-Khaṭīb, 92, 436
Ibn Khātima, Abū Ja'far Aḥmad ibn 'Alī, 92, 436
Ibn al-Khaṭṭāb, Umar, 223
Ibn Khuthaym, Rabī', 407
Ibn al-Qārih, 369–70
Ibn Qutayba, Abū Muḥammad 'Abdallāh ibn Muslim, 222–23, 366, 383, 405, 436
Ibn Qutayba, Salm, 405
Ibn Sa'īd, 33, 436
Ibn Sayāba, Ibrāhīm, 404
Ibn Ṭufayl, Abū Bakr Muḥammad, 354, 370–71, 436
Ibn al-Walīd al-Ṭurṭūshī, Muḥammad, 405
Ibn Wāsi', Muhammad, 407
Ibn Yaḥyā, Ja'far, 226
Ibn Ya'qūb, Ibrāhīm al-Isrā'īlī al-Ṭurṭūshī, 363, 436
Ibn Zā'ida, Ma'n, 405
Ibn Zubayr, 404
ideas, dissemination of, 25, 40, 46, 48–49, 54, 63, 77, 248–52, 345, 351–53, 366
al-Idrīsī, Abū 'Abdallāh Muḥammad ibn Muḥammad, 32, 436
al-'Ijlī, Muwarriq, 404
impaling, 231
imperialism, European, 16–18, 24–26, 48–49, 54–55, 64, 76–77, 82–84, 106–8, 123–24, 165–69, 181, 244–46, 291–94, 418

cultural effects of, 63–64, 68, 190–91
resistance to, 117, 170, 174, 244, 248–57, 251, 306, 315–22
Imru ul Qais ibn Hujr, 370
incest, 5, 27
India, x, xii, 5, 45, 48, 66, 71–72, 127, 141–43, 291, 328, 338, 351, 352
  colonial, 25, 53, 64, 68, 103, 326, 419
  missionaries in, 100–101
  Muslim travelers in, 84–85, 90–91, 141–43
  stereotypes of, 7–10, 17, 24
industry, 42, 49, 162–63, 326, 343–48, 423
intellect, stereotypes of, 7–10, 17–20, 30–31, 123–24, 244–46
intellectuals, 49, 247–48, 263–64
interpreters, 62, 80–81, 95–96, 116, 129–31, 145–47, 151–55, 160, 162, 174, 200, 297, 333, 412
Al-'Iqd al-Farīd (Ibn 'Abd Rabbihi), 363
Iran, xi, xii, 3, 6–9, 24, 26, 66–67, 222–23, 270, 276, 283, 328, 338, 352, 407–8
  diplomacy of, 127, 129–30, 132–34, 160–65, 173–74, 265–66, 300, 335
  food of, 71, 90, 376–77, 382
  Jews in, 108–10, 163
  literature of, 211–12, 224–25, 353–54, 371–72, *374,* 408–10, 431, 432
  oil in, 174, 265, 343–44
  revolution in, 120–21, 218, 248–52, 260–66, 418, 426
  stereotypes of, 6–9, 11–12, 117–18, 187
  Western influence in, 57, 237, 419–20
Iraq, 7–8, 164, 220–21, 282, 291, 306–8, 311, 319–20, 340, 381
Ireland, 31–35, 44, 291, 419
Irving, T. B., 185
Iṣfahān, 90
Islam, xiv–xv, 23–24, 66, 76, 90, 209–10, 239, 247, 367
  afterlife in, 72, 224–25, 269, 271–73, 277–78
  conversion to, 77–78, 87–89, 101, 137n, 181, 280
  fundamentalist, 57, 120–21, 181, 251, 262–66, 319–20, 426–27
  martyrs for, 228, 264, 269, 321
  militant sects of, 66, 270, 276–79, 319–20, 415, 426–27
  modern challenges to, 120–21, 181, 240, 260, 427–28
  political interpretations of, 15, 218–19, 222–23, 260–64, 269, 296–99
  stereotypes of, 3–4, 11–14, 48, 103, 105–6, 169–70, 179–80
  women and, 179–87, 209–10, 412
  as world religion, x, xiii, 17, 75–78, 352–53, 426–27
Islamic Revolution (Iran), 120–21, 218, 257, 260–66, 426

Israel, 119–20, 171–73, 247–48, 260, 266, 320, 418–26, 430
Israeli, Isaac, 355–57, 436
Israelites, 71–72, 115, 127, 217–18, 271, 279, 415
  see also Jews
Istanbul, iv, 37, 112–13, 127–28, 130, 135, 138–42, 206–8, 228, 231, 259, 309, 331–36, 359–60, 377–78, 390–95
  revolutionary politics in, 252–56
  Sultan's court in, 139–41, 155–57, 196, 289, 359–60
  western residents in, 53n, 79, 128, 155, 157, 160, 387–88, 390–93, 419
  women's quarters of, 196–201, 412
Italian language, 67, 70, 147
Italy, 67, 91, 127–28, 274, 309–14, 417–18, 434

al-Jabartī, 'Abd al-Raḥmān, 190–91, 292–94, 436
al-Jāḥiz, 'Amr ibn Bahr, 132, 282, 328, 404, 436
al-Jahshiyārī, Abū 'Abdallāh Muḥammad ibn 'Abdūs, 221–22, 436
Jamali, Fadhel, 171
James VI, King of Scotland (James I of England), 284–86
Japan, 248, 251, 420
Jarvis, Claude Scudamore, 18, 436
Jaurès, Jean, 52
jealousy, 179, 191, 366, 391
Jemāl Pasha, 302–3, 436
Jericho, 115
Jerusalem, 70, 74, 80, 115–16, 119–20, 159, 247, 254, 275n, 276, 310, 320
  civil order in, 94–95, 171–73, 298–99
  pilgrimages to, 23, 76, 99–100, 116
Jesuits, 100–101, 437
Jevdet, Abdullah, 244, 436
Jevdet Pasha, 239–40, 242–43, 436
jewels, 85, 141–42, 204, 278, 328, 338, 365
Jews, xiv–xv, 71–72, 75–76, 93, 96–98, 129–30, 163, 218, 240, 246, 257, 280, 399–402
  customs of, 375, 396, 409, 415
  nationalism of, see Zionism
  occupations of, 108–10, 330–31, 336, 338, 357, 359–60, 377
  prejudice against, 3, 5, 9, 13, 18–19
  sanctions against, 96, 108–10, 116, 299, 420
  see also Israel
Jezzar Pasha, 232
jihād, 64, 75–76, 220, 222, 269–73, 296–97, 319–20, 325–27
Johnson, Samuel, 20, 323, 339
Jones, Sir William, 145, 436
Jordan, 171–73, 175, 302, 381, 423–24
jurisprudence, 109–10, 229–37, 243, 247, 250–51, 262–63, 280–82, 301, 410, 432

justice, 217, 222–23, 228–29, 241, 405, 410
Juvenal (Decimus Junius Juvenalis), 3, 5, 436

Ka'abah, 111–12, 321
Kainardji, Treaty of (1774), 297
Kanık, Orhan Veli, 321–22, 428, 437
Kapudan Pasha, 391–93
Katel (feast of mourning), 110
Kemal, Namık, 192, 241, 437
Kemalist Revolution (Turkey), 257–60
Kennan, George F., 169–71, 437
khanate, Tatar, 134
Khāqānī (poet), 372
kharatch, see poll tax
Khayyám, Omar, 371
Khója Mimí Beg, Gházi, 289
Khomeini, Imam Ruhullah, 120, 260–64, 437
Kinglake, Alexander William, 83, 93–94, 106–8, 437
Kirkbride, Sir Alec, 171–73, 423–24, 437
Kirli Hasan Páshá, 287
Kissinger, Henry A., 175, 437
Kitab al-Bulhan (tract), 414
Knights of Jerusalem (military order), 274–75
Knolles, Richard, 144
Koçu Bey, Mustafa, 228–29, 437
koltuk ceremony, 192–93
koshub (dessert), 393
Kurdish peoples, xiii, 16, 427
Kurze Beschreibung der Gantzen Turckey, Die (Happelius), vi, 268
Kuwait, 345

Lane, Edward, 208–9, 437
language, ix–xiv, 17–18, 34, 61–72, 101–2, 192, 245–46, 429–33
  commercial, 63–64, 67–71
  diplomatic, 28–29, 127, 129–30, 134–45, 153–54, 157
  literary, xiii–xiv, 28, 55, 61, 69–70, 78, 118, 182, 210–11, 352–54
  local, 17, 108, 130, 147, 301, 304, 390, 419
  military, 64, 68–69, 269–70, 312, 423–24
  religious, 6, 61–62, 64, 72, 78, 102, 194, 353–54
  scientific, 63, 65, 77, 351–53, 359
Latin, 61–62, 64–65, 351, 354, 376, 406, 429
Latin America, 37, 246, 326, 352
Lawrence, Thomas Edward, 17, 301, 303–8, 422–23, 437
laws, 49, 181, 202, 217–18, 232–36, 247, 325, 333
  dietary, 5, 11, 23, 32, 35, 105, 273, 375–76, 392–93
  reform of, 239–41, 243, 259–60, 302

laws (*cont.*)
    religious understanding of, 202, 209–10,
        218, 228–28, 232, 262–63, 269–72,
        296–97, 338, 341, 361, 366
    of war, 70, 269, 273, 293, 296
    see also freedom; government
Layard, Sir Henry, 243, 344
lazaretti, 91, 93, 148–49
Lebanon, 80, 248, 261, 303, 316–19, 426
Leopold I, Holy Roman Emperor, 35–36,
    189, 290
Lepanto, Battle of (1571), 284–87
Lesseps, Ferdinand Marie, Vicomte de,
    82
Levant Company, British, 138, 146, 151,
    331–34, 336
Levantines, 18–19, 130–31, 151–53, 157,
    181
Levni (painter), *36*
Libya, 121–23, 310–14, 418, 426, 437
Liman von Sanders, Otto Viktor Karl, 51,
    301–2, 437
literacy, 49, 187, 194, 217, 239, 360–61
literature, xiii–xiv, 28, 55, 118, 345–48,
    394, 399–412
    of travel, xvi, 76, 78–79, 83, *97,* 106,
        111, 154, 210, 236–37, 353–54
    see also poetry
Lloyd George, David, 246, 422
Lokotsch, Karl, 68–69
London, 136–37, 161–62, 419–20
Lorimer, D. L. R., 343
Lothar I, Holy Roman Emperor, 136
Louis IX, King of France, 278–79
Louis XIV, King of France, 297
Louis Napoléon (Napoléon III), 294, 412
Lowther, Gerard, 253
Loyola, Saint Ignatius, 99–100, 437
Luther, Martin, 4, 13
Lyon, Richard, 159

al-Ma‘arrī, Abu'l-‘Alā', 354, 369–70, 437
McCullagh, Francis, 252–55
MacDonald, Ramsay, 52–53, 420
Machiavelli, Niccolò, 228, 267, 274–75,
    437
MacKereth, Gilbert, 165–68, 437
MacWhirter, Reverend, 236–37
Madden, Richard Robert, 155–56, 202–8,
    437
Mahkemeh (tribunal), 209
Mahmud II, Sultan, 240–41
maisir (game), 367–68
Malta, 80–81, 335
Mamluks, 291–92
al-Ma'mūn, King, 226–27
Manchester, 162–63
Manes, Diego, 100
manners, 44–45, 50–55, 81–84, 97–98,
    102–4, 198–200, 204, 333, 345–46,
    365, 390

in diplomatic relations, 52–53, 69–70,
    138–45, 148–51, 155–58, 164, 200,
    304–5, 390–93
political freedom and, 52–53, 191–92
table, 376, 378–81, 383–84, 386, 391–93
Manoglu, 142–43
al-Mansūr, Caliph, 223
Maqāmāt (al-Harīrī), 324
al-Maqrīzī, Taqī al-Dīn Ahmad ibn ‘Alī,
    329, 437
Mardam, Jamil, 171–72
marriage, 7, 29, 141, 179–80, 192–93,
    200–202, 204–6, 208–10, 226, 406
    interfaith, 190, 201
    precepts for, 183–86, 189, 409
    see also polygamy
Martin, Father, 101
martyrdom, 264, 269, 321
Marx, Karl, 294–99, 437
al-Mas‘ūdī, Abu'l-Hasan ‘Alī ibn
    al-Husayn, 30, 437
mathematics, 63, 72, 351
Maugham, Viscount, 339–41
Maximilian of Bavaria, Elector, 289
Mecca, 23, 70, 76, 87, 105–6, 111–12, 218,
    254, 319, 426, 433
media, xiv, 19–20, 173, 247–48, 249, 264,
    294–95, 307
medicine, 70, 81, 84, 91–92, 110, 202–3,
    206–7, 222, 352–53, 355–59, 363, 379,
    435
Medina, 23, 70, 105–6, 111, 218, 319, 433
Mediterranean, xii, 76, 284–86, 331
Medjid, Sultan Abdul, 157–58
Mehmed IV, Sultan, 141–43, *268*
Mehmed Efendi, 37, 364, 384, 438
Meinertzhagen, Richard, 422, 438
Melos, Gulf of, 335–36
Melville, Herman, xvi, 112, 160, 438
Mendoza, Bernardino de, 334–35, 438
Mersa Matruh, Egypt, 311–13
Meshullam da Volterra, Rabbi, 96–98, 438
Mesopotamia, xii, 217, 306, 344, 422
Middle East:
    climate of, 81, 169–70, 205, 359, 367
    geography of, xii–xiv, 48, 105, 170
    holy sites in, *74,* 75, 115, 297–99
    nationalism in, 165–68, 171–74, 248–60,
        305–10, 417–23, 426
    power and authority in, 106–7, 123–24,
        217–18, 219–20, 225, 238–39, 247–48,
        254, 392–94
    religious minorities in, 23–24, 48, 75,
        96–98, 108–10, 116, 130, 163, 180–81,
        235, 239–40, 272, 280–82, 295–99,
        304–5, 357, 387–88, 417
    revolutionary movements in, 26, 57,
        120–21, 218, 241, 248–66, 300–310,
        417–20
    scientific innovations of, 48, 63, 72,
        351–57

tourism in, 76, 80–84, 93–94, 106–8, 110–19, 123–24
as trading center, x, 23–24, 105, 325–26, 335–36, 338, 343
Western enclaves in, 32–33, 127–28, 130, 155, 160, 296–99
Westernization of, 55–57, 170, 180, 190–91, 218, 233, 237–40, 263–65, 353
Mihri Hatun, 213, 438
al-Miknāsī, Muḥammad ibn 'Uthmān, 38, 438
Miller, Judith, 121–23, 438
missionaries, 48–49, 100–101, 158–59
Mohacs, Battle of (1526), 288
Mohammed Páshá, 288
Mohieddin, Zakaria, 315
monarchy, 49, 197–98, 217–29, 240–41, 254–55, 282, 405–6, 433
see also government
monasteries, 297–99
money, 47, 81, 146, 220, 225–26, 235, 324–25, 331, 336, 347, 389, 404, 407–8
Mongols, 377
Montagu, Lady Mary Wortley, 79, 179, 200–201, 203, 205, 364, 366–67, 389–90, 438
Montesquieu, Charles Louis de, 55
Moors, x, 269–70, 299
Morocco, xi, 15, 24, 422
Mosadeq, Muhammad, 173–74
Moscati, Sabatino, 399
Moses, 217, 279, 285
mosques, 74, 92–93, 98, 220–21, 317, 394, 426
Mosul District, Iraq, 307–8, 435
Mu'āwiya, Caliph, 220, 223
al-Mubarrad, Abu'l-'Abbās Muḥammad ibn Yazīd, 402, 438
Mubashshir ibn Fātik, 398, 406–7
muezzins, 64, 98–99, 113, 394, 409
Muhammad, Prophet, xiv–xv, 65, 101, 120, 180, 209, 218, 270, 280, 292, 319, 321, 408, 415
sayings attributed to, xv, 4, 6–7, 219–20, 222, 269, 272–73, 327–28, 379, 402, 436, 439
Muḥammad Shāh, 160–61
Mujīr (poet), 372
al-Muktafi billah, Caliph, 136
al-Mulk, Niẓām, 132–34, 282–83
Munif, Abdelrahman, 345–48, 438
Muqaddam Ajudanbashi, Ḥusayn Khan, 160–61
al-Muqaddasī, Shams al-Dīn, 8, 438
al-Muqtadir, Caliph, 87
Murad III, Sultan, 136–38, 394
Murad IV, Sultan, 395
murder, 96, 208, 230, 234–35, 277–79, 391, 396
Mūsā, Suleymān, 308

music, 5, 53, 62, 71, 118, 138–40, 163, 191, 198, 203–5, 253, 353, 363–65, 388, 389, 390, 393
Mussolini, Benito, 311–15
Mustafa Páshá, Zádeh, 287, 289
musta'min (safe-conduct bearer), 281–82
mysticism, 62, 100, 180, 186

Nadīm, 'Abdallāh, 48–49, 438
el-Nahas, Mustafa, 315–16
Na'ima (historian), 141–43, 287–89, 438
Naipaul, V. S., 120–21
al-Najīb (secretary), 329
names, 429–31
Naples, 135–36, 201, 232
Napoléon I, Emperor of France, 42, 102, 105, 190, 291–92, 438
Napoléon III, Emperor of France, 294, 412
Napoleonic wars, 42, 190–91, 237, 291–94, 331
Nāsir al-Dīn Shah, 161, 300
Nasser, Gamel Abdel, 175, 425–26, 443
nationalism, 165–68, 171–74, 248–60, 305–10, 417–23, 426
navies, 76, 201, 272, 284–86, 296, 312, 330, 391
Navigations, Peregrinations, and Voyages Made into Turkey, The (Nicolay), 178, 359–60
Nelson, Horatio Lord, 291
Netherlands, 63, 128, 270, 337
newspapers, 45–47, 51–52, 173, 192, 238–39, 249, 294–95, 319, 393, 419
New Testament, xv, 15, 40, 61–62, 93, 271, 353, 375
Newton, Sir Isaac, 65
Nicolay, Nicolas, 178, 359–60, 438
Nicolson, Sir Harold, 163–65, 438
Nightingale, Florence, 16, 209, 239, 438
Nile, xii, 87, 95, 111, 190–91
Nīsābūrī, Shāh Mahmūd, 60
nisba (descriptor), 431
Nixon, Richard, 175
Niẓāmī-i'Arūdī, 366, 438
Noeldeke, Theodore, 368, 438
Nokrashi Pasha, 171–72
nomadism, 27, 67, 367–68
North Africa, x, 8, 15, 63, 75, 181, 251, 275–76, 309–19, 326, 381
Northern peoples, stereotypes of, 30–31
numbers, 34, 72, 351–52
Nutting, Sir Anthony, 424, 438
al-Nuwayrī, Shihāb al-Dīn Aḥmad ibn 'Abd al-Wahhāb, 188, 405, 439

oaths, 206, 333
obedience, 180, 183–85, 188, 190–91, 202, 217–23, 231–32, 236, 244, 247–48, 261–65
Ockley, Simon, 354

Odysseus (Charles Eliot), 209–10, 439
oil, 56, 122, 174, 265, 306, 340, 342–48, 424
Okeley, W., 102, 439
Old Man of the Mountain, 276–79
    see also Assassins
Old Persian language, xiv, 71
Old Testament, xiv–xv, 61–62, 72, 110,
    127, 217–18, 271, 279, 325, 343–44,
    353, 375, 399–400
Oman, 340
Orientalism, 77, 123–24, 145, 340–41
Osborn, Francis, 197–98, 361
Ottoman Empire, xii, 18, 69–71, 76, 93–94,
    127–31, 228–35, 248–49, 252–60, 292,
    300–309, 411–12
    Christian subjects of, 75, 96–98, 116,
        130, 235, 239–40, 295–99, 301, 388,
        417
    commercial contacts with, x, 42, 68,
        128, 136–37, 146, 296–97, 329–44,
        387–88, 394–95
    corruption in, 232–34, 237–39, 297–98,
        300–302, 309, 394
    diplomatic missions to, x, 51, 129,
        136–41, 144–47, 153–56, 196–97, 200,
        390–93, 412, 420–21
    embassies of, 24–25, 129, 417
    envoys from, 24, 127, 141–43, 148–51
    Jews in, 96–98, 108–10, 116, 130, 163,
        235, 239–40, 336, 388
    military forces of, 16, 63–64, 75–76, 201,
        233, 258–59, 284–94, 300–303, 309,
        336, 391, 418–20
    reform in, 157–58, 181, 192, 218,
        228–29, 233, 237–44, 290–91, 303,
        411–12
    republicanism denounced by, 39–42,
        238, 244
    women in, 106–7, 178, 181–82, 192,
        196–210, 390

Paget, Sir Bernard, 317–19
Pahlavi, Reza Shah, 66, 163–65, 174n, 261,
    263–65
Palestine, x, 23, 75, 115–16, 159, 171–73,
    261, 269, 301, 303, 437
    Arab-Jewish conflict in, 18, 246, 311,
        420–25
Palestine Liberation Organization (PLO),
    266
Palgrave, William Gifford, 395–95, 439
pan-Arabism, 171–73, 175, 248, 425
pan-Islamism, 251, 258, 260
pan-Turkism, 258, 309
papacy, 29–30, 134, 274, 284, 326
papal bulls, 329–30, 335
paper, 84, 352
paradise, 71–72, 224–25, 272–73, 327
Paris, 26, 37–38, 41–42, 45–48, 191–92,
    243, 364, 383–84, 412
Parliament, British, 294, 317–18, 339–41

parody, 142–43, 399–400
Patriarch of Constantinople, 296
Patton, George S., Jr., 19–20, 439
Peçevi, Ibrahim, 393–95, 439
Pera, 79, 155, 160
    see also Istanbul
perfume, 29, 327, 337, 390
Persia, see Iran
Persian language, xiii–xiv, 6–7, 61–72,
    101, 147, 182, 211–12, 250, 431
Pertev Pasha, 287
Pescia, Antonio da, 95
Peter the Hermit, 274
petitions, 129, 151–52, 227, 236, 253,
    293
philosophy, 34, 43, 54, 63, 77, 84, 102–3,
    224, 353, 359, 362
Pickthall, Marmaduke, 116–17, 439
pilgrimage, 13, 23, 70, 75–76, 229, 409
    first-hand accounts of, 76, 87–88, 94–96,
        99–100, 111–12, 433, 441
Piperi, Januli, 335–36
piracy, 15, 76, 97–98, 101–2, 135, 296,
    326
Pisa, 275, 328–29
Pius V, Pope, 67
plague, 91–93, 206–7
Plagued by the West (Āl-e-Aḥmad), 56–57,
    432
Plato, 146
Plutarch, 344, 439
poetry, 10–12, 28, 69–70, 118, 180,
    211–13, 320–21, 353, 366–68, 371–72,
    382, 385, 394–95, 428
    political, 123–24, 224–25, 249, 255–57
police, 162, 232–35, 239, 244, 262, 292,
    301, 303
poll tax, 272, 280, 296
polygamy, x, 12, 90, 141, 179, 197–98,
    202, 204–6, 208–9, 409
Porte, 130, 149–50, 153–56, 235, 295–98,
    390
    see also Ottoman Empire
Porter, Sir James, 128, 146–48, 439
postal systems, xi, 46–47
poverty, 23, 116, 150–51, 174, 226–27,
    237
prayer, 82–83, 85–87, 92, 113, 222, 225,
    272, 317, 328, 387, 407–8
preaching, 186, 394, 404
Precious Necklace, The (Ibn ʻAbd
    Rabbihi), 363
prediction, xv, 159, 260, 415–16
    see also prophets and prophecy
prejudice, ix–x, xiv–xv, 3–20, 78, 83–84
    anti-European, 24, 30–31, 51, 101, 106,
        108, 275
    anti-Jewish, 3, 5, 9, 13, 96–98, 108–10,
        240
    western, 3–4, 10–20, 68–69, 103,
        123–24, 239, 245–46, 300, 337

pride, 83, 139, 189, 227, 259, 381
  in diplomacy, 27–28, 129, 139, 143–47,
    149–51, 154–57, 175
  stereotypes of, 12, 43, 103, 108
prophets and prophecy, xv, 154, 159,
    217–18, 260, 356, 413–29, *414*
prostitution, 5, 38, 190, 210
proverbs and sayings, 4, 6–7, 83, 103, 127,
    219–20, 222, 269, 272–73, 302, 325,
    327–28, 400–410
Prussia, 36–37, 299
publishing, 44–46, *398,* 406
  see also media; newspapers
punishment, xi, 43, 109, 123–24, 145–46,
    151–52, 230–37, 253, 262–63, 280–82,
    292–94, 382–83
  capital, 76, 93, 205, 230–32, 235–37,
    240–41, 270, 280–81, 293, 305
  in political theory, 220–21, 223, 229
  of women, 183–86, 197, 205, 281, 409

Qaddafi, Muammar, 121–23, 426
qadis (judges), 64, 204–5, 229, 233–34,
    247, 292, 387–88, 408–10
Qala'un, Sultan, 329
al-Qalqashandī, Abu'l-'Abbās Aḥmad,
    134–36, 283–84, 439
al-Qalyūbī, Aḥmad ibn Aḥmad, 189, 383,
    439
al-Qāsim, Sāmiḥ, 320–21, 439
al-Qazwīnī, Zakariyyā ibn Muḥammad,
    33–34, 439
quarantine, 80, 91–94
Al Quds al-Arabi (newspaper), 319–20
Qur'ān, xv, 8, 12, 23, 28, 34, 40, 87, 92,
    183–86, 194, 279, 292, 295–96, 353,
    371, 431
  political teachings of, 15, 218–19, 232,
    269, 271–72

rabbinic writings, 129–30, 218–19, 375,
    399–402, 413
race, pseudoscience of, 65–66, 438
Rafsanjani, Faezeh, 266
Rafsanjani, Hashimi, 265–66
railroads, 161, 342–43
Ramadan, 231
rape, 201, 341
Rashīd al-Dīn Faḍlallah, 34–35, 439
rayahs (protected Christians), 241,
    296–97
Reagan, Ronald, 120, 122–23
Rejeb he, Ambassador, 141–42
religion, 5–7, 18, 23–24, 27, 48, 54, 84,
    116, 222, 254, 361, 366, 408
  devotion to, 30, 39–40, 43, 62, 102,
    105–6, 112, 170, 190, 265, 274
  governments challenged by, 217–18,
    228–29, 251–52
  language of, 61–62, 64, 72, 102,
    399–400

territorial claims of, 75–76, 269–72,
    274–75, 298–99
Rendel, Sir George William, 167–68, 439
republicanism, 38–42, 49, 52, 238, 241, 244
Rescript of 1856, Imperial (Ottoman),
    239–40
Resmi, Ahmed, 37, 439
Revolutionary Guards (Iran), 261–62
Reynolds, G. B., 343–44
Reza Shah, *see* Pahlavi, Reza Shah
Rhodes, 99, 135, 275
Riad es Solh, 171
rice, 376–77, 382, 392–93
robbery, 95–98, 109, 221, 234, 237
Robinson Crusoe (Defoe), 354
Roger II, King of Sicily, 275–76
Romans, ancient, xi, xiii, 3, 61, 72, 75,
    127–29, 218, 315, 408
Rome, 5–6, 25, 34, 232, 273, 292
Rommel, Erwin, 310, 312–16
Rothschild family, 163
Rousseau, Jean-Jacques, ix, 39, 55
Rūdagī, Abū 'Abdallāh Ja'far, 211–12,
    224–25, 439
rumor, 19–20, 247
Russia, x, 63, 77, 170, 238, 248–51,
    265–66, 269, 294–300, 335, 337–38,
    342, 412, 417
Russian language, 65, 67, 72, 431–32
Russian Orthodox church, 18, 76, 298
Russo-Japanese War (1904–5), 248
Rycaut, Sir Paul, 14, 128, 144–45, 198–200,
    199, 216, 290, 336, 439

sabbath, 3, 5, 62, 352, 375
Sackville-West, Vita, 163
Sadat, Anwar el-, 314–16, 425–26, 439
Sadullah Pasha, 243, 439
safe-conduct, 95, 136, 280–82
Said Agha, 194
Ṣā'id ibn Aḥmad al-Andalusī, 31, 439
Said Pasha, 243, 439
Saint-Priest, Comte de, 337
Saladin, x, 33, 275, 328–29, 430
Salahaddin Bey, 51
Sale, George, 183
Ṣāliḥ, Prophet, 415
Salisbury, Robert Arthur, Marquess of,
    243, 439
Sallustius Neoplatonicus, 5
Sanā'ī (poet), 371
Sanderson, John, 230–31, 439
Sanhedrin, 129, 401
Saracens, xi, 5–6, 11, 195–96, 230, 274,
    282, 329–30, 386–87
Sarwar, Al-Haj Hafiz Ghulam, 183–84
Satan, 40, 62, 204, 320, 378
satire, 143, *242,* 305, 399, 408–10
Saud, King of Saudi Arabia, 424
Saudi Arabia, 319–20, 340–41, 345–46,
    380, 424, 427

Saxe, Count Maurice de, 290–91, 439
sayings, *see* proverbs and sayings
Scappi, Bartolomeo, 67
Schacht, Hjalmar, 66
scholars and scholarship, xv, 34, 43–44, 63, 77, 308, 352–55, 362, 366–67
Schumacher, E. F., 121
science, 31, 34, 44, 46, 49, 77, 84, 238, 351–62
    experimentation in, 352–53, 359
    language of, 63, 65, 355
    medical, 84, 91–92, 110, 352, 355–60, 363, 379
Scotland, 31, 44–45, 393, 419
Scrope, Stephen, 406–7
Selim III, Sultan, 129
Semitic peoples, 17–18, 301, 351
Semlin, Hungary, 93–94
Seneca, Lucius Annaeus, 3, 440
Sennaar, women of, 207
sensuality, 6–8, 41, 179, 188–89, 192, 203–6, 283–84
    fear of, 51, 190–91, 394–95
    stereotypes of, 11–12, 14–15, 57, 72, 117–18
seraglio, 72, 139–41, 196–200, 231, 359–61
Sercambi, Giovanni, 354
Serkhúsh Ibrahim Páshá, 289
servants, 10, 45, 80–82, 94, 105–6, 123, 156–57, 356, 384, 405–6, 411
sexual practices, 84, 185, 191, 198–200, 204–6, 341, 383, 409–10
Shaarawi, Huda, 47, 194, 440
al-Sha'bī, 405
Shah-Jahan I, Emperor, 141
Shāhnāma (Firdawsī), *350*
Shakespeare, William, 4, 10–11, 67, 373
Shaw, George Bernard, 13, 177
al-Shaybānī, Muḥammad ibn al-Ḥasan, 281–82, 440
Shaykh al-Jabal (Old Man of the Mountain), 276–79
    see also Assassins
el-Shazly, Saad, 247–48, 426–27, 440
Shemaya, Rabbi, 219
Shems (merchant), 394
Shi'ism, 265
Shimon ben Elázar, Rabbi, 401
ships, 31–32, 38, 99–100, 104–5, 325, 334–36, 339, 342–43, 344
    see also navies
Shirley, Edward (pseudonym), 283–84, 440
Shu'ayb, Prophet, 415
al-Shujā'ī, Vizier, 329
Sicily, xi, 63, 269, 275–76, 334, 352
sickness, 81, 91–94, 99, 293, 356–60
el Sidari, Abdul Azziz, 341
Sigoli, Simone, 195–96, 386–87, 440
Sikhs, 291
Sinán Páshá, 287–89

al-Ṣīn wa'l Hind, Akhbār, 84–85
Siyavush Pasha, Grand Vizier, 136–38, 287
skin color, ix, 7–8, 10, 30–31, 90, 187–89, 207, 369
Slade, Sir Adolphus, 157–58, 238–41, 391–93, 417, 440
slavery, 10, 76, 110, 180–81, 236, 280–81, *324*, 325–26, 395, 405
    suppression of, 107, 129, 181, 210, 338–41, 385
    victims' accounts of, 85–88, 101–2
    women in, 91, 104–7, 142, 187–88, 191, 197–98, 200, 202, 204–8, 210, 418–19
Slavs, xi, 8, 30, 432
smoking, 114, 204, 206, 377–78, 393–96
Smyrna, 112–13, 422
Socrates, 146, *398*
soldiers, 16, 24–25, 41–42, 225, 250, 339
    in revolutionary upheavals, 250, 252–53
Solomon, King of Israel, 325
Sophianos, Theodore, 32–33
Soviet Union, 122, 181, 247, 260–61, 265, 423–24
Spain, 25, 37–38, 91, 128, 148–51, 179, 284–86, 326, 332, 334–35, 337, 365
    Islamic, x–xi, 63, 76, 269, 275, 352
Spanish language, 65, 70, 406, 431–32
spices, 326, 332, 390
spies, 42, 76, 95, 132–34, 157, 197, 232, 270, 279–84, 315–16
sports and games, 68, 133, 196, 289, 368, 394
Staël, Madame de, 180
Stalin, Joseph, 314
Stark, Freya, 345, 440
Storrs, Sir Ronald, 246, 440
students, Middle Eastern, 24–26
Sudan, 315, 320
Suez, 106–7, 123, 171–72, 344
Suez Canal, 82, 310
suicide, 269, 273, 277–78, 426
Süleyman the Magnificent, Sultan, *126*, 297, 433
el Sulk, Riza Bey, 303
Sunnī Muslims, 90
surme (makeup), 203–4
al-Suyūṭī, Jalāl al-Dīn, 405, 440
Syria, x, 3, 8, 16, 80, 102–4, 114–15, 159, 171–73, 201–2, 232–33, 291, 301–3, 311, 381
    commerce in, 32–33, 103, 232, 301, 336
    Crusaders in, 25, 32–33, 66, 270, 274–77, 308, 357
    independence sought by, 165–68, 302, 316–19

Tabaristan, 187
al-Ṭahṭāwī, Rifā'a Rāfi', 26, 45–47, 384–85, 440
Talaat Efendi, 365, 420–21
Taliban movement, 26, 57

Talleyrand-Périgord, Charles-Maurice de, 42
Talmud, 399–400, 413
Tamīm, King of Tunisia, 276
targum (translation), 130
Tatars, x–xi, 134, 198, 269–70, 335
Tathqif (manual), 134
al-Tawḥīdī, Abū Ḥayyān, 9, 403, 405, 440
taxation, 38, 85, 128, 220, 226–27, 237–39, 376
   of religious minorities, 96, 109–10, 272, 280, 387–88
tea, 377, 385
technology, 120–21, 259, 337, 343–48, 352, 361–62, 423
Tehran, 120–21, 163–65, 249–52, 266, 419–20
terrorism, 119–20, 122, 266, 276–79, 319–20, 426–27
textiles, 33, 35, 63, 195, 325–27, 330, 332, 338
Thabit (physician), 357
Thackeray, William Makepeace, xvi, 12, 158–59, 237–38, 437, 440
al-Thawrī, Sufyān, 404
Thomas, Lowell, 308
Thousand and One Nights, The, 114, 354, 433
timekeeping, 98–99, 118–19, 351–52
Times (London), 419
tin, 33, 329, 334–35
Tippoo Sahib, 291
tobacco, 377, 393–96, *396*
Tobruk, Battle of (1942), 310, 312
Tocqueville, Alexis de, 15, 440
Tomson, James, 331–32
Torah, 40, 93
Tott, Baron François de, 233–35, 390–91, 440
Tott, Madame de, 390–91
Toynbee, Arnold J., 307–8, 440
trade, *see* commerce and trade
translation, 17–18, 25–26, 55, 63, 136, 147, 167, 224, 297, 307, 352–54, 367, 371, *398,* 400
   scriptural, 72, 129, 183–85
   see also interpreters
transportation, 19–20, 46–47, 66–67, 89, 161, 303, 338, 340–43
travel, ix, xi, xvi, 23–26, 73–124
   dangers of, 32–33, 91–98, 100–102
   literature of, xvi, 76, 78–79, 83, *97,* 106, 111, 154, 179–80, 210, 236–37
   provisions for, 80–81, 96, 104–5
   religious, 13, 23–24, 75–76, 87–88, 94–96, 99–101
   restrictions on, 75, 91–95, 206, 239, 280–81
   by women, 79, 179–80, 190, 200–201, 203, 205, 210, 412

treaties, 128, 137–38, 146–47, 165–66, *242,* 288, 295–97, 316
Tripartite Conference (1945), 316
Tripoli, 310
Truman, Harry S., 173–74
Tülümen, Turgut, 265–66, 440
Tunisia, 276, 310
turbans, 10, 64, 81, 96, 252, 285, 360, 395
Turkey, modern, 194–95, 252–60, 265–66, 309, 422–23, 430, 432
   see also Ottoman Empire
Turkish baths, 81, 116, 203–5
Turkish language, xiii, 26, 61–72, 101, 147, 182, 212–13, 353–54, 429–31
Turkish peoples, x–xi, 103, 269–70, 299
   courage of, 8–10, 14, 16, 40, 97, 235, 309
   stereotypes of, 7–11, 13–14, 18–19, 70, 187, 238–41, 302
al-Ṭurṭūshī, Abū Bakr, 226–27, 441
al-Tūsī, Abu'l-Abbās, 223
Ṭūsī, Naṣir al-Dīn, 9, 437, 441
Twain, Mark, xvi, 12, 112–15, 441
Tyler, John, 420
Tyre, 277–78, 303

'Ubayd-i Zākānī, 355, 372, 383, 408–10, 441
al-'Ula'ī, Shu'ayb, 407
ulema (council), 141, 228, 249–50, 292, 295, 320, 387, 394–95
al-'Umarī, Ṣubḥī, 308
United Arab Republic, 424–26
   see also Egypt
United States, 119, 122–23, 158–59, 170–71, 173–75, 247, 260, 265, 316, 319–20, 417, 420, 424–25
   oil politics of, 174, 340, 342–43
universities and colleges, 259, 263–64, 352, 355, 360–61
Urban II, Pope, 274–75
Usāma ibn Munqidh, 32–33, 357, 441

Vasif Efendi, 148–51, 365, 439, 441
veiling, 180, 190, 192–93, 203, 205
Venice, 91, 128, 135–36, 275, 284, 328–31, 334–36
Versailles Peace Conference (1919), 246, 307–8, 421–22
Vichy France, 311, 433
Victoria, Queen of England, 113
Vienna, 25, 63, 76, 189, 200, 287, 290, 336, 361–62, 365
Vikings, 25, 27–29
Vogüé, Eugène-Melchior, Vicomte de, 116, 441
Volney (Constantin François Chasseboeuf), 102–4, 201–2, 232–33, 441
Voltaire, ix, 4, 39, 55, 336–38

Waddāḥ ibn Ismā'īl (Waddāḥ al-Yaman), 211, 441

war, x–xii, 16, 63, 276–323, 339–40, 353,
    367, 418–19
  avoidance of, 70, 127, 300, 316–19,
    421–22, 425–26
  commerce stimulated by, x, 63, 75,
    325–26, 328–30
  deception in, 68–69, 134, 272, 402
  espionage in, 157, 270, 281–82,
    315–16
  holy, x, 23, 64, 75–76, 220, 222, 229,
    269–73, 296–97, 319–20, 325–30
  of independence, 130, 171–73, 300–309,
    315–16, 420–24
  language of, 64, 68–69, 269–70, 284,
    292, 312, 423–24
  laws of, 70, 269, 273, 293, 296
  of national unification, 48, 217, 309, 417
  naval, 76, 272, 280–81, 284–87, 296,
    312, 330, 342
  spoils of, 272–73, 287, 290, 313–14
  of territorial expansion, 75–76, 217,
    269–70, 273, 284–90
  see also jihād
Warburton, Eliot, 80–82, 108, 441
War of Independence, Greek, 130
War of Independence, Israeli, 171–73,
    423–24
War of Independence, Turkish, 309
Washington, George, 4, 14
al-Wāsitī (painter), 324
water, 217, 313, 379, 383
al-Waṭwāṭ, Muḥammad ibn Ibrāhīm
    al-Kutubī, 404, 407–8, 441
Wavell, Archibald Lord, 310
wealth, 49, 149, 265, 306, 327–28, 331,
    366–67, 405
weapons, 95–97, 158, 171–72, 217, 225,
    253, 280–81, 290, 353, 371, 419, 427
  traffic in, x, 33, 134, 150, 325–26,
    329–30, 335–36
weddings, 192–93, 195–96, 205
Weizmann, Chaim, 421–22
Wesley, John, 4, 13
West, concept of, xi–xii, 23–26, 54–57, 265
Westernization, 55–57, 170, 180, 190–91,
    218, 233, 237–40, 263, 353
West-Östliche Diwan (Goethe), 70
Wiet, Gaston, 367, 441
William, Archbishop of Tyre, 277–78, 441
Willibald, Saint, 282, 441
Wilson, Arnold, 343–44, 441

wine, 33, 45, 81, 106, 235, 367, 371, 376,
    382–83, 387–89, 392–93, 409
witnesses, 109, 219, 233–34, 281, 396, 410
women, 7, 28–29, 84, 135–36, 177–213,
    227, 391, 396, 410, 412
  beauty of, 7, 28, 45, 107, 187–89, 191,
    203–5, 272–73, 364
  education of, 179, 187, 192, 194,
    198–99
  enslavement of, 91, 104–7, 142, 187–88,
    191, 197–98, 200, 202, 204–8, 210,
    418–19
  faith of, 7, 186, 369
  marriageability of, 7, 160, 189, 197, 201
  modesty of, 50–51, 189–91, 202, 405
  occupations of, 32, 37–38, 57, 106, 163,
    192, 209, 283–84, 331
  punishment of, 183–86, 197, 205, 281,
    409
  rights of, xi, 29, 170, 179–82, 194–95,
    201–2, 205–6, 208–09
Wood, Richard, 159
wool, 33, 35, 325, 332, 419
World War I, 51–52, 300–309, 321, 365,
    418–19
World War II, 309–19, 438

Xenophon, 71

Yalta Conference (1945), 316
al-Yaman, Waddāḥ, 211, 441
al-Yamanī, Shaykh Aḥmad ibn
    Muḥammad, 220–21, 441
Yemen, 225, 324, 341, 377
Yohanan, Rabbi, 413
Yose ben Judah, Rabbi, 401
Young Turk movement, 244, 248–49, 252,
    255–57, 418, 436
Yussuf Bey, 242
Yūsuf (poet), 225

Zafrulla Khan, Muhammad, 185
Zama, Plains of, 292
Zanj (African people), 8, 85–88, 188
Zapolya, Stephen, 126
Zerín Oghlí, 288–89
zero, 72
Zionism, 260, 420–23, 426
Ziyād (Ibn Abīh), 220–21
Zoroastrianism, 342
Zulfikar Aga, 142–43

PERMISSION
ACKNOWLEDGMENTS

Grateful acknowledgment is made to the following for permission to reprint previously unpublished material:

HAMID ALGAR: Excerpts from *Islam and Revolution* by Imam Khomeini, translated by Hamid Algar. Reprinted by permission of the translator.

AMERICAN MIDEAST RESEARCH: Excerpt (approximately 413 words) from *The Arab Military Option* by General Saad El-Shazly. Copyright © 1986 by American Mideast Research. Reprinted with permission.

THE ATHLONE PRESS, LONDON: Excerpt from a letter dated November 9, 1785, from *The Correspondence of Jeremy Bentham,* edited by Timothy L. S. Sprigge and Ian R. Christie. Reprinted by permission of The Athlone Press, London.

GEORGES BORCHARDT, INC. AND THE ORION PUBLISHING GROUP: Excerpt from *The Complete War Memoirs of Charles de Gaulle: Volume I: The Call to Honor* by Charles de Gaulle (New York: DaCapo, 1955). Copyright © 1955 by Simon and Schuster, Inc. Originally published in France as *L'Appel.* Copyright © 1954 by Librairie Plon. Reprinted by permission of Georges Borchardt, Inc., and The Orion Publishing Group, Ltd.

COLUMBIA UNIVERSITY CENTER FOR IRANIAN STUDIES: Excerpts from *Plagued by the West (Gharbzadegi)* by Jalāl Al-e Aḥmad, translated by Paul Sprachman. Reprinted by permission of Columbia University Center for Iranian Studies.

COLUMBIA UNIVERSITY PRESS VIA COPYRIGHT CLEARANCE CENTER: Excerpt from *A History of Deeds Done Beyond the Sea* by William of Tyre, translated by Emily Atwater Babcock and A. C. Krey. Copyright © 1943 by Columbia University Press. Reprinted by permission of Columbia University Press via Copyright Clearance Center.

DEBRETT'S PEERAGE, LTD.: Excerpt from *Debrett's Manners and Correct Form in the Middle East* by Sir Donald Hawley, KCMG, MBE. Reprinted by permission of Debrett's Peerage, Ltd.

DOUBLEDAY, A DIVISION OF RANDOM HOUSE, INC., AND THE SEVEN PILLARS OF WISDOM TRUST: Excerpts from *The Seven Pillars of Wisdom* by T. E. Lawrence. Copyright © 1935 by T. E. Lawrence. Reprinted by permission of Doubleday, a division of Random House, Inc., and The Seven Pillars of Wisdom Trust.

EDITIONS MAISONNEUVE ET LAROSE: Excerpt from *Introduction à la litterature arabe* by Gaston Wiet. Translated by Bernard Lewis by permission of Editions Maisonneuve et Larose.

EDITIONS MERCURE DE FRANCE, PARIS: Excerpts from *Consultation aux Pays d'Islam* by George Duhamel. Translated by Bernard Lewis by permission of Editions Mercure de France, Paris.

THE ESTATE OF SIR ANTHONY NUTTING: Excerpt from "A-Mid-East Settlement Is Imperative" by Sir Anthony Nutting (*The New York Herald Tribune,* July 31, 1958). Reprinted by permission of The Estate of Sir Anthony Nutting.

FARRAR, STRAUS & GIROUX, LLC.: Excerpt from *Know Thine Enemy: A Spy's Journey into Revolutionary Iran* by Edward Shirley. Copyright © 1997 by Edward Shirley. Reprinted by permission of Farrar, Straus & Giroux, LLC.

THE FEMINIST PRESS AND VIRAGO PRESS, LTD.: Excerpts from *Harem Years: The Memoirs of an Egyptian Feminist* by Huda Shaarawi, translated by Margot Badran. Copyright © 1987 by Margot Badran. Reprinted by permission of The Feminist Press and Virago Press, Ltd.

HARCOURT, INC., AND THE SOCIETY OF AUTHORS AS THE LITERARY REPRESENTATIVES OF THE E. M. FORSTER ESTATE: "Salute to the Orient" from *Abinger Harvest* by E. M. Forster. Copyright © 1936 and renewed 1964 by E. M. Forster. Reprinted by permission of Harcourt, Inc., The Provost and Scholars of King's College, Cambridge, and The Society of Authors as the literary representatives of the E. M. Forster Estate.

HARPERCOLLINS PUBLISHERS, INC.: Excerpt from *In Search of Identity: An Autobiography* by Anwar el-Sadat. English translation copyright © 1978 by Harper & Row, Publishers, Inc. Reprinted by permission of HarperCollins Publishers, Inc.

HER MAJESTY'S STATIONERY OFFICE: Excerpt from *The Parliamentary Debates, Fifth Series, Volume CCXXV, House of Lords Official Report,* 7th Volume of Session 1959–1960, July 11, 1960–October 27, 1960 (London: Her Majesty's Stationery Office). Reproduced under the terms of Crown Copyright Policy Guidance issued by HMSO.

DAVID HIGHAM ASSOCIATES, LTD.: Excerpts (3 pages) from *The Travels of Ibn Battūta,* Volumes I, II and III by Ibn Battūta, translated by H. A. R. Gibb (London: The Hakluyt Society, 1958, 1962, 1971); excerpt from *Ciano's Diary 1939–1943* by Count Galeazzo Ciano (London: William Heinemann, 1947); excerpt from *The Travels of John Sanderson in the Levant 1584-1602* by Ralph Fitch, edited by Sir William Foster (London: The Hakluyt Society, 1931). Reprinted by permission of David Higham Associates, Ltd.

HOUGHTON MIFFLIN COMPANY AND CURTIS BROWN LTD., LONDON, ON BEHALF OF THE ESTATE OF SIR WINSTON CHURCHILL: Excerpts from *Triumph and Tragedy,* Volume IV of *The Second World War* by Winston S. Churchill. Copyright © 1953 by Houghton Mifflin Company. Copyright renewed 1981 by The Honourable Lady Sarah Audley and The Honourable Lady Mary Soames. Reprinted by permission of Houghton Mifflin Company and Curtis Brown Ltd., London, on behalf of the Estate of Sir Winston Churchill.

HOUGHTON MIFFLIN COMPANY: Excerpt from *War As I Knew It* by George S. Patton, Jr. Copyright © 1941 by George S. Patton, Jr. All rights reserved. Reprinted by permission of Houghton Mifflin Company.

HUTCHINSON PUBLISHING GROUP, A DIVISION OF RANDOM HOUSE UK: Excerpts from *Arabesque* by Princess Musbah Haidar. Reprinted by permission of Hutchinson Publishing Group Ltd/The Random House Archive and Library.

INSTITUT ET MUSÉE VOLTAIRE, GENEVA: Excerpt from *Voltaire's Correspondence,* Vol. 78, 79 by Voltaire, edited by Theodore Besterman. Translated by Bernard Lewis by permission of Institut et Musée Voltaire, Geneva.

JOHN MURRAY (PUBLISHERS) LTD.: Excerpt from *Desert and Delta* by C. S. Jarvis; excerpt from *A Crackle of Thorns: Experiences in the Middle East* by Sir Alec Kirkbride; excerpt from *Baghdad Sketches* by Freya Stark. Reprinted by permission of John Murray (Publishers) Ltd.

JOURNAL OF THE PAKISTAN HISTORICAL SOCIETY: Excerpt from "Embassy of Queen Bertha to Caliph al-Muktafi billah in Baghdad 293/906" by Shihāb al-Dīn Ahmad ibn 'Abdallah al-Awhadī, edited and translated by M. Hamidullah from *Journal of the Pakistan Historical Society* 1, 1953.

ALFRED A. KNOPF, A DIVISION OF RANDOM HOUSE, INC.: Excerpt from *Among the Believers: An Islamic Journey* by V. S. Naipaul. Copyright © 1981 by V. S. Naipaul. Reprinted by permission of Alfred A. Knopf, a division of Random House, Inc.

LITTLE, BROWN AND COMPANY, INC.: Excerpt from *White House Years* by Henry Kissinger. Copyright © 1979 by Henry A. Kissinger. Reprinted by permission of Little, Brown and Company, Inc.

THE NEW REPUBLIC: Excerpt from "Getting Even" by Uriel Dann from the June 3, 1991, issue of *The New Republic.* Copyright © 1991 by The New Republic, Inc. Reprinted by permission of *The New Republic.*

OFFICES OF THE ROYAL HISTORICAL SOCIETY: Excerpts from *The Diaries of Edward Henry Stanley, 15th Earl of Derby (1826–1893) Between September 1869 and March 1878,* Volume IV, edited by John Vincent; excerpt from *The Letter-Journal of George Canning, 1793–1795,* edited by Peter Jupp. Reprinted by permission of the Offices of the Royal Historical Society.

OXFORD UNIVERSITY PRESS, LTD.: Excerpts from *The Complete Letters, Volume I, 1708–1720* by Lady Mary Wortley Montagu, edited by Robert Halsband; excerpt from *The Turkish Letters of Ogier Ghiselin de Busbecq* by Ogier Ghiselin de Busbecq, translated by Edward Seymour Forster (Oxford: Clarendon Press, 1927); excerpt from *South-West Persia: A Political Officer's Diary 1907–1914* by Sir Arnold Wilson; excerpt from *Arabic Literature*, first edition, by Sir Hamilton Gibb. Reprinted by permission of Oxford University Press, Ltd.

PRINCETON UNIVERSITY PRESS: Excerpt from *Kitāb al-I'tipār* by Usāma ibn Munqidh, edited by P. K. Hitti. Copyright © 1930 by Princeton University Press. Translated by Bernard Lewis by permission of Princeton University Press.

PUTNAM BERKELEY, A DIVISION OF PENGUIN PUTNAM, INC., AND THE ORION PUBLISHING GROUP, LTD.: Excerpt from *Orientations* by Ronald Storrs. Copyright © 1937 by Ronald Storrs; excerpt from *Vita and Harold: The Letters of Vita Sackville-West and Harold Nicolson*, edited by Nigel Nicolson. Copyright © 1992 by Harold Nicolson. Reprinted by permission of Putnam Berkeley, a division of Penguin Putnam, Inc., and The Orion Publishing Group, Ltd.

RANDOM HOUSE, INC.: Excerpt from *Cities of Salt* by Adbelrahman Munif, translated by Peter Theroux. Copyright © 1987 by Cape Cod Scriveners Company. Reprinted by permission of Random House, Inc.

ROUTLEDGE: Excerpts by David Azulai and Rabbi Meshullam da Volterra from *Jewish Travellers*, translated by Elkan Nathan Adler. Reprinted by permission of Routledge.

SIMON AND SCHUSTER, INC., AND THE WYLIE AGENCY, INC.: Excerpt from *God Has Ninety-nine Names: Reporting from a Militant Middle East* by Judith Miller. Reprinted by permission of Simon and Schuster, Inc., and The Wylie Agency, Inc.

STUDIUM BIBLICUM FRANCISCANUM: Excerpt from *Visit to the Holy Places of Egypt, Sinai, Palestine and Syria in 1384* by Lionardo Frescobaldi, Simone Sigoli and Giorgio Gucci, translated by Fr. Theophilis Bellorini, O.F.M, and Fr. Eugene Hoade, O.F.M. Reprinted by permission of Studium Biblicum Franciscanum.

TALEBAN ISLAMIC MOVEMENT: "Working Women: A View from Afghanistan" from www.taleban.com. Copyright © 1999 by the Taleban Islamic Movement. Reprinted by permission.

THE WESTMINSTER PRESS/JOHN KNOX PRESS: Excerpts from *Christians in the Arab East* by Robert Brenton Betts. Reprinted by permission of The Westminster Press/John Knox Press.

W. W. NORTON & COMPANY, INC.: Excerpts from *Present at the Creation: My Years in the State Department* by Dean Acheson. Copyright © 1987 by Dean Acheson. Reprinted by permission of W. W. Norton & Company, Inc.

YALE UNIVERSITY PRESS AND ROUTLEDGE: Excerpts from *The Book of Government or Rules for Kings* by Nazām al-Mulk. Reprinted by permission of Yale University Press and Routledge.

ILLUSTRATIONS

page 2 Collection Israel Museum, Jerusalem.

page 22 The Nasil M. Heeramaneck Collection, the Los Angeles County Museum of Art, gift of Joan Palevsky (M.73.5.333).

page 36 By permission of the British Library O.R. 1960-11-12-02.

page 60 Istanbul University Library, Istanbul.

page 74 Victoria and Albert Picture Gallery, the Victoria and Albert Museum; reproduced from the Library of Congress.

pages 97, 324 © Bibliothèque Nationale de France.

pages 126, 288 The Topkapi Palace Museum, Istanbul.

page 140 The Bridgeman Art Library International Ltd., New York.

pages 186, 414 © Bodleian Library, Oxford, U.K.

page 350 The Nasil M. Heeramaneck Collection, the Los Angeles County Museum of Art, gift of Joan Palevsky (M.73.5.591).

page 358 The Metropolitan Museum of Art. The Cora Timken Burnett collection of Persian miniatures and other Persian art objects. Bequest of Cora Timken Burnett, 1957 (57.51.21).

page 374 Courtesy of the Arthur M. Sackler Museum, Harvard University Art Museums, promised gift of Mr. and Mrs. Stuart Cary Welch, Jr. Partially owned by the Metropolitan Museum of Art and the Arthur M. Sackler Museum, Harvard University, 1988. (Acc. #1988.460.3, Surr. ID #13224).

ABOUT THE AUTHOR

Internationally recognized as one of our century's greatest historians of the Middle East, BERNARD LEWIS is the author of *The Middle East: A Brief History of the Last 2,000 Years,* a National Book Critics Circle Award finalist; *The Emergence of Modern Turkey; The Muslim Discovery of Europe;* and *The Arabs in History,* among other seminal books in a long and distinguished career. His books have been translated into over twenty languages. A fellow of the British Academy, a member of the American Philosophical Society and the American Academy of Arts and Sciences, and a correspondent of the Institut de France, he is Cleveland E. Dodge Professor Emeritus of Near Eastern Studies at Princeton University and was a long-term member of the Institute for Advanced Study.